TECHNOLOGY
AT YOUR SERVICE

Ralph De Arazoza

Introduction to Computers—CIS 110
Special Edition for Wake Technical Community College

Mc
Graw
Hill
Education

2 3 4 5 6 7 8 9 0 BRP BRP 19 18 17 16

ISBN-13: 978-1-260-00700-8
ISBN-10: 1-260-00700-6

Solutions Program Manager: Tricia Wagner
Project Manager: Connie Kuhl
Cover Photo Credits:
87834631.tif – n/a
guy_highangle.tif © Jupiterimages
stk158045rke.tif © Stockbyte
140410733.tif © winterling

About the Author

Ralph De Arazoza is an Associate Professor of Technology at Miami Dade College, where he has been teaching for over 10 years. His areas of specialization include computer concepts, office applications, web development, photo editing, animation, and computer ethics. He has developed several face-to-face and online courses, including an advanced web programming course covering jQuery and mobile website development.

Prof. De Arazoza's teaching philosophy centers on the way students experience and use technology. His energetic lectures instill a passion for technology in his students, encouraging them to explore what this field has to offer. He also serves as the advisor for the MDC Computer Club, whose members hold a variety of technology workshops and compete in various local and state tournaments throughout the year.

When he is not teaching and working with students, Prof. De Arazoza prepares and writes content for publishers for various types of products such as test banks, exercises, digital presentations, instructor manuals, and chapter revisions. In his spare time he enjoys collecting (and tasting) wine, science fiction, trivia, and just about any type of comedy.

Dedication

For all the educators who have inspired me and the students who continue to motivate me.

Acknowledgments

I would first like to thank my family and friends for their support and encouragement throughout this process. I am especially grateful to my mother and brother, whose expertise on Mac systems proved to be invaluable. I would also like to thank my colleagues at Miami Dade College for their advice and assistance with various topics in this book. A final thanks goes to everyone at McGraw-Hill who continuously encouraged me and helped make this endeavor possible.

Table of Contents

CHAPTER 4
The Internet 94

CHAPTER 5
Networking & Security 132

CHAPTER 6
Changing the World 164

Selected Materials from "*Microsoft® Office 2016: In Practice*" *1e*, by Randy Nordell, Kathleen Stewart, Annette Easton and Pat Graves.

`OFFICE`

WORD

Word and Excel Capstone Projects
See Resources in SIMnet

POWERPOINT

Word, Excel, and PowerPoint Capstone Projects
See Resources in SIMnet

Preface

Before You Begin

If you are reading this textbook, it is likely that you are enrolled in an introductory computing course. Like many students in this type of course, you will soon find yourself taking notes, creating documents, and completing a variety of exercises on your computer. Before you do any of those things, there are a few tools that you should consider using to help you throughout your course.

The companion website to this book (see link below) contains information on where to find these tools. In addition, there are links that provide help on using these tools and tips on how to get the most out of them.

TEXTBOOK RESOURCES

You should become familiar with the online resources available for this textbook.

Companion website

The companion website is located at **techatyourservice .com**. It contains a variety of material that you will find interesting and useful. Here are just a few examples:

- **Before you begin.** Links and tips that cover the tools discussed in this preface.
- **More online.** Throughout the book, you will see "more online" boxes that direct you to the textbook's website. In this section of the site, you will find many useful tips and bonus material that pertain to the section of the book you are currently reading.
- **Videos.** These are links to useful videos or animations that help explain various concepts or contain step-by-step instructions for different activities.
- **Careers.** This section will have up-to-date information on various technology careers, including salary ranges.
- **LearnSmart.** This textbook will feature McGraw-Hill's innovative LearnSmart technology, which presents a study plan of questions that are tailored just for you!

Social media

Find your textbook on various social media sites to receive up-to-date technology news and updates to the book. The course website contains links to:

- Facebook.
- Google+.
- Twitter.

TAKING NOTES

Many students currently take notes in and out of class by writing them on paper or typing them into Microsoft Word. Although these methods may work just fine for you, consider the following tools and the advantages they offer.

Tools

- **Evernote.** Considered one of the premier note-taking apps, it is available on most mobile devices. There are also versions for your Windows or Mac computer. You can type a variety of notes, record reminders, and take/attach photos to your notes. Multiple notebooks can help you keep track of several classes, recipes, wish lists, and anything else you want to remember.
- **Google Docs.** Now part of Google Drive, these are web-based tools that let you create documents, spreadsheets, and presentations without installing any software. Google makes it very easy to type, format, and share notes. Apps are available for a variety of mobile devices.

Write notes, record audio, take photos, and clip websites with Evernote.

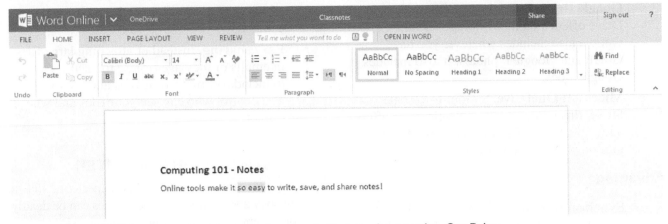

Microsoft Word Online allows you to create documents that can be saved to OneDrive.

- **Microsoft Office Online.** Microsoft now offers mini versions of Word, Excel, and PowerPoint online. These apps are similar to Google Docs, but may seem more familiar to those who have used Microsoft's Office programs before. They may also be desirable if your course includes exercises in MS Office.

Advantages

- **Instant save.** Notes are saved online as you type. If you lose power or your computer crashes, there is no need to worry . . . your notes are safe.
- **Searching.** Digital notes can be searched in the same way that you search websites. Type in a word or two and it will find any page in your notes that contains that word. This is much faster than flipping through pages in a notebook!
- **Easy access.** There is no need to copy your notes from a school's computer to yours, for example, because they are saved online. All you need to access your notes is connection to the Internet.
- **Multiple devices.** These notes are accessible on any Internet-connected device, including your tablet or smartphone.
- **Collaboration.** Share notes with classmates and work together on the same document.

SAVING YOUR WORK

If you have a computer lab or classroom at your school, it is likely that you use a small USB flash drive to save and transport your files. Although these devices are useful, there are more convenient ways

to save your work and keep the files synchronized among all the computers you use.

Tools

- **Dropbox.** This is one of the premier Internet storage and synchronization tools. Save files in a special folder in your computer and it instantly gets uploaded to your account. Manage your files on the website or on the mobile app. Free accounts start at a few gigabytes, but can increase significantly if you refer your friends.

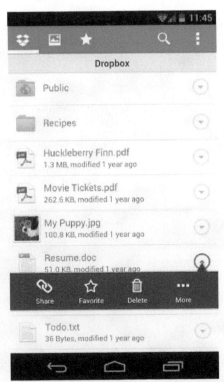

Dropbox app lets you view your photos, documents, and more from a mobile device.

- **Google Drive.** Similar to Dropbox, Google Drive offers a bit more storage because Google also includes whatever you have in Gmail and Google+ photos. It also includes Google Docs.
- **Microsoft OneDrive.** Similar to Google Drive, this new service from Microsoft offers a few gigabytes of storage and excellent integration with Office Online.

Advantages

- **Synchronization.** Each of these tools will install a special folder on your desktop/laptop computer. Anything you place in that folder is instantly uploaded to your online account so that you can access it from anywhere. Any changes you make to your files will trigger synchronization, ensuring that your files are always up-to-date in all of your computers. This is extremely useful for those who have multiple computers or are just tired of carrying around a portable storage device.
- **Access anywhere.** Your important files are accessible no matter where you are. All three of these tools have apps that can be installed on your desktop/laptop and mobile devices. In addition, they have websites that are easy to use, allowing you to open your files without the need to install the app on another computer.
- **Easy sharing.** Instead of attaching large files in emails or messages, these tools allow you to include a link to your files and photos. You control who can see your files and who cannot.

PROTECTING YOUR COMPUTER

Nothing can ruin your computing experience like a virus or spyware. Although some viruses can be deadly for your computer, many infections can slow down your system or steal valuable information from you.

It is true that Mac computers rarely get viruses; however, infections have started to rise as the Mac's popularity increases. If you have Windows, it is crucial that you have a reliable and active antivirus installed. While Windows itself offers basic protection, it simply isn't enough against today's sophisticated attacks. If you do not have an up-to-date antivirus running on your system, you can easily install one of these free tools today:

Tools

- AVG AntiVirus Free.
- Avast Free Antivirus.
- Avira Free Antivirus.

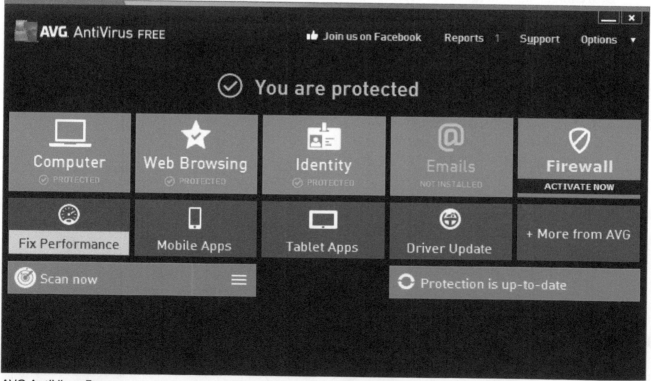

AVG AntiVirus Free.

TECHNOLOGY
AT YOUR SERVICE
Ralph De Arazoza

1

INTRODUCTION

Chapter Overview

This chapter covers the fundamentals of computing. You will discover the different types of computers that exist today and learn how they are being used in a variety of organizations. In addition, you will explore several mobile devices and wearable technology that are transforming many aspects of today's society.

PART 1:
The World of Technology

Regardless of your experience with computers, you probably have been blown away by how quickly technology progresses. This rapid change leads to amazing developments in medicine, engineering, and other fields. At the same time, it also frustrates many individuals who feel as if they are always playing "catch up" with technology. Whether it is figuring out which mobile device to purchase or how best to protect sensitive information, many individuals feel overwhelmed and confused. This book aims to ease this frustration by increasing your **digital literacy**— a broad understanding of computer and information technology, along with the ability to use it well. Once you become familiar with the world of technology, you will be ready to use it in every aspect of your life: work, education, communication, and even entertainment.

Technology Is Everywhere

Computers have drastically changed the way we do everything in our society. You could probably come up with a long list of reasons computers are important to most individuals and organizations. Many of these reasons likely have to do with information, which is something that computers allow us to create and access at very fast speeds. In addition, computers support the technology and infrastructure that allows us to communicate this information to anyone in the world.

It would be impossible to list all the ways in which computers are being used today. Therefore, this section will focus on just a few of the roles computers have in society.

HOME

Today, many American families own multiple computers, all sharing an Internet connection in their homes. While some families might share a larger computer at a desk, low prices have made it easier for many individuals (especially students) to have their own portable computer, which they use both in and out of their home. In addition to computers, technology now allows us to manage many aspects of our home life, from controlling our TVs and sound systems to monitoring security cameras from a remote location. Let's look at some of the activities that home users can engage in with the power of technology:

- **Communication.** The power of the Internet allows computer users to communicate with people all over the world. Friends and family members can stay in touch with one another more easily than ever before. A variety of services, such as Facebook and Instagram, make it simple to share updates and special moments with everyone in your social circle.

- **Business work done at home.** Thanks to computers and Internet connections, more people are working from home than ever before. Many users connect to their employer's systems from home. Computers also are making it easier for people to start their own home-based businesses.

- **Schoolwork.** Today's students are increasingly reliant on computers, particularly for researching information online. Electronic books are replacing printed books, and easy-to-use software makes it possible for students to create polished documents and presentations. Even grade school students are using computers to learn how to read and complete basic math problems.

- **Entertainment.** Computers and video game consoles offer a variety of entertainment options, from solitaire to realistic sports and action games. People can play games alone, with a friend or family member, or go online to play with tens of thousands of others in a single, massive fantasy world. Computers can also serve as media centers, storing music, videos, and movies for on-demand playback on other computers, consoles, and televisions throughout the home.

Many students use a portable computer at home and at school.

- **Creativity.** Art, music, photography, and creative writing—these once required publishers and marketing efforts to reach a vast audience. Now, with blogs, personal web pages, and social media, people can create just about anything and share it with a large number of individuals.

- **Finances and shopping.** Computers and personal finance software can make it easy to manage your budget. Home users rely on their computers for paying bills and making investments. They also use computers to spend what they earn, shopping online for everything from cars to collectibles.

HEALTH CARE

Here are a few examples of how computers are changing the way organizations and health care providers help individuals feel better:

- **Procedures.** A variety of medical procedures now involve computers, from ultrasound and magnetic resonance imaging (MRI) to laser eye surgery and fetal monitoring. Surgeons can use robotic surgical devices to perform delicate operations and even to conduct surgeries remotely.

- **Research.** The care we all receive has been improved drastically over the years because of the research capabilities offered by computers.

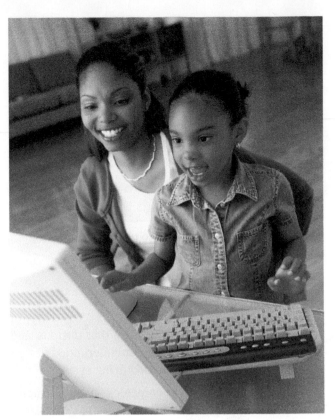

Computers offer education and entertainment for many families.

Powerful systems have helped researchers discover new medications and treatments. Also, robotic technology and implantable computer chips are currently helping a variety of patients, from those who have lost a limb to individuals who suffer seizures or tremors.

- **Training.** Various technologies are being used to train students in the health sciences. One example is an automated "dummy" that simulates a real patient with a variety of conditions.

- **Medical records.** Most hospitals, doctors, and pharmacies have turned to electronic medical records. This makes it easier to search for something specific in your medical history, as well as share it with another health care provider who is also caring for you.

INDUSTRY

Today, large businesses use a variety of technologies to run their operations. Corporate headquarters are filled with employees using connected computers, while production facilities might use computer-controlled robotics to manufacture products. Here are just a few ways computers are applied to industry:

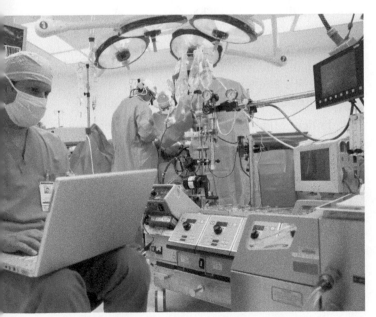

Computers help in nearly all aspects of health care, from electronic medical records to controlling machines for surgeons.

Police officers use computers to quickly access vital information.

- **Design.** Nearly any company that designs and makes products can use a computer-aided design or computer-aided manufacturing system.

- **Shipping.** Freight companies need computers to manage the thousands of ships, planes, trains, and trucks that are moving goods at any given moment. In addition to tracking vehicle locations and contents, computers can manage maintenance, driver schedules, invoices and billing, and many other activities.

- **Process control.** Modern assembly lines can be massive, complex systems, and a breakdown at one point can cause chaos throughout a company. Sophisticated process-control systems can oversee output, check the speed at which a machine runs, and analyze inventory, all with very little human interaction.

- **Administration.** Computers now help a wide range of office workers complete their tasks more quickly and efficiently. For example, accountants use sophisticated software to track income and expenses, while a human resources specialist keeps track of all employee records. Managers can use computers to oversee a variety of business operations and keep track of employee performance.

- **Marketing.** In order to compete and sell products or services, most businesses need to advertise. Computers help companies produce everything from flyers and coupons to sophisticated television commercials.

GOVERNMENT

Not only is government a big consumer of technology, but government also helps to develop it as well. As you will learn in Chapter 4, the U.S. government played a key role in developing the Internet. Today, computers play a crucial part in nearly every level of government, from federal agencies to your local police.

- **Military.** Some of today's most sophisticated technology exists because it was developed and funded by the military. A few of the earliest computers were created for combat or defense functions, such as improving radar and rocket technology. Today, the military uses computers for a variety of reasons including combat simulation, research, defense, and controlling unmanned aerial vehicles (drones).

- **Security.** Colossus, the first programmable electronic computer, was used by the British during World War II to help crack many coded messages being sent to the German army. Today, government agencies such as the CIA and NSA use large, sophisticated computer systems to gather intelligence. The United States Cyber Command is also involved with security, protecting crucial systems and networks against computer-based attacks.

- **Taxes.** The Internal Revenue Service uses computers to calculate the tax bills for millions of individuals and corporations. In addition, the IRS encourages taxpayers to file their tax returns electronically via the Internet.

- **Police.** Many police forces consider computers to be just as important as guns and ammunition. Today's police cruisers are equipped with laptop computers and wireless Internet connections that enable officers to search through millions of records instantly.

Basic Terms in Computing

Now that you are familiar with the variety of tasks that computers can be used for, it is time to learn basic terminology used in the world of computers and technology.

WHAT IS A COMPUTER?

In the simplest terms, a **computer** is a device that accepts input, processes data, and can output or store the result of its actions. All computers, regardless of their size, purpose, or type, follow this definition. Let us take a closer look at the elements in this definition:

- **Input** refers to user entries or activities that tell the computer what to do. Input can take a variety of forms, such as the text you type with your keyboard or finger movements on the touchscreen of a mobile device.

- **Processing** is the ability of a computer to perform actions based on instructions from the user or a program. As you already know, a computer can complete a variety of tasks including financial calculations and handling the graphics for a video game.

- **Output** refers to the processed results that a computer sends out to you. Typically, the results appear on the computer's screen or on a printed piece of paper.

- **Storage** is the ability of a computer to hold or remember the information it processes. Some storage is temporary, such as the data held by your computer's RAM, or memory. Most storage, however, is permanent; it will remain there until you erase it.

These four operations are part of a process called the **information processing cycle** (see Figure 1.1). In Chapter 2, you will explore a variety of devices that perform the functions in this cycle.

Hardware refers to the parts that make up a computer system.

Figure 1.1 **The Information Processing Cycle**

HARDWARE

The physical devices that make up a computer system are called **hardware**. Hardware is any part of the computer you can touch. Processors, monitors, and keyboards are all examples of hardware. These parts will be discussed in more detail throughout Chapter 2.

SOFTWARE

A **computer program** is a set of instructions that directs the computer to perform a variety of tasks. These instructions are written in a computer programming language such as C++, Java, and Visual Basic. The term **software** refers to one or more of these programs that are packaged together for a unified purpose. Some software, such as the Windows or Mac OS *operating systems,* exists primarily to help the computer run and manage its resources. Other types of software known as applications or *apps* enable users to perform a variety of activities. These include creating documents, playing games, or communicating with others. A variety of software that can be purchased or downloaded (retrieved) from the Internet will be discussed throughout Chapter 3.

DATA

Data consist of individual facts or pieces of information. Suppose for a moment that you are a traffic engineer who is working on a proposal to lower the speed limit on a neighborhood street. You might collect facts (data) about the speed of each car and any accidents that you observed on that road. Choosing the right data to examine and process is a big part of making the computer an effective tool.

There is a difference between information and data. Information describes concepts, facts, and ideas that people find useful. Data are raw materials that we use in the creation of information. In the example above, the individual speeds are not very useful when considered by themselves. But when we average them using computer software and give them context in our proposal, we produce useful information. Others can read the proposal and gain an understanding of what is going on in that neighborhood's street.

NETWORKS

A **network** allows users to communicate and share information between computers. A computer network is what allows multiple employees to access information about customers or products from a central computer. It also allows friends and family to have a live conversation with each other, even if they live in different parts of the world. Computers in a traditional network are connected by cables; however, more computers are now being connected via **wireless networks**, whereby communication takes place using radio waves. **Wi-Fi** is the current standard for wireless networks and Internet connectivity.

Networks allow many users to connect to a central computer to access information and communicate.

Regardless of how computers connect, networks have transformed the way in which we communicate at home and at work. We will discuss networking in more detail in Chapter 5.

THE INTERNET

The largest network in the world is known as the **Internet**, which connects billions of people and organizations throughout the world. Many of you likely go "online" every day and perhaps own a home computer or mobile device that is permanently connected to the Internet. If you have not used the Internet, you have probably heard of some of its capabilities.

Most individuals use the Internet to access web pages on the **World Wide Web (WWW)**. These pages can contain a seemingly unlimited variety of information, from news and sports to updates from your family and social circle. Another popular use of the Internet is electronic mail, or **email**, which allows messages to be sent to electronic mailboxes in an instant. The fastest-growing areas of the Internet are cloud computing and social media. **Cloud computing**, simply put, allows you to store your files and use various applications in an online account. **Social media** refers to a variety of websites and services that allow individuals to share photos, news, and thoughts on just about anything. Friends, family, and co-workers often connect by using social media. We will explore all aspects of the Internet in more detail throughout Chapter 4.

The Internet and World Wide Web offer a variety of services.

Categories of Computers

Computers, just like vehicles, come in all sorts of sizes and can serve a variety of purposes. In the same way that the automobile industry separates cars and vans into distinct categories, the computer industry also uses categories to differentiate between various types of computers. The enormous computers that fill an entire room within a large business are clearly different from those you can stick inside your pocket. As we explore all of these categories, keep in mind that the line between some categories is very thin and can change as new devices are released by manufacturers.

PERSONAL COMPUTERS

The computers that you are likely familiar with are those meant to be used by only one person at a time. Those computers have historically been known as **personal computers (PCs)** or microcomputers. However, in recent times, the term "PC" most commonly refers to personal computers that run the Windows operating system. Although Apple's line of desktop and laptop computers are technically personal computers, no one would ever refer to them as PCs. Instead, they call them "Macs." It is also important to note that the term *mobile device*, and not PC,

An all-in-one desktop computer.

is used to refer to the latest tablets and smartphones, even though they are, of course, computers that are intended for personal use. We will be exploring mobile devices in detail throughout Part 2 of this chapter. For now, let us turn our attention to desktop and laptop computers.

DESKTOP COMPUTERS

The computer that has been traditionally found on the desks in many offices and homes is the **desktop computer**. This computer received its name a few decades ago when it was originally designed to lie flat on top of your desk, with the monitor, or screen, being placed on top of it. Today, most desktop computers are in the form of towers that are usually placed below the desk. Others are available as **all-in-one computers** that have all of the hardware integrated with the monitor.

Today, the desktop is losing ground to various portable computers, which have become both powerful and affordable. However, many individuals still prefer having a desktop system that has a larger monitor and more comfortable keyboard. In addition, tower-based systems can be custom-built by anyone who knows how to purchase and connect the pieces. Various power users, such as gamers, will often take advantage of this option to get the exact configuration that best meets their needs.

LAPTOP COMPUTERS

Laptop computers are portable computers that contain all of the components of a desktop computer in a single, integrated unit. Also known as notebook computers, laptops possess a folding monitor that can rest flat against an area containing the keyboard and other hardware components. They also include wireless

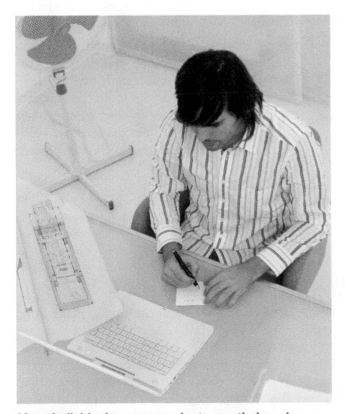

Many individuals now use a laptop as their main computer.

capabilities that allow users to connect to the Internet at a variety of locations. A rechargeable battery keeps them powered for a few hours, and they can be connected directly to a power outlet when the battery runs out.

Laptops are fully functional personal computers. They can use the same software and accomplish most of the same tasks as a desktop computer. Because of this, many individuals have chosen to buy a laptop as their primary computer; they use it when they are home and when they are on the go. Let us now take a look at a few varieties of laptops that possess unique qualities:

- **Netbooks** are small and inexpensive laptops that have reduced processing power and lack a DVD drive. They are designed for budget shoppers who will use the computer primarily for browsing the web and basic office tasks, such as creating documents. These types of computers are losing popularity because the prices of regular laptops have dropped to historic lows.

This convertible laptop can be used as either a tablet or a regular laptop.

- **Ultraportable computers** are thin, lightweight laptops that possess strong processing power. They are more powerful than netbooks, but also more expensive. Many weigh less than four pounds and are often touchscreen capable in order to take advantage of the Windows 8 interface. Apple's MacBook Air competes with Intel-based Ultrabooks in this category.

- **Convertible laptops** are lightweight laptop computers that allow users to swivel or detach the touchscreen monitor. This gives users maximum flexibility, allowing them to switch between a laptop and tablet experience based on their needs. We will discuss tablet computers in more detail later in this chapter.

- **Chromebooks** are lightweight laptops that run Google's Chrome operating system. These are usually the most affordable laptops, partly because they contain very little storage inside the computer. Google encourages users to store most of their information in an online Google account, which means that an Internet connection is often needed.

Narrow blade servers are suitable for side-by-side installation in a server rack.

More **Online:** *Do you want your laptop battery to last longer? Visit the companion website to learn the answer to this and other common laptop-related questions.*

MULTI USER COMPUTERS

Some computers, such as those that manage large retail stores or airline reservation systems, are designed to work with many people at the same time. These larger, **multi-user computers** manage a variety of services for businesses and organizations. They act as the central computer in a network, allowing personal computers to connect to them in order to access information or software stored inside of them.

NETWORK SERVERS

A **network server** is a powerful computer with special software and equipment that enables it to function as the primary computer in a network. Though their exact functions are different from organization to organization, network servers all have the basic task of making files, software, and in some cases, other computer hardware available to many users at any given time. For example, a network server might run the email services accessed by all employees, while another server manages the company's website.

Often, the requests from the network grow so large and complex that a single server cannot handle the job by itself. In such cases, network server computers are linked to share the load. In some cases, dozens or even hundreds of individual servers work together to manage data processing requests. When set up in such groups—sometimes called *clusters* or *server farms*—network servers must be arranged in a space-saving manner. Each computer is reduced to a thin unit called a **blade server**, which can slide in and out of a rack that holds many of its companion servers. In these large networks, server groups are often serving different purposes or supporting a certain set of users.

MAINFRAME COMPUTERS

Mainframe computers are very large and powerful systems used in organizations where a heavy amount of processing and user requests need to be handled. A state's government, for example, might use a mainframe to store information about drivers, vehicles, and driver's licenses. Some school districts and colleges use these computers to manage records related to employees, students, and courses. Large businesses, such as international banks and airlines, might use several mainframes to handle the millions of transactions that are performed on a daily basis.

Engineer working on a mainframe computer.

NASA's supercomputer fills this entire room.

SUPERCOMPUTERS

Supercomputers are the largest and most powerful computers in the world. These enormous machines, which often fill warehouse-sized rooms, can link hundreds of thousands of processors. Supercomputers are ideal for handling large and highly complex problems that require extreme calculating power. NASA, for example, will use supercomputers to conduct modeling and simulations for upcoming missions. Others might be involved in forecasting weather, performing nuclear research, and even breaking codes on behalf of a government agency.

> More **Online:** *What is the fastest computer in the world? What does it do? Visit the companion website to find out.*

EMBEDDED SYSTEMS

All of the computers you have learned about so far are general-purpose computers—they can be used for just about anything. In contrast, **embedded systems** are limited computers because they are placed inside devices that require specific computing functions. Embedded systems manage a variety of functions inside modern cars, military equipment, medical imaging devices, and several home appliances. In this section, we will explore a few examples of these systems.

E-BOOK READERS

Electronic books (e-books) are digital books that are stored on a computing device. These books can contain a mix of text, illustrations, and photos,

much like a traditional, paper-based book. Although e-books can be read on a variety of computers, several companies have created special **e-book readers**, or e-readers, to make it convenient for individuals to store many of their books. Compared to tablet computers, these devices are much lighter, affordable, and enjoy a longer battery life. They have unique screens featuring crisp black text that is capable of being read in even the brightest outdoor conditions. Because of these features, many individuals find e-book readers to be much more comfortable for extended reading than regular tablet computers. However, their limited processors prevent these devices from being used for much more than reading books. Examples of e-readers include:

- Amazon Kindle
- Barnes & Noble Nook

GAMING CONSOLES

For decades, video game systems have provided countless hours of excitement for children (and adults) in front of the TV. However, today's **gaming consoles** are complete entertainment systems, offering Internet connectivity, movie rentals, photo storage, and many other services in addition to video games. Many consoles are also Blu-ray disc players, which allow you to watch high-definition movies stored on these discs.

The Amazon Kindle e-book reader offers easy reading in all lighting levels.

A variety of input devices are available for these consoles, ranging from game controllers and musical instruments to sophisticated video cameras that can capture the body's movements during an exercise routine. Example consoles include:

- Sony PlayStation 4 (PS4)
- Microsoft Xbox One
- Nintendo WiiU

SMART TVS

Many new TVs are being manufactured with the ability to use your home's Internet connection to bring you a variety of services. These **smart TVs** can connect to a variety of online services such as Netflix, Amazon, and Pandora to let you watch movies and listen to music from your accounts. Many of these TVs also offer connectivity with your home computers and mobile devices. This allows you to easily access videos, photos, and music on these devices without the need to plug in cables or storage devices to your TV.

If you are not ready to replace your current television, a variety of **streaming players** can add many of these "smart" features to almost any TV. These small, affordable devices connect to your TV and wireless home network. For those who have newer gaming consoles, it is unlikely that you will need a streaming player since these consoles include many of the same online services. Examples of streaming players include:

- Roku
- Apple TV

Sony PlayStation 4 gaming console with controller and camera.

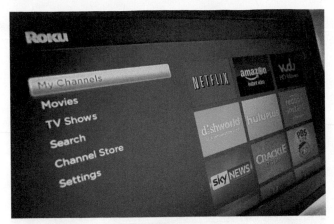

The small Roku streaming player can turn a TV into a smart TV.

HOME AUTOMATION

In addition to entertainment systems, many other areas in your home can benefit from embedded computers. We are currently seeing an increase in **home automation**, where many household activities are being automated or controlled from a distance (often using mobile devices as remote controls). The following are some examples of what home automation offers:

- **Security.** Surveillance cameras, home alarms, and door locks can now be activated or monitored from any device that has an Internet connection.

- **Temperature.** New generations of thermostats contain sophisticated programming that can manage the temperature automatically based on your schedule/routine and energy-saving goals.

- **Lighting.** The lights throughout your home can be turned on and off from a mobile device. They

Home automation allows individuals to remotely manage and automate their home's lighting, temperature, security systems, and various smart appliances.

can also be automated with motion detectors, allowing them to turn off automatically whenever you leave a room.

- **Appliances.** Many of today's appliances have embedded systems that manage touchscreen interfaces and control a variety of internal functions. Some homeowners have also purchased automated vacuum cleaners that use advanced sensors to clean large areas and avoid obstacles.

More **Online:** Visit the companion website to learn more about the convenience and energy-saving features of the Nest thermostat.

PART 2:
The Mobile User

In the previous section, we explored laptop computers that provide a portable computing experience. However, for true mobility, nothing beats having a computer that can fit in your pocket or be worn as eyeglasses. The ability to bring a computer with you no matter where you go offers a large number of benefits and conveniences. In this section, we will learn about a variety of mobile devices and explore how they are changing the way we learn, work, communicate, and live.

Mobile devices come with various sensors, such as a compass and GPS.

Mobile Devices

Mobile devices are lightweight, handheld computers that offer a variety of software and communication services for mobile users. They generally have touchscreen interfaces as the primary form of input and use unique programs known as *apps*. These apps allow users to do everything from viewing web pages and sending email to reading books and getting driving directions. Many apps are dedicated to personal organization, allowing us to manage our contacts, calendar, to-do list, personal notes, and alarms. We will explore many apps and the software that powers these devices in Chapter 3.

Mobile devices have many features in common that make them useful at home or on the go. Let's look at some of these features before we explore the various types of mobile devices.

- **Cameras.** Take photos and videos with cameras located on both sides of these devices.
- **Microphone and speakers.** Listen to music, have conversations, and speak commands.

- **Wireless connectivity.** Connect to the Internet and hands-free devices.
- **Internal sensors.** Accelerometers and gyroscopes can sense even the smallest movements in the device, while a compass and GPS prevent you from getting lost.

TABLET COMPUTERS

The **tablet computer**, or tablet, is a mobile device that typically ranges from 7 to 10 inches in size. They are currently the fastest-growing category of computers. Users find them to be an affordable and lightweight tool for reading electronic books, performing research, watching movies, and staying in touch with friends and family. The most popular tablet is the iPad from Apple, which took the world by storm when it was introduced in 2010. It has since received competition from a variety of Android-based devices and, more recently, from Microsoft. We will discuss the differences between these mobile operating systems in Chapter 2.

SMARTPHONES

A **smartphone** is a combination mobile phone and handheld computer. Most smartphone users are permanently connected to the Internet via a monthly data plan that keeps them online almost anywhere they go. They rely heavily on their smartphone throughout the day to stay up-to-date with news, weather, traffic, email, and updates from their friends. Smartphones are also receiving heavy use as cameras, allowing individuals to record all types of events without the need to carry a separate camera.

Tablets are available in a variety of sizes.

In addition to making phone calls, smartphones offer countless services for mobile users.

Google Glass provides a wide range of information in your field of vision.

Apple transformed the smartphone market with the release of its revolutionary iPhone in 2007. Since then, various Android-based devices have given Apple some serious competition. One of these devices, the Samsung Galaxy Note, shocked the industry with its large 5.3-inch screen. This phone, along with a few larger ones that have been developed recently, falls into a new category known as the **phablet**. This name, which is a mix of the terms "phone" and "tablet," is appropriate given that the size of these devices falls somewhere between a traditional smartphone and a 7-inch tablet.

> More **Online:** *Can your phone be used on another company's mobile network? Does your SIM card have anything to do with this? Visit the companion website for the answers to these common smartphone questions.*

WEARABLE TECHNOLOGY

Wearable technology refers to computing devices that are worn on various parts of the body. Although they are not as powerful or sophisticated as mobile devices, these computers can provide many useful services with minimal effort from the user. Most will synchronize with your smartphone to access the information that it will display to you. The following are a few examples of technology that you can wear:

- **Eyeglasses.** Google's Glass has captured the imagination of millions. These eyeglasses provide users with visual information directly in front of their right eye. Many of the alerts that you would receive on a smartphone or tablet now appear right before you. In addition, you can take photos and videos of whatever you are looking at. Soon, these glasses will be able to provide a full **augmented reality** experience, where the real world is supplemented with computer-generated information. For example, the name of a landmark would appear electronically in your field of vision when you look directly at it. To communicate with these glasses, you simply speak your command or use a variety of finger movements on the right side of the frame.

- **Wristwatch.** A "smart" watch essentially acts as a digital assistant on your wrist. In addition to the time and date, these watches display useful alerts and incoming messages from your smartphone. Some also add health-related features such as monitoring your heart rate or counting the number of steps taken on a recent walk. They accept user input via buttons, small touchscreen interfaces, and/or voice commands.

Hands-Free Computing

The ability to communicate with a device without using your hands is known as **hands-free computing**. This technology became popular about a decade ago when individuals looked for ways to make extended cell phone conversations more comfortable. Using a short-range wireless technology known as **Bluetooth**, calls could be made with a wireless headset worn on the ear or the hands-free systems in some cars. In addition to Bluetooth, many mobile devices now support voice input as a hands-free way to issue commands and dictate messages. Hands-free computing has a couple of benefits—convenience and safety.

CONVENIENCE

Many individuals feel that it is difficult to type quickly on the small, on-screen keyboards of most mobile devices. By using your voice, you can send messages, initiate web searches, and even request a direct answer to many common questions. Apple's Siri, Microsoft's Cortana, and Google's Voice Search are three products that respond to a variety of voice commands on mobile devices. Their ability to understand you is made possible by a technology known as speech recognition, which will be discussed further in Chapter 2.

SAFETY

It can be dangerous to use mobile devices during various activities, especially when driving a car. In fact, many state governments have passed laws restricting the way you use mobile devices while driving. Instead of holding a smartphone while talking or texting, it is safer to use hands-free technology. Many new cars have buttons on the steering wheel that allow you to make and receive calls. Together with a microphone and the speakers of your car, you can have conversations while keeping your hands on the wheel. In addition, many smartphones and car dashboards include the ability to read incoming messages and driving directions out loud, thereby eliminating the need to look at the screen. Although it is best to avoid any distractions when driving, hands-free technology will let you keep your eyes on the road.

Hands-free systems allow you to keep your hands on the wheel while driving.

Safety and Courtesy

In addition to distracted driving, other risks arise from the widespread adoption of mobile devices. Furthermore, many social interactions are changing because of the constant use of these devices. Let's look at a few of these issues.

DEVICE DAMAGE

This may seem obvious, but mobile devices are not designed to handle frequent drops or crushing weight. The glass itself is surprisingly strong; however, you have probably seen a few people with cracked screens. The best way to avoid damage to your mobile device is to buy a protective case. Some of these are affordable, thin, and light, but they may not offer the best protection for those who have slippery fingers. If you want the best protection, invest in a bulkier and/or waterproof case.

One additional option to consider is an extended warranty or insurance plan. Many individuals keep their smartphones for about two years because of the way wireless contracts are structured. If your phone comes with only a one-year warranty, you will be left with a gap of one year. If you cannot afford the extra insurance, find out if your credit card comes with an extended warranty plan. Many cards come with a benefit that will extend the warranty of your purchases up to one year.

LOSS AND THEFT

Mobile devices are small and valuable. This puts them at risk of being stolen, especially because users tend

A protective case can help prevent damage from drops.

to leave them behind in restaurants, classrooms, and even restrooms. Although the monetary loss hurts, worse is having a thief go through your personal information. Imagine all the photos, emails, and personal data that can be found by looking through your apps. And if you use your mobile device for work, the organization that employs you will also be put at risk. To avoid these problems, make sure that you use both of these tools:

- **Lock screens**, which are the start screens of mobile devices, allow users to set a password, PIN, or other security measure in order to access the device. Be sure you use this feature and configure the automatic lock based on your personal habits and tendency to lose the device.

- **Remote wipe** utilities allow users to erase their mobile device if it is lost or stolen. These utilities typically require that you log into a website to issue the remote wipe command.

WIRELESS SECURITY

Many mobile users rely on wireless connections available at schools, libraries, and various businesses in their city. For maximum security, always ask an employee for the name of the wireless network that you should connect to. Once connected, be careful with the websites and apps that you use. Casual browsing is fine, but transmitting sensitive information may be risky if the wireless connection is not secure. We will cover security issues in more detail throughout Chapter 5.

Protect your personal information by adding security on your device's lock screen.

Observe common courtesy when using mobile devices around others.

RUDENESS

While personal and equipment safety are fairly straightforward concepts, the same cannot be said about courtesy to others when using mobile devices. It is true that different individuals and societies disagree on what is considered rude behavior. In addition, a behavior that may be acceptable when having lunch with co-workers will be unacceptable during a business meeting with the same people. Chapter 6 addresses computing ethics and proper online behavior. For now, a few general guidelines will help you start thinking about courteous mobile computing.

PHONE AND VOICE VOLUME

This topic is fairly straightforward. As a general rule, always put your phone on vibrate mode when in public or in the company of other individuals. When in a very quiet environment, such as a classroom or meeting, be aware that a vibrating phone on a table can still be a distraction. In addition, be aware of the volume of your voice if using your phone in a public area such as a grocery store or medical office. Don't speak any louder than you would to someone who is standing next to you. If you must speak louder, go outside.

COFFEE SHOP COURTESY

Don't make the coffee shop your new office or study center unless you've been invited to do so. If you sit down and spread your notebook computer, mobile device, and books across a four-person table, you're occupying a lot of space that the owners may have hoped could be used by more than a single person. If you plan to occupy that table for hours, consider whether that cup of coffee is adequate "rent" for the

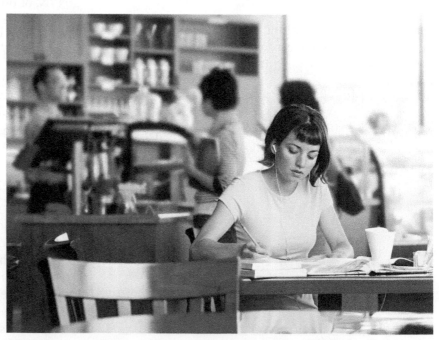

Be mindful of both the coffee shop owner and other customers when studying for extended periods.

time and space you are using. Lastly, always be sure to check for those who are standing, waiting for a table to clear so that they can enjoy their food and drinks.

MESSAGING WHILE MAD

Mobile devices give individuals the opportunity to communicate with almost anyone in a matter of seconds. This capability can be a big problem if a person decides to send a message or post a social network comment while upset. For most individuals, it is psychologically easier to send an angry electronic message than it is to call or yell in someone's face. To spare hurt feelings and reduce your risk of losing a friend (or your job), give yourself a few minutes to think clearly before clicking "send."

DIVIDING ATTENTION

No mobile behavior is as widespread and controversial as dividing your attention between your device and those around you. Generally, using your mobile device while engaged in a face-to-face interaction signals a lack of interest in the person you are interacting with. Other times, such as when placing an order or paying for goods, your mobile device may distract you from the fact that others are waiting in line behind you. Unless you are waiting for an urgent message or phone call, it is best to put your mobile

Unfortunately, mobile devices make it a little too easy to send messages when upset.

device away during class, meetings, dinners, and many other social situations that demand your undivided attention.

Some have argued that mobile devices are slowly changing our conception of what is rude behavior. For example, many of your friends or family members may not think twice if you quickly check a notification on your smartphone. However, if you start to send messages back and forth or engage in a long conversation, your behavior will likely be deemed unacceptable. To be polite, always ask those who are close to you how they feel about mobile devices. You may find that your friends enjoy having online social interactions at the same time that you are all having conversations in person. In fact, part of the fun may be discussing a crazy photo or video that a mutual friend posted. As long as you consider the feelings and preferences of those you are with, common sense will likely help you judge when the use of your mobile device is appropriate.

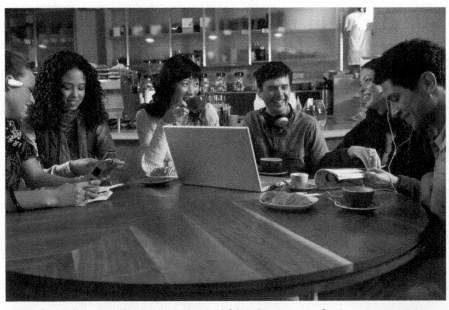

Rules for using mobile devices around friends can vary from one group to another.

Computing in New Ways

Mobile and wearable technology is changing many aspects of our lives. Having an always-on Internet connection and a countless number of apps has transformed the way we communicate and stay in touch. In addition, a world of knowledge is accessible in an instant, enabling you to make better decisions as you go through your day. In this section, we look at innovative and popular activities that are made possible by the widespread adoption of mobile devices. We will continue exploring apps and online services throughout Chapters 3 and 4.

LOCATION-BASED SERVICES

If you allow it, your mobile device can identify and report your location through the use of GPS, cell phone towers, and nearby wireless access points. This allows many organizations to offer you **location-based services (LBS)** through apps installed on your mobile device. The Yelp app, for example, informs you which restaurants are close to you and how others have rated them. You can even "check in" to a variety of businesses to let your friends know where you are and receive potential discounts from those businesses. Another benefit of LBS is the ability to receive driving directions based on your current location. Through the use of apps such as Google Maps, your mobile device can perform many of the navigation functions of a stand-alone GPS unit.

Some have concerns with location-based services, especially when it comes to privacy. They worry

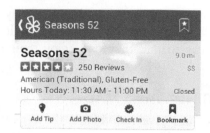

Check in and find nearby restaurants with the Yelp app.
Source: Yelp app

about the safety of the individuals who share their whereabouts and the data gathering being done by various companies. We will cover many of these issues in Chapter 6.

REAL-TIME INFORMATION

Real-time information refers to any information that is delivered to you immediately after it is created. Mobile devices allow individuals throughout the world to report events as they witness or experience them. They also offer a platform for opinions on just about anything, from a reality TV show to a politician's speech. The service known as Twitter has become the go-to service for real-time information. You can follow individuals and organizations that you find interesting or you can search for specific keywords related to the event that you want to know more about. Whether it is reactions to a big play in a sports game or an emergency in a location near you, Twitter will often have information before other sources.

Weather apps also offer real-time information, with radar images and weather data receiving continuous updates. The traffic reports offered by various map and navigation apps also make use of real-time data. A series of icons or colored lines indicate areas that are currently congested, allowing you to change your route before reaching the problem area.

CROWDSOURCING

Many of the companies that offer traffic data on your mobile device do not always use traditional sources such as news and police reports. Many turn to **crowdsourcing**, which is the gathering of information from a large group of people. Because many of us have location-based services on our devices, the speed of our cars can be used to determine areas where traffic is slow. In addition, apps such as Waze rely on users to report accidents, construction areas, and even gas prices. The more information that users provide, the better the app becomes for everyone.

The Waze navigation app combines location-based services, real-time data, and crowdsourcing.

MOBILE PAYMENTS

Your mobile device is now capable of becoming your digital wallet, freeing you from having to carry so many things with you at all times. Using a wireless technology known as **NFC** (near field communication), many smartphones can now be tapped on special payment devices to complete your purchase at select stores. All you need to do is save your bank or credit card information in an app such as Google Wallet. The payment device at the store will then process the transaction as if you had swiped your debit or credit card. Google Wallet can also store promotions and coupons electronically. The following are some additional ways in which mobile devices are making payments easier:

- **Sending money.** The apps of several banks now offer the capability to send anyone money, transferring a designated amount from your bank account to theirs.

- **Receiving payments.** For those who need to accept credit cards on a continuous basis, devices such as Square plug into your mobile device and allow customers to swipe their credit card like they would anywhere else. A companion app processes the payment and keeps track of all your transactions.

SOCIAL AND SHARING

For many individuals, the mobile device has become the primary tool for sharing events and

The Square credit card reader and mobile app turns a smartphone into a payment device.

communicating with friends and family. Many popular services and apps allow us to stay in touch with one another.

COMMUNICATION AND MESSAGING

Mobile communication is instantaneous: Individuals can send and receive information from others in real time. This allows mobile users to easily relay what they see and feel at the moment, as well as respond to questions quickly from wherever they are. Many users have messaging capabilities on their cell phones and smartphones that are offered by wireless providers. The **Short Message Service (SMS)** allows you to send text messages of 160 characters to any other cell phone user. The more versatile **Multimedia Messaging Service (MMS)** allows you to attach a variety of media such as photos and short videos.

There are new alternatives to these services on smartphones and tablets. Companies such as Google and Apple, along with many social media websites, offer messaging services that use your Internet connection. You no longer need to pay for a text messaging plan as long as all of the individuals that you communicate with install the same free messaging tool. Many of these services also offer free video calling capabilities that allow you to have video conversations with anyone in the world. You can message and talk as much as you wish using the following

Google's Hangouts app allows you to send messages, share photos, and make video calls.

apps, but be mindful of your data limits if you are not connecting via Wi-Fi.

- **Apple iMessage.** Exclusive to users of Apple's computers and mobile devices, this free service lets you send text messages, photos, and videos to any other user of this service.

- **WhatsApp.** Free for the first year, this messaging service has become very popular worldwide as the main substitute for SMS. Setup is easy, as it uses your current phone number and scans your contact list for other WhatsApp users. Text, photo, and video messaging are all available.

- **Videoconferencing tools.** If you prefer having a video conversation using your mobile device, several reliable services work on a variety of computers. Two of the most popular free tools are Skype and Google Hangouts, both of which provide complete messaging services in addition to video conversations. Apple offers a competing tool known as FaceTime that can be used exclusively by owners of Apple devices.

SOCIAL NETWORKING

Social networking services make it easy for friends and family to share updates and special events with each other. While messaging services target specific people, social networking allows users to post a message, photo, or video that can be viewed by anyone in their social circle. Some individuals even allow the general public to view some of their content.

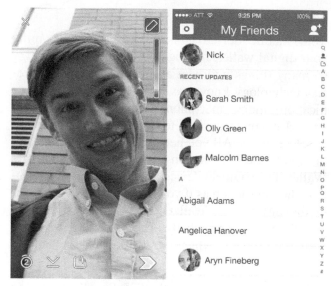

Snapchat users often share silly, casual, and private photos that are deleted after their receipt.

The following are some popular services that allow mobile users to share just about anything.

- **Full-featured social networking.** The largest social networks that offer a variety of features are Facebook and Google+. We will cover their features in more detail throughout Chapter 4.

- **Photo and video.** Instagram and Vine have become popular for making it easy to share photos and short videos with friends. Instagram also allows users to apply special effects to shared photos, adding excitement to this popular social activity.

- **Short-duration sharing.** The newcomer to the social networking market is Snapchat. This service allows users to send messages, photos, and videos to other individuals that are deleted within seconds of receipt. This has become popular for sending casual or humorous photos that users do not want to post permanently in a larger social network. It has also been the source of controversy as some individuals have used it to share illicit content. This issue, along with privacy concerns related to social networking, will be discussed in Chapter 6.

STREAMING MEDIA

Streaming media refers to music and movies that are delivered on demand from an online source. The streaming process allows you to begin enjoying your music and movies while they are still being transmitted. Although you can stream using a variety of

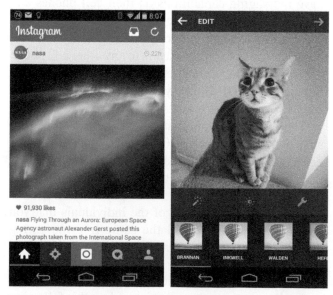

Instagram's app lets you edit photos and share them online.

devices at home, high-speed mobile networks now allow individuals to watch movies and listen to music from almost anywhere. The following are a few examples of these streaming services.

MUSIC

Mobile devices have become today's portable music players, allowing you to store and play back your purchased music files. However, if you are low on storage space or desire more variety, you should consider streaming music. There are two general ways in which to stream music. One way is to upload your purchased music files to a service that allows you to stream them back via an Internet connection. Google Play Music, Amazon Cloud Drive, and Apple iCloud are some examples of these "music locker" services. The more popular method is to subscribe to a service that offers a large collection of music. Some of these require a monthly paid subscription, while others are ad-supported. The following are examples of these services, broken down into two categories:

- **Personalized radio stations.** These services will deliver music based on your personal preferences. If you indicate which song or artist you like, they will play songs that are similar to your choice. Pandora is the most popular service in this category. Other companies, such as iHeartRadio, offer the ability to listen to thousands of actual radio stations in addition to your customized stations. Some companies, such as Songza, even use music experts (instead of automated systems) to develop playlists that match a variety of tastes, moods, and situations.

iHeartRadio allows you to listen to various radio stations or create your own based on any song or artist.

- **On-demand songs.** Instead of delivering songs that you are *likely* to enjoy, a variety of on-demand services offer you the ability to play any song you want. Companies such as Spotify offer instant access to millions of songs, allowing you to listen to whatever you want at any given moment.

MOVIES AND VIDEOS

Most individuals enjoy streaming videos and movies on their TVs. However, mobile devices are also becoming popular video and movie players, especially in areas such as airports where one might need extended entertainment. The following are a few examples of streaming video services.

- **Netflix** is by far the most popular service for streaming movies. For a low monthly fee, you can watch as many movies and shows as you desire from the company's large collection.

- **Hulu** specializes in TV shows, offering episodes that can be seen as early as the day after they air. The paid Hulu Plus service offers a large selection of TV episodes and streaming on just about every device.

- **YouTube.** The most popular video sharing site offers millions of videos that have been submitted by users. You can find a wide range of selections including music videos from your favorite artists or cooking videos that you can watch in your kitchen while preparing your next meal.

FITNESS & HEALTH

The sensors inside many mobile devices allow various apps to track your activity, such as counting the number of steps you take per day. In addition to mobile apps that make it easy to track your fitness and health, there are a variety of new devices that you can wear or use on the go.

Hulu Plus lets you stream current-season TV shows on your mobile devices.

FITNESS APPS

You can choose from various fitness apps based on your desired type and level of activity. Those that act as pedometers will count the number of steps that you take. Whether you run or walk, apps can help you keep track of your activity goals for each day. Other apps focus on providing instructions for those that use workout equipment such as machines and weights. Many apps offer cloud synchronization so that your fitness data over time is available wherever you need it. And if you need motivation and support, some apps will help you connect with your social network so that others can see your progress and cheer you on. Examples of these apps include:

- Accupedo
- RunKeeper
- Jefit

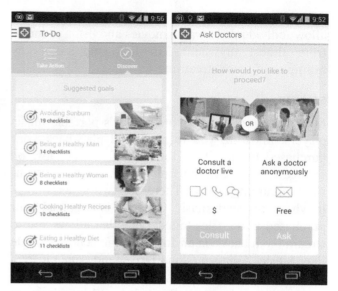

The HealthTap app offers health information and lets you connect with thousands of doctors.

HEALTH APPS

Health apps are often used to record and monitor information about your diet, vital signs, and medications. You can receive tips on improving your diet and health based on the information you enter daily. A few apps will even monitor your sleep by using the sensors in your device to measure how often you snore and move around. Many apps provide medical information at your fingertips including details on medications, symptoms, and how to treat a variety of conditions. Some even offer advice from actual physicians, allowing you to read answers to previously asked questions or engage in a virtual private consultation with a doctor for a small fee. Apps in this category include:

- HealthTap
- SleepBot
- Lose It!

FITNESS DEVICES

If you do not own a mobile device or do not want to bring it along on your daily run, you can still choose from a variety of wearable fitness devices. Some can be clipped onto your clothing while others are worn on the wrist. Like many fitness apps, these can measure the number of steps, distance traveled, and calories burned on a daily basis. Some, such as the Fitbit Flex, can even measure your sleep quality. Although many of these fitness devices offer websites and apps for tracking your activity, some can synchronize your data with existing fitness apps. Popular fitness devices include:

Accupedo (left) keeps track of your steps and calories burned, while SleepBot (right) monitors your sleep quality.

- Fitbit Flex
- Nike+ FuelBand

HEALTH DEVICES

Many are predicting an explosion of mobile health devices that help monitor your vital signs or make basic diagnoses. One such device, the Scanadu Scout, can measure multiple vital signs with a simple 10-second scan on your forehead. Your temperature, blood pressure, oxygen levels, and more will then be transferred to your mobile device for easy storage and tracking.

More **Online:** *Many of us sit in front of a computer for long periods and don't get enough physical activity. Visit the companion website for tips on health and fitness in a digital age.*

The Fitbit Flex wristband tracks your activity, calories burned, and sleep quality.

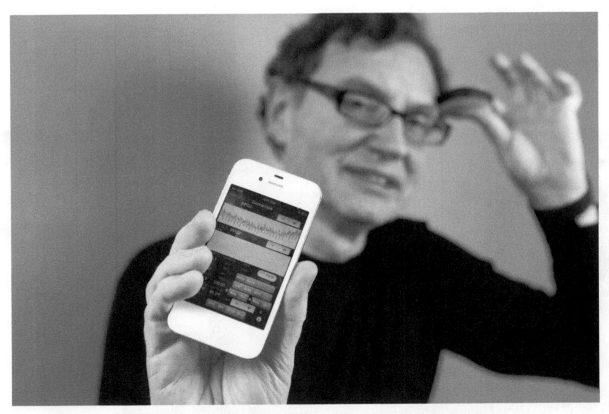

The Scanadu Scout is able to measure multiple vital signs with a simple 10-second scan.

Mobile Cloud Services

In the preface of this book, we discussed some useful cloud services that allow you to harness the power of the Internet to take notes and store schoolwork online. However, these services can do much more. For the mobile user, it means never having to experience the frustration of leaving a file at home or at work. In addition, these services allow anyone to take advantage of powerful online computers to complete a variety of activities from their mobile device. Although many applications and online services will be discussed in future chapters, the following sections will give you an idea of how cloud computing has transformed the way we access and create information.

ACCESS TO YOUR DATA

Many people confront the challenge of storing data that they can use in more than one place. For example, you might start working on a document at the office, but would like to finish it at home using your tablet. Perhaps you have music, photos, or other files on your home computer that you would like to access on your smartphone when you are away from home. All this is now possible through various **cloud storage** services, whereby your files can be stored online and accessed from any Internet-connected device. If you desire, these files can even be synchronized on all of your computers for offline access. The following services, which were discussed in the preface, all offer free apps on mobile devices and include several gigabytes of free storage.

- Dropbox
- Google Drive
- Microsoft OneDrive
- Apple iCloud

CLOUD APPLICATIONS

The preface also mentioned a few services that let you create a variety of notes and documents. These **cloud collaboration** tools allow individuals to view, edit, and share documents. These services help employees work on business documents, seeing each other's edits in real-time. They also allow families to share grocery lists, vacation documents, and much more. The following services are recommended:

- Evernote
- Google Docs
- Microsoft Office Online

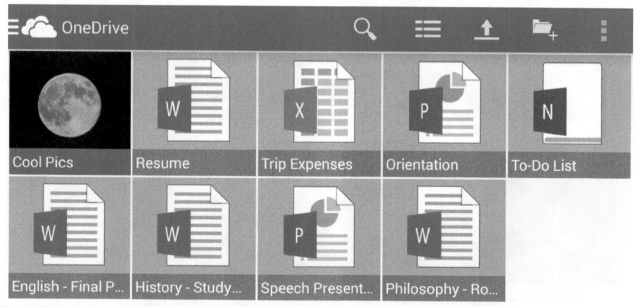

Microsoft OneDrive is a cloud service that allows you to create and store a variety of files online.

In addition to document creation, cloud computing has brought a variety of useful services to the mobile user. The following are just a few of these.

INSTANT TRANSLATION

Just a few years ago, you either needed to flip through a book or use expensive software to translate a foreign language. Today, services such as Google Translate can convert typed or spoken words into almost any foreign language. If you travel to another country, you can use this app to instantly translate what you hear into English words that appear on your screen.

INSTANT IDENTIFICATION

Another way to use the power of cloud computing is in photo identification. Google Goggles is a free mobile app that allows you to point your camera at just about anything—landmarks, artwork, and even bar codes—for the purpose of identifying what that object is. This is possible because of Google's large collection of images and its powerful computers. Once Google finds the object, it can help you find additional information on it or locate the stores that sell it.

> More **Online:** *Google's Goggles and Translate apps can transform the travelling experience. Visit the companion website for some tips on these and other useful travel apps.*

CLOUD GAMING

Mobile games have become extremely popular over the years. However, most of these games are installed and played on your device; they have nothing to do

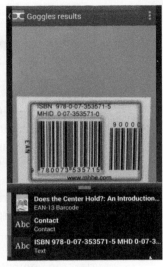

Google's Goggles app will identify almost anything you view with your camera, from artwork to a textbook's barcode.

with the cloud. Several companies, such as OnLive, are changing this by storing the games on their servers and allowing you to play over the cloud. Whether it is on your laptop or mobile device, all you need is the OnLive software to get started. After installing it, you can choose from hundreds of games that can be played using your Internet connection.

THE POWER OF THE CLOUD

These three services clearly demonstrate the power of cloud computing. Any user with a simple smartphone and an Internet connection can use the power of large computers to accomplish a variety of tasks. Cloud computing has truly transformed many aspects of our lives—and many argue this is just the beginning. We will continue discussing software and cloud services throughout the textbook.

KEY TERMS

all-in-one computer, 9
augmented reality, 15
blade server, 11
Bluetooth, 16
Chromebook, 10
cloud collaboration, 26
cloud computing, 8
cloud storage, 26
computer, 7
computer program, 7
convertible laptop, 10
crowdsourcing, 20
data, 7
desktop computer, 9
digital literacy, 4
electronic book, 11
e-book reader, 12
email, 8
embedded system, 11
gaming console, 12
hands-free computing, 16

hardware, 7
home automation, 13
information processing cycle, 7
input, 7
Internet, 8
laptop computer, 9
location-based service (LBS), 20
lock screen, 17
mainframe computer, 11
mobile device, 14
Multimedia Messaging Service (MMS), 21
multi-user computer, 10
netbook, 10
network, 8
network server, 11
NFC, 21
output, 7
personal computer (PC), 9
phablet, 15

processing, 7
real-time information, 20
remote wipe, 17
Short Message Service (SMS), 21
smart TV, 12
smartphone, 14
social media, 8
social networking, 22
software, 7
storage, 7
streaming media, 22
streaming player, 12
supercomputer, 11
tablet computer, 14
ultraportable computer, 10
wearable technology, 15
Wi-Fi, 8
wireless network, 8
World Wide Web (WWW), 8

Review Questions

MULTIPLE CHOICE

1. Someone who possesses _____ has a broad understanding of computer technology and is able to use it well.

 a. augmented reality
 b. data
 c. digital literacy
 d. real-time information

2. Which of the following are thin, lightweight laptops that possess strong processing power and are more expensive than typical laptops?

 a. Ultraportable computers
 b. Netbooks
 c. Blade servers
 d. All-in-one computers

3. Which of the following allows users to switch between a laptop and tablet experience?

 a. Netbook
 b. All-in-one computer
 c. Convertible laptop
 d. Phablet

4. Which types of computers are ideal for handling highly complex problems that require extreme calculating power?

 a. Network servers
 b. Supercomputers
 c. Desktop computers
 d. Embedded systems

Review Questions (continued)

5. Which of the following is an e-book reader?
 a. Chromebook
 b. Roku
 c. Samsung Galaxy Note
 d. Amazon Kindle

6. Which of the following is a popular streaming service that specializes in TV shows, especially those that have been aired recently?
 a. Yelp
 b. Twitter
 c. Netflix
 d. Hulu

7. The most popular _____ is the iPad from Apple.
 a. smartphone
 b. tablet
 c. ultraportable computer
 d. gaming console

8. The gathering of information from a large group of people is known as:
 a. real-time information
 b. location-based services
 c. crowdsourcing
 d. augmented reality

9. Because of a technology known as _____, many smartphones can now be tapped on special payment devices to complete a purchase at select stores.
 a. Bluetooth
 b. streaming
 c. MMS
 d. NFC

10. Which of the following is NOT a cloud storage service?
 a. OnLive
 b. Google Drive
 c. Dropbox
 d. Microsoft OneDrive

FILL IN THE BLANK

11. _____ computers are very large and powerful systems used in organizations where a heavy amount of processing and user requests need to be handled.

12. _____ consist of individual facts or pieces of information.

13. A(n) _____ is a combination mobile phone and handheld computer.

14. Although it is best to avoid any distractions when driving, _____ technology will at least let you keep your eyes on the road.

15. A(n) _____ allows users to communicate and share information between computers.

16. _____ computers are personal computers that have all of the hardware integrated with the monitor.

17. Many network servers come in the form of thin units known as _____ servers, which can slide in and out of a rack that holds many of its companion servers.

18. _____ allow various apps to recommend nearby restaurants or let you check-in at the establishment where you are currently located.

19. When using _____, your files can be stored online and accessed from any Internet-connected device.

20. Google's Glass provides a basic _____ experience, where the real world is supplemented with computer-generated information.

TRUE / FALSE

21. The physical devices that make up a computer system are known as software.

22. Chromebooks have very little internal storage, relying mainly on cloud storage.

23. If you do not have a smart TV, a streaming player can bring a variety of online services to your TV.

24. The app known as Spotify is used by small businesses to accept mobile payments.

25. Google Goggles is a service that will identify many of the objects and barcodes that you point your mobile device's camera at.

SHORT ANSWER

26. Name and define the four fundamental operations that all computers must be able to do.

27. List and briefly describe four ways in which computers are used in health care.

28. Describe four ways in which to automate your home.

29. List and briefly describe four ways in which computers are used by various parts of the government.

30. Describe at least three ways in which you can safeguard your mobile device and the information contained inside of it.

31. Name at least two apps that allow you to send messages to other users without the need to use your phone's SMS service.

32. Name at least two apps that allow you to upload photos and share them with your social networks.

33. List and briefly describe at least two apps that let you stream music.

34. List and briefly describe two apps and two devices that help you stay healthy and fit.

35. Name three services that allow you to create notes or documents online to collaborate with others.

Research Exercises

INSTRUCTIONS

Go beyond the book by performing research online to complete the exercises below.

1. Millions of individuals are "cutting the cord," cancelling their cable service in favor of streaming services such as Netflix and Hulu. What are some of the advantages of doing this? What are the disadvantages? Would you do it? Defend your answers and be sure to provide pricing evidence.

2. What sort of video surveillance products are available for individuals who wish to monitor their home using the Internet or a mobile device? Provide examples of solutions that are sold in stores as well as those that are installed by professional home security/alarm companies.

3. What are some of the advantages of using a Chromebook? What are some disadvantages? Would you buy one? Defend your answers.

Research Exercises (continued)

4. A variety of medical devices can be swallowed or implanted to treat various conditions. Name at least two of these and describe the technology behind them.

5. The dashboards in many modern cars are starting to look and feel like mobile devices. Find two cars from different automobile companies that have app-like interfaces and describe some of their features. How do they connect to the Internet? What type of hands-free services do they offer?

6. Google Glass is an extremely innovative technology, but it is raising some privacy concerns. What are these concerns? Do you agree with them? Defend your answers.

7. The U.S. military isn't the only organization using drones. Many local police departments have started to use them. What are some of their applications? Do you support their use over the United States? Would you be in favor of companies and individuals using drones? Defend your answers.

8. What is wireless charging? How does it work? Which devices can currently be charged using this technology (list three examples)? In the future, could an entire home be charged without wires or power cables?

2
HARDWARE

Chapter Overview

The various categories of computers share many fundamental components that allow them to process and store information, receive input, and deliver output. In this chapter, you will learn not just how computers work, but also how to choose the best devices to meet your personal or business needs.

PART 1:
Inside the Computer

As a user, you likely see computers as mere tools that help you accomplish a variety of tasks. Few people have the time to stop and wonder what makes these amazing machines work. The only time most people concern themselves with what is inside the computer is when something goes wrong.

Like any machine, a computer is a collection of parts. What may surprise you is that a personal computer has only about a dozen parts. Learning about these computer components and their basic functions will improve your ability to both purchase the right computer and understand the cause of various problems when they arise.

System Unit and Motherboard

We will begin our tour of the computer with the two parts that comprise the bulk of the machine: the system unit and the motherboard. Although all computers (even your smartphone) have circuit boards and some sort of outer shell/casing, we will be focusing on desktop computers for this section.

SYSTEM UNIT

The main component of a desktop computer is the **system unit**, which is the case that houses the

The system unit contains various internal devices.

computer's critical parts, such as the processing and storage devices. This part has historically been available in two forms: a horizontal desktop and a vertical tower. There are also all-in-one systems, such as the iMac, where the system unit is integrated with the monitor (screen).

Tower cases, which have been predominant for over a decade, are available in a variety of sizes, colors, and styles. Some have unique designs and colorful lighting that make them popular with gaming and multimedia enthusiasts.

If you were to purchase a system unit by itself, you would find that it is mostly empty on the inside. However, a few components either included or commonly purchased with the system unit are:

- **Drive bays.** Tower-based system units include several drive bays that hold the internal storage devices of your computer, such as the hard drive and the DVD drive.

- **Power supply.** This component is responsible for providing power to all the parts inside the system unit. When you plug a power cable into the back of your tower, you are essentially connecting it to the power supply. If you purchase a power supply separately, be sure to note the number of watts, which determines how many devices it can provide power to.

The system unit of all-in-one computers are integrated with the screen.

- **Cooling fans.** You may find one or more cooling fans responsible for cooling the inside of your computer. Many of the components inside a computer generate a great deal of heat. Without proper cooling, a computer could overheat and malfunction. Dust is an enemy of both electronic components and fans, so if necessary, use a can of compressed air to clean your computer periodically.

All parts of a computer connect to the motherboard.

MOTHERBOARD

The **motherboard** is the largest circuit board in a personal computer. It contains a variety of slots, connectors, and plugs for hooking up all the other parts of a computer, from the storage devices on the inside to the keyboard and monitor on the outside. All data travels through wires located throughout the motherboard's surface, and several **chipsets** act as traffic directors for all this data. Today's motherboards also contain specialized microchips that handle tasks such as video and sound output, as well as network communication. Nevertheless, some users may still choose to purchase add-on circuit boards known as **expansion cards** in order to improve the performance of their system's video or sound.

PORTS

At the back of your system unit, you will likely find a variety of plugs, or **ports**. These ports are typically part of the motherboard, located on the side that faces the back of the case. You may also find ports on the front of your system unit or on the sides of laptop computers. The most popular of these plugs

Ports are used to connect external devices.

is the small, rectangular **USB port**, which is used to connect almost all of today's external devices. This port has undergone a variety of improvements over the years (current version is 3.0) to increase the speed at which information can be transferred to external storage devices. Although the USB port is the most predominant, we will be looking at other specialty ports in upcoming sections of this chapter.

CPU and Memory

Most of the "action" inside any computer occurs between the main processor and the various types of memory. These components are the primary factors in the overall speed and performance of your computer.

CPU

The **central processing unit (CPU)**, or microprocessor, is the main processor of a computer. It is responsible for organizing and carrying out instructions to produce a desired output. It can perform a diverse number of operations, from finding a name in your smartphone's contacts to handling the complex calculations required by today's engineers. For this reason, it is often nicknamed "the brain" of the computer.

The CPU is plugged into a special socket on the computer's motherboard. Because modern CPUs generate a great deal of heat when they operate, they require their own cooling units. These consist of large blocks of heat-conducting metal that are pressed

tightly against the CPU and cooling fans to whisk the heat from the metal. All this makes the CPU look like a very large unit inside your computer, yet the chip itself is just a thin wafer that is a fraction of an inch across.

When you shop for a new computer, the CPU will often be one of the first components listed in the specifications. Because it has such an impact on performance, you are likely to see several pieces of information about the processor. Here are a few:

- **Brand and model.** Intel and AMD dominate the market for desktop and laptop computers. Next to these manufacturers' names you will find a series and model, such as Intel's i7-3630QM or AMD's A8-4500M. Don't let all of this intimidate you. It is no different from understanding the various models of a car, such as BMW's X5 xDRIVE35i. For mobile devices, you will find companies such as Apple, Qualcomm, and Texas Instruments producing ARM-based processors. These types of chips generally produce less heat and use less power—characteristics that are crucial for mobile devices.

- **Multiple cores.** Most of today's microprocessors have several processors, or **cores**, inside a single chip. A dual-core processor can be twice as efficient as a traditional processor, given that it can handle twice the work at any given moment. Many of today's processors have more than two cores, with four, six, and even eight becoming common.

- **Clock rate.** A CPU's **clock rate** measures the frequency or speed at which it can process instructions. This speed is measured in *hertz,* which is equal to one instruction cycle per second. Today's processors have reached the

The processor model, such as this Intel Core i3, is often featured prominently on a computer.

gigahertz (GHz) mark, capable of processing billions of instructions per second. Although looking at the number of gigahertz is a tempting way to compare two computers or processors, it isn't always that easy. Since various factors can affect overall speed, experts depend on a series of performance tests known as benchmarks to compare processors.

The CPU is the green square at the bottom center, inserted into a socket on the motherboard.

More **Online:** Visit the companion website to learn more about various benchmarks and how they can help you decide between two different devices.

MEMORY

In a computer, **memory** is a general term for electronic chips that store data and program instructions that can be accessed quickly by the CPU. Many users confuse memory and storage, especially now that we have storage devices called "memory cards." This will all be cleared up in the next few pages as we contrast

the various memory and storage technologies. In this section, we will be exploring several types of memory used in personal computers, starting with the one you are likely familiar with already: RAM.

RAM

The most noticeable type of memory for a user is the temporary workspace known as **random access memory (RAM)**. Whenever you actively work on something using your computer, that work is temporarily stored in RAM. For example, right now you may have a résumé or school paper that is stored somewhere on your computer. When you open this document in Microsoft Word to work on it, both the Word program and the document will be copied into RAM. When you save the document and close Word, it is removed from RAM but remains safe on a storage device (see Figure 2.1).

RAM is considered to be volatile because its contents change often and will disappear if the computer loses power or is restarted. This is one of the fundamental differences between this temporary memory and your more permanent storage devices such as hard drives, DVDs, and SD cards. Let us now turn to a few details you should know about RAM:

- **Memory modules.** RAM consists of a set of chips mounted on a small circuit board called a memory module. These modules are then inserted into special slots on the motherboard. This is important to know when purchasing a computer as the number of available slots can affect your ability to add more RAM. Computers typically have anywhere from one to four slots.

RAM modules are inserted into slots on the motherboard.

- **Type and speed.** There are a large variety of RAM types and speeds. Consider the following example: DDR3 1333. The first part, *DDR3,* indicates the type of RAM. The *1333* represents the speed at which it can transmit data to the CPU. The main reason to know these details is to ensure that you purchase the correct RAM if you are planning on upgrading your computer.

- **Capacity.** Each RAM module can hold a specific amount of information, typically one to eight gigabytes. The higher your overall capacity, the more programs and files you can open and work on at once. This allows you to have a fast and smooth experience when switching from one program or browser tab to another.

OTHER TYPES OF MEMORY

Although RAM is the most popular type of memory, a modern computer would not function properly without a few other types of memory.

- **Read-only memory (ROM)** is a small chip that contains device-specific information. The instructions on this chip are known as **firmware**, and they handle a computer's basic functions when it is powered on. On PCs, these instructions are commonly known as the *BIOS*. Currently, the "read-only" portion is a bit misleading, as most of these chips can be electronically reprogrammed via a process called *flashing*. This allows for a variety of activities, from receiving an important update from your computer manufacturer to installing a customized operating system on Android mobile devices.

- **Cache** refers to a form of high-speed memory that stores a small, frequently used set of instructions and data. It is located inside modern CPUs.

A document is copied from the hard drive (storage) to RAM (memory) when you open it.

The document is removed from RAM and sent back to the hard drive when you save and close it.

Figure 2.1 How RAM Works.

- **Virtual memory** is not actual memory, but rather a portion of your hard drive that is being used as RAM. Your operating system uses this tactic when your opened programs and files do not fit into RAM. It takes portions of them and, without you noticing, moves them onto your hard drive. The only time you may be aware of it is when you experience a tiny delay in switching from one open program to another that had been temporarily placed in virtual memory. This is because accessing RAM is much faster for a computer than accessing your storage devices.

More **Online:** *Both PCs and Macs have a tool that lets you see how much RAM and CPU your open programs are currently using. Visit the companion website to learn more about these tools.*

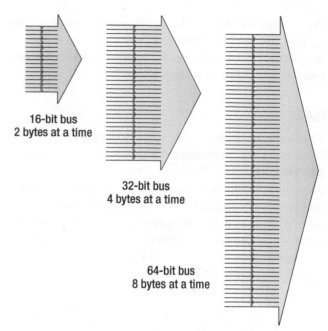

16-bit bus
2 bytes at a time

32-bit bus
4 bytes at a time

64-bit bus
8 bytes at a time

Wires (buses) carry electrical signals known as bits. Eight bits are equal to one byte.

Storage

As you have already learned, the purpose of storage is to hold programs and data permanently, even when the computer is turned off. The devices that can read, write, and erase data are called **drives**. The physical locations where things are stored are known as storage **media**. For example, your DVD discs are known as storage media, while the device that you insert them into is the drive. Let us now explore all of the various storage devices used by modern computers, as well as the units of measurement that describe their capacity.

STORAGE UNITS

The most fundamental unit of computing is the **bit**, which is typically represented as an *on* (1) or *off* (0) value. This is because digital, electrical devices can truly only "understand" the concept of being on or

off. Consider for a moment that you are a wire (or *bus*) on a circuit board. Essentially, all that could possibly make sense to you is that there is electricity flowing through you at a given moment or that there isn't. It is the sequence or order of these bits that is interpreted and processed into meaningful information. Many storage devices also use this 0 and 1 system to remember all types of information, from letters to colors.

When it comes to describing a computer's storage or memory, we commonly use the unit known as the **byte**, which is simply a collection of eight bits. The eight is significant because it is the amount of space required to store a single character, such as a letter or number. In modern computing, the size of our files and programs are so large that it is helpful to use terms such as kilobyte (KB), megabyte (MB), gigabyte (GB), and terabyte (TB) to describe the

TABLE 2.1 MEMORY AND STORAGE UNITS

Unit	Approximate Value	Actual Value (bytes)
Kilobyte (KB)	1,000 Bytes	1,024
Megabyte (MB)	1,000 KB	1,048,576
Gigabyte (GB)	1,000 MB	1,073,741,824
Terabyte (TB)	1,000 GB	1,099,511,627,776

values (see Table 2.1). In a world dominated by computers, it is crucial that you memorize these storage units much like you did inches and feet when you were young.

MAGNETIC STORAGE

In the 1940s, when electronic computers were beginning to appear, researchers realized that a computer would not be able to remember or store anything if it relied solely on electrical components. With a loss of power, every component would lose its charge and all data would be lost. The development of magnetic storage allowed data to be represented by magnets, which can hold their position or pattern to represent 0's and 1's without electricity. The following are some examples of magnetic storage devices:

- The **hard drive** (also known as the hard disk), is the primary storage device of a personal computer. While most use magnetic disks, some may use solid state technology, which will be discussed later in this section. Practically all desktop and laptop computers have an internal hard drive. You can also buy an external hard drive to store additional information or make copies of your irreplaceable data. These external drives are very portable and typically connect to the USB port

Inside the hard drive are a stack of disks and a magnetic read/write head.

on a computer. Both types of hard drives are currently capable of storing a few terabytes of data.

- **Tape drives**, which use magnetic tape to store data, are popular for organizations that have large quantities of information to back up or archive. You might find these drives organized into giant tape libraries that can hold thousands of terabytes of archived information.

OPTICAL STORAGE

In addition to the hard drive, most personal computers sold today include at least one form of optical storage. These devices use lasers to read data from or write data to the reflective surface of an optical disc. Bits are represented by changing the reflectivity of small areas on the disc.

TYPES OF OPTICAL DISCS

The primary difference between the various optical discs is the amount of data that they can store. Over the years, researchers have been able to increase the capacity of optical discs while keeping their physical size the same. This allows you to insert old discs, such as CDs, in the newer DVD or Blu-ray drives. You are likely familiar with many of the following optical discs:

- **Compact discs (CDs)** are capable of storing up to 700 MB of data. Although most commercial music is still sold as CDs, this type of disc is not used much in today's computers.

- **Digital versatile discs (DVDs)** can store either 4.7 or 8.5 GB of data. The larger amount is possible because DVDs allow data to be recorded on two layers within the disc. Most of today's software and standard-definition movies are sold as DVDs.

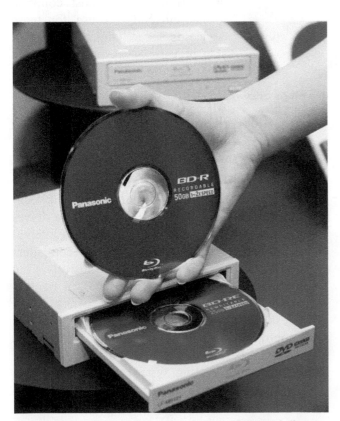

The Blu-ray drive reads various types of optical discs.

- The latest optical technology is the **Blu-ray disc (BD)**, which typically stores 25 or 50 GB of data. This is enough to hold an entire high-definition movie, as well as the video games used in the newest PlayStation and Xbox consoles. A new type of disc, the BD-XL, can store over 100 GB of data by using three or four layers per disc.

RECORDING TECHNOLOGY

All three types of discs, along with the drives they are inserted into, have a series of designations that let you know about their read, write, and erase capabilities. If you see the word ROM after any of them, it means they are read only. A designation of −R or +R means the blank disc can only be recorded to once. However, the initials −RW, +RW, or −RE indicate that the disc can be recorded and erased. The process of recording to a blank disc is known as *burning*.

SOLID STATE STORAGE

The future of data storage may well be solid state storage, which relies on a special kind of flash memory chip to permanently store data. Since this technology uses memory chips for storage, it has no moving parts like hard drives or optical drives. Consequently, the devices can perform read, write, and erase operations at much quicker speeds. Their lack of mechanical parts also results in a much smaller size and less power consumption, which makes them ideal for ultraportable computers, mobile devices, and a variety of gadgets. Although this type of storage is the most expensive (cost per gigabyte), prices are falling at a quick

A USB flash drive plugs into a USB port.

This smartphone has a slot for a micro SD card.

Solid state memory cards come in a variety of sizes.

pace while storage capacities increase to hundreds of gigabytes. The following devices use this new type of technology:

- A **USB flash drive** is the small storage stick that plugs into a USB port. You have likely used one of these to transfer files between computers or store copies of important files.

- The tiny and flat **memory cards** are used to store data in tablets, smartphones, and devices such as digital cameras and digital photo frames. The most common format currently in use for these devices is Secure Digital (SD), available in various speeds and storage capacities. Smaller versions of SD are known as mini and micro SD. All of these cards can be easily removed from a device and inserted into a memory card reader, which is usually a small slot on your computer or printer.

- Many hard drives now use flash memory instead of the more traditional magnetic technology. These are known as **solid state drives (SSDs)**, and they can be found as both internal and external drives. Ultraportable computers will often use this technology exclusively, even though the storage capacity is only a fraction of what a traditional hard drive offers. Many desktop and laptop computers use a different approach, whereby they include a large traditional hard drive and a small SSD that only stores the operating system. This allows Windows, for example, to load and operate much faster than if it ran off a magnetic hard drive.

PART 2:
Input and Output

As you remember from Chapter 1, input refers to user entries or activities that tell the computer what to do, while output refers to the processed data that a computer sends out. Input and output devices are evolving in variety and sophistication just as rapidly as the computer itself. In this section, you'll explore some of these devices.

Input

Computers are data processing marvels, but they first need to receive information from the outside world. Sights, sounds, words, and commands are received by input devices and then converted into a digital format that can be processed by the computer. In this section, you will explore the latest versions of input devices that help computers gather information from a variety of sources.

THE KEYBOARD

For most individuals, the keyboard is still the primary input device for entering text and numbers. Nearly all computers come with some sort of keyboard. Your desktop computer likely came with a wired keyboard that is connected via a USB cable. Laptop computers have an integrated keyboard, while tablets and smartphones include a touchscreen keyboard. Alternative keyboards include:

Ergonomic keyboards are designed to ease the strain of typing for long periods.

This wireless keyboard also functions as a protective cover for the tablet.

- **Wireless keyboards.** These keyboards do not require a physical connection and can communicate with your computer via Bluetooth wireless technology. These keyboards come in a variety of sizes and can connect to all types of computers, from desktops and smart TVs to a wide range of mobile devices.

- **Ergonomic keyboards.** Individuals who type for extended periods often suffer from hand and wrist strain. **Ergonomic keyboards**, which are designed to be comfortable and tailored for the human body, have angled keys and a palm rest at the base to keep your wrists straight.

- **Keyboard covers.** These keyboards snap directly onto a tablet and can serve as a protective cover as well. They are very thin and can communicate with your tablet via wireless technology. They are very useful to those that type extensively on this mobile device.

CATEGORIES OF KEYS

The quantity, types, and location of keys vary greatly among keyboards. The traditional, 104-key arrangement for Windows-based desktops is different from the ones used with Macs, laptop computers, and mobile devices. This section will explore the most common categories of keys used today.

- **Alphanumeric keys.** These refer to the main set of keys that allow you to input letters, numbers, and punctuation. The most common arrangement of these keys is referred to as the QWERTY (pronounced KWER-tee) layout because of the first six letters near the top left.

- **Modifier keys.** These keys, such as SHIFT, modify the input of other keys when held down. The CTRL, ALT, FN, and WINDOWS keys are commonly used for **keyboard shortcuts**, which are keystrokes that can quickly perform an operation within software. Mac computers have similar keys, which are labeled as CONTROL, OPTION, and COMMAND.

Mac wireless keyboard.

More **Online:** Visit the companion website to learn a variety of keyboard shortcuts for Windows and Mac.

- **Function keys.** These keys, which are labeled F1, F2, and so on, are used to perform an action within a program. Each function key's purpose depends on the program you are using. For example, in many programs, F1 is the help key.
- **Cursor control keys.** These navigation keys, such as the four arrows near the bottom right, let you move around the screen without using a mouse. In many programs that display what you type, a mark on the screen indicates where the characters you type will be entered. This mark, called the **cursor** (or insertion point), appears on the screen as a blinking vertical line, a small box, or some other symbol to show your place in a document or command line.
- **Numeric keypad.** This area is very useful for numeric entry and calculations, as it contains the numbers 0 to 9 and four basic mathematical operators (+, −, *, and /). The numeric keypad is typically located on the right side of a standard desktop keyboard or larger laptop computers. It is often absent on computers with smaller keyboards.

Common categories of keys on a PC (Windows) keyboard.

POINTING DEVICES

As a user, you interact with most computer software via an on-screen pointer, which is typically in the form of an arrow. Several types of pointing devices can be used to move the pointer and issue commands at the pointer's location. Commands are issued by using the following basic operations:

- **Clicking.** Pressing and releasing the left mouse button. This is often used to select an object or option on the screen.

- **Double-clicking.** Pressing and releasing the left mouse button twice in rapid succession. This is typically done to desktop icons.

- **Right-clicking.** Pressing and releasing the right mouse button. In Windows, this operation will bring up a shortcut menu.

- **Dragging.** Holding down a button while moving the mouse. This is usually used to move objects.

- **Scrolling.** Most pointing devices have a scroll wheel, which can be used to scroll, or move, information up or down on your screen.

- **Gestures.** Many new devices support the use of various **gestures**, or finger movements, to accomplish various tasks. For example, bringing your thumb and index together in a pinching motion can be used to zoom in and out.

Optical mouse (left) and trackball (right) are both similar pointing devices.

MOUSE

The **optical mouse** is the most common pointing device for desktop computers. For PCs, an optical mouse will include a left and right button, a scroll wheel in the middle, and a light-emitting mechanism at the bottom to sense movement. Some mice include additional, programmable buttons, while others allow special gestures to be performed directly on their curved surface. Like keyboards, a mouse can be connected using a USB cable or via wireless technology.

TRACKBALL

A **trackball** is a pointing device that works like an upside-down mouse. You rest your index finger or thumb on an exposed ball, then place your other fingers on the buttons. To move the pointer around the screen, you roll the ball with your finger. Because you move this ball and not the whole device, a trackball requires less space than a mouse.

TOUCHPAD

The **touchpad** is a stationary, rectangular pointing surface that is typically found on laptop computers. The movement of a finger across the small, touch-sensitive surface is translated into pointer movement on the screen. Touchpads sometimes include two buttons that perform the same functions as mouse buttons. However, most touchpads now support various types of taps and gestures on their surface that can accomplish much more than the two traditional buttons.

Laptop touchpads support various types of taps and gestures.

TOUCHSCREEN TECHNOLOGY

Touchscreens accept input by allowing the user to place a fingertip directly on the computer screen. Your fingers can be used to perform a variety of taps and gestures to accomplish different tasks. This technology has become the primary way in which we interact with our tablets and smartphones. In addition, many newer laptop computers are including touchscreens to take advantage of the Windows 8 tiled interface. You will also find these monitors in many types of businesses where a simple interface is important, such as restaurants, retail stores, and ticketing kiosks.

Most of today's devices use *capacitive* touchscreens, which means that they detect the position of your finger by detecting the electrical current present in your body. This is why you cannot use most of these devices when you are wearing gloves. Alternatively, some monitors use *resistive* touchscreens, which detect the pressure of your touch. These work well in restaurants or outdoor environments where dirt and liquids would create problems for other types of input devices.

An airport check-in kiosk uses a touchscreen interface.

STYLUS

A **stylus** is a pen-like input tool that is used with a variety of touchscreen devices. You may have used one of these when signing for a delivered package or when paying for goods at many retail stores. Some tablets and smartphones come with a stylus that can be used for input or writing notes and annotations by hand. If desired, these devices can then use handwriting recognition to convert what you wrote into typewritten text.

Artists who draw images on a computer often use a stylus in conjunction with special **graphics tablets**, which offer extra-sensitive touch surfaces that translate an artist's motions into drawings on the computer screen. These styluses often have a variety of special features, such as the ability to erase parts of the drawing when used upside-down.

A stylus can be used on a graphics tablet.

SCANNERS

Computers may never see in the same way that humans do, but optical technologies allow computers to use light as a source of input. A **scanner** is a device that uses optical technology to convert objects that it analyzes into a digital format. Various types of scanners are used for homes and businesses:

- **Document scanners.** These scanners specialize in scanning large quantities of documents in a short amount of time. They can usually hold and process dozens of papers per minute. Businesses will often use them to go "paperless" by converting long, physical documents (such as contracts or medical records) into a digital format stored in the computer. Once scanned, a technology known as **optical character recognition (OCR)** can translate the document image into text that can be edited and formatted.

- **Flatbed scanners.** These scanners have a glass surface that allows you to scan almost any object, from a page in a textbook to an old photo album. Many of these scanners now include a **document feeder**, which is a tray that allows you to scan several sheets of paper automatically. These types of scanners are often integrated into multifunction printers (see page 53).

Handheld barcode scanner.

QR code.

- **Barcode scanners.** These scanners are used to scan the barcode labels that uniquely identify most products sold today. They are used by many businesses to maintain inventory, track packages, or speed up the purchasing process for customers. Some of these scanners are handheld while others, such as those in many grocery stores, are flatbed models.

There are other types of product codes that do not use the traditional black bars. One of these, called **QR codes**, appears as a square filled with dots and lines. One of the most popular uses for these codes is to direct a smartphone to open a specific web address by simply pointing its camera at it.

Document scanner.

Flatbed scanner.

- **RFID scanners.** An **RFID tag** is a tiny chip or label that contains electronically stored data. Special RFID scanners use radio frequencies to read the data stored in these tags. Although a bit more expensive than paper-based barcodes, RFID tags can be scanned from longer distances and at higher speeds. For example, many of the automated toll collection systems in use today allow scanners installed throughout a highway to read the RFID tag inside vehicles. The tag stores a unique account number that allows the government's computers to find the driver's account and deduct the appropriate toll payment. RFID has many other applications that range from inventory control at large facilities to implantable chips that help identify the owner of a lost pet. It is worth noting that RFID tags are not GPS devices, and cannot therefore be used for tracking movement or location.

- **Scanner apps.** These software-based scanners use the camera on a mobile device to perform the scan. Because tablet and smartphone cameras have become very sharp, these apps can produce very clear scans of your documents. This allows you to input important documents and receipts into your mobile device in widely used formats such as Adobe PDF.

MULTIMEDIA INPUT

Practically all of today's computers are equipped with complete **multimedia** capabilities, which means that they can input and output sound, music, images, and

This tiny RFID tag can be implanted under the skin.

video. Let's take a look at the input devices that make this possible.

MICROPHONE

While desktop computers typically require a separate, physical microphone or headset, most laptop and mobile computers have one that is built-in. Common uses for microphones include Internet voice calling and capturing the audio portion of a video recording or conversation. A capability that is receiving increased attention is **speech recognition**, which is a computer's ability to recognize human speech. Using fast processors, sophisticated software, and an incredibly large volume of data, computers have become quite accurate in detecting exactly what we are saying. Two of the most popular speech recognition programs, Apple's Siri and Google's Search app, are enabling individuals to use their voice, rather than a keyboard, to issue commands and search for information on their mobile devices. Various professionals, such as doctors, are also using speech recognition to dictate information in locations or environments where typing on a keyboard would be difficult or obtrusive.

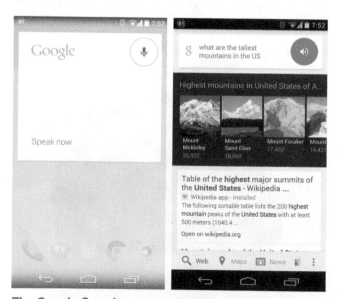

The Google Search app uses speech recognition.

More **Online:** Are you using all the capabilities of speech recognition on your mobile device? Visit the companion website to learn more about voice commands and searches.

DIGITAL CAMERA

Digital cameras are portable devices that electronically capture and store still images and video. They come in all shapes and sizes, from ultra-slim models that fit in your pocket to larger DSLR cameras that capture professional-quality images. In addition, most mobile devices now include one or two integrated cameras. They have become so sophisticated in the last few years, many individuals use their smartphone or tablet as their primary camera. Just be aware that the camera in the front of your mobile device will capture images at a lower quality than the one in the back.

Most digital cameras can store hundreds or thousands of high-resolution images. This depends on both the size of the storage media used and the number of **megapixels** used for the photo. Higher megapixel cameras can capture more detail, but they will produce a larger image file on your storage media. If you are running low on storage space in your local or cloud storage account, you can try taking photos with fewer megapixels or use an application that can reduce the size of your photos.

VIDEO CAMERAS

As you have already learned, digital cameras can capture video in addition to still images. You will also find video input capabilities in the cameras that are integrated into many laptop computers, tablets, and smartphones. For those who want to capture video on their desktop computers, a **webcam** is an affordable solution. This small video camera, which is typically attached to your monitor, is commonly used for online

Digital SLR cameras are used by those who desire the highest photo quality.

video chats or conversations. Businesses often use more sophisticated versions of webcams to engage in **videoconferencing**, where multiple individuals hold meetings and converse using internal networks or the Internet.

Some video cameras are used by homes and businesses for security and surveillance. If they are connected to a computer with Internet access, video can be recorded and even viewed from a remote location. Other video cameras, commonly known as camcorders, allow individuals and professionals to record high-quality video that can be played or edited on a computer. These cameras usually possess large viewing screens and excellent zoom capabilities. Recently, many gaming consoles have started to include video cameras that can capture the body's movement and even detect facial expressions.

TV TUNERS

A **TV tuner** is a device that can capture television signals for viewing on a computer. Some TV tuners are in the form of internal cards for your desktop computer, while others are small, external USB devices. They usually have a coaxial port where you connect a cable from your home's antenna or a cable box. Many individuals are using TV tuners as **digital video recorders (DVR)** to record television shows for future playback. Although many cable companies include DVR capabilities with their cable boxes, individuals who do not have cable subscriptions can still

Videoconferencing uses sophisticated versions of webcams.

record local television stations in HD by using affordable antennas and TV tuners.

OTHER INPUT DEVICES

Individuals and businesses use countless specialty devices to get information into a computer. These range from music instruments and mixers that can help musicians produce and edit songs digitally to ultrasound devices that help medical professionals see what is going on inside your body. This section will focus on just a few widely used input devices that fall into their own category.

GAME CONTROLLERS

Whether you are playing games on a computer or a gaming console, you will often use a **game controller** as your primary input device. Most modern controllers are small, wireless devices designed to be held with both hands. They provide an array of buttons, which perform a variety of functions, and analog sticks that are used for movement. Some even include internal sensors that can detect subtle movements of the device. With the Nintendo Wii, for example, a swinging motion with the controller in your hand can simulate the swing of a golf club or tennis racket. As previously mentioned, many gaming consoles now

Xbox One works with a game controller and Kinect video camera.

combine controllers and video cameras to make your entire body into a source of input.

BIOMETRICS

Biometrics refers to the measurement of patterns or characteristics found in the human body. Various biometric input devices are now being used to authenticate, or identify, an individual when accessing a device. For most people, this technology is much more convenient than remembering a password or carrying an identification card.

- **Fingerprint scanners** detect the unique patterns and swirls of an individual's finger. These scanners are now integrated with many portable computers so that users can log in with a quick press or swipe of their finger.

- **Facial recognition** is a biometric technology that looks for unique measurements in an individual's face. Mobile users can often gain access to their device by looking into the front-facing camera. In secure areas, such as airports, cameras can scan many individuals at one time and sophisticated software can detect if one of those individuals is present in a criminal or terrorist database.

Other parts of the body are increasingly being used for identification. These include the colored part of the eyes (iris), the particular geometry of the hand, and even the unique pattern of your DNA. While many have raised legitimate concerns about biometrics and privacy, it is important to remember that most consumer and business systems only record measurements and do not actually store photos of your fingerprints, for example.

The Face Unlock feature for Android smartphones is an example of biometrics.

Output

One of the most critical things a computer can do is to provide a solution or an answer. We give computers input because we want a result, or output. In this section, we will explore the latest versions of output devices that help computers produce audio, visual, and physical information.

MONITORS

The monitor is an electronic display device, or screen, used to output text and graphics to the user. The earliest monitors could only display black and one other color, such as green or amber. Today's monitors display 16.7 million colors. Two important hardware devices determine the quality of the image you see on any monitor: the monitor itself and the video controller. Both will be explored in this section.

MONITOR TERMINOLOGY

To fully understand the different types of monitors, it is necessary to review basic display terminology. In addition, these terms will help you make a better decision when shopping for a new device.

- **Pixels.** A monitor's screen is divided into millions of tiny dots, called **pixels**. Each pixel has a unique address, which the computer uses to locate the pixel and control its appearance.

- **Size.** The size of a monitor is measured in diagonal inches. As a general rule, buy the largest monitor that fits your budget and your workspace.

- The **resolution** of a monitor refers to the number of pixels that it can display on the screen. A monitor with a maximum resolution of

2560 pixels
1440 pixels

A monitor's resolution is the number of pixels that can fit horizontally and vertically on the screen.

1920x1080 will display up to 1,920 pixels in each row (horizontally) and up to 1,080 pixels in each column (vertically). Although a higher resolution will produce a sharper image, screen elements will appear to shrink because of these tightly packed pixels. Your operating system will allow you to set an ideal resolution for both your monitor and your eyes.

- The **response time** of a monitor is the amount of time (in milliseconds) that it takes for a pixel to change from black to white. Lower values are ideal for the smooth display of fast-moving images, such as those in video games.

- The **contrast ratio** of a monitor measures how close the monitor can get to the brightest white and the darkest black. This ratio will be represented with two numbers, such as 1000:1. Monitors with a larger ratio will produce higher-quality images. Manufacturers can list figures for either the static (still images) contrast ratio or the dynamic (moving images) contrast ratio.

- **Viewing angle.** Most monitors produce the best picture when viewed from a position near the center of the screen. However, many monitors will promote their large viewing angles, which indicate how far to the sides a user can be before the picture fades or blurs.

Darker Black — Brighter White

The monitor on the right has a higher contrast ratio, resulting in a darker (deeper) black and a brighter white.

Flat-planel displays

CRT monitor

Flat-panel monitors have replaced the older CRT monitors.

TYPES OF MONITORS

Most monitors today are flat-panel monitors. They are thin, lightweight, and energy efficient. The older **CRT monitors**, which were large and bulky because they used cathode-ray tube (CRT) technology, are rarely used today. The two common types of flat-panel monitors are described below.

- **LCD.** An **LCD (liquid crystal display) monitor** contains a light source and a screen of special crystals placed in the monitor between the user and the light source. By default, the crystals do not allow light to shine through them; however, the crystals shift when electricity is applied to them, allowing light to pass through. By switching on specific pixels of crystals, patterns can be drawn on the monitor. LCD monitors use transistors to control the display of each pixel on the screen.

- **LED.** This newer technology, which also uses liquid crystals, changes the way LCD monitors are illuminated. **LED monitors** are lit by a grid of tiny electronic lights called light emitting diodes (LEDs). These lights respond to an electric current, and replace the standard backlight technology of traditional LCD monitors. This allows LED monitors to be thinner, lighter, and more energy-efficient. In addition, they tend to have better contrast ratios, response times, and viewing angles. Most monitors and mobile devices today use LED.

More **Online:** *Did you know that the improper use of monitors may cause eye and neck strain? Visit the companion website to learn how to prevent discomfort and injuries related to computer use.*

High-end video cards are purchased by individuals who use graphics-intensive software.

VIDEO CARDS

The quality of the images that a monitor can display is defined as much by the **video card** (or graphics card) as by the monitor itself. The video card is an intermediary device between the CPU and the monitor. It contains a processor, video-dedicated memory, and other circuitry necessary to process and send information to the monitor. In many newer computers, the video circuitry is built directly into the motherboard, eliminating the need for a separate card.

- The **graphics processing unit (GPU)** is the video card's microprocessor. The speed and

quality of this chip, along with the RAM on the card, determines the relative power of the video card. Various applications are so graphics-intensive that they require a great deal of dedicated memory and processing power. Therefore, many individuals in the video industry, as well as those who enjoy the latest, graphics-intensive games, will shop for high-end (and expensive) video cards that have the best GPUs on them. NVIDIA and AMD are popular GPU manufacturers.

- **Connectors.** Video cards can include various types of connectors for your monitor or TV. The oldest of these is the VGA (or D-sub) connector, which contains 15 pins arranged in three rows. After this came the DVI connector, which became the standard for digital video on most computers and monitors. The newest connector is HDMI, which carries both digital video and sound. Although HDMI connectors are available on many monitors, you may be more familiar with them in HDTVs.

SOUND SYSTEMS

Today, nearly any new computer includes a complete sound system, with a microphone, speakers, and a sound card or processor. Sound systems are especially useful to people who use their computer to create or use multimedia products, watch videos, listen to music, engage in videoconferencing, or participate in online activities.

SPEAKERS

Speakers are included on practically all of today's computers. They can range from tiny ones that are integrated with your monitor or mobile device, to

A sound card offers several connectors for surround-sound speakers.

full surround-sound systems that include a variety of speakers and subwoofers. Many computer users prefer listening to audio through headphones or a headset, rather than using speakers. Most systems include a convenient jack to accept a headset plug.

SOUND CARD

A computer's **sound card** is a circuit board that converts sound from analog to digital form, and vice versa, for recording or playback. Analog signals, such as those from your voice, are accepted from a microphone and converted into digital data for the computer to process. Inside the computer, digital data representing music can be sent to the sound card and converted to electrical current that speakers can play. Similar to video cards, many new computers provide a sound subsystem directly on the motherboard and do not require a separate sound card for audio output. Separate sound cards are primarily used in computers by users who require specialized or premium sound output.

With the appropriate software, you can do much more than simply record and play back digitized sound. Sound editing programs provide a miniature sound studio, allowing you to create, mix, and edit everything from today's electronic music to complex multi-instrumental symphonies.

PRINTERS

Over the past decade, the variety of available printing devices has exploded, serving the needs of the average home and office user, as well as those of the publishing and manufacturing industries. Choosing

A surround-sound speaker system includes speakers and a subwoofer.

the right printer requires knowledge of both printing terminology and the various categories of printers.

PRINTER TERMINOLOGY

Before exploring the different types of printers, it is important to review some basic terminology and various factors that you should consider before making your purchase.

- **Image quality.** Image quality, also known as print resolution, is usually measured in **dots per inch (dpi)**. If, for example, a printer's resolution is 600 dpi, this means it can print 600 columns of dots and 600 rows of dots in each square inch of the page. The more dots per inch a printer can produce, the higher its image quality. A school paper or business document will look good when printed at 300 dpi, but a high-quality photo may need resolutions of 1200 dpi and perhaps higher. Most modern printers can produce output with at least 1200 dpi.

- **Speed.** Printer speed is measured in the number of **pages per minute (ppm)** the device can print. Most printers have different ppm ratings for black and color printing because color graphics generally take longer to print. Be careful when comparing page-per-minute rates. Printer manufacturers and retailers often quote the speed for draft printing (a lower-quality, lower-resolution way of printing text). A printer might be able to print 35 to 40 pages per minute in draft mode but only 5 or 6 per minute at full quality.

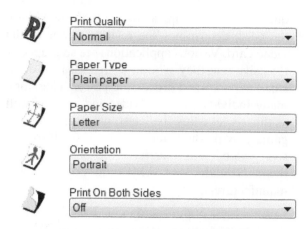

You can change various settings any time you print.

- **Duplexing.** The ability to automatically print to both sides of a piece of paper is known as **duplexing**. Various industries rely on duplexing to produce a wide range of printouts such as magazines, manuals, and catalogs.

- **Materials.** The price of new printers has fallen dramatically in recent years, while their capabilities and speed have improved just as dramatically. However, the cost of printing materials remains expensive. Consider the replacement cost of items such as ink cartridges and specialty paper, and how often you'll likely have to replace them.

More **Online:** *Visit the companion website to learn about various ways to save money on printing supplies, including information on how to recycle them.*

Recycling printer cartridges can be good for the environment and your wallet.

TYPES OF PRINTERS

Printers are divided into a variety of categories, separated by both their mechanisms and the materials used in printing.

- **Dot matrix printers** create output by striking an inked ribbon against paper using metal pins. Although they are still produced, they date to the 1970s and produce output that is inferior to other categories of modern printers. However, because of the hard impact they make on paper,

they are the only printers that can produce carbon-copy or pressure-sensitive forms (think of an auto lease contract). While this need is important to a few types of businesses, these types of printers are rarely used today.

- **Inkjet printers** create an image directly on the paper by spraying ink through tiny nozzles. The nozzles are mounted on a carriage that slides back and forth across the page, applying in the desired pattern as the page is fed through the printer. Color inkjet printers have four ink nozzles: cyan (blue), magenta (red), yellow, and black. These four colors (often referred to as CMYK) are used in almost all color printing because it is possible to combine them to create any color. Inkjet printers typically use one cartridge for black, and either one cartridge for each color or a single cartridge that contains the three colored nozzles. Although these printers have become very affordable (and the standard for homes), the replacement cost of cartridges can dramatically increase their expense over time.

- **Laser printers** create output by using a laser that is aimed at a rotating drum. Toner, which is a powder composed of tiny particles of ink, then sticks to the drum in the places the laser has charged. Lastly, with pressure and heat, the

Laser printers produce sharp quality text output.

toner is transferred off the drum onto the paper. A processor and memory are built into the printer to interpret the data that it receives from the computer and to control the laser. Many laser printers are monochrome, which means that they can only print in black. Such printers meet the needs of many businesses, which is generally to produce documents. However, there are now many affordable color laser printers that produce stunning output. They work like a single-color model, except that the process is repeated four times and a different toner color (CMYK) is used for each pass. Because of their sharp quality text output and fast printing speeds, laser printers are often preferred by businesses.

- **Multifunction printers** combine either inkjet or laser printing capabilities with scanning, photocopying, and faxing capabilities. These affordable, all-in-one devices are popular in home offices and small businesses because they remove the need for several separate pieces of equipment. The only downside is that if this device malfunctions, a business will lose multiple capabilities all at once.

This multifunction printer can also scan, copy, and fax.

A dye-sub card printer (left) and a thermal label printer (right) both use heat to create images.

- **Dye-sublimation (dye-sub) printers** use a process where by colored dyes are heated and then diffuse on specialty paper or other materials. This technology is often used to create lab-quality photos, as well as the images found on plastic ID cards.

- **Thermal printers** apply heat to special thermal paper, turning select areas black to produce text and basic graphics. They are often used to create receipts and labels.

- **3D printers** are unique in that they can create a three-dimensional object made of various materials. Although several technologies exist for accomplishing this, the rapid growth is in commercially available printers that use several types of polymers, or plastics. Initially, a 3D model is created on a computer using special software. When it is transferred to the printer, a nozzle will heat special plastic material until it melts. This nozzle will expel the liquid in a series of layers, which quickly hardens into solid form. There are countless applications for 3D printing that range from the creation of plastic toys at home to producing equipment and parts for astronauts that are stationed on another planet.

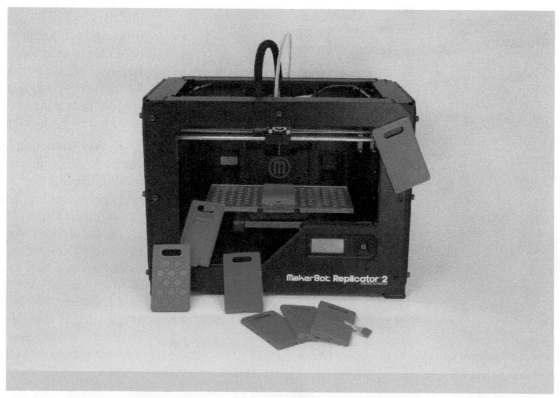

This 3D printer can create almost any plastic object, such as these custom cases for smartphones.

OTHER OUTPUT TECHNOLOGY

Monitors, speakers, and printers are by far the most common devices used to deliver computer output to a user. Many other devices, however, can provide output for more specialized applications.

PROJECTORS

Digital projectors are used to project digital images and video onto a large screen where they can be viewed by an audience. Projectors can be placed on a table or permanently mounted on a wall or ceiling. They can accept data to output directly from a computer, a local network, or even a USB flash drive. Some projectors are often used with **interactive whiteboards**, whereby a user can interact with the images projected on a screen or whiteboard.

Interactive whiteboard combines with a digital projector.

HAPTIC TECHNOLOGY

The communication of vibration, motion, or physical resistance to a user is called **haptics** or **haptic feedback**. Haptic technology can enhance audio or video output from computers to make them more relevant or noticeable. One of the most common devices using haptic technology is the smartphone, which can buzz for incoming calls or be triggered by a specific action within an app. Game controllers for consoles and PCs commonly use haptic feedback to increase the sense of immersion for users who are driving, flying, or shooting things on the screen. In modern flight simulators, haptics are sometimes used in the handheld control systems to provide feedback to pilots. Robotic control systems can also employ haptic feedback. For example, the controls for a robotic arm that handles radioactive or toxic materials might use haptic technology to let operators feel resistance as they move the controls to twist, squeeze, and lift with the robotic arm.

Flight simulators often use haptic feedback in the pilot's controls.

KEY TERMS

3D printer, 54
biometrics, 48
bit, 38
Blu-ray disc (BD), 40
byte, 38
cache, 37
central processing unit
 (CPU), 35
chipset, 35
clock rate, 36
compact disc (CD), 39
contrast ratio, 49
core, 36
CRT monitor, 50
cursor, 42
digital camera, 47
digital projector, 55
digital versatile disc
 (DVD), 39
digital video recorder
 (DVR), 47
document feeder, 45
dot matrix printer, 52
dots per inch (DPI), 52
drive, 38
duplexing, 52
dye-sublimation printer, 54
ergonomic keyboard, 41

expansion card, 35
facial recognition, 48
fingerprint scanner, 48
firmware, 37
game controller, 48
gesture, 43
graphics processing unit
 (GPU), 50
graphics tablet, 44
haptic feedback, 55
hard drive, 39
inkjet printer, 53
interactive whiteboard, 55
keyboard shortcut, 42
laser printer, 53
LCD monitor, 50
LED monitor, 50
media, 38
megapixel, 47
memory, 36
memory card, 40
motherboard, 35
multifunction printer, 53
multimedia, 46
optical character recognition
 (OCR), 45
optical mouse, 43
pages per minute (PPM), 52

pixel, 49
port, 35
QR code, 45
random access memory
 (RAM), 37
read-only memory
 (ROM), 37
response time, 49
resolution, 49
RFID tag, 46
scanner, 45
solid state drive (SSD), 40
sound card, 51
speech recognition, 46
stylus, 44
system unit, 34
tape drive, 39
thermal printer, 54
touchpad, 43
touchscreen, 44
trackball, 43
TV tuner, 47
USB flash drive, 40
USB port, 35
video card, 50
videoconferencing, 47
virtual memory, 38
webcam, 47

Review Questions

MULTIPLE CHOICE

1. Which of the following is a pointing device that can be useful if you have very limited space on your desk?

 a. Trackball
 b. Stylus
 c. GPU
 d. Controller

2. Which type of printer should you purchase if your company needs to print employee ID cards?

 a. Dot matrix
 b. Laser
 c. Dye-sub
 d. Thermal

Review Questions (continued)

3. Which type of memory is nothing more than the use of your hard drive when you are running out of RAM?
 a. ROM
 b. Cache
 c. BIOS
 d. Virtual memory

4. You are shopping for a new computer online. The description lists the following: "Intel i7 3630QM." What part of the computer does that refer to?
 a. RAM
 b. CPU
 c. Solid state drive
 d. Monitor

5. If you want to know the maximum number of pixels that a monitor can display on the screen, you would look at its:
 a. contrast ratio
 b. response time
 c. resolution
 d. size

6. Both fingerprint scanners and facial recognition are examples of:
 a. biometrics
 b. haptics
 c. firmware
 d. ergonomics

7. _____ is the primary storage device of a personal computer.
 a. RAM
 b. ROM
 c. The DVD drive
 d. The hard drive

8. The quality of a printer's output is measured in:
 a. PPM
 b. DPI
 c. OCR
 d. CRT

9. Which optical disc typically holds 25 GB or 50 GB of data?
 a. DVD
 b. Blu-ray
 c. CD
 d. SD card

10. Which type of keyboard is designed to be comfortable and help reduce the chance of hand and wrist strain?
 a. Multimedia
 b. Biometric
 c. Interactive
 d. Ergonomic

FILL IN THE BLANK

11. The _____ of a desktop computer is the case that houses the computer's critical parts, such as the processing and storage devices.

12. The _____ is the largest circuit board in a personal computer.

13. The ability to automatically print to both sides of a piece of paper is known as _____.

14. _____ are unique in that they can create a three-dimensional object made of various materials.

15. The most fundamental unit of computing is the _____, which is typically represented as a 1 or a 0.

16. _____ is the temporary workspace of a computer. It stores the content you are currently working on.

17. A(n) _____ is a device that can capture television signals for viewing on a computer.

18. The USB _____ is the most popular type of plug found on desktop and laptop computers.

19. _____ combine either inkjet or laser printing capabilities with scanning, photocopying, and faxing capabilities.

20. A technology known as _____ can translate the image of a scanned document into text that can be edited and formatted.

TRUE / FALSE

21. One gigabyte is larger than one terabyte.

22. Without proper cooling, a computer could overheat and malfunction.

23. Modern ROM chips can be electronically reprogrammed.

24. Because of their high speeds and the sharp-looking text they produce, dot matrix printers are preferred by modern businesses.

25. With speech recognition, it is possible to issue commands and search for information by speaking into your mobile device.

SHORT ANSWER

26. Other than in video games, where might you find haptic technology being used?

27. Why are LED monitors replacing the more traditional LCD monitors?

28. List five modifier keys that you would find on a laptop computer running Windows.

29. Why do some computers include a small, solid state hard drive in addition to the large, magnetic hard drive?

30. What is the difference between RAM and storage? Use an example to support your answer.

31. Describe a product that can protect your tablet computer and help you type on a surface that is more comfortable than the screen.

32. What are gestures? Give one example of a gesture commonly used on touchpads or touchscreens.

33. Other than gestures, list and briefly describe five operations that can be performed with pointing devices such as the mouse.

34. Which expansion card do gamers and individuals in the video industry normally purchase to improve their graphics? What types of components are found on this card?

35. What is the difference between a document scanner and a flatbed scanner? Why would a business choose a document scanner?

Research Exercises

Go beyond the book by performing research online to complete the exercises below.

1. Experts are claiming that 3D printers are going to change a variety of industries. Name at least two of these industries and provide a few examples of the products that will be 3D printed.

2. Several types of LED technology are used in monitors, TVs, and mobile devices. Name these technologies and briefly describe the differences.

3. List the required steps for changing the resolution on your desktop or laptop computer. If you do not own these types of computers, find the steps for a machine that runs Windows 8.

4. List the required steps for changing your printing options to consume less ink. If you do not own a printer, find the steps for Windows 8 and a printer of your choice.

5. Why is it important to recycle printer cartridges? Find a store near you that is willing to accept empty cartridges and offer discounts on the purchase of new cartridges.

6. Many large organizations and cloud providers use enormous data centers for their storage needs. Find at least one of these large data centers and describe their processing and storage needs.

7. List the steps for identifying the RAM and storage capacities of your computer. Record the type of computer you have along with these capacities.

8. Gaming consoles are not the only systems that can accept input through the movement of your body. Find at least three other devices that can track the movement of your hands, eyes, or other body parts without the need to touch the input device.

3

SOFTWARE

Chapter Overview

This chapter provides an overview of the software that operates today's computers. You will also learn about a variety of software that individuals use for productivity, education, and entertainment. You'll also gain an understanding of how the computer can help you manage and organize your important files, such as documents, photos, and music.

PART 1:
System Software

As you learned in Chapter 1, software contains computer programs that instruct the computer to complete a variety of tasks. Without software, a computer would not know what to do after you power it on. Furthermore, we would find little use for a computer if it weren't for the wide range of software that exists today. Two broad categories of software will be discussed in this chapter:

- **Application software** is any type of software that is made for you, the user. It allows individuals to complete a variety of work and school-related tasks. In addition, the software that you use for entertainment—managing music, editing photos, playing games, and so on—also falls under application software.

- **System software** refers to any software that is created for the operation, maintenance, and security of a computer. Most users take this software for granted, especially if it was included with their computer. However, it is crucial for the proper operation and well-being of your system. In this section, we will explore the various categories of system software.

Operating Systems

The purpose of an **operating system (OS)** is to manage the flow of data between hardware components and allow the user to communicate with the computer. It also supports all the other software that is installed in that computer. This is why the operating system must be loaded before any other software during the computer's start-up or **boot process**.

To better illustrate the function of an operating system, imagine a situation where you need to copy an image from a web page and save it in your hard drive. Typically, this operation only requires one or two simple clicks of your pointing device. However, behind the scenes, the operating system has to manage many components and resources. First, it has to manage your connection to the Internet. Next, it must support the software that we use to browse websites. Lastly, it has to interpret your clicks and ensure that it creates a perfect copy of the image on the hard drive. It doesn't always get noticed, but the operating system is performing countless services in the background that allow users and applications to complete their tasks. Let us now look at some key concepts and features related to operating systems.

- **Compatibility.** Because all software runs on top of the operating system, each has to be programmed to work with a specific operating

Operating systems perform a variety of functions such as managing your Internet connection and saving image files on your storage devices.

system. If, for example, you buy accounting software for your Windows-based Dell laptop, it is unlikely to work on your Mac computer. However, it will work just fine on your HP desktop computer because it too runs Windows. Computers that have the same operating system are said to be **compatible** with each other because they can support the same software.

- **GUI.** You generally interact with a computer using various mouse operations or hand gestures. This is because modern operating systems have a **graphical user interface (GUI)**, allowing users to communicate via graphical elements on the screen. GUI elements include objects such as windows, icons, menus, and buttons. This is in contrast to computers that use a **command-line interface**, which requires users to memorize and type a series of commands. For home users, this older type of interface was phased out over 20 years ago.

- **Multitasking.** The ability to run multiple programs at the same time is known as **multitasking**. A modern operating system will, for example, allow you to work on a document in one window while researching information online in another. This is in contrast to older operating systems such as Microsoft DOS (1980s) in which you could only use one program at a time.

- **32 vs. 64-bit.** You may encounter two versions of the same operating system that differ only in their bit numbers. If you recall from Chapter 2, a bit refers to the 0s and 1s that represent data in its most fundamental form. A 32-bit operating system is intended to work with older 32-bit processors, which can only handle 4 GB of RAM. The newer processors are 64-bit, making them more powerful and capable of supporting much more RAM. The 64-bit operating systems are created to work with these types of processors, which are quite prevalent in today's computers.

- **Device drivers.** Operating systems com -municate with most hardware components using **device drivers**. These programs, which are usually downloaded and installed automatically, instruct the operating system how to use or "drive" a newly installed device.

"Tux" the penguin is the logo most often associated with the Linux operating system.
Source: Linux

Unix uses a command-line interface.

SERVER OPERATING SYSTEMS

The operating systems for desktops, laptops, and mobile devices are generally intended for a single user at any given time. Because of this, they are not well suited to be installed on powerful servers, which manage a variety of functions and resources for many organizations today. Server operating systems must have the capability to handle the connections and requests of large numbers of users at the same time. They must also be very stable as they manage many critical aspects of organizations such as banks, universities, and airlines. You may not have worked directly with the following operating systems, but you have definitely used the resources they support.

UNIX

Unix (or UNIX), which dates to 1969, runs many of the world's most powerful servers. Although Unix may not be as easy to use or configure as Windows, for example, it is very powerful and extremely stable. Since its development, Unix has been operated by a command-line interface. Although there are several GUIs that can now be added to Unix, many system administrators prefer to use it by typing quick commands. Today, you will find many variants of Unix, with Oracle's Solaris being one of the most popular.

LINUX

Linux is an open source, Unix-like operating system that was created by Linus Torvalds in 1991. It is considered to be **open source** because it can be freely distributed and modified. Its popularity has exploded and thousands of users participate in the global community that has built up around this OS. This community invites Linux users and developers to contribute modifications and enhancements, and it freely shares information about Linux-related issues.

Even though Linux is free, companies may choose to sell their own versions of Linux. These companies, such as Red Hat, typically include customer service and support as part of the price, which is desired by most businesses that use Linux. Currently hundreds of Linux variants, or *distributions,* are available commercially or as a free download. Linux has grown at a very rapid pace and can be found in millions of servers worldwide. There are also desktop versions, which will be discussed later in this section.

> More **Online:** *Visit the companion website to learn more about Linux and its various distributions.*

WINDOWS SERVER

Although Microsoft has been making operating systems since the early 1980s, it wasn't until the mid to late 1990s that its server products gained any significant popularity. Today, Microsoft's Windows Server operating system is widely used in businesses of all sizes to manage users and a variety of services. It employs a GUI that is very similar to the desktop version of Windows. The newest version, Windows Server 2012, matches the style of Microsoft's other operating systems such as Windows 8 and Windows Phone.

DESKTOP OPERATING SYSTEMS

The operating systems used on desktop and laptop computers are likely the ones that you know best. Although Windows and Mac OS are dominant for these types of computers, we will explore a few others that are starting to get noticed.

MICROSOFT WINDOWS

Windows is Microsoft's operating system for personal computers. It has the largest market share of any competitor, with one version or another appearing on roughly 90 percent of the world's personal computers. Hundreds of PC manufacturers sell Windows-based computers. In addition, anyone can build a desktop computer using the same parts as those found in popular brands of PCs. As long as you install Windows on your machine, it will be compatible with any other PC.

Windows has undergone dramatic transformations since its introduction in the mid-1980s. The latest version is Windows 8, which is intended to unify the desktop/laptop experience with those of Microsoft's tablets and smartphones. It can run mobile-style apps in the area known as the **Start screen**, while running traditional Windows software in the more familiar **desktop**. The Start screen has replaced the older icons on the desktop with new **live tiles** that can display real-time information such as the current weather, news, or social media updates.

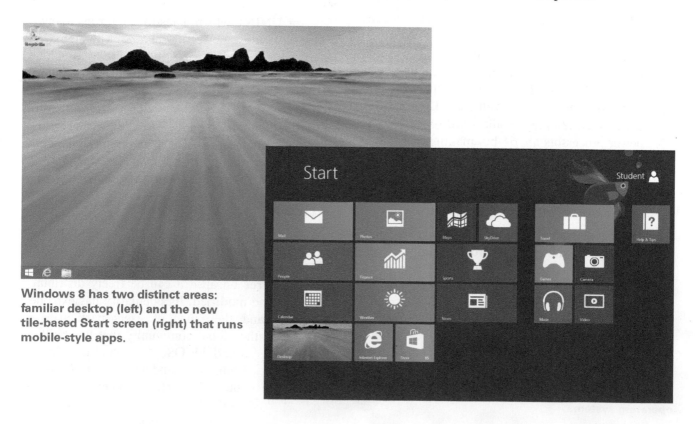

Windows 8 has two distinct areas: familiar desktop (left) and the new tile-based Start screen (right) that runs mobile-style apps.

MAC OS

Mac OS is the operating system used for computers sold by Apple. "Mac" refers to the Macintosh brand name of computer, introduced by Apple in 1984. At the time, Apple's GUI was revolutionary. Macs were quickly adopted by many schools and individuals in the graphics, music, and design industries. However, most businesses never switched to Macs, opting to keep their IBM PCs. This, along with Apple's reluctance to allow any other manufacturer to build Mac-compatible computers, partially explains why PC usage spread quickly and became the computers used by most individuals and businesses today. Some also cite cost as a factor, with Macs generally being more expensive than similarly equipped PCs.

The current Mac operating system, OS X, has gone through multiple versions over the years, each with its own nickname such as "Mountain Lion" or "Yosemite." Recent versions have increased the Mac's integration with Apple's other products, which is especially beneficial to individuals who own an iPhone and/or iPad. Though OS X and Windows share similar features and functions, they each have a distinctly different style and operation. Although most computer owners stick with Windows, users who purchase a Mac cite some key advantages of owning these types of computers:

- **Stability.** Mac computers seem to be more stable and suffer from fewer issues than PCs. This is partly due to the programming that lies at the heart of OS X. Another reason has to do with Apple being in control of both the hardware and software powering their computers. This is in contrast with Windows, which can end up on hundreds of different systems, including ones that individuals build for themselves.

- **Fewer viruses.** Macs rarely get infected by computer viruses and other malicious programs. This is because viruses can only target one operating system. Since Windows is found on many more machines, individuals who want to create chaos will generally write malicious programs for Windows-based computers.

- **Included software.** OS X includes various applications that a wide range of individuals find very useful. These include iPhoto, iMovie, and GarageBand, which allow users to create and edit photos, videos, and music.

Apple's OS X has a distinctive "dock" at the bottom and menu bar at the top.

- **Unified ecosystem.** Apple manufactures popular smartphones, tablets, and laptops. If you own at least two of these devices, you can experience a unified "ecosystem." Your devices work well with each other and all of your data is seamlessly synchronized to the cloud using Apple's iCloud service. Apple controls its ecosystem tightly to ensure a comfortable, worry-free experience for its users. Both Microsoft and Google are building competing ecosystems for their devices.

- **Support.** Many users argue that Apple's customer service is second to none. One of the reasons for this claim is that you can simply walk into an Apple store and get help from various experts that work at the "Genius Bar."

- **It runs Windows.** This fact surprises many people, including some Mac users. Because Macs are now powered by Intel processors, it is possible to purchase and install Windows on a Mac computer. Using the Boot Camp program, users can decide whether to boot up their Mac using Windows or OS X. By running Windows, a user no longer has issues when switching to Mac—all existing Windows software will work!

If you want to learn more about the various Mac devices, turn to the buying guide in the appendix of this book.

DESKTOP LINUX

Although Linux is widely used on servers, many distributions have been aimed at desktop computers. Various companies, such as Ubuntu, are trying to lure Windows and Mac users with their friendly interfaces and familiar features. It also doesn't hurt that the operating system is free. If you want to try Linux before replacing your current OS, many versions can be run directly off a USB drive. If you do decide to make the switch, you will find a surprisingly good operating system and many free, open source applications waiting for you.

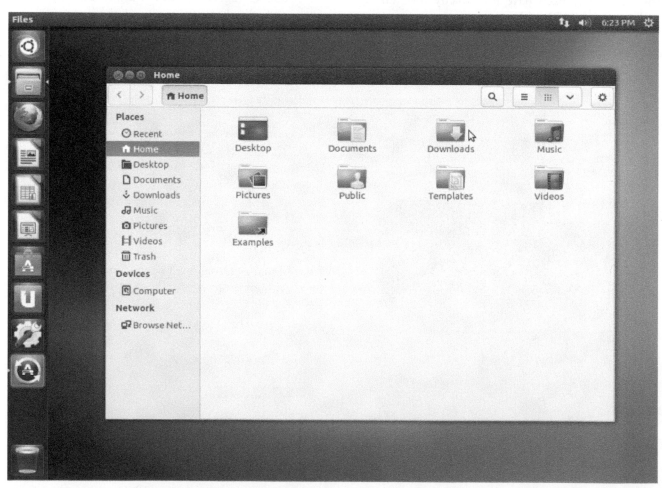

Ubuntu Linux for desktops has familiar GUI elements.

CHROME OS

The newest member of this group of operating systems is Google's Chrome OS. In essence, the Chrome web browser will be running your computer. Therefore, an Internet connection is required to get the most out of this operating system. All of the available apps are those that work with the Chrome browser. Your services, from file storage to document creation, are those offered by Google. With this operating system, you will be fully immersed in Google's ecosystem.

At the moment, Chrome OS is available on a few small, ultraportable computers. Their prices are lower than Windows or Mac laptops, and Google even offers 100 GB of free cloud storage for those who purchase these systems. Overall, Chrome OS–based laptops are attractive options for individuals (such as students) who enjoy Google's various services and find themselves near a wireless access point at all times.

MOBILE OPERATING SYSTEMS

Various operating systems are made solely to operate tablets and smartphones. Most of their features revolve around the needs of mobile users, who require quick access to information and notifications of incoming messages and daily reminders. These operating systems support mobile apps, which are

Chrome OS, with its Google apps at the bottom left, is included in this Samsung Chromebook.

generally fast, touch friendly, and require little storage space. The following are the four most popular operating systems for mobile devices.

iOS

The iOS operating system powers Apple's iPhone and iPad. It is considered to be a very friendly and stable operating system, largely due to Apple's tight control of the hardware and software ecosystem. Apple practically set the standards for a user-friendly interface with the debut of the iPhone in 2007. Since then, Apple has added a variety of features including messaging, videoconferencing, and cloud storage that are exclusively available for Apple users. More recently, the Siri speech recognition system has made a big impact on the way many users interact with their mobile device. In addition to these built-in features, you can download over a million apps from the App Store to extend your device's functionality.

ANDROID

Like Linux, Android is an open source operating system. Although Google owns Android and manages the Google Play Store for apps, it allows any manufacturer to use and modify this operating system for their devices. This is why you see Android-based smartphones and tablets from companies such as Samsung, Motorola, and HTC. Google also has its own line of "Nexus" Android devices that many individuals seek because they contain the pure, unaltered versions of this operating system. Android versions use numbers (e.g., 4.2.2), but they are popularly referred to by the names of various sweets, such as "Jelly Bean" and "Ice Cream Sandwich." Each version brings a wide range of improvements, some of which rival or even

The "BlinkFeed" home screen of the HTC One demonstrates how much Android can be customized.

exceed the features of iOS. One unique feature is the ability to add **widgets**, which are much larger than icons and provide automatically updating information without the need to open an app.

The open source nature of Android allows any programmer to alter it and add innovative features. Many individuals and groups even release their own Android versions, or *ROMs,* that can replace the one you have on your device. To allow this, your phone must be *rooted,* which involves a series of steps that give you full access and control over your device. This type of access is necessary for *flashing* a custom ROM as your new operating system. Although this will void the phone's warranty, many individuals are willing to take the risk in order to replace their inferior version of Android with a more useful one.

More **Online:** *Visit the companion website to learn more about Android customization and flashing ROMs.*

BLACKBERRY

The BlackBerry operating system can be found on a variety of BlackBerry smartphones. These phones achieved tremendous popularity a few years ago with the small, physical keyboards that were integrated into these devices. Since then, iOS and Android devices have come to dominate the market. Nevertheless, BlackBerry devices are still enjoyed by those who became accustomed to sending messages and email on those keyboards.

WINDOWS RT AND WINDOWS PHONE

Although Microsoft waited several years to create a mobile OS that could compete with iOS and Android, its recent efforts have received significant attention. Microsoft uses two operating systems for its mobile devices: Windows Phone and Windows RT. Windows Phone, as the name implies, powers smartphones created by several manufacturers such as Nokia. This OS features frequently updating live tiles on the home screen that are similar to those in the new Windows 8 Start screen. Microsoft also incorporated these tiles in Windows RT, which is used in its new Surface tablets.

Microsoft has received praise for giving users a unified experience on Windows-based smartphones, tablets, laptops, and desktops. At the same time, it has also received some criticism. Since Windows RT looks the same as the Start screen of Windows 8, some users have become confused. In a nutshell, Windows RT is made to compete with iOS and Android. Devices running Windows RT, such as the Microsoft Surface RT, are limited to running mobile-style apps much like their competitors' tablets. However, computers running Windows 8 can run both Windows RT apps and traditional Windows software, including those made for older versions of Windows such as 7 and XP. Windows 8 is what powers Microsoft's Surface Pro devices and most of the laptops and desktops sold today.

Microsoft's "Live Tiles" are present on Windows smartphones (right), Surface tablets (left), and Windows 8 computers.

Utilities

As you just learned, operating systems are responsible for managing your hardware and allowing you to easily communicate with your computer. Historically, desktop operating systems included only the most fundamental programming, allowing users to complete basic tasks such as managing files and opening programs. Little by little, programmers began to create a variety of **utilities** that enhanced or extended the operating system's capabilities. In some cases, these utilities offered features not provided by the operating system. Among these were utilities that protect your computer from viruses and increase your storage space through compression. As operating systems were improved and updated, the functionality of popular utilities started to be included with subsequent releases of the OS. Although today's operating systems include many of the utilities covered in this section, some users still choose to install third-party utility software.

SECURITY UTILITIES

The purpose of **security software** is to keep you, your computer, and your personal information safe from a variety of threats. With millions of infections and intrusions yearly, home users and businesses can no longer afford to be without basic security software. Many types of security software can be purchased individually or even downloaded for free from several reliable companies. Others are available as a **security suite**, which is essentially a bundle of programs that accomplish a variety of security-related tasks. Many

Security suites often bundle several security utilities into one package.

individuals opt for these types of suites since one software title (with one interface) can take care of all of their security needs. We will cover all aspects of computer security throughout Chapter 5. For now, let's look at some of the software that can provide a variety of security services.

ANTIVIRUS

A virus is one of many types of computer programs that are created to harm your computer or steal valuable information. Collectively, all malicious programs are referred to as **malware**. Although recent versions of Windows include some level of malware protection, you should consider one of the following tools to protect your desktop and laptop computers from all types of malware:

- **Paid:** Norton AntiVirus, Bitdefender Antivirus Plus
- **Free:** AVG Anti-Virus Free, Avast Free Antivirus, Avira Free Antivirus

FIREWALL

A software-based **firewall** is dedicated to examining and blocking Internet traffic. Most desktop operating systems, including recent versions of Windows and Mac OS, include a firewall utility that is usually activated for you. Although several security suites will include a firewall, it is rarely necessary for you to purchase a separate one. Businesses also use firewalls, but their needs are usually more complex.

ENCRYPTION

Encryption is the process of scrambling your data or storage devices to make them unreadable by anyone who doesn't have the proper key. This key

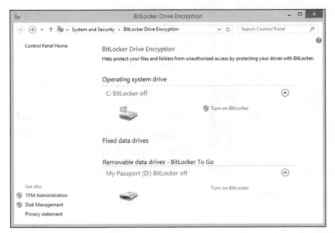

Encryption utilities can protect drives or individual files.

can be a password, PIN, or even a card. Encryption can be useful to prevent someone from gaining access to your data, such as a USB flash drive that you accidentally left at school. Both Windows 8 and Mac OS include an encryption utility for your drives.

PASSWORD MANAGEMENT

Remembering countless passwords for all of your accounts can be frustrating, but it is dangerous to reuse passwords for multiple websites and services. With information being stolen at an alarming rate, you cannot risk a thief having access to many of your accounts. Although many web browsers include a password storage utility, they are limited to services that you visit with that browser. LastPass is a secure and reliable password management utility that stores all of your passwords on each of your computers, including mobile devices. If you can remember one master password, you will have instant access to every account login and password you have ever created. In addition, this tool can also help you generate strong passwords so that you don't have to come up with your own each time.

PARENTAL CONTROL

Parental control utilities allow parents to set a variety of limits on their children's Internet usage.

Password management utilities help you remember passwords and will generate new ones as well.

Parents can set time limits, block adult content, and even receive reports on their child's activity. Both Windows and Mac OS have a variety of parental control utilities. If you desire a separate one, Net Nanny has been a popular choice for over a decade.

VIRTUAL MACHINES

A **virtual machine** is a special environment that allows you to run an operating system on top of another operating system. The operating system that runs in this virtual environment will think it is your primary OS with all the capabilities to manage hardware and run other programs. This is useful for individuals who wish to test a different operating system or for those that have software that requires an operating system other than the one that runs their computer. Earlier in the chapter you learned that you could try Linux by running it off a USB drive. An alternative way is to install and run Linux in a virtual machine, which allows it to run normally inside a window of your current operating system. The software that allows you to run a virtual machine is usually referred to as **virtualization software**. VirtualBox from Oracle (free) is a good choice for individuals, while businesses often use products from VMware.

Virtualization software (left) allows one operating system (Ubuntu Linux on the right) to run inside another.

STORAGE OPTIMIZATION

Most of what you store inside a computer is located in the hard drive. Therefore, if this component is not functioning efficiently, it can impact the speed at which the operating system stores and retrieves data. Furthermore, many of your other storage devices might need occasional troubleshooting to solve a variety of issues. Whether it is fixing an SD card that is seemingly unreadable to helping you make files smaller, these utilities are all crucial aspects of managing storage.

DISK FORMATTING

Preparing a storage device for use by an operating system is known as **formatting**. It is possible that you have never gone through this process yourself. The computers you buy at the store come preformatted with the operating system already installed for you. Furthermore, many portable storage devices come formatted in a manner that allows them to be used in a variety of computers. However, if you are setting up a new hard drive, you might have to format it before writing data to it. Additionally, devices such as SD cards and USB flash drives may become corrupted and can only be saved by formatting them. Although all data gets erased during formatting, there are times when we simply have no choice.

Formatting utilities, which are included with operating systems, are capable of performing several functions that are crucial to storage devices. The following are a few that you should become familiar with:

- **Partitioning.** Dividing a hard drive into multiple sections is known as **partitioning**. Although many hard drives just have one large partition, others might be split into two or three sections. One common reason for doing this is to create a recovery partition that allows you to restore your computer to its factory settings. Since your computer's manufacturer doesn't want you to store anything in this area, it sections it off to make it look like a separate storage device that is clearly labeled.

- **File system.** The **file system** of a storage device, which is configured after partitioning, determines how the operating system manages the space on the device. For PCs, there are two popular file systems: FAT and NTFS. Since FAT enjoys more widespread compatibility with other operating systems, it is often used on removable devices such SD cards and USB flash drives. However, your primary hard drive uses the more powerful and secure NTFS. Other operating systems, such as Mac OS, Unix, and Linux, use distinct file systems for the hard drive.

The Recovery (D:) drive on this computer is nothing more than a partition on the main hard drive.

More **Online:** *Do you have an SD card or USB flash drive that can no longer be read by your computer? Visit the companion website to learn how you can recover your precious data from these drives.*

DEFRAGMENTATION AND OPTIMIZATION

At some point, most magnetic hard drives become cluttered with thousands and thousands of file fragments to the point where there are no large areas of empty space available. If the operating system needs to write a large file, it must separate the large file into smaller parts and write them in areas scattered throughout the disk surface. Reading a file that is fragmented in that manner takes extra time because the read/write head of the drive needs to keep repositioning itself.

Operating systems typically contain a **disk defragmentation** or optimization utility, which will reorganize files and fragments to place related ones nearer to each other. Reading from the disk surface will now occur far more quickly because the file portions are all next to each other. You should always follow your operating system's recommendation to either automate or run this utility periodically. If you have a solid state drive, fragmentation is not an issue because these drives do not possess read/write heads. Nevertheless, these utilities will optimize them in a different way to ensure that they are working as efficiently as possible.

DISK CLEANUP

Operating systems and many other programs (such as web browsers) create temporary files during their operation. These files, which are necessary for a variety of reasons, take up space on your hard drive just like any other files. Operating systems generally make an effort to clean up this data. However, if you want to clear these temporary files yourself for storage, performance, or privacy reasons, you should run a **disk cleanup** utility. Most operating systems and web browsers include these utilities.

FILE COMPRESSION

The process of making a file smaller than its original size is known as **file compression**. Compression utilities use a variety of techniques that can "squeeze" one or more files into a smaller, compressed file. They are often unusable when compressed, but they

The Optimize Drives utility in Windows 8 can improve your computer's performance.

definitely occupy less space on your storage devices. Many users choose to compress several files into one for the sake of easy transport, especially when attaching them to an email message. It is better to attach one compressed file than many separate files.

Most operating systems contain a file compression utility. The most popular format for compression is known as *ZIP*. In Windows, these files are represented by an icon that looks like a folder with a zipper on it. Less popular is the compression known as *RAR*, which requires separate utility software to create and open. Regardless of the compression type, always be sure to remove or extract the files from their compressed container before using them.

BACKUP

A **backup** is a copy of one or more files (or entire storage devices) that is made in case the originals become lost or damaged. Ideally, the backup should be made to a separate storage device in case your computer is severely damaged or stolen. Creating a backup can be as simple as copying important files to a DVD or external USB drive. However, there are many backup utilities that can automate this process to make it easier for the user. Most operating systems include at least one backup utility. Windows 8 uses utilities known as System Restore and File History that can help you recover files or restore your system to a previous moment in time. Mac OS has a similar backup utility that is known as Time Machine. Regardless of which tool you use, it is *crucial* that you get into the habit of creating

This compressed (zipped) file in Windows contains five files.

frequent backups. You never know when a disaster could strike you or your business, causing you to lose irreplaceable files.

CLOUD BACKUP

With many homes and businesses now having access to high-speed Internet connections, many users are choosing to store their backups online. **Cloud backup** providers are companies that provide utility software that creates automated backups to an online account. The advantage of creating online backups is twofold.

- **Safety.** An online account is probably the safest place for your backups. If, for example, some thieves were to enter your home, they might steal both your computer and the USB drive that contains your backups. A cloud storage account is immune from theft, fires, and other disasters that could hit your home or business.

- **Accessibility.** As you have already learned, the files that you store in the cloud can usually be accessed from any device that is connected to the Internet. This is not the case with physical backups, which are stored in your home or business.

Apple's Time Machine utility backs up your Mac automatically to an external drive.

Cloud backup providers typically charge an annual fee that varies based on how much data (and how many computers) you have to back up. The types of files that are usually backed up are your irreplaceable data files—documents, music, photos, and videos. It is not necessary to back up your operating system or application software because you likely have those on DVDs or you are able to simply download them again. There are dozens of cloud backup providers, with Carbonite being one of the most popular.

DISK WIPING AND RECOVERY

Most individuals believe that the files they delete from their portable storage devices and recycle bins are gone forever. This is not entirely true, as it is possible to recover all or parts of these files using recovery utilities. While these utilities may help you bring back an important file, they can also be used by those who purchase or obtain access to used computers. For this reason, it is crucial to use disk wiping utilities to remove all traces of your files from computers you are selling or giving away (see Research Exercise 1). For mobile devices, this can often be accomplished via a *factory reset* option.

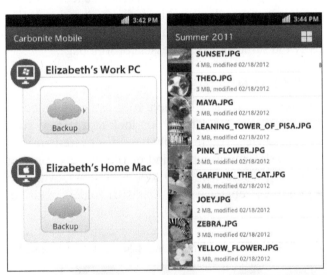

Many cloud backup tools allow you to access your home or office computer's backups from a mobile device.

File Management

Before we explore application software in the next section, let us first learn about one of the most important activities that we engage in with our system software: file management. Although many of the terms and examples used in this section are for Windows-based computers, most of what you will learn can also be applied to other operating systems.

FILES AND FOLDERS

The most fundamental components of storage that users interact with are the files. Before computers, homes and businesses used quite a bit of paper. These papers could contain almost anything—letters, financial reports, building instructions, musical notes, and even photos. In essence, papers contained information or instructions that were crucial to the individuals using them. Computer files are similar. They can contain the instructions of a computer program or the data that you care to store, from school papers to vacation photos and videos. Because of their importance, computers offer us a variety of ways to store and organize our files. This structure, known as the **file hierarchy**, consists of several components:

- **Drives** refer to your storage devices. They can store both folders and files.

- **Folders** are containers that can store files or other folders. When a folder is located inside another folder, it is referred to as a *subfolder*. In some operating systems, folders may be referred to as *directories*.

- **Files** can be located inside drives, folders, or subfolders. When they are located on a drive without being inside any folder, they are often said to be in the **root directory** of that drive.

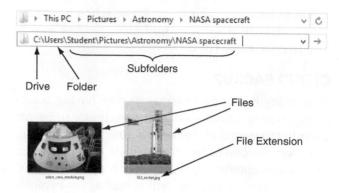

Figure 3.1 Example of a File Path Windows can display the current location, or path, in different ways, as shown in the two address bars at the top.

THE PATH

A file **path** is a complete address that describes the exact location of a file. Each operating system uses a unique path that contains words and symbols to describe drives, folders, and files. Figure 3.1 compares the address that Windows displays to the user with the actual path of that file. If the path looks a little familiar to you, it is likely because you have seen a similar notation in the address bar of your web browser. This is not a coincidence. Much of the Internet was designed by individuals using Unix-based computers, which use paths that look practically the same as the addresses for web pages.

FILE EXTENSIONS

As you have already learned, files can contain computer programs or data. If you look at a file on your storage device, you probably have discovered various ways to determine what kind of file you are looking at. One possible way is to look at its **icon**, which is a graphical representation of a file, folder, or drive.

TABLE 3.1 COMMON FILE EXTENSIONS

File Extension	Description
.exe	Windows executable file
.jpg, .png, .gif	Image files
.mp3, .m4a	Music files
.mp4, .avi, .mov	Video files
.pdf	Adobe PDF document
.docx, .xlsx .accdb, .pptx	Microsoft Word, Excel, Access, PowerPoint
.zip	Compressed ZIP file

That icon might contain a "W" indicating that it is a Word file or it might display the logo of your favorite video game. In addition, many operating systems will reveal the file type when you select the file. If the previous two options are not available (such as in an email attachment), it is useful to understand the **file extension**—a short, unique sequence of characters located after the file's name that indicate the file type. File extensions are always located after a period (dot) that follows the file's name. All files have this, even if your operating system doesn't display it at all times. Table 3.1 shows some common file extensions.

FAVORITE LOCATIONS

Most operating systems help you manage special folders that contain popular file types such as documents, music, photos, and videos. Mac OS will display these as *favorites* while Windows uses the term *libraries*. In Windows, these libraries display both your personal folders and public folders that are accessible to anyone that uses your machine. Although Windows also displays favorites, this area is used for other folders on the computer such as your downloads and your desktop (yes, the desktop is just another folder on your computer).

Every user account created on a computer will have unique folders created for that account. If other individuals use your computer, they will see document, music, and image folders that are unique to them. You don't see those folders in your favorites/library; you see your own. This helps users avoid the distraction of seeing countless files that do not belong to them. Now, if you want to share files with those who use your computer, you can place the files in a public or shared folder that is viewable by everyone.

MANAGING YOUR FILES

Now that you know what files, folders, and drives are, it is time to explore a variety of things that you can do with them. In Windows, files are managed with a tool known as *File Explorer*. On a Mac, that tool is known as *Finder*. No matter which tool you use, the basic file management operations are usually the same.

CREATING FOLDERS

File managers contain a feature that allows you to create folders and subfolders in a specific location. This is an important operation that helps keep similar files organized. If you have a folder with images, for example, you could create subfolders for categories such as birthdays, vacations, and holidays. Document folders could also be organized with subfolders for your various classes and personal files at home.

COPYING AND MOVING FILES

One of the advantages of computer files and folders is the ease with which we can copy or move them from one location to another. For example, you might choose to copy photos from a friend's USB flash drive onto your computer's hard drive. Alternatively, a teacher might choose to move a set of student documents from a parent (main) folder into a subfolder for a particular semester. Regardless of what method an individual uses for copying or moving, there are certain concepts that are important to know:

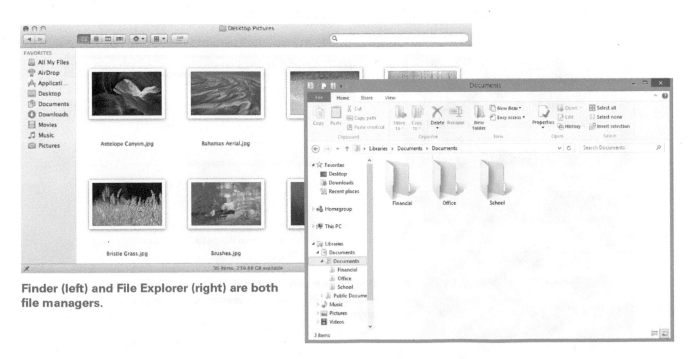

Finder (left) and File Explorer (right) are both file managers.

- **Clipboard.** In the real world, you often move an item by grabbing with your hands and then placing it in a new location. A computer also needs a temporary location for things that are being moved or copied, and that location is known as the **clipboard**. This clipboard is managed by RAM and the operating system.

- **Copy.** The **copy** command places a copy of the object (or objects) that are currently selected into the clipboard.

- **Cut.** The **cut** command removes the selected object (or objects) from their current location and places them into the clipboard.

- **Paste.** The **paste** command takes whatever is currently in the clipboard and places it in the location where this command is issued. Copy and paste will end up making a copy, while cut and paste is used to move something to a new location.

Windows 8 Recycle Bin holds deleted files.

DELETING AND RECOVERING FILES

When you no longer need a file or a folder, you can use the **delete** command to remove it from your drive. On most operating systems, files deleted from the hard drive go to a location that helps you recover those files that were erased by accident. On Windows it is known as the *Recycle Bin,* while on Mac OS it is called the *Trash.* Depending on your settings, files deleted from removable storage devices may not be sent here. Also keep in mind that while files remain in this second-chance location, you have not truly freed up any storage space on your computer. Therefore, be sure to clear these deleted files periodically.

SEARCHING FOR FILES

Most operating systems are trying to reduce the frustration of searching through countless folders or menus to find specific files. With Mac OS and Windows 8, you can type any search text and the operating system will find any files that contain this text. In addition, these operating systems will also search through programs, settings, and even the web in order to display relevant results alongside your files. In Windows, the *Smart Search* feature can be activated by typing on the Start screen, while Mac's *Spotlight* feature can be accessed from the menu bar or the Finder window.

Windows 8 (left) and Mac OS (right) allow you to initiate file and web searches from just about anywhere.

PART 2:
Application Software

The software that most individuals and businesses purchase and use on a daily basis is known as application software. Tens of thousands of software titles are available for purchase and download for the various operating systems in use today. Before we cover some of the most popular categories of applications, let us first explore the various ways in which this software is sold and distributed.

Acquiring and Installing Software

All individuals and businesses have a variety of options when acquiring software. While mobile users download apps directly from their device, a business with hundreds of computer systems might sign a special contract with the software company. Home users typically purchase a DVD or an electronic download from companies such as Amazon. Once the software is acquired, it must first be **installed**—set up by the operating system—before it can be used.

Before deciding to purchase or install software, one must be aware of the license that governs the software's use. A **software license** is a contract from the software creator that specifies the rules for using this software. This is in addition to federal **copyright law**, which gives software creators a variety of rights and privileges over their creative work. There are many types of licenses, with some being customized to meet the needs of a large business. The following terminology and license categories will help you gain a better understanding of the software acquisition and installation processes.

END-USER LICENSE AGREEMENT

An **end-user license agreement (EULA)** is the typical license that a user must agree to before installing software. Most EULAs take the form of an electronic notification that appears when starting the installation process. The user then has a choice to accept or decline the terms of this agreement. Although many users ignore these agreements and accept them blindly, you should read some of the basic usage and privacy notices before proceeding with the installation.

Most of the software and apps that individuals install are intended for one user at a time. In other words, you usually cannot take that same DVD, for example, and install it on the computers of all your friends and family members. Unless the software comes with a license that permits installation on multiple devices (typical for most antivirus software), you must limit your installation to only your machine. Other licenses allow you to install the software on all the machines that you use, such as your desktop and laptop or your tablet and smartphone. All of these variations demonstrate how important it is that you familiarize yourself with the license agreement.

VOLUME LICENSE

It would be inefficient for a medium or large business to purchase or download multiple copies of software to install on each employee's computer. For this reason, software companies usually offer a **volume license**, which allows companies to install the software on multiple machines. Businesses can buy a license for a certain number of users, or they can negotiate a package that includes maintenance and support. Software companies will usually offer a discount for volume licenses.

An end-user license agreement (EULA) must be accepted before installing software.

SUBSCRIPTION MODEL

Certain types of software, such as those for professional graphics and design, can reach or exceed $1,000 per copy. To ease the burden of paying that much at one time, many software companies have started to offer subscriptions. With the **subscription model**, users pay a fixed amount of money per month to use the software. Some subscriptions are done on a month-to-month basis while others require an annual commitment. Once the user stops paying, the software will no longer work. This is enforced by having the software check the user's online account for payment verification periodically, usually once per month.

Users must evaluate whether the subscription model will save them money for the period in which they need this software. In addition, some of these subscriptions include many added benefits, from installation on multiple computers for the family to a variety of cloud services. Adobe, for example, charges students and teachers about $1,000 for its large collection of graphics and design software. However, the monthly subscription that allows you to access the same software is only $30 per month and it also includes a generous cloud storage account. If you only need to use this software for a year, then the savings are easy to see.

SHAREWARE / TRIAL SOFTWARE

Some software is free to download and install, but will stop working as intended after about 30 days. This software is known as **shareware** or trial software. To keep using the software after the trial period, you must purchase a full version or a code that can be entered into the software. This software is very popular with users, as they get to try it for free before they commit to paying for it.

FREEWARE

Freeware is software that is free to use without any specified time restrictions. Although it doesn't cost anything, it is still protected by a license and by copyright law. Many programmers that are just starting out might offer their software for free to establish a fan base. However, even large companies might offer freeware, knowing that they can make money using methods such as these:

- **Promoting the paid version.** Many free software titles, such as antiviruses, do everything possible to promote the paid version that has more features. You will often see promotions for this full version while you are installing or using the free version.

- **Viewing content.** Some free software is required to view files or content created by the paid version. For example, the free Adobe Flash Player is required to view the web-based animated content and movies created with Adobe Flash Professional. Adobe hopes that users who view these animations online will become inspired to purchase the professional tool that can create them.

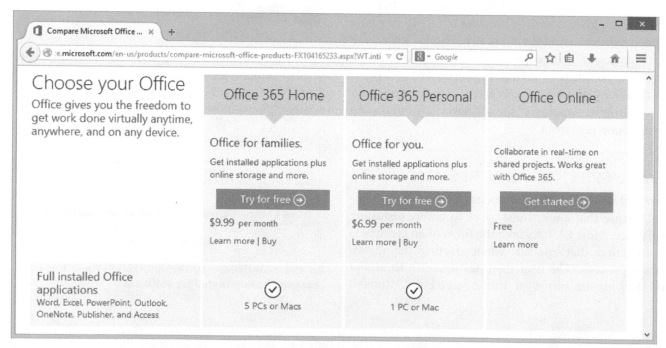

Microsoft offers various subscription plans for Office 365.

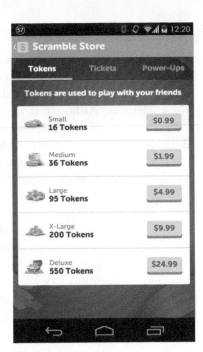

Free apps often include advertisements or offer in-app purchases.

- **Advertising.** Although some desktop software contains advertisements or third-party toolbars, this method has become most popular for mobile devices. You may have noticed that many free apps have small, rectangular advertisements at the bottom. These developers get money from the viewing and/or clicking of the ad. Many others sell a version of the app without the ads, hoping that users will pay a few dollars to get rid of that permanent advertisement.

- **In-app purchases.** The last way in which free software can make money is by offering users the chance to purchase a variety of things within the program. Games, for example, might offer desirable characters or objects with a one-time purchase.

OPEN SOURCE SOFTWARE

Earlier in this chapter, you explored a variety of open source software such as Linux and VirtualBox. Although they can be obtained legally for free, programs such as these are governed by licenses. One of the most famous open source licenses is the *GNU General Public License (GPL),* which ensures that a particular program and any of its derivatives (modified versions) remain free to distribute. In addition, its programming code can be examined and modified by anyone. For many, open source is more than free software: It is a philosophical movement that hopes to change the way we acquire, use, and share software.

CLOUD AND WEB-BASED APPLICATIONS

Powerful web and cloud technology enables anyone to use various types of software that do not require installation. **Web-based applications** are programs that run directly on your web browser. This technology allows you to play games, edit documents, and even create basic drawings without leaving your web browser. Although you can use services such as Evernote, Google Docs, and Microsoft Office Online on your browser, it is often more convenient to install a mobile app that offers quicker and more convenient access on your mobile device. Regardless of where you use them, your settings and data are saved because they are located on remote servers.

Types of Applications

Many categories of application software are used for a wide range of purposes, from entertaining and educating children to running the day-to-day operations of a business. Although it would be impossible to cover all types of applications, this section will introduce you to those that are widely used. Unless otherwise stated, these applications are primarily for servers, desktop, and laptop computers.

OFFICE SOFTWARE

Office software includes some of the most popular programs that help businesses efficiently carry out tasks such as writing letters, analyzing sales figures, and scheduling meetings. The same software helps students create reports and presentations for class. Often, several office programs are bundled as a unit known as an **office suite**. Although these suites have traditionally been made for desktop and laptop users, many have started to offer mobile and cloud-based versions (see Chapter 1). The following are some of the most popular office suites:

- **Microsoft Office.** The popular office suite from Microsoft can be found in most homes and organizations.

- **LibreOffice.** This free and open source office suite is gaining popularity and can be used on Windows, Mac OS, and Linux.

- **iWork.** Apple's office suite allows you to create documents, spreadsheets, and presentations on Mac OS and iOS devices.

LibreOffice is a complete open source office suite.

More **Online:** *Can mobile devices open the files created with desktop office suites? Visit the companion website to learn more about file compatibility.*

WORD PROCESSING

Word processing software provides tools for creating and editing all kinds of text-based documents. In addition, this software allows you to format your document by changing the appearance of text and the layout of each page. These capabilities allow you to create anything from simple one-page letters and résumés to large reports and publications containing separate chapters, a table of contents, and an index. These programs also enable you to add photos, graphics, tables, and various other elements to each page. This makes it easy to create eye-catching documents such as newsletters, flyers, and brochures. Popular titles in this software category include:

- Microsoft Word
- Corel WordPerfect
- LibreOffice Writer
- iWork Pages

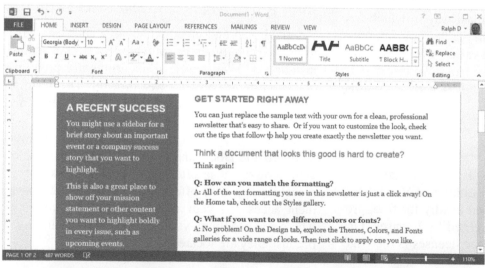

Microsoft Word includes many sample documents with attractive formatting and layouts to help you get started.

SPREADSHEET

Spreadsheet software is used for entering, calculating, and analyzing sets of numbers. These programs also create charts and graphs that are based on the selected set of numbers. Spreadsheets have a wide range of uses, from managing a teacher's grade book to performing complex analysis on a company's sales figures. One of a spreadsheet's most powerful purposes is to answer "what if" questions for a variety of scenarios. For example, a company can preview the financial consequences of changes such as price increases or rising fuel costs. This is made possible by this software's ability to instantly recalculate totals and redraw charts the moment any number is changed. Popular titles in this software category include:

- Microsoft Excel
- LibreOffice Calc
- iWork Numbers

Microsoft Excel allows you to create charts and perform complex calculations.

DATABASE MANAGEMENT

A computer **database** is simply an organized method for storing information. Practically every business and organization relies on databases for the storage and quick retrieval of information. For example, an online store selling electronics would have the need to store data about customers, suppliers, employees, inventory, sales, and shipping. Each of those categories has different types of associated data. A customer *record,* for example, might include each person's name, address, and payment information. However, the records for each product in their inventory would include different attributes such as model number, manufacturer, price, and quantity on hand. Databases have to be able to create connections, or *relationships,* between different types of data in order to create transactions and generate meaningful information for this company. To create and manage such complex databases, businesses can use software known as a **database management system (DBMS)**. The software best suited for an organization often depends on its size and needs:

- **Small businesses and individuals:** Microsoft Access or LibreOffice Base.

- **Medium to large businesses:** Microsoft SQL Server or Oracle Database.

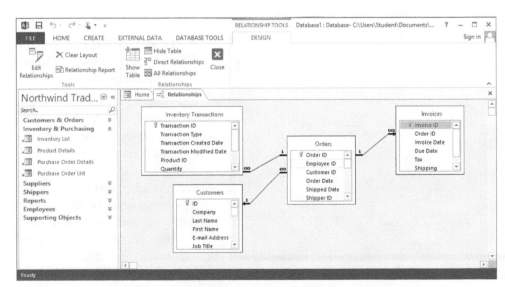

Microsoft Access creates relationships between different types of data.

PRESENTATION

Presentation software enables users to create electronic slide-shows that are used to present information. Each slide in the presentation can contain a combination of text, images, charts, videos, and other elements that are arranged in an appealing layout. These slides are then shown in sequence to support the individual who is speaking in front of an audience. The content of these slides often comes from other office software. A presenter might copy some text from a document and a chart from a spreadsheet to create a brief summary for an upcoming meeting. The alternative, which is showing a long document or spreadsheet with small text, is not very appealing when trying to relay information to an audience using a digital projector. The most popular titles for presentation software are:

- Microsoft PowerPoint
- LibreOffice Impress
- iWork Keynote

Microsoft PowerPoint helps you create eye-catching presentations.

PERSONAL INFORMATION MANAGEMENT

A **personal information manager (PIM)** is software designed to keep individuals organized. You can use a PIM to manage your contacts, create appointments and meetings, set up reminders, and keep track of various to-do lists. A PIM also provides email capabilities that allow you to send messages to any one of your contacts. Most office workers, from employees to managers, use a PIM on a daily basis. In fact, some offices coordinate most of their activities through PIM software. It can automatically determine the best times for meetings and available rooms simply by scanning everyone's schedule. Let's take a look at a few categories and examples of PIM software.

- **Traditional.** The most popular PIM software for business is Microsoft Outlook, which often connects to a Microsoft Exchange Server that stores and manages all this information.

- **Open source.** Mozilla Thunderbird and Zimbra Desktop are popular choices.

- **Cloud based.** Google, Microsoft, and Apple all offer PIM services. These can be accessed on the web and on mobile devices. Some organizations have started to use premium versions of these cloud services, relieving their need to buy servers that manage employee or student email, calendars, contacts, and even documents.

Microsoft Outlook manages email, appointments, contacts, and tasks to keep you organized.

ACCOUNTING & FINANCE

The software in this category helps businesses and individuals with a variety of finance-related tasks. With powerful reporting, this software makes it easy to see where your money is going and it helps improve the way you or your business manages both income and expenses.

BUSINESS ACCOUNTING

Accounting software helps businesses manage all aspects of their company's finances. It keeps records of every transaction between customers and suppliers, generating a variety of invoices and forms. The software can keep track of all business contacts and maintain your entire inventory. It also manages the employee payroll, making it easy to calculate taxes and report information to the IRS. Software in this category includes:

- Intuit QuickBooks
- Sage 50 Accounting
- Xero (cloud based)

PERSONAL FINANCE

Personal finance software helps individuals and families manage their budget. It keeps track of all your expenses and helps you create a budget that works with your income. Many programs will even connect to your financial institutions to download transactions and make sure they match your entries in the software. If you tend to have trouble with your finances, the following software can help you get out of debt and change the way you manage your money:

- **Desktop and mobile.** Intuit Quicken and YNAB both offer desktop software that synchronizes with your mobile app. You can enter transactions or view your budget from wherever you are.

- **Cloud based.** Mint is the most popular cloud-based financial application. Once you log into your financial accounts using this website, it practically does all the work for you. Both the web-based service and the mobile app are free.

TAX PREPARATION

Tax preparation software allows individuals to prepare their income taxes and file electronically (e-file)

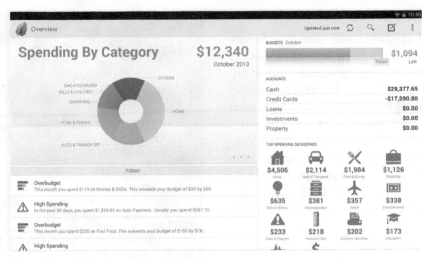

Mint can help you manage your personal finances on multiple devices.

with the IRS. This type of software is usually available in several versions that vary depending on the complexity of your tax return. Some companies even offer free web-based tax preparation if your income is lower or you meet specific requirements. The following are the most popular desktop programs in this category:

- Intuit TurboTax
- H&R Block

CREATIVE AND MULTIMEDIA

As you remember, *multimedia* is a term that encompasses a variety of media such as music, graphics, photos, and video. Individuals and businesses use different types of software to create, edit, and publish these types of files. Although Macs are the preferred systems for those in these fields, PCs are capable of producing the same type of files. When it comes to multimedia software, Adobe dominates the field.

Before we explore the various categories of multimedia, it is important to note that operating systems include applications that allow you to view (and sometimes create) many of these files. **Media players** refer to applications that allow you to listen to music and play videos. In addition, you will find several image viewers that allow you to view image slideshows and manage photo galleries on desktop and mobile operating systems.

DRAWING

For those who need to create graphics from scratch, a variety of drawing programs are available. Those based on **bitmap graphics**, such as Microsoft Paint, will record your drawings on a pixel-by-pixel basis. Your bitmap or *raster* graphics can then be saved in popular formats such as JPG, GIF, and PNG. However, any attempt to make these images larger than their original size will result in blurriness and distortion.

Vector graphics, on the other hand, rely on mathematics to generate and manipulate a variety of shapes. This allows you to increase or decrease the size of your graphics without any distortion. Drawing programs based on these types of graphics are well suited for work when accuracy and flexibility are important. Practically all professional-level artwork, from company logos to animated characters, is created with vector-based drawing tools. The following are popular choices:

- Adobe Illustrator
- CorelDRAW
- Inkscape (open source)

Adobe Illustrator uses vector graphics to help you create artwork.

GRAPHICS EDITING

Graphics editing software, which is sometimes referred to as image or photo editing software, contains bitmap-based tools that are used primarily to edit images. Individuals will often use this software to remove blemishes and imperfections in photos or add special effects to any type of image. Many mobile and web-based applications allow amateurs to improve or apply cool effects to any of the photos they take with their digital cameras. However, for more professional programs, consider one of the following:

- Adobe Photoshop
- GIMP (open source)

Apple's Final Cut Pro helps you edit videos, their accompanying sound, and apply special effects.

VIDEO EDITING

Video editing software is used to edit and produce a variety of videos. Amateurs can use simple (and free) applications such as Apple's iMovie and Windows Live Movie Maker to create vacation movies and fun slideshows from their photos. Professionals use more sophisticated tools to edit and export videos for use in movies, TV, and even websites. Popular video editing programs include:

- Adobe Premiere
- Apple Final Cut Pro

CAD / 3D MODELING

A variety of professionals now turn to software to create both two and three-dimensional designs. **Computer aided design (CAD)** software aids architects, engineers, and many others who need to create a digital model of an object. For example, before a city starts construction on a new bridge, a digital version will be created using CAD software that contains all the specifications for the bridge in a visual format. **3D modeling software**, on the other hand, is typically used by professional artists and animators who need to create three dimensional graphics and characters for advertisements, video games, cartoons, and movies. The following are some of the most popular software titles in these categories:

Autodesk's 3ds Max helps artists create and animate realistic 3D models.

- **CAD.** Autodesk's AutoCAD has been the industry standard CAD and drafting tool for over two decades.
- **3D modeling.** Autodesk offers two products for professional 3D modeling and animation: Maya and 3ds Max. For an open source alternative, many use Blender for their 3D needs.

AUDIO EDITING & PRODUCTION

It is likely that you have used one or more programs designed to play and organize your music collection. Software such as Apple's iTunes allows home users to manage their music and playlists, purchase new songs, or *rip* existing music from their CDs into a digital format such as MP3. This software is very different from those used by musicians and sound engineers. These professionals use audio production software to compose, edit, and mix music or sound effects. Although performers usually record their music at a professional studio, much of the editing and enhancements can now occur on the computer. Additionally, much of today's electronic music can be composed using this software. Musicians can sample pieces of other songs or create sounds that are replicas of those produced by a variety of musical instruments. Some examples of this software are:

- Avid Pro Tools (the industry standard).
- Apple GarageBand (included with Mac OS).
- Audacity (open source sound editor).

DESKTOP PUBLISHING

Desktop publishing software is used by professionals to create works that require complex layouts and contain a mix of text and graphics. Magazines, newspapers, and textbooks are all created with this type of software. Popular titles include:

- Adobe InDesign
- QuarkXPress

WEB DEVELOPMENT

Although there are now countless ways to create a website, professionals who need to manage complex sites will often use web development software. In addition to a variety of design and programming tools, these programs also help the web developer publish the site to a web server. The following are some popular tools:

- Adobe Dreamweaver
- Microsoft Visual Studio

EDUCATION & ENTERTAINMENT

Some of the most popular software titles for the home are those that either educate or entertain us. Thousands of programs teach children how to read and do basic math. Older students often purchase software that offers tutoring in a specific subject or helps prepare them for a variety of standardized exams. One of the fastest-growing categories of educational software is those that help teach a foreign language. Programs

such as Rosetta Stone include a variety of advanced features such as the ability to detect whether you are pronouncing a word correctly.

For entertainment, there are many categories of games created for both desktop computers and mobile devices. These range from simple action games and puzzles to complete fantasy worlds that can be played online with millions of other individuals. Many feel that the future of gaming will involve **virtual reality**, where humans can experience realistic environments that are simulated by computers. A variety of headsets and machines have already been developed for playing games. Others can be used to train individuals such as pilots or soldiers, or even allow individuals to travel virtually to any other place in the world.

VERTICAL MARKET

Vertical market software is created for a specific industry such as health care or insurance. Unlike most of the applications you studied in this section, this software is not intended for general use. It is tailored for one specific type of company or role. For example, the software used by pharmacies needs to track inventory, process patient prescriptions, and communicate electronically with doctors and hospitals. No business would have use for such software except for pharmacies. Companies that sell this type of software generally create a license or contract that includes installation, setup, training, and support.

LARGE BUSINESS

It would be difficult to operate a large business if many of its core functions were managed by different types of software. **Enterprise resource planning (ERP)** systems bring together many types of business functions into one software solution. It can handle tasks as diverse as manufacturing and quality control to accounting and human resources. Managers can also use it for **project management** functions, where a sophisticated plan is created and tracked to achieve a variety of goals. Some ERP systems also integrate **customer relationship management (CRM)** capabilities that allow sales departments to manage call centers, support customers, and keep track of sales commissions.

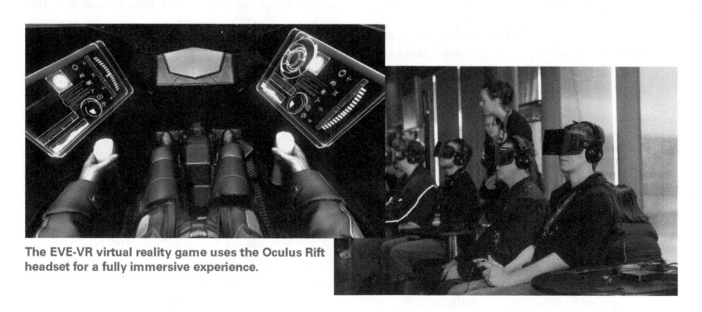

The EVE-VR virtual reality game uses the Oculus Rift headset for a fully immersive experience.

Software Development

Now that you have explored a variety of software, we will consider how it is all created. As you remember from Chapter 1, software is made from computer programs that contain detailed instructions for the computer. To create successful software, computer programmers go through a series of steps known as the **software development life cycle (SDLC)**. This cycle takes programmers from the idea and planning stages through the actual programming, testing, and maintenance of the software. In this section, we will explore some fundamental concepts in computer programming by taking a quick tour of the typical development stages.

PLANNING

Like most things you do on a daily basis, software development begins with an idea and a plan. Programmers must come up with a detailed description of the tasks they want their software to accomplish.

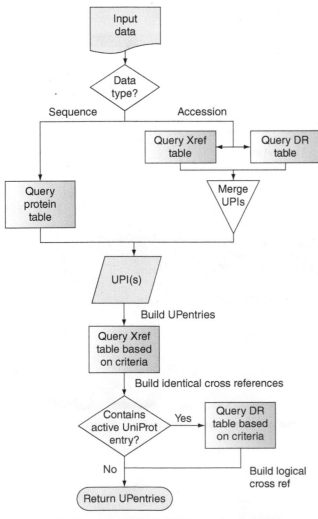

Figure 3.2 Flowchart Tracing Steps of a Program

They will come up with a series of steps, known as an **algorithm**, that describes exactly what each portion of their program is supposed to do. This algorithm is often represented visually as a **flowchart**, which uses special symbols to trace the steps of the program (see Figure 3.2). Once programmers have developed their algorithms and flowcharts, they essentially have a blueprint or guide that will allow them to start writing their program.

If you have trouble understanding this stage of development, imagine for a moment the process that you go through to cook and eat hamburgers for dinner. Not only do you need to come up with an idea of what you want to eat, you must also create a plan for successfully preparing the hamburgers. From heating the grill to cutting vegetables while the hamburgers cook, you probably have developed a series of steps that you follow to prepare this or any other meal. For more complex dishes, you likely have a recipe with detailed ingredients, notes, and steps that you must review before you start cooking. That is the sort of planning that programmers must engage in before they start to work on the actual coding of the program.

CODING

In this phase, the programmer will begin the process of converting the algorithms and flowcharts into an actual computer program, a process known as **coding**. The code created by these programmers is written in one of many computer programming languages that contain their own vocabulary and grammar (syntax), much like English, Spanish, and practically every other language. Although these programming languages use many words that you would immediately recognize, they also use complex symbols and sequences that require a great deal of training to master. The following are some of the most popular programming languages for creating computer software:

- C++
- Java
- Visual Basic
- Python

Many programmers today use an **integrated development environment (IDE)**, which is software that helps them build their computer programs. This software, such as Microsoft Visual Studio, provides a variety of tools and features that can increase the programmer's speed and accuracy. In addition, these IDEs contain a **compiler**, which is a program that translates a specific programming language into a machine language that can be processed by the CPU.

Once a computer program is compiled, the IDE will produce an **executable file** that can be run by the operating system on a user's computer.

> More **Online:** *Several websites offer fun and interactive tutorials on programming for free. Visit the companion website to learn more.*

TESTING AND MAINTENANCE

In the same way that you test and adjust a recipe to make it as perfect as possible, software must also go through a process after it is created. First, a programmer will look for errors, or **bugs**, by testing the software under a series of conditions. The process of finding and fixing these bugs is known as *debugging*. Once this phase is over, programmers might want to test the software in real-world conditions. They will release a **beta version** to a limited audience that will test it on their systems. Programmers can now collect information from these users about any errors that were encountered.

Once the software is deemed ready, it is released to the general public. However, no software is truly free of bugs. Errors and security vulnerabilities will continue to be found and programmers will "patch" them by offering **software updates** to users. It is crucial that you download and install all software updates (especially for the operating system) the moment they are released. Most software does this automatically, requiring only an occasional restart of the program or your computer. Some updates may also include improvements and new features that many users desire. Programmers will continue to update and maintain the software until the company decides to no longer support this software or one of its particular versions.

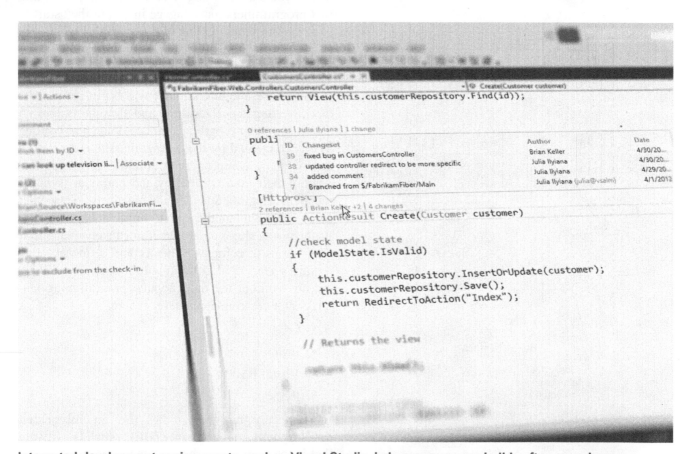

Integrated development environments, such as Visual Studio, help programmers build software and apps.

KEY TERMS

Review Questions

MULTIPLE CHOICE

1. Operating systems communicate with most hardware components using:

 a. compilers

 b. device drivers

 c. algorithms

 d. widgets

2. Collectively, all malicious programs are referred to as:

 a. malware

 b. bugs

 c. vectors

 d. CRM

3. A(n) _____ is a special environment that allows you to run an operating system on top of another operating system.

 a. file system
 b. virtual machine
 c. widget
 d. IDE

4. Which of the following is a DBMS that you might find a large business using?

 a. Oracle
 b. Excel
 c. QuickBooks
 d. AutoCAD

5. Which of the following is NOT an office suite?

 a. Microsoft Office
 b. Apple iWork
 c. Adobe Creative
 d. LibreOffice

6. Dividing a hard drive into multiple sections is known as:

 a. formatting
 b. defragmentation
 c. compression
 d. partitioning

7. Which type of software is used for entering, calculating, and analyzing sets of numbers, as well as creating graphs and charts?

 a. Word processing
 b. Spreadsheet
 c. Database
 d. Presentation

8. A(n) _____ is software designed to keep individuals organized.

 a. CRM
 b. ERP
 c. IDE
 d. PIM

9. Which of the following is NOT a popular computer programming language?

 a. Exchange
 b. C++
 c. Visual Basic
 d. Java

10. Which of the following products would you choose if you wanted to edit videos?

 a. Apple Final Cut Pro
 b. Adobe Photoshop
 c. Adobe InDesign
 d. Microsoft Visual Studio

FILL IN THE BLANK

11. The purpose of a(n) _____ is to manage the flow of data between hardware components and allow the user to communicate with the computer.

12. _____ is the process of scrambling your data or storage devices to make them unreadable by anyone who doesn't have the proper key.

13. A(n) _____ is the typical license that a user must agree to before installing software.

14. The ability to run multiple programs at the same time is known as _____.

15. A(n) _____ is a copy of one or more files that is made in case the originals become lost or damaged.

Review Questions (continued)

16. A file _____ is a complete address that describes the exact location of a file.

17. A computer _____ is simply an organized method for storing information.

18. Modern operating systems have a(n) _____, allowing users to communicate via graphical elements on the screen.

19. Many feel that the future of gaming will involve _____, where humans can experience realistic environments that are simulated by computers.

20. _____ software aids architects, engineers, and many others who need to create a digital model of an object.

TRUE / FALSE

21. Application software is made for the computer's proper operation, while system software aims to make users more productive.

22. The most popular format for file compression is known as CRM.

23. In some operating systems, folders may be referred to as directories.

24. With a subscription model, users pay a fixed amount of money per month in order to use software.

25. A programmer or software company will often release a beta version in order to test software in real-world conditions.

SHORT ANSWER

26. Name four operating systems used in mobile devices. Are any of those open source?

27. List and describe at least three ways in which freeware could still make money.

28. Describe the operations used to copy and move files using a file manager.

29. List six different file extensions and describe the type of file they belong to.

30. Describe two unique features of open source software. In addition, provide at least three examples of open source software.

31. Name and describe the two distinct areas of Windows 8.

32. Name two examples of paid security suites and two examples of free ones.

33. List two reasons for using file compression.

34. Name one cloud backup provider and describe two advantages of using cloud backups.

35. What type of software do businesses use to keep track of monetary transactions? How about individuals? Provide at least two examples of each type of software.

Research Exercises

Go beyond the book by performing research online to complete the exercises below.

1. Find at least one utility that can help you recover files that you thought had been permanently deleted. Find another utility that can permanently wipe data in high-security environments.

2. Which settings or activities accelerate the draining of the battery in a mobile device? Name at least three. Find one utility (app) that claims to increase the battery life of your mobile device.

3. Find any software title or suite that offers both traditional purchasing and a subscription. Compare the two options, assuming that you will use the software for two years. Which do you feel is a better deal? Why?

4. List and describe at least three accessibility features in your operating system.

5. Discuss the philosophy of the free and open source movement. Do you agree with this philosophy? Defend your answer.

6. Compare the applications that are included with Windows and Mac OS X. Are the offerings of one operating system superior to those of the other? Provide a few examples in your response.

7. Find and list five free mobile apps, each in a different category. Why is each of them offered for free?

8. While most software is protected by a license and copyright law, others are protected by a patent. How can software qualify for patent protection? What sort of problems has this created for technology companies? Are there any proposals that aim to remedy these problems?

4

THE INTERNET

- Reflecting on how many email accounts you have and what you are using them for.
- Comparing search engines and looking for personalized search results.
- Performing research on net neutrality and considering the impact of services that generate a large amount of Internet traffic.
- Reflecting on the way you use social networking sites.
- Using Twitter to quickly access headlines and important events around you.
- Discussing advertising practices on the web, social media, and mobile apps.
- Finding reliable sources in search engine results.
- Exploring the growth of community-based question and answer websites.

Chapter Overview

Just as the personal computer revolutionized the way the world solves problems and completes tasks, the Internet has changed how the world learns and communicates. This chapter provides basic information about the structure of the Internet and discusses an array of services that the Internet provides to its users.

PART 1:
Internet Basics

In Chapter 1, you learned that the Internet is the largest network in the world. It connects billions of people and organizations, with millions of new users joining each year. Thanks to the Internet, virtually any computer on any network can communicate with any other computer on any other network. These connections allow users to exchange messages, have live conversations, share data and programs, and access enormous amounts of information.

The Internet has become so important that its proper use is considered an essential part of computer competency. Mastering the Internet is one of the first things you should do if you want to get the most from your computing experience. In this chapter, you will learn about the Internet's history and its major components, and gain a broad overview of how we connect and what we do while we're online.

The Internet connects billions of people and organizations all over the world.

History and Structure

The following section will help you understand how the Internet came to be and which organizations are responsible for its development and maintenance.

DEFENSE DEPARTMENT RESEARCH

The seeds of the Internet were planted in 1969, when the Advanced Research Projects Agency (ARPA) of the U.S. Department of Defense began connecting computers at four universities in the western United States. The resulting network was called **ARPANET**. One goal of this early project was to create a large computer network with multiple paths—in the form of telephone lines—that allowed researchers in one location to access the computing resources at another location. This was crucial because, at that time, the number of powerful computers that could be used for advanced research was very small.

ARPANET expanded from the original four universities quite rapidly. By 1971, 18 locations had access (see Figure 4.1). The network jumped across to Europe in 1973, connecting a system in Norway to ARPANET. It kept growing through the early 1980s with continued funding from ARPA.

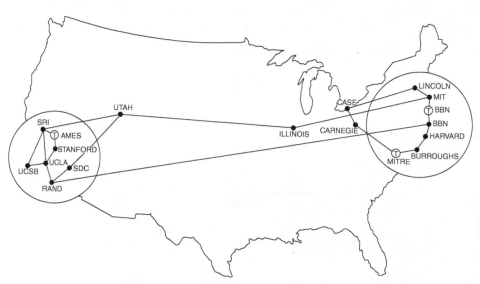

Figure 4.1 The Reach of ARPANET in 1971.

CREATING STANDARDS

We human beings set rules for almost everything we do, from playing sports to dispensing medication. We do this so that everyone knows which procedures to follow. In a similar manner, computers that communicate over a network must follow certain rules to ensure that the transmission is sent properly and understood. These rules are known as communication **protocols**.

The protocols at the heart of Internet communication are known as **TCP/IP** (Transmission Control Protocol/Internet Protocol). Developed in 1973, TCP/IP created standards for transmitting packets (units of data) to ensure that future networks would be able to communicate with existing networks such as ARPANET. TCP/IP sets rules for both the transport of these packets and the addressing system for a network. Today, every computer or device that is on the Internet needs an **IP address** that uniquely identifies it. The most widespread addressing system is known as IPv4; however, it is slowly being replaced by the newer IPv6 system, which offers many more possible addresses (see Figure 4.2).

SCIENCE RESEARCH & EDUCATION

Participation on ARPANET was limited to the handful of institutions and researchers that supported ARPA's research goals. Other U.S. government agencies and researchers decided to work on their own networks starting in the early 1980s. Among them was the National Science Foundation (NSF), which created **CSNET** in 1981 to bring together researchers in the field of computer science. By 1986, approximately 165 university, industrial, and government computer research groups belonged to this network.

In 1986, the NSF established connections between five supercomputing centers that were available to anyone who wanted to use them for academic research. The NSF created a new high-speed network called **NSFNET** that could transmit data at 25 times the speed of CSNET. In addition, it created connections to smaller regional networks, other agencies' networks, CSNET, and ARPANET. The young Internet was finally taking shape as this new interconnected "network of networks."

192.168.1.101

fe80::d14b:58c:1e50:217f

Figure 4.2 **IPv6 addresses (bottom) offer many more combinations than IPv4 (top).**

COMMERCIAL USE

As NSFNET traffic grew rapidly in the late 1980s, the organization realized that it would need help from the private sector to upgrade the network. Various companies, including IBM, provided equipment and established new telecommunications networks to help improve the Internet. As years went by, these companies continued to upgrade existing networks and create new **backbones**, which refer to the connections that carry most of the Internet's traffic. By 1995, there were about 100,000 connected networks throughout the United States, with several backbones operated by private telecommunication companies. Based on this success, the NSF

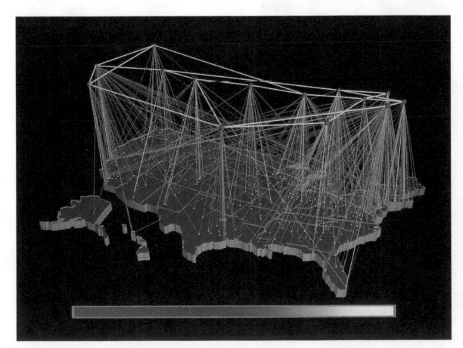

Visualization of the NSFNET T1 backbone and client networks (Sept 1991). The backbone is represented by the white lines connecting the red dots. The colored client networks represent data flow into the backbone.

decided to stop funding NSFNET and leave the Internet in the hands of the private sector.

Interest in the Internet exploded in the mid to late 1990s. A network that had been started by the Department of Defense had now found its way into millions of businesses and homes. Expansion continued through the rest of the world, eventually becoming the standard way in which individuals communicated and shared information. The most recent growth has been in the mobile sector, where many companies compete to become your provider for the "always on" Internet connection in your pocket.

WHO OWNS THE INTERNET?

Today, the Internet connects multiple networks and over 2 billion users around the world. It is a huge, decentralized, and cooperative community; no single person or group controls the network. Many telecommunications companies provide the infrastructure in a particular region, and these companies connect with each other at various points to ensure their users have a global reach. It is up to each country's government to determine whether it will regulate or censor the content that ends up reaching the businesses and homes within its boundaries. If the government decides to censor, it typically will ask the regional telecommunication company to filter the incoming content before sending it out to the rest of the country.

FREEDOM AND OPENNESS

The concepts of free expression and censorship are hot topics around the world. Many have argued that it is the Internet's independence and free flow of information that makes it the universally powerful tool it has become. If you can use a computer and if the computer is connected to the Internet, you are not only free to use the resources posted by others but also free to create information of your own. Although several organizations (such as The Internet Society and the W3C) propose standards for Internet-related technologies and appropriate use, these organizations almost universally support the Internet's openness and lack of centralized control.

Overview of Internet Services

The Internet acts as a carrier for several different services, each with its own distinct features and purposes. Think of the Internet as the road upon which many different types of vehicles travel. The roads in your city allow various services to reach you, from UPS and FedEx deliveries to emergency vehicles that can save your life. In a similar manner, you can enjoy services such as websites, email, and online games because the Internet provides the infrastructure that can carry this type of information. Let's look at some of the popular services that exist because of the Internet.

THE WORLD WIDE WEB (WWW)

The **World Wide Web** (also known as the web or WWW) is a global system of linked, hypertext documents. The hypertext in these documents refers to text that is capable of acting as a **hyperlink**, or connector, to another piece of text or document. While these

The Internet is decentralized. Small networks connect to larger networks, which in turn connect to each other.

hyperlinks were originally limited to specially coded text, it eventually became possible to use images and videos as hyperlinks. Web-based documents are normally referred to as **web pages**. Several related pages that connect to each other are referred to as a **website**. These sites are typically located, or hosted, on servers known as **web servers**. It is these servers that deliver a requested web page to your computer using a protocol known as **HTTP** (hypertext transfer protocol).

The web traces its origin to a proposal made by Tim Berners-Lee in 1989. He envisioned a large collection of documents, all stored in different places but all linked in some manner. These linked documents would create a sort of "web" of interconnected information. If you extend that collection of documents and their links to cover the entire globe, you would have a "world wide web" of information. In 1990, this proposal was realized when the first web page was created and placed on the first web server. It was a simple document, containing only black text and hyperlinks. The language used by this first page, **HTML** (hypertext markup language), is still used in pages today along with newer languages such as CSS and JavaScript.

As with all computer technology, the web has continued to evolve since its creation. The web pages you see today can contain music, photos, videos, and even games. In the second half of this chapter, we will take a closer look at all the activities we engage in on the World Wide Web.

More **Online:** *Visit the companion website to see the first web page created by Tim Berners-Lee while he was working at CERN.*

PARTS OF A URL

Home and business addresses throughout the world must follow certain standards (house number, postal code, etc.) to make physical visits and deliveries easier. Web pages also have a standard addressing system known as a **URL** (uniform resource locator), which allows them to be located on the Internet. Most users arrive at a specific address by clicking a link that connects them there. Other times, users can type it directly into a web browser if they know the full URL. It is important to pay attention to URLs, as they can often reveal a great deal about the site that you are on. Use Figure 4.3 and the following list to gain a better understanding of a URL's components.

The HTML and CSS code (below) are converted by the web browser into an attractive web page (above).

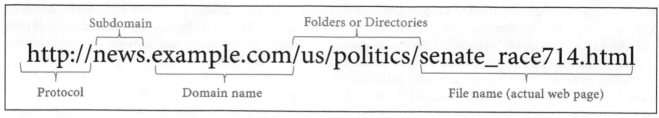

http://news.example.com/us/politics/senate_race714.html

Subdomain — Folders or Directories — Protocol — Domain name — File name (actual web page)

Figure 4.3 **The parts of a URL.**

- **Protocol.** The http:// portion of a URL represents the standard web protocol. If you see **HTTPS** instead, it means that a secure, encrypted connection has been established, such as when shopping or logging in to your bank.

- **Domain.** The **domain name** uniquely identifies a site and a brand on the web. Examples include *apple.com*, *whitehouse.gov*, and *red-cross.org*. The first part indicates the unique domain name, while the second half, known as a top-level domain (TLD), indicates the type of site. "Com," for example, is commercial, while "gov" represents a site from the government. Although a few rules are strictly enforced, organizations are generally allowed to use any domain and TLD they want. In fact, anyone can purchase a domain for less than $20 a year.

1&1 DOMAINS

Got a great idea? Get a great domain!

.com	$14.99	first year	$7.99*
.us	$14.99	first year	$7.99*
.info	$14.99	first year	$0.99*

Companies compete to become your domain name registrar.

- **Subdomain.** The **subdomain** of a URL is located just before the domain. It usually indicates a specific subdivision or server within a large site. While "www" is the most popular, sites such as yahoo.com have subdomains for each of their services. When you see *sports.yahoo.com*, for example, you know that you are in the sports section of that site. Many scammers take advantage of the subdomain to trick users into thinking that a site is legitimate. For example, if you accidently land on a site whose URL is *microsoft.example.com*, do not believe that you are on a Microsoft-related site because of the subdomain. Whoever owns *example.com* is allowed to add subdomains with any name, including those that could trick users.

- **Folders and file.** The last part of a URL will list the folders and subfolders (or directories) where the web page file is located. Remember that a web page is nothing more than a file that contains code for the web browser. Like all files on a computer, they are stored on a disk and possibly located within a folder/subfolder structure.

ELECTRONIC MAIL SERVICES

Electronic mail, more commonly called **email**, is a system for exchanging messages through a computer network. People often use email to send and receive messages containing only text. However, email can also contain images, and practically any type of file can be attached to a message. Because of its versatility, email has become an important and widely used form of communication, particularly in the workplace.

Email started to gain popularity a few years after the launch of ARPANET. Its growth has continued, with practically every employee and Internet user having an email account. Unfortunately, that growth has also come with an increase in **spam**, which is unsolicited email that is sent in bulk. This "junk" mail is not only a nuisance and a waste of network resources, but it also can contain links to dangerous

websites. Fortunately, many companies have become quite good at filtering out spam so that you don't see it while going through your inbox. Nevertheless, if you don't recognize the sender or if the content of the message is suspicious (even from someone you know), you should delete the email immediately.

More **Online:** *Is it "e-mail" or "email"? Do I capitalize "internet" and "web"? Visit the companion website to discover the answers and the reasons behind them.*

WEB-BASED EMAIL

It is typical for individuals to have an email account at work and one that is issued by their Internet service provider. However, many choose to create additional, free accounts on the websites of companies such as Google, Microsoft, or Yahoo. These companies offer free web-based email services that are usually supported by advertisements. You can check this email from just about anywhere, including your mobile device.

It is often useful to create at least two of these free accounts. One should be given out to a limited number of people, such as friends and family. This one will have all of your important messages and very little spam. The other can be given out to just about anyone, including businesses that want to send you newsletters and special offers via email. You can check this one when you have extra time or want to look for a particular coupon.

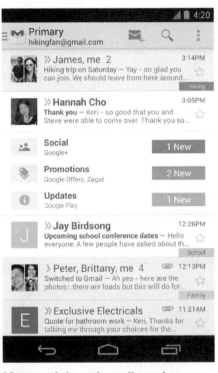

Many web-based email services, such as Gmail, offer mobile apps.

EMAIL COMPONENTS AND ACTIONS

Although you likely have used email, you may not be familiar with certain aspects of it. Understanding all parts of an email will help you communicate more effectively and ensure that you don't make a mistake when sending messages at work. The following are the parts of every email message:

- **To.** This contains the email address of the primary recipient(s) of your message. This address typically contains the name of an individual and the organization that provides the email, separated by the "@" symbol (e.g., liz_williams@example.com).

- **Cc.** The section known as **Cc**, or carbon copy, is used to send a copy of your message to individuals other than your primary recipient. For example, suppose that you are part of a four-member committee. If you want to send some ideas for the next meeting to the chair of the committee, you would place her email address in the "To" area. However, since you want to offer other committee members the chance to comment on your ideas, but they are not the primary target of your message, you would place their email addresses in the "Cc" section. Another popular use of "Cc" is when you want another individual, such as a supervisor, to be notified, or "copied," on an email message that you are sending to someone else.

- **Bcc.** Any email address placed in the **Bcc**, or blind carbon copy, will be invisible to the recipients of your message. It is common to use Bcc when sending email to a large group of people, especially if you want to protect the privacy of the recipients' email address. It also prevents individuals from having to scroll through a very long list of recipients when reading the message.

- **Subject.** The subject of an email indicates the topic or purpose of your message. Be sure to always fill this box, as it makes it easy for individuals to know what a message is about before opening it. If the subject contains the letters "re," it indicates that the message is a **reply**, or response. If it contains "fw," it means that the message has been **forwarded**, or re-sent, after its initial transmission. Be sure to use good judgment when forwarding email or replying to a group of individuals. Always consider the privacy of the original sender and be considerate with other people's time. They may not appreciate

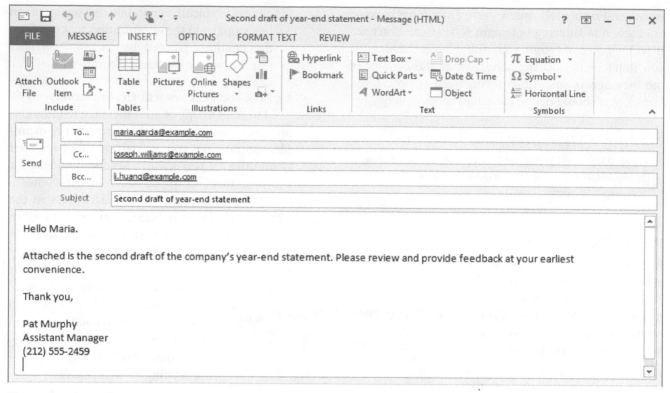

The parts of an effectively written email message.

receiving a large number of messages that are not relevant to them.

- **Body.** The body of an email message contains the text that you want your recipient to read. Most email accounts also support the placing of images alongside your text. At the bottom of the message, most individuals add a *signature,* which typically contains their name, title, and contact information.

- **Attachments.** If you want to include a file with your message, you must place it in the **attachments** area. Always try to attach small files, as the recipient may have an email account that has size limits and restrictions. Whenever possible, place your files in a cloud storage account so that you can simply send a link to those files in the message area of your email.

USING EMAIL PROPERLY & EFFECTIVELY

The previous section introduced the parts of an email and some tips on how to use them effectively. In addition, other guidelines and best practices should be followed to communicate properly and effectively with others, especially in business. Although many of these guidelines are not official, some general rules of conduct are expected by those who use email.

One of the most important rules to observe with respect to email is the proper use of your account. Never use your work or school email for anything other than their respective purposes. Not following this could violate policies set forth by that organization. Furthermore, you don't know how long you will be at that particular institution, so if you start using that email for personal activities, you could eventually lose access to those messages. Besides this major rule, there are other guidelines that you should follow for good email etiquette:

- **Language.** Use traditional spelling and grammar in most, if not all, workplace and school communication. Unless your message is for a friend or family member, avoid using the type of abbreviations and casual tone you might use in text messages.

- **Tone.** It is often difficult to sense sarcasm and other emotions in a written email. Although you can use **emoticons** (symbols representing emotions) in casual messages, you should be

careful with the tone of your writing when sending email at school or work. It is also important to note that writing in ALL CAPITAL LETTERS indicates to the reader that you are shouting.

- **Be brief.** Always be mindful of how busy the recipient of your email might be. Make your messages brief, yet clear enough to convey your thoughts. If you have quite a bit to say, a conversation may be better than an email message.

REAL-TIME COMMUNICATION

Generally, an email message arrives at its destination just a few seconds after you send it. However, you must wait an indefinite amount of time until the recipient decides to check email, open your message, and write a reply. This is acceptable when communicating with your supervisor or professor, but it may not be best when trying to converse with a friend. For this reason, many individuals today prefer various forms of **real-time communication**, where messages and conversations between two or more people occur instantaneously. This section will cover some of the most popular tools that individuals use to converse in real time.

INSTANT MESSAGING

Instant messaging is the act of having an online, text-based conversation with one or more individuals. Unlike an email, which can be read by the recipient at any time, instant messengers engage individuals in a

Skype offers instant messaging, video calling, and VoIP services.

live conversation. During conversations, you will see some sort of icon showing that the other person is typing. And before starting a conversation, an icon or status message will notify you of the person's availability to chat. Some of the earliest forms of this communication were the instant messengers and chat rooms of America Online (AOL). Today, instant messaging is built into many web-based email and social networking sites. Companies such as Google, Facebook, and Microsoft (Skype) all have popular instant messaging services. Some require that you go to a particular website while others offer a downloadable program that lets you chat without going to the web. There are also many instant messaging apps for mobile devices, some of which were discussed in Chapter 1.

VIDEO CALLING AND CONFERENCING

If you prefer to have a conversation using voice and video, then a video calling or videoconferencing service would meet your needs. This is quite useful for having conversations with friends and family that do not live near you, or having a meeting with employees located in a different office. Like instant messaging, these conversations occur in real time much like a face-to-face conversation. If both you and the other individual have an account with the same service, such as Google Hangouts or Skype, you can usually talk for as long as you want, regardless of where you both live. Much like instant messaging tools, these services are often available directly through your web browser, as desktop software, or as a mobile app. Most of these services are free; however, many business users pay for videoconferencing services that offer more features and support for a larger number of participants.

VOICE OVER IP (VOIP)

Voice over Internet Protocol (VoIP) translates analog voice signals into digital data and uses the Internet to transport the data. VoIP systems can connect to the telephone network, allowing you to place a call to another individual's phone from your computer or Internet-connected phone. Companies such as Vonage and MagicJack allow you to use your existing Internet connection and home telephones to make calls. However, many users are opting to pay for a package from their Internet provider that includes VoIP. Other companies, such as Skype, offer affordable calling

packages (local and long distance) in addition to free video calling. Regardless of which option you choose, VoIP allows many individuals to cancel their traditional phone service and make all calls using their Internet connection. Just be sure to consider all the advantages and disadvantages, including the possibility of being without a home phone if you lose power or Internet connectivity.

BROADCASTS & STREAMING MEDIA

As you learned in Chapter 1, streaming media refers to music and movies that are delivered on demand from an online source. Netflix is the most popular streaming service, delivering movies and TV shows to your computer, entertainment system, or mobile device. Various reports have indicated that Netflix often accounts for over 30 percent of all Internet traffic in North America.

Other types of content take advantage of streaming. A **webcast** is the broadcast of various types of media over the web. Many stations, from radio to TV, will broadcast music, news, sports, and other content live on the web for anyone who wishes to listen or watch. In addition, many individuals and organizations create original content on the web since it is affordable and accessible. You can find many *channels* on YouTube, for example, that contain web-only content. Some of them are very high quality and intend to compete with many of the shows and videos you watch on TV.

Some types of broadcasts are referred to as **podcasts**. Many of these are typically prerecorded and can be downloaded from a variety of sources, including Apple's iTunes. Because you can subscribe

The White House offers a variety of podcasts.

to a podcast, future episodes will be downloaded automatically by your system.

FILE SHARING

An important service offered by the Internet is the ability to transfer files anywhere in the world. The most popular method for file transfer today is known as **peer-to-peer (P2P)** file sharing. This method uses a distributed network of individual users instead of a central server to transfer files. Specialty software allows an individual's computer to identify other computers in the distributed network and access their shared files directly and independently. Requesters seeking a specific file may find multiple copies within the peer-to-peer network and request a copy from a participating computer with the most efficient connection.

The BitTorrent protocol has recently become very popular for sharing large files, such as software or full-length videos and movies. BitTorrent uses a P2P design that makes large numbers of user connections and requests small pieces of the desired file from each of them. This allows a large amount of data to be **downloaded**, or received, by the requesting machine without relying on just one connection to one sender. It also allows requesters to become senders. As soon as a data piece has been downloaded to the requester's computer, that piece is made available to be **uploaded**, or sent, to others who need it.

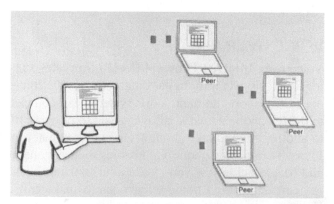

A BitTorrent user downloads parts of a file from other users. After receiving a piece, this user can then provide it to others.

Many companies have adopted P2P technology as a quick means of transporting files. This is true for a large number of software companies that distribute software and updates to millions of users at a time. Instead of overwhelming their servers on any given day, they use BitTorrent networks to allow the file to be distributed more efficiently from users to users. In addition, many amateur artists and musicians can also use this service to quickly share their work with anyone in the network. Unfortunately, P2P networks are also used for illegally sharing copyrighted works such as movies, books, music, and software. We will discuss illegal sharing and violation of copyright law in the first half of Chapter 6.

ONLINE CLASSES

The Internet makes it easy to send video and other multimedia content anywhere in the world. Because of this, it is possible to deliver educational content such as classroom broadcasts or complete online courses. Some of these classes are designed to supplement classroom education. For example, if a professor wants students to hear a specific lecture from the professor at another school, videoconferencing equipment can be set up to watch the lesson live in the classroom. Other classes are completely available online, allowing students to be anywhere in the world while they learn. While this may seem desirable, online classes generally require students to be

self-motivated and not fall victim to the distractions at the location where they log into the course.

Some universities even offer entire accredited degree programs online. Students learn via online lecture notes or presentations using a **learning management system (LMS)** such as Blackboard Learn. They use this system to complete exams, turn in work, and communicate with their instructor and classmates. Some traditional universities offer degrees that use a combination of face-to-face and online classes, while others offer their services exclusively over the Internet. Universities are also experimenting with blending classroom and online components, where you meet with your class in person on one day, but meet online for the other.

Students who simply want to learn and do not require course credit can now enroll in a **massive open online course (MOOC)**. These are huge online courses offered for free by a variety of universities, including prestigious ones such as Princeton, Harvard, and MIT. Their aim is to offer high-quality content to millions of individuals throughout the world who do not have the opportunity to attend select classes at these universities. If you enroll in one of these classes, you might discover that tens of thousands of students are registered along with you.

ONLINE GAMES

The Internet offers more than the games you download to your mobile device or play on websites. For many years, it has been possible to connect gaming consoles such as the PlayStation and Xbox to the Internet in order to play with (or against) other players. For PCs, a category of games known as **MMORPGs** (massively multiplayer online role-playing games) has experienced rapid growth. In these games, millions of players connect to various servers to team up with other players in very large virtual worlds. While some games can be played using a web browser, most require the purchase and installation of software.

Coursera offers hundreds of noncredit MOOCs from a variety of universities.

Connecting to the Internet

Now that you know many of the services that the Internet has to offer, it is time to explore the ways in which users connect to this global network. We will begin with some basic terms related to data communication and Internet connectivity.

Every type of Internet service requires a connection and monthly payment to an **Internet service provider (ISP)**. These are usually telecommunications companies that offer homes and businesses access to the Internet. These companies have connections to an Internet backbone or a higher-level ISP (see Figure 4.4). When choosing an ISP, you will often be given a choice of various speeds. The speed at which data travels to and from the ISP is measured in **bits per seconds (bps)**. As speeds have increased, so have the units. A kilobit is a thousand bits, while a megabit is a million bits. Keep these units in mind as we compare the various types of Internet connections.

DIAL-UP

The first way in which most users connected to the Internet was using a **dial-up** connection with their phone line. Back then, many computers would include a **modem**, which is a device that can convert digital information from a computer into the analog sound waves that could be transmitted over the phone lines. The computer was essentially making a phone call to another computer that would then convert the sound waves back into digital form. The most popular dial-up service was America Online (AOL). Not only did the service connect most users in the 1990s, but it also offered software and services to make things easier for first-time Internet users.

Only a minority of users in North America continue to use dial-up. One of the biggest drawbacks was the maximum speed of 56 Kbps (kilobits per second), which made it difficult to download larger files and load pages with many images. Additionally, a dial-up user will essentially tie up the phone line for the house, making it impossible for family members to make or receive phone calls.

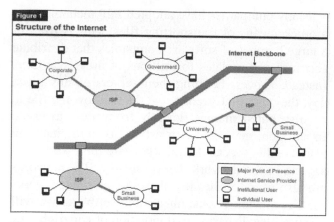

Figure 4.4 ISPs connect users to the Internet.

BROADBAND

The term **broadband** is used to describe any digital data connection that can transmit information faster than standard dial-up by using a wider band of frequencies. For homes, the ISP will usually provide a router or **residential gateway**, which is a device that connects your home's network to the Internet. The following are the most common types of broadband:

- **DSL.** With a digital subscriber line, or DSL, companies use the same telephone lines already present in your home. Telecommunication companies simply upgraded their networks to handle digital data instead of analog voice signals.

- **Cable.** If you already subscribe to a cable TV package in your home, you can add Internet connectivity to that package. The same technology that carries hundreds of TV channels can also transmit Internet signals.

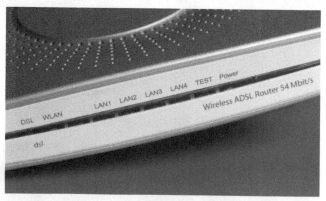

A DSL router acts as a residential gateway.

Max Turbo	Max Plus	Max	Elite	Pro
DOWNSTREAM SPEEDS UP TO **24** MBPS	DOWNSTREAM SPEEDS UP TO **18** MBPS	DOWNSTREAM SPEEDS UP TO **12** MBPS	DOWNSTREAM SPEEDS UP TO **6** MBPS	DOWNSTREAM SPEEDS UP TO **3** MBPS
$66/mo.*	$56/mo.*	$51/mo.*	$46/mo.*	$41/mo.*

ISPs usually offer various home packages at different speeds.

- **Satellite.** If you live in an area where companies do not offer DSL or cable, you can purchase a special dish and connect to the Internet via satellite. This same dish can also give you access to hundreds of TV channels.

- **Fiber-optic communication.** Several companies, such as Verizon and Google, have begun to promote fiber-optic technology for the home. This means that data travels using light pulses through an optical fiber instead of through the traditional copper wires. Most telecommunication companies use the better-performing fiber-optic technology throughout their networks, but the extension of this technology directly to homes and businesses is fairly new. That is what makes services such as Verizon's FiOS unique and very desirable.

More **Online:** *Visit the companion website to learn how to test your Internet connection speed at home or on your mobile device.*

Many individuals wonder which of the various services they should use for Internet access. In most cases, it comes down to pricing and special offers. Ask what sort of discount is available if you bundle services such as TV, Internet, and a wireless plan for your mobile device. For many users, speed is the biggest factor. Depending on the area in which you live, one broadband technology might offer a faster connection than the other. While 1.5 to 3 Mbps might be sufficient for most Internet activities, those who desire high-definition video or engage in heavy downloading will likely want 6 to 12 Mbps speeds.

MOBILE

The use of mobile devices for Internet connectivity is increasing daily. If you are at home, you will typically use your existing wireless network to access the Internet from a tablet or smartphone. However, when you are on the go, you will need a mobile **data plan** that allows you to connect to the Internet using a cellular network. These data plans, which often limit the amount of data you can send and receive per month, are measured in megabytes (MB) or gigabytes (GB). If you go over your limit during any month, you will be required to pay an additional charge for the extra data usage.

Many terms are used to describe the type and speed of mobile networks. The general terms are 3G and 4G, which simply represent a generation number. The one you connect to is determined by your mobile device, your area, and the wireless carrier (company) that you choose. Although it is obvious that 4G is an improvement over 3G, the various subcategories of 4G (e.g., LTE and WiMAX) make it difficult to define a specific speed range.

MOBILE HOTSPOTS

A **mobile hotspot** refers to a device that can connect to a mobile network and offer Internet access to multiple devices near it. This device can be either a smartphone or a stand-alone hotspot device such as

the MiFi. If your smartphone is the device, all you need to do is pay for a data plan as described in the previous section. Then, use the **tethering** feature to make your phone act as a wireless access point. Any computer that is near it, from a laptop to a tablet, can now connect to your smartphone and use its Internet access. Although many smartphones are capable of doing this, most carriers charge an extra fee for this service.

If you do not own a smartphone or do not wish to use it for tethering, you can purchase a mobile hotspot device from most wireless companies. This small device, which requires a mobile data plan, can be taken almost anywhere to provide wireless Internet access to a group of people. This is useful if you and a group of friends or family members frequently find yourselves in locations that do not offer free wireless Internet. It is worth noting that the term "hotspot" is also used to refer to a location or business that offers wireless Internet access. We will discuss wireless technology further in Chapter 5.

Web Browsers

To view web pages, you need special software known as a **web browser**. Web browsers are so important that practically all desktop and mobile operating systems now include one. In this section, you will discover some of the features and settings of popular web browsers.

INTRODUCTION

A web browser has two fundamental purposes. First, it helps you find and retrieve a web page that you are interested in viewing. Second, when the page arrives at your computer, the browser translates the code that web pages are made of into the attractive layouts you see today. Although all browsers can handle today's web programming languages, it is possible for a page to look slightly different from one browser to the next. The following are some of the popular (and free) web browsers used today:

- Apple Safari
- Google Chrome
- Microsoft Internet Explorer
- Mozilla Firefox

AT&T mobile hotspot device.

BROWSER BASICS

Each web browser may offer unique features and capabilities. However, all of them have several components in common. These are important for the understanding and effective use of a web browser. Observe Figure 4.5 as you review the following components.

ADDRESS BAR

The address bar of a web browser displays the URL of the web page you are currently looking at. Users can enter a new URL into this area to navigate to a new page. Newer browsers also use this area to allow users to initiate a web search.

NAVIGATION BUTTONS

Browsers contain various navigation buttons that let you easily move between web pages. Here are a few examples:

- **Back.** This button takes you to the previous web page that you were viewing.
- **Forward.** This button returns you to the page you were on before clicking the *back* button.
- **Stop.** If a page is taking too long to load, you can click the *stop* button to give up the attempt to load it.
- **Refresh.** This is often used immediately after clicking the *stop* button. It will ask the browser to make another attempt to retrieve and display that page. Another popular use for the *refresh* button is to request the most current information (such as news or weather) for the page you are currently on.
- **Home.** You are allowed to configure the **home page**, or starting page, for each browser. Clicking this button will return you to this specific page.

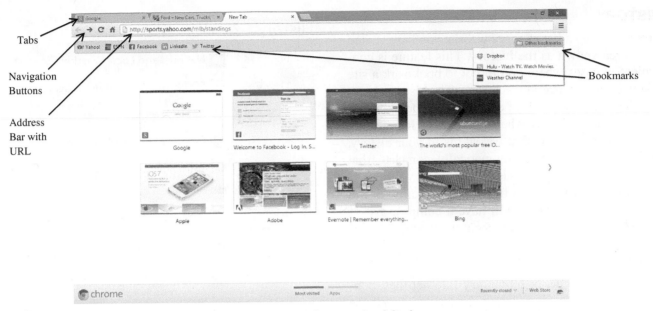

Tabs

Navigation
Buttons

Address
Bar with
URL

Bookmarks

Figure 4.5 Google's Chrome web browser showing frequently visited pages.
Source: Google Plus

TABS

Several years ago, web browsers would open an additional window if you wanted to view a second web page on your computer. As you can imagine, this got a bit messy if you wanted to open many web pages at a time, such as when performing research for a school project. All newer browsers use a **tabbed browsing** interface, which allows you to have multiple web pages open in one browser window. You can navigate between these pages by clicking its tab at the top of the browser window.

It is not uncommon for users to have a dozen or more tabs open at any given time. If your browser or computer malfunctions, browsers such as Google Chrome will remember every one of the tabs you had open and will restore them immediately when the browser is reopened. Furthermore, Chrome will allow you to access these tabs from a remote location as long as you log into the browser with your unique user ID and password.

> More **Online:** *Visit the companion website to learn useful shortcuts for tabs and other common browser operations.*

CONVENIENCE AND PRIVACY

There are various features and settings in web browsers that offer many conveniences to users. However, these same features could also be seen as a privacy threat by some users. Although Internet-related privacy issues will be discussed in Chapter 6, this section will offer a brief introduction to these browser features.

BOOKMARKS/FAVORITES

If you visit a website or page that you would like to remember for the future, you can add it to your browser's **bookmarks** or favorites. This area will remember the exact URL of any page and offers you easy one-click access to it. Browsers let you organize related bookmarks into various folders. In addition, you can also add your most important bookmarks to a special toolbar near the top of the browser window. The main privacy issue with bookmarks occurs when someone borrows your computer or watches you while you use it. For example, if you are married and you added a bookmark for a specific piece of jewelry at a famous store, it may spoil the surprise if your spouse sees it when opening the bookmarks area of the browser.

HISTORY

Browsers keep a list of every website you have visited in an area known as the **history**. This feature is convenient in cases where you forgot to bookmark a site that you visited several weeks ago. The history shows you the name and URL of every site you have visited. It also comes in handy when typing the URL of a site in the address bar. If that website is in your history, then the browser will automatically complete that URL for you. The privacy issue here is very similar to that of bookmarks. The difference is that anyone who accesses your computer will have a complete list of every site you have been to recently.

CACHE

The browser **cache**, or temporary Internet files, contains every single page, image, and video for all the web pages you have recently retrieved. Recall that the history only remembers the name and URL of the site. The cache, which is usually stored for a few weeks on your hard drive, contains the actual files. Browsers keep these files so that frequently visited pages can be loaded faster. This occurs because many of the larger files, such as images, can be loaded locally from your hard drive instead of having to be retrieved from the Internet. Law enforcement agencies typically look at the cache to see what content a suspect has been looking at online.

COOKIES

The small data files known as **cookies** are one of the most misunderstood features of the web. Most websites ask the browser to create and keep these files so that they can remember users and their preferences the next time they visit the site. If all websites behaved ethically, everyone would likely welcome these cookies. However, many companies use cookies to track users' habits as they go from one site to the next. To better understand cookies, it is important to distinguish between the two fundamental types:

- **First-party cookies.** These cookies can only be created and read by the actual website you are visiting.

History

11:59 PM	TWC	National and Local Weather Forecast,
11:59 PM		ESPN: The Worldwide Leader In Sports
11:58 PM		Apple www.apple.com
11:58 PM		Evernote \| Remember everything with
11:57 PM	Y!	Yahoo! ☆ www.yahoo.com
11:57 PM		Sign In login.live.com
11:57 PM		Twitter ☆ twitter.com
11:57 PM	in	World's Largest Professional Network
11:56 PM	f	Welcome to Facebook - Log In, Sign L
11:56 PM		Bing www.bing.com
11:56 PM		Google www.google.com

A browser's history shows the name and URL of every site visited.

Companies such as Amazon often request that the browser make cookies that allow the company to remember your name and ID when you return to the site. Other companies, such as UPS, use cookies to remember the selections you made when first visiting the site. It would be annoying to users if they had to select their country every time they navigated to the UPS site. With cookies, UPS can read that preference and immediately direct users to the site tailored for the country they are from.

- **Third-party cookies.** These cookies are typically created by marketing and advertising companies that work with the website you are visiting. For example, suppose that you visit the websites of two different car manufacturers who happen to employ the same advertising company. Besides receiving first-party cookies from the car companies, you will also receive third-party cookies from the advertising companies.

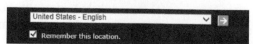

UPS uses cookies to store your selected location.

While the second car company is not allowed to read the cookie from the first car company, the advertising company can read the cookies issued from both sites! This allows the company to effectively track you because it knows which of its partner's websites you have visited. Gathering general information about your online activity allows advertisers to generate ads that better target your interests. This sort of tracking makes many individuals uncomfortable, even though personal or secure information is not being collected.

PLUG-INS AND EXTENSIONS

A browser **plug-in** is a separate program that allows your web browser to play several types of multimedia content. The most popular plug-in is Adobe Flash Player, which is required to watch many videos and play games in the browser. Most plug-ins are offered as free downloads.

A browser **extension** is also a separate program, but its purpose is to add a variety of useful features to the web browser. These include activities such as sending instant messages or playing mobile-style games from your browser window. Many of the programs discussed in this book, from Evernote to Google Hangouts, also create browser extensions to make their programs more convenient to use.

Web browsers allow you to clear all of your browsing history, cache, and cookies.

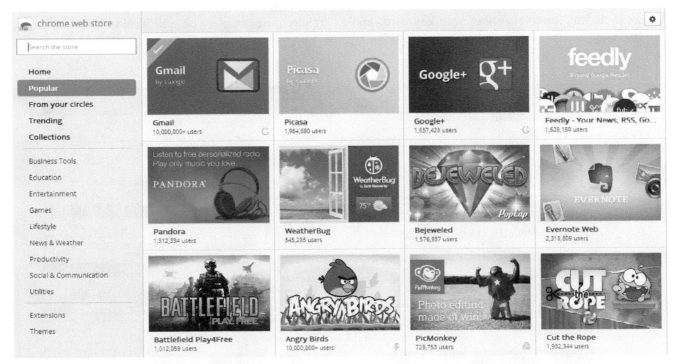

The Chrome Web Store offers thousands of browser extensions.

PART 2:
Exploring the Web

You have just learned about a variety of services that exist because of the Internet. In this section, we will focus mostly on activities that individuals engage in on the World Wide Web.

Finding Information

One of the most important reasons individuals use the web is to find information. This ranges from today's news and weather to school or work-related research. This section will cover the most common ways in which we search for information and the websites that help us find what we are looking for.

SEARCH ENGINES

Search engines are sophisticated services that store the URLs of millions of web pages and most of the content on those pages. When users type specific keywords into the search engine, they will receive an organized list of matching sites, images, and news articles that contain those keywords. The order of the search results can be based on a variety of factors including the relevance of your keywords and the website's popularity. Recently, search engines have begun to personalize the results for users, taking into account your current location, social networks, and previous searches. You will learn more about effective online searches and research later in this chapter.

Search engines continuously index, or *crawl,* the web's contents, finding new sites and revisiting existing ones in order to update their database of sites. In some cases, search engines can identify new information (for example, news stories) within a few minutes of it being published. There are several search engines, but two currently dominate the market. Google has firmly established itself as the leader, but Microsoft's Bing is a worthy alternative for finding what you need on the web.

> More **Online:** *Microsoft offers rewards for using its Bing search engine. Visit the companion website to learn more.*

WEB PORTALS

A **web portal** is a website that provides a variety of useful information and services to visitors. Yahoo and MSN are both popular web portals that many users have as their browser's home page. When you load Yahoo, for example, you will have today's headlines,

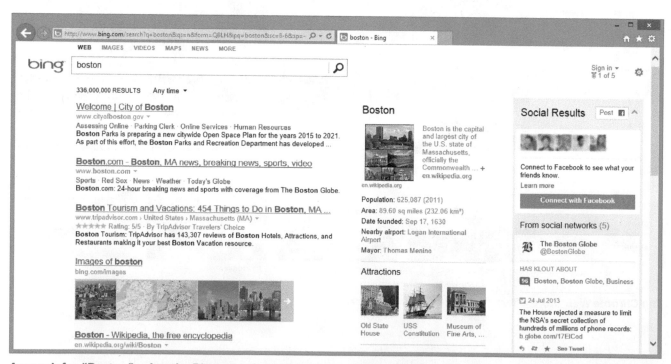

A search for "Boston" using the Bing search engine returns these results.

local weather, sports scores, and financial data all on the home page of that site. In addition, you can access a general search engine, web-based email, free online games, and the Flickr photo-sharing site with just one click. Companies invest millions of dollars to run a portal, hoping that one large website will provide most of a user's information-based needs. Their motivation is essentially the same as that of any TV network: If they keep you from turning the channel (or leaving the site), you will see more advertisements.

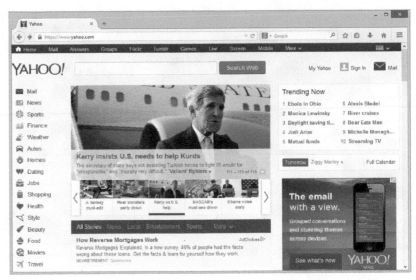

Yahoo is a web portal that offers useful information and a variety of services.

NEWS

The web has changed the way we learn about current events. All the major news organizations, from CNN and Fox to *The Wall Street Journal* and *Time* magazine, now place many of their articles, photos, and videos on the web. This makes it easy to scroll through a large number of headlines, stopping to read the ones you find most interesting. Most news websites are supported by advertisements; however, a few premium news sources may charge a monthly or annual fee to access some of their content. You can also use a search engine to browse a variety of news sources that contain the keywords you entered.

Many users are finding creative ways to read today's news. The first is by using a mobile app known as a **news aggregator**. These tools, such as Flipboard and the Windows 8 News app, allow you to pick a variety of news sources in different categories. It will then present them to you in a magazine-style interface for easy reading. In essence, you are designing your own magazine that delivers the exact types of news and topics that you want to read each day. The other creative way to get news is to simply follow popular news sources on social networks. That way, you will see an occasional headline or breaking news mixed in with updates from your friends and family.

More **Online:** *RSS feeds also allow users to gather news from multiple sources. Visit the companion website to learn more.*

MAPS & BUSINESS INFORMATION

Many individuals use the web to learn more about a business. By typing the name of the business in most search engines, you can quickly retrieve that organization's website, contact information, operating hours, a detailed map, and even user reviews. Bing, for example, will show you reviews from Yelp, which is one of the most popular review sites in the world. Alternatively, you can go directly to Yelp's website or app whenever you need any type of business information. Like search engines, Yelp can detect your general location to give you results that are nearby.

Internet-based map tools have been incredibly powerful in the last few years. Google's map service, for example, will show you detailed road

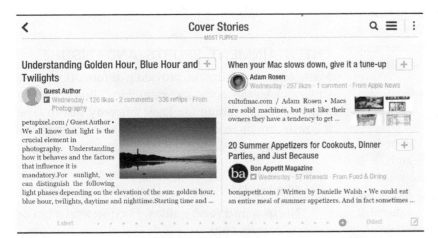

Flipboard's app displays news from various sources in a magazine-style format.

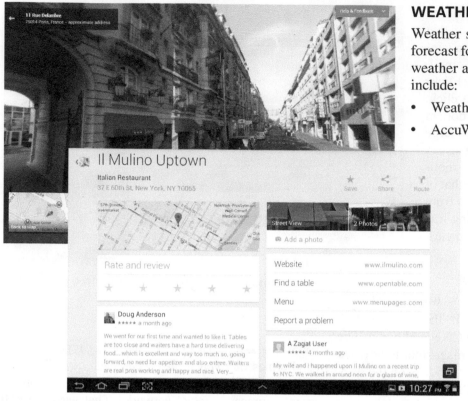

Google Maps offers traffic information and business details (below), and Street View (above) lets you drive virtually through many cities in the world.

WEATHER

Weather services now provide a detailed forecast for several days along with severe weather alerts and radar maps. Examples include:

- Weather Channel (weather.com)
- AccuWeather (accuweather.com)

JOBS

If you are looking for a job, several websites can help you search through large listings. In addition, they will help you prepare and upload your résumé for employers that want to browse for candidates. Two popular sites are

- Monster (monster.com)
- Indeed.com

TRAVEL

One type of travel site contains tips and reviews that help guide you while planning your trip. Some of these offer expert reviews and recommendations (e.g., frommers.com and fodors.com), while others allow individual travelers to rate their experiences (e.g., tripadvisor.com). Both can be crucial for helping you avoid bad hotels and attractions. In addition to review sites, travelers also use online travel agencies as part of their travel research. These services help you find and book flights, hotels, and cars.

- Expedia (expedia.com)
- Orbitz (orbitz.com)
- Priceline (priceline.com)

and satellite maps for any address in the world. It also offers turn-by-turn driving directions, traffic information, and details on any business on the map. One of its most powerful features is *Street View,* which shows you almost any part of the map as if you were driving through that street. This was made possible by Google sending out hundreds of specially equipped vehicles that contained a 360-degree camera. This has become useful for individuals who wish to see an unfamiliar business on the outside in order to find it easier when they drive to it. Others use Street View to learn more about cities they have never been to, essentially taking a virtual drive through it from the comfort of their home!

OTHER USEFUL INFORMATION

Although search engines can often provide or lead you to useful information with a simple search, it is often more efficient to search within reliable websites that specialize in one area or category. The following sections will briefly describe these areas and then list a few popular websites that also have mobile apps.

ENTERTAINMENT, SPORTS, AND LEISURE

Many sites specialize in providing information for a variety of leisure activities, including following every major sport or reading the latest celebrity gossip. The following are three examples of these types of sites:

- **Sports.** ESPN.com or Yahoo Sports (sports.yahoo.com).
- **Movies.** IMDB.com or RottenTomatoes.com.
- **Recipes and food guides.** Foodnetwork.com or Allrecipes.com.

FORUMS

Many companies and specialty websites offer **forums**, or discussion boards, where individuals can ask questions and reply to each other. This is often a great place to find solutions to specific issues or learn what everyday users think about a product or service. Many forums are moderated, or supervised, by a company's employees or experts in a particular subject.

The Social Web

The popularity of using the Internet for sharing personal thoughts, opinions, and details on events in one's life has skyrocketed in recent years. The term **social media** refers to the tools and services on the Internet that allow anyone to create and share different types of information. This can include text, photographs, music, and even videos. In addition to sharing, individuals also use social media to interact, collaborate, and build (or strengthen) relationships with others.

The desire people have to share information, along with the Internet's ability to connect people around the world, led to both the development of social media and the phenomenon commonly known as **Web 2.0**. In the early years of the web, only larger organizations and tech-savvy individuals created web pages that users simply viewed. Web 2.0 refers to a new way to use the web, whereby any user can create and share content, as well as provide opinions on existing content. These user contributions and opinions have dramatically changed and personalized large portions of the content available on the web. This section will explore some of those changes by providing an overview of a few social media categories.

COMMENTING AND RATING

Social media websites are not the only ones that encourage the creation of user-generated content. A variety of companies, from news organizations to retailers, now allow users to write comments on practically every page of the site. This allows individuals to provide their opinion or review on any article or product. In addition, there is usually a way for other users to rate any one of those comments. This will elevate opinions and reviews that are popular, while lowering or hiding those that are not. In many cases,

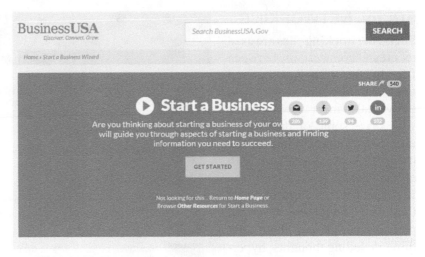

Social share buttons such as "Like" help websites gauge the popularity of their content.

you will find company representatives or site owners engaging users through these comments, answering some of their questions or even addressing concerns and complaints.

Websites use a variety of methods to gauge user interest and opinion. Facebook uses the now-famous "like" system, while Google+ uses a "+1" button. Others may use a star-rating system, such as music review sites and Yelp. Twitter popularized a system that uses the **hashtag** symbol (#) to mark keywords or topics in a message. As more people use hashtags, such as #election or #cats, it increases the likelihood that the keyword becomes a trending topic. In addition to ratings, many services also pay attention to how many times an item has been shared by its users. Funny or fascinating content, for example, is said to go **viral** when it is shared again and again over a short period. This usually causes it to be noticed by a large number of Internet users and even reported by news organizations. Some content can become so popular and widespread over time that it ends up becoming an **Internet meme**. These popular, cultural items can range from a funny phrase or expression, to an activity that many photograph or record themselves doing.

> More **Online:** *Both social media and instant messaging have popularized many abbreviations and Internet slang. Visit the companion website to learn more about these.*

SOCIAL NETWORKING

Social networking sites are used to create connections between friends, family members, and organizations. They also help individuals meet new people who share some of their interests. Social networking allows users to keep up-to-date with events happening around the world and in the lives of those they care about. Any user can post, or submit, just about anything including thoughts, hyperlinks, and photos. They do so with the intention of sharing them with one or more individuals. For example, if you have photos of a major event, such as your graduation, nothing beats social networking's ability to share those photos with all the people in your life and allow them to provide their thoughts on this important event.

Facebook's mobile app lets you stay in touch.

FACEBOOK AND GOOGLE+

Facebook and Google+ are two examples of large-scale social networking services that invite users to share any type of information with others. New users create a free account and are then prompted to provide a wide range of personal data and preferences. This includes information such as their name, contact information, relationship status, college attended, as well as their favorite movies, books and music. Along with personal data, these sites encourage users to invite people they know and add them to their list (or circle) of friends. Essentially, everything these services do is aimed at collecting as much data from as many users as possible. The goal is to look for trends and preferences that can be used to provide you with targeted advertisements. As you remember, many applications and services that you use for free are powered by advertising money.

FRIENDS AND CIRCLES

Facebook calls connected people friends and refers to the group of friends as a user's friends list. Google+ uses a similar system, except it refers to connections as people in your "circles." Both allow users to control who can read a particular post. For example, if you post photos from a family gathering, you may only want to share those with your family members. Conversely, a general thought you may have about a current event might be OK to share with all of your friends or even the general public.

Users can make new connections by searching the system for names of people or organizations that they wish to connect with. Social networks also provide their users with suggestions for new connections based on your existing contacts, preferences, and interests. In Facebook, a friend link is established only by mutual consent: Both users must accept. However, Google+ allows you to follow any person you want, making only that person's public posts available for you to read. Both treat the pages of businesses and celebrities in a similar manner, allowing users to follow or "like" these pages in order to keep track of their posts. Once you have set up a network of friends and chosen a few pages to follow, all of their posts will show up in a single feed on your account.

Google+ organizes your connections into various social circles.
Source: Google Plus

PROFESSIONAL NETWORKING

LinkedIn is similar to other social networks, but it is designed with a strictly business-oriented focus. Most of a user's profile is related to education, professional experience, and other items that one might find on a résumé. Your connections might be co-workers or professionals that you met at a seminar. When recommending new connections, LinkedIn considers several factors such as present and past employers, types of employment, region, and the user's existing network of connections. When posting on LinkedIn, items such as vacation photos, links to funny or controversial websites, and details about relationship problems are largely considered inappropriate by the user community. Instead, you might see individuals posting notifications of upcoming events such as conferences and online seminars.

LinkedIn encourages participants to provide endorsements and recommendations for others in their network. Recommendations are free-form notes that identify something exceptional about the individual based on the writer's experience as a co-worker, employee, or manager of this individual. These recommendations can serve as a significant set of professional references for job seekers looking within their online network for new employment.

BLOGGING

A **blog** (web log) is a web page or small website that contains a series of chronological posts and comments. These posts can contain just about anything, from the thoughts of an individual to updates from the executives of a large organization. It can be a work that stands on its own or a portion of a large corporate website. Blogs tend to have a sort of personal tone that would be inappropriate in more formal areas of a business website. In most cases, the Internet community is encouraged to comment on the posts of the blog's writer, or *blogger*.

WordPress has become the most popular blogging tool. Individuals can create a free account, choose the site's theme, and start writing within minutes. A blog's purpose can cover a wide range of topics such as politics, sports, movies, video games, music, creative writing, and much more. Besides creating their own work, bloggers can follow other bloggers that they find interesting. Some bloggers have gone on to become quite famous, moving on to careers in journalism or expanding their small blog to a popular news or entertainment destination. These large blogs, such as Engadget or The Huffington Post, are often difficult to distinguish from standard news websites.

Tumblr is a popular microblogging service.

> More **Online:** *Visit the companion website to learn more about WordPress and other services that allow you to create your own blog or website.*

MICROBLOGGING

A **microblogging** service, which is essentially a short-form blog, is one where users share brief thoughts, links, and multimedia. Much like regular blogs, individuals can follow their favorite blogs and write comments or responses to any post they read. One of the leading microblogging services is Tumblr. It takes seconds to make an account and start posting. A typical Tumblr blog might be about sharing art, funny photos, or creative recipes. If you visit Tumblr, you will notice that a photo is at the center of most posts, with links or brief comments written underneath.

TWITTER

No microblogging service has become as popular or as important as Twitter. This service is specifically designed to encourage people to make short, frequent posts about news, thoughts, and events. The service restricts posts, referred to as *tweets,* to a maximum of 140 characters, requiring people to become more concise in expressing themselves. In addition to text, Twitter allows posts to contain photos and links. The company also owns a mobile video app known as Vine that allows users to record six-second clips that can be posted to their Twitter account.

Although a Twitter account can be set to private, the majority of users post messages with the intent of making them public. Much like other social networks, you can follow any other Twitter user so that their tweets appear on the home page of your account. Many celebrities and politicians use Twitter to send messages to their fans, while news columnists and bloggers use the service to express thoughts on current events in between longer pieces they publish on their main sites. Businesses use Twitter to announce anything from new products and services to daily discounts.

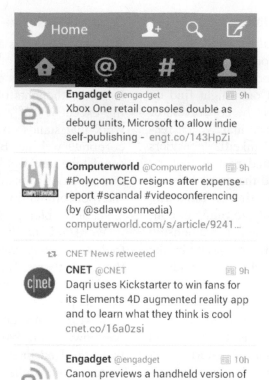

Twitter limits messages to 140 characters.

Twitter has become important for a variety of reasons. First, the short-form messages can be read quickly, allowing individuals to gather a wide range of information in a short amount of time. By scrolling down a few times, you can get a glimpse of today's headlines, information on new product releases, and thoughts from your close friends and favorite celebrities. Furthermore, because tweets can be written quickly, individuals are encouraged to report anything interesting that they see. This can include everything from eyewitness reports of an accident to viewers' thoughts and opinions on a live TV show. Because so many individuals post publically on Twitter, news organizations and businesses use the service to get a feel for how the public is reacting to an event. It is strongly recommended that you learn how to use Twitter, as it has become an indispensable tool for the transmission of information, thoughts, and ideas all over the world.

SPECIALTY SHARING

All the social media services that have been discussed so far allow users to contribute practically any type of information they desire. However, many services specialize in one particular type of media, focusing all of their energy in making one aspect of social sharing the best it can be. The following are some of these services.

VIDEOS

When it comes to social video, no service is as large or popular as YouTube. In a nutshell, YouTube provides a library of user-contributed videos to watch. The clips cover almost any topic you might think of, including snippets of TV shows, instructional videos, funny animals, and an endless variety of individuals

YouTube lets users upload, watch, and share a variety of videos.

talking or singing into a video camera. And speaking of singing, some musicians and artists use YouTube as the primary method for airing new songs or music videos. YouTube is also host to a rising number of business videos and original shows with a high production value.

Many people visit YouTube seeking a specific video or topic, and they can find them quickly by initiating a search. The service also provides lists of recommended and popular videos as determined by visitor ratings and a user's past viewing history. As with other forms of social media, YouTube lets users create a free account in order to upload content, provide comments on videos, and subscribe to the "channels" of their favorite users. With respect to sharing, YouTube allows videos to be embedded, or inserted, in many other websites such as blogs and social networks.

PHOTOS AND IMAGES

Some services specialize in the sharing of photographs. Although these sites often provide unique features for photo enthusiasts, part of their attraction lies in the omission of the excessive features found in larger social networking sites. At a minimum, these sites allow users to easily upload photos from their computers and mobile devices to create online albums at no cost. They can be kept privately in your account, or they can be shared with specific friends or even the general public. Once your photos shared, other users can comment on them. In addition, these services offer various tools to fix or enhance your photos with various effects. They can also be **tagged**, or marked, with keywords, faces, and your current location. Two of

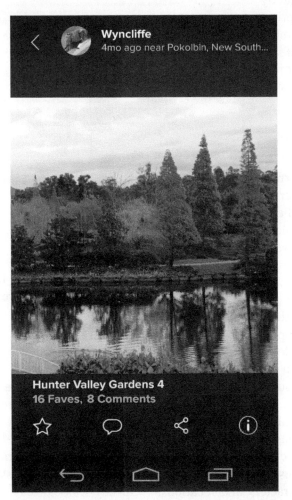

Flickr lets you capture, share, and comment on photos.

the most popular services in this category are Instagram and Flickr.

A few other services offer unique features for sharing images. One of those is DeviantArt, which is the largest online social network for artists. From illustrations to professional photography, DeviantArt allows users to showcase their artwork, sell prints, and connect with other users and fans. Another popular service is Pinterest, which allows users to collect images and content from the web and organize them in a digital pin board. Any image gathered, along with your notes, is known as a pin. You then place related pins on a single board, which allows you to organize various things such as favorite recipes or a wish list of items. Pinterest encourages users to connect with others to share pins and spread good ideas.

NEWS AND LINKS

Social news sites, such as Reddit, encourage users to share links to news and other interesting content they find on the web. Users can comment and vote on the submissions of others, turning these sites into a sort of conversation about trending topics. The best submissions get voted up by users, making it easy to tell what content is hot at the moment. In addition to links, Reddit is also famous for hosting AMA (Ask Me Anything) sessions, where celebrities and politicians, including the president of the United States, answer questions from Reddit's users in a live session.

BOOKS AND DOCUMENTS

Reading has now become a social activity, thanks in part to sites such as Scribd. Authors of books, business

documents, how-to guides, and even comic books can submit their work to Scribd for free or paid distribution. The site will rank what's hot based on how many users are reading or sharing that book. If you are a user, you can view and even download a significant amount of free content. However, some content must be purchased individually based on the author's selling price. If you plan to read a large number of documents and books that are not free, Scribd offers a premium subscription that includes many of these items for a single price.

WIKIS

A **wiki** is a collaborative information site that relies on the Internet community to both create and edit content. Wikis encourage people with subject knowledge to contribute at their convenience, adding to or fixing pages where information is missing or incorrect. The ongoing process of collaborative contributing and editing is designed to produce increasingly accurate and rich content over time.

Wikipedia is the most popular of these sites, offering millions of encyclopedia-style articles for free. In addition, you can find wikis all over the web that cover subjects such as video games, comic books, movies, finance, gardening, cooking, and much more. If, for example, you play a popular video game that has millions of users, you might find a fast-growing wiki that covers that particular game. Users will post articles that contain information about the game's characters and locations, along with guides and hints that help you complete the game.

The content on wikis can change rapidly based on current events. For example, if a country holds an election and new leader is elected, that leader's name will appear within minutes in the Wikipedia article for that country. In a traditional encyclopedia, that change would not have been made until next year's edition! Unfortunately, this benefit is also the curse of wiki-based sites. Because anyone (including those with bad intentions) can contribute and edit, you will find the occasional error or misleading information

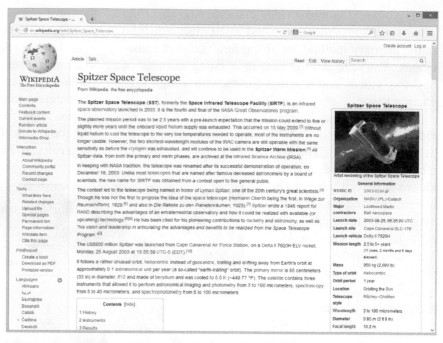

Wikipedia contains millions of articles with photos, quick facts, and links to other content.

inside wiki articles. If this knowledge is crucial for your job or one of your classes, be sure to double-check that particular fact on another reliable site. We will discuss effective online research later in this chapter.

Electronic Commerce

The web has become a global vehicle for electronic commerce (**e-commerce**), creating new ways for businesses to interact with one another and their customers. E-commerce means doing business online, such as when a consumer buys a product over the web instead of going to a store to buy it. You can go online to buy a book, lease a car, shop for groceries, buy insurance, and rent movies. You can get pizza delivered to your door without picking up the phone and even check the status of your order while you wait.

These kinds of transactions are only a fraction of what e-commerce entails. In fact, the vast majority of e-commerce activities do not involve consumers. They are conducted among businesses, which have developed complex networking systems dedicated to processing orders, managing inventories, and handling payments. In this section, you will learn about many of the ways in which money, goods, and services are exchanged online.

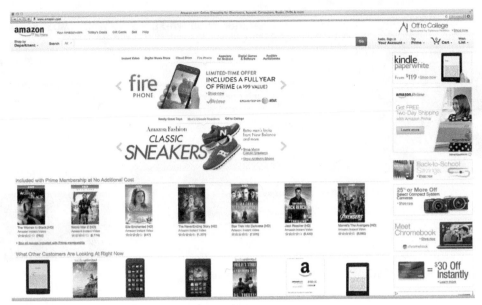

Amazon sells just about everything, and it can make recommendations based on your interests.

BUSINESS TO CONSUMER (B2C)

Tens of thousands of online businesses cater to the needs of consumers. Online shopping is the process of buying a product or service through a website. These types of websites provide information about products, take orders, receive payments, and provide on-the-spot customer service. Even if you have never shopped online, you have probably heard of Amazon.com, the web's largest store. Amazon sells everything, from books and movies to groceries and kitchen appliances. In addition to goods, you can also purchase a variety of services all over the web. These range from weekly food delivery to legal consultation from a licensed attorney. Before choosing an online merchant, be sure to use a search engine to scan for the lowest online price for the specific product you are interested in purchasing.

THE SHOPPING EXPERIENCE

Most online retailers offer a detailed catalog of products and services, usually with various photos and lengthy descriptions. This is important because consumers don't have the luxury of holding the product or reading information on the box. In addition, many retailers offer consumer or expert reviews on the product, allowing you to make an informed decision. Whenever you are ready to purchase an item, you place it inside an electronic "shopping cart." This will keep track of every item you want while you continue to shop for other items. Shopping carts are easy to modify, allowing you to remove items or change quantities with a few clicks. Once you are done shopping, you move to the checkout process where payment and shipping information must be entered. If you have already bought from this retailer before, it is likely that your payment and shipping information is already stored and the checkout can be completed with as little as one click.

PAYMENT AND SHIPPING

Most online merchants offer a variety of ways to pay for goods and services. Although electronic checks and debit cards are often accepted, it is always better to pay with a credit card that offers protection in case your computer or the merchant's site is compromised. Many argue that the best way to pay is by using an **online payment service** such as PayPal or Google Wallet. In a nutshell, you give these companies information about your bank and credit card accounts. You then use these services to pay for anything online or to transfer money to other individuals. This adds an extra layer of security and convenience for online payments. With respect to tax, you must check your state's law regarding online purchases. In many cases, online retailers in one state will not collect tax from consumers who are in a different state.

The last step of the purchase is making an arrangement for shipping. Many companies offer a variety of services, from next-day delivery to free shipping that uses a slower and more economical transit method.

Apple iPad 3rd Generation 16GB, Wi-Fi, 9.7in - White (MD328LL/A), Works Great!

★★★★☆ 125 product reviews

Item condition: **Used**

"Please read the entire auction description for complete details on this item, thanks. WE ONLY SHIP " ... Read more

Time left: **29m 6s**

Current bid: **US $306.89** [25 bids]

Enter US $311.89 or more

Additional coverage available

Seller information

_____ (34954) m8

99.8% Positive feedback

Save this seller

See other items

Visit store:

ebay deals

VERY

An auction on eBay for a used iPad.

For websites that belong to a company with a physical presence in your city, you are often given the opportunity to pick up your items at the store. Regardless of shipping method, you can usually track the progress of your order and shipment online so that you know exactly when it will arrive. If your product is defective or otherwise unsatisfactory, most retailers will offer various ways to contact them such as email or online chats. Be sure to always read a company's return policy before making your purchase.

CONSUMER TO CONSUMER (C2C)

Many websites provide a variety of mechanisms that allow any individual to sell new or used goods to another individual. Amazon, for example, will often show you used versions of a product that you are currently viewing on the site. These are sold by other companies or individuals who are using Amazon as a way to reach millions of potential customers. Amazon keeps a small commission of every sale made through its site.

Auction sites offer a twist on the traditional shopping experience. A familiar example is eBay, a large and comprehensive auction site that allows buyers to bid and compete for an endless variety of new and used goods. Sellers post a starting price and a length of time to run the auction. Like Amazon, eBay will keep a small commission of the final selling price of the good or service. To help build trust between users of its service, eBay uses a feedback system for rating buyers and sellers. As transactions are completed, both the buyer and seller each enter a short description of the selling experience for others to

see. Repeat buyers and sellers take their reputation seriously and generally strive to show that they are reliable. Many other online merchants, such as Amazon, use this feedback system whenever they allow individuals and smaller companies to sell goods on their site.

BUSINESS TO BUSINESS (B2B)

As its name implies, a business-to-business (B2B) transaction is one that takes place between companies; consumers are not involved. E-commerce has given companies an entirely different way to conduct business with each other. Using powerful websites and online databases, companies can track inventory, order products, send invoices, and receive payments. In addition, they can form online partnerships to collaborate on product designs, sales and marketing campaigns, and much more. The following are some examples of the sort of transactions companies can complete over the Internet:

- Auto repair shops can order parts from a wide range of suppliers.
- Stockbrokers and financial institutions can buy stocks and other commodities.
- Lenders can request a consumer's credit information from a credit-reporting agency.

ONLINE BANKING

The efficiency of online transactions has been an attractive way for banks to reduce costs and add services. With online banking, customers can securely

log into their bank's website and perform a variety of financial transactions. Users can pay bills, view monthly statements, and transfer money around the clock. A variety of companies, from cable TV providers to banks that issue car loans and credit cards, encourage their customers to establish regular automatic payments online. This allows these companies to automatically deduct each month's bill from the customer's bank account, eliminating the hassle of writing checks and possibly missing a payment deadline.

ADVERTISING

Advertising is one of the driving forces of both the Internet and many types of mobile software. Some advertising is done by online companies to promote their business or the products they offer. Other advertisements are created by traditional companies, from movie studios to car manufacturers. Either way, one of the top commodities that fuels advertising is consumer data, preferences, and trends. In a nutshell, advertising companies, search engines, and social media sites want to know more about their users and their Internet activities. These companies will look for patterns in a user's browsing habits so that they can deliver ads that the user will find appealing. The more these advertising agencies know about

consumers, the better they can represent the companies that hire them.

One of the most common ways in which to advertise is via email. Companies can create their own mailing lists from customers that have expressed interest or they can purchase lists of email addresses from a variety of sources. Another type of advertisement is a **banner ad**. These thin, rectangular ads are commonly placed across the top or on the sides of a web page. Once in a while, you may still stumble upon a "pop-up" ad that opens in a new window; however, since most browsers now have **pop-up blockers** built-in, few companies use this type of advertisement today.

The traditional practice of web advertising involved charging a certain amount of money for placement of the ad. However, many companies now prefer a model called **pay-per-click**, where advertisers pay for their ads only when a website visitor clicks on the ad to go to the advertiser's site. Google's AdWords is an example of the pay-per-click model. When a user of its search engine types a certain keyword or phrase, Google will display relevant advertisements along the side of the regular search results. Companies pay Google a certain amount of money per click based on the popularity of the keywords. Google also creates partnerships with many websites to display these ads, giving them a share of the profit when users click on

them. Now that you know how popular pay-per-click can be, you may want to consider clicking on the ads of your favorite search engines, websites, or mobile apps; after all, it is the primary way in which you can support those who create and maintain these services.

Effective Online Research

Online research is an everyday activity, whether you're a student or you are looking for do-it-yourself tips for a home improvement project. Finding information on the web can often be a straightforward process thanks to powerful and intelligent search engines. However, on many occasions, users have trouble finding the information they need or they spend an excessive amount of time looking for it. Other times, a large number of sites claim to have the information, but your instincts tell you that the sites may be unreliable. In this section, we will explore some useful search tips and discuss how to properly cite websites for your schoolwork or professional research.

SEARCHING TECHNIQUES

Search engines have become quite good at figuring out what you are trying to ask and displaying information that is relevant to your search. However, if you are new to searching on the web or sometimes have trouble finding what you want, you may want to consider the following tips:

Reliable online sources can complement traditional resources.

- **Keyword quantity.** Type as few keywords as needed to express the topic you are looking for. Complete sentences are usually not necessary.

- **Common words and names.** If you are searching for the rock band known as Boston, you will likely get many results and maps for the city of Boston. Add words such as "band" to give the search engine a bit more information. For common names, add the city where the person is from or perhaps the type of work they do.

- **Search modifiers.** If you are still having trouble finding what you need, try using a few search modifiers. Placing quotes (" ") around a group of words will force the search engine to find pages where the words appear together. You can also type a minus sign (-) in front of any word that you do not want in the search results.

More **Online:** *Did you know that many search engines can solve math problems, convert units, and provide instant definitions? Visit the companion website to learn additional search engine tips and tricks.*

USING RELIABLE SITES

There are plenty of helpful and useful websites around the world, but there are also many sites that are designed to be misleading or are simply put together by someone with flawed information or a specific agenda. Furthermore, many users (intentionally or unintentionally) spread rumors and incorrect information via email and social networks. They will even provide a link to a site that contains that misinformation. Unfortunately, many web users believe that if the website and information *seem* reliable, then the information must be correct.

Although you might find experts disagreeing about the reliability of a few specific websites, you should consider some general criteria when judging a site's credibility. As a general rule, you should always try to use websites whose writers and publishers are expected to meet professional standards. When possible, use a site owned by an organization that you are familiar with or one that is cited often by other reliable sites. Avoid websites that have long domain names with many hyphens or a series of common search words; they are usually created just to rank highly on search engines and direct traffic to their

site. (See Figure 4.6 for examples of what to watch for.) The following are a few categories of sites that are generally credible.

NEWS ORGANIZATIONS

Professional journalists are expected to meet standards for information gathering and fact checking. Many of them work for large news organizations that exist as TV networks, magazines, or local newspapers. Their sites are usually formal and complex with well-written and unbiased articles. They will have an "about" section that explains who they are and how long they have been in business. In general, avoid websites that appear to be heavily biased, are poorly designed or organized, and contain an excessive number of text-based advertisements.

ACADEMIC JOURNALS

Academic journals are written by professors and researchers in specific areas of study. These journals require that articles be reviewed by the researchers' peers. Ask your school's library or an instructor for guidance about which journals in a particular field are highly respected. Articles in most academic journals are available online either directly or through database services.

GOVERNMENT SITES

Most of what the federal and state governments do these days is posted online. From laws to public records, you can find quite a bit of reliable information on government websites. In addition, government agencies hire experts in statistics and other fields to gather accurate data. The Census Bureau, NASA, and the Department of Energy are just a few of the agencies offering a wealth of reliable information online.

REFERENCE SITES

The major encyclopedias and dictionaries obtain their information from subject-matter experts. Although some can be searched online for free, others require a subscription. It is possible that your school offers access through your library. Ask your school's librarian for details, as well as advice on the best references sites in your field of interest.

IS WIKIPEDIA RELIABLE?

You have already learned that Wikipedia is an online encyclopedia that can be edited by anyone. Although many of the articles are written and edited by experts, you cannot be 100 percent certain that the specific information you need comes from a credible source. Because of this, it is not a good idea to use Wikipedia as a source for schoolwork or professional research. However, Wikipedia is a great starting point for gaining a general understanding of a topic. In addition, many parts of a Wikipedia article contain a citation to a reliable site. Follow that link to the original source, find the information you need, and then use this reliable website as a source in your paper.

CITATION AND PLAGIARISM

The web has such an abundance of useful information that it has created a great deal of temptation for students. With a simple mouse click, users can copy large chunks of text from a web page and paste it in their schoolwork. Obviously, such activity is highly unethical. Turning in the work of another as if it were your own or failing to cite the source of your work is known as **plagiarism**. It is considered a great offense

1 Introducing Titan | The World's #1 Open Science **Supercomputer**
www.olcf.ornl.gov/titan/
U.S. **supercomputer** at Tenn. lab is world's fastest. A **supercomputer** at the government's Oak Ridge National Laboratory in Tennessee has been named the ...

2 U.S. Lab's "Titan" Named World's Fastest **Supercomputer**
news.nationalgeographic.com/news/.../121029-titan-fastest-**supercomput** ...
Oct 29, 2012 - But another U.S. **government** machine, Sequoia, has topped the world ... A few dozen **supercomputers** around the world have used GPU and ...

3 Intel Federal LLC to Propel **Supercomputing** Advancements for the ...
newsroom.intel.com › All Places › Intel Newsroom
Jul 13, 2012 - NEWS HIGHLIGHTS Intel Federal LLC wins $19 million contract to apply new approaches to extreme-scale computing research and ...

4 San Diego **Supercomputer** Center: SDSC's Gordon: A Non ...
www.sdsc.edu › News Center
Jun 6, 2013 - When the San Diego **Supercomputer** Center (SDSC) at the ... Available for use by industry and **government** agencies, Gordon is part of the ...

5 Met Office needs **supercomputers**, say MPs - Central **government** ...
central-**government**.government**computing**.com/.../mps-report-met-offic... ▾
Feb 21, 2012 - Met Office needs **supercomputers**, say MPs. Met Office needs 'step-change' in computing capacity, says science and technology committee.

6 NSA Utah Data Center - Serving Our Nation's Intelligence Community
nsa.gov1.info/utah-data-center/ ▾
The AES 256-bit encryption key is the standard for top-secret US **government** ... a classified **supercomputer** designed specifically for cryptanalysis targeting the ...

Reliable:
(1) Government agency / lab
(2) Trusted news magazine
(3) Press release from well-known company
(4) News from a research university

Questionable:
(5) Unknown site; It seems domain and subdomain were created just to capture specific search keywords.
(6) The ".info" TLD reveals that this is not a government site. Ignore the "nsa" and "gov1" portions.

Figure 4.6 Searching for reliable sites.

in both school and professional writing. Many schools now use software, such as Turnitin, to scan students' papers for plagiarism and excessive copying from the web. If you are going to use facts and quotes from websites, always be sure to properly cite them using the method required by your instructor. If you need help creating a proper citation, you can use free sites such as EasyBib.com and BibMe.org.

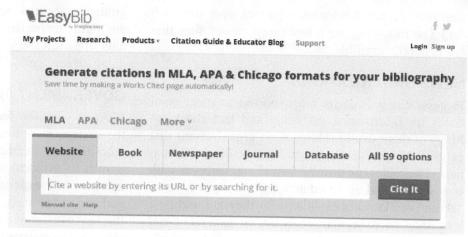

EasyBib can help you prepare citations.

KEY TERMS

Review Questions

MULTIPLE CHOICE

1. Which of the following networks, which began with just four universities, is the earliest ancestor of the Internet?

 a. NSFNET

 b. CSNET

 c. ARPANET

 d. TCP/IP

2. _____ translates analog voice signals into digital data and uses the Internet to transport the data.

 a. P2P

 b. Tethering

 c. VoIP

 d. Microblogging

Review Questions (continued)

3. The _____ language, which was used in the first web page, is still being used today alongside other languages.
 - a. HTML
 - b. HTTP
 - c. TCP/IP
 - d. BPS

4. Yahoo and MSN are both examples of:
 - a. blogging sites
 - b. e-commerce sites
 - c. social networking
 - d. web portals

5. When sending email to a large number of individuals, placing their addresses in the _____ field will prevent all those addresses from being seen by the recipients.
 - a. CC
 - b BCC
 - c. HTTP
 - d. HTTPS

6 Which part of a URL identifies a site and a brand on the web?
 - a. Protocol
 - b. Domain name
 - c. Directory
 - d. Backbone

7. Which of the following is NOT a high-speed Internet connection for homes?
 - a. 4G
 - b. DSL
 - c. Cable
 - d. Satellite

8. A(n) _____ is a huge, noncredit, online course that is offered for free by a variety of universities.
 - a. blog
 - b. LMS
 - c. forum
 - d. MOOC

9. A(n) _____ is a collaborative information site that relies on the Internet community to both create and edit content.
 - a. wiki
 - b. tag
 - c. meme
 - d. aggregator

10. Which of the following is NOT a web browser?
 - a. Safari
 - b. Skype
 - c. Chrome
 - d. Firefox

FILL IN THE BLANK

11. The _____ is the largest network in the world.

12. _____ file sharing uses a distributed network of individual users instead of a central server to transfer files.

13. To access the Internet from home you must connect to a(n) _____, which typically involves making monthly payments to a telecommunications company.

14. The _____ is a global system of linked, hypertext documents.

15. A(n) _____ is a discussion board where individuals can ask questions and reply to each other.

16. _____ sites, such as Reddit, encourage users to share links to news and other interesting content they find on the web.

17. Junk mail, or _____, is unsolicited email that is sent in bulk.

18. A(n) _____ is a web page or small website that contains a series of chronological posts and comments.

19. The term _____ is used to describe any digital data connection that can transmit information faster than standard dial-up by using a wider band of frequencies.

20. _____ is the act of having an online, text-based conversation with one or more individuals.

TRUE / FALSE

21. HTTP and HTTPS are the heart of Internet communication, setting rules for the transport and addressing of packets.

22. The asterisk symbol (*) is often used to mark keywords or topics in a social post or tweet.

23. 192.168.1.101 is an example of an IP address.

24. Google's Street View shows you almost any part of a map as if you were driving through a particular street.

25. No single person or group controls the Internet. It is a decentralized and cooperative community.

SHORT ANSWER

26. Contrast first-party cookies with third-party cookies. Which one of these raises privacy concerns for many individuals?

27. What are the differences between B2C, C2C, and B2B?

28. Describe three guidelines that should be followed for good email etiquette.

29. List and briefly define five navigation buttons found in most web browsers.

30. How are social networking sites different from professional networking sites?

31. List four categories of reliable sites and provide an example or brief description of each.

32. Describe three types (or models) of advertising on the web.

33. What are the differences between browser bookmarks, history, and cache?

34. Why has Twitter become such an important service? List three reasons.

35. What is the difference between a browser plug-in and a browser extension? Provide one example of each.

Research Exercises

Go beyond the book by performing research online to complete the exercises below.

1. How many email accounts do you currently use? Do you have a specific use or purpose for each of these? Provide details and examples.

2. Search for the following three things on both Google and Bing: (a) a local restaurant; (b) a famous athlete or celebrity; (c) any electronic product or appliance. List a few similarities and differences between the results. In addition, consider which results were personalized for you.

3. What is *net neutrality*? Do you believe that the U.S. government should enforce this principle? Should an ISP have the right to add surcharges for companies that generate a great deal of Internet traffic (e.g., Netflix) or desire higher priority for their data within the ISP's network? Provide examples and defend your answers.

4. How do you normally use social networking sites? What sort of content do you read? What do you post? What criteria do you consider when adding people to your friends list or circles?

5. If you do not have a Twitter account, create one. Add a few news organizations and any individuals you are interested in following. What do you think of this service? Do you find it useful? Do you ever see yourself posting any tweets? Defend your answers.

6. What do you think of the advertisements that you see on websites, social media, and apps? Do you pay attention to them? Do you ever click on them? Why or why not?

7. Using a search engine, perform a search for the following phrase: *United States economy*. Look through several pages of results and identify three reliable sites and three questionable sources. List the URLs of these sites and briefly explain why they are or are not reliable.

8. The popularity of community-based question and answer websites has been increasing over the years. Do you use services such as Yahoo Answers, Quora, Stack Exchange, and Answers.com? Why or why not? Are the answers provided on these sites reliable? Defend your answers and be sure to list the advantages and disadvantages of using these sites.

5

NETWORKING & SECURITY

Chapter Overview

One of the most powerful aspects of computing is the capability to communicate and send information through networks. Whether it is a classroom, building, or the Internet, networks have changed the way individuals learn, work, run organizations, and stay in touch with each other. However, networks have also brought a variety of security concerns with them. To protect your information, it is important to understand networks and their risks.

PART 1:
Networking and Information Systems

As you learned in Chapter 1, a **network** allows users to communicate and share information between computers and various devices. For years, organizations have understood the importance of connecting computers. Homes also enjoy the benefits of networks, allowing families to transfer files between computers and share the Internet connection wirelessly throughout their home. And of course, networking equipment supports the entire Internet, facilitating the near-instant delivery of video, images, music, documents, and all types of information.

Networks go hand in hand with software systems to connect users and distribute computing power and storage. Together, the software and network hardware create information systems to properly serve both provider and user. Hospitals, for example, need to store, find, and retrieve information about their patients' records from every computer in the building. In addition, they also use complex information networks to manage employee data, inventories, and payment and billing records. In this chapter, you will learn about these types of information networks, as well as the hardware and software that support them.

Computer Networks

Computer networks are set up for a variety of reasons. They come in many forms and sizes, from a small home network to complex ones that connect multiple

The hard disk in this server is a shared storage device. The network's users can access data or applications stored on the server.

A computer network lets users share access to data and applications.

A network can connect computers in offices, homes, and classrooms.

offices over a wide geographic area. Large networks can also connect smaller networks, as is the case with the Internet.

BENEFITS OF USING NETWORKS

Networks let multiple users access shared data, programs, and hardware devices almost instantly. For example, many organizations will purchase just one or two printers because they know that any user on the network will be able to print to them. It would cost that organization much more to purchase a separate printer for each individual.

Along with the ease of sharing devices, networks open up new ways to share data and applications that were not practical or possible in the past. In any business, several workers may need to use the same information at any given time. They might also need to simultaneously use a program that is installed on a server. This capability is important for many types of software, such as those that manage the entire company's customer service capabilities.

Communication is another key benefit of networks. In a company, employees can use internal messaging, mail, and videoconferencing systems to communicate with each other. They can also work together on documents that are stored on a server, making edits and placing comments on the work of a fellow employee. The other essential component to communication is access to the Internet. Whether you are at home, school, or the office, the power of networking can make it easy for you to communicate with almost anyone in the world. Without networks,

the instant messages and photo sharing that we now take for granted would simply not be possible.

COMMON TYPES OF NETWORKS

To understand the different types of networks and how they operate, you need to know how networks are structured. The two main types of networks are local area networks (LANs) and wide area networks (WANs).

LOCAL AREA NETWORKS

A **local area network (LAN)** is a data communication system consisting of multiple devices that are relatively near each other and are physically connected using cables or wireless media. Any network that exists within a room, a single building, or even a group of adjacent buildings, is considered to be a LAN. It is often helpful to connect separate LANs so they can communicate and exchange data. Though a LAN can make a connection to other networks in the public environment (such as the Internet), that public connection itself is not part of the LAN.

WIDE AREA NETWORKS

A **wide area network (WAN)** is the connection of two or more central computers or LANs, generally across a wide geographical area. For example, a company may have its corporate headquarters and manufacturing plant in one city and its marketing office in another. Each site needs resources, data, and programs locally, but it also needs to share data with the other sites. To accomplish this feat of data communication, the company can attach devices that connect over public utilities to create a WAN. Though it is common for a WAN to be made up of interconnected LANs, it is not a requirement.

INTRANET AND EXTRANET

Some organizations offer an internal version of the Internet, called an **intranet**. An intranet uses the same software and service structure as the Internet, but it contains only the company's private information. It usually limits access to employees within the company. One common use of an intranet is the ability to manage and share company documents using a web application such as Microsoft's SharePoint.

Organizations can also create an **extranet** to share some of its intranet resources with people outside the organization. This can include selected contractors and partners that have ongoing business with the company. A company could also use an extranet to allow employees to access their intranet from another

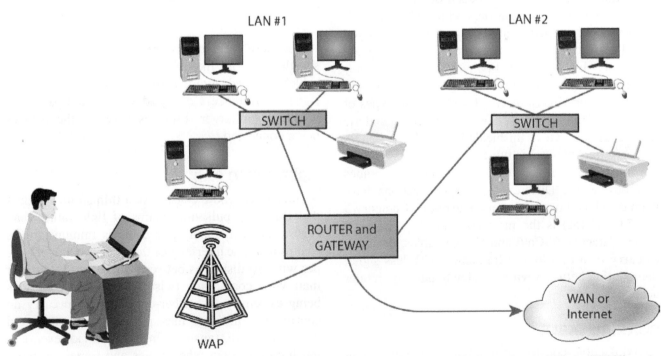

Networks are often complex, with wireless users, multiple LANs, and a connection to other buildings (WAN) and the Internet.

location. Access to an extranet is possible only if you have a valid username and password, and your identity determines which parts of the extranet you can view.

SPEED AND RELIABILITY

When comparing networks and the equipment used to create them, two factors are generally considered. The first is the maximum distance that data can reliably travel without **attenuation**, which is the loss of intensity and clarity of the data signal being transmitted. The second factor is **bandwidth**, which is the amount of data that can be transmitted over a given amount of time. For modern networks, bandwidth is measured in either megabits per second (Mbps) or gigabits per second (Gbps).

WIRED NETWORKS

The means used to link parts of a computer network are referred to as **network media**. The network uses the media to carry data from one **node**, or connection point, to another. This section will introduce the most common types of wires used as network media.

TWISTED-PAIR CABLE

Twisted-pair cable normally consists of four pairs of wires that are twisted around each other. Each copper wire is insulated in plastic, and all wires are collectively bound together in a layer of plastic that you would refer to as the network cable. Some cables are known as shielded twisted-pair (STP) because they contain a metal sheath that surrounds all the wires in order to reduce interference. However, most types of twisted-pair cables do not have this shielding and are therefore referred to as unshielded twisted-pair (UTP).

For wired networks, twisted-pair cable is by far the most common medium in use today for homes and businesses. Different wire specifications have been developed over the years. Currently, Category 5 (Cat5 or Cat5e) is the most common type of UTP cable. Category 6 (Cat6 and Cat6a) cables, designed to carry data at a higher frequency with less signal degradation between wires, is slowly gaining greater acceptance.

COAXIAL CABLE

Coaxial cable consists of a single copper wire that is surrounded by insulation and a wire mesh shield.

The most common types of wires for networks are (left to right) twisted-pair, coaxial, and fiber-optic cables.

All of these components are located inside a plastic sheath that looks like many cable TV wires. Coaxial cable's main advantage is that it is less susceptible to signal interference. Compared with twisted-pair wire, it allows for larger distances between the devices being connected.

FIBER-OPTIC CABLE

A **fiber-optic cable** consists of a thin strand of glass that transmits pulsating beams of light rather than electric current. Fiber-optic cable is immune to the electromagnetic interference that is a problem for copper wire, so distances between nodes can be greater than with coaxial or twisted-pair cables. Besides being extremely fast, fiber-optic cable can carry an enormous number of messages simultaneously and is a very secure transmission medium. However, it is much costlier than other cables and somewhat more vulnerable to damage in installation.

WIRELESS NETWORKS

Some types of networks do not require physical media for communication between nodes. **Wireless networks** use radio signals that travel through the air to transmit data. These signals operate on either the 2.4 GHz or 5 GHz bands. Practically all homes now use wireless technology for both networking and Internet access. Many businesses use it too, especially restaurants and cafes that offer Internet access, or hotspots, to their customers.

To create a wireless LAN, a **wireless access point (WAP)** is needed. All nodes connect to the device in order to communicate wirelessly. Mobile devices and laptops typically include wireless capabilities. However, most desktop computers require an internal or external **wireless adapter** to connect to a WAP.

A wireless access point.

WI-FI

The most popular standard for wireless networking is called 802.11 or **Wi-Fi**. This technology has gone through several revisions in order to increase its bandwidth and maximum range. As a general rule, Wi-Fi signals can reach about 100 to 200 feet indoors. However, that can be heavily affected by barriers such as the walls and floors of buildings. The following are the various specifications for Wi-Fi, which are essentially different letters added after 802.11:

- **802.11b:** up to 11 Mbps.
- **802.11g:** up to 54 Mbps.
- **802.11n:** up to 600 Mbps (most popular).
- **802.11ac:** can exceed 1 Gbps (>1000 Mbps).

PACKETS

Data moves though networks in structures known as **packets**, which are pieces of a message broken

down into small units by the sending device and reassembled by the receiving device. Machines that communicate over a network must follow certain rules to ensure that the packets are sent, received, and interpreted properly, and that data integrity, or accuracy, is guaranteed. These rules are known as communication **protocols**. As you learned in Chapter 4, TCP/IP is currently the most popular protocol and the driving force behind the Internet.

Packets increase transmission efficiency and reduce the chances for a lost or broken transmission. Because a message's packets do not have to be received in any particular order, individual packets can be sent separately through whichever paths in the network are most efficient at the time of transmission. Different networks format packets in different ways, but most packets have two parts:

1. **Header.** This first part of a packet contains information needed by the network. It will have the address of the node that sent the packet (the source) and the address of the node that will receive the packet (the destination). The network reads each packet's header to determine where to send the packet and, in some cases, the best way to get it to its destination. The header also contains control data that helps the receiving node reassemble a message's packets in the right order.

2. **Payload.** The second part of a packet contains the actual data being transmitted between the two nodes.

A wireless USB adapter.

NETWORK TOPOLOGIES

The **topology** of a network is the logical layout of the cables and devices that connect the nodes of the network. A network's topology aims to improve packet efficiency by reducing collisions, which occur when multiple nodes try to transmit data at the same time. If two packets collide, they are either discarded or returned to the sender to be retransmitted in a timed sequence.

Network designers consider several factors when deciding which topology or combination of topologies to use: the type of computers and cabling (if any) in place, the distance between computers, the degree of reliability needed, the speed at which data must travel around the network, and the cost of setting up the network. The following are some of the basic topologies that are used for computer networks (see Figure 5.1).

BUS TOPOLOGY

A network with a bus topology arranges the network nodes in a series, linking one node to the next via a single cable. A special device, called a *terminator*, is attached at the cable's start and end points to stop network signals so they do not bounce back down the cable. This topology's main advantage is that it uses the least amount of cabling. However, extra circuitry and software are used to keep data packets from colliding with one another. Also, a broken connection can bring down all or part of the network.

STAR TOPOLOGY

With a star topology, all nodes are connected to a hub (a type of linking device, described in the next section) and communicate through it. Data packets travel through the hub and are sent to the attached nodes, eventually reaching their destinations. In a star topology, a broken connection between a node and the hub does not affect the rest of the network. If the hub is lost, however, all nodes connected to that hub are unable to communicate. The star topology is the most common type used today.

RING TOPOLOGY

The ring topology connects the network's nodes in a circular chain, with each node connected to the next. The last node connects to the first, completing the ring. Each node examines data as it travels through the ring. If the packet is not addressed to the node

Figure 5.1 Types of network topologies.

examining it, that node passes it to the next node. If the ring is broken at or between nodes, the entire network may be unable to communicate.

MESH TOPOLOGY

In a mesh topology, a cable runs from every computer to every other computer. If you have four computers, you need six cables—three coming from each computer to the other computers. The big advantage to this arrangement is that data can never fail to be delivered. If one connection goes down, there are other ways to route the data to its destination. The downside to this topology is that all of these extra connections may end up being redundant, unused, or underused. The mesh topology is the least-used network topology and the most expensive to implement.

NETWORK HARDWARE

Transmission media are necessary to make a network, but wires alone are not enough. Hardware must be present at each node to translate, send, and receive the packets. The device at each node that performs translation and transmission is the **network interface card (NIC)**, which is also known as a network adapter card or network card. Historically, the NIC was a separate circuit board that was added to most computers. Today, the NIC hardware is integrated into a computer's motherboard and in network-ready printers. The NIC includes a port where data cables can be connected. In most networks, these data cables eventually lead to a variety of linking devices that can connect multiple nodes and ensure that data gets to the right place. These linking devices are described below.

Many companies require large quantities of network hardware.

REPEATER

A **repeater** is used to prevent attenuation when packets are traveling long distances. It receives each packet, ensures that it is intact, and retransmits it down the line toward the next node at full-signal strength.

HUB

A **hub** provides multiple ports for connecting nodes. When it receives a packet from one port, it transmits the packet without modification to all the other nodes to which the hub is connected. Although all nodes receive the packet, they will ignore it; only the node that is the actual target of the packet will accept it.

SWITCH

A **switch** is similar to a hub, but it is aware of the exact address or identity of all the nodes attached to it. Because it can determine the identity of each node, it is able to send packets directly and only to the correct destination. Because it is not merely rebroadcasting in all directions like a hub would do, the chance for packet collisions and retransmission is greatly reduced. This increases the efficiency of the network. Switches can also allow multiple conversations between nodes to take place simultaneously. For example, two computers can deliver data to each other while two different computers send messages back and forth. This is possible because the switch can keep the packet flow of each conversation separate.

ROUTER

A **router** is a complex device that stores the routing information for networks. It looks at each packet's header to determine where the packet should go and then determines the best route for the packet to take toward its destination. Routers also provide increased

A switch can connect many computers in a LAN.

security for the LAN they link. Because routers receive all packets and transmissions, they can detect and ignore attempts by unauthorized users to break into the local network. By refusing to acknowledge inquiries and attempts to access local computers, the router both prevents the attacks and provides no confirmation that the local computers even exist beyond the router.

Routers are usually connected to at least two networks. This is typically two LANs or WANs, or a LAN and the network of its Internet service provider. The wireless access points that are used in homes contain integrated routers, as do the devices that ISPs typically provide for Internet connectivity. In fact, many ISPs are now giving users a wireless broadband router that serves all the networking and Internet functions a home user needs. Most home routers also come with a built-in switch, which allows computers on a small, wired LAN to communicate without the need to buy a separate switch.

> **More Online:** *Visit the companion website to learn more about Cisco, a company that makes many of the routers used today.*

GATEWAY

In its simplest form, a **gateway** is a node on a network that serves as an entrance to another network. Gateways are needed because packets from different types of networks have different kinds of information in their headers, and the information can be in various formats. The gateway can take a packet from one type of network, read its header, and then add a second header that is understood by the second network (see Figure 5.2). The gateway also handles the configuration and maintenance of the various WAN or Internet addresses required to connect and relay information outside of the LAN. Each computer on the LAN can simply point to the gateway's network address without needing to know exactly where to find things on the Internet. In a small business or home network, the gateway is usually the router. That is why your ISP might refer to your broadband device as the "gateway" or "wireless gateway" device.

BRIDGE

A **bridge** is a device that connects two LANs or two segments of the same LAN. A bridge looks at the information in each packet header and forwards data traveling from one LAN to another. This is different from routers and gateways, which generally connect two different types of networks.

PUTTING IT ALL TOGETHER

Just as a network protocol sets a standard for the structure of the data to be transmitted, standards must exist for the hardware as well. This ensures that all the hardware—NICs, cables, linking devices—can all properly connect to each other. A number of physical transmission standards have been developed over the years. Of these, Ethernet is by far the most common.

Ethernet is a standard for local area networks. It provides a variety of specifications for the equipment and protocols used in a network. Most network installations use an Ethernet star topology with twisted-pair cables that plug into the RJ45 port located on many devices. However, Ethernet can also use fiber-optic cables, generally when communicating over longer distances. Originally, Ethernet was only capable of a 10 Mbps transmission speed. Now, Fast Ethernet can reach 100 Mbps, while Gigabit Ethernet transmits at 1 Gbps (1000 Mbps).

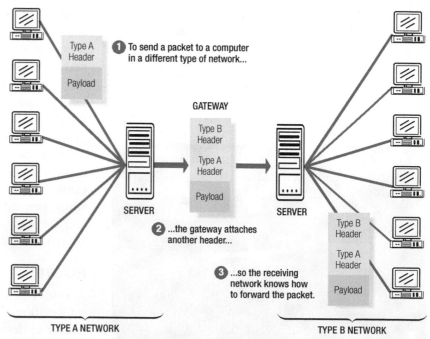

Figure 5.2 **How a gateway sends a packet from one type of network to another.**

Types of Information Systems

Network hardware and software provide an unparalleled vehicle for making connections between users, whether they are in the same room or around the world. Along with those connections, networks provide an ideal platform on which to build systems that actively collect, manage, and share information. An **information system (IS)** is a complex system for acquiring, storing, organizing, using, and sharing data and information. The basic purpose of any information system is to help its users get value from the information in the system, regardless of the type of information stored or the type of value desired. Information systems, therefore, can be designed to help people harness many kinds of information in countless ways. In this section, you will learn about the various types of information systems used today.

OFFICE AUTOMATION SYSTEMS

In organizations of any size, basic office work such as maintaining project schedules, keeping records of meetings, and handling correspondence can become extremely time-consuming and labor intensive. Collaborating with co-workers, serving customers, and dealing with suppliers require the sharing of accurate information as varied as phone numbers, meeting minutes, work schedules, and volumes of correspondence. If these types of information are scattered about the office on pieces of paper, it is easy to make mistakes, lose a key piece of information, or fall behind on recordkeeping or filing tasks.

For gathering, storing, and making available the kinds of information needed in an office environment, many organizations set up a type of information system known as an **office automation system**. This system uses computers and/or networks to perform various operations, such as word processing, accounting, document management, or communications. Office automation systems are designed to manage information and, more importantly, to help users handle certain information-related tasks more efficiently.

Using office automation tools frees workers at all levels from performing redundant and mundane tasks, allowing time for handling more mission-critical jobs such as planning, designing, and selling. Because office automation systems integrate different functions, information can be shared across applications such as a customer database, scheduling software, and a spreadsheet. This reduces the errors and time spent copying data from one program to another. While many companies use traditional office suite software for office automation, some have started to use cloud services such as Microsoft's Office 365 or Google Apps for Business.

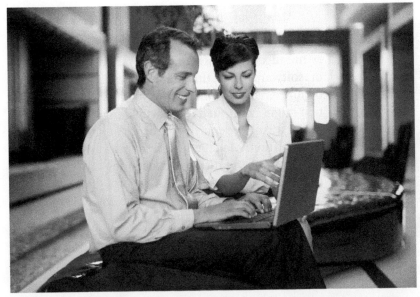

Office automation systems allow sales employees to stay up to date on appointments and access important documents on the go.

TRANSACTION PROCESSING SYSTEMS

A transaction is a complete information operation. Transactions can be one-step events, such as adding a new piece of information to a database. They can also be more complex and require many steps, such as the process of selling a product online. The information system that handles the processing and tracking of transactions is called a **transaction processing system (TPS)**.

EXAMPLE OF A TRANSACTION

Consider the process of withdrawing cash at an automated teller machine (ATM). From your perspective, this involves a single transaction: you put in your card and take your money,

with the understanding that the $60 in your hand has been removed from your account. However, this transaction is actually a series of smaller, linked transactions:

- Before any money is transferred, the ATM verifies your identity by reading your ATM card's magnetic stripe, requesting a PIN from you, passing that information to your financial institution, and receiving authorization to proceed.

- When you select an amount to withdraw, the ATM forwards that amount to your bank and requests authorization to dispense the cash. Your bank verifies the amount in your account and (assuming your balance is sufficient) places a hold on the funds in the amount of the withdrawal. It then authorizes the ATM to dispense the cash.

- The ATM counts out the requested cash, makes it available to you, and internally records its operation.

- The ATM notifies the bank that the cash was successfully distributed.

- The bank changes the hold on your funds to an actual debit, and the amount in your account is reduced.

THE IMPORTANCE OF TPS

What seemed like a single ATM transaction to you is actually broken down into this longer, behind-the-scenes list. This process allows the overall transaction (you getting your money) to be monitored and, in the event of an error, identifies precisely what went

Withdrawing money from an ATM triggers a series of behind-the-scenes transactions.

wrong and where. If the ATM's power goes out before it can dispense your cash, the bank will eventually release the hold on your funds because it will be able to determine that the ATM never gave it to you. If the ATM dispenses cash but its communication network crashes immediately afterward, the bank will be able to compare the ATM's log with the unfinished transaction and properly debit your account.

A transaction processing system is designed specifically to work with completing the basic transactions and monitoring the overall transaction for success and failure. Some transaction processing systems have sophisticated abilities to undo the unfinished parts of a failed transaction, correcting databases and performing other tasks to bring information back to the state it was in before the broken transaction began.

MANAGEMENT INFORMATION SYSTEMS

A **management information system (MIS)** is a set of software tools that enables managers to gather, organize, and evaluate information. This information might be limited to a particular group of employees or a single department, or it can cover the entire organization. Management information systems meet the needs of the different categories of managers by producing different kinds of reports drawn from the organization's database. An efficient MIS summarizes vast amounts of business data into information that is useful to each type of manager. Since different individuals have particular ways to express and understand information, a good MIS will allow the

Management information systems analyze data to give managers information about company operations.

same data to be displayed in a variety of ways, such as columns of numbers, line graphs, and bar graphs. That allows digital thinkers to see the numbers, while 3D visual analysts can see a picture of how those numbers relate.

MIS EXAMPLES

Within any business, managers at different levels need access to the same type of information, but they may need to view the information in different ways. At a call center, for example, a supervisor may need to see a daily report detailing the number of calls received, the types of requests made, and the production levels of individual staff members. However, a mid-level manager, such as a branch manager, may need to see only a monthly summary of this information shown in comparison to previous months, with a running total or average.

Managers at different levels also need very different types of data. A senior manager, such as a chief financial officer, is responsible for a company's financial performance. This individual would view the company's financial information, in detail, on a regular basis. However, a front-line manager who oversees daily production may receive little or no financial data. This individual would need to access production data and summaries. Ultimately, the challenge in each scenario is the same: to get the right information to the right person at the right time, and in a format that is useful and appropriate.

Business managers often use decision support systems to access and analyze data.

DECISION SUPPORT SYSTEMS

A **decision support system (DSS)**, which is a special application that collects and reports certain types of data, can help managers make better decisions. Decision support systems are useful tools because they give managers highly tailored, highly structured data about specific issues. Many decision support systems are spreadsheet or database applications that have been customized for a certain business. These powerful systems can import and analyze data in various formats, such as flat database tables or spreadsheets, two-dimensional charts, or multidimensional "cubes" (meaning several types of data and their interrelationships can be graphically shown). They can quickly generate reports based on existing data and update those reports instantly as data change.

Decision support systems can combine and correlate information from multiple locations. Business managers often use decision support systems to access and analyze data in the company's transaction processing system. In addition, these systems can include or access other types of data, such as stock market reports or data about competitors. By compiling this kind of data, the decision support system can generate specific reports that managers can use in making mission-critical decisions.

DSS EXAMPLES

Some questions in business or management can be difficult to answer without some kind of assistance. Of the four colors of T-shirts that a shirt company produces, how many of each should be made in the latest production run? How many salmon should the local fishery controller allow fishers to catch before halting the season's activity? Without the proper information, answers to these questions are simply guesswork.

Decision support systems can help the shirt manufacturer collect and analyze buying trends, not only of its own T-shirts but also of the marketplace in general. It can also look for guidance when forecasting what current products will sell in the near future and what new product opportunities might be profitable. The fishery manager can collect data such as estimates of the current salmon population, historical population trends, the number of applications for fishing licenses, and so forth, in order to predict what level of fishing will be sustainable.

ACTIVE VERSUS PASSIVE

Decision support systems can be active or passive. A *passive* system simply collects and displays data in the format requested. An *active* system collects the data but also makes recommendations as to the best decision. Because few people are willing to blindly trust the recommendations of a program, active decision support systems are often used cooperatively, where users review the recommended decisions along with the data.

EXPERT SYSTEMS

An **expert system** is a type of information system that performs analytical tasks traditionally done by a human. It will typically ask a series of questions and then take specific actions based on the responses to those questions. To do this, an expert system requires a large collection of human expertise in a specific area. Detailed information is compiled from the human experts on:

- Ways that problems are considered.
- Steps that are taken to diagnose problems.
- Actions taken to find solutions.
- The reasoning for the actions.

HOW THEY WORK

The information gathered from human experts is entered into a highly detailed database, called a knowledge base. A program called an inference engine accepts information about the problem or question being analyzed and uses the knowledge base to select the most appropriate response or follow-up question.

Basic expert systems are typically little more than preset question and answer sequences, using simple yes or no answers to move along its list. Sophisticated expert systems may use new information to reevaluate the problem from the start. They also contain a feedback process that refines the data in the knowledge base. As users report success and failure during the diagnostic process, the expert system can learn more efficient diagnostic paths. For example, an expert system diagnosing network problems may, over time, discover that most of the faults involve malfunctioning network adapter cards in employees' personal computers. Based on the new data, the system changes its analysis path to focus first on testing those parts.

EXPERT SYSTEM EXAMPLES

Although expert systems mimic the routine decision-making process of experts, they cannot be as innovative as humans because they are simply machines following instructions. Consequently, expert systems are most useful in situations where a given set of circumstances always calls for the same kind of response. For example, an expert system can monitor the inventory levels for a grocery store chain. When the system determines that inventory of a product falls below a given level, it can automatically order a new shipment of the product from a supplier. In air traffic control, an expert system can be configured to issue a warning to ground controllers and pilots when two aircraft are on a collision course or flying too near one another. In education, expert systems are used to create adaptive exams or educational products that adjust the questions or material delivered based on a student's performance. McGraw-Hill's LearnSmart suite is one example of this new type of adaptive software.

Adaptive educational products, such as McGraw-Hill's LearnSmart Advantage, use extensive data and sophisticated programming to deliver a customized experience.

Supporting Information Systems

Many types of information systems, such as complex transaction processing systems, often need to be available without fail every moment of every day. They also require the storage and quick access of hundreds of terabytes of information. In this section, you will explore many of the requirements of information systems and both the hardware and software that support them.

REDUNDANT AND FAULT-TOLERANT HARDWARE

With a typical home or small business computer, most hardware failures cause the computer to crash. If the hard drive malfunctions or the CPU overheats after a cooling fan fails, the computer stops running. If network hardware such as a router breaks, network traffic is disrupted and the connection to the Internet will be lost. While these kinds of events are frustrating to homes and businesses, it isn't the end of the world for them. However, for certain types of organizations, any large-scale failure can result in catastrophic losses.

MISSION-CRITICAL SYSTEMS

Some types of organizations cannot afford to experience any type of extended systems malfunction. If computers running life-support systems at a hospital crashed, for example, many patients could lose their lives. Even small amounts of computer downtime at

A RAID offers redundancy by linking several disk drives.

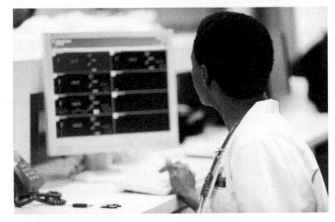

Many systems at hospitals are mission-critical. Their failure could be catastrophic.

a major stock exchange or in an air defense system could have dire consequences. These types of systems are called **mission-critical** because they must run without failure or with nearly instant recovery from failure.

It is simply not possible to construct computer hardware and software that can never fail. Therefore, mission-critical hardware and software systems have been designed to continue operating without interruption when components and programs fail. Such systems are known as **fault-tolerant** computers because they are able to continue their operation even when problems are present.

One of the ways fault tolerance is accomplished is via redundancy. **Redundant** computers have multiple hardware systems performing the same task at the same time. A fully redundant computer will have multiple system units, each with their own motherboard, CPU, memory, and hard drives. The computers execute software instructions in lockstep, meaning all CPUs and supporting hardware execute the same instruction at the same time. When one of the CPUs produces a different result (or no result, if it breaks), it is declared to have failed. The remaining hardware systems continue to operate without the failed unit until it can be fixed.

RAID

Even in computer systems that aren't mission-critical, extra disk drives are sometimes used as a way to provide a countermeasure against data loss.

A **redundant array of independent disks (RAID)** is a storage system that links any number of disk drives (a disk array) so that they act as a single disk. A RAID's capabilities are based on many different techniques, but there are three basic types:

- **Striping.** Also known as *RAID 0,* striping gives the user rapid access by spreading data across several disks. Striping alone, however, is used to boost data access performance and does not provide redundancy. If one of the disks in a striped array fails, the data is lost, because it's not being duplicated on any of the other disks.

- **Mirrored system.** Also known as *RAID 1,* this type writes data onto two or more disks simultaneously. This creates a complete copy of all the information on multiple drives, thereby preventing data loss if one drive fails.

- **Striping with parity.** Most commonly implemented as *RAID 5,* this strategy spreads data across several disks. However, it adds the safety of redundancy because the system stores parity information (a type of error-correcting code) that can be used to reconstruct data if a disk drive fails.

Scalable systems can be upgraded as an organization grows.

SCALABLE AND INTEROPERABLE SYSTEMS

Most businesses plan to expand over time, and computer systems need to be able to grow with the organization. Many company directors find it unacceptable to start from scratch with new computer and software systems every time the company outgrows its current system, and many information systems cannot practically be redesigned and replaced. Scalable systems address this issue because they can be incrementally expanded as the need arises. **Scalability** is the capacity to provide increasing amounts of computing power, storage, and/or software. Scalable systems allow organizations to buy affordable systems that meet their current computing needs and gradually increase their computing capability only as needed.

Many information systems need to interact with other systems. The efficiency of a tool manufacturer's accounting system, for example, can be greatly enhanced if it has access to the company's inventory and order-entry systems. **Interoperability** is the ability of each organization's information system to work with the other, sharing both data and services. Interoperability is also required by information

systems that allow partnership and customer-vendor relationships between organizations. Though interoperability is often viewed at a software level, hardware interoperability is just as critical. When different types of computer systems are involved, a common interface is needed so that those systems can effectively communicate.

DATABASES

Most information systems attempt to organize data and information in ways that make it easier for users to find what they need. Databases are a fundamental building block for the storage, retrieval, and analysis of a company's data. This section will discuss some of the ways in which organizations manage large volumes of data for use in their information systems.

DATA WAREHOUSES

Many organizations keep track of large volumes of information. For a company such as Amazon, this will include details on every product sold, account information for all customers, and a detailed record

of every order made on its website. Behind the scenes, the company would also need to keep records for all employees and suppliers. All of this information is generally stored or archived in a central repository known as a **data warehouse**. This enormous digital warehouse contains data gathered from multiple databases.

Data warehouses contain information from both the present and the past. Because it is an archive, businesses can access it to look for historical data that can be useful in creating a variety of graphs and reports. For example, Amazon's current database of products would naturally show the price of a product today. That price is displayed next to the product on the website. However, a data warehouse would contain that product's price at different points in time, which might be useful to a manager who is looking at Amazon's pricing when compared to that of its competitors. Another manager might use that data to analyze the correlation between the price of the product and the number of sales generated at different points in time. With such a large volume of correlated data, organizations can perform a great deal of analysis by using a data warehouse.

DATA MINING

Large databases that support information systems can provide an ideal environment for **data mining**, which is the discovery of new patterns or relationships between data. Businesses can tap into consumer and sales data to find trends, new sales opportunities, and signs of waning interest in their customers' behavior. Amazon.com, for example, uses data mining to predict what product a customer might like in order to feature it when the customer logs in and begins to browse. Governments can correlate and analyze data from many different areas to track needs and spending, look for possible disease outbreaks, and identify potential security threats. And as you learned in Chapter 4, advertising companies, search engines, and social media sites continuously look for patterns in the browsing habits of their users so that they can deliver ads that they will find appealing.

The Centers for Disease Control and Prevention uses large databases and tools to look for patterns that might signal a possible outbreak.

DATA VALIDATION

For information systems to be effective, the databases that support them must be as free of errors as possible. One method for checking and improving the reliability of data is called **data validation**. This is the process of safeguarding against erroneous or duplicate data by checking what is entered and, in some cases, placing restrictions on how the data is entered. Data validation is often accomplished by specifying format or range requirements at data entry. Zip code fields, for example, may require that the entry contain exactly five numeric characters. Email fields will look for required elements, such as the "@" sign, and ensure that the entire entry looks like a properly formatted email address. If an entry does not meet the rules enforced by the database, the entry will be rejected.

Data validation can also occur with information that has already been collected. For example, a government agency might want to make sure that a particular piece of information is spelled or formatted consistently throughout all its databases. It might also look for items that seem unusual. For example, if someone is listed as a felon in a criminal database, that person should not be listed in the database of active voters.

Security

You are aware that cars are stolen every day, so you probably take measures to reduce the risk of losing yours. These include locking the doors, parking in a well-lit area, and perhaps using a car alarm. In the same way, you should be aware of the various threats facing your computer and personal information. By taking precautionary steps, you can safeguard not only your hardware, software, and irreplaceable files, but also your privacy and safety.

Safeguarding data, computers, and information systems is crucial to both individuals and businesses. The first step to good computer security for everyone is awareness. Individuals and organizations should understand all of the dangers that threaten their systems and sensitive information. Only then can appropriate measures be taken to safeguard them. This section introduces you to some of the most common threats in the world of technology and shows you how to protect yourself from them.

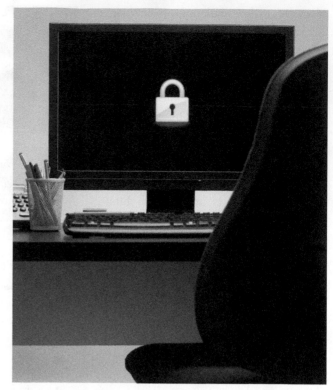

Safeguarding data, computers, and information systems is crucial to both individuals and businesses.

Basic Security Concepts

Any discussion of computer security is likely to use terms such as threats, risks, and countermeasures. This section will explore many of these terms and how they affect the security of various systems.

THREATS AND VULNERABILITIES

The entire purpose of computer security is to eliminate or protect against threats. A **threat** is anything that can cause harm. In the context of computer security, threats can be as varied as a burglar, a computer virus, an earthquake, or a simple user error.

By itself, a threat is not harmful unless it exploits an existing vulnerability. A **vulnerability** is a weakness that has not been protected against threats, thereby making it open to harm. For instance, the presence of a car thief is a threat; however, if there are no cars on the street to steal, the threat is meaningless to those in the neighborhood. Similarly, a vulnerability is relevant only if a threat is likely to be present. Your expensive hat is vulnerable to being blown away by a gust of wind, but unless you are outdoors on a windy day, that vulnerability is not a concern.

UNDERSTANDING THREATS

We gauge the danger of a threat by a combination of factors:

- The probability of a threat.
- The degree of vulnerability.
- The penalty or injury that may occur if the threat succeeds in causing harm.

Threats that are very likely to cause harm, or threats that cause very negative consequences if unchecked, are much more likely to be guarded against. Most people wear a seat belt when driving their car, not because they are likely to crash every time they drive, but because the threat of severe injury in that unlikely event makes us cautious. Although a seat belt doesn't guarantee our safety 100 percent of the time, it is much better than ignoring the threat of harm because you believe it will never happen to you. This is true for computer systems just as much as it is for cars.

When people think of the ways their systems can be threatened, they may think only of damage to the

hardware or the loss of some data. In reality, computer systems and those that use them can be harmed in many ways. Indeed, individuals themselves can suffer the consequence of poor security. Identity theft, humiliation, and even physical harm can result if individuals don't understand the threats to their security and privacy.

RISK ASSESSMENT

When protecting your computer system, it pays to think in the broadest possible terms about the types of harm that could affect you. This allows you to better assess the risk. A nasty virus or hacker can wipe out your programs as well as your data, but the risk may be greater than just that incident. If your PC is connected to a network, other systems on the network could suffer similar problems. Damages to your home or office from disasters such as a fire or flooding can easily extend to your computer, everything stored on it, and possibly even backup copies of data.

A practical and accurate **risk assessment**, where you identify and examine possible threats, is critical to being able to safeguard a system. Unfortunately, many individuals and businesses can err when assessing risks. For example, suppose that you always use your last name or date of birth as your password (a very bad idea). However, you are so fearful of an identity thief breaking into your computer that you install a complex security system in both your home and your computer. While that is not a bad idea, the risk of your password being discovered is higher from someone simply guessing it than it is from

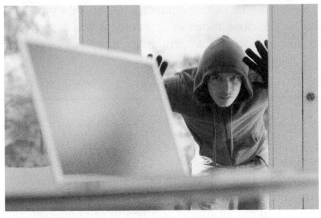
Computer systems face many threats.

sophisticated break-ins. So, when companies ask that you create complex or strong passwords, they are simply helping you understand how risky an easily guessable password is.

Other times, solutions to problems can lead to greater problems. Requiring that your company's users change their passwords every few days might seem like a great idea. However, you may not notice that many employees are writing their ever-changing password on sticky notes in their office for fear of forgetting them. The risk of passwords being located in such a visible place is greater than the risk of letting employees use the same password for a longer period. When it's time to assess risks, consider as many factors as possible and try to be realistic about where the biggest threats lie.

Network administrators must assess risks when configuring systems and creating security policies.

COUNTERMEASURES

For any threat, there is some action or plan you can employ to guard yourself against the risk. Any step you take to ward off a threat is called a **countermeasure**. For example, regularly backing up your data is a countermeasure against the threat of data loss, much like an antivirus is a countermeasure against computer viruses. There are generally two classes of countermeasures:

- One type of safeguard protects the computer system from physical hazards such as theft, vandalism, power problems, and natural disasters.

- The other type of countermeasure is concerned with protecting data and software from threats such as viruses and hackers.

The remainder of this chapter will focus on introducing the various types of threats and the appropriate countermeasures that will help safeguard both your systems and precious data.

Safeguarding Hardware

Many threats can physically damage your computer or network equipment. Some of these are environmental in nature, such as those caused by power fluctuations, fire, and water damage. Others involve misuse by the individual operating the equipment or an unexpected breakdown of a faulty piece of hardware. And of course, a computer system can disappear if it is lost to theft. This section will explore these physical threats and the measures you can take to protect your computer hardware.

A surge protector offers necessary protection for your computer.

POWER PROBLEMS

The electricity supplied to computer hardware is critical to its operation. Problems such as power fluctuations and power failures can affect computers in a variety of ways. Let's take a closer look at these.

POWER FLUCTUATIONS

Power levels that rise and fall can produce unpredictable behavior in, or cause damage to, sensitive computer components. A computer's system unit has its own power supply that is designed to strictly regulate the power fed to the motherboard, CPU, and other internal parts. This makes the power supply especially vulnerable to problems with incoming electricity. When a system unit's power supply malfunctions due to an electrical surge, for example, it can simply shut off (causing a power failure) or it can go out with an eruption of electrical smoke and a massive power surge that ruins delicate components on the motherboard. Devices outside the computer, such as network hardware, printers, and external drives, may also be at risk from inconsistent power.

Power problems can arise for many reasons. People commonly think electrical storms are the primary cause of power interruptions, but storms are actually one of the least likely causes. A more likely source is the house or building itself. Disturbances from high-demand equipment such as air conditioners, space heaters, dryers, and copy machines can produce fluctuations. Old wiring in houses may also produce an inconsistent power feed.

POWER FAILURE

The complete loss of power, which can occur during a power outage in a particular neighborhood, may not cause component failure. However, it can cause the loss of unsaved work when the failure occurs. In addition, it can interrupt an important activity such as a videoconference with company executives or the ability to support customers that are contacting your business.

POSSIBLE COUNTERMEASURES

There are a couple of common countermeasures for the threat of lost or uneven power. For all hardware, a **surge protector** (or surge suppressor) is an inexpensive product that guards connected equipment against large power spikes or surges that may infrequently occur. This is an absolutely necessary piece of equipment, and every single one of your devices should be connected to a surge protector. This includes computers, monitors, printers, and even modern TVs and gaming consoles. Surge protectors are common products available at electronics and hardware stores. Check the packaging carefully to make sure you are actually buying a surge protector and not a many-to-one extension cord that looks the same but lacks protection against power surges.

Problems with both power fluctuations and power failure can be minimized by adding another kind of hardware known as an **uninterruptible power supply (UPS)**. A UPS contains both a surge protector and rechargeable battery, allowing it to handle

any type of power issue for your computer. When the power fails, the battery contains enough power to run a computer system for a given amount of time. Depending on the size of the UPS and the needs of the user, this can range from a few minutes (good enough to save your work) to several hours if you need to keep your business operational. If you include a UPS unit for your network hardware, such as your router, you can maintain your connection to the Internet even when the lights go out.

THEFT AND ACCIDENTS

Both theft and vandalism can result in the total loss of the system and the data it contains. The financial loss may be high if you have to repair or replace many of your components. If you have stored sensitive information on the computer, the thief could use it to compromise your financial, professional, or personal safety. This fact makes it even more crucial that individuals take the proper precautions to protect their computers from intentionally destructive acts.

An uninterruptible power supply (UPS) can provide battery power in case of power failure.

THEFT COUNTERMEASURES

In principle, keeping hardware in a secure area can help to protect it from theft and vandalism. If it is difficult to get to the hardware or carry it off without being noticed, the computer hardware is safer. At home, keeping your home secure protects everything in your house including the computer. At work, you can use a variety of locks that help reduce the chance of hardware being stolen. One of the most popular types of locks, known as the Kensington lock, involves a steel cable and security device that attaches to a special oval slot on most laptop computers. By tying this steel cable around a desk, it makes it difficult for a thief to remove these lightweight portable computers. Locks can also be used to keep a tower's system unit from being opened, which guards against an office thief removing components such as hard drives and RAM modules.

This Kensington lock uses a steel cable to help safeguard a laptop computer.

ACCIDENTS AND DISASTERS

Accidental harm is much harder to address, but it is no less of a threat. Dropping your laptop or mobile device can crack the screen or make the computer unusable. Other accidents, such

as spilling liquids, can cause electrical damage to your system. If hardware gets wet, turn it off or unplug it immediately and leave it off until it is dry. Individuals and businesses must also consider natural disasters such as fires and earthquakes. Although there is little that can protect a system from major calamities, steps can be taken to protect valuable data. One of those involves making regular backups, which will be discussed later in this chapter.

More **Online:** *Do you have a mobile device that has a cracked screen or other type of damage? Visit the companion website to learn more about repairing these devices.*

ENVIRONMENTAL HAZARDS

Most individuals likely consider it obvious that water and extreme heat can damage electrical components. However, the environmental hazard that surprises many people is dust. This nuisance can clog cooling systems such as fans, which in turn may cause hardware to overheat. Fans are present in the system units of both tower and laptop computers, and they are often used to cool processors.

It is important to remove dust regularly from your system unit. With the computer unplugged, use a can of compressed air to whisk away dust from fans and anywhere else it has accumulated. Never use a vacuum cleaner to remove dust. Monitors can be gently dusted with a microfiber cloth or a manufacturer-approved

A malware infection can cause all sorts of headaches for individuals and businesses.

A can of compressed air helps keep fans and components free of dust.

cleaning solution, but never use glass cleaner or materials such as facial tissue or paper towels.

Safeguarding Data

When many individuals think of their computer, they likely think of that machine that contains their irreplaceable photos and documents. Organizations also think of their systems in this way, knowing that the precious data held by the computers is invaluable to their daily operations. Furthermore, many organizations, such as online stores and schools, hold large amounts of personal user information that simply cannot fall into the wrong hands. You have already learned that theft and other disasters can cause data loss. In this section, we will explore additional threats to computer data along with the countermeasures that can keep data safe.

MALWARE

As you learned in Chapter 3, **malware** refers to several types of malicious computer programs that are created to harm computer systems and their users. Malware is the most common threat to data and security. The exact goals of malware vary greatly, but most of the time it attempts to steal information, destroy data, harm the flow of data through a network, or take control of some of a computer's functions.

Malware is not always noticeable by the user. In fact, most forms of malware do not want to be recognized by you or your anti-malware utilities. The longer the activity can remain a secret, the more

damage it can do. The only time malware will make itself known is when it is designed to trick you into doing something more dangerous. For example, one popular scam is to issue an alert message warning users that they are infected or have committed some sort of crime. That message will then prompt users to install something that looks like a fix (it isn't) or pay for something they don't need. This type of scam is often referred to as **scareware** (or ransomware) because its goal is to scare the user into doing exactly what the thief wants.

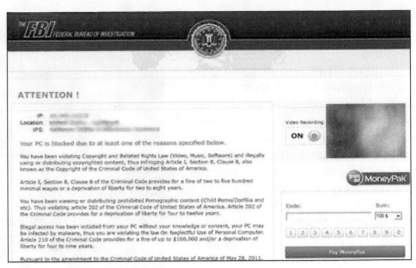

This "scareware" infection attempts to collect money from users by claiming to be the FBI.

VIRUS

A **virus** is a type of malware that is attached to a host file and has the ability to replicate, or copy, itself. A virus can be found in many types of files, from executable programs to Microsoft Office files. Users can unknowingly receive a computer virus via file-sharing services and email attachments, or when copying infected files from someone else's computer. When a recipient opens an infected file, the virus will activate itself and find more files to infect. It will also do the damage it was intended to do, which can be as extreme as making your operating system unusable.

WORM

A **worm** is a type of malware that self-replicates and spreads through computers and networks. Unlike a virus, a worm is a fully contained program that is not attached to a host file. Furthermore, a worm does not require that a user take an action such as opening a file. It can spread on its own rather quickly, usually by exploiting a vulnerability in an operating system or some other software. Some of the worst worms in history have infected millions of computers in a matter of hours.

TROJAN HORSE

A **Trojan horse** (or Trojan) is a program that disguises itself as an interesting, useful, or desirable program in order to gain access to your system. Users often download Trojans from a compromised website, file-sharing service, or even an email attachment. When the user installs this software, it will often work as intended so that the user will not suspect anything. However, the Trojan will do its damage behind the scenes by installing something sinister or changing the settings on your operating system.

SPYWARE

One type of malware that has rapidly grown in use is **spyware**, which is designed to report activity on your computer to another party. Spyware can record individual keystrokes (using *keyloggers*), visited websites, and other types of activities. It does this to obtain personal information such as passwords, account numbers, browsing history, and just about anything that might be useful to a thief or unethical marketing company. Once spyware has data to report, the program transmits the data back to its creator via the Internet. Most spyware is spread via Trojan horses or some other software that the user accidentally installed.

HACKING

In the early days of computing, a "hacker" was an individual who possessed advanced skills, often making a computer do something that it wasn't originally intended to do. Today, a **hacker** generally refers to an individual who uses a computer and/or network to commit a variety of crimes. Such crimes, from creating viruses to disrupting computer networks, are often referred to as **cybercrimes**. Hackers that commit these crimes are known as "black hat" hackers in

order to distinguish them from non-criminal (or "white hat") forms of hacking.

Individuals engage in hacking for many reasons. One of those is curiosity. Many hackers break into networks and systems just to see if they can do it. Another reason is theft. Because so much personal and financial information is stored in computers, breaking into them can yield a bounty of credit card and social security numbers. **Hacktivism**, which has a social or political agenda behind it, has become a popular reason to hack in recent years.

No form of hacking is as dangerous as **cyberterrorism**, which is an attack that seeks to create large-scale chaos and damage to a country's infrastructure. At the moment, most hacking incidents between countries have focused on spying. However, experts believe that it is only a matter of time before major warfare begins to occur between Internet-connected systems. In fact, there has already been one incident where a foreign power was suspected of attacking the nuclear facility of another by creating a very specific type of worm.

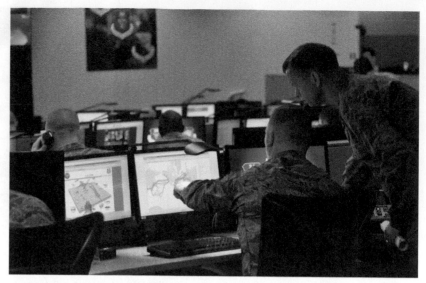

These Air Force "cyber warriors" help defend the nation's infrastructure from attacks.

CONDUCTING ATTACKS

Hackers use a variety of tools and techniques to look for vulnerabilities that they can exploit. However, hackers rarely use their own computers to conduct attacks. They often use malware to open communication ports on the computers of thousands of users, making them available for control by the hacker.

The HTTPS protocol secures your web activity from hackers who may be monitoring your communication.

Computers infected and compromised in this way are known as **zombies** because they are under external control. Massive networks of zombies, known as **botnets**, can be used by the hacker to spread malware, send spam, and conduct carefully orchestrated network attacks.

One popular type of network attack, known as a **distributed denial-of-service (DDoS)** attack, allows hackers to shut down or block access to websites and other network resources by overwhelming them with requests. And because the attacks come from millions of infected computers instead of the one owned by the hacker, it makes it difficult to know who was responsible. Unfortunately, users who are part of these botnets will usually have no idea that their computer has been compromised.

MONITORING COMMUNICATIONS

Sometimes hackers don't need to break into a system to get what they need. There are various ways hackers can "listen in" on unsecured network traffic to get valuable data. That is why, for example, many websites use the *https* protocol to encrypt communication that contains financial or personal information. It is also why many wireless routers ask that you set up a password.

One type of danger that you should be aware of is known as a **rogue hotspot**. Hackers will set up their own wireless access points at popular areas such as

airports. When users turn on their mobile devices or laptops to look for a free hotspot, they may inadvertently connect to the hacker's hotspot. Once that happens, that hacker can intercept much of those users' communication. When at a location such as an airport, hotel, or coffee shop, always ask an employee for the name of that location's official wireless access point.

DATA THEFT

Many hacking incidents target the databases of large online businesses. Hackers are usually looking for user account data and credit card information. These companies will typically alert you if your account has been compromised, and most credit card companies will not hold you responsible for fraudulent charges that result from this incident. However, if hackers ever get a hold of additional information, such as your social security number and date of birth, they can do much more damage.

The worst type of data theft for an individual is known as **identity theft**. Hackers will essentially assume your identity and begin to open new bank accounts under your name. As you can imagine, this can create years of headaches for the individuals whose identity is stolen. Besides caution, one of the best countermeasures against identity theft is checking your credit report regularly. Since there are three credit reporting agencies and consumers are allowed one free report per year, it is recommended that you get one report from one company every four months.

> More **Online:** *Visit the companion website to learn how to get free annual credit reports from a trusted source.*

PASSWORD THEFT

Hackers often do their damage by figuring out a user's login and password for a specific account. Besides using spyware, a hacker can discover your password by attempting combinations that are used by many individuals. Studies have shown that a frightening number of users have easy-to-guess passwords such

The Federal Trade Commission (FTC) offers consumer information on scams and identity theft.

as "123456" or "password." We will discuss the creation of a strong password in the upcoming section on countermeasures.

Besides stealing your account information, hackers can do something equally dangerous if they gain access to your email account. They can send malware or a link to a compromised website to everyone in your address book. Because you are trusted by many of your friends and family members, they will let their guard down when they receive an email from you. They will likely download the infected file or visit the malicious website because they believe you are making a recommendation.

SOCIAL ENGINEERING

Social engineering is a form of hacking that focuses on deceiving individuals into giving away the information that the thief needs. Although technical expertise can be used, the most important skill needed is the ability to manipulate and trick other people. The following are two popular types of social engineering:

- **Pretexting** is gaining someone's trust by pretending you are someone else. Hackers have been able to gain valuable information over the phone or via instant message by pretending that they work for a bank or a company's tech support department.

- **Phishing** involves luring individuals into entering personal information into a website controlled by the hacker. This scam involves two steps. First, the hacker must make a website that

looks like the login page of a popular site such as Facebook or PayPal. Second, the hacker will send an alarming email to millions of users asking them to sign into the site by following the bad link. Hundreds of thousands of individuals have fallen prey to this scam.

Hackers can use other tactics that require very little technical expertise. For example, going through the trash or simply looking at someone's desk can yield valuable information. Hackers also can gain quite a bit of information from what you post on social networks and online forums.

MALWARE AND HACKING COUNTERMEASURES

You have just learned many of the consequences of being infected by malware or having your personal information accessed by a hacker. Before we get to specific countermeasures, it is worth noting that nothing is more important than education and awareness. For example, there is nothing that you can install or configure that can protect you from a pretexting scam. However, being aware that the scam exists will allow you to be more vigilant and cautious about giving away account information to someone who is not verified. For other social engineering attacks, items such as a $20 paper shredder can go a long way to protecting you or your company. Let's now turn to some specific countermeasures against malware and hacking.

Classic countermeasures, such as a paper shredder, education, and awareness, can help prevent social engineering attacks.

SECURITY UTILITIES

In Chapter 3, you learned about various utility programs that can protect you and your computer. Below is a quick summary of what you learned in that section:

- **Anti-malware.** This software helps protect your computer from various types of malware.

- **Firewall.** This utility examines and blocks Internet traffic in order to protect your private network. Firewalls are present in most operating systems and many types of routers.

- **Encryption.** Many types of software and devices use encryption to scramble your data or communication, making it unreadable by anyone who doesn't have the proper key.

KEEPING SOFTWARE UP-TO-DATE

Both operating systems and application software issue updates to fix vulnerabilities and bugs in the programming. Whenever your operating system or browser issues an update, you should apply it immediately. Putting it off for weeks or even days can make your system susceptible to an attack. Remember, both malware and hackers often gain access to a system via security vulnerabilities.

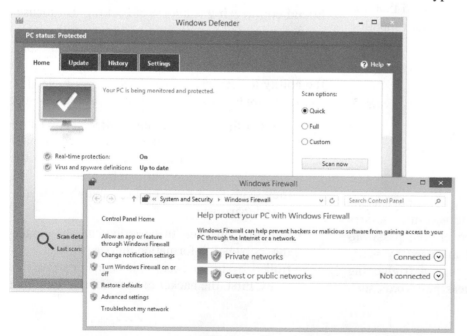

Windows 8 includes basic security utilities such as Windows Defender (anti-malware) and Windows Firewall.

Figure 5.3 A VPN encapsulates packets for a more secure connection.

PROTECTING COMMUNICATION

You can protect your communication from being monitored by hackers. One method of protection involves the proper configuration of your wireless router. Always be sure to use *WPA2* encryption, which requires a password when connecting to your router and makes your wireless transmissions unreadable by hackers. When choosing a password, come up with something unique that you wouldn't mind sharing with a friend or family member. After all, they will likely want to connect to your wireless router when they come to your home.

A popular way for both individuals and businesses to increase the security of a network connection is by using a **virtual private network (VPN)**. A VPN employs a method called "tunneling" in which each packet from the sending computer is encapsulated within another packet before being sent over the Internet (see Figure 5.3). When you use a VPN, all of your activity will first pass through the secure connection between your computer and a VPN server before traveling to the Internet. This effectively shields your data traffic from nearby hackers who would otherwise be monitoring your unsecured communication. A VPN is often required for users who wish to access a company's private network (extranet) over an Internet connection.

PROPER AUTHENTICATION

Individuals and companies use two important principles to deter hackers and block the unauthorized access to

Access cards are often used for authentication.

information. The first is known as **authentication**, where an individual must confirm his or her identity. The second, known as **authorization**, gives individuals a certain level of access based on who they are. As you can imagine, a company's president is authorized to view much more information than a part-time mail room employee.

Three general strategies are used to authenticate individuals:

1. *What you know.* This typically refers to passwords or PINs that an individual must memorize.

2. *What you have.* In some cases, this can refer to a credit or debit card that allows individuals to access their money. For employees, it is often a special card or badge that is used to access certain systems or secure areas of a building.

3. *Who you are.* As you learned in Chapter 2, various parts of your body can be used as a biometric input device. Many systems are now authenticating individuals by scanning their unique fingerprint, iris, or face.

For most users, nothing is more important than having a **strong password** that is difficult to guess or crack by thieves. Strong passwords are long and use a mix of uppercase and lowercase letters, numbers, and at least one symbol such as a dash or period. In addition, you should never use the same password for multiple websites or devices. It is also very

dangerous to leave your passwords in a visible location or to give them out to anyone. If you are fearful of forgetting all of your passwords, use a secure password management tool such as LastPass (see Chapter 3).

USE CAUTION ONLINE

As was stated before, nothing beats general awareness or common sense when it comes to protecting yourself and your data. Given the popularity of the web and social media sites, many thieves are turning to those services to look for useful information. Although there are many dangers on the Internet, a few general rules can help you avoid many problems:

- Avoid clicking suspicious links in email messages or social networking sites. If possible, always open a new browser window/tab and type the address yourself. This will help you avoid phishing attacks.

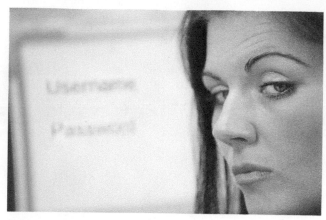

Exercise caution online, especially when it comes to your usernames and passwords.

- Never trust anyone that contacts you without warning and claims to be from tech support or customer service. Instead, ask for the telephone extension and call the toll-free number (or use the chat tool) for that business yourself.
- Avoid downloading software from file-sharing services. Many thieves use the temptation of free (illegal) software to lure individuals into downloading malware. Download software only from trusted sources, such as the websites of the companies that make the software or well-known companies such as Amazon.

BACKUPS

Very few countermeasures are as effective as making regular backups of data. No one truly knows when, or how, data may be lost. A simple disk error can do just as much damage as a hacker might do. And even the most experienced computer user occasionally deletes a file or folder by accident. When such events happen, information can be recovered quickly if data was backed up properly and regularly. In addition to data recovery, backups can also be used to access the previous version of a file.

There are many ways to create backups and archives of data. Large organizations have historically used a **tape library**, which is a large storage unit for magnetic tape drives. Many of these libraries are so vast, modern facilities use robotic arms to store and retrieve the tapes. Smaller businesses and individuals often turn to external hard drives and optical discs for their backup needs. However, nothing is more popular at the moment than cloud storage and backup services.

Fermi National Accelerator Laboratory, part of the U.S. Department of Energy, has a massive tape library.

As you learned in Chapter 3, cloud backups are immune from many of the problems that affect physical backups such as theft and damage. Furthermore, many cloud backup tools are incredibly easy to use. This makes them extremely attractive to both home users and businesses. Cloud storage accounts such as Google Drive, Microsoft One-Drive and Dropbox make a copy of your files the moment you save them in a specific folder in your computer. Cloud backup solutions such as Carbonite and CrashPlan also make things easy for users by performing continuous backups as the contents of a computer are changed. And of course, there is the added convenience of being able to access your backups from these services using any Internet-connected device.

Individuals and businesses are increasingly turning to cloud backup solutions such as CrashPlan.

KEY TERMS

attenuation, 136
authentication, 157
authorization, 157
bandwidth, 136
botnet, 154
bridge, 140
coaxial cable, 136
countermeasure, 149
cybercrime, 153
cyberterrorism, 154
data mining, 147
data validation, 147
data warehouse, 147
decision support system
 (DSS), 143
distributed denial-of-service
 (DDoS), 154
Ethernet, 140
expert system, 144
extranet, 135
fault-tolerant, 145
fiber-optic cable, 136
gateway, 140
hacker, 153
hacktivism, 154
hub, 139
identity theft, 155

information system (IS), 141
interoperability, 146
intranet, 135
local area network (LAN), 135
malware, 152
management information
 system (MIS), 142
mission-critical, 145
network, 134
network interface card
 (NIC), 139
network media, 136
node, 136
office automation system, 141
packet, 137
phishing, 155
pretexting, 155
protocol, 137
RAID, 146
redundant, 145
repeater, 139
risk assessment, 149
rogue hotspot, 154
router, 139
scalability, 146
scareware, 153
social engineering, 155

spyware, 153
strong password, 157
surge protector, 150
switch, 139
tape library, 158
threat, 148
topology, 138
transaction processing
 system (TPS), 141
Trojan horse, 153
twisted-pair cable, 136
uninterruptible power supply
 (UPS), 150
virtual private network
 (VPN), 157
virus, 153
vulnerability, 148
wide area network
 (WAN), 135
Wi-Fi, 137
wireless access point
 (WAP), 137
wireless adapter, 137
wireless network, 137
worm, 153
zombie, 154

Review Questions

MULTIPLE CHOICE

1. The _____ topology, where nodes connect to a hub, is the most common type used today.

 a. bus
 b. star
 c. ring
 d. mesh

2. Which type of information system handles the processing and tracking of transactions?

 a. Office automation system
 b. MIS
 c. TPS
 d. DSS

3. Which of the following Wi-Fi standards is the fastest?

 a. ac
 b. b
 c. g
 d. n

4. Some organizations offer an internal version of the Internet, called a(n):

 a. intranet
 b. extranet
 c. botnet
 d. Ethernet

5. A(n) _____ is a storage system that links any number of disk drives so that they act as a single disk.

 a. NIC
 b. RAID
 c. WAP
 d. IS

6. Which type of malware is a fully contained program that self-replicates and spreads through networks?

 a. Spyware
 b. Trojan horse
 c. Virus
 d. Worm

7. _____ is the amount of data that can be transmitted over a given amount of time.

 a. Attenuation
 b. Bandwidth
 c. Topology
 d. Striping

8. A _____ is similar to a hub, but it is aware of the exact address or identity of all the nodes attached to it.

 a. repeater
 b. bridge
 c. router
 d. switch

9. Hackers often set up their own wireless access points in popular areas with the hope that users connect to them. These are known as:

 a. Trojan horses
 b. zombies
 c. botnets
 d. rogue hotpots

10. A(n) _____ cable consists of a thin strand of glass that transmits pulsating beams of light rather than electric current.

 a. fiber-optic
 b. twisted-pair
 c. coaxial
 d. Ethernet

FILL IN THE BLANK

11. In its simplest form, a(n) _____ is a node on a network that serves as an entrance to another network.

12. Networks must follow rules, known as communication _____, to ensure that data is sent, received, and interpreted properly.

13. A(n) _____ is a type of information system that performs analytical tasks traditionally done by a human.

14. Network media helps carry data from one _____, or connection point, to another.

15. The network standard known as _____ uses a star topology with twisted-pair cables that plug into the RJ45 port located on many devices.

16. A(n) _____ is a complex system for acquiring, storing, organizing, using, and sharing data and information.

17. Data moves through networks in structures known as _____, which are pieces of a message broken down into small units by the sending device and reassembled by the receiving device.

18. A(n) _____ employs a method called "tunneling" in which each packet from the sending computer is encapsulated within another packet before being sent over the Internet.

19. A(n) _____ is the device that all nodes connect to in order to communicate wirelessly.

20. _____ computers are ones that have multiple hardware systems performing the same task at the same time.

Review Questions (continued)

TRUE / FALSE

21. A decision support system can include or access other types of data, such as stock market reports or data about competitors.

22. Scalability is the ability of each organization's information system to work with the other, sharing both data and services.

23. A Kensington lock is an effective countermeasure against phishing threats.

24. Wireless networks use radio signals that travel through the air in order to transmit data.

25. For mission-critical systems, technology companies construct computer hardware and software that can never fail.

SHORT ANSWER

26. With respect to computer security, what is the difference between a threat and a vulnerability?

27. Define data warehouse and provide one example of how it can be used.

28. What is the difference between a surge protector and a UPS? In your response, be sure to indicate the types of threats they help minimize.

29. Describe the difference between a LAN and a WAN, and provide one example of each.

30. Define social engineering and provide two examples or techniques it employs.

31. What are the original and modern meanings of "hacker"? Are there different types of hackers? What is the most dangerous form of hacking?

32. List and describe three countermeasures (security utilities) against malware and hacking.

33. What are the three general strategies used to authenticate individuals? Include one example of each.

34. Define data mining and provide one example of how a retail company might use it.

35. What are zombies and botnets? What can hackers do with them?

Research Exercises

Go beyond the book by performing research online to complete the exercises below.

1. Suppose that you wanted to set up a media server in your home for wireless streaming to any other computer or mobile device. How would you go about doing this? What sort of hardware would you purchase? Is a Windows HomeGroup required?

2. Compare the cloud-based office automation systems of Microsoft and Google. What are some of their benefits? Which would you choose if you were a business? Defend your answers.

3. Explore the use of expert systems in the health-care industry. Provide at least two examples of how they are used and the benefits they offer.

4. Consider the data mining practices of search engines, social networking sites, and retailers. Do you agree with the way they gather, use, and share data? Why or why not?

5. Go to the configuration screen of your wireless router. What settings does it offer that help maximize security? Provide at least three examples. If you do not own a wireless router, find this information for any wireless router of your choosing.

6. Suppose that a website requires an eight-character password of your choosing. Provide at least three examples of weak passwords along with three examples of strong passwords. Explain the reasoning or evidence for your examples.

7. Evaluate the strengths and weakness of the following authentication categories: passwords, access cards, and biometrics. Then consider which one(s) you would use if you were in charge of security at a medium-size office with approximately 150 employees.

8. Name two reliable news sources or labs that test many of the anti-malware products on the market. What sort of tests do they run? Which paid and free products received the highest scores this year? Based on this research, which anti-malware utility would you install on your system? Defend your answer.

6

CHANGING THE WORLD

Chapter Overview

This chapter will help you understand how technology is changing the way we work, socialize, and live. You will learn how your online behavior can affect other individuals and even hurt your chances to find (or keep) a job. You will also learn the effects that technology has had on the environment and people all over the world. Lastly, you will be introduced to emerging technologies such as robotics and automated systems, and learn how they are impacting our jobs and our lives.

PART 1:
Legal and Ethical Issues

The advent of personal computing technology has undeniably taken the world by storm. In just a few short decades, personal and mobile computers have changed the way people interact almost everywhere on the planet. There was a time when our actions might have affected only a few dozen people around us. Today, our online behavior can either impact or be visible to thousands (or even millions) of individuals and businesses around the globe.

It is no surprise that the ethical use of computing technology is a pressing issue. The discussion of computing ethics should seem very familiar and serve as a reinforcement of lessons that were learned in childhood. Topics such as lying, stealing, and bullying are being revisited in the Information Age even though most individuals understand these behaviors outside of computing. In addition to these traditional topics, technology presents some new issues. This portion of the chapter will discuss and clarify some unethical computing practices that are common in the digital world, as well as some penalties that exist for violating computer-related laws.

Introduction to Ethics

Ethics is the philosophical study of morality. It is a rational analysis of the voluntary, moral choices that individuals make. When you study and apply ethics, you must provide a well-reasoned justification for why something is wrong. Stating that you did or didn't do something because a friend or family member told you so isn't sufficient justification. This is especially true of computer ethics. You cannot excuse the illegal downloading of music, for example, by stating that all of your friends do it too. If you believe that this activity is morally acceptable, you must provide rational justifications for it.

LEGAL CONSEQUENCES

Many activities that are unethical are also illegal. As you know there are laws for crimes such as stealing, cheating on taxes, and hurting other people. In the same manner, there are legal consequences for technology crimes such as hacking and sharing copyrighted files. Although it is useful to know the legal consequences of various actions, many individuals act ethically not because there is a law; rather, they do so because it is the right thing to do. Unfortunately, some individuals choose to act unethically if they believe they can get away with it.

EMPATHY

One of the factors that can significantly affect a person's ethical outlook and behavior is **empathy**, the ability to recognize, understand, and share the feelings of others. Empathy requires that we ask ourselves that age-old question that we've all heard many times: "How would you feel if that happened to you?" Applying this sort of question to ethical situations can help us see them more clearly and may even modify our behavior. Throughout this lesson, take time to not just understand the mechanical aspects of unethical behavior and the legal penalties, but also to practice being empathetic. Ethics can involve many gray areas and unanswered questions, but you may be surprised at how often a gray area resolves into clearer situations that seem right or wrong when you understand the perspective of others.

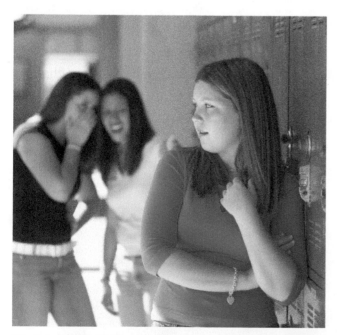
Many unethical behaviors, from gossiping to bullying, now affect online users.

Piracy and Copyright Law

One of the most widespread forms of unethical computer use is piracy. In the world of computing, **piracy** means acquiring or exchanging copies of protected digital creations without payment to or permission from their creator. These creations often include software, photos, music, and movies. Piracy doesn't need to involve profit to be illegal. Sharing digital products without consent is considered piracy even if they are given away. Let's take a close look at the laws and ethics that govern piracy.

INTELLECTUAL PROPERTY

It can be a bit challenging to understand the products over which the piracy battle is being fought. It is much easier to picture the theft of a TV from a store than the theft of an MP3 music file. If someone makes a copy of a music file and shares it online, the original file is still in the same place. This makes it less obvious that a theft has occurred. Even so, legal concepts have been created and refined to help protect **intellectual property**, or products of the mind. While ideas, designs, and expressions of creativity may not have much (or any) physical form, they can be quite valuable.

The U.S. government fights piracy and protects intellectual property.

The Internet has increased the piracy of intellectual property such as music.

Centuries ago, individuals began to see the value of their ideas. While those ideas began as books and inventions, today they extend to music, photos, software, and many other creative works. Society rewards creative individuals and companies by protecting their works for a limited time. This grants them exclusive right to, among other things, sell their works and make a living off of them. If only one person bought a song, for example, and immediately made a copy for everyone on the Internet, that musician would be robbed of the opportunity to make money off her creative property. If society wants creative people to keep producing, it is in our interest to reward those individuals, not steal from them.

COPYRIGHT AND FAIR USE

One of the foundation blocks of intellectual property law is the **copyright**, a legal concept that grants rights and control to the owner of any published work. A creative product such as a book, song, or photograph is generally considered to be published when it is made available to the public for consumption. This includes retail releases, public performances, art exhibits, and even uploading to YouTube or a blog. Once that occurs, the author is protected and now has the exclusive right to sell, distribute, copy, and perform the work. It is through licensing, which you learned about in Chapter 3, that a copyright holder can grant usage or distribution rights to others.

Copyright protection lasts for a very long time, usually 70 years after the death of the author. Therefore, it is safe to assume that most of the things you see on the Internet are still under protection. This includes websites, photos, music, videos, and software. If, for example, you download a photo from a Google search result and place it on your business website, you will likely be guilty of copyright infringement. It is always safe to ask authors for their permission if you want to use their creative work somewhere else. The only exception is works that are in the **public domain**, which means that they can be downloaded and used without obtaining permission. Works go into the public domain when their copyright expires. They also include most works created by the government and any items that an author purposely released into the public domain.

FAIR USE

Copyright law contains an exception known as **fair use**, which provides for a limited set of circumstances where others can use portions of copyrighted material without first obtaining permission. Some of these circumstances include education, commentary, criticism, and parody. People can use small excerpts from a larger work in reviews and observations, so long as the review is genuine and not just a disguised means of unauthorized reproduction. Although determining fair use can sometimes be difficult, there are four questions that should be asked when considering whether it applies:

Educators and students can often use portions of copyrighted material under the fair use provision.

Many images that come from government websites are in the public domain.

1. *What is the nature of the use?* Educational use and commentary are more acceptable than a for-profit use.

2. *What is the nature of the work?* Copying from a news article (nonfiction) is more acceptable than a popular song or major network TV show (works of fiction).

3. *How much of the work is being copied?* Using only a few seconds of a song or video is more acceptable than copying the entire thing.

4. *How will the copy affect the market?* If you are claiming fair use just to avoid paying for a book, song, or movie, then fair use will likely not apply. Remember, the reason for the existence of copyright law is to protect authors and allow them to profit from their creations.

There is no easy formula to figure out if fair use applies. Mostly, it is a common sense review of the fair use criteria. For example, if you are a teacher who photocopies three pages of a 500-page book for your class, you are likely covered under fair use. But if you upload an entire song or movie to your blog and write a short comment for it, you will not be covered unless you have permission from the creator of the song or movie.

THE IMPACT OF PIRACY

Examples of piracy are common and varied. In most cases, it is everyday users that upload or distribute copyrighted works on the Internet. Popular songs are frequently exchanged via file-sharing services

such as BitTorrent. Software can often be found with modifications that disable **DRM (digital rights management)** technology such as copy protection and authenticity checks. Even TV shows and movies can be viewed at various websites that are not authorized to display or distribute them.

With piracy, both the provider and receiver are generally considered to be part of the crime. Individuals have been caught and prosecuted both for sharing material online and for copying it from a pirate site. Many services have also been prosecuted and shut down for facilitating copyright violations. Because so many computer users illegally engage in piracy, media companies report billions of dollars in annual revenue loss. The impact to artists, companies, and the economy is clearly substantial.

ALTERNATIVES TO PIRACY

There are many ways to enjoy your favorite songs, TV shows, and movies without resorting to piracy. Although many media companies need to modernize the way they distribute content, there have been major improvements over the years. The following are just some of the methods in which you can enjoy content in an affordable manner while still supporting your favorite artists.

PURCHASING ONLINE

You can purchase a digital copy of almost anything at various websites. Companies such as Apple, Amazon, and Google will sell you music, movies, books, and software that you can enjoy for as long as you wish. Songs cost about a dollar each, making it easy to own a permanent version of the music you love most. Furthermore, they can usually be copied and enjoyed on all of your devices such as laptops, tablets, and smartphones.

DIGITAL RENTALS

Instead of purchasing items such as movies, you can rent them for about two days. This is more convenient than driving to a video store to pick up the latest release. Apple, Amazon, and Vudu are popular services for renting movies and TV shows.

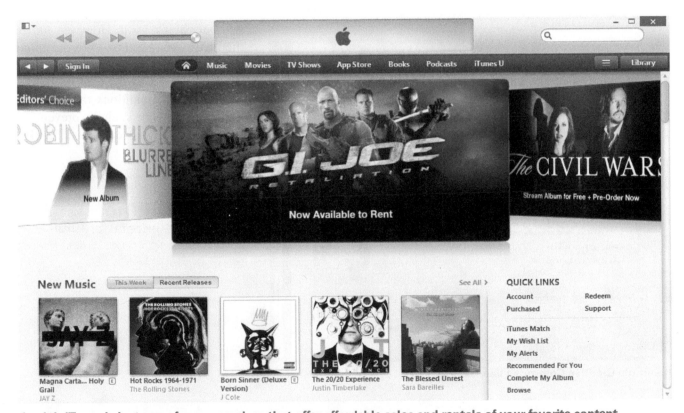

Apple's iTunes is just one of many services that offer affordable sales and rentals of your favorite content.

AD-SUPPORTED STREAMING

For music, many are turning to streaming services that are supported by advertisements. These companies, such as Pandora and Spotify, pay royalties to artists and music labels that are financed by the advertising companies. In a similar manner, video services such as Hulu use advertisements to support the free viewing of recent TV episodes. If using any type of mobile app that only uses banner ads, consider clicking them every now and then to support the creators of the app.

Streaming services such as Pandora often use ads to pay for music royalties.

SUBSCRIPTION SERVICES

Many of the free streaming services also offer a paid subscription option that eliminates advertisements or offers additional features. Your monthly payment to services such as Netflix, Hulu Plus, Amazon Prime, and Spotify Premium will help support the streaming company and your favorite artists. In addition, you get a variety of perks including faster shipping with Amazon and a larger catalog of TV shows with Hulu Plus.

CREATIVE COMMONS

A **Creative Commons** license allows authors to set conditions for the free use and distribution of their work. Most of these licenses require, at a minimum, that the user provide **attribution**, or credit, to the author wherever the work is used. For example, if you download an image that has a Creative Commons license, you can freely place it on your blog without paying for it. However, under the image, you need to write the name of the artist or photographer so that he or she receives full credit for the image. Other conditions that may be set by the author include preventing any modifications, derivative works, or commercial use.

More **Online:** Visit the companion website for links to Creative Commons websites.

A sample Creative Commons license.

Personal Conduct

When we first begin to use computers and the Internet, we do not generally receive the same sort of guidance as we do at school, work, or even when growing up. Most people simply join in and participate, whatever their age, and either learn as they go or simply do whatever they want. That last approach, to do whatever one wants without regard for consequences, can cause a great deal of harm to your social, professional, and online reputation. It can also cause harm, inconvenience, and distress for others. While the Internet can accommodate many different styles of behavior and points of view, some actions are undeniably unethical and should be avoided without exception.

NETIQUETTE

The term **netiquette**, or Internet etiquette, refers to the set of online behaviors that are considered polite and proper. For the most part, the behaviors that find their way onto various netiquette lists are the same ones that we regard highly in our day-to-day interactions with others. Politeness, courtesy, and respect are highly prized, while abusive speech and rude behavior are discouraged. Interacting with others online may seem different because we do not always see the faces of other individuals. However, the consequences of our negative actions are still very real.

In Chapter 4, you learned a variety of rules and best practices for using email. Many of these also apply to various Internet activities such as posting on discussion forums and social networks. However, because online discussions tend to be more casual and often anonymous, many people engage in unacceptable behavior. The following are just a few examples.

POSTING AND SEARCHING

The user community has certain expectations when posting a question or message to a discussion forum. First, it is important to post your message in the correct forum of the website, as there are often several categories to choose from. In addition, each forum has many **threads**, which are essentially topics that contain related posts. Placing your message in the correct thread will maximize your chances of getting a reply. If creating your own thread, be sure to use a descriptive and informative subject. Most importantly, understand the general topics being discussed in a particular forum. Posting a message that

When it comes to online experiences, most individuals learn as they go.

is completely off topic or appears to be promoting something may be considered spam. And just like spam for email, this behavior is not welcomed and could get your account suspended on this website.

It is also important to search the forum thoroughly to check if your question has already been answered. Many websites also have **frequently asked questions (FAQ)** areas that should be checked for common questions and their responses. If you cannot find your question anywhere, go ahead and ask it; however, do not keep posting your question over and over. If it went unanswered, it means the user community likely does not know the answer.

ANGER, FLAMING, AND TROLLING

Anyone can get angry or frustrated on a forum or social network. The problem is that getting angry on

the Internet is very different from yelling at someone in person. Angry words posted online will always outlive your anger because of the permanent nature of things written on the Internet. Even if you delete your message, there is a record of it somewhere. If you are skeptical, you may want to check how many celebrities and athletes have had to apologize for a message that they thought had been erased.

Online social interactions that exhibit anger and/or insults are known as **flaming**. You often see this type of behavior on forums or online games, where a user becomes enraged at another user. This is different from **trolling**, which is usually just the act of being annoying and antagonistic. Regardless of the type of nuisance, many feel that these behaviors occur because individuals forget that there is a human being on the other end, receiving the hateful message.

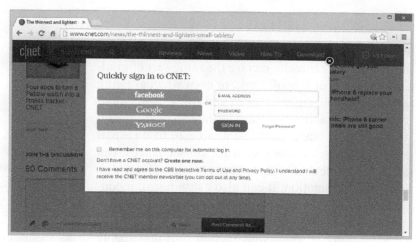

Sites that support discussions, such as CNET, often require users to log in or use their real name to reduce trolling.

CYBERBULLYING

Sometimes, anger and aggression can go too far on the Internet. Repeated hostile behavior with intent to harm another individual is known as **cyberbullying**. This can include actions such as intimidation and humiliation, often with the intention of ruining a person's reputation or causing psychological trauma. Children and teenagers are particularly vulnerable. In many cases, the bullying and taunting

Sending email containing potentially offensive jokes to the people at work can be inappropriate and risky.

that goes on in person might extend online, or vice versa.

Many teenagers have had to seek therapy because of cyberbullying and, in a few extreme cases, even committed suicide. Because of the prevalence of cyberbullying, many states have passed laws banning this type of online harassment. Whether or not it is illegal in your state, these actions are highly unethical and very harmful. Even a playful prank, such as posting an embarrassing photo or video against someone's wishes, can cause distress that you may not be able to predict.

USE OF HUMOR

Humor requires the right audience to be funny. Before you send or post a joke, make sure it will be appropriate for the readers and that the joke (especially if posted publically) will not come back to haunt you. This is equally true of photos, videos, and any other content posted under your real name or social networking account.

Sending email containing funny jokes to the people at work, for example, is more risky than it sounds. If the joke contains potentially offensive content, the sender's reputation in the company could suffer. Even if no one takes offense, the sender risks being reprimanded or fired for behavior that goes against acceptable use policies.

ACCEPTABLE USE POLICIES

An **acceptable use policy (AUP)** is a document containing an organization's policies for the ethical, secure, and appropriate use of computing resources.

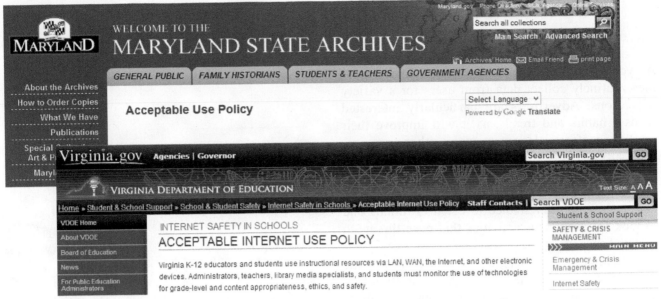

MARYLAND

Search all collections

Main Search Advanced Search

Archives' Home Email Friend print page

GENERAL PUBLIC FAMILY HISTORIANS STUDENTS & TEACHERS GOVERNMENT AGENCIES

About the Archives
How to Order Copies
What We Have
Publications
Special ...
Art & P...
Maryl...

Acceptable Use Policy

Select Language
Powered by Google Translate

Virginia.gov Agencies | Governor

Search Virginia.gov GO

VIRGINIA DEPARTMENT OF EDUCATION

Text Size A A A

Home » Student & School Support » School & Student Safety » Internet Safety in Schools » Acceptable Internet Use Policy Staff Contacts | Search VDOE GO

VDOE Home
About VDOE
Board of Education
News
For Public Education Administrators

INTERNET SAFETY IN SCHOOLS
ACCEPTABLE INTERNET USE POLICY

Virginia K-12 educators and students use instructional resources via LAN, WAN, the Internet, and other electronic devices. Administrators, teachers, library media specialists, and students must monitor the use of technologies for grade-level and content appropriateness, ethics, and safety.

Student & School Support
SAFETY & CRISIS MANAGEMENT
MAIN MENU
Emergency & Crisis Management
Internet Safety

Most organizations, from government agencies to libraries, have an acceptable use policy.

They can be useful tools for protecting an organization and creating a legal framework for punishing wrongdoers. Some AUPs are simply a comprehensive statement of policy so that the institution's point of view is made clear. Others are framed as an agreement or contract that individuals are required to sign or agree to before being given access to computer-related resources. Although many different types of organizations use them, AUPs generally have a few common elements:

- Outlawing the use of computing resources to commit crimes, such as hacking and piracy.

- Restricting particular services, such as file-sharing, on their networks.

- Banning inappropriate and unethical behavior, and guidelines for the organization's netiquette.

- Stressing the importance of security, especially the creation of a strong password.

- Explaining the ownership and privacy of email, storage, and other resources that you have access to. Typically, companies reserve the right to monitor your email, web activity, and files stored on company equipment.

ACCEPTABLE USE AT SCHOOL

In addition to the above, your school might also add guidelines regarding the appropriate use of specific computers. What might be acceptable in the lab of a network security course might not be acceptable in the library's computers. Your school may also list the sort of online actions that are prohibited because they would constitute academic dishonesty.

ACCEPTABLE USE AT WORK

One of the most popular policies enforced by businesses is the ban on using computers for anything that isn't related to an employee's work. Many organizations understand the temptation of activities such as social networking and how they can hurt an employee's productivity. They use a variety of techniques, including monitoring, to ensure employees remain on task. We will discuss employee monitoring in the next section.

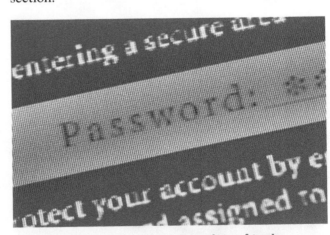

Acceptable use policies cover a variety of topics including the security of your account.

Privacy and Surveillance

One of the hottest topics in computer ethics pertains to the privacy of individuals in the Information Age. As you have already learned, many online companies routinely collect data from users for a variety of reasons. Advertisers are particularly interested in user habits and trends, as it will improve their marketing efforts. However, many other organizations are also interested in what you are doing on the computer. Businesses often monitor employees for productivity and security reasons. Governments also engage in surveillance to catch criminals and to look for suspicious activities that pose threats to national security.

Individuals often disagree when it comes to the need for privacy. Some people are naturally social and will post almost anything about their lives online. Others agree to exchange privacy for certain benefits, such as consenting to having their bags inspected in exchange for better airline security. On the flip side, many are often shocked when they learn what information is routinely collected about them and do everything in their power to retain their privacy or anonymity. In this section, you will learn about the variety of ways in which data is collected, so that you can decide for yourself what steps (if any) to take if you are interested in protecting your privacy.

More **Online:** *Visit the companion website for information about nonprofit organizations that fight for privacy rights and individual liberties.*

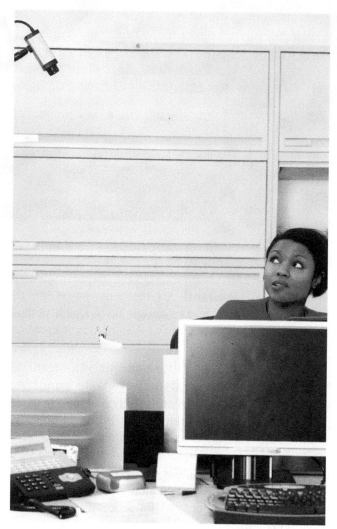
Is the Information Age threatening our privacy?

Companies often monitor their employees' online activity while at work.

EMPLOYEE MONITORING

Most organizations feel that employees should focus solely on producing work and value for the business during the time they are being paid. With that in mind, it should not be surprising to discover that many employers are nervous about the negative impact that computers might have on worker productivity. The same Internet that can be used to access cloud-based business programs and shared documents can also be used to check Facebook activity, share copyrighted files, and view pornography. For employers, these activities can translate into reduced work output, security problems on the network, or even criminal liability.

As you already know, most companies use AUPs to inform employees about the behaviors and practices that are forbidden. A large number of companies

will also use software that can either block particular Internet services or monitor what employees do on their computer. By checking **logs** (files that record activities and events) periodically, employers can determine whether there was inappropriate use by an employee. Organizations may also check the company-issued email account periodically if they suspect that an employee is violating the AUP or putting the company at risk.

ETHICS AND LEGALITY OF MONITORING

There is some debate as to whether employee monitoring has a positive outcome for a company. While cameras and monitoring software can force employees to remain productive, evidence shows that excessive surveillance lowers morale. Employees with low morale are less productive than those who are happy and motivated. Often, the chance to have a little fun with co-workers and discuss a recent sports game or fun weekend event can raise the spirits of an entire office. The difference today is that conversations that used to occur around a water cooler, for example, may now occur on a social networking site. Many have argued that as long as employees finish their work and remain productive, there is little harm in letting them unwind and stay in touch with the online world for a few minutes each day.

Everyone generally agrees about one aspect of monitoring: Employers should always inform employees about what kind of monitoring the company will engage in. This shows respect for the employee's privacy as no one will be caught off guard by monitoring devices. Also clear is the legality of monitoring.

Should employers treat conversations by the water cooler differently than those that occur online?

Various court cases have demonstrated that employers are generally within their rights to restrict Internet access at work and monitor employee use of the company's computing resources.

MONITORING ONLINE ACTIVITY

Many organizations do not restrict their monitoring to the workplace. They may check the public, online activity of their employees for anything that could harm the company. This includes statements that insult the company or executives, as well as those that may reveal company secrets. In addition, employee photos that can embarrass or hurt the reputation of a company are also deemed to be harmful. Many employees, from fast-food workers to corporate executives, have been fired for something they posted online because it made their company look negative or careless in the eyes of the public.

Organizations also check online activity before they hire employees. Your words, photos, and videos can say quite a bit about you. Anything you post online can affect your ability to get that initial interview. Many companies now specialize in gathering data about individuals on behalf of organizations such as businesses, universities, and government agencies.

GOVERNMENT SURVEILLANCE

Many government agencies such as the NSA and FBI monitor the Internet and mobile activities of individuals all over the world. They do this for national security purposes or as part of a criminal investigation. Laws such as the Patriot Act and the Foreign Intelligence Surveillance Act (FISA) give the government

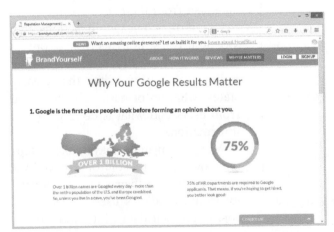

Since your online image could affect your job prospects, services such as BrandYourself help you manage it.

broad surveillance powers. In addition, law enforcement can request warrants and require that online companies turn over records including your email messages, search history, and social networking activity.

For hundreds of years, individuals in a society have had to trade some privacy for the purpose of security and enforcement of laws. What is being continually debated is how much of that privacy should be given up, especially by those who have committed no crime. Like many privacy-related debates, it often comes down to how much personal information you are willing to place on the Internet. In addition, you should keep in mind that you and your devices usually leave **digital footprints**, which is a trail of your data, activity, and even the locations where devices are used.

Agencies such as the NSA can monitor Internet and mobile activity.

ONLINE/SOCIAL RISKS

The most important thing to know about sharing anything online is this: Nothing posted to social media services or anywhere else on the Internet should be considered private. Many social media users feel that their right to privacy is being violated or abused by many online companies. Unfortunately, this is more of a misunderstanding on the part of the user than a legitimate concern. Although services such as Facebook allow users to control access to their personal information, you must remember that this data is stored on the systems owned by these companies. In addition, friends who can see your photos, videos, and status messages can copy, store, and forward that information to others.

Social media companies typically include conditions for using the service, in which each user grants permission to use the information in certain ways. Furthermore, automated programs run by social media companies and search engines can easily find, organize, and store the information that they find. This information can then be sent to marketing companies or partners who find usage patterns and trends very useful for their business. The more information they know about you or the users of a particular site, the more relevant the ads they can display to users.

ETHICS AND ONLINE COMPANIES

Most online companies have started to take privacy very seriously. Some companies, such as banks, are legally required to consider privacy. And when it comes to the privacy of children, various laws keep companies from taking advantage of them. However, many companies fear backlash from their users or the news media if they engage in actions that violate privacy. For this reason, online companies typically have a **privacy policy** on their websites that clearly states what information is collected from users and what is done with that information.

Many companies have taken steps to allow users to control various privacy settings on their services. Google, for example, allows users to view and control all their data with a tool known

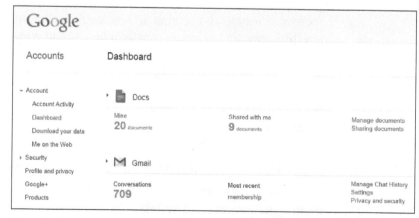

Google Dashboard allows users to control privacy settings and manage their data on Google's various services.

as Google Dashboard. Here, users can see everything from email messages to their YouTube and search activity. Online services also allow users to delete their personal information and accounts. However, even if you were to delete everything on your social media accounts, there is no assurance that this information is completely gone. Remember, anyone from your friends to search engines that gather public posts could still have some content that you thought was gone forever. Therefore, the only means for truly keeping information private is to not share it at all.

ETHICS OF SHARING

You have already read about how your words or photos can come back to haunt you later, both personally and in your career. It is also important to realize that anything you share online can hurt the individuals you care about. Compromising photographs, such as those showing a group of friends at a wild party, should not be posted to social media sites if they could be embarrassing or devastating to the lives of others. If you really want to post it, ask the individuals in the photo for permission.

PRIVACY TOOLS

In most cases, you can safeguard your privacy by following the advice in this chapter and using the security tools discussed in Chapter 5. However, when

When sharing photos and videos, always be considerate of those who appear in them.

it comes to leaving digital footprints, you should be aware of a few additional tools.

- **Private browsing** is a feature of all modern browsers that will delete your history, cache, and cookies the moment you close the private window. This is ideal if you are using a computer that is not yours.

- **Do not track** is a browser feature that attempts to stop websites from automatically sharing details about your visit with other companies. However, this is simply a request and websites are not obligated to obey it.

- **Anonymity software**, such as Tor and Anonymizer, will help mask your IP address from websites. This can help protect your privacy when visiting a website that does not have a privacy policy, as it will not allow that particular company to keep your real IP address in its records.

For regular browsing, you can control your desired privacy through various settings, such as keeping history for only a certain number of days. Browsers also include a feature that will delete all of your browsing history with a single click.

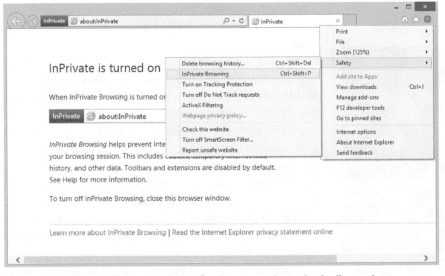

Internet Explorer offers a variety of privacy settings, including private browsing.

Global and Environmental Issues

Many of the ethical issues discussed in the previous section focused on actions that individuals and organizations should avoid in order to be ethical. However, ethics involves more than those things we shouldn't do. Ethics also tells us those things that we ought to do in order to help other people and even our planet. The following section will offer many examples of how individuals and organizations are using technology to change our world for the better.

SOCIAL AND POLITICAL CHANGE

In the last few years, technology has become an important tool for revolution and social action. Uprisings against governments have been started by and chronicled with Twitter updates and YouTube video clips. Rebels have used mobile devices and social media to coordinate their actions and receive information to aid their cause. Oppressive governments have been caught by surprise by how quickly socially sensitive information can spread through these channels. In fact, some leaders have been so terrified by the power of the Internet that they have shut it off during times of turmoil.

In the United States, most politicians now have social media accounts and often engage their constituents through them. They will also use the Internet for

Mobile devices and social media have been used in various political demonstrations and uprisings.

raising money and campaigning. The White House even has a petition form on its website, promising to address any issue from citizens if it receives enough signatures online. Social media also receives extensive use by individuals, groups, and organizations that want to advance a social or political agenda. On several occasions, unpopular proposals in Congress have been withdrawn due to the coordinated outrage shown on social media.

THE DIGITAL DIVIDE

The **digital divide** refers to the technology gap that exists between different social and economic classes. Many experts believe that without access to technology such as computers and the Internet, certain groups may fall behind when it comes to education and the ability to find a job. Because technology has become so important, many U.S. cities offer public access to computers in libraries and schools. In addition, various charities collect used computers that can be donated to homes that do not have one. One particular organization, One Laptop Per Child (OLPC), is taking this idea further by placing affordable, durable laptops in the hands of children all over the world. It is hoped that these laptops can engage students in both education and communication with others, empowering them to improve themselves and the lives of those in their community.

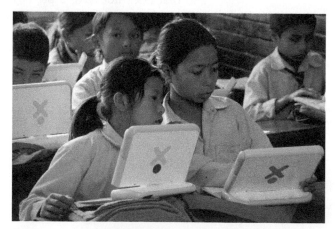

One Laptop Per Child (OLPC) places these laptops in the hands of children around the world.

WHISTLEBLOWING

Whistleblowing is the act of alerting the public about harmful activities that are being hidden by an organization. These activities can range from the production of harmful chemicals to deceiving the U.S. government or its people. Since most companies keep electronic records of just about anything, evidence is often easy for potential whistleblowers to find. However, before someone can ethically blow the whistle and turn against their organization, a few questions should be considered:

- Have I alerted my supervisor and, if needed, the top-level managers of the organization?

- Is the activity in question illegal or likely to cause harm to the public?

- Do I have documented proof of the activities that will cause this alleged harm?

Many state and federal governments have laws that protect the job and safety of whistleblowers, preventing them from being fired for identifying illegal or unethical behavior within the company. Even so, retaliatory action is often a real consequence for the whistleblower, whether it manifests itself as reassignments to lower-priority roles in the company or isolation from co-workers who no longer wish to associate with the whistleblower.

WHISTLEBLOWING CONTROVERSY

The Internet has given whistleblowers a new forum for alerting the public of misconduct. WikiLeaks is

WikiLeaks, which offers whistleblowers an anonymous way to submit evidence of wrongdoing, has received significant media attention due to high-profile leaks.

a global, online organization that offers whistleblowers an anonymous way of posting information and submitting evidence. It has become a very polarizing service, with some singing its praises while others criticize its decision to release many private documents and communications belonging to various countries.

Blowing the whistle may not always be the ethical thing to do. Some have argued that recent whistleblowers against the U.S. government have put lives in danger and hurt the standing of their country in the eyes of others. While the debate rages as to whether they should or shouldn't have blown the whistle, it is important for potential whistleblowers to look at the big picture. They must consider whether the outcome of their actions might be worse than the harm they were trying to prevent. In addition, they must explore all possible options for addressing the harm being done by an organization before making details of the problem public.

ENVIRONMENTAL PROBLEMS AND SOLUTIONS

As the years pass, our society finds itself increasingly concerned with the effect we have on the global environment. Technological advances have accelerated our use of resources and contributed to various global problems such as pollution. However, technology has also helped us to better understand a variety of issues facing the planet.

NASA uses satellite imagery and software to track sea ice thickness and look for trends in climate change.

Satellites orbiting Earth are providing us with a wealth of data about air and water pollution. Data stations on the planet's surface as well as in orbit allow us to measure changes in climate and global temperature with unprecedented precision. Computers now provide sophisticated simulations to test "what-if" climate change scenarios, along with heavy-duty data analysis that aids scientists in developing solutions. Technology also helps us create or improve environmentally friendly energy solutions such as solar and wind power.

Green computing follows the reduce, reuse, and recycle model.

GREEN COMPUTING

Green computing concentrates on reducing the environmental impact of computers and their widespread use. Many computers consume a great deal of electricity to operate. And like other metal and plastic creations, they do not disappear very quickly in a landfill. As billions of people put computers or other devices into use, the cost to the global environment becomes significant. To help lower that impact, green computing follows the "reduce, reuse, recycle" model that has been promoted for decades in environmental initiatives. Let's take a closer look at what this model entails.

REDUCING ENVIRONMENTAL IMPACT

Green computing has emerged as a new way to consider the manufacture and operation of computers to reduce their environmental impact. Designs that

The EPA offers information on recycling and donating electronic devices.

yield even a fractional reduction in a computer's power consumption can cause a substantial reduction in the global demand for electricity. Computers and their components, such as CPUs and monitors, are being developed to run on less power. Operating systems use **power management** utilities to place computers and devices in low-power states when they are not being used. These states include:

- **Sleep**, which uses only enough electricity to keep the contents of your RAM active.

- **Hibernate**, which saves more electricity by copying the contents of RAM to your hard drive. RAM can now be powered off since the hard drive does not require power to remember its content.

Companies that use heavy computing resources also strive to reduce their environmental impact. In fact, it is common for the websites of many large organizations to promote their environmental initiatives. These range from recycling programs to the improved management of their large servers and networks. Many organizations have reduced the amount of technology purchased and used because of the increased reliance on shared, cloud computing resources.

WASTE & RECYCLING

Some local and international programs collect old computers to be refurbished and redistributed to individuals or schools that do not have access to computers. Most population centers now have a municipal or private program that encourages the recycling of old and broken computers and peripherals. Those centers can resell working parts and strip gold or other useful metals from components for recycling. In addition, many retailers offer recycling programs for computers, mobile devices, and printer cartridges, often offering discounts if you trade something in.

One of the most significant activities that helps reduce waste is going **paperless**. Both companies and individuals are using technology to lower their consumption and reliance on paper. Throughout this book, you have learned of the countless benefits offered by technology. As time goes on, you will find many types of organizations, including schools and hospitals, eliminating paper from their facilities.

PART 2:
Changes at Work

As the computer revolution began decades ago, people often wondered if their job might someday require computer expertise. Given the explosion in the use of technology, individuals are no longer asking themselves this question; instead, they are finding themselves using computers on a daily basis. In fact, the more appropriate question for today's graduates and job applicants to ponder is what sort of hardware and software they should master in order to do their job.

This section will focus on more than the use of technology in various types of businesses. You will learn how technology has changed not just the way we work, but also what type of work we do and where we can do it. You will also learn about the growing fields of robotics and artificial intelligence, and the ways they are changing many aspects of business and education. Lastly, you will explore the various computing careers that are responsible for developing and supporting most of the technology used today.

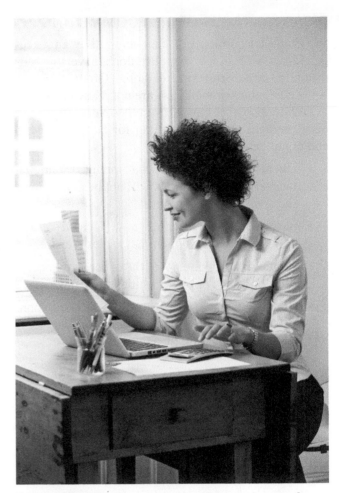

Telecommuting allows individuals to work away from the office.

Workplace Changes

In Chapter 1, you learned about the various ways in which organizations use computers. From health care to law enforcement, technology allows workers to do their jobs quickly and effectively. However, technology has also allowed organizations to engage in certain activities that were practically impossible before the advent of powerful computers and networks. This section will introduce some of these activities and discuss their advantages and disadvantages.

TELECOMMUTING

Telecommuting is the process of working for a company without being physically present at the company's office. The term describes a wide variety of remote work practices, from working at home occasionally to living in a different country than the company you work for. Powerful home computers, mobile devices, and high-speed Internet have made telecommuting possible for millions of individuals.

To be effective as a telecommuter, a worker must become self-disciplined enough to complete work efficiently and avoid distractions. Telecommuters also need to have the computer hardware, software, and connectivity required to get the job done properly. Employers will often provide some of this technology and a VPN so that the remote worker can access the company's network securely. In addition, video-conferencing applications can make it easy for that employee to have conversations with supervisors and join in on team meetings.

ADVANTAGES OF TELECOMMUTING

When a particular job is capable of being completed from home, employees often jump at the chance. Companies should also be excited by some of the advantages that telecommuting offers. These include:

- The ability to hire or keep workers whose schedule or location would make it impossible for them to work at the company's offices.

- Reduced costs for office space and utilities.

- Improved employee morale, which can boost productivity and loyalty.

DISADVANTAGES OF TELECOMMUTING

Although telecommuting can seem like an exciting idea, some employees just don't have the self-discipline or a distraction-free home. On the flip side, some companies or managers are not ready or capable of having employees away from the main office. The disadvantages of telecommuting for both employees and organizations include:

- Clients and managers that prefer traditional face-to-face interactions will not be able to have them with remote workers.

- Sensitive information is now located at the employee's home, which may be less secure.

- Employees who are not at the office may receive inferior wages or opportunities for promotion.

- Employees may find themselves working more hours, especially if their supervisor feels as if they are always "on the clock."

EMPLOYEE AVAILABILITY

The last point made in the previous section marks a growing problem for many employees, not just

Distractions at home may cause problems for telecommuters.

remote ones. A large number of office workers and executives now have mobile devices that are capable of retrieving company email and receiving instant messages. This creates an expectation of being available at all times, ready to read a message or answer a quick question. Technology has made work easier in many ways, but it also has individuals working more hours than ever.

OUTSOURCING

In addition to allowing employees to work from home, technology has made it possible for companies to outsource many of their functions or services. **Outsourcing** occurs when an organization transfers some aspect of its business to a third party. For example, many companies choose not to have an accounting department; instead, they hire an outside accounting firm to handle their finances. With networking technology, such as extranets, it is very simple for this firm to access the company's sales and expense figures as if they were in the same office.

OFFSHORING

When companies outsource functions to another country, it is referred to as **offshoring**. Some of the most popular uses of offshoring are the call centers and live support tools that handle customer service for an organization. With high-speed networks, an employee located in India, for example, can access customer data and support files that may be located in the United States. In addition to customer

High-speed networks allow call centers to be located anywhere.

support, many companies outsource manufacturing for various devices and components. Most of the mobile devices used today are manufactured in China, with some components coming from Japan or South Korea. Computing and communication technology make many aspects of the global economy possible.

Automation and Emerging Technologies

You have already learned various ways in which technology has changed the way we work. Perhaps none has had a more significant impact than automation. Computers and robots are now performing many jobs that used to be performed by humans. However, these tools, along with other emerging technologies, are creating new jobs and helping organizations all over the world tackle some of the biggest issues facing us today. This section will explore automation and many of these emerging technologies.

AUTOMATION

Automation occurs when computers or machines can perform the work that was once done by a human. In some cases, the machine completely replaces a human worker. For example, large robotic arms now handle many aspects of a car's assembly, a process that used to take several people to complete. In other cases, the automation can help individuals complete their work faster or free them to do other tasks. This is especially true for small-business owners, who can enjoy more free time with the help of systems

These robotic arms bring automation to manufacturing.

Automated checkout systems are being used at many stores.

that manage inventory and other business functions automatically.

Automated systems offer many benefits to organizations and individuals. However, sometimes the advantages for a company can result in lost jobs or job shifts. For example, a large number of Americans were employed in manufacturing 60 years ago. Today, very few people are needed for those types of jobs. More people are now working in service industries and in the creation or support of those automated systems.

USES FOR AUTOMATION

Both computers and automated machines are used in a variety of roles. Often, they increase an organization's productivity. Others can be used to save people's lives. The following are some examples of where you will find these types of systems today:

- Areas where pinpoint accuracy is required, such as in the manufacture of microprocessors.

- Tasks that require long hours of physical work or extreme strength.

- Activities or locations that are too dangerous for humans, such as cleanup efforts in a toxic area or search and rescue operations in a catastrophe.

- Activities that involve fixed or predictable transactions, such as checkout lines and course registration.

ROBOTICS

During early robotic research, machines were limited to performing a single and specific task with consistency and precision. Robotic arms, for example,

could be taught to position themselves over an object, grasp that object, move it to a new location, and set the object down. While that accomplishment may not seem like much in retrospect, it required the development of machinery that could be programmed and manipulated in precise ways. As you have learned, companies such as car manufacturers found these specific and repetitive tasks quite useful.

The complexity and sophistication of robots has increased dramatically over the years. This has coincided with an improvement in computing technology such as faster processors and more sophisticated programming. Their ability to understand their environment has greatly improved, as evidenced by affordable robots that can vacuum your home. As time goes on, you will see improvements in both their intelligence and range of motion.

HUMANOID ROBOTS

Humanoid robots are those that are created to imitate the appearance or capabilities of humans. New technology in robot construction is exploring ways to simulate a variety of human movements, such as running or shaking someone's hand. In addition, various sensors can perform functions similar to our eyes and ears. Some humanoid robots, like Honda's ASIMO, can already perform a variety of activities that require a great deal of balance and range of motion. It can jog, climb stairs, and even kick a ball. Furthermore, it can recognize stationary and moving objects, and understand certain kinds of human input such as spoken words and gestures.

Honda's ASIMO humanoid robot displays human-like movement.

There are many applications for humanoid robots. They may be used to perform a variety of activities that are too risky for humans, such as traveling in space for long periods and exploring the surface of other planets. We can also use these robots as caretakers for elderly or disabled individuals, providing 24/7 oversight for those who wish to stay in their homes instead of moving to assisted-living facilities. And because these robots continue to look and act more like humans, it makes it easier, psychologically, for individuals to relate to them.

More **Online:** Visit the companion website to learn more about robots, including some that you can build or program yourself.

ARTIFICIAL INTELLIGENCE

Artificial intelligence (AI) involves the development of intelligent systems. These systems can include anything from sophisticated programs that answer

NASA Robonaut 2 can work alongside astronauts or perform tasks that are too dangerous for humans.

questions to futuristic robots that can think and act like humans. Though the sciences of AI and robotics are very different, some of the futuristic products and accomplishments we envision involve contributions from both of them.

WHAT IS INTELLIGENCE?

Superficially, intelligence can be defined as the processes used in learning, problem solving, and communication. However, not everyone agrees on an exact definition. Philosophers, scientists, psychologists, programmers, and many others have struggled to create a precise and comprehensive definition of intelligence. And even if a standard model for human intelligence were created, the model might not cover the behavior of other species that are normally considered to be intelligent.

Equally ambiguous is the notion of when a machine can be classified as being intelligent. One popular test of a machine's ability to think is known as the **Turing test**. It was developed by Alan Turing, who was a very influential figure in the development of computer science as a discipline. In his test, a computer would be said to exhibit intelligence if it could imitate humans and deceive an interrogator in the way it responded to a variety of questions. Although no system has exhibited this type of intelligence yet, various supercomputers such as IBM's Watson now have an astounding capability to understand complex questions and quickly find the answers using large databases of information.

IBM's Watson system displays remarkable intelligence when it comes to research.

AI APPLICATIONS

Many types of programs attempt to imitate a certain type of human intelligence. One system may act as a personal sales consultant that can make recommendations based on what it knows about you (e.g., Amazon.com). Another might focus on understanding human languages and the way we ask questions (e.g., Apple's Siri and Google's Voice Search). Expert systems, which you learned about in Chapter 5, are often regarded as intelligent for their ability to provide expert answers to specific types of questions.

As stated earlier, AI and robotics can often come together to produce fascinating results. If robots are to act as caretakers, companions, and explorers, they must possess enough intelligence to handle a variety of tasks on their own. Furthermore, they must be able to "think outside the box" when an unexpected situation occurs. The good news is that we already have software and devices that can recognize our faces, follow verbal commands, and provide personalized recommendations. Little by little, these abilities will be integrated into robots that have a wide range of motion and can be made to look like us. Many feel that it is just a matter of time before a truly intelligent, humanoid robot is developed.

Many robots are being made to look like humans (Einstein, in this case) and imitate many of our facial expressions.

EMERGING TECHNOLOGIES

It would be an impossible task to list all the technology being developed and researched today. Most areas of study and activity,

from sports to space exploration, are continually being improved and aided by emerging technologies. To make our task easier, let's focus on just a few areas where emerging technologies are aiming to improve the lives of humans.

BIOTECHNOLOGY

Biotechnology is an application of biology that uses living organisms to manufacture new products or improve existing ones. Computing technology is being used by researchers in this field to develop new medications, map human genes, and increase crop yields. There are many exciting areas of research in biotechnology, some of which aim to cure a variety of diseases or engineer organisms that help fight pollution.

NANOTECHNOLOGY

Nanotechnology involves the creation or manipulation of matter at the smallest possible scale. Researchers from a variety of fields are creating new types of materials, devices, and even computer circuits by working directly with molecules and atoms. At the moment, nanotechnology is being used to develop effective drug delivery systems that can better target problem areas while reducing side effects. Many dream of a day when tiny, nanoscale robots can be injected into the body to repair damaged tissue or deliver compounds directly into human cells. Others eagerly await the arrival of the *quantum* computer, which will be millions of times faster than today's

Researchers use DNA sequencing technology to find genes that may cause cancer.

devices. This is because their atoms can represent data in states beyond the two bits (0's and 1's) of today.

HUMAN ENHANCEMENT

Technology can be integrated with biological systems in various ways to repair or improve human functions. For those who have lost a limb, engineers have developed robotic prosthetics that can perform a variety of movements by simply projecting a thought to them. Others act as a sort of exoskeleton that can help paralyzed individuals walk again using motorized leg attachments. Researchers have also discovered ways to make computer chips interact with various areas of the body and brain to help those who suffer from conditions such as Parkinson's or blindness. Some chips are even able to record new memories, helping those who have suffered damage to parts of the brain or have early-stage memory loss.

It is just a matter of time before technology begins to be used in healthy individuals who wish to enhance one or more parts of their body. A variety of implants could be used to give someone superhuman strength, vision, and even brain function. Biotechnology will one day be able to modify a person's genes before they are born, allowing parents to "customize" their child, so to speak. Some futurists even believe that human memories can one day be copied and stored into a computer, allowing that person to achieve a sort of immortality. Ethicists are already debating many of these topics, feeling that some of these developments are not far away.

Advanced technology is allowing amputees to control a robotic arm as if it were their natural one.

Computer Careers

As you have learned throughout this book, many types of computing technology support organizations today. This technology changes rapidly, with new hardware, software, and Internet features being released continuously. This has created a strong demand for professionals who can develop and maintain these systems. The following section will introduce you to various careers and positions in the information technology field.

> More **Online:** *Visit the companion website for up-to-date information on computer careers and salaries.*

Software engineers create diagrams in order to visualize systems.

SOFTWARE ENGINEER

A **software engineer** is responsible for the development of computer software. Some of these engineers take on the role of a **systems analyst**, who specializes in developing plans and recommendations that meet the software and system needs of an organization. Regardless of their role, these individuals are experts in one or more computer programming languages and have a good understanding of the software that runs on (or manages) various computer systems. In addition to designing and developing software, those with computer programming skills may find careers in specific areas such as:

- **Game development.** Today's video games are quite complex and require programming for user interaction, realistic motion and physics, and even intelligent character behavior.

Web developers are often responsible for the programming and graphics of today's websites.

- **Mobile app development.** Different considerations go into making apps for mobile users, such as ensuring that a program works well with a smaller, touchscreen interface.

DATABASE ADMINISTRATOR

A **database administrator (DBA)** is responsible for configuring, maintaining, and securing an organization's database. Given the explosion in data storage and analysis, this field is growing rapidly. Some of the duties of a DBA include:

- Developing and designing a database.
- Installing and configuring a database server.
- Optimizing a database for maximum performance and security.
- Creating backups of data and restoring those backups when necessary.

WEB DEVELOPER

A **web developer** creates and maintains websites for organizations. Web developers are trained in web programming languages and are often responsible for connecting the company's website to a database. Because websites have become such a crucial component of an organization's marketing efforts, many developers have added skills or branched out into additional areas of specialization. Some of these include:

- **Search engine optimization (SEO)** involves improving the ranking of a website when users enter relevant keywords in a search engine.

- **Graphic design** skills, such as editing photos and designing layouts, have become an important skill for creating websites.
- Many positions, such as **social media strategist**, are being created for experts in sales and marketing using the web and various social media tools.

NETWORK ADMINISTRATOR

A **network administrator** is responsible for configuring and maintaining networks and communication systems. In addition, they are responsible for securing a company's infrastructure from internal and external threats. Some of their duties include:

- Installing and updating network software.
- Managing network hardware.
- Creating and configuring user accounts.
- Configuring and securing Internet, intranet, and extranet connections.

SUPPORT SPECIALIST

A **computer support specialist** excels when it comes to installing, configuring, and supporting computer systems. Most companies have the need for a **help desk** department that can quickly repair and troubleshoot systems, as well as provide technical support to employees. Some of a support specialist's duties include:

- Installing and configuring new computer hardware.
- Troubleshooting and repairing hardware of all types.

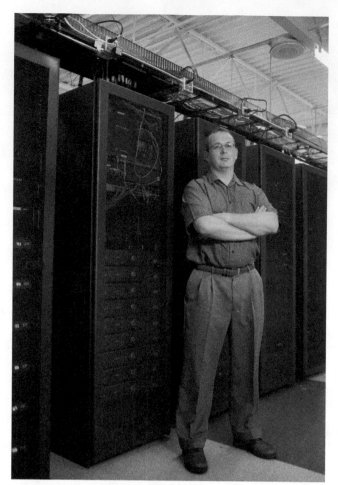

Network administrators are in charge of the configuration and security of an organization's network.

- Troubleshooting problems with the operating system and other company software.
- Providing support to employees or customers.

INFORMATION SYSTEMS MANAGER

Information systems managers are responsible for managing a diverse team of IT professionals that include programmers, network administrators, and many others. In addition to overseeing employees, they make top-level decisions regarding the purchasing of software and hardware for an organization. These individuals often possess a wide range of knowledge in information technology fields, along with experience or a degree related to business and management.

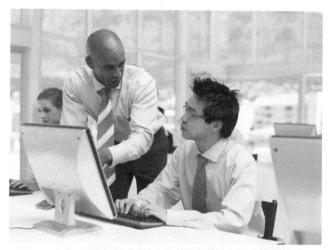

Information systems managers supervise other IT personnel and make top-level decisions.

KEY TERMS

acceptable use policy (AUP), 172
anonymity software, 177
artificial intelligence (AI), 184
attribution, 170
automation, 183
biotechnology, 186
computer support specialist, 188
copyright, 167
Creative Commons, 170
cyberbullying, 172
database administrator (DBA), 187
digital divide, 178
digital footprints, 176
digital rights management (DRM), 169
do not track, 177

empathy, 166
ethics, 166
fair use, 168
flaming, 172
frequently asked questions (FAQ), 171
graphic design, 188
green computing, 180
help desk, 188
hibernate, 180
humanoid robot, 184
information systems manager, 188
intellectual property, 167
log, 175
nanotechnology, 186
netiquette, 171
network administrator, 188
offshoring, 182

outsourcing, 182
paperless, 180
piracy, 167
power management, 180
privacy policy, 176
private browsing, 177
public domain, 168
search engine optimization (SEO), 187
sleep, 180
social media strategist, 188
software engineer, 187
systems analyst, 187
telecommuting, 181
thread, 171
trolling, 172
Turing test, 185
web developer, 187
whistleblowing, 179

Review Questions

MULTIPLE CHOICE

1. A(n) _____ license allows authors to set conditions for the free use and distribution of their work.

 a. public domain
 b. acceptable use
 c. DRM
 d. Creative Commons

2. _____ is a feature of all modern browsers that will delete your history, cache, and cookies the moment you close the browser.

 a. Do not track
 b. Intellectual property
 c. Green computing
 d. Private browsing

3. One of the foundation blocks of intellectual property law is the _____, a legal concept that grants rights and control to the owner of any published work.

 a. copyright
 b. attribution
 c. netiquette
 d. acceptable use policy

4. Which of the following fields involves the creation or manipulation of matter at the smallest possible scale?

 a. Biotechnology
 b. Nanotechnology
 c. Artificial intelligence
 d. Robotics

Review Questions (continued)

5. _____ is the act of being annoying and antagonistic in areas such as online forums.
 a. Piracy
 b. Whistleblowing
 c. Flaming
 d. Trolling

6. _____ occurs when computers or machines can perform the work that was once done by a human.
 a. Automation
 b. Outsourcing
 c. Offshoring
 d. Green computing

7. _____ involves the development of intelligent systems.
 a. AI
 b. DRM
 c. SEO
 d. DBA

8. _____ is the act of alerting the public about harmful activities that are being hidden by an organization.
 a. Outsourcing
 b. Whistleblowing
 c. Green computing
 d. Turing

9. Many websites have _____ areas that should be checked for common questions and their responses.
 a. DRM
 b. AUP
 c. SEO
 d. FAQ

10. In the world of computing, _____ means acquiring or exchanging copies of protected digital creations without payment to or permission from their creator.
 a. trolling
 b. flaming
 c. piracy
 d. attribution

FILL IN THE BLANK

11. The term _____ refers to the set of online behaviors that are considered polite and proper.

12. Online companies typically have a(n) _____ on their websites that clearly state what information is collected from users and what is done with that information.

13. _____ is the ability to recognize, understand, and share the feelings of others.

14. The _____ refers to the technology gap that exists between different social and economic classes.

15. You might find a computer support specialist at a company's _____, troubleshooting systems and providing technical support to employees.

16. _____ is the philosophical study of morality.

17. A(n) _____ is responsible for configuring, maintaining, and securing an organization's database.

18. Repeated hostile behavior with intent to harm another individual is known as _____.

19. Legal concepts have been created and refined to help protect _____, which are essentially products of the mind.

20. _____ concentrates on reducing the environmental impact of computers and their widespread use.

TRUE / FALSE

21. If a company hires an outside organization to handle its accounting, it is engaged in outsourcing.

22. It is illegal for social networking companies to share profile and usage information with marketing companies they are partnered with.

23. Copyright protection lasts for approximately 15 years after the author applies for it.

24. For a computer, "sleep" mode uses less electricity than "hibernate" mode.

25. Some humanoid robots can already jog, climb stairs, recognize objects, and understand human speech.

SHORT ANSWER

26. List five elements that are typically found in acceptable use policies.

27. How can your online activity affect your ability to find or maintain employment?

28. Briefly describe the four factors that must be considered for "fair use."

29. What sort of Internet surveillance does the U.S. government engage in? Name two laws that give government agencies broad surveillance powers.

30. Describe at least three ways in which you can recycle and reduce computing-related waste.

31. Suppose that you wanted to watch a Hollywood movie or the entire season of a TV show. List four legal ways in which you could view this content.

32. List three advantages of telecommuting.

33. Describe three ways in which social media have been used to help bring about political or social change.

34. Is it legal for a company to monitor employees while they work? Is it ethical? Defend your answers.

35. List four ways in which technology can be integrated with biological systems to repair or improve human functions.

Research Exercises

INSTRUCTIONS

Go beyond the book by performing research online to complete the exercises below.

1. Find YouTube's policies or guidelines on uploading music and videos protected by copyright law. What does YouTube it say? What does YouTube do when a copyright violation is reported?

2. Perform additional research on the government's use of sophisticated computers to monitor communications. What did you find? Do you agree with this type of surveillance? Defend your answers.

3. Name two nonprofit organizations that support privacy rights. What are some of the issues they are currently fighting? Describe at least three of these issues.

4. Find at least three local organizations and/or retailers near you that can recycle or reuse your unwanted devices. Describe the services they provide and consider which one(s) you will use in the future.

5. Find an organization that can analyze your DNA and generate reports on your health risks and ancestry. Would you use this service? Why or why not?

6. Do you believe it is ethical for researchers to create intelligent robots? Discuss some of the pros and cons of the development of these machines.

7. Consider the implications of using a smartphone for work. What are some of the advantages and disadvantages? Is it ethical for employees to be contacted outside of work hours? Defend your answers.

8. Perform research on any emerging technology (such as biotech) that can improve or enhance human lives. Describe one example of a technology that is already in place and another example of a technology that is in development. Do you support such research? Is there a line that shouldn't be crossed with respect to improving or modifying humans that are otherwise healthy? Defend your answers.

Buying Guide

Many people feel lost or overwhelmed during the computer buying process. There are many categories of computers for individuals, from desktops and laptops to tablets and smartphones. And within each category are countless devices with a wide range of specifications and prices. Unfortunately, no one-size-fits-all recommendation can apply to everyone. And to make matters more complicated, specifications and prices change rapidly in this industry as new hardware and devices are continually released.

This buying guide contains recommendations for the typical student. It assumes that you are still in school and are interested in using a computer wherever you go, including at home and on campus. As you read the list below, please note that it is arranged *in order of priority*. In other words, the first category is the most important, followed by the second, and so on. If you are interested in more up-to-date information, check the companion website for this book.

1. All-Purpose Laptop

The best device to meet all of your computing needs is an all-purpose laptop. It is small enough to take to school, but powerful enough to be your primary computer at home. If you plan on using it extensively at home, you should consider connecting it to a TV or external monitor for comfort. Many individuals also buy a larger keyboard and external mouse. The following are some of the specifications and prices you should be looking for in a Windows-based system:

- **Price:** $450 to $750
- **CPU:** Intel Core i3 or i5; AMD A-Series
- **RAM:** 4 GB to 8 GB
- **Hard drive:** 500 GB to 750 GB
- **Monitor:** 15 to 17 inches, touchscreen preferable for Windows 8

ALTERNATIVE: CONVERTIBLE ULTRABOOK

Choose this option if you need two specific things: a very lightweight laptop and a tablet computer. These laptops will either convert to a tablet or will allow you to detach the screen for use as a tablet. Expect the following differences:

- **Price:** $800+
- **Monitor:** 11 to 13 inches, touchscreen
- **Weight:** 2.5 to 3.5 pounds

2. Smartphone

Choosing a smartphone starts with your budget. If you are interested in the lowest possible price, your wireless carrier likely offers several Android, iOS, and Windows devices for free (or close to free) with a two-year wireless contract. These phones are slightly older models, yet still excellent smartphones that are capable of running any app.

If you are willing to pay more to get the latest and greatest, expect to pay around $200 (with a two-year contract). You can choose from the best devices offered by manufacturers, running the latest mobile operating systems. When choosing between mobile OS, be aware that Apple and Android devices have more available apps than those running Windows. In addition, be sure to compare some of the following specifications:

- **Camera quality:** Megapixels can guide you, but be sure to check the web for reviews on the camera's overall performance. Consider color accuracy, image sharpness, and low-light performance.
- **Screen size:** Newer smartphones are coming out with bigger screens, with some getting close to six inches. Consider how well it fits in your hand and whether a large screen is useful for your smartphone activities.
- **PPI:** The number of pixels-per-inch will indicate how sharp or crisp objects appear on your screen.
- **Battery life:** Find out how long the battery is expected to last on a single charge.
- **Storage:** If you plan to install many apps and store large numbers of photos and music, you should consider 16 GB to 32 GB. Also check if the phone allows you to add an external SD card. Lastly, remember that many of your files can be stored in the cloud, reducing the need for high storage amounts.

3. Tablets

Tablets are very hot at the moment. That being said, purchase one only if you absolutely need one. Consider what activities would be significantly easier or convenient with a tablet. Keep in mind that quality tablets with larger screens can be pricey, and many of their functions can be performed by your laptop or smartphone. If you do decide to purchase one, consider the same specifications as smartphones but with a few differences:

- **Screen size:** This ranges from 7 to 10 inches. The bigger the screen, the pricier the tablet.
- **Price:** Expect to pay around $200 for smaller tablets and $400 to $500 for larger ones.
- **Operating system:** It is often best to choose the same OS as your smartphone, as you will not need to buy the apps all over again.

4. Desktop (All-In-One)

Desktops, which were once the standard computers for the home, are losing popularity quite quickly. Laptops and mobile devices are now preferred, and users often have little motivation to sit down in one place and use desktop computers for extended periods. That being said, if you want to have a family computer that many can share or you desire maximum comfort when using a computer, a desktop may be desirable. Consider the following specifications for your all-in-one desktop computer:

- **Price:** $600 to $900
- **CPU:** Intel Pentium-based or Core i3/i5
- **RAM:** 4 GB to 8 GB
- **Hard Drive:** 500 GB to 1 TB
- **Monitor:** 20- to 24-inch touchscreen

Macs and Chromebooks

The prices given for both laptops and desktops have assumed the purchase of a Windows-based computer. Apple's Mac computers are generally more expensive than their Windows counterparts. As you have learned in this textbook, Apple makes excellent computers that are powerful, reliable, and user-friendly. Choose a Mac only if you can afford it or wish to be part of the Apple "ecosystem" along with your smartphone and/or tablet. With respect to Chromebooks, they are typically the most affordable category of laptops. However, they are best suited as a secondary device unless your computing needs are very light and limited mostly to online activities.

3D modeling software Used by professional artists and animators who need to create three dimensional graphics and characters for advertisements, video games, cartoons, and movies.

3D printer A printer that can create a three-dimensional object made of various materials.

A

Acceptable use policy (AUP) A document containing an organization's policies for the ethical, secure, and appropriate use of computing resources.

Algorithm A series of steps that describe exactly what each portion of a program is supposed to do.

All-in-one computer Computers that have all of the hardware integrated with the monitor.

Anonymity software Software that helps mask your IP address from websites.

Application software Software that allows individuals to complete a variety of work and school-related tasks. Entertainment software and most mobile apps are also in this category.

ARPANET A predecessor to the Internet, this government-funded network connected four U.S. universities in 1969.

Artificial intelligence (AI) Involves the development of intelligent systems or machines that possess capabilities such as learning, problem solving, and communication.

Attachment A file attached to an email message.

Attenuation The loss of intensity and clarity of a transmitted data signal.

Attribution Credit to the author of a work wherever it is used.

Augmented reality An experience where the real-world is supplemented with computer-generated information.

Authentication A security measure used to confirm an individual's identity.

Authorization A security measure used to give individuals a certain level of access based on who they are.

Automation The use of computers or machines to perform the work that was once done by a human.

B

Backbone Refers to the connections that carry most of the Internet's traffic.

Backup A copy of one of more files (or entire storage devices) that is made in case the originals become lost or damaged.

Bandwidth In networks, it refers to the amount of data that can be transmitted over a given amount of time.

Banner ad A thin, rectangular advertisement that is commonly placed across the top or on the sides of a web page.

Bcc Stands for "blind carbon copy," and is used to send a copy of an email to recipients who will remain invisible to other recipients of the message.

Beta version An early version of a computer program used to test the software in real-world conditions.

Biometrics The measurement of patterns or characteristics found in the human body.

Biotechnology An application of biology that uses living organisms to manufacture new products or improve existing ones.

Bit A fundamental unit of computing that is represented as an on (1) or off (0) value.

Bitmap graphic A type of image that is represented by individual pixels.

Bits per second (bps) A unit of measurement used to track the speed at which data travels to and from the ISP.

Blade server A thin unit that can slide in and out of a rack that holds many of its companion servers.

Blog A web page or small website that contains a series of chronological posts and comments.

Bluetooth A short-range wireless technology used in devices such as hands-free systems.

Blu-ray disc (BD) The latest optical storage technology, which typically stores 25 or 50 GB of data.

Bookmarks A list of favorite websites or pages.

Boot process The start-up process of a computer, which includes loading the operating system from the disk.

Botnets Massive networks of zombies that can be used by a hacker to spread malware, send spam, and conduct carefully orchestrated network attacks.

Bridge A device that connects two LANs or two segments of the same LAN; looks at the information in each packet header and forwards data traveling from one LAN to another.

Broadband Any digital data connection that can transmit information faster than standard dial-up by using a wider band of frequencies.

Bugs Errors in a software program.

Byte The unit of memory or storage that represents eight bits. It is the amount of space required to store a single character, such as a letter or number.

C

Cache (browser) Also known as temporary Internet files, the browser cache stores every single page, image, and video for all the web pages you have recently retrieved.

Cache (memory) A form of high-speed memory that stores a small, frequently used set of instructions and data. It is located inside modern CPUs.

Cc Stands for "carbon copy," and is used to send a copy of your message to individuals other than your primary recipient.

Central processing unit (CPU) The main processor of a computer. It is responsible for organizing and carrying out instructions to produce a desired output.

Chipset A part of a motherboard that acts as a traffic director for data.

Chromebook A line of lightweight laptops that run Google's Chrome operating system.

Clipboard A temporary holding space in the computer's memory for data that is being copied or moved.

Clock rate The frequency or speed at which CPUs process instructions.

Cloud backup Utility software that creates automated backups to an online account.

Cloud collaboration The ability to view, edit, and share documents online.

Cloud computing The ability to store your files and use various applications in an online account.

Cloud storage The ability to store your files online and access them from any Internet-connected device.

Coaxial cable A cable that consists of a single copper wire that is surrounded by insulation and a wire mesh shield.

Coding The process of converting algorithms and flowcharts into an actual computer program.

Command-line interface A way to interact with computers that requires users to memorize and type a series of commands.

Compact disc (CD) A type of optical storage technology that is capable of storing 700 MB of data.

Compatible The condition whereby two computers can use the same software because they run the same operating system.

Compiler A program that translates a specific programming language into a machine language that can be processed by the CPU.

Computer A device that accepts input, processes data, and can output or store the result of its actions.

Computer aided design (CAD) Software that aids architects, engineers, and many others who need to create a digital model of an object.

Computer program A set of instructions that directs the computer to perform a variety of tasks.

Computer support specialist An individual who is responsible for installing, configuring, and supporting computer systems.

Contrast ratio Measures how close the monitor can get to the brightest white and the darkest black.

Convertible laptop Lightweight laptop computers that allow users to swivel or detach the touchscreen monitor.

Cookie A small data file created by a web browser that remembers your preferences for a specific website.

Copy A command that places a copy of the selected object (or objects) into the clipboard.

Copyright A legal concept that grants rights and control to the owner of any published work.

Copyright law A federal law that gives software creators a variety of rights and privileges over their creative work.

Core An individual processor inside a chip.

Countermeasure Any step you take to ward off a threat.

Creative Commons A license that allows an author to set conditions for the free use and distribution of their work.

Crowdsourcing The gathering of information from a large group of people.

CRT monitors Rarely used today, these large and bulky displays used cathode-ray tube (CRT) technology.

CSNET An early computer network created in 1981 to bring together researchers in the field of computer science.

Cursor A mark on the screen indicating where the characters you type will be entered; also known as "insertion point."

Customer relationship management (CRM) Software that allows sales departments to manage call centers, support customers, and keep track of sales commissions.

Cut A command that removes the selected object (or objects) from their current location and places them into the clipboard.

Cybercrime The use of a computer and/or network to commit a variety of crimes, such as creating viruses or disrupting networks.

Cyberbullying An online form of aggression that involves repeated hostile behavior with intent to harm another individual.

Cyberterrorism A dangerous form of hacking that seeks to create large-scale chaos and damage to a country's infrastructure.

D

Data Individual facts or pieces of information.

Database An organized method for storing information.

Database administrator (DBA) An individual who is responsible for configuring, maintaining, and securing an organization's database.

Database management system (DBMS) Software that allows users to create and manage complex databases.

Data mining The discovery of new patterns or relationships between data.

Data plan A subscription that allows individuals to connect to the Internet using a cellular network.

Data validation A method for checking and improving the reliability of data.

Data warehouse A central repository where records from multiple databases are stored.

Decision support system (DSS) A special application that collects and reports certain types of data, thus helping managers make better decisions.

Delete A command that removes a file from your drive.

Desktop The traditional starting area on GUI-based operating systems.

Desktop computer A personal computer that has been traditionally found on the desks in many offices and homes. Most are in the form of a tower.

Device driver Programs that allow operating systems to communicate with hardware.

Dial-up An older type of Internet connection that uses analog signals over a phone line.

Digital camera Portable devices that electronically capture and store still images and video.

Digital divide The technology gap that exists between different social and economic classes.

Digital footprints A trail of your data, activity, and the locations where devices are used.

Digital literacy A broad understanding of computer and information technology, and the ability to use it well.

Digital projector A device that projects digital images and video onto a large screen where they can be viewed by an audience.

Digital rights management (DRM) Technologies used to protect copyrighted material.

Digital versatile disc (DVD) A type of optical storage technology that is capable of storing 4.7 or 8.5 GB of data.

Digital video recorder (DVR) A device that allows you to record television shows for future playback.

Disk cleanup A utility that clears out temporary files that take up space on your hard drive.

Disk defragmentation An optimization utility that will reorganize files and fragments to place related ones nearer to each other.

Distributed denial-of-service (DDoS) A network attack that attempts to shut down or block access to websites or other network resources by overwhelming them with requests.

Do not track A browser feature that attempts to stop websites from automatically sharing details about your visit with other companies.

Document feeder A tray that allows you to scan several sheets of paper automatically.

Domain name The portion of a URL that uniquely identifies a site and a brand on the web.

Dot matrix printer A printer that creates output by striking an inked ribbon against paper using metal pins.

Dots per inch (DPI) A measurement of image quality for printers.

Download To receive data.

Drive A computer's storage devices.

Duplexing The ability to automatically print to both sides of a piece of paper.

Dye-sublimation printer A printer that uses a process where colored dyes are heated and then diffuse on specialty paper or other materials.

E

E-book reader A device that makes it convenient for individuals to store and read many electronic books.

E-commerce Doing business online.

Electronic book Digital book that is stored on a computing device.

Email A system for exchanging messages through a computer network.

Embedded system Limited computers that are placed inside devices that require specific computing functions.

Emoticon A symbol that represents an emotion in casual messages.

Empathy The ability to recognize, understand, and share the feelings of others.

Encryption The process of scrambling your data or storage devices to make them unreadable by anyone who doesn't have the proper key.

End-user license agreement (EULA) The typical license that a user must agree to before installing software.

Enterprise resource planning (ERP) A system that brings together many types of business functions into one software solution.

Ergonomic keyboard A keyboard that's designed to be comfortable and tailored for the human body, with keys that are angled and a palm rest at the base in order to keep your wrists straight.

Ethernet The most common physical standard for local area networks.

Ethics The philosophical study of morality.

Executable file A file that can be run by the operating system on a user's computer.

Expansion card Add-on circuit boards that improve the performance of a system's video or sound.

Expert system A type of information system that performs analytical tasks traditionally done by a human, using sequences of questions to ask and actions to take based on the responses to those questions.

Extension A program used to add a variety of useful features to the web browser.

Extranet A service that allows organizations to share some of its intranet resources with people outside the organization.

F

Facial recognition A biometric technology that looks for unique measurements in an individual's face.

Fair use An exception to copyright law that provides for a limited set of circumstances where others can use copyrighted material without first obtaining permission.

Fault-tolerant Systems that are able to continue their operation even when problems are present.

Fiber-optic cable A high-speed cable that consists of a thin strand of glass that transmits pulsating beams of light rather than electric current.

File The most fundamental component of storage that users interact with. A file can contain the instructions of a computer program or the data that you care to store.

File compression The process of making a file smaller than its original size.

File extension A short, unique sequence of characters located after a file's name that indicate the file type.

File hierarchy The way a computer organizes files, consisting of drives, folders, and files.

File system The way in which the operating system views and manages the space on a storage device.

Fingerprint scanner A biometric technology that can detect the unique patterns and swirls of an individual's finger.

Firewall A software utility dedicated to examining and blocking Internet traffic.

Firmware Instructions placed on a chip that contain device-specific information.

Flaming Online social interactions that exhibit anger and/or insults.

Flowchart A chart that uses special symbols to trace the steps of a program's development.

Folder A container that can store files or other folders. Also known as a directory.

Formatting The process of preparing a storage device for use by an operating system.

Forums Discussion boards where individuals can ask questions and reply to each other.

Forward To re-send an email after its initial transmission.

Freeware Any software that is free to use without any specified time restrictions.

Frequently asked questions (FAQ) A list of common questions and their responses on a website.

G

Game controller An input device for a computer game.

Gaming consoles Complete entertainment systems that offer Internet connectivity, movie rentals, photo storage, and many other services in addition to video games.

Gateway A node on a network that serves as an entrance to another network. It helps one network understand the packet headers from another network.

Gesture A type of finger movement that can accomplish various tasks on specialized input devices.

Graphic design The art or skill of editing photos and designing layouts.

Graphical user interface (GUI) A type of operating system interface that allows users to communicate with the computer via graphical elements on the screen.

Graphics processing unit (GPU) A video card's microprocessor.

Graphics tablet A tool that offers extra-sensitive touch surfaces that translate an artist's motions into drawings on the computer screen.

Green computing The principle of reducing the environmental impact of computers.

H

Hacker In the negative sense, this term refers to an individual who uses a computer and/or network to commit a variety of crimes, such as creating viruses and disrupting computer networks.

Hacktivism Hacking with a social or political agenda.

Hands-free computing The ability to communicate with a device without using your hands.

Haptic feedback The communication of vibration, motion, or physical resistance to a user; also called "haptics."

Hardware The physical devices that make up a computer system.

Hard drive The primary storage device of a personal computer.

Hashtag A symbol (#) to mark keywords or topics in a message.

Help desk A department at a company that can repair and troubleshoot systems, as well as provide technical support to employees.

Hibernate A computer state that saves electricity by copying the contents of RAM to your hard drive.

History A list of every website you have visited, kept by your web browser.

Home automation The technology that allows various household activities to be automated or controlled from a distance.

Home page The starting page for a web browser.

HTML Hypertext markup language. It is used to create web pages.

HTTP Hypertext transfer protocol. It helps web servers deliver a requested page to a user's computer.

HTTPS A secure, encrypted version of HTTP.

Hub A basic network device that provides multiple ports for connecting nodes.

Humanoid robot A robot that is created to imitate the appearance or capabilities of humans.

Hyperlink A word or picture users can click on to immediately jump to another location within the same document or to a different web page.

I

Icon A graphical representation of a file, folder, or drive.

Identity theft A type of crime in which criminals essentially assume your identity and begin to open new bank accounts under your name.

Information processing cycle The series of steps the computer follows to receive input, process the data according to instructions from a program, display the resulting output to the user, and store the results.

Information system (IS) A complex system for acquiring, storing, organizing, using, and sharing data and information.

Information systems manager A person responsible for managing a diverse team of IT professionals that include programmers, network administrators, and many others.

Inkjet printer A type of printer that creates an image directly on the paper by spraying ink through tiny nozzles.

Input User entries or activities that tell the computer what to do.

Install The process of having software set up by the operating system so that it can be used.

Instant messaging (IM) The act of having an online, text-based conversation with one or more individuals.

Integrated development environment (IDE) Software that helps developers build their computer programs.

Intellectual property Products of the mind such as ideas, designs, and expressions of creativity that may not have any physical form.

Interactive whiteboard A large screen that allows a user to interact with the images projected on it.

Internet The largest network in the world, it connects billions of people and organizations throughout the planet.

Internet meme Online content that has become very popular and widespread over time.

Internet service provider (ISP) Telecommunications companies that offer Internet access to homes and businesses.

Interoperability The ability of each organization's information system to work with the other, sharing data and services.

Intranet An internal version of the Internet containing information that is restricted to a particular company's employees.

IP address A unique set of numbers and/or letters that uniquely identifies every computer or device on the Internet.

K

Keyboard shortcuts Keystrokes that can quickly perform an operation within software.

L

Laptop computer A portable computer that contains all of the components of a desktop computer in a single, integrated unit. It is also known as a notebook computer.

Laser printer A fast, high-quality printer that creates output by using a laser that is aimed at a rotating drum.

LCD monitor A common type of flat-panel monitor that contains a light source and a screen of special crystals placed in the monitor between the user and the light source.

Learning management system (LMS) A system that offers students the ability to complete exams, turn in work, and communicate with their instructor and classmates.

LED monitor A thinner, lighter, and more energy-efficient type of LCD monitor that is lit by a grid of tiny electronic lights called light emitting diodes.

Live tile A graphical element on the Windows 8 Start screen that can display real-time information such as the current weather, news, or social media updates.

Local area network (LAN) A data communication system consisting of multiple devices that are relatively near each other and are connected using cables or wireless media.

Location-based services (LBS) Services that can give you certain information based on where you are physically located.

Lock screen The start screen of a mobile device that allows the user to set a variety of security measures.

Log A file that records activities and events.

M

Mainframe computer Very large and powerful systems used in organizations where a heavy amount of processing and user requests need to be handled.

Malware A generic term to describe various kinds of malicious programs created to harm a computer or steal valuable information.

Management information system (MIS) A set of software tools that enables managers to gather, organize, and evaluate information.

Massive open online course (MOOC) Huge online courses offered for free by a variety of universities.

Media The physical locations, such as discs, where things are stored.

Media player An application that allows you to listen to music and play videos.

Megapixel A unit of graphic ???resolution equivalent to one million pixels.

Memory General term for electronic chips that store data and program instructions that can be accessed quickly by the CPU.

Memory card A type of solid state storage used to store data in tablets, smartphones, and other electronic devices.

Microblogging A short-form blog where users share brief thoughts, links, and multimedia.

Mission-critical Systems that must run without failure or with nearly instant recovery from failure.

MMORPG Stands for "massively multiplayer online role-playing game" and lets millions of players connect to various servers to team up with other players in very large virtual worlds.

Mobile device Lightweight, handheld computers that offer a variety of software and communication services for mobile users.

Mobile hotspot A device that can connect to a mobile network and offer Internet access to multiple devices near it.

Modem A device that can convert digital information from a computer into the analog sound waves that can be transmitted over phone lines.

Motherboard The largest circuit board in a personal computer. It contains a variety of slots, connectors, and plugs for hooking up all the other parts of a computer.

Multifunction printer A device that combines either inkjet or laser printing capabilities with scanning, photocopying, and faxing capabilities.

Multimedia The capacity of a computer to input and output sound, music, images, and video.

Multimedia Messaging Service A service offered by wireless companies that allows cell phone users to attach and send a variety of media to other users.

Multitasking The ability to run multiple programs at the same time.

Multiuser computer A computer that's designed to work with many people at the same time.

N

Nanotechnology The creation or manipulation of matter at the smallest possible scale.

Netbook A small and inexpensive laptop that has reduced processing power and lacks a DVD drive.

Netiquette The set of online behaviors that are considered polite and proper.

Network A connection between computers that allows users to communicate and share information.

Network administrator A person responsible for configuring and maintaining networks and communication systems.

Network interface card (NIC) A computer component that translates and transmits network packets.

Network media The means used to link parts of a computer network.

Network server A powerful computer with special software and equipment that enables it to function as the primary computer in the network.

News aggregator An app that allows you to pick a variety of news sources and read them in a magazine-style interface.

NFC A wireless technology (near field communication) that lets your mobile device communicate over very short distances, such as when paying for goods on wireless payment devices.

Node A connection point within a network.

NSFNET A high-speed network created by the National Science Foundation in 1986 that established connections to smaller regional networks, other agencies' networks, CSNET, and ARPANET.

O

Office automation system A type of information system that is designed to manage information in an office environment and help users handle certain information-related tasks more efficiently.

Office suite A bundle of programs that help businesses efficiently carry out tasks such as writing letters, analyzing sales figures, and scheduling meetings.

Offshoring A company's outsourcing of certain business functions to another country.

Online payment service A company that offers a secure and convenient way to pay for online goods and services.

Open source A type of software license that permits the source code to be freely distributed and modified.

Operating system Software that manages the flow of data between hardware components and allows the user to communicate with the computer.

Optical character recognition (OCR) Technology that can translate a scanned document image into text that can be edited and formatted.

Optical mouse The most common pointing device for desktop computers, it includes a left and right button, a scroll wheel in the middle, and a light-emitting mechanism at the bottom to sense movement.

Output The processed results that a computer sends to you.

Outsourcing An organization's transfer of some aspect of its business to a third party.

P

Packet Pieces of a message broken down into small units by the sending device and reassembled by the receiving device in a network.

Pages per minute (PPM) A measure of printer speed.

Paperless The use of technology by companies and individuals to lower their consumption and reliance on paper.

Parental control Utilities that allow parents to set a variety of limits on their children's Internet usage.

Partitioning Dividing a hard drive into multiple sections.

Paste A command that places the contents of the clipboard into the location where this command is issued.

Path A complete address that describes the exact location of a file.

Pay-per-click Payment model where advertisers pay for their ads only when a website visitor clicks on the ad to go to the advertiser's website.

Peer-to-peer (P2P) A file transfer method that uses a distributed network of individual users instead of a central server to transfer files.

Personal computer A computer that is meant to be used by only one person at a time; also called "microcomputer."

Personal information manager (PIM) Software that is designed to keep individuals organized via the management of contacts, appointments, to-do lists, and email.

Phablet A mix of the terms "phone" and "tablet," this term is given to very large smartphones.

Phishing Luring individuals into entering personal information into a website controlled by a hacker.

Piracy Acquiring or exchanging copies of protected digital creations without payment to or permission from their creator.

Pixel Tiny dots on a display screen, each with its own unique address, that the computer uses to locate it and control its appearance.

Plagiarism Turning in the work of another as if it were your own or failing to cite the source of your work.

Plug-in A separate program that allows your web browser to play several types of multimedia content.

Podcast A type of prerecorded webcast that users typically subscribe to for future streaming or automatic downloading.

Pop-up blocker A browser feature that automatically blocks advertisements that attempt to open in a new, "pop-up" window.

Port A plug on a computer that is used to connect external devices.

Power management The ability to place computers and devices in low-power states when they are not being used.

Presentation software A category of software that enables users to create electronic slideshows that are used to present information.

Pretexting Gaining someone's trust by pretending you are someone else.

Privacy policy A website's written statement that clearly states what information is collected from users and what is done with that information.

Private browsing A feature of all modern browsers that will delete your history, cache, and cookies the moment you close the private window.

Processing The ability of a computer to perform actions based on instructions from the user or a program.

Project management A sophisticated plan used by businesses to track and achieve a variety of goals.

Protocol A set of rules or standards that must be followed by computers that wish to communicate over a network.

Public domain A term that refers to creative works whose copyright has expired or never existed in the first place. These works can be freely used without permission.

Q

QR code A scannable product code, which appears as a square filled with patterns of dots and lines, that typically directs users to a website.

R

RAID A storage system that links any number of disk drives (a disk array) so that they act as a single disk.

Random access memory (RAM) A type of memory that temporarily stores the data and programs that a computer is currently using.

Read-only memory (ROM) A small chip that contains device-specific information and handles a computer's basic functions when it is powered on.

Real-time communication When messages and conversations between two or more people occur instantaneously.

Real-time information Any information that is delivered to you immediately after it is created.

Redundant Computers that have multiple hardware systems performing the same task at the same time.

Remote wipe The ability to completely erase a mobile device if it is lost or stolen.

Repeater A network device used to prevent attenuation when packets are traveling long distances.

Reply Abbreviated "re" in the subject line of emails, this indicates that the message is a reply, or response.

Residential gateway A device that connects your home's network to the Internet.

Resolution The number of pixels that are displayed on the screen.

Response time The amount of time in milliseconds that it takes for a pixel to change from black to white.

RFID tag A tiny chip or label containing electronically stored data that can be accessed wirelessly.

Risk assessment Identifying and examining possible threats to a computer system.

Rogue hotspot A wireless access point set up by a hacker in a public area to intercept users' communication.

Root directory The location on a drive that is outside of any folders or directories.

Router A complex device that stores the routing information for networks. It looks at each packet's header to determine where the packet should go, then determines the best route for the packet to take toward its destination.

S

Scanner A device that uses optical technology to convert objects that it analyzes into a digital format.

Scareware A type of scam whose goal is to scare the user into doing exactly what the thief wants.

Scalability The capacity to provide increasing amounts of computing power, storage, and/or software.

Search engine optimization (SEO) The process of improving the ranking of a website when users enter relevant keywords in a search engine.

Search engine A sophisticated combination of hardware and software that stores the URL of millions of web pages and most of the content on those pages. When users type specific keywords into the search engine, they will receive an organized list of matching sites, images, and articles that contain those keywords.

Security software Programs that help keep you, your computer, and your personal information safe from a variety of threats.

Security suite A bundle of programs that accomplish a variety of security-related tasks.

Shareware Software that is free to download and install, but will stop working after a trial period unless the user purchases the software.

Short Message Service (SMS) A service offered by wireless companies that allows cell phone users to send text messages of 160 characters to any other user.

Sleep A computer state that uses only enough electricity to keep the contents of your RAM active.

Smartphone A device that combines the functions of a mobile phone and a handheld computer.

Smart TV A TV that offers connectivity to a variety of online services to let you watch movies and listen to music. Many also connect to other computing devices in your home.

Social engineering A form of hacking that focuses on deceiving individuals into giving away the information that the thief needs.

Social media A variety of websites and services that allow individuals to share photos, news, and thoughts with other individuals.

Social media strategist An expert in sales and marketing who uses the web and various social media tools.

Social Networking Websites that are used to create connections between friends, family members, and organizations, thereby allowing individuals to share information and receive updates from those in their social circles.

Social news Websites that encourage users to share links to news and other interesting content they find on the web.

Software One or more computer programs that are packaged together for a unified purpose.

Software development life cycle (SDLC) A series of steps that take programmers from the idea and planning stages through the actual programming, testing, and maintenance of software.

Software engineer A person responsible for the development of computer software.

Software license A contract from the software creator that specifies the rules for using this software.

Software updates Software patches used to fix errors and security vulnerabilities.

Solid state drive (SSD) A small and fast type of hard drive that uses flash memory instead of the more traditional magnetic technology.

Sound card A circuit board that converts sound from analog to digital form and vice versa for recording or playback.

Spam Unsolicited email that is sent in bulk.

Speech recognition A computer's ability to recognize human speech.

Spreadsheet software Software used for entering, calculating, and analyzing sets of numbers. This software is also used for creating charts.

Spyware Malware that reports activity on your computer to another party.

Start screen The new default screen in Windows 8, it can run mobile-style apps and display live tiles that show real-time information.

Storage The ability of a computer to hold or remember the information it processes.

Streaming media Music and movies that are delivered on demand from an online source.

Streaming player A small, affordable device that allows you to stream videos and music using your TV and wireless home network.

Strong password A password that is difficult for thieves to guess or crack.

Stylus A pen-like tool used to input information directly into a variety of touchscreen devices.

Subdomain A portion of a URL that usually indicates a specific subdivision or server within a large site.

Subscription model A payment method for software that has users pay a fixed amount of money per month in order to use the software.

Supercomputer The largest and most powerful type of computer in the world, they are ideal for handling large and highly complex problems that require extreme calculating power.

Surge protector An inexpensive product that guards connected equipment against large power spikes or surges that may infrequently occur.

Switch A network device that is similar to a hub, but it is aware of the exact address or identity of all the nodes attached to it, thereby increasing the efficiency of the network.

Systems analyst A person who specializes in developing plans and recommendations that meet the software and system needs of an organization.

System software Any program created for the operation, maintenance, and security of a computer.

System unit The case that houses the computer's critical parts, such as its processing and storage devices.

T

Tabbed browsing An interface that allows you to have multiple web pages open in one browser window.

Tablet computer A mobile device that typically ranges from 7 to 10 inches in size.

Tag Data attached to a photo, such as keywords, faces, and the location where it was taken.

Tape drive A storage device that uses magnetic tape to back up or archive large amounts of data.

Tape library A large storage unit that houses multiple tape drives.

TCP/IP The protocols at the heart of Internet communication.

Telecommuting The process of working for a company without being physically present at the company's office.

Tethering A feature that makes a phone act as a wireless access point.

Thermal printer A printer that applies heat to special thermal paper, turning select areas black to produce text and basic graphics.

Thread In a forum, a topic that contains related posts.

Threat Anything that can cause harm.

Topology The logical layout of the cables and devices that connect the nodes of the network.

Touchpad A stationary, rectangular pointing surface that is typically found on laptop computers.

Touchscreen A technology found on monitors and mobile devices that accepts input by allowing the user to perform a variety of finger taps and gestures directly on the screen.

Trackball A pointing device that works like an upside-down mouse.

Transaction processing system (TPS) A type of information system that handles the processing and tracking of transactions.

Trojan horse A program that disguises itself as an interesting, useful, or desirable program in order to gain access to your system.

Trolling A type of social interaction where a user acts in an annoying and antagonistic manner.

Turing test A test for artificial intelligence that measures a system's ability to hold a human-like conversation.

TV tuner A device that can capture television signals for viewing on a computer.

Twisted-pair cable A cable that consists of four pairs of wires that are twisted around each other. Each copper wire is insulated in plastic, and all wires are collectively bound together in a layer of plastic.

U

Ultraportable computer A thin, lightweight laptop that possesses strong processing power.

Uninterruptible power supply (UPS) A device that contains both a surge protector and rechargeable battery, allowing your computer system to run for a limited amount of time during a power failure.

Upload To send data.

URL A standard addressing system that allows web pages to be located on the Internet.

USB flash drive A small, solid state storage device that plugs into a USB port.

USB port A small, rectangular port which is used to connect almost all of today's external devices.

Utilities Programs that enhance or extend the operating system's capabilities or offer new features not provided by the operating system itself.

V

Vector graphic A type of image that relies on mathematics, which allows users to increase or decrease the size of the image without any distortion.

Vertical market software Software that is created for a specific industry such as health care or insurance.

Video card An intermediary device between the CPU and the monitor that contains a processor, video-dedicated memory, and other circuitry.

Videoconferencing Voice and video communication that allows multiple individuals to hold meetings and converse over a network.

Viral When funny or fascinating content is shared again and again over a short period.

Virtual machine A special environment that allows users to run an operating system on top of another operating system.

Virtual memory A portion of your hard drive that is being used as RAM.

Virtual private network (VPN) A type of connection that increases the security of network communication by employing a method called "tunneling," whereby each packet from the sending computer is encapsulated within another packet.

Virtual reality An experience where humans can interact with realistic environments that are simulated by computers.

Virtualization software The software that allows you to run a virtual machine.

Virus A type of malware that is attached to a host file and has the ability to replicate, or copy, itself.

Voice over Internet Protocol (VoIP) Translates analog voice signals into digital data and uses the Internet to transport the data; can connect to telephone networks and digital sources such as PCs.

Volume license A license that allows companies to install software on multiple machines.

Vulnerability A weakness that has not been protected against threats, thereby making it open to harm.

W

Wearable technology Computing devices that are worn on various parts of the body.

Web 2.0 A term that refers to a new way to use the web, whereby any user can create and share content, as well as provide opinions on existing content.

Web browser Software that helps you find and retrieve a web page that you are interested in viewing.

Web developer A person who creates and maintains websites for organizations.

Web page A web-based document.

Web portal A website that provides a variety of useful information and services to visitors.

Web server A server that hosts websites.

Web-based application A program that runs directly on your web browser.

Webcam A small video camera, typically attached to a monitor, that is commonly used for online video chats or conversations.

Webcast The broadcast of various types of media over the web.

Website Several related web pages that connect to each other.

Whistleblowing The act of alerting the public about harmful activities that are being hidden by an organization.

Wide area network (WAN) The connection of two or more central computers or LANs, generally across a wide geographical area.

Widget A small screen element that provides automatically updating information without the need to open an app.

Wi-Fi The most popular standard for wireless networking; also called "802.11."

Wiki A collaborative information site, such as Wikipedia, that relies on the Internet community to both create and edit content.

Wireless access point (WAP) Connects single or multiple PCs in the wireless environment.

Wireless adapter A piece of hardware that is plugged into a desktop computer to gain Wi-Fi access.

Wireless network A type of connection whereby communication takes place using radio waves.

Word processing software Software that provides tools for creating, editing, and formatting all kinds of text-based documents.

World Wide Web A global system of linked, hypertext documents known as web pages.

Worm A type of malware that self-replicates and spreads through computers and networks without the need to attach to a host file.

Z

Zombie An infected and compromised computer that is under the external control of a hacker, usually without the knowledge of the computer's owner.

Front Matter

Page x (top center): Google; p. x (top left): Source: Facebook; p. x (top right): Source: Twitter; p. x (bottom right): Source: Evernote; p. xi (top): Source: Microsoft; p. xi (bottom right): Google; p. xii: Source: AVG.

Chapter 1

Page 2: Gandee Vasan/Stone/Getty Images; p. 4: Rubberball/Punchstock; p. 5 (bottom left): ERproductions Ltd/Blend Images ; p. 5 (top right): JLP/Sylvia Torres/Flame/Corbis; p. 6: David R. Frazier Photolibrary, Inc.; p. 7: Michael Spence/Alamy; p. 8 (bottom left): Ian McKinnell/Photographer's Choice/Getty Images; p. 8 (top right): Digital Vision/Getty Images; p. 9 (top right): David Caudery/Official Windows Magazine via Getty Images; p. 9 (bottom left): Image Source/Getty Images; p. 10 (bottom left): John Kershaw/Alamy; p. 10 (top right): AP Images/Julie Jacobson; p. 11 (top right): NASA; p. 11 (bottom left): Jan Woitas/dpa/picture-alliance/Newscom; p. 12 (top right): Future Publishing/Getty Images; p. 12 (bottom left): Simon Dawson/Bloomberg/Getty Images; p. 13 (top right): Source: Comcast; p. 13 (top left): Patrick T. Fallon/Bloomberg via Getty Images; p. 14 (bottom left): Jacek Lasa/Alamy; p. 14 (top right): Stacy Walsh Rosenstock/Alamy; p. 15 (top left): AP Images/Mark Lennihan; p. 15 (top right): Krista Kennell/ABACAUSA/Newscom; p. 16: Daniel Acker/Bloomberg/Getty Images; p. 17 (top right): Steve Carroll/Alamy; p. 17 (bottom left): Source: Android; p. 17 (bottom left): Source: Android; p. 18 (bottom right): Juice Images/Alamy; p. 18 (top center): mage 100/PunchStock; p. 19 (bottom left): Thomas Northcut/Riser/Getty Images; p. 19 (top right): Ingram Publishing; p. 20 (bottom left): Source: Waze; p. 20 (bottom left): Source: Waze; p. 20 (top right): Source: Yelp; p. 21 (bottom left): Source: Google; p. 21 (top right): Courtesy of SquareUp. Photo By Dwight Eschliman; p. 22 (bottom left): Source of interface image: Instagram; Source of photo: NASA; p. 22 (bottom left): Source: Instagram; p. 22 (top right): Snapchat; p. 23 (top right): Source: iheartradio; p. 23 (bottom left): Source: Hulu; p. 24 (top right): Source: Healthtap; p. 24 (bottom left): Source: Accupedo; p. 24 (bottom left): Source: Sleepbot; p. 25 (bottom): Kim Kulish/Corbis News/Corbis; p. 25 (top right): Gavin Roberts/Tap Magazine /Getty Images; p. 26: Source: Microsoft; p. 27: Source: Google.

Chapter 2

Page 32: Victor Habbick Visions/Science Photo Library/Corbis; p. 34 (bottom left): AP Images; p. 34 (top right): Kitch Bain/age fotostock; p. 35 (bottom left): Ludovit Repko/Alamy; p. 35 (top right): Alamy; p. 36 (top right): AP Images/Paul Sakuma; p. 36 (bottom left): © Keith Eng 2007 /McGraw-Hill Companies; p. 37: Simon Belcher/Alamy; p. 39 (bottom left): AP Images/Itsuo Inouye; p. 39 (top right): Digital Stock/Corbis; p. 40 (bottom left): © McGraw-Hill Education; p. 40 (top right): Maciej Latałło/Alamy; p. 40 (center): © Keith Eng 2007 / McGraw-Hill Companies; p. 41 (top right): Gavin Roberts/Official Windows Magazine via Getty Images; p. 41 (bottom left): JG Photography/Alamy; p. 42: Erkan Mehmet/Alamy; p. 43 (bottom left): goldy/Getty Images; p. 43 (top right): Photodisc/Getty Images; p. 43 (top right): Source: Microsoft; p. 44 (top right): Thinkstock/Getty Images; p. 44 (bottom left): Creative Crop/Digital Vision/Getty Images; p. 45 (bottom left): Epson; p. 45 (bottom right): Epson; p. 45 (top right): Digital Stock/Corbis; p. 46 (bottom left): Source: Google; p. 46 (top right): Don Farrall/Getty Images; p. 47 (top right): Joby Sessions/Digital Camera Magazine /Getty Images; p. 47 (bottom left): Photodisc/Getty Images; p. 48 (top right): AP Images/ Al Powers/Invision/AP,

File; p. 48 (bottom left): Source: Google; p. 49 (bottom left): Seth Joel/Photographer's Choice RF/Getty Images ; p. 49 (top right): © iStockphoto.com/Signature/rustemgurler; p. 049 (inset)(bottom left): NASA; p. 50 (bottom left): AP Images/PRNewsFoto/NVIDIA Corporation; p. 50 (top left): Roy Wylam/Alamy; p. 50 (top center): David Cook/Alamy; p. 50 (top right): Ingram Publishing /Alamy; p. 51 (top right): Zoonar/Vladimir Blinov/Alamy; p. 51 (bottom left): HANDOUT/KRT/Newscom; p. 52 (top right): Source: Microsoft; p. 52 (bottom left): ermingu/Getty Images; p. 53 (bottom left): Stephen VanHorn/Alamy; p. 53 (top right): Ryan McVay/Getty Images; p. 54 (top right): AWM concepts/Alamy; p. 54 (bottom): AP Images/GLOBE NEWSWIRE; p. 54 (top left): evolis; p. 55 (bottom): NASA; p. 55 (top right): Smart Technologies.

Chapter 3

Page 60: Jorg Greuel/Photodisc/Getty Images; p. 62: NASA; p. 63 (bc): Linux; p. 63 (top right): Ivan Voras/Wikimedia; p. 64: Source: Microsoft; p. 65: Source: Apple; p. 66: Source: Ubuntu; p. 67 (top right): AP Images/Google; p. 67 (bottom left): David Paul Morris/Bloomberg/Getty Images; p. 68 (bottom): Source: Microsoft; p. 68 (bottom right): Nokia; p. 69 (top right): Source: Norton Security; p. 69 (bottom left): Source: Microsoft; p. 70 (top right): Source: Starbucks; p. 70 (top right): Source: LastPass; p. 70 (bottom left): Source: Ubnuntu; p. 71: Source of interface image: Microsoft; Source of logo: Hewlett-Packard; p. 72 (top right): Source: Microsoft; p. 73 (top right): Source: Apple; p. 73 (bottom left): Google; p. 74 (top right): Source: Microsoft; p. 74 (top right): Source: NASA; p. 75 (bottom): Source: Apple; p. 75 (bottom left): Source: Microsoft; p. 76 (bottom right): Source: Apple; p. 76: Source: Microsoft; p. 77: Source; WinRAR; p. 78: Source: Microsoft; p. 79 (top): Source: AccuWeather; p. 79 (top right): Source: Weather Channel; p. 80 (top right): Source: LibreOffice; p. 80 (bottom): Source: Microsoft; p. 81, p. 82: Source: Microsoft; p. 83: Google; p. 84 (top right): Source: Adobe; p. 84 (bottom left): Source: Apple; p. 85: Source: Autodesk; p. 86 (center left): EVE-VR; p. 86 (center right): EVE-VR/Oculus VR; p. 88: Source: Microsoft.

Chapter 4

Page 94: David Malan/Photographer's Choice RF/Getty Images; p. 96: Dieter Spannknebel/Photodisc/Getty Images; p. 97: Donna Cox and Robert Patterson, courtesy of the National Center for Supercomputing Applications (NCSA) and the Board of Trustees of the University of Illinois; p. 98: Copyright 2002 The Regents of the University of California; p. 99: EPA (Environmental Protection Agency); p. 100: 1and1.com; p. 101: Google; p. 102: Source: Microsoft; p. 103: Skype; p. 104 (bottom left): BitTorrent; p. 104 (top right): Whitehouse.gov; p. 105: Coursera; p. 106 (bottom right): ©iStockphoto.com/rbouwman; p. 106 (top right): Mark A. Ibele/lao.ca.gov; p. 107: Source: AT&T; p. 108: AP Images/AT&T; p. 109: Google; p. 110 (top right): Source: Google; p. 110 (bottom): Source: UPS; p. 111: Source: Google; p. 112: Source: Bing; p. 113 (bottom left): Source: Flipboard; p. 113 (inset)(top right): AP Images/Brian Snyder, Pool; p. 113 (main)(top right): © 2014 Yahoo. YAHOO! and the YAHOO! logo are registered trademarks of Yahoo.; p. 114: Google; p. 115: Source: BusinessUSA; p. 116: Google; p. 117: Source: Tumblr; p. 118 (top center): Source: Twitter; p. 118 (bottom left): Source: Youtube; p. 119: Source: Flickr; p. 120: Wikipedia; p. 121: Top Sites/Alamy; p. 122: "These materials have been reproduced with the permission of eBay Inc." © 2014 EBAY INC. ALL RIGHTS RESERVED; p. 123: Notebookcheck http://www.notebookcheck.com/; p. 124: Larry Williams/Jay Newman/Getty Images; p. 125: Source: Google; p. 126: Source: EasyBib.

Chapter 5

Page 132: Tetra Images/Getty Images; p. 134: Colorblind/Cardinal/Corbis; p. 136: Phil Degginger/The Image Bank/Getty Images; p. 137 (top right): Sheval/Alamy; p. 137 (bottom left): vetkit/YAY Media AS/Alamy; p. 139 (top right): Arthur Kwiatkowski/Getty Images; p. 139 (bottom left): Jacus/Getty Images; p. 141: Paul Bradbury/OJO Images/Getty Images; p. 142 (top right): Jetta Productions/Iconica/Getty Images; p. 142 (bottom left): Duncan Smith/Photodisc/Getty Images; p. 143: Steve Cole/Getty Images; p. 144 (main): McGraw-Hill Education; p. 144 (inset): FilippoBacci/Getty Images; p. 145 (bottom left): Sehenswerk/Alamy; p. 145 (top right): PhotoAlto/Odilon Dimier/Getty Images; p. 146: Andrew Holt/Photographer's Choice RF/Getty Images; p. 147: CDC; p. 148: Martin Poole/Getty Images; p. 149 (top right): Image Source/Getty Images; p. 149 (bottom left): Erik Isakson/Getty Images; p. 150: Amos Morgan/Jupiter Images; p. 151 (bottom left): Handout/MCT/Newscom; p. 151 (top right): Schneider Electric; p. 152 (top right): Rob Wilkinson/Alamy; p. 152 (bottom left): Jose Luis Pelaez Inc/Blend Images/Getty Images; p. 153: Federal Bureau of Investigation; p. 154 (bottom left): Source: Chase; p. 154 (top right): Air Force; p. 155: Federal Trade Commission; p. 156 (bottom left): Source: Microsoft; p. 156 (top right): CMCD/Getty Images; p. 157: Brand X Pictures/Jupiterimages; p. 158 (bottom left): Fermi National Accelerator Laboratory; p. 158 (top right): James Lauritz/Digital Vision/Getty Images; p. 159: CrashPlan.

Chapter 6

Page 164: Bloomimage/Corbis; p. 166: SW Productions/Getty Images; p. 167 (top right): Federal Bureau Of Investigation; p. 167 (bottom left): Comstock Images/Getty Images; p. 168 (bottom left): Andersen Ross/Digital Vision/Getty Images; p. 168 (top right): NASA; p. 170 (bottom left): Creative Commons; p. 170 (top right): Source: Pandora; p. 171: Somos/Veer/Getty Images; p. 172 (top right): Source: CNET; p. 172 (bottom left): Allison Michael Orenstein/The Image Bank/Getty Images; p. 173 (top): Maryland State Archives; p. 173 (bottom right): Comstock/Jupiterimages; p. 173 (top): © 2014 by the Commonwealth of Virginia Department of Education. All rights reserved. Reproduced by permission.; p. 174 (top right): Paul Bradbury/The Image Bank/Getty Images; p. 174 (bottom left): Image Source/Getty Images; p. 175 (bottom left): Brand Yourself; p. 175 (top right): Comstock/PunchStock ; p. 176 (bottom left): Google; p. 176 (top right): National Security Agency; p. 177 (bottom left): Source: Microsoft; p. 177 (top right): Stockbyte/Getty Images; p. 178 (top right): Sallie Pisch/Demotix/Demotix/Demotix/Corbis News/Corbis; p. 178 (bottom left): VAN CAKENBERGHE TO/SIPA/Newscom; p. 179 (bottom left): NASA; p. 179 (top right): WikiLeaks; p. 180 (top center): Tanja Niesen/Westernd61/Corbis; p. 180 (bottom left): EPA (Environmental Protection Agency); p. 181: Klaus Vedfelt/ The Image Bank/Getty Images; p. 182 (bottom left): Plush Studios/DH Kong/Blend Images/Getty Images; p. 182 (top right): BananaStock/Jupiterimages; p. 183 (top right): AP Images/Roland Weihrauch/picture-alliance/dpa; p. 183 (bottom left): Aaron Roeth Photography/McGraw-Hill; p. 184 (top right): Jason Kempin/WireImage/Getty Images; p. 184 (bottom left): NASA; p. 185 (top right): Ben Hider/Stringer/Getty Images; p. 185 (bottom left): Hanson Robotics; p. 186 (bottom left): © 2014 The Johns Hopkins University/Applied Physics Laboratory. All Rights Reserved. For permission to use, modify, or reproduce, contact the Office of Technology Transfer at JHU/APL.; p. 186 (top right): National Cancer Institute; p. 187 (bottom left): Simion Marian/Alamy; p. 187 (top right): nullplus/Getty Images; p. 188 (bottom left): Stockbyte/Gettyimages; p. 188 (top right): Purestock/SuperStock.

Core, 36
Corel WordPerfect, 80
CorelDRAW, 84
Cortana, 16
Countermeasures, 149–150, 156
CPU. *See* Central processing unit (CPU)
CrashPlan, 159
Creative and multimedia software, 83–85
Creative Commons, 170
CRM. *See* Customer relationship management (CRM)
Crowdsourcing, 20
CRT monitor, 50
Cursor, 42
Cursor control keys, 42
Customer relationship management (CRM), 86
Cut, 76
Cyberbullying, 172
Cybercrime, 153
Cyberterrorism, 154

D

Data, 7–8
Data mining, 147
Data plan, 107
Data theft, 155
Data validation, 147
Data warehouse, 146–147
Database, 81
Database administrator (DBA), 187
Database management system (DBMS), 81
DBA. *See* Database administrator (DBA)
DBMS. *See* Database management system (DBMS)
DDoS. *See* Distributed denial-of-service (DDoS)
Debugging, 88
Decision support system (DSS), 143–144
Definitions (glossary), 195–204
Defragmentation and optimization, 71–72
Delete, 76
Deleting and recovering files, 76
Desktop, 64
Desktop computer, 9
Desktop Linux, 66
Desktop operating system, 64–67
Desktop publishing software, 85
DeviantArt, 119
Device driver, 63
Dial-up connection, 106
Digital camera, 47
Digital divide, 178
Digital footprint, 176
Digital literacy, 4
Digital projector, 55
Digital rentals, 169
Digital rights management (DRM), 169
Digital SLR camera, 47
Digital subscriber line (DSL), 106
Digital versatile disc (DVD), 39
Digital video recorder (DVR), 47
Directory, 74
Discussion board, 115
Disk cleanup, 72
Disk defragmentation, 72
Disk formatting, 71
Disk wiping and recovery, 73
Distributed denial-of-service (DDoS), 154
Distributions, 64
Divided attention, 19
DNA sequencing technology, 186
Do not track, 177
Document feeder, 45
Document scanner, 45
.docx, 74
Domain name, 100
Dot matrix printer, 52–53
Dots per inch (dpi), 52
Double-clicking, 43
Download, 104
dpi. *See* Dots per inch (dpi)
Dragging, 43
Drawing programs, 84
Drive, 38, 74
Drive bays, 34
DRM. *See* Digital rights management (DRM)

Dropbox, 26, 159
Drug delivery system, 186
DSL. *See* Digital subscriber line (DSL)
DSS. *See* Decision support system (DSS)
Dual-core processor, 36
Duplexing, 52
Dust, 152
DVD. *See* Digital versatile disc (DVD)
DVI connector, 51
DVR. *See* Digital video recorder (DVR)
Dye-sub card printer, 54
Dye-sublimation (dye-sub) printer, 54

E

E-book, 11–12
E-book reader, 12
E-commerce, 120–124
 advertising, 123–124
 business to business (B2B), 122
 business to consumer (B2C), 121
 consumer to consumer (C2C), 122
 online banking, 122–123
 payment and shipping, 121–122
 shopping, 121
EasyBib.com, 126
eBay, 122
Education and entertainment software, 85–86
Education sites, 105
Electronic book (e-book), 11–12
Electronic commerce. *See* E-commerce
Email, 8, 100–103
 advertising, 123
 ALL CAPS, 103
 attachments, 102
 Bcc, 101
 body, 102
 Cc, 101
 netiquette, 102–103
 reply/forward, 101
 spam, 100
 subject line, 101
Embedded system, 11
Emerging technologies, 185–186
Emoticons, 102
Empathy, 166
Employee availability, 182
Employee monitoring, 174–175
Encryption, 69, 156
Encryption utilities, 69–70
End-user license agreement (EULA), 77
Engadget, 117
Enter and editing keys, 42
Enterprise resource planning (ERP), 86
Environmental hazards, 152
Environmental problems, 179–180
Ergonomic keyboard, 41
ERP. *See* Enterprise resource planning (ERP)
Errors (in computer program), 88
ESPN.com, 114
Ethernet, 140
Ethics, 166. *See also* Legal and ethical issues
EULA. *See* End-user license agreement (EULA)
EVE-VR virtual reality game, 86
Evernote, 26, 79, 111
.exe, 74
Executable file, 88
Expansion card, 35
Expedia, 114
Expert system, 144
Extension, 111
Extranet, 135

F

Face unlock feature, 48
Facebook, 103, 115, 116
FaceTime, 22
Facial recognition, 48
Factory reset, 73
Fair use, 168
Fan, 152
FAQ. *See* Frequently asked questions (FAQ)
Fast Ethernet, 140

FAT, 71
Fault-tolerant computer, 145
Favorites, 75, 109
Fermi National Accelerator Laboratory, 158
Fiber-optic cable, 136
File, 74
File compression, 72
File extensions, 74–75
File hierarchy, 74
File History, 72
File management, 74–76
 copying and moving files, 75–76
 creating folders, 75
 deleting and recovering files, 76
 favorite locations, 75
 file extensions, 74–75
 file hierarchy, 74
 files and folders, 74
 managing your files, 75
 path, 74
 searching for files, 76
File path, 74
File system, 71
Finder, 75
Fingerprint scanner, 48
FiOS, 107
Firewall, 69, 156
Firmware, 37
First-party cookies, 110
FISA. *See* Foreign Intelligence Surveillance Act (FISA)
Fitbit Flex, 24, 25
Fitness and health, 23–25
Fitness apps, 24
Flaming, 172
Flashing, 37
Flashing ROMs, 68
Flat-panel monitor, 50
Flatbed scanner, 45
Flickr, 119
Flight simulator, 55
Flipboard, 113
Flowchart, 87
fodors.com, 114
Folder, 74
Folder creation, 75
Foodnetwork.com, 114
Foreign Intelligence Surveillance Act (FISA), 176
Foreign language software, 85–86
Formatting utilities, 71
Forums, 115
Forward, 101
Fragmentation, 71–72
Freeware, 78–79
Frequently asked questions (FAQ), 171
Friends and circles, 116
frommers.com, 114
Full-featured social networking, 22
Function keys, 42

G

Game controller, 48
Game development (as career), 187
GarageBand, 65, 85
Gateway, 140
GB. *See* Gigabyte (GB)
Gbps. *See* Gigabits per second (Gbps)
Gestures, 43
.gif, 74
Gigabit Ethernet, 140
Gigabits per second (Gbps), 136
Gigabyte (GB), 38
GIMP, 84
Global and environmental issues, 178–180
Glossary, 195–204
GNU General Public License (GPL), 79
Google, 103, 107, 112, 169
Google+, 115, 116
Google Adwords, 123
Google Chrome, 109
Google Dashboard, 176
Google Docs, 26, 79
Google Drive, 26, 159

Windows 10, Office 2016, and File Management

CHAPTER OVERVIEW

Microsoft Office 2016 and Windows 10 introduce many new features, including cloud storage for your files, Office file sharing, and enhanced online content. The integration of Office 2016 and Windows 10 means that files are more portable and accessible than ever when you use *OneDrive*, Microsoft's free online cloud storage. The new user interface for Office 2016 and Windows 10 allows you to work on tablet computers and smartphones in a consistent working environment that resembles that of your desktop or laptop computer.

STUDENT LEARNING OUTCOMES (SLOs)

After completing this chapter, you will be able to:

SLO Intro.1 Explore the features of Windows 10 (p. 214).

SLO Intro.2 Use the basic features of Office 2016 and navigate the Office 2016 working environment (p. 222).

SLO Intro.3 Create, save, close, and open Office files (p. 229).

SLO Intro.4 Customize the view and display size in Office applications and work with multiple Office files (p. 237).

SLO Intro.5 Print, share, and customize Office files (p. 240).

SLO Intro.6 Use the *Ribbon*, tabs, groups, dialog boxes, task panes, galleries, and the *Quick Access* toolbar (p. 245).

SLO Intro.7 Use context menus, mini toolbars, keyboard shortcuts, and function keys in Office applications (p. 249).

SLO Intro.8 Organize and customize Windows folders and Office files (p. 254).

CASE STUDY

Throughout this book you have the opportunity to put into practice the application features that you are learning. Each chapter begins with a case study that introduces you to the Pause & Practice projects in the chapter. These Pause & Practice projects give you a chance to apply and practice key skills in a realistic and practical context. Each chapter contains three to five Pause & Practice projects.

American River Cycling Club (ARCC) is a community cycling club that promotes fitness. ARCC members include recreational cyclists who enjoy the exercise and camaraderie as well as competitive cyclists who compete in road, mountain, and cyclocross races throughout the cycling season. In the Pause & Practice projects, you incorporate many of the topics covered in the chapter to create, save, customize, manage, and share Office 2016 files.

213

Pause & Practice Intro-1: Customize the Windows *Start* menu and *Taskbar*, create and save a PowerPoint presentation, create a folder, open and rename an Excel workbook, and use Windows 10 features.

Pause & Practice Intro-2: Modify the existing document, add document properties,

customize the Quick Access toolbar, export the document as a PDF file, and share the document.

Pause & Practice Intro-3: Copy and rename files, create a folder, move files, create a zipped folder, and rename a zipped folder.

SLO INTRO. 1

Using Windows 10

Windows 10 is the ***operating system*** that controls computer functions and the working environment. Windows 10 uses the familiar ***Windows desktop, Taskbar***, and ***Start menu***, and you can customize the working environment. You can install traditional applications (***apps***), such as Microsoft Office, to your computer. Also, you can add modern apps from the Microsoft Store similar to how you add an app to your smartphone. Your ***Microsoft account*** is used to store your Microsoft settings, download apps from the Microsoft Store, and connect you to Microsoft Office, *OneDrive*, and *Office Online*.

Windows 10

The Windows 10 operating system controls interaction with computer hardware and software applications. ***Windows 10*** has a revised user interface that utilizes an updated ***Start menu***, where you can select and open a program. Alternatively, you can use the *Taskbar* on the Windows desktop, which has the familiar look of previous versions of Windows. When you log in to Windows 10 using your Microsoft account, it synchronizes your Windows, Office, and ***OneDrive*** cloud storage among computers.

Microsoft Account

In Windows 10 and Office 2016, your files and account settings are portable. In other words, your Office settings and files can travel with you and be accessed from different computers. You are not restricted to a single computer. When you sign in to Windows 10 using your Microsoft account (user name and password), Microsoft uses this information to transfer your Windows and Office 2016 settings to the computer you are

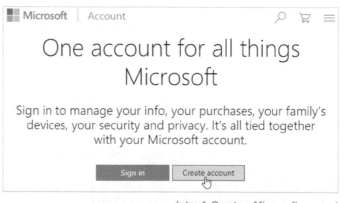

Intro-1 Create a Microsoft account

using. Your Microsoft account not only signs you in to Windows and Office but also to other free Microsoft online services, such as *OneDrive* and ***Office Online***. If you don't have a Microsoft account, you can create a free account at https://signup.live.com (Figure Intro-1).

Windows Desktop and Taskbar

The Windows desktop is the working area of Windows. When you log in to Windows, the desktop displays (Figure Intro-2). The *Taskbar* displays at the bottom of the desktop. You can open programs and folders from the *Taskbar* by clicking on an icon on the *Taskbar* (see Figure Intro-2). You can pin apps and other Windows items, such as the *Control Panel* or *File Explorer*, to the *Taskbar* (see "Customize the Taskbar" later in this section).

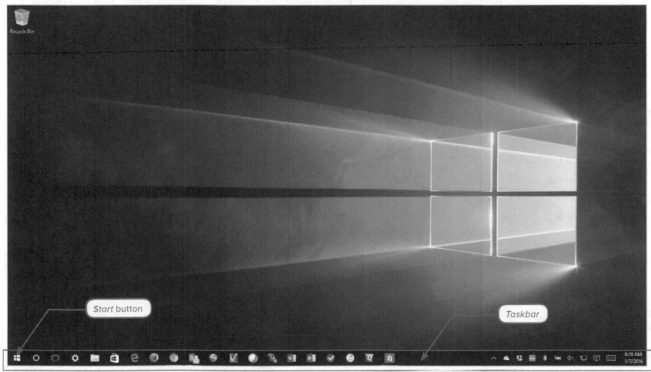

Intro-2 Windows desktop and *Taskbar*

Intro-3 Windows *Start* menu

Start Menu

Windows 10 utilizes a redesigned *Start* menu (Figure Intro-3), that you open by clicking the ***Start button*** located in the bottom left of the *Taskbar*. From the *Start* menu, you can open programs, files, folders, or other Windows resources. The *Start* menu is divided into two main sections. The left side of the *Start* menu displays ***Most Used*** items, buttons to open the ***File Explorer*** and ***Settings*** windows, the ***Power*** button, and ***All apps***, which displays an alphabetical listing of all applications installed on your computer. The right side of the *Start* menu displays apps as tiles (large and small buttons) you can click to open an application or window.

You can customize which apps and items appear on either side of the *Start* menu, arrange and group apps on the *Start* menu, resize the *Start* menu, and display the *Start* menu as a **Start page** when you log in to Windows (similar to the *Start* page in Windows 8 and 8.1). See "Customize the Start Menu" later in this section for information about customizing the *Start* menu.

Add Apps

Windows 10 uses the term *apps* generically to refer to applications and programs. Apps include the Windows 10 Weather app, Microsoft Excel program, Control Panel, Google Chrome, or *File Explorer*. Many apps are preinstalled on a Windows 10 computer, and you can add apps to your computer. You can install an app such as Office 2016 or Quicken by downloading it from a web site or from a program DVD. These are referred to as *traditional apps*.

The *Microsoft Store* app is preinstalled on Windows 10 computers. You can also install apps such as Netflix, Trip Advisor, and The Weather Channel from the Microsoft Store. These apps are referred to as *modern apps* and look and function similar to apps you install on your smartphone. Many apps in the Microsoft Store are free and others are available for purchase.

▶HOW TO: Add an App from the Microsoft Store

1. Click the **Start** button to open the *Start* menu.
2. Click the **Store** button (tile) to open the Microsoft Store app (Figure Intro-4).
 - If the *Store* tile is not available on the *Start* menu, click **All apps** on the *Start* menu, scroll down, and click **Store** in the alphabetic listing of all apps.
3. Select an app in the Microsoft Store (Figure Intro-5).
 - The Microsoft Store has different categories of apps.
 - You can search for apps by typing key words in the *Search* box in the upper right.
 - When you select an app, a description and screen shots of the app displays.
4. Click the **Free**, **Free trial**, or price button to install the app.
 - You must have a payment method stored in your Microsoft account to purchase apps from the Microsoft Store.
5. Click **Open** to open the installed app.
 - When you install an app, the app is listed in the *Recently added* area on the *Start* menu and *All apps* list of applications.

Intro-4 *Store* button on the *Start* menu

Intro-5 Install an app from the Microsoft Store

Customize the Start Menu

When you start using Windows 10 or after you have installed either traditional or modern apps, you can customize what appears on your *Start* menu and resize the *Start*

Task View

A new feature to Windows 10 is *Task View*. *Task View* displays all open apps and windows as tiles on your desktop, and you can choose which item to display or close. This feature is very helpful when you have multiple items open and want to select or close one.

▶**HOW TO: Use Task View**

Intro-17 *Task View* button on the *Taskbar*

1. Click the **Task View** button on the *Taskbar* (Figure Intro-17).
 - All open apps and windows display on the desktop (Figure Intro-18).

Intro-18 *Task View* with open apps and windows displayed on the desktop

2. Select the app or window to open or close.
 - Click a tile to open an app. The app opens and *Task View* closes.
 - Click the **X** in the upper right corner of an app to close an app. *Task View* remains open when you close an app.

Settings

In Windows 10, the *Settings* window is the redesigned *Control Panel* (although the *Control Panel* is still available). The *Settings* window is where you change global Windows settings, customize the Windows environment, add devices, and manage your Microsoft account. Click the **Settings** button on the *Taskbar* or *Start* menu to open the *Settings* window (Figure Intro-19). The following categories are available in the *Settings* window:

Intro-19 *Settings* window

- **System**: Display, notifications, apps, and power
- **Devices**: Bluetooth, printers, and mouse
- **Network & Internet**: Wi-Fi, airplane mode, and VPN
- **Personalization**: Background, lock screen, and colors
- **Accounts**: Your account, sync settings, work, and family
- **Time & Language**: Speech, region, and date
- **Ease of Access**: Narrator, magnifier, and high contrast
- **Privacy**: Location and camera
- **Update & Security**: Windows Update, recovery, and backup

> ### MORE INFO
>
> If you can't find an item in *Settings*, use the *Search* dialog box (*Find a setting*) in the upper right corner and type key words. If *Settings* is not available on the *Taskbar*, you can find it in the *All apps* list on the *Start* menu.

Action Center

The ***Action Center*** in Windows 10 provides a quick glance of notifications and buttons to open other commonly used settings and features in Windows. The *Action Center* displays notifications such as emails and Windows update notifications. Or you can click an action button to turn on or off features or open other windows or apps such as the *Settings* menu (*All Settings* button) or OneNote (*Note* button). Click the **Action Center** button on the right side of the *Taskbar* to open the *Action Center* pane on the right side of your screen (Figure Intro-20).

Intro-20 *Action Center*

Using Office 2016

Office 2016 includes common software applications such as Word, Excel, Access, and PowerPoint. These applications give you the ability to work with word processing documents, spreadsheets, presentations, and databases in your personal and business projects.

Office 2016 and Office 365

Microsoft Office is a suite of personal and business software applications (Figure Intro-21). ***Microsoft Office 2016*** and ***Microsoft Office 365*** are the same software products; the difference is how you purchase the software. Office 2016 is

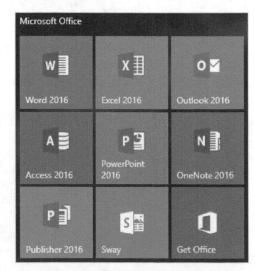

Intro-21 Microsoft Office application tiles on the *Start* menu

the traditional model of purchasing the software, and you own that software for as long as you want to use it. Office 365 is a subscription that you pay monthly or yearly, similar to how you purchase Netflix or Spotify. If you subscribe to Office 365, you automatically receive new versions of the software when they are released.

The common applications typically included in Microsoft Office 2016 and 365 are described in the following list:

- *Microsoft Word*: Word processing software used to create, format, and edit documents such as reports, letters, brochures, and resumes.
- *Microsoft Excel*: Spreadsheet software used to perform calculations on numerical data such as financial statements, budgets, and expense reports.
- *Microsoft Access*: Database software used to store, organize, compile, and report information such as product information, sales data, client information, and employee records.
- *Microsoft PowerPoint*: Presentation software used to graphically present information in slides such as a presentation on a new product or sales trends.
- *Microsoft Outlook*: Email and personal management software used to create and send email and create and store calendar items, contacts, and tasks.
- *Microsoft OneNote*: Note-taking software used to take and organize notes, which can be shared with other Office applications.
- *Microsoft Publisher*: Desktop publishing software used to create professional-looking documents containing text, pictures, and graphics such as catalogs, brochures, and flyers.

Office Desktop Apps, Office Universal Apps, and Office Online

Office desktop apps are the full-function Office 2016 or 365 programs installed on your computer (PC or Mac). Both Office 2016 and Office 365 are considered Office desktop apps. Because of the increased popularity and capabilities of tablets and mobile devices, Office software is also available for both tablets and smartphones. *Office universal apps* are the Office 365 programs that can be installed on tablets or other mobile devices. Office universal apps do not have the full range of advanced features available in Office desktop applications, but Office universal apps provide users the ability to create, edit, save, and share Office files using many of the most common features in the Office suite of programs.

> **MORE INFO**
> Office universal apps are also referred to as *Office mobile apps*.

Intro-22 *Office Online*

Office Online is free online software from Microsoft that works in conjunction with your Microsoft account and *OneDrive* (Figure Intro-22). With *Office Online*, you can work with Office files online through a web browser, even on computers that do not have Office 2016 or 365 installed. This is a useful option when you use a computer at a computer lab or use a friend's computer that does not have Office installed.

You can access *Office Online* from your *OneDrive* web page to create and edit Word documents, Excel workbooks, PowerPoint presentations, and OneNote notebooks. *Office Online* is a scaled-down version of Office 2016/365 and not as robust in terms of features, but you can use it to create, edit, print, share, and collaborate on files. If you need more advanced features, you can open *Office Online* files in Office 2016.

▶HOW TO: Create an Office Online File

1. Open an Internet browser Window, navigate to the *OneDrive* web site (www.onedrive.live.com), and log in to *OneDrive*. If you are not already logged in to *OneDrive*, use the following steps.

 - Click the **Sign in** button, type your Microsoft account email address, and click **Next**.
 - Type your Microsoft account password and click **Sign in** to open your *OneDrive* page.

 Intro-23 Create an Office Online file from your online *OneDrive* page

2. Click the **New** button and select the type of *Office Online* file to create (Figure Intro-23).

 - A new file is created and opens in the *Office Online* program.
 - The new file is saved in your *OneDrive* folder (both online and on your computer).

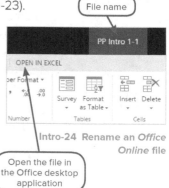

3. Rename the file by clicking on the file name at the top of the file, typing a new file name, and pressing **Enter** (Figure Intro-24).

 - You can also click the **File** tab to open the *Backstage* view, select *Save As*, and choose **Save As** or **Rename**.
 - Click the **OPEN IN *[OFFICE APPLICATION]*** button (for example **OPEN IN EXCEL**) to open the file in the Office desktop application (see Figure Intro-24).

 Intro-24 Rename an *Office Online* file

4. Close the browser tab or window to close the file.

 - *Office Online* automatically saves the file as you make changes.

Open an Office Desktop Application

When using Windows 10, you open an Office desktop application by clicking the application tile on the *Start* menu or the application icon on the *Taskbar*. If your *Start* menu and *Taskbar* do not have the Office applications displayed, click the **Start** button, select **All apps**, and select **Word 2016**, **Excel 2016**, **Access 2016**, or **PowerPoint 2016** to launch the application (Figure Intro-25).

You can also use *Cortana* to quickly locate an Office desktop app (Figure Intro-26).

Intro-25 Open an Office desktop app from the *All apps* area on the *Start* menu

Intro-26 Use *Cortana* to find and open an app

Office Start Page

Most of the Office applications (except Outlook and OneNote) display a ***Start page*** when you launch the application (Figure Intro-27). From this *Start* page, you can create a new blank file (for example a Word document, an Excel workbook, an Access database, or a PowerPoint presentation), create a file from an online template, search for an online template, open a recently used file, or open another file. These options vary depending on the Office application.

Intro-27 Excel *Start* page

▶**HOW TO:** Use the Office Start Page

1. Open a file listed in the *Recent* area on the left side of the *Start* menu by clicking the file to open. The file opens in the working area of the Office application.

 • The *Recent* area on the left side of the *Start* page lists files you have recently used and files that are pinned to the *Start* page.

2. Open a new blank file by clicking the **Blank [file type]** tile (*Blank workbook, Blank document,* etc.) to the right of the *Recent* area.

 • You can also press the **Esc** key to exit the *Start* page and open a new blank file.

3. Open an existing file that is not listed in the *Recent* area by clicking the **Open Other Workbooks** link (Figure Intro-28). The *Open* area on the *Backstage* view displays.

 • Click the **Browse** button to open the *Open* dialog box where you can locate and open a file.
 • You can also select a different location, *OneDrive* or *This PC*, and select a file to open.

4. Open a template by clicking a template file on the right or searching for templates.

 • Search for a template by typing key words in the *Search* area on the *Start* page.
 • Click a link to one of the categories below the *Search* area to display templates in that category.

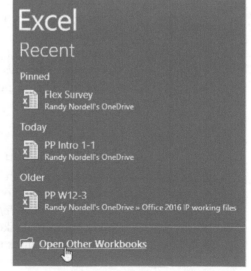

Intro-28 *Open Other Workbooks* link on the *Start* page

5. Pin a frequently used file to the *Start* page by clicking the **Pin** button.
 - The *Pin* button is on the right side of items listed in the *Recent* area and at the bottom right of templates displayed in the *Templates* area (to the right of the *Recent* area).
 - Pinned files display at the top of the *Recent* area.

Intro-29 *Backstage* view in Excel

Backstage View

Office incorporates the ***Backstage view*** into all Office applications (including *Office Online* apps). Click the **File** tab on the *Ribbon* to open the *Backstage* view (Figure Intro-29). *Backstage* options vary on the different Office applications. The following list describes common tasks you can perform from the *Backstage* view:

- ***Info***: Displays document properties and other protection, inspection, and version options.
- ***New***: Creates a new blank file or a new file from a template or theme.
- ***Open***: Opens an existing file from a designated location or a recently opened file.
- ***Save***: Saves a file. If the file has not been named, the *Save As* dialog box opens when you select this option.
- ***Save As***: Opens the *Save As* dialog box.
- ***Print***: Prints a file, displays a preview of the file, or displays print options.
- ***Share***: Invites people to share a file or email a file.
- ***Export***: Creates a PDF file from a file or saves as a different file type.
- ***Close***: Closes an open file.
- ***Account***: Displays your Microsoft account information.
- ***Options***: Opens the *[Application] Options* dialog box (for example *Excel Options*).

Office Help—Tell Me

In all the Office 2016/365 applications, ***Tell Me*** is the new help feature (Figure Intro-30). This new help feature displays the commands in the Office application related to your search. The *Help* feature in older versions of Office displayed articles describing the feature and how to use it. The new *Tell Me* feature provides command options that take you directly to a command or dialog box. For example if you type *PivotTable* in the *Tell Me* search box in Excel, the results include the option to open the *Create PivotTable* dialog box, as well as other options such as *Recommended PivotTables* and *Summarize with PivotTable*.

Intro-30 *Tell Me* search box

▶HOW TO: Use Tell Me

1. Place your insertion point in the **Tell Me** search box at the top of the *Ribbon* (see Figure Intro-30).

2. Type key words for the command or feature for which you are searching.

3. Select an option from the list of displayed search results (Figure Intro-31).

 • When you select a search result, it may apply a command, open a dialog box, or display a gallery of command choices.

Intro-31 *Tell Me* search results

> ▶ **ANOTHER WAY**
>
> **Alt+Q** places the insertion point in the *Tell Me* dialog box.
> The previous *Help* feature is still available in Office 2016/365. Press **F1** to open the *Help* dialog box.

Mouse and Pointers

If you are using Office on a desktop or laptop computer, use your mouse (or touch pad) to navigate around files, click tabs and buttons, select text and objects, move text and objects, and resize objects. The following table lists mouse and pointer terminology used in Office:

Mouse and Pointer Terminology

Term	Description
Pointer	When you move your mouse, the pointer moves on your screen. A variety of pointers are used in different contexts in Office applications. The following pointers are available in most of the Office applications (the appearance of these pointers varies depending on the application and the context used): • **Selection pointer:** Select text or an object. • **Move pointer:** Move text or an object. • **Copy pointer:** Copy text or an object. • **Resize pointer:** Resize objects or table columns or rows. • **Crosshair:** Draw a shape.
Insertion point	The vertical flashing line indicating where you type text in a file or text box. Click the left mouse button to position the insertion point.
Click	Click the left mouse button. Used to select an object or button or to place the insertion point in the selected location.
Double-click	Click the left mouse button twice. Used to select text.
Right-click	Click the right mouse button. Used to display the context menu and the mini toolbar.
Scroll	Use the scroll wheel on the mouse to scroll up and down through your file. You can also use the horizontal or vertical scroll bars at the bottom and right of an Office file window to move around in a file.

Touch Mode and Touch Screen Gestures

The new user interface in Windows 10 and Office 2016 has improved touch features to facilitate the use of Windows and the Office applications on a tablet computer or smartphone. On tablets and smartphones, you use a touch screen rather than using a mouse, so the process of selecting text and objects and navigating around a file is different from a computer without a touch screen.

In Office 2016/365, *Touch mode* optimizes the Office working environment when using a computer with a touch screen to provide more space between buttons and commands. Click the **Touch/Mouse Mode** button on the *Quick Access* toolbar (upper left of the Office app window) and select **Touch** from the drop-down list to enable *Touch* mode (Figure Intro-32). To turn off *Touch* mode, select **Mouse** from the *Touch/Mouse Mode* drop-down list.

Intro-32 Turn on *Touch* mode

Quick Access toolbar

> **MORE INFO**
>
> The *Touch/Mouse Mode* button displays on the *Quick Access* toolbar when using a touch-screen computer.

The following table lists common gestures used when working on a tablet or smartphone (these gestures vary depending on the application used and the context):

Touch Screen Gestures

Gesture	Used To	How To
Tap	Select text or an object or position the insertion point. Double tap to edit text in an object or cell.	
Pinch	Zoom in or resize an object.	
Stretch	Zoom out or resize an object.	
Slide	Move an object or selected text.	
Swipe	Select text or multiple objects.	

> **MORE INFO**
>
> Window 10 has a *Tablet mode* that optimizes all of Windows and apps for touch screens. When you turn on the *Tablet mode* feature in Windows, the *Touch mode* in Office apps turns on automatically. Click the **Action Center** button on the Windows *Taskbar* and click the **Tablet mode** button to turn on this feature in Windows.

Creating, Saving, Closing, and Opening Files

Creating, saving, opening, and closing files is primarily done from the *Start* page or *Backstage* view of the Office application you are using. These areas provide you with many options and a central location to perform these tasks. You can also use shortcut commands to create, save, and open files.

Create a New File

When you create a new file in an Office application, you can create a new blank file or a new file based on a template (in PowerPoint, you can also create a presentation based on a theme). On the *Start* page, click **Blank [file type]** to create a new blank file in the application you are using (in Word, you begin with a blank document; in Excel, a blank workbook; in Access, a blank desktop database; and in PowerPoint, a blank presentation).

> **HOW TO:** Create a New File from the Start Page

1. Open the Office application you want to use. The *Start* page displays when the application opens (Figure Intro-33).

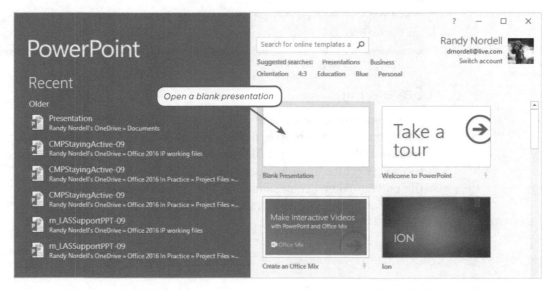

Intro-33 *Start* page in PowerPoint

2. Click **Blank [file type]** or select a template or theme to use for your new blank file. A new file opens in the application you are using.
 - The new file is given a generic file name (for example *Document1*, *Book1*, or *Presentation1*). You can name and save this file later.
 - When creating a new Access database, you are prompted to name the new file when you create it.
 - A variety of templates (and themes in PowerPoint only) display on the *Start* page, but you can search for additional online templates and themes using the *Search* text box at the top of the *Start* page.

> MORE INFO
>
> **Esc** closes the *Start* page and takes you into the Office application (except in Access).

If you have been using an application already and want to create a new file, you create it from the *Backstage* view. From the *Backstage* view, the new file options are available in the *New* area.

▶HOW TO: Create a New File from the Backstage View

1. Click the **File** tab to display the *Backstage* view.
2. Select **New** on the left to display the *New* area (Figure Intro-34).
3. Click **Blank [file type]** or select a template or theme to use in your new blank file. A new file opens in the application.
 - The new file is given a generic file name (*Document1*, *Book1*, or *Presentation1*). You can name and save this file later.
 - When you are creating a new Access database, you are prompted to name the new file when you create it.

Intro-34 *New* area on the *Backstage* view in PowerPoint

ANOTHER WAY

Ctrl+N opens a new file from within an Office application. In Access, **Ctrl+N** opens the *New* area in the *Backstage* view.

Save a File

In Access, you name a file as you create it, but in Word, Excel, and PowerPoint, you name a file after you have created it. When you save a file, you type a name for the file and select the location to save the file. You can save a file on your computer, an online storage location such as *OneDrive*, or portable device, such as a USB drive.

Intro-35 *Save As* area on the *Backstage* view in PowerPoint

▶HOW TO: Save a File

1. Click the **File** tab to display the *Backstage* view.
2. Select **Save** or **Save As** on the left to display the *Save As* area (Figure Intro-35).
 - If the file has not already been saved, clicking *Save* or *Save As* takes you to the *Save As* area on the *Backstage* view.
3. Click the **Browse** button to open the *Save As* dialog box (Figure Intro-36).
 - You can also select a different location (*OneDrive* or *This PC*) and select a folder from the list of folders at the right to open the *Save As* dialog box.
4. Select a location to save the file in the *Folder* list on the left.

Intro-36 *Save As* dialog box

5. Type a name for the file in the *File name* area.
 - By default, Office selects the file type, but you can change the file type from the *Save as type* drop-down list.
6. Click **Save** to close the dialog box and save the file.

> ANOTHER WAY

Ctrl+S opens the *Save As* area on the *Backstage* view when a file has not been named. If a file has already been named, **Ctrl+S** saves the file without opening the *Backstage* view.

> MORE INFO

If you save a file in *OneDrive*, you have access to that file from any computer with Internet access. Also, you can share and collaborate on files stored in *OneDrive*. *OneDrive* is one of the folders in the *Save As* dialog box.

Create a New Folder When Saving a File

When saving files, it is a good idea to create folders to organize your files. Organizing your files in folders makes it easier to find your files and saves you time when you are searching for a specific file (see *SLO Intro.8: Organizing and Customizing Folders and Files* for more information on this topic). When you save an Office file, you can also create a folder in which to store that file.

> **HOW TO:** Create a New Folder When Saving a File

1. Click the **File** tab to display the *Backstage* view.
2. Select **Save As** on the left to display the *Save As* area.
3. Click **Browse** to open the *Save As* dialog box.
4. Select a location to save the file in the *Folder* list on the left.
5. Click the **New Folder** button to create a new folder (Figure Intro-37).
6. Type a name for the new folder and press **Enter**.

Intro-37 Create a new folder

> ANOTHER WAY

F12 opens the *Save As* dialog box (except in Access). On a laptop, you might have to press **Fn+F12**. See more about the *Fn* (Function) key in *SLO Intro.7: Using Context Menus, the Mini Toolbars, and Keyboard Shortcuts*.

Save As a Different File Name

After you have saved a file, you can save it again with a different file name. If you do this, you have preserved the original file, and you can continue to revise the second file for a different purpose.

▶**HOW TO:** Save as a Different File Name

1. Click the **File** tab to display the *Backstage* view.
2. Select **Save As** on the left to display the *Save As* area.
3. Click the **Browse** button to open the *Save As* dialog box.
4. Select a location to save the file in the *Folder* list on the left.
5. Type a new name for the file in the *File name* area.
6. Click **Save** to close the dialog box and save the file.

Office 2016 File Types

When you save an Office file, by default Office saves the file in the most recent file format for that application. You also have the option of saving files in older versions of the Office application you are using. For example, you can save a Word document as an older version to share with or send to someone who uses an older version of Word. Each file has an extension at the end of the file name that determines the file type. The *file name extension* is automatically added to a file when you save it. The following table lists common file types used in the different Office applications:

Office File Types

File Type	Extension	File Type	Extension
Word Document	.docx	Access Database	.accdb
Word Template	.dotx	Access Template	.accdt
Word 97-2003 Document	.doc	Access Database (2000-2003 format)	.mdb
Rich Text Format	.rtf	PowerPoint Presentation	.pptx
Excel Workbook	.xlsx	PowerPoint Template	.potx
Excel Template	.xltx	PowerPoint 97-2003 Presentation	.ppt
Excel 97-2003 Workbook	.xls	Portable Document Format (PDF)	.pdf
Comma Separated Values (CSV)	.csv		

Close a File

You can close a file using the following different methods:

- Click the **File** tab and select **Close** on the left.
- Press **Ctrl+W**.
- Click the **X** in the upper right corner of the file window. This method closes the file and the program if only one file is open in the application.

When you close a file, you are prompted to save the file if it has not been named or if changes were made after the file was last saved (Figure Intro-38). Click **Save** to save and close the file or click **Don't Save** to close the file without saving. Click **Cancel** to return to the file.

Open an Existing File

You can open an existing file from the *Start* page when you open an Office application or while you are working on another Office file.

▶**HOW TO:** Open a File from the Start Page

1. Open an Office application to display the *Start* page.

2. Select a file to open in the *Recent* area on the left (Figure Intro-39). The file opens in the Office application.

 - If you select a file in the *Recent* area that has been renamed, moved, or on a storage device not connected to the computer, you receive an error message.

3. Alternatively, click the **Open Other [file type]** (for example *Open Other Presentations*) (see Figure Intro-39) link to open the *Open* area of the *Backstage* view (Figure Intro-40).

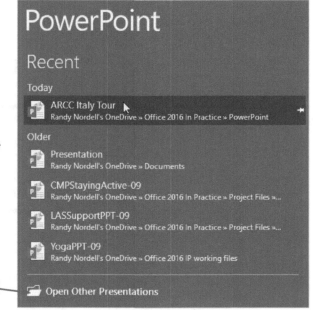

Intro-39 Open a file from the *Start* page

Intro-40 *Open* area on the *Backstage* view

4. Click the **Browse** button to open the *Open* dialog box (Figure Intro-41).

5. Select a location from the *Folder* list on the left.

6. Select the file to open and click the **Open** button.

 - If the file opens in *Protected View*, click the **Enable Editing** button to allow you to edit the file.

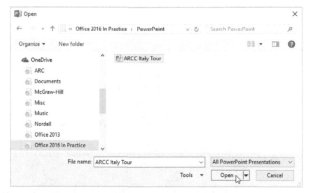

Intro-41 *Open* dialog box

When working on a file in an Office application, you might want to open another file. You can open an existing file from within an Office application from the *Open* area on the *Backstage* view.

> **HOW TO:** Open a File from the Backstage View

1. Click the **File** tab from within an open Office application to open the *Backstage* view.
2. Click **Open** on the left to display the *Open* area on the *Backstage* view (see Figure Intro-40).
3. Click the **Browse** button to open the *Open* dialog box (see Figure Intro-41).
 - You can also select a file to open from the list of *Recent* files on the right of the *Open* area on the *Backstage* view.
4. Select a location from the *Folder* list on the left.
5. Select the file to open and click the **Open** button.
 - If the file opens in *Protected View*, click the **Enable Editing** button to allow you to edit the file.

You can also open a file from a *File Explorer* folder. When you double-click a file in a *File Explorer* folder, the file opens in the appropriate Office application. Windows recognizes the file name extension and launches the correct Office application.

PAUSE & PRACTICE: INTRO-1

For this project, you log in to Windows using your Microsoft account, customize the Windows *Start* menu and *Taskbar*, create and save a PowerPoint presentation, create a folder, open and rename an Excel workbook, and use Windows 10 features.

File Needed: ***ARCC2018Budget-Intro.xlsx*** *(Student data files are available in the Library of your SIMnet account)*
Completed Project File Names: ***[your initials] PP Intro-1a.pptx*** and ***[your initials] PP Intro-1b.xlsx***

1. Log in to Windows using your Microsoft account if you are not already logged in.
 a. If you don't have a Microsoft account, you can create a free account at https://signup.live.com.
 b. If you are using a computer on your college campus, you may be required to log in to the computer using your college user name and password.
2. Customize the *Start* menu to include Office 2016 apps. If these apps tiles are already on the *Start* menu, skip steps 2a–e. You can pin other apps of your choice to the *Start* menu.
 a. Click the **Start** button at the bottom left of your screen to open the *Start* menu.

b. Click **All apps** at the bottom left of the *Start* menu (Figure Intro-42). The list of apps installed on the computer displays on the left side of the *Start* menu.

c. Locate and right-click **Access 2016** and select **Pin to Start** (Figure Intro-43). The app displays as a tile on the right side of the *Start* menu.

d. Repeat step 2c to pin **Excel 2016**, **PowerPoint 2016**, and **Word 2016** apps to the *Start* menu.

e. Display the *Start* menu and drag these Office app tiles so they are close to each other.

f. Click the **Start** button (or press the **Esc** key) to close the *Start* menu.

Intro-42 *All apps* button on the *Start* menu

3. Use *Cortana* and the *Start* menu to pin Office 2016 apps to the *Taskbar*.

a. Click the **Cortana** button (to the right of the *Start* button) on the *Taskbar* and type Access. *Cortana* displays content matching your search.

b. Right-click the **Access 2016** option near the top of the *Cortana* pane and select **Pin to taskbar** (Figure Intro-44). The app pins to the *Taskbar*.

c. Click the **Start** button to open the *Start* menu.

d. Right-click the **Excel 2016** tile on the right side of the *Start* menu, click **More**, and select **Pin to taskbar**. The app pins to the *Taskbar*.

e. Use either of the methods described above to pin the **PowerPoint 2016** and **Word 2016** apps to the *Taskbar*.

f. Drag the Office apps on the *Taskbar* to rearrange them to your preference.

Intro-43 Pin Access 2016 app to *Start* menu

Intro-44 Use *Cortana* to find an Office app and pin it to the *Taskbar*

4. Create a PowerPoint presentation and save the presentation in a new folder.

a. Click the **PowerPoint 2016** app tile on your *Start* menu to open the application.

b. Click **Blank Presentation** on the PowerPoint *Start* page to create a new blank presentation.

c. Click the **Click to add title** placeholder and type American River Cycling Club to replace the placeholder text.

d. Click the **File** tab to open the *Backstage* view and click **Save As** on the left to display the *Save As* area.

e. Click **Browse** to open the *Save As* dialog box (Figure Intro-45).

f. Select a location to save the file from the *Folder* list on the left. If the *OneDrive* folder is an option, select **OneDrive**. If it is not, select the **Documents** folder in the *This PC* folder. You can also save to a portable storage device if you have one.

g. Click the **New Folder** button to create a new folder.

h. Type American River Cycling Club as the name of the new folder and press **Enter** (Figure Intro-46).

i. Double-click the **American River Cycling Club** folder to open it.

Intro-45 *Save As* area on the *Backstage* view in PowerPoint

j. Type [your initials] PP Intro-1a in the *File name* area.

k. Click **Save** to close the dialog box and save the presentation. Leave the file and PowerPoint open.

5. Open an Excel file and save as a different file name.

a. Return to the Windows *Start* menu.

b. Click the **Excel 2016** app button on the *Taskbar* to open it.

c. Click the **Open Other Workbooks** link on the bottom left of the Excel *Start* page to display the *Open* area of the *Backstage* view.

d. Click **Browse** to open the *Open* dialog box (Figure Intro-47).

e. Browse to your student data files and select the **ARCC2018Budget-Intro** file.

f. Click **Open** to open the workbook. If the file opens in *Protected View*, click the **Enable Editing** button.

g. Click the **File** tab to open the *Backstage* view.

h. Click **Save As** on the left to display the *Save As* area and click **Browse** to open the *Save As* dialog box.

i. Locate the **American River Cycling Club** folder (created in step 4h) in the *Folder* list on the left and double-click the folder to open it.

j. Type [your initials] PP Intro-1b in the *File name* area.

k. Click **Save** to close the dialog box and save the workbook. Leave the file and Excel open.

6. Use the *Tell Me* feature in Excel to find a command.

a. Click the **Tell Me** search box on the *Ribbon* of the Excel window and type PivotTable (Figure Intro-48).

b. Click **PivotTable** to open the *Create PivotTable* dialog box.

c. Click the **X** in the upper right corner of the *Create PivotTable* dialog box to close it.

7. Open the *Microsoft Store* app, the *Action Center*, and the *Settings* window.

a. Click the **Cortana** button and type Microsoft Store.

b. Click **Store** at the top of the *Cortana* pane to open the *Store* app.

c. Click **Apps** in the top left and browse the available apps in the Microsoft Store.

d. Click the **Minimize** button in the upper right corner of the *Store* window to minimize this app (Figure Intro-49). The app is still open, but it is minimized on the *Taskbar*.

e. Click the **Action Center** button on the right side of the *Taskbar* to display the *Action Center* pane at the right (Figure Intro-50).

Intro-46 Create a new folder from the *Save As* dialog box

Intro-47 *Open* area on the *Backstage* view

Intro-48 Use the *Tell Me* feature to find a command

Intro-49 *Minimize* button on an app window

Intro-50 Windows 10 *Action Center*

f. Click **All settings** to open the *Settings* window.

g. Click the **Find a setting** search box, type **Printer**, and view the search results.

h. Click the **Minimize** button to minimize the *Settings* windows to the *Taskbar*.

8. Use the *Task View* feature to open and close apps and windows.

a. Click the **Task View** button on the left side of the *Taskbar* (Figure Intro-51). All of the open apps and windows are tiled on the Windows desktop.

b. Click the **Store** app to open it. *Task View* closes and the *Store* app displays on your Windows desktop.

c. Click the **Task View** button again.

d. Click the **X** in the upper right corner to close each open app and window. You may be prompted to save changes to a file.

e. Click the **Task View** button again or press **Esc** to return to the desktop.

Intro-51 *Task View* button on the *Taskbar*

SLO INTRO. 4 **Working with Files**

When you work with Office files, a variety of display views are available. You can change how a file displays, adjust the display size, work with multiple files, and arrange the windows to view multiple files. Because most people work with multiple files at the same time, Office makes it easy and intuitive to move from one file to another or to display multiple document windows at the same time.

File Views

Each of the different Office applications provides you with a variety of ways to view your document. In Word, Excel, and PowerPoint, the different views are available on the *View tab* (Figure Intro-52). You can also change views using the buttons on the right side of the *Status bar* at the bottom of the file window (Figure Intro-53). In Access, the different views for each object are available in the *Views* group on the *Home* tab.

Intro-52 *Workbook Views* group on the *View* tab in Excel

Intro-53 PowerPoint views on the *Status* bar

The following table lists the views that are available in each of the different Office applications:

File Views

Office Application	Views	Office Application	Views
Word	*Read Mode* *Print Layout* *Web Layout* *Outline* *Draft*	**Access** *(Access views vary depending on active object)*	*Layout View* *Design View* *Datasheet View* *Form View* *SQL View* *Report View* *Print Preview*
Excel	*Normal* *Page Break Preview* *Page Layout* *Custom Views*	**PowerPoint**	*Normal* *Outline View* *Slide Sorter* *Notes Page* *Reading View* *Presenter View*

Change Display Size

You can use the **Zoom** feature to increase or decrease the display size of your file. Using *Zoom* to change the display size does not change the actual size of text or objects in your file; it only changes the size of your display. For example, if you change the *Zoom* level to 120%, you increase the display of your file to 120% of its normal size (100%), but changing the display size does not affect the actual size of text and objects in your file. You could also decrease the *Zoom* level to 80% to display more of your file on the screen.

You can increase or decrease the *Zoom* level several different ways. Your *Zoom* options vary depending on the Office application you are using.

- **Zoom level** *on the Status* bar (Figure Intro-54): Click the + or − button to increase or decrease *Zoom* level in 10% increments.

Intro-54 *Zoom* area on the *Status* bar in PowerPoint

- **Zoom group** *on the View tab* (Figure Intro-55): The *Zoom* group includes a variety of *Zoom* options. The options vary depending on the Office application.
- **Zoom dialog box** (Figure Intro-56): Click the **Zoom** button in the *Zoom* group on the *View* tab or click the **Zoom level** on the *Status* bar to open the *Zoom* dialog box.

Intro-55 *Zoom* group in Excel

> **MORE INFO**
>
> The *Zoom* feature is only available in Access in *Print Preview* view when you are working with reports.

Manage Multiple Open Files and Windows

When you are working on multiple files in an Office application, each file is opened in a new window. You can **minimize** an open window to place the file on the Windows *Taskbar* (the bar at the bottom of the Windows desktop), **restore down** an open window so it does not fill the entire computer screen, or **maximize** a window so it fills the entire computer screen. The *Minimize, Restore Down/Maximize,* and *Close* buttons are in the upper right of a file window (Figure Intro-57).

Intro-56 *Zoom* dialog box in Word

> **MORE INFO**
>
> You can open only one Access file at a time. If you open another Access file, the first one closes.

Intro-57 Window options buttons

- *Minimize*: Click the **Minimize** button (see Figure Intro-57) to hide the active window. When a document is minimized, it is not closed. It is minimized to the *Taskbar* so the window is not displayed on your screen. Place your pointer on the application icon on the Windows *Taskbar* to display thumbnails of open files. You can click an open file thumbnail to display the file (Figure Intro-58).
- *Restore Down/Maximize*: Click the **Restore Down/Maximize** (see Figure Intro-57) button to decrease the size of an open window or maximize the window to fill the entire screen. This button toggles between *Restore Down* and *Maximize*. When a window is restored down, you can change the size of a window by clicking and dragging a border of the window. You can also move the window by clicking and dragging the title bar at the top of the window.
- *Close*: Click the **Close** button (see Figure Intro-57) to close the window. If there is only one open file, the Office application also closes when you click the *Close* button on the file.

Intro-58 Display minimized file on the *Taskbar*

You can switch between open files or arrange the open files to display more than one window at the same time. The following are several methods to do this:

- *Switch Windows button*: Click the **Switch Windows** button [*View* tab, *Window* group] (not available in Access) to display a drop-down list of open files. Click a file from the drop-down list to display the file.

> **ANOTHER WAY**
>
> Click the Windows **Task View** button on the *Taskbar* to tile all open windows and apps on the desktop.

- *Windows Taskbar*: Place your pointer on an Office application icon on the Windows *Taskbar* to display the open files in that application. Click a file thumbnail to display it (see Figure Intro-58).
- *Arrange All button*: Click the **Arrange All** button [*View* tab, *Window* group] to display all windows in an application. You can resize or move the open file windows.

Snap Assist

The *Snap Assist* feature in Windows provides the ability to position an open window to the left or right side of your computer screen and fill half the screen. When you snap an open window to the left or right side of the screen, the other open windows tile on the opposite side where you can select another window to fill the opposite side of the computer screen (Figure Intro-59).

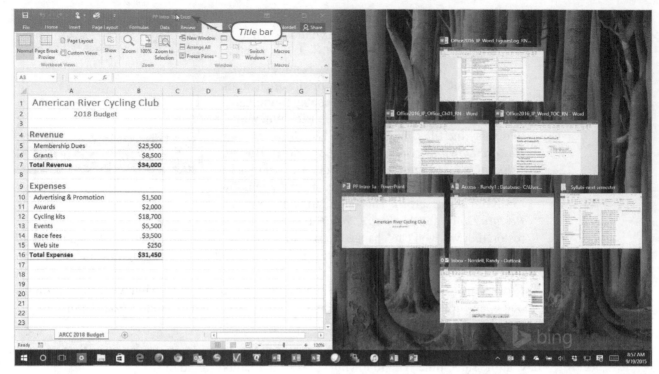

Intro-59 Windows *Snap Assist* feature

HOW TO: Use Snap Assist

1. Click the **title bar** of an open window.
2. Drag it to the left or right edge of the computer screen and release the pointer.
 - The window snaps to the side of the screen and fills half of the computer screen (see Figure Intro-59).
 - The other open windows and apps display as tiles on the opposite side.
 - If you're using a touch screen computer, you can use *Snap Assist* by pressing and holding the title bar of an open window and dragging to either side of the computer screen.
3. Select a tile of an open window or app to fill the other half of the screen.

> **MORE INFO**
>
> *Snap Assist* also allows you to snap a window to a quadrant (quarter rather than half) of your screen. Drag the **title bar** of an open window to one of the four corners of your computer screen.

SLO INTRO. 5

Printing, Sharing, and Customizing Files

On the *Backstage* view of any of the Office applications, you can print a file and customize how a file is printed. You can also export an Office file as a PDF file in most of the Office applications. In addition, you can add and customize document properties for an Office file and share a file in a variety of formats.

Print a File

You can print an Office file if you need a hard copy. The *Print* area on the *Backstage* view displays a preview of the open file and many print options. For example, you can choose which page or pages to print and change the margins of the file in the *Print* area. Print settings vary depending on the Office application you are using and what you are printing.

▶ **HOW TO:** Print a File

1. Open the file you want to print from a Windows folder or within an Office program.
2. Click the **File** tab to open the *Backstage* view.
3. Click **Print** on the left to display the *Print* area (Figure Intro-60).
 - A preview of the file displays on the right. Click the **Show Margins** button to adjust margins or **Zoom to Page** button to change the view in the *Preview* area. The *Show Margins* button is only available in Excel.
4. Change the number of copies to print in the *Copies* area.
5. Click the **Printer** drop-down list to choose from available printers.
6. Customize what is printed and how it is printed in the *Settings* area.
 - The *Settings* options vary depending on the Office application you are using and what you are printing.
 - In the *Pages* area (*Slides* area in PowerPoint), you can select a page or range of pages (slides) to print.
 - By default all pages (slides) are printed when you print a file.
7. Click the **Print** button to print your file.

Intro-60 *Print* area on the *Backstage* view

▶ **ANOTHER WAY**

Press **Ctrl+P** to open the *Print* area on the *Backstage* view.

Export as a PDF File

Portable document format, or ***PDF***, is a specific file format that is often used to share files that are not to be changed or to post files on a web site. When you create a PDF file from an Office application file, you are actually exporting a static image of the original file, similar to taking a picture of the file.

The advantage of working with a PDF file is that the format of the file is retained no matter who opens the file. PDF files open in the Windows Reader app or Adobe Reader, which is free software that is installed on most computers. Because a PDF file is a static image of a file, it is not easy for other people to edit your files. When you want people to be able to view a file but not change it, PDF files are a good choice.

1. Open the file you want to export as a PDF file.

2. Click the **File** tab and click **Export** to display the *Export* area on the Backstage view (Figure Intro-61).

3. Select **Create PDF/XPS Document** and click the **Create PDF/XPS**. The *Publish as PDF or XPS* dialog box opens.

 - XPS (XML Paper Specification) format is an alternative to a PDF file. XPS is a Microsoft format and is not widely used.

4. Select a location to save the file.

5. Type a name for the file in the *File name* area.

6. Click **Publish** to close the dialog box and save the PDF file.

 - A PDF version of your file may open. You can view the file and then close it.

Intro-61 *Export* a file as a PDF file

> ▶ MORE INFO
>
> Microsoft Word can open PDF files, and you can edit and save the file as a Word document.

Document Properties

Document properties are hidden codes in a file that store identifying information about that file. Each piece of document property information is called a ***field***. You can view and modify document properties in the *Info* area of the *Backstage* view.

Some document properties fields are automatically generated when you work on a file, such as *Size*, *Total Editing Time*, *Created*, and *Last Modified*. Other document properties fields, such as *Title*, *Comments*, *Subject*, *Company*, and *Author*, can be modified. You can use document property fields in different ways such as inserting the *Company* field in a document footer.

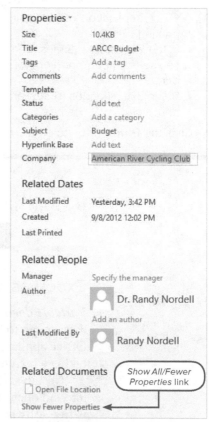

1. Click the **File** tab and click **Info**. The document properties display on the right (Figure Intro-62).

2. Click the text box area of a field that can be edited and type your custom document property information.

3. Click the **Show All Properties** link at the bottom to display additional document properties.

 - Click **Show Fewer Properties** to collapse the list and display fewer properties.
 - This link toggles between *Show All Properties* and *Show Fewer Properties*.

4. Click the **Back** arrow to return to the file.

Intro-62 Document properties

Share a File

Windows 10 and Office 2016 have been enhanced to help you share files and collaborate with others. The *Share* area on the *Backstage* view lists different options for sharing files from within an Office application. When you save a file to your *OneDrive*, Office provides a variety of options to share your file (Figure Intro-63). The two main sharing options are ***Share with People*** and ***Email***. Within these two categories, you have a variety of ways to share a file with others. Your sharing options vary depending on the Office application you are using. The following list describes the sharing options available in the Office applications:

Intro-63 *Share* options on the *Backstage* view

- ***Word***: *Share with People*, *Email*, *Present Online*, and *Post to Blog*
- ***Excel***: *Share with People* and *Email*
- ***Access***: No *Sharing* option on the *Backstage* view
- ***PowerPoint***: *Share with People*, *Email*, *Present Online*, and *Publish Slides*

▶HOW TO: Share a File

1. Click the **File** tab to open the *Backstage* view and select **Share** on the left.
 - If your file is not saved in *OneDrive*, you are directed to first save the file to the cloud (*OneDrive*). Click the **Save to Cloud** button and save your file in *OneDrive*.
 - If your file is not saved to *OneDrive*, you will not have all available sharing options.

2. Share a *OneDrive* file with others by clicking **Share with People** on the left and then clicking the **Share with People** button on the right (see Figure Intro-63).
 - The *Backstage* view closes and the *Share* pane opens on the right side of the file (Figure Intro-64).
 - Alternatively, click the **Share** button in the upper right corner of the Office application window to open the *Share* pane (Figure Intro-65).
 - Type an email address in the *Invite people* text box. If you want to share the file with more than one person, separate email addresses with a semicolon.
 - Select **Can edit** or **Can view** from the permission drop-down list, which controls what others can do with your file.
 - You can include a message the recipients will receive.
 - Click the **Share** button below the message to send a sharing email to recipients.
 - Alternatively, click the **Get a sharing link** option at the bottom of the *Share* pane to create an *edit link* or *view-only link* (Figure Intro-66). You can then copy the sharing link and email it to others or post it in an online location.

Intro-64 *Share* pane

Intro-65 *The Share button* opens the *Share* pane

Intro-66 *Get a sharing link* options in the *Share* pane

Intro-67 *Email* share options in the *Share* area on the *Backstage* view

3. Share a file through email by clicking the **Email** button on the left side of the *Share* area on the *Backstage* view and selecting an option (Figure Intro-67).

- These *Email* share options use Microsoft Outlook (email and personal management Office application) to share the selected file through email.
- The *Email* share options include *Send as Attachment*, *Send a Link*, *Send as PDF*, *Send as XPS*, and *Send as Internet Fax*.
- A description of each of these *Email* share options are provided to the right of each option.

> ▶ **MORE INFO**
>
> Sharing options are also available if you save files to other online storage locations such as Dropbox and Box.

Program Options

Using the program options, you can apply global changes to the Office program. For example, you can change the default save location to your *OneDrive* folder or you can turn off the *Start* page that opens when you open an Office application.

 Click the **File** tab and select **Options** on the left to open the **[Program] Options** dialog box (Word Options, Excel Options, etc.) (Figure Intro-68). Click one of the categories on the left to display the category options on the right. The categories and options vary depending on the Office application you are using.

Intro-68 *Excel Options* dialog box

Using the Ribbon, Tabs, and Quick Access Toolbar

You can use the *Ribbon*, tabs, groups, buttons, drop-down lists, dialog boxes, task panes, galleries, and the *Quick Access* toolbar to modify your Office files. This section describes different tools you can use to customize your files.

The Ribbon, Tabs, and Groups

The ***Ribbon***, which appears at the top of an Office file window, displays the many features available to use on your files. The *Ribbon* is a collection of ***tabs***. On each tab are ***groups*** of features. The tabs and groups that are available on each Office application vary. Click a tab to display the groups and features available on that tab.

Some tabs always display on the *Ribbon* (for example the *File* tab and *Home* tabs). Other tabs are ***context-sensitive***, which means that they only appear on the *Ribbon* when you select a specific object. Figure Intro-69 displays the context-sensitive *Table Tools Field* tab that displays in Access when you open a table.

Intro-69 Context-sensitive *Table Tools Fields* tab displayed

Ribbon Display Options

The *Ribbon* displays by default in Office applications, but you can customize how the *Ribbon* displays. The ***Ribbon Display Options*** button is in the upper right corner of an Office application window (Figure Intro-70). Click the **Ribbon Display Options** button to select one of the three options:

- ***Auto-Hide Ribbon***: Hides the *Ribbon*. Click at the top of the application to display the *Ribbon*.
- ***Show Tabs***: *Ribbon* tabs display. Click a tab to open the *Ribbon* and display the tab.
- ***Show Tabs and Commands***: Displays the *Ribbon* and tabs, which is the default setting in Office applications.

Intro-70 *Ribbon Display Options*

> **MORE INFO**
>
> **Ctrl+F1** collapses or expands the *Ribbon*.

Buttons, Drop-Down Lists, and Galleries

Groups on each of the tabs contain a variety of ***buttons***, ***drop-down lists***, and ***galleries***. The following list describes each of these features and how they are used:

- ***Button***: Applies a feature to selected text or object. Click a button to apply the feature (Figure Intro-71).

- **Drop-down list**: Displays the various options available for a feature. Some buttons are drop-down lists only, so when you click one of these buttons the drop-down list of options appears (Figure Intro-72). Other buttons are **split buttons**, which have both a button you click to apply a feature and an arrow you click to display a drop-down list of options (Figure Intro-73).
- **Gallery**: Displays a collection of option buttons. Click an option in a gallery to apply the feature. Figure Intro-74 is the *Styles* gallery. You can click the **More** button to display the entire gallery of options or click the **Up** or **Down** arrow to display a different row of options.

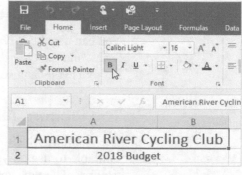

Intro-71 *Bold* button in the *Font* group on the *Home* tab

Up and *Down* buttons

More button

Intro-74 *Styles* gallery in Word

Intro-72 *Orientation* drop-down list

Intro-73 *Merge & Center* split button—button and drop-down list

Click the arrow on a split button to display the drop-down list

Dialog Boxes, Task Panes, and Launchers

Not all of the features that are available in an Office application are displayed in the groups on the tabs. Additional options for some groups display in a **dialog box** or **task pane**. A **launcher**, which is a small square in the bottom right of some groups, opens a dialog box or displays a task pane when you click it (see Figure Intro-76).

- **Dialog box**: A new window that opens to display additional features. You can move a dialog box by clicking and dragging the title bar, which is the top of the dialog box where the title is displayed. Figure Intro-75 shows the *Format Cells* dialog box that opens when you click the *Alignment* launcher in Excel.

Intro-75 *Format Cells* dialog box

Intro-76 *Clipboard* pane

menu. When you *pin* an app to the *Start* menu, the app tile remains on the right side of the *Start* menu. Pin the apps you most regularly use, unpin the apps you don't want to display on the *Start* menu, and rearrange and resize apps tiles to your preference.

▶HOW TO: Customize the Start Menu

1. Move an app tile by clicking and dragging the app tile to a new location on the *Start* menu. The other app tiles shuffle to accommodate the placement of the app tile.

2. Remove an app tile from the *Start* menu by right-clicking the app tile you want to remove and selecting **Unpin from Start** from the context menu (Figure Intro-6).

 - The app tile is removed from the *Start* menu, but the program or task is not removed from your computer.

Intro-6 Unpin an app from the *Start* menu

3. Pin an app tile to the *Start* menu by clicking **All apps** at the bottom of the *Start* menu, right-clicking the app to pin, and selecting **Pin to Start** (Figure Intro-7).

 - Drag the newly added app tile to the desired location on the Start menu.

Intro-7 Pin an app to the *Start* menu

4. Resize an app tile by right-clicking the app tile, selecting **Resize**, and selecting **Small**, **Medium**, **Wide**, or **Large**.

 - Some apps only have *Small*, *Medium*, and *Wide* size options.

5. Turn on or off the live tile option by right-clicking the app tile and selecting **Turn live tile on** or **Turn live tile off**.

 - Live tile displays rotating graphics and options on the app tile. When this option is turned off, the name of the app displays on the tile.

6. Uninstall an app by right-clicking the app you want to uninstall and selecting **Uninstall**.

 - Unlike the unpin option, this option uninstalls the program from your computer, not just your *Start* menu.

7. Resize the *Start* menu by clicking and dragging the top or right edge of the *Start* menu.

8. Use a full screen *Start* menu by clicking the **Start** button to open the *Start* menu, selecting **Settings** to open the *Settings* window, clicking the **Personalization** button, clicking the **Start** option at the left, selecting **Use Start full screen**, and clicking the **X** in the upper right to close the *Settings* window (Figure Intro-8).

 - The *Start* menu expands to the full screen when opened.

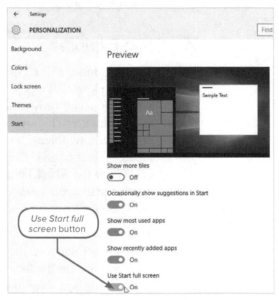

Intro-8 Use full screen *Start* menu

Customize the Taskbar

The *Taskbar* is located at the bottom of the Windows desktop, and you can quickly open an app by clicking a button on the *Taskbar* rather than opening it from the *Start* menu. You can customize the *Taskbar* by pinning, unpinning, and rearranging apps on the *Taskbar*.

1. Pin an app to the *Taskbar* by clicking the *Start* menu, right-clicking an app, clicking **More**, and selecting **Pin to taskbar** (Figure Intro-9).
 - You can also pin an app to the *Taskbar* from the *All apps* list in the *Start* menu.
2. Unpin an app from the *Taskbar* by right-clicking an app on the *Taskbar*, and selecting **Unpin from taskbar** (Figure Intro-10).
 - You can also unpin apps from the *Taskbar* by right-clicking the app in the *Start* menu, clicking **More**, and selecting **Unpin from taskbar**.
3. Rearrange apps on the *Taskbar* by clicking and dragging the app to the desired location on the *Taskbar* and release.

Intro-9 Pin an app to the *Taskbar*

Intro-10 Unpin an app from the *Taskbar*

> **MORE INFO**
>
> If using a touch screen, you can press and hold an app on the *Start* menu or *Taskbar* to display the app options.

File Explorer

The redesigned *File Explorer* in Windows 10 is a window that opens on your desktop where you can browse for files stored on your computer (Figure Intro-11). You can open a file or folder, move or copy items, create folders, and delete files or folders. Click the **Start** button and select **File Explorer** to open a *File Explorer* window.

The *File Explorer* has different areas:

Intro-11 *File Explorer* window

- *Navigation pane*: The *Navigation* pane displays folders on the left. The ***Quick access*** area at the top of the *Navigation* pane displays shortcuts to favorite folders. You can pin or unpin folders in the *Quick access* area of the *Navigation* pane.
- *Navigation buttons*: The navigation buttons (*Back, Forward, Recent location,* and *Up*) are located directly above the *Navigation* pane and below the *Ribbon*. Use these buttons to navigate a File Explorer window.
- *Folder pane*: When you select a folder in the *Navigation* pane, the contents of the folder displays in the *Folder* pane to the right of the *Navigation* pane. Double-click a folder or file in the *Folder* pane to open it.
- *Ribbon*: The *Ribbon* at the top of the *File Explorer* is collapsed by default. When you click a tab on the *Ribbon*, it expands to display the options on the tab. The main tabs of

the *Ribbon* are ***File***, ***Home***, ***Share***, and ***View***. Other context-sensitive tabs open when you select certain types of files. For example, the *Picture Tool Manage* tab opens when you select a picture file.

- ***Quick Access toolbar***: The *Quick Access* toolbar is above the *Ribbon*. From the *Quick Access* toolbar, you can click the **New Folder** button to create a new folder or **Properties** to display the properties of a selected file or folder. You can add buttons, such as *Rename*, to the *Quick Access* toolbar.
- ***Search***: The *Search* text box is located on the right of the *File Explorer* window below the *Ribbon*. Type key words in the *Search* text box to find files or folders.

OneDrive

OneDrive is a cloud storage area where you can store files in a private and secure online location that you can access from any computer. When you store your files in *OneDrive*, the files are actually saved on both your computer and on the cloud. *OneDrive* synchronizes your files so when you change a file it is automatically updated on the *OneDrive* cloud.

With Windows 10, the ***OneDrive folder*** is one of your storage location folder options, similar to your *Documents* or *Pictures* folders (Figure Intro-12). You can save, open, and edit your *OneDrive* files from a *File Explorer* folder. Your *OneDrive* folder looks and functions similar to other Windows folders.

In addition to the *OneDrive* folder on your computer, you can also access your *OneDrive* files online using an Internet browser such as Microsoft Edge, Google Chrome, or Mozilla Firefox. When you access *OneDrive* online using a web browser, you can upload files, create folders, move and copy files and folders, and create Office files using *Office Online* (*Office Online* is discussed in *SLO Intro.2: Using Office 2016*).

Intro-12 *OneDrive* folder in a *File Explorer* window

Intro-13 Log in to *OneDrive* online

▶**HOW TO: Use OneDrive Online**

1. Open an Internet browser window and navigate to the *OneDrive* web site (www.onedrive.live.com), which takes you to the *OneDrive* sign in page.
 - You can use any Internet browser to access *OneDrive* (Microsoft Edge, Google Chrome, Mozilla Firefox).
2. Click the **Sign in** button, type your Microsoft account email address, and click **Next**.
3. Type your Microsoft account password and click **Sign in** (Figure Intro-13). You are taken to your *OneDrive* page.
 - If you are on your own computer, check the **Keep me signed in** box to stay signed in to *OneDrive* when you return to the page.

- The different areas of *OneDrive* are listed under the *OneDrive* heading on the left (Figure Intro-14).
- Click **Files** to display your folders and files in the folder area.
- At the top of the page, buttons and drop-down menus list the different actions you can perform on selected files and folders.

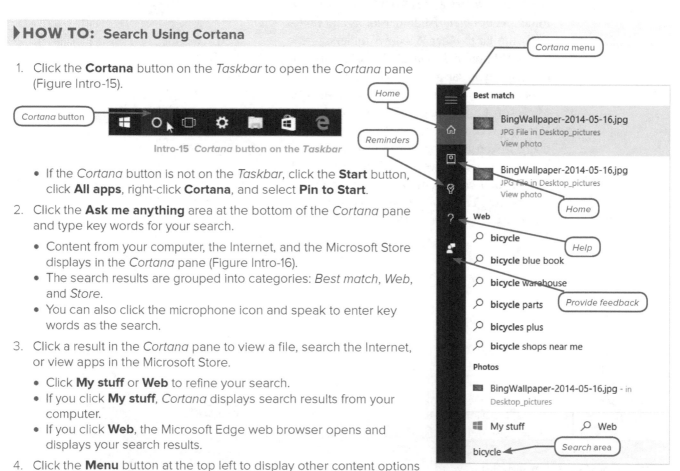

Intro-14 *OneDrive* online environment

Cortana

In addition to using the search tools in the *File Explorer*, you can also use **Cortana**, which is new in Windows 10. While the search feature in the *File Explorer* searches only for content on your computer, *Cortana* searches for content on your computer, on the Internet, and in the Microsoft Store. You can either type key words for a search or use voice commands to search for content.

When you open *Cortana*, other content, such as weather, upcoming appointments, and popular news stories, displays in the *Cortana* pane.

▶HOW TO: Search Using Cortana

1. Click the **Cortana** button on the *Taskbar* to open the *Cortana* pane (Figure Intro-15).

 Intro-15 *Cortana* button on the *Taskbar*

 - If the *Cortana* button is not on the *Taskbar*, click the **Start** button, click **All apps**, right-click **Cortana**, and select **Pin to Start**.

2. Click the **Ask me anything** area at the bottom of the *Cortana* pane and type key words for your search.

 - Content from your computer, the Internet, and the Microsoft Store displays in the *Cortana* pane (Figure Intro-16).
 - The search results are grouped into categories: *Best match*, *Web*, and *Store*.
 - You can also click the microphone icon and speak to enter key words as the search.

3. Click a result in the *Cortana* pane to view a file, search the Internet, or view apps in the Microsoft Store.

 - Click **My stuff** or **Web** to refine your search.
 - If you click **My stuff**, *Cortana* displays search results from your computer.
 - If you click **Web**, the Microsoft Edge web browser opens and displays your search results.

4. Click the **Menu** button at the top left to display other content options in the *Cortana* pane (see Figure Intro-16).

 - The other content options are *Home*, *Notebook*, *Reminders*, *Help*, and *Feedback*.

Intro-16 Use *Cortana* to search your computer, the Internet, and the Microsoft Store

- **Task pane**: Opens on the left or right of the Office application window. Figure Intro-76 shows the *Clipboard* pane, which is available in all Office applications. Task panes are named according to their feature (for example *Clipboard* pane or *Navigation* pane). You can resize a task pane by clicking and dragging its left or right border. Click the **X** in the upper right corner to close a task pane.

ScreenTips

ScreenTips display descriptive information about a button, drop-down list, launcher, or gallery selection. When you place your pointer on an item on the *Ribbon*, a *ScreenTip* displays information about the selection (Figure Intro-77). The *ScreenTip* appears temporarily and displays the command name, keyboard shortcut (if available), and a description of the command.

Intro-77 *Align Left ScreenTip*

Radio Buttons, Check Boxes, and Text Boxes

Dialog boxes and task panes contain a variety of features you can apply using ***radio buttons***, ***check boxes***, ***text boxes***, ***drop-down lists***, and other buttons (Figure Intro-78).

- **Radio button**: A round button you click to select one option from a list of options. A selected radio button has a solid dot inside the round button.
- **Check box**: A square button you click to select one or more options. A check appears in a check box you have selected.
- **Text box**: An area where you can type text.

A task pane or dialog box may also include drop-down lists or other buttons that open additional dialog boxes. Figure Intro-78 shows the *Page Setup*

Intro-78 *Page Setup* dialog box in Excel

dialog box in Excel, which includes a variety of radio buttons, check boxes, text boxes, drop-down lists, and other buttons that open additional dialog boxes (for example the *Print* and *Options* buttons).

Quick Access Toolbar

The ***Quick Access toolbar*** is located above the *Ribbon* on the upper left of each Office application window. It contains buttons to apply commonly used commands such as *Save*, *Undo*, *Redo*, and *Open* (Figure Intro-79). The *Undo* button is a split button. You can click the

Intro-79 *Quick Access* toolbar

button to undo the last action performed or you can click the drop-down arrow to display and undo multiple previous actions.

Customize the Quick Access Toolbar

You can customize the *Quick Access* toolbar to include features you regularly use, such as *Quick Print*, *New*, and *Spelling & Grammar*. The following steps show how to customize the *Quick Access* toolbar in Word. The customization process is similar for the *Quick Access* toolbar in the other Office applications.

▶HOW TO: Customize the Quick Access Toolbar

1. Click the **Customize Quick Access Toolbar** drop-down list on the right edge of the *Quick Access* toolbar (Figure Intro-80).
2. Select a command to add to the *Quick Access* toolbar. The command displays on the *Quick Access* toolbar.
 - Items on the *Customize Quick Access Toolbar* drop-down list with a check mark are commands that are displayed on the *Quick Access* toolbar.
 - Deselect a checked item to remove it from the *Quick Access* toolbar.
3. Add a command that is not listed on the *Customize Quick Access Toolbar* by clicking the **Customize Quick Access Toolbar** drop-down list and selecting **More Commands**. The *Word Options* dialog box opens with the *Quick Access Toolbar* area displayed (Figure Intro-81).
4. Click the **Customize Quick Access Toolbar** drop-down list on the right and select **For all documents** or the current document.
 - If you select *For all documents*, the change is made to the *Quick Access* toolbar for all documents you open in Word.
 - If you select the current document, the change is made to the *Quick Access* toolbar in that document only.
5. Select the command to add from the alphabetic list of commands on the left and click the **Add** button.
 - If you can't find the command you're looking for, click the **Choose commands from** drop-down list and select **All Commands**.
 - The list on the right contains the commands that display on the *Quick Access* toolbar.
6. Rearrange commands on the *Quick Access* toolbar by selecting a command in the list on the right and clicking the **Move Up** or **Move Down** button.
7. Click **OK** to close the *Word Options* dialog box.

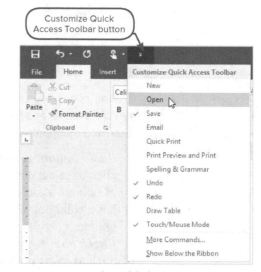

Intro-80 Add a command to the *Quick Access* toolbar

Intro-81 Customize the *Quick Access* toolbar in the *Word Options* dialog box

SLO INTRO. 7

Using Context Menus, the Mini Toolbars, and Keyboard Shortcuts

Most of the commands you use for formatting and editing your files display in groups on the tabs. But many of these features are also available using content menus, mini toolbars, and keyboard shortcuts. You can use these tools to quickly apply formatting or other options to text or objects.

Context Menu

A **context menu** displays when you right-click text, a cell, or an object such as a picture, drawing object, chart, or *SmartArt* (Figure Intro-82). The context menu is a vertical list of options, and the options are context-sensitive, which means they vary depending on what you right-click.

Context menus include options that perform an action (*Cut* or *Copy*), open a dialog box or task pane (*Format Cells* or *Hyperlink*), or display a drop-down list of selections (*Filter* or *Sort*).

Mini Toolbar

The **mini toolbar** is another context menu that displays when you right-click or select text, a cell, or an object in your file (see Figure Intro-82). The

Intro-82 Context menu and mini toolbar

mini toolbar is a horizontal rectangular menu that lists a variety of formatting options. These options vary depending on what you select or right-click. The mini toolbar contains a variety of buttons and drop-down lists. The mini toolbar typically displays above the context menu. The mini toolbar automatically displays when you select text or an object, such as when you select a row of a table in Word or PowerPoint.

Keyboard Shortcuts

You can also use a **keyboard shortcut** to quickly apply formatting or perform commands. A keyboard shortcut is a combination of keyboard keys that you press at the same time. These can include the **Ctrl**, **Shift**, **Alt**, letter, number, and function keys (for example **F1** or **F7**). The following table lists common Office keyboard shortcuts.

Common Office Keyboard Shortcuts

Keyboard Shortcut	Action or Displays	Keyboard Shortcut	Action or Displays
Ctrl+S	Save	Ctrl+Z	Undo
F12	*Save As* dialog *box*	Ctrl+Y	Redo or Repeat
Ctrl+O	*Open* area on the *Backstage* view	Ctrl+1	Single space
Shift+F12	*Open* dialog box	Ctrl+2	Double space
Ctrl+N	New blank file	Ctrl+L	Align left
Ctrl+P	*Print* area on the *Backstage* view	Ctrl+E	Align center
Ctrl+C	Copy	Ctrl+R	Align right
Ctrl+X	Cut	F1	*Help* dialog box
Ctrl+V	Paste	F7	*Spelling* pane
Ctrl+B	Bold	Ctrl+A	Select All
Ctrl+I	Italic	Ctrl+Home	Move to the beginning
Ctrl+U	Underline	Ctrl+End	Move to the end

> **MORE INFO**
> See Appendix A for additional Office 2016 keyboard shortcuts.

Function Keys on a Laptop

Intro-83 Function key

When using a laptop computer, function keys perform specific Windows actions on your laptop, such as increase or decrease speaker volume, open Windows *Settings*, or adjust the screen brightness. So when using a numbered function key, such as **F12** as a shortcut to open the *Save As* dialog box in an Office application, you may need to press the ***function key*** (**Fn** or **fn**) on your keyboard in conjunction with a numbered function key to activate the command (Figure Intro-83). The *function key* is typically located near the bottom left of your laptop keyboard next to the *Ctrl* key.

PAUSE & PRACTICE: INTRO-2

For this project, you work with a document for the American River Cycling Club. You modify the existing document, add document properties, customize the *Quick Access* toolbar, export the document as a PDF file, and share the document.

File Needed: ***ARCCTraining-Intro.docx*** *(Student data files are available in the* Library *of your SIMnet account)*
Completed Project File Names: *[your initials] PP Intro-2a.docx* and *[your initials] PP Intro-2b.pdf*

1. Open Word 2016 and open the ***ARCCTraining-Intro*** file from your student data files. If the file opens in *Protected View*, click the **Enable Editing** button.

2. Save this document as [your initials] PP Intro-2a in the *American River Cycling Club* folder in your *OneDrive* folder.
 a. In *Pause & Practice Intro-1*, you created the *American River Cycling Club* folder in *OneDrive* or other storage area. Save this file in the same location.
 b. If you don't save this file in *OneDrive*, you will not be able to complete steps 7 and 9 in this project.

Intro-84 Apply *Double underline* to selected text.

3. Use a button, drop-down list, and dialog box to modify the document.
 a. Select the first heading, "**What is Maximum Heart Rate?**"
 b. Click the **Bold** button [*Home* tab, *Font* group].
 c. Click the **Underline** drop-down arrow and select **Double underline** (Figure Intro-84).
 d. Click the **launcher** in the *Font* group [*Home* tab] to open the *Font* dialog box (Figure Intro-85).
 e. In the *Size* area, select **12** from the list or type 12 in the text box.
 f. In the *Effects* area, click the **Small caps** check box to select it.
 g. Click **OK** to close the dialog box and apply the formatting changes.
 h. Select the next heading, "**What is Target Heart Rate?**"
 i. Repeat steps 3b–g to apply formatting to selected text.

Intro-85 *Font* dialog box

4. Add document properties.
 a. Click the **File** tab to display the *Backstage* view.
 b. Select **Info** on the left. The document properties display on the right.
 c. Click the **Add a title** text box and type ARCC Training.
 d. Click the **Show All Properties** link near the bottom to display additional document properties.
 e. Click the **Specify the subject** text box and type Heart rate training.
 f. Click the **Specify the company** text box and type American River Cycling Club.
 g. Click the **Back** arrow on the upper left to close the *Backstage* view and return to the document.

5. Customize the *Quick Access* toolbar.
 a. Click the **Customize Quick Access Toolbar** drop-down arrow and select **Open** (Figure Intro-86).
 b. Click the **Customize Quick Access Toolbar** drop-down arrow again and select **Spelling & Grammar**.

Customize Quick Access Toolbar button

Intro-86 *Customize Quick Access Toolbar* drop-down list

c. Click the **Customize Quick Access Toolbar** drop-down arrow again and select **More Commands**. The *Word Options* dialog box opens (Figure Intro-87).

d. Select **Insert Comment** in the list of commands on the left.

e. Click the **Add** button to add it to your *Quick Access* toolbar list on the right.

f. Click **OK** to close the *Word Options* dialog box.

g. Click the **Save** button on the *Quick Access* toolbar to save the document.

Intro-87 Customize the *Quick Access* toolbar in the *Word Options* dialog box

6. Export the file as a PDF file.

a. Click the **File** tab to go to the *Backstage* view.

b. Select **Export** on the left.

c. Select **Create PDF/XPS Document** and click the **Create PDF/XPS** button. The *Publish as PDF or XPS* dialog box opens (Figure Intro-88).

d. Select the **American River Cycling Club** folder in your *OneDrive* folder as the location to save the file.

e. Type [your initials] PP Intro-2b in the *File name* area.

f. Deselect the **Open file after publishing** check box if it is checked.

g. Select the **Standard (publishing online and printing)** radio button in the *Optimize for* area.

h. Click **Publish** to close the dialog box and create a PDF version of your file.

Intro-88 *Publish as PDF or XPS* dialog box

7. Get a link to share a document with your instructor. If your file is not saved in *OneDrive*, skip steps 7 and 9.

a. Click the **Share** button in the upper right of the Word window. The *Share* pane opens on the right side of your document.

b. Click **Get a sharing link** at the bottom of the *Share* pane.

c. Click the **Create an edit link** button.

d. Click **Copy** to copy the edit link (Figure Intro-89).

Intro-89 Copy a sharing link

8. Save and close the document (Figure Intro-90).

American River Cycling Club
www.arcc.org Cycling...a way of life info@arcc.org

WHAT IS MAXIMUM HEART RATE?

The maximum heart rate is the highest your pulse rate can get. To calculate your **predicted maximum heart rate**, use this formula:

(Example: a 40-year-old's predicted maximum heart rate is 180.)

Your actual maximum heart rate can be determined by a graded exercise test. Please note that some medicines and medical conditions might affect your maximum heart rate. If you are taking medicines or have a medical condition (such as heart disease, high blood pressure, or diabetes), always ask your doctor if your maximum heart rate/target heart rate will be affected.

WHAT IS TARGET HEART RATE?

You gain the most benefits and decrease the risk of injury when you exercise in your target heart rate zone. Usually this is when your exercise heart rate (pulse) is 60 percent to 85 percent of your maximum heart rate. Do not exercise above 85 percent of your maximum heart rate. This increases both cardiovascular and orthopedic risk and does not add any extra benefit.

When beginning an exercise program, you might need to gradually build up to a level that is within your target heart rate zone, especially if you have not exercised regularly before. If the exercise feels too hard, slow down. You will reduce your risk of injury and enjoy the exercise more if you don't try to over-do it.

To find out if you are exercising in your target zone (between 60 percent and 85 percent of your maximum heart rate), use your heart rate monitor to track your heart rate. If your pulse is below your target zone (see the chart below), increase your rate of exercise. If your pulse is above your target zone, decrease your rate of exercise.

	Age	Predicted Max Heart Rate	Target Heart Rate (60-85% of Max)
MAX AND TARGET HEART RATES	20	✓ 200	120-170
	25	✓ 195	117-166
	30	✓ 190	114-162
	35	✓ 185	111-157
	40	✓ 180	108-153
	45	✓ 175	105-149
	50	✓ 170	102-145
	55	✓ 165	99-140
	60	✓ 160	96-136
	65	✓ 155	93-132
	70	✓ 150	90-128

Intro-90 PP Intro-2a completed

9. Email the sharing link to your instructor.
 a. Using your email account, create a new email to send to your instructor.
 b. Include an appropriate subject line and a brief message in the body.
 c. Press **Ctrl+V** to paste the link to your document in the body of the email.
 d. Send the email message.

Organizing and Customizing Folders and Files

The more you use your computer to create and use files, the more important it is to stay organized. You can use *folders* to store related files, which makes it easier for you to find, edit, and share your files. For example, you can create a folder for the college you attend. Inside the college folder, you can create a folder for each of your courses. Inside each of the course folders you might create a folder for student data files, solution files, and group projects. Folders can store any type of files; you are not limited to Office files.

Create a Folder

In *SLO Intro.3: Creating, Saving, Closing, and Opening Files*, you learned how to create a new folder when saving an Office file in the *Save As* dialog box. You can also create a Windows folder using *File Explorer*. You can create folders inside other folders.

▶HOW TO: Create a Windows Folder

1. Click the **Start** button and select **File Explorer** to open a *File Explorer* window.
 - Your folders and computer locations are listed on the left.
2. Select the location in the *Navigation* pane on the left where you want to create a new folder.
3. Click **Home** tab, and click the **New folder** button [*New* group]. A new folder is created (Figure Intro-91).
 - The *New Folder* button is also on the *Quick Access* toolbar in the *File Explorer* window.
4. Type the name of the new folder and press **Enter**.

Intro-91 Create a new Windows folder

▶ **ANOTHER WAY**

Ctrl+Shift+N creates a new folder in a Windows folder.

Move and Copy Files and Folders

Moving a file or folder is cutting it from one location and pasting it in another location. Copying a file or folder creates a copy of it, and you can paste in another location so the file or folder is in two or more locations. If you move or copy a folder, the files in the folder are moved or copied with the folder. Move or copy files and folders using the *Move to* or *Copy to* buttons on the *Home* tab of *File Explorer*, keyboard shortcuts (**Ctrl+X**, **Ctrl+C**, **Ctrl+V**), or the drag-and-drop method.

To move or copy multiple folders or files at the same time, press the **Ctrl** key and select multiple items to move or copy. Use the **Ctrl** key to select or deselect multiple non-adjacent files or folders. Use the **Shift** key to select a range of files or folders. Click the first file or folder in a range, press the **Shift** key, and select the last file or folder in the range to select all of the items in the range.

▶HOW TO: Move or Copy a File or Folder

1. Click the **Start** button and select **File Explorer** to open a *File Explorer* window.
2. Select a file or folder to move or copy.
 - Press the **Ctrl** key to select multiple files or folders.
3. Click the **Home** tab in the *File Explorer* window.
4. Click the **Move to** or **Copy to** button [*Organize* group] and select the location where you want to move or copy the file or folder (Figure Intro-92).

Intro-92 Move or copy a selected file or folder

 - If the folder you want is not available, select **Choose location** to open the *Move Items* or *Copy Items* dialog box.
 - To use the keyboard shortcuts, press **Ctrl+X** to cut the file or folder or **Ctrl+C** to copy the file or folder from its original location, go to the desired new location, and press **Ctrl+V** to paste it.
 - To use the drag-and-drop method to move a file or folder, select the file or folder and drag and drop to the new location.
 - To use the drag-and-drop method to copy a file or folder, press the **Ctrl** key, select the file or folder, and drag and drop to the new location.

> ### ANOTHER WAY
> Right-click a file or folder to display the context menu where you can select **Cut**, **Copy**, or **Paste**.

Rename Files and Folders

You can rename a file or folder in a *File Explorer* window. When you rename a file or folder, only the file or folder name changes, and the contents of the file or folder do not change.

▶HOW TO: Rename a File or Folder

1. Click the **Start** button and select **File Explorer** to open a *File Explorer* window.
2. Select the file or folder you want to rename.
3. Click the **Rename** button [*Home* tab, *Organize* group] (see Figure Intro-92).
4. Type the new name of the file or folder and press **Enter**.

> ### ANOTHER WAY
> Select a file or folder to rename, press **F2**, type the new name, and press **Enter**. You can also right-click a file or folder and select **Rename** from the context menu.

Delete Files and Folders

You can also easily delete files and folders. When you delete a file or folder, it is moved from its current location to the ***Recycle Bin*** on your computer where deleted items are stored. If a file or folder is in the *Recycle Bin*, you can restore this item to its original location or move it to a different location. You also have the option to permanently delete a file or folder; the item is deleted and not moved to the *Recycle Bin*. If an item is permanently deleted, you do not have the restore option.

▶HOW TO: Delete Files and Folders

1. Open a *File Explorer* window and select the file or folder you want to delete.
 - You can select multiple files and folders to delete at the same time.
2. Click the **Delete** drop-down arrow [*Home* tab, *Organize* group] to display the list of delete options (Figure Intro-93).
 - The default action when you click the *Delete* button (not the drop-down arrow) is *Recycle*.
3. Delete a file by selecting **Recycle**, which moves it to the *Recycle Bin*.
 - *Recycle* deletes the item(s) and moves it to the *Recycle Bin*.
 - When you *Recycle* an item, you are not by default prompted to confirm the deletion. Select **Show recycle confirmation** from the *Delete* drop-down list to receive a confirmation dialog box each time you delete or recycle an item.
4. Permanently delete a file by selecting **Permanently delete**. A confirmation dialog box opens. Click **Yes** to confirm the deletion.
 - *Permanently delete* deletes the item(s) from your computer.

Intro-93 Delete selected folder

> ▶ **ANOTHER WAY**
>
> Press **Ctrl+D** or the **Delete** key on your keyboard to recycle selected item(s).
> Press **Shift+Delete** to permanently delete selected item(s).

Create a Zipped (Compressed) Folder

If you want to share multiple files or a folder of files with classmates, coworkers, friends, or family, you can *zip* the files into a ***zipped folder*** (also called a ***compressed folder***). For example, you can't attach an entire folder to an email message, but you can attach a zipped folder to an email message. Compressing files and folders decreases their size. You can zip a group of selected files, a folder, or a combination of files and folders, and then share the zipped folder with others through email or in a cloud storage location such as *OneDrive*.

▶HOW TO: Create a Zipped (Compressed) Folder

1. Open a *File Explorer* window.
2. Select the file(s) and/or folder(s) you want to zip (compress).
3. Click the **Zip** button [*Share* tab, *Send* group] (Figure Intro-94). A zipped folder is created.
 - The name of the zipped folder is the name of the first item you selected to zip. You can rename this folder.
 - The icon for a zipped folder looks similar to the icon for a folder except it has a vertical zipper down the middle of the folder.

Intro-94 Create a zipped folder

Extract a Zipped (Compressed) Folder

If you receive a zipped folder via email or download a zipped folder, save the zipped folder to your computer and then you can *extract* its contents. Extracting a zipped folder creates a regular Windows folder from the zipped folder.

▶HOW TO: Extract a Zipped (Compressed) Folder

1. Select the zipped folder to extract.
2. Click the **Compressed Folder Tools** tab.
3. Click the **Extract all** button (Figure Intro-95). The *Extract Compressed (Zipped) Folders* dialog box opens (Figure Intro-96).
4. Click **Extract** to extract the folder.
 - Both the extracted folder and the zipped folder display in the folder where they are located.
 - If you check the **Show extracted files when complete** check box, the extracted folder will open after extracting.

Intro-95 Extract files from a zipped folder

Intro-96 *Extract Compressed (Zipped) Folders* dialog box

For this project, you copy and rename files in your *OneDrive* folder on your computer, create a folder, move files, create a zipped folder, and rename a zipped folder.

Files Needed: *[your initials] PP Intro-1a.pptx*, *[your initials] PP Intro-1b.xlsx*, *[your initials] PP Intro-2a.docx*, *[your initials] PP Intro-2b.docx*, and **ARCC_Membership-Intro.accdb** *(Student data files are available in the* Library *of your SIMnet account)*
Completed Project File Names: *[your initials] PP Intro-1a.pptx*, *[your initials] PP Intro-1b.xlsx*, *[your initials] PP Intro-2a.docx*, *[your initials] PP Intro-2b.docx*, *[your initials]PP Intro-3.accdb*, and **ARCC Italy Tour-2018** (zipped folder)

1. Copy and rename a file.
 a. Click the Windows **Start** button and click **File Explorer** to open a *File Explorer* window. If *File Explorer* is not available on the *Start* menu, use *Cortana* to find and open a *File Explorer* window.
 b. Browse the *File Explorer* window to locate your student data files.
 c. Select the **ARCC_Membership-Intro** file.
 d. Click the **Copy to** button [*Home* tab, *Organize* group] and select **Choose location** from the drop-down list to open the *Copy Items* dialog box.
 e. Browse to locate the *American River Cycling Club* folder you created in *Pause & Practice: Intro-1.*
 f. Select the **American River Cycling Club** folder and click the **Copy** button to copy the **ARCC_Membership-Intro** file to the *American River Cycling Club* folder (Figure Intro-97). The *Copy Items* dialog box closes and the file is copied.

Intro-97 *Copy Items* dialog box

 g. In the open *File Explorer* window, browse to locate the *American River Cycling Club* folder and double-click the folder to open it.
 h. Click the **ARCC_Membership-Intro** file in the *American River Cycling Club* folder to select it.
 i. Click the **Rename** button [*Home* tab, *Organize* group], type [your initials] PP Intro-3 as the new file name, and press **Enter** (Figure Intro-98).

2. Create a new folder and move files.
 a. With the *American River Cycling Club* folder still open, click the **New folder** button [*Home* tab, *New* group] (see Figure Intro-98).
 b. Type ARCC Italy Tour as the name of the new folder and press **Enter**.

Intro-98 Rename a file

c. Select the *[your initials] PP Intro-1a* file.

d. Press the **Ctrl** key, select the *[your initials] PP Intro-1b*, *[your initials] PP Intro-2a*, *[your initials] PP Intro-2b*, and *[your initials] PP Intro-3* files, and release the **Ctrl** key. All five files should be selected.

e. Click the **Move to** button [*Home* tab, *Organize* group] and select **Choose location** to open the *Move Items* dialog box (Figure Intro-99).

f. Browse to locate the *ARCC Italy Tour* folder in the *Move Items* dialog box.

g. Select the **ARCC Italy Tour** folder and click the **Move** button to move the selected files to the *ARCC Italy Tour* folder.

h. Double-click the **ARCC Italy Tour** folder to open it and confirm the five files are moved.

i. Click the **Up** or **Back** arrow above the *Navigation* pane to return to the *American River Cycling Club* folder (see Figure Intro-99).

3. Create a zipped folder.

 a. Select the **ARCC Italy Tour** folder.

 b. Click the **Zip** button [*Share* tab, *Send* group]. A zipped (compressed) folder is created.

 c. Place the insertion point at the end of the zipped folder name, type –2018, and press **Enter** (Figure Intro-100).

4. Email the zipped folder to your instructor.

 a. Use your email account to create a new email to send to your instructor.

 b. Include an appropriate subject line and a brief message in the body.

 c. Attach the **ARCC Italy Tour-2018** zipped folder to the email message and send the email message.

Intro-99 Move selected files to a different folder

Intro-100 Create a zipped folder

Chapter Summary

Explore the features of Windows 10 (p. 213).

- **Windows 10** is a computer operating system.
- A **Microsoft account** is a free account you create. When you create a Microsoft account, you are given an email address, a **OneDrive** account, and access to **Office Online**.
- The **Windows desktop** is the working area of Windows 10 and the **Taskbar** displays at the bottom of the desktop. You can rearrange icons on and pin applications to the *Taskbar*.
- Use **Start menu** in Windows 10 to select a task. You can pin applications to the *Start* menu and customize the arrangement of apps.
- **Most Used** items, **File Explorer**, **Settings**, the **Power** button, and **All apps** options display to the left of the *Start* menu.
- **Apps** are the applications or programs installed on your computer. App buttons are arranged in tiles on the Windows 10 *Start* menu.
- The **Microsoft Store** is a Windows 10 app you use to search for and install apps on your computer.
- You can install both **traditional apps** and **modern apps** in Windows 10.
- You can customize the *Start* menu and *Taskbar* to add, remove, or arrange apps.
- The *File Explorer* is a window that displays files and folders on your computer.
- *OneDrive* is the cloud storage area where you can store files in a private and secure online location.
- In Windows 10, the **OneDrive folder** is one of your file storage location options.
- You can access your *OneDrive* folders and files using an Internet browser window.
- **Cortana** is a search tool in Windows 10 used to locate information on your computer and the Internet.
- **Task View** displays all open apps and windows as tiles on your desktop where you can select an app or window to display or close.
- **Settings** is the redesigned *Control Panel* where you change many Windows settings.

- The **Action Center** displays notifications and buttons to open many common Windows settings and features.

Use the basic features of Office 2016 and navigate the Office 2016 working environment (p. 222).

- **Office 2016** is application software that includes **Word**, **Excel**, **Access**, **PowerPoint**, **Outlook**, **OneNote**, and **Publisher**.
- *Office 2016* and **Office 365** include the same application products, but they differ in how you purchase them.
- **Office desktop apps** are the full-function Office 2016 or 365 products you install on your laptop or desktop computer.
- **Office universal apps** are a scaled-down version of Office applications you install on a tablet or mobile device.
- **Office Online** is free online software that works in conjunction with your online *Microsoft* account.
- When you open each of the Office applications, a **Start page** displays where you can open an existing file or create a new file.
- In the **Backstage view** in each of the Office applications, you can perform many common tasks such as saving, opening an existing file, creating a new file, printing, and sharing.
- **Tell Me** is the Office help feature that displays Office commands related to specific topics.
- Use the mouse (or touch pad) on your computer to navigate the pointer on your computer screen. Use the pointer or click buttons to select text or objects.
- When using Office 2016 on a touch-screen computer, use the touch screen to perform actions. You can choose between **Touch Mode** and **Mouse Mode** in Office applications.

Create, save, close, and open Office files (p. 229).

- You can create a new Office file from the *Start* page or *Backstage* view of the Office application you are using.
- When you save a file for the first time, assign the file a file name.

- You can create folders to organize saved files, and you can save a file as a different file name.
- A variety of different file types are used in each of the Office applications.
- You can close an Office file when you are finished working on it. If the file has not been saved or changes have been made to the file, you are prompted to save the file before closing.
- In each of the Office applications, you can open an existing file from the *Start* page or from the *Open* area on *Backstage* view.

Intro.4 Customize the view and display size in Office applications and work with multiple Office files (p. 237).

- Each Office application has a variety of display views.
- You can select an application view from the options on the **View tab** or the view buttons on the **Status bar**.
- The **Zoom** feature changes the display size of your file.
- You can **minimize**, **restore down**, or **maximize** an open Office application window.
- You can work with multiple Office files at the same time and switch between open files.
- **Snap Assist** enables you to arrange an open window on one side of your computer screen and select another window to fill the other side of the screen.

Intro.5 Print, share, and customize Office files (p. 240).

- You can print a file in a variety of formats. The *Print* area on the *Backstage* view lists your print options and displays a preview of your file.
- You can export a file as a **PDF (portable document format)** file and save the PDF file to post to a web site or share with others.
- **Document properties** store information about a file.
- You can share Office files in a variety of ways and allow others to view or edit shared files. To share a file with others, save the file in *OneDrive*.

- Program options are available on the *Backstage* view. You can use the program options to apply global changes to an Office application.

Intro.6 Use the *Ribbon,* tabs, groups, dialog boxes, task panes, galleries, and the *Quick Access* toolbar (p. 245).

- The **Ribbon** appears at the top of an Office window. It contains **tabs** and **groups** with commands to format and edit files.
- The **Ribbon Display Options** provides different ways the *Ribbon* displays in Office applications.
- Within groups on each tab are a variety of **buttons**, **drop-down lists**, and **galleries**.
- **Dialog boxes** contain additional features not always displayed on the *Ribbon*.
- Click the **launcher** in the bottom right corner of some groups to open a dialog box for that group.
- A **ScreenTip** displays information about commands on the *Ribbon*.
- Dialog boxes contain **radio buttons**, **check boxes**, **drop-down lists**, and **text boxes** you can use to apply features.
- The **Quick Access toolbar**, which contains buttons that allow you to perform commands, displays in all Office applications in the upper left.
- You can add or remove commands on the *Quick Access* toolbar.

Intro.7 Use context menus, mini toolbars, keyboard shortcuts, and function keys in Office applications (p. 249).

- A **context menu** displays when you right-click text or an object. The context menu contains different features depending on what you right-click.
- The **mini toolbar** is another context menu that displays formatting options.
- You can use **keyboard shortcuts** to apply features or commands.
- Some of the numbered **function keys** perform commands in Office applications. On laptops, you may have to press the function key (**Fn** or **fn**) to activate the numbered function keys.

261

Intro.8 Organize and customize Windows folders and Office files (p. 254).

- **Folders** store and organize your files.
- You can create, move, or copy files and folders. Files stored in a folder are moved or copied with that folder.
- You can rename a file to change the file name.
- When you delete a file or folder, it is moved to the **Recycle Bin** on your computer by default. Alternatively, you can permanently delete files and folders.
- You can **zip** files and/or folders into a **zipped (compressed) folder** to email or share multiple files as a single file.
- When you receive a zipped folder, you can **extract** the zipped folder to create a regular Windows folder and access its contents.

Check for Understanding

The SIMbook for this text (within your SIMnet account) provides the following resources for concept review:

- Multiple choice questions
- Short answer questions
- Matching exercises

For these projects, you use your *OneDrive* to store files. If you don't already have a Microsoft account, see *SLO Intro.1: Using Windows 10* for information about creating a free personal Microsoft account.

Guided Project Intro-1

For this project, you organize and edit files for Emma Cavalli at Placer Hills Real Estate. You extract a zipped folder, rename files, manage multiple documents, apply formatting, and export as a PDF file. [Student Learning Outcomes Intro.1, Intro.2, Intro.3, Intro.4, Intro.5, Intro.6, Intro.7, Intro.8]

Files Needed: ***CavalliFiles-Intro*** (zipped folder) *(Student data files are available in the* Library *of your SIMnet account)*
Completed Project File Names: ***PHRE*** folder containing the following files: ***BuyerEscrowChecklist-Intro***, ***CavalliProspectingLetter-Intro***, *[your initials]* ***Intro-1a.accdb***, *[your initials]* ***Intro-1b.xlsx***, *[your initials]* ***Intro-1c.docx***, and *[your initials]* ***Intro-1d.docx***

Skills Covered in This Project

- Copy and paste a zipped folder.
- Create a new folder in your *OneDrive* folder.
- Extract a zipped folder.
- Move a file.
- Rename a file.
- Open a Word document.

- Use *Task View* to switch between two open Word documents.
- Save a Word document with a different file name.
- Change display size.
- Use a mini toolbar, keyboard shortcut, context menu, and dialog box to apply formatting to selected text.
- Export a document as a PDF file.

1. Copy a zipped folder and create a new *OneDrive* folder.
 a. Click the Windows **Start** button and click **File Explorer** to open the *File Explorer* window. If *File Explorer* is not available on the *Start* menu, use *Cortana* to find and open the *File Explorer* window.
 b. Browse in the *File Explorer* window to locate your student data files.
 c. Select the ***CavalliFiles-Intro*** zipped folder from your student data files and press **Ctrl+C** or click the **Copy** button [*Home* tab, *Clipboard* group] to copy the folder.
 d. Select your ***OneDrive*** folder on the left of the *File Explorer* window, and click the **New folder** button [*Home* tab, *New* group] to create a new folder. If you don't have *OneDrive* available, create the new folder in a location where you store your files.
 e. Type PHRE and press **Enter**.
 f. Press **Enter** again to open the *PHRE* folder or double-click the folder to open it.
 g. Press **Ctrl+V** or click the **Paste** button [*Home* tab, *Clipboard* group] to paste the copied ***CavalliFiles-Intro*** zipped folder in the *PHRE* folder.

2. Extract a zipped folder.
 a. Select the ***CavalliFiles-Intro*** zipped folder.
 b. Click the **Compressed Folder Tools Extract** tab and click the **Extract all** button. The *Extract Compressed (Zipped) Folders* dialog box opens.
 c. Uncheck the **Show extracted files when complete** box if it is checked.
 d. Click the **Extract** button (Figure Intro-101). The zipped folder is extracted, and the *PHRE* folder now contains two *CavalliFiles-Intro* folders. One folder is zipped and the other is a regular folder.

e. Select the zipped **CavalliFiles-Intro** folder and click the **Delete** button [*Home* tab, *Organize* group] to delete the zipped folder.

3. Move and rename files.
 a. With the *PHRE* folder still open, double-click the **CavalliFiles-Intro** folder to open it.
 b. Click the first file, press and hold the **Shift** key, and click the last file to select all four files.
 c. Press **Ctrl+X** or click the **Cut** button [*Home* tab, *Clipboard* group] to cut the files from the current location (Figure Intro-102).
 d. Click the **Up** arrow to move up to the *PHRE* folder.
 e. Press **Ctrl+V** or click the **Paste** button [*Home* tab, *Clipboard* group] to paste and move the files.
 f. Select the **Cavalli files-Intro** folder and press **Delete** to delete the folder.
 g. Select the **CavalliPHRE-Intro** file and click the **Rename** button [*Home* tab, *Organize* group].
 h. Type [your initials] Intro-1a and press **Enter**.
 i. Right-click the **FixedMortgageRates-Intro** file and select **Rename** from the context menu.
 j. Type [your initials] Intro-1b and press **Enter**.

4. Open two Word documents and rename a Word document.
 a. Press the **Ctrl** key and click the **BuyerEscrowChecklist-Intro** and **CavalliProspectingLetter-Intro** files to select both files.
 b. Press the **Enter** key to open both files in Word. If the files open in *Protected View*, click the **Enable Editing** button.
 c. Press the **Task View** button on your *Taskbar* (Figure Intro-103). All open windows display as tiles on your desktop.
 d. Select the **BuyerEscrowChecklist-Intro** document.
 e. Click the **File** tab to open the *Backstage* view and select **Save As** on the left.
 f. Click the **Browse** button to open the *Save As* dialog box.
 g. Type [your initials] Intro-1c in the *File name* text box and click **Save**. The file is saved in the *PHRE* folder.
 h. Click the **X** in the upper right corner of the Word window to close the document. The *CavalliProspectingLetter-Intro* document remains open.

5. Change display size and edit and rename a Word document.
 a. Press the **Task View** button on your *Taskbar* and select the **CavalliProspectingLetter-Intro** document.

Intro-101 Extract a zipped folder

Intro-102 *Cut* files to move from a folder

Intro-103 *Task View* button on the *Taskbar*

b. Click the **Zoom In** or **Zoom Out** button in the bottom right of the document window to change the display size to **120%** (Figure Intro-104).

c. Select "**Placer Hills Real Estate**" in the first body paragraph of the letter and the mini toolbar displays (Figure Intro-105).

d. Click the **Bold** button on the mini toolbar to apply bold formatting to the selected text.

e. Select "**Whitney Hills resident**" in the first sentence in the second body paragraph and press **Ctrl+I** to apply italic formatting to the selected text.

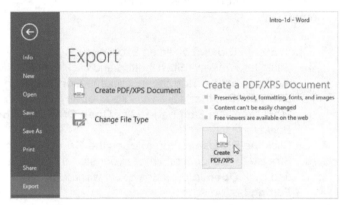

Intro-105 Use the mini toolbar to apply formatting

f. Select the text that reads "**Emma Cavalli**," below "Best regards,".

g. Right-click the selected text and select **Font** from the context menu to open the *Font* dialog box.

h. Check the **Small Caps** box in the *Effects* area and click **OK** to close the *Font* dialog box.

i. With "**Emma Cavalli**" still selected, click the **Bold** button [*Home* tab, *Font* group].

j. Click the **File** tab, select **Save As** on the left, and click the **Browse** button to open the *Save As* dialog box.

k. Type [your initials] Intro-1d in the *File name* text box and click **Save**.

6. Export a Word document as a PDF file.

a. With the ***[your initials] Intro-1d*** still open, click the **File** tab to open the *Backstage* view.

b. Select **Export** on the left, select **Create PDF/XPS Document** in the *Export* area, and click the **Create PDF/XPS** button (Figure Intro-106). The *Publish as PDF or XPS* dialog box opens.

c. Deselect the **Open file after publishing** check box if it is checked.

d. Select the **Standard (publishing online and printing)** radio button in the *Optimize for* area.

e. Type [your initials] Intro-1e in the *File name* text box and click **Publish**.

f. Click the **File** tab to open the *Backstage* view and select **Save** on the left.

g. Click the **X** in the upper right corner of the Word window to close the document and Word.

7. Your *PHRE* folder should contain the files shown in Figure Intro-107.

Intro-106 Export as a PDF file

Intro-107 Intro-1 completed

Guided Project Intro-2

For this project, you modify an Excel file for Hamilton Civic Center. You create a folder, rename a file, add document properties, use *Tell Me* to search for a topic, share the file, and export a file as a PDF file.
[Student Learning Outcomes Intro.1, Intro.2, Intro.3, Intro.5, Intro.6, Intro.7, Intro.8]

File Needed: ***HCCYoga-Intro.xlsx*** *(Student data files are available in the* Library *of your SIMnet account)*
Completed Project File Names: ***[your initials] Intro-2a.xlsx*** and ***[your initials] Intro-2b.pdf***

Skills Covered in This Project

- Open Excel and an Excel workbook.
- Create a new folder.
- Save an Excel workbook with a different file name.
- Add document properties to a file.
- Use *Tell Me* to search for a topic.
- Open a Word document.
- Share a file.
- Export a file as a PDF file.

1. Open Excel 2016 and open an Excel workbook.
 a. Click the Windows **Start** button and click **Excel 2016** to open this application. If Excel 2016 is not available on the *Start* menu, click the **Cortana** button on the *Taskbar*, type Excel, and then click **Excel 2016** in the search results to open it.
 b. From the Excel *Start* page, click **Open Other Workbooks** to display the *Open* area of the *Backstage* view.
 c. Click the **Browse** button to open the *Open* dialog box.
 d. Browse to the location where your student data files are stored, select the ***HCCYoga-Intro*** file, and click **Open** to open the Excel workbook. If the file opens in *Protected View*, click the **Enable Editing** button.

2. Save a file as a different file name in your *OneDrive* folder.
 a. Click the **File** tab to open the *Backstage* view and select **Save As** on the left.
 b. Click the **Browse** button to open the *Save As* dialog box.
 c. Select the **OneDrive** folder on the left and click the **New folder** button to create a new folder (Figure Intro-108). If *OneDrive* is not a storage option, select another location to create the new folder.
 d. Type HCC and press **Enter**.
 e. Double-click the **HCC** folder to open it.
 f. Type [your initials] Intro-2a in the *File name* area and click **Save** to close the dialog box and save the file.

Intro-108 Create a new folder from the *Save As* dialog box

3. Add document properties to the Excel workbook.
 a. Click the **File** button to open the *Backstage* view and select **Info** on the left if it is not already selected. The document properties displays on the right.
 b. Place your insertion point in the *Title* text box ("Add a title") and type Yoga Classes as the worksheet title.

c. Click the **Show All Properties** link at the bottom of the list of properties to display more properties (Figure Intro-109).

d. Place your insertion point in the *Company* text box and type Hamilton Civic Center as the company name.

e. Click the **Back** arrow in the upper left of the *Backstage* window to return to the Excel workbook.

4. Use *Tell Me* to search for a topic.

a. Click the **Tell Me** search box at the top of the *Ribbon* and type Cell formatting (Figure Intro-110).

b. Select **Get Help on "Cell formatting"** to open the *Excel 2016 Help* dialog box.

c. Click the first result link to display information about the topic.

d. Click the **Back** arrow to return to the search list.

e. Click the **X** in the upper right corner to close the *Excel 2016 Help* dialog box.

Intro-110 Use *Tell Me* to search for a topic

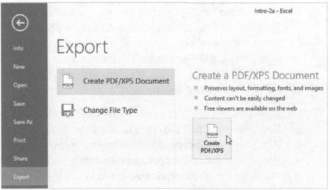

Intro-109 Add document properties

5. Share an Excel workbook with your instructor. If your file is not saved in *OneDrive*, skip step 5.

a. Click the **Share** button in the upper right of the Excel worksheet. The *Share* pane opens on the right side of the worksheet (Figure Intro-111).

b. Type your instructor's email address in the *Invite people* area.

c. Select **Can edit** from the drop-down list below the email address if it is not already selected.

d. Type a brief message in the body text box.

e. Click the **Share** button.

f. Click the **X** in the upper right corner of the *Share* pane to close the pane.

g. Press **Ctrl+S** to save the worksheet.

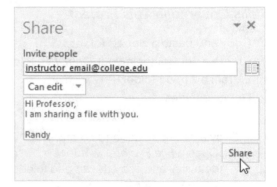

Intro-111 *Share* pane

6. Export an Excel file as a PDF file.

a. Click the **File** tab to open the *Backstage* view.

b. Select **Export** on the left, select **Create PDF/XPS Document** in the *Export* area, and click the **Create PDF/XPS** button (Figure Intro-112). The *Publish as PDF or XPS* dialog box opens.

c. Deselect the **Open file after publishing** check box if it is checked.

Intro-112 Export as a PDF file

d. Select the **Standard (publishing online and printing)** radio button in the *Optimize for* area.

e. Type [your initials] Intro-2b in the *File name* text box and click **Publish**.

7. Save and close the Excel file.

a. Click the **File** tab to open the *Backstage* view and select **Save** on the left.

b. Click the **X** in the upper right corner of the Excel window to close the file and Excel.

Independent Project Intro-3

For this project, you organize and edit files for Courtyard Medical Plaza. You extract a zipped folder, delete a folder, move files, rename files, export a file as a PDF file, and share a file.
[Student Learning Outcomes Intro.1, Intro.2, Intro.3, Intro.5, Intro.8]

File Needed: *CMPFiles-Intro* (zipped folder) *(Student data files are available in the Library of your SIMnet account)*
Completed Project File Names: *[your initials] Intro-3a.pptx*, *[your initials] Intro-3a-pdf.pdf*, *[your initials] Intro-3b.accdb*, *[your initials] Intro-3c.xlsx*, and *[your initials] Intro-3d.docx*

Skills Covered in This Project

- Copy and paste a zipped folder.
- Create a new folder in your *OneDrive* folder.
- Extract a zipped folder.
- Delete a folder.
- Move a file.
- Rename a file.
- Open a PowerPoint presentation.
- Export a file as a PDF file.
- Open a Word document.
- Share a file.

1. Copy a zipped folder and create a new *OneDrive* folder.

a. Open a *File Explorer* window, browse to locate the **CMPFiles-Intro** zipped folder in your student data files and copy the zipped folder.

b. Go to your *OneDrive* folder and create a new folder named Courtyard Medical Plaza within the *OneDrive* folder. If *OneDrive* is not a storage option, select another location to create the new folder.

2. Paste a copied folder, extract the zipped folder, and move files.

a. Paste the zipped folder in the *Courtyard Medical Plaza* folder.

b. Extract the zipped folder and then delete the zipped folder.

c. Open the **CMPFiles-Intro** folder and move all of the files to the *Courtyard Medical Plaza* folder.

d. Return to the *Courtyard Medical Plaza* folder to confirm the four files were moved.

e. Delete the **CMPFiles-Intro** folder.

3. Rename files in the *Courtyard Medical Plaza* folder.

a. Rename the **CMPStayingActive-Intro** PowerPoint file to [your initials] Intro-3a.

b. Rename the **CourtyardMedicalPlaza-Intro** Access file to [your initials] Intro-3b.

c. Rename the **EstimatedCalories-Intro** Excel file to [your initials] Intro-3c.

d. Rename the **StayingActive-Intro** Word file to [your initials] Intro-3d.

4. Export a PowerPoint file as a PDF file.

a. From the *Courtyard Medical Plaza* folder, open the *[your initials] Intro-3a* file. The file opens in PowerPoint. If the file opens in *Protected View*, click the **Enable Editing** button.

 b. Export this file as a PDF file. Don't have the PDF file open after publishing and optimize for **Standard** format.

 c. Save the file as **[your initials] Intro-3a-pdf** and save in the *Courtyard Medical Plaza* folder.

 d. Close the PowerPoint file and exit PowerPoint.

5. Share a file with your instructor. If your files are not saved in *OneDrive*, skip step 5.

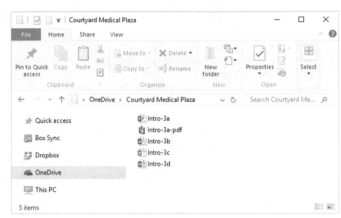

 a. Return to your *Courtyard Medical Plaza* folder and open the **Intro-3d** file. The file opens in Word. If the file opens in *Protected View*, click the **Enable Editing** button.

 b. Open the *Share* pane.

 c. Type your instructor's email address and select **Can edit** from the permission drop-down list.

 d. Type a brief message and **Share** the file.

 e. Close the *Share* pane.

 f. Save and close the document and exit Word.

6. Close the *File Explorer* window containing the files for this project (Figure Intro-113).

Intro-113 Intro-3 completed

Independent Project Intro-4

For this project, you modify a Word file for Life's Animal Shelter. You create a folder, rename a document, add document properties, modify a document, create a sharing link, export a document as a PDF file, and create a zipped folder.
[Student Learning Outcomes Intro.1, Intro.2, Intro.3, Intro.5, Intro.6, Intro.7, Intro.8]

File Needed: **LASSupportLetter-Intro.docx** *(Student data files are available in the Library of your SIMnet account)*
Completed Project File Names: **[your initials] Intro-4a.docx**, **[your initials] Intro-4b.pdf**, and **LAS files** (zipped folder)

Skills Covered in This Project

- Open a Word document.
- Create a new folder.
- Save a file with a different file name.

- Apply formatting to selected text.
- Add document properties to the file.
- Create a sharing link.
- Export a file as a PDF file.
- Create a zipped folder.

1. Open a Word document, create a new folder, and save the document with a different file name.
 a. Open Word 2016.
 b. From the Word *Start* page, open the **LASSupportLetter-Intro** document from your student data files. If the file opens in *Protected View*, click the **Enable Editing** button.
 c. Open the **Save As** dialog box and create a new folder named LAS in your *OneDrive* folder. If *OneDrive* is not a storage option, select another location to create the new folder.

 d. Save this document in the *LAS* folder and use [your initials] Intro-4a as the file name.

2. Apply formatting changes to the document using a dialog box, keyboard shortcut, and mini toolbar.
 a. Select "**To**:" in the memo heading and use the launcher to open the *Font* dialog box.
 b. Apply **Bold** and **All caps** to the selected text.
 c. Repeat the formatting on the other three memo guide words "**From**:," "**Date**:," and "**Subject**:".
 d. Select "**Life's Animal Shelter**" in the first sentence of the first body paragraph and press **Ctrl+B** to apply bold formatting.
 e. Select the first sentence in the second body paragraph ("**Would you again consider** . . .") and use the mini toolbar to apply **italic** formatting.

3. Add the following document properties to the document:
Title: Support Letter
Company: Life's Animal Shelter

4. Get a link to share this document with your instructor and email your instructor the sharing link.
 a. Open the *Share* pane and click **Get a sharing link** at the bottom of the *Share* pane.
 b. Create an edit link to send to your instructor.
 c. Copy the edit link.
 d. Open the email you use for this course and create a new email message to send to your instructor.
 e. Type your instructor's email address, include an appropriate subject line, and type a brief message in the body of the email message.
 f. Paste (**Ctrl+V**) the sharing link in the body of the email message and send the message.
 g. Click the **Task View** button on the Windows *Taskbar* and select the *Intro-4a* document to display this document.
 h. Close the *Share* pane.
 i. Use the **Save** command on the *Quick Access* toolbar to save the file before continuing.

7. Export this document as a PDF file.
 a. Export this file as a PDF file. Don't have the PDF file open after publishing and optimize for **Standard** format.
 b. Save the file as [your initials] Intro-4b and save in the *LAS* folder.
 c. Save and close the document and exit Word.

8. Create a zipped folder.
 a. Using *File Explorer*, open the *LAS* folder in your *OneDrive* folder.
 b. Select the two files and create a zipped folder.
 c. Rename the zipped folder LAS files.

9. Close the open *File Explorer* window (Figure Intro-114).

Intro-114 Intro-4 completed

Challenge Project Intro-5

For this project, you create folders to organize your files for this class and share a file with your instructor.
[Student Learning Outcomes Intro.1, Intro.5, Intro.8]

Files Needed: Student data files for this course
Completed Project File Name: Share a file with your instructor

Using *File Explorer*, create *OneDrive* folders to contain all of the student data files for this class. Organize your files and folders according to the following guidelines:

- Create a *OneDrive* folder for this class.
- Create a *Student data files* folder inside the class folder.
- Copy and paste the student data files in the *Student data files* folder.
- Extract student data files and delete the zipped folder.
- Create a *Solution files* folder inside the class folder.
- Inside the *Solution files* folder, create a folder for each chapter.
- Create a folder to store miscellaneous class files such as the syllabus and other course handouts.
- Open one of the student data files and share the file with your instructor.

Challenge Project Intro-6

For this project, you save a file as a different file name, customize the *Quick Access* toolbar, share a file with your instructor, export a file as a PDF file, and create a zipped folder.
[Student Learning Outcomes Intro.1, Intro.2, Intro.3, Intro.5, Intro.6, Intro.8]

File Needed: Use an existing Office file
Completed Project File Names: *[your initials] Intro-6a* and *[your initials] Intro-6b*

Open an existing Word, Excel, or PowerPoint file. Save this file in a *OneDrive* folder and name it [your initials] Intro-6a. If you don't have any of these files, use one from your Pause & Practice projects or select a file from your student data files.

With your file open, perform the following actions:

- Create a new folder on OneDrive and save the file to this folder using a different file name.
- Customize the *Quick Access* toolbar to add command buttons. Add commands such as *New*, *Open*, *Quick Print*, and *Spelling* that you use regularly in the Office application.
- Share your file with your instructor. Allow your instructor to edit the file.
- Export the document as a PDF file. Save the file as [your initials] Intro-6b and save it in the same *OneDrive* folder as your open file.
- Zip the files in the folder.

WORD

Microsoft® Office

IN PRACTICE

word

Creating and Editing Documents

CHAPTER OVERVIEW

Microsoft Word (Word) has been and continues to be the leading word processing software in both the personal and business markets. Word improves with each new version and is used for creating and editing personal, business, and educational documents. Word allows you to create letters, memos, reports, flyers, brochures, and mailings without a vast amount of computer knowledge. This chapter covers the basics of creating and editing a Word document.

STUDENT LEARNING OUTCOMES (SLOs)

After completing this chapter, you will be able to:

SLO 1.1 Create, save, and open a Word document (p. 277).

SLO 1.2 Customize a document by entering and selecting text, using word wrap, and using *AutoComplete*, *AutoCorrect*, and *AutoFormat* features (p. 281).

SLO 1.3 Enhance a document using paragraph breaks, line breaks, spaces, and non-breaking spaces (p. 284).

SLO 1.4 Edit a document using cut, copy, paste, the *Clipboard*, and the undo, redo, and repeat features. (p. 289).

SLO 1.5 Customize a document using different fonts, font sizes, and attributes (p. 292).

SLO 1.6 Enhance a document using text alignment and line and paragraph spacing (p. 302).

SLO 1.7 Finalize a document using Word's research and proofing tools (p. 306).

SLO 1.8 Apply custom document properties to a document (p. 310).

CASE STUDY

Throughout this book you have the opportunity to put into practice the application features that you are learning. Each chapter begins with a case study that introduces you to the Pause & Practice projects in the chapter. These Pause & Practice projects give you a chance to apply and practice key skills realistic and practical context. Each chapter contains three to five Pause & Practice projects.

Placer Hills Real Estate (PHRE) is a real estate company with regional offices throughout central California. PHRE encourages agents to use standard formats for their business documents. This ensures consistency in document appearance while also allowing agents to personalize their correspondence to customers and colleagues. In the Pause & Practice projects in this chapter, you create a business document related to the real estate business.

WORD

Pause & Practice 1-1: Create a business letter in block format with mixed punctuation.

Pause & Practice 1-2: Edit the business letter using copy, paste, and *Format Painter*. Modify the font, font size, color, style, and effects of selected text.

Pause & Practice 1-3: Finalize the business letter by modifying line spacing and paragraph spacing, changing paragraph alignment, translating text, using research and proofing tools, and adding document properties.

> **MORE INFO**
>
> *Appendix B* (online resource) contains examples of business documents.

SLO 1.1 **Creating, Saving, and Opening Documents**

In Microsoft Word, you can create a variety of document types. Your creativity and knowledge of Word enables you to create, edit, and customize high-quality and professional-looking documents. You can create Word documents from a new blank document, from existing Word templates, or from existing documents. Word allows you to save documents in a variety of formats.

Create a New Document

All new documents are based on the ***Normal template*** (*Normal.dotm*). When you create a new Word document, a blank document displays in the Word window. This document has default fonts, font sizes, line and paragraph spacing, and margins, all of which are controlled by the *Normal* template.

> **HOW TO: Create a New Document**
>
> 1. Click the **File** tab to open the *Backstage* view.
> - When you first open Word, the *Start* page is displayed. You can open a new blank document from the *Start* page.
> 2. Click the **New** button (Figure 1-1).
> 3. Select **Blank document**. A new blank document opens in Word.

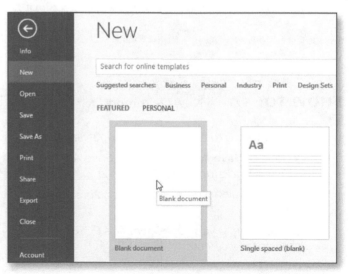

1-1 Open a new blank document

> **ANOTHER WAY**
>
> **Ctrl+N** opens a new blank document.

Save a Document

When you create a blank document, Word automatically assigns a generic file name to this document, such as *Document1*. Save all your new documents using the **Save As dialog box**. You can save a Word document in a variety of file formats. By default, a Word document is saved as a **.docx** file. Other types of Word files are discussed throughout this text. The following table lists some of the more commonly used file formats.

Save Formats

Type of File	File Extension	Uses
Word Document	.docx	Standard Word 2016 document
Word Macro-Enabled Document	.docm	Word document with embedded macros
Word 97-2003 Document	.doc	Word document that is compatible with previous versions of Microsoft Word
Word Template	.dotx	Create a new document based upon a template
Word Macro-Enabled Template	.dotm	Create a new document based upon a template with embedded macros
Portable Document Format (PDF)	.pdf	Similar to a picture of a document that is used to preserve the formatting of a document
Rich Text Format (RTF)	.rtf	Generic file format that can be read by many different types of word processing programs while retaining the basic format of the document
Plain Text	.txt	Files contain only text with no special formatting and can be opened with most word processing programs
Open Document Text	.odt	Format used in the Open Office word processing program

▶ HOW TO: Save a New Document

1. Click the **File** tab to open the *Backstage* view.
2. Click **Save** or **Save As** to display the *Save As* area on the *Backstage* view (Figure 1-2).
3. Select the location where you want to store your document.
 - You can save to your *OneDrive*, *This PC*, or other storage device.

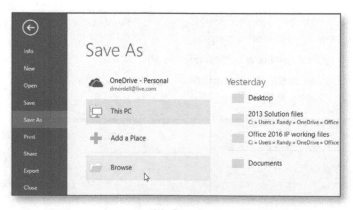

1-2 *Save As* area of the *Backstage* view

4. Click the **Browse** button or select a recently used folder in the *Folders* area on the right to open the *Save As* dialog box (Figure 1-3).

5. In the *Save As* dialog box, browse to the location on your *OneDrive*, computer, USB drive, or other storage device to save the file.

6. Type the file name in the *File name* area.

7. Click the **Save** button.

1-3 *Save As* dialog box

> **ANOTHER WAY**
>
> **F12** opens the *Save As* dialog box. When using a laptop computer, you might have to press the **Fn** (Function) key and the **F12** key to open the *Save As* dialog box.

After you have named and saved a document, you can save changes to the document without opening the *Save As* dialog box in the following ways:

- Press **Ctrl+S**.
- Click the **Save** button on the *Quick Access* toolbar.
- Select **Save** from the *Backstage* view.

Save As a Different File Name

You can save a document as a different name by opening the *Save As* dialog box and typing a new file name. When you save a file with a different file name, the original document is not changed and is still available. Saving with a different file name creates a new version of the original document, but the new document has a different file name.

> **HOW TO: Save As a Different File Name**

1. Click the **File** tab to open the *Backstage* view.

2. Click the **Save As** button to display the *Save As* area.

3. Click the **Browse** button or select a recent folder to open the *Save As* dialog box (see Figure 1-3).
 - From within Word (not the *Backstage* view), you can also press **F12** to open the *Save As* dialog box.
 - On some laptops, you might have to press the **Fn** (Function key) and the **F12** key to open the *Save As* dialog box.

4. In the *Save As* dialog box, browse to a location to save the file.

5. Type the file name in the *File name* area.

6. Click the **Save** button.

 MORE INFO

Avoid saving too many different versions of the same document. Rename only when you have a good reason to have multiple versions of a document.

Open a Document

You can open an existing document from your computer, *OneDrive*, other storage location, or an attachment from an email. After you open a document, you can edit the content and save the changes to the document.

▶ HOW TO: Open a Document

1. Click the **File** tab to open the *Backstage* view.
2. Click the **Open** button to display the *Open* area on the *Backstage* view.
3. Select the location where the document is stored.
 - You can click **Recent** and select a document on the right to open it.
 - You can also open a document from *OneDrive* or *This PC*.
4. Select a file or folder to open it or click **Browse** to open the *Open* dialog box (Figure 1-4).
5. Select the file and click the **Open** button.
 - If the document opens in *Protected View*, click the **Enable Editing** button.

1-4 **Open** *dialog box*

▶ ANOTHER WAY

Ctrl+F12 opens the *Open* dialog box. Some laptops require **Fn+Ctrl+F12**.

Pin a Frequently Used Document

If you use a document frequently, you can pin it to the *Open* area on the *Backstage* view. Pinned documents appear at the top of the *Recent* documents list so you can quickly open the document. In the *Open* area on the *Backstage* view, click **Recent** and then click the **Pin** icon to the right of a file name to add the document to the *Pinned* area (Figure 1-5). Pinned files display in the *Pinned* area of the *Start* page and *Open* area of the *Backstage* view. Click the pinned file to open it.

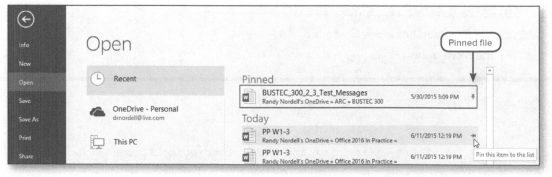

1-5 The *Pinned* area in the *Open* area on the *Backstage* view

Share and Export Options

Word 2016 provides you with sharing and export options. To share a document, you must first save the document to *OneDrive*. You can also export a Word document to PDF format.

From the **Share** (Figure 1-6) and **Export** areas of the *Backstage* view, you have the following options:

- *Share with People* [*Share* area]
- *Email* [*Share* area]
- *Present Online* [*Share* area]
- *Post to Blog* [*Share* area]
- *Create PDF/XPS Document* [*Export* area]
- *Change File Type* [*Export* area]

1-6 *Share* area of the *Backstage* view

SLO 1.2

Entering and Selecting Text

When creating or editing a document, you can type new text, insert text from another document, or copy text from a web page or another document. It is important to understand how to enter text, use word wrap, select text, show or hide formatting symbols, and use *AutoComplete* and *AutoCorrect* options to create professional-looking documents.

Type Text and Use Word Wrap

Word inserts text at the point in the document where the insertion point is flashing. By default, text is aligned at the left margin and the text wraps to the next line when it reaches the right margin, which is called **word wrap**. Press **Enter** to begin a new paragraph or line of text.

Show/Hide Formatting Symbols

The **Show/Hide** feature allows you to display or hide the formatting symbols in your document. By default, *Show/Hide* is turned off and formatting symbols do not display in your document. When the *Show/Hide* feature is turned on, you can see paragraph breaks, line breaks, spaces, tabs, and other formatting symbols that help you create clean documents and edit existing documents (Figure 1-7).

1-7 Document with *Show/Hide* turned on

Click the **Show/Hide** button in the *Paragraph* group on the *Home* tab to toggle on and off *Show/Hide* (Figure 1-8). These symbols do not print, but they allow you to see the formatting that is in the document when you view it on your screen.

Show/Hide button

1-8 Show/Hide button

▶ ANOTHER WAY

Ctrl+Shift+8 turns on and off *Show/Hide*.

▶ MORE INFO

When editing a document that has inconsistent formatting, begin by turning on **Show/Hide**.

Select Text

Word allows you select words, lines, sentences, paragraphs, or the entire document so you can apply formatting, copy, move, or delete selected text. You do this by clicking and dragging the pointer over the desired text, but there are a variety of additional quick methods to select text. The following table lists ways to select text.

Selecting Text

Select	Method
Word	Double-click the word.
Line	Click in the *Selection* area, which is to the left of the left margin. Your pointer becomes a right-pointing arrow.
Multiple lines of text	Click in the *Selection* area and drag up or down.
Sentence	Press **Ctrl+Click**. Hold down the **Ctrl** key and click the sentence.
Paragraph	Double-click in the *Selection* area to the left of the paragraph.
Multiple paragraphs	Click in the *Selection* area to the left of the first line of the paragraph and drag down.
Entire document	Press **Ctrl+A** or **Ctrl+Click** in the *Selection* area. You can also click the **Select** button [*Home* tab, *Editing* group] and choose **Select All**.
Non-adjacent text	Select text, press and hold the **Ctrl** key, and select non-adjacent text.

▶ ANOTHER WAY

F8 is the selection function key.

Press once: Use the arrow keys to select text.
Press twice: Select word.
Press three times: Select sentence.
Press four times: Select paragraph.
Press five times: Select entire document.

Press **Esc** to turn off **F8** selection.

AutoComplete

When you type a day, month, or date, Word uses the *AutoComplete* feature to automatically complete typing the day, month, or date for you, which saves you a few key strokes and allows you to be more efficient and accurate when entering dates. As you begin to type the date, Word displays the information in an *AutoComplete tag* (Figure 1-9). Press **Enter** to accept the *AutoComplete* entry. If you do not want this *AutoComplete* entry, keep typing and the *AutoComplete* entry disappears.

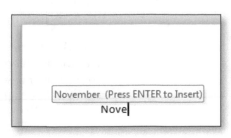

1-9 *AutoComplete* tag

AutoCorrect and AutoFormat

When you're typing, do you ever misspell a word by transposing letters or omitting a letter or adding a letter? Because we all regularly make typing mistakes, the *AutoCorrect* feature recognizes and corrects commonly misspelled words and some grammatical errors. Word automatically makes the following corrections:

- Eliminates two initial capitals in a word
- Capitalizes the first letter of a sentence
- Capitalizes the first letter of table cells
- Capitalizes the names of days
- Corrects accidental usage of the *Caps Lock* key
- Changes fractions such as 3/4 to ¾ and numbers such as 2nd to 2nd.

Word's *AutoFormat* controls the formatting of items such as numbered and bulleted lists, fractions, ordinal numbers, hyphens and dashes, quotes, indents, and hyperlinks. For example, when you type 3/4 followed by a space, *AutoFormat* automatically changes the format of the fraction to ¾.

AutoCorrect Smart Tag

When Word automatically makes a correction or formatting change, you have the option to accept the change, undo the change, stop Word from making the change, or control *AutoCorrect* using the *AutoCorrect Options* dialog box. If you keep typing, the change is accepted. Often when Word automatically corrects a word, you don't even recognize that a change has been made.

If you do not want to accept a change, you can click the *AutoCorrect Options smart tag* on the changed word to open the *AutoCorrect Options* menu (Figure 1-10). For example, when you type reference initials at the end of a business letter, Word automatically capitalizes the first letter. You can undo this automatic capitalization by clicking on the *AutoCorrect Options* smart tag and selecting **Undo Automatic Capitalization**.

1-10 *AutoCorrect Options* smart tag

> ### ANOTHER WAY
> Press **Ctrl+Z** to reverse an automatic correction made by Word.

Add Custom AutoCorrect Entry

The *AutoCorrect* dialog box allows you to customize how Word automatically corrects and formats items in a document. In this dialog box, you can also add custom items to the *AutoCorrect* menu. For example, you can add a custom entry to the *AutoCorrect* menu to correct a misspelled word or type your name every time you type your initials.

> ▶ **HOW TO:** Add a Custom AutoCorrect Entry

1. Click the **File** tab to open the *Backstage* view.
2. Choose the **Options** button to open the *Word Options* dialog box.
3. Click the **Proofing** button on the left.
4. Select the **AutoCorrect Options** button. The *AutoCorrect* dialog box opens (Figure 1-11).
5. Type the text you want to replace in the *Replace* box.
6. Type the word(s) to replace the original text in the *With* box.
7. Choose **Add** to add this custom *AutoCorrect* entry.
 - You can delete *AutoCorrect* entries in the *AutoCorrect* dialog box by selecting the entry and clicking **Delete**.
 - You can also add exceptions to *AutoCorrect* by clicking the **Exceptions** button.
8. Click **OK** to close the *AutoCorrect* dialog box.
9. Click **OK** to close the *Word Options* dialog box.

1-11 *AutoCorrect* dialog box

> **SLO 1.3**

Using Paragraph Breaks, Line Breaks, and Non-Breaking Spaces

It is essential to create attractive and readable documents. Using paragraph and line breaks allows you to break up a document into more readable chunks of information. The different types of breaks can be used for different purposes when you are formatting documents.

Paragraph Breaks

The **Enter** key inserts a **paragraph break** and is marked by a **paragraph symbol** that displays at the end of each paragraph when *Show/Hide* is turned on (Figure 1-12). Use paragraph breaks to control the amount of white space between paragraphs of text within a document.

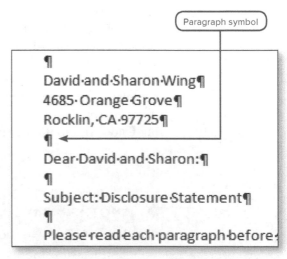

1-12 Paragraph breaks after and between lines

Many formatting features, such as indents, numbering, bullets, text alignment, line spacing, and paragraph spacing, are applied to an entire paragraph. For example, if your insertion point is within a paragraph and you change the line spacing to double space, double spacing is applied to that paragraph only. It is not applied to the entire document or just the line where the insertion point is located. For more on line and paragraph spacing, see *SLO 1.6: Changing Text Alignment, Line Spacing, and Paragraph Spacing*.

Line Breaks

*You can use **line breaks*** to control breaks between lines or sentences of text. The distinction between a paragraph break and a line break is that when line breaks are used, the text separated by line breaks is treated as one paragraph. Press **Shift+Enter** to insert a line break.

You can use line breaks within a numbered or bulleted list to allow for multiple lines of text on separate lines and blank lines between the text without creating a new number or bullet (Figure 1-13). When *Show/Hide* is turned on, the line break symbol is different from the paragraph symbol.

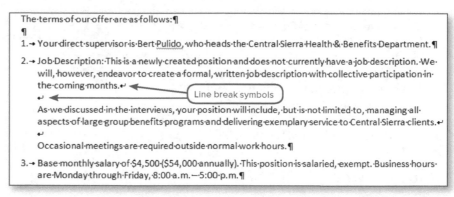

1-13 Line breaks used in a numbered list

Spaces and Non-Breaking Spaces

Spaces are included between words. Use the *spacebar* to insert a space. Current practice now dictates one space after most punctuation marks, including periods, commas, semi-colons, and ending quotation marks. Do not use spaces after a beginning quotation mark, before or after a hyphen in a hyphenated word, or when using a dash.

There might be times when you are typing a document and word wrap separates words that you want to keep together. For example, you might want to keep a person's first and last name or a date together on the same line. In this case, you can use a *non-breaking space* to keep these words together. To insert a non-breaking space, press **Ctrl+Shift+Spacebar** between words rather than inserting a regular space. In Figure 1-14, there is a non-breaking space between 8:00 and a.m., which keeps this information together.

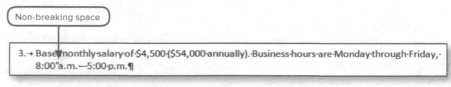

1-14 Non-breaking space used to keep text together

In this project, you create a block format business letter for Emma Cavalli, a realtor consultant for Placer Hills Real Estate. In a block format business letter, all lines begin at the left margin. For more examples of business documents, see *Appendix B* (online resource).

File Needed: None
Completed Project File Name: *[your initials] PP W1-1.docx*

1. Open a new document.
 a. Click the **File** tab, click **New**, and click **Blank document**. You can also click **Blank document** on the *Start* page when you open Word.

2. Save the document.
 a. Click the **File** tab to open the *Backstage* view.
 b. Click **Save** on the left and then click **Browse** to open the *Save As* dialog box (Figure 1-15).
 c. Browse to the location on your computer or storage device to save the document.
 d. Type [your initials] PP W1-1 in the *File name* area.
 e. Click **Save** to save the document.

1-15 *Save As* dialog box

> **ANOTHER WAY**
>
> **F12** opens the *Save As* dialog box. When using a laptop computer, you might have to press the **Fn** (Function) key and the **F12** key to open the *Save As* dialog box.

3. Create an *AutoCorrect* entry.
 a. Click the **File** tab to open the *Backstage* view and select **Options** on the left to open the *Word Options* dialog box.
 b. Click the **Proofing** button on the left and select **AutoCorrect Options** to open the *AutoCorrect* dialog box (Figure 1-16).
 c. Click the **AutoCorrect** tab if it is not already selected.
 d. Type Cavali in the *Replace* area.
 e. Type Cavalli in the *With* area.
 f. Click the **Add** button to add the *AutoCorrect* entry.
 g. Click **OK** to close the *AutoCorrect* dialog box.
 h. Click **OK** to close the *Word Options* dialog box.

4. Click the **Show/Hide** button [*Home* tab, *Paragraph* group] to turn on the *Show/Hide* feature.

1-16 Add an *AutoCorrect* entry

5. Type the current date on the first line of the document. Type the date in month, day, year format (e.g., September 1, 2018).
 a. If the *AutoComplete* tag appears, press **Enter**, and the month is automatically inserted (Figure 1-17).
 b. Continue typing the rest of the date; press **Enter** if the *AutoCorrect* tag displays the current date.
 c. Press **Enter** two times after typing the date.

September (Press ENTER to Insert)
Septe|

1-17 *AutoComplete* tag

6. Type the inside address, salutation, and subject line of the letter.
 a. Type David and Sharon Wing and press **Shift+Enter** to insert a line break.
 b. Type 4685 Orange Grove Road and press **Shift+Enter** to insert a line break.
 c. Type Rocklin, CA 97725 and press **Enter** to insert a paragraph break.
 d. Type Dear Mr. and Mrs. Wing: as the salutation and press **Enter**.
 e. Type Subject: Disclosure Statement as the subject and press **Enter**.

> **MORE INFO**
>
> In the salutation of a business letter, use "Dear" followed by a courtesy title (e.g., Mr., Mrs., Ms., Miss, or Dr.) and the person's last name.

7. Type the body paragraphs of the business letter and insert a non-breaking space.
 a. Type the following paragraph and press **Enter** once at the end of the paragraph. You will not need to press *Enter* at the end of each line since word wrap automatically moves text to the next line as you reach the right margin.

 Please read each paragraph before signing the disclosure statement documents. As you fill out the required disclosure packet, it is critical to the transmission of sale that you give as much information as possible about your residence, no matter how small or insignificant. Please use additional paper if necessary and make a notation to that fact.

 b. Type the following second paragraph and press **Enter** once at the end of the paragraph.

 If there is information about the neighborhood or neighbors that you as a buyer would want to know about, be sure to reveal that information. Be sure to address those types of questions on the Real Estate Transfer Disclosure Statement, item #11 on page 2.

 c. Delete the space between the words "Real" and "Estate" in the second paragraph and press **Ctrl+Shift+Spacebar** to insert a non-breaking space between.

8. Type the closing lines of the business letter.
 a. With your insertion point on the blank line below the second body paragraph, type Best regards, and then press **Enter** two times.

b. Type Emma Cavalli and press **Shift+Enter** to insert a line break.

c. Type Realtor Consultant and press **Shift+Enter** to insert a line break.

d. Type Placer Hills Real Estate and press **Enter** to insert a paragraph break.

e. Type your initials in lowercase letters and press **Shift+Enter** to insert a line break. Word automatically capitalizes the first letter because it is the first letter in a new paragraph.

f. Click the **AutoCorrect Options** smart tag and select **Undo Automatic Capitalization** (Figure 1-18) or press **Ctrl+Z** to undo automatic capitalization.

1-18 *AutoCorrect Options* smart tag

g. On the blank line below the reference initials, type Enclosure. An enclosure notation indicates to the reader that something is enclosed with the letter.

9. Press **Ctrl+S** to save the document (Figure 1-19). You can also save the document by clicking the **Save** button on the *Quick Access* toolbar or in the *Backstage* view.

10. Click the **File** tab and select **Close** (or press **Ctrl+W**) to close the document.

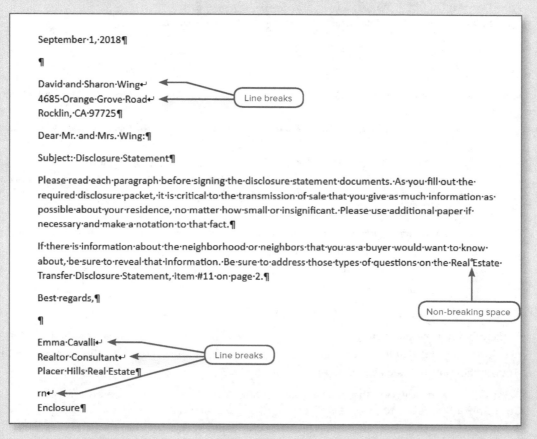

1-19 PP W1-1 completed

Moving and Copying Text

Editing is an important phase in document creation. Editing involves not only proofreading and correcting grammar and spelling mistakes but also arranging text within a document, which can include cutting, copying, and pasting. Word makes it easy to move and copy information within a document or between multiple documents.

Move Text

Moving is actually removing text from one location (cutting) and placing it in another location (pasting). There are two methods you can use to move text: *drag and drop* or *cut and paste*.

> **ANOTHER WAY**
>
> Press **Ctrl+C** to copy.
> Press **Ctrl+X** to cut.
> Press **Ctrl+V** to paste.

▶HOW TO: Move Text Using Drag and Drop

1. Select the text you want to move.
 - Refer to the *Select Text* section in *SLO 1.2: Entering and Selecting Text* for methods of selecting text.
2. Click and hold the selected text with your pointer.
3. Drag the text to the desired new location and release the pointer (Figure 1-20).

Drag pointer

If there is information about the neighborhood or neighbors that you as a buyer would want to know about, be sure to reveal that information. Be sure to address those types of questions on the Real Estate Transfer Disclosure Statement, item #11 on page 2.¶

Make note on the disclosure statement if you have had any work done with or without permits. Some examples include a gas spa, a new water heater, or a wholehouse fan where a trus may have been cut. If you had granate counters installed, that does not require a permit.¶

1-20 Move using drag and drop

There are a variety of ways to move text using cut and paste:

- *Cut and Paste buttons*: Click the **Cut** and **Paste** buttons in the *Clipboard* group on the *Home* tab.
- *Shortcut commands*: Press **Ctrl+X** to cut and **Ctrl+V** to paste.
- *Context menu*: Right-click the selected text to display this menu.

▶HOW TO: Move Text Using Cut and Paste

1. Select the text you want to move.
2. Click the **Cut** button [*Home* tab, *Clipboard* group].
 - You can also press **Ctrl+X** or right-click the selected text and choose **Cut** from the context menu.
3. Place your insertion point in the desired location.
4. Click the **Paste** button [*Home* tab, *Clipboard* group].
 - You can also press **Ctrl+V** or right-click and choose from one of the *Paste Options* from the context menu. *Note: See the* Paste Text and Paste Options *section below for the different paste options available.*

Copy Text

An efficient method of inserting text into a document is to copy it from another location, such as a web page or a different document, and paste it into your document. Copying text leaves the text in its original location and places a copy of the text in a new location.

You can *copy* text by using the drag-and-drop method or the ***Copy*** and ***Paste*** buttons. Use the drag-and-drop method when copying text within the same document. The drag-and-drop method for copying is similar to the method for moving, except that you press the **Ctrl** key when dragging the text to be copied to an additional location.

> ### ▶ HOW TO: Copy Text Using Drag and Drop
>
> 1. Select the text you want to copy.
> 2. Press the **Ctrl** key and click and hold the selected text with your pointer.
> - A+ (plus sign) appears next to your pointer, indicating this text is being copied.
> 3. Drag to the desired new location and release the pointer (Figure 1-21). Release the **Ctrl** key after you have released the pointer.

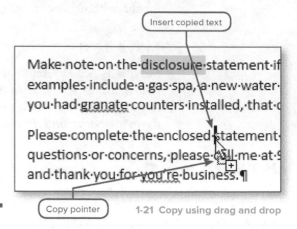

1-21 Copy using drag and drop

Copying text using the following copy and paste method is similar to moving text using the cut and paste method:

- ***Copy and Paste buttons***: Press the **Copy** and **Paste** buttons in the *Clipboard* group on the *Home* tab.
- ***Shortcut commands***: Press **Ctrl+C** to copy and **Ctrl+V** to paste.
- ***Context menu***: Right-click the selected text to display this menu.

Paste Text and Paste Options

You might want to paste plain text without formatting into a document, or you might want to merge the format from the source document into the new document. Word provides multiple paste options.

You have three primary paste options when you use the *Paste* button in the *Clipboard* group (Figure 1-22) or from the context menu:

- ***Keep Source Formatting***: Retains formatting from source document (the document where the text was copied)
- ***Merge Formatting***: Merges formatting from source document and current document
- ***Keep Text Only***: Pastes only unformatted text

The default paste option is *Keep Source Formatting*. In addition to these paste options, there are other context-specific paste options that are available when you paste information from lists, tables, or graphic objects.

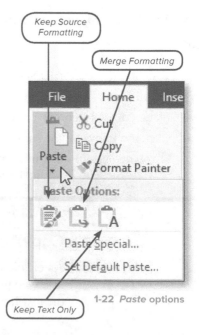

1-22 *Paste* options

> ### ▶ MORE INFO
> If you have trouble with the format of pasted text, try pasting the text as plain text and formatting the text *after* you have pasted it into the document.

Clipboard Pane

When you copy or cut an item from a document, Word stores this information in the ***Clipboard***. From the *Clipboard*, you can select a previously copied item and paste it into a document. When Word is open, the *Clipboard* stores multiple items copied from Word documents and also items from web pages or other documents. The *Clipboard* stores text, pictures, tables, lists, and graphics.

The ***Clipboard pane*** displays all of the items stored in *Clipboard*. To display the *Clipboard* pane, click the **Clipboard** launcher in the bottom right corner of the *Clipboard* group on the *Home* tab (Figure 1-23). The *Clipboard* pane displays on the left side of the Word window and stores up to 24 copied items.

1-23 *Clipboard* launcher

> **MORE INFO**
>
> The ***launcher*** (also referred to as the ***dialog box launcher***) is referred to throughout this text. Click the launcher in the bottom right corner of a group to open a dialog box or pane for additional options.

▶**HOW TO: Use the Clipboard Pane to Paste Text**

1. Select the text you want to copy or cut and click the **Copy** or **Cut** button [*Home* tab, *Clipboard* group].
 - You can also press **Ctrl+C** to copy or **Ctrl+X** to cut selected text.
2. Place your insertion point in the document where you want to paste the text.
3. Click the **Clipboard** launcher to open the *Clipboard* pane on the left side of the Word window (see Figure 1-23).
4. Click the item to paste or click the drop-down arrow to the right of the item and choose **Paste** (Figure 1-24). The selected content from the *Clipboard* is inserted in the document.
 - *Paste All* pastes all of the items in the *Clipboard* at the insertion point in the document.
 - *Clear All* empties the content of the *Clipboard*.
5. Click the **X** in the upper right corner of the *Clipboard* pane to close it.

1-24 *Clipboard* pane

Undo Change

You can undo, redo, or repeat previous actions. All of these commands are available on the ***Quick Access toolbar***, which is above the *Ribbon* on the upper left.

When you click the ***Undo*** button, the last action you performed is reversed. You can undo multiple actions by clicking the **Undo** drop-down arrow to the right of the button and selecting the action to undo (Figure 1-25). For example if you select the third item in the list to undo, the previous two items will also undo.

1-25 *Undo* button on the *Quick Access* toolbar

Redo and Repeat Change

The **Redo** and **Repeat** features are similar to the undo feature. The same button is used for both of these commands, and it is context sensitive. Depending on the previous action performed, the button is either *Redo* or *Repeat*.

When you use the *Undo* button, the *Redo* button is activated so you can redo the previous change (Figure 1-26).

When you perform an action or apply formatting in a document, the *Repeat* button is activated (the icon changes) so you can repeat the previous action or formatting (Figure 1-27). For example, if you need to copy the date or a name into a document in multiple places, you can use the *Repeat* feature to accomplish this task quickly and accurately.

1-26 *Redo* button on the *Quick Access* toolbar

1-27 *Repeat* button on the *Quick Access* toolbar

> **ANOTHER WAY**
>
> Press **Ctrl+Z** to undo.
> Press **Ctrl+Y** to redo or repeat.

SLO 1.5

Changing Fonts, Font Sizes, and Attributes

Word has many features that you can use to customize the appearance of the text within a document. You can change the font and font size; add styles such as bold, italics, and underlining; change the case of the text; add font and text effects; adjust the scale, spacing, and position of text; and change the default font settings. You can use buttons in the *Font* group on the *Home* tab, the *Font* dialog box, and the mini toolbar to apply formatting to text.

Font and Font Size

There are two main categories of fonts: serif and sans serif. **Serif fonts** have structural details (flair) at the top and bottom of most of the letters. Commonly used serif fonts include Cambria, Times New Roman, and Courier New. **Sans serif fonts** have no structural details on the letters. Commonly used sans serif fonts include Calibri, Arial, and Century Gothic.

Font size is measured in **points** (pt.); the larger the point, the larger the font. Most documents use between 10 and 12 pt. font sizes. Titles and headings generally are larger font sizes.

When creating a new document, you can choose a font and font size before you begin typing, and it applies to the entire document. If you want to change the font or font size of existing text, you must first select the text before applying the change.

> **MORE INFO**
>
> The default font and font size in Microsoft Word are *Calibri* and *11 pt.*, respectively.
> Font size of 72 pt. is approximately 1" in height.

1. Select the text you want to change.
2. Click the **Font** drop-down list to display the list of available fonts (Figure 1-28).
 - The *Font* drop-down list has three sections: *Theme Fonts*, *Recently Used Fonts*, and *All Fonts*.
3. Select the font you want to apply to the selected text.
4. Click the **Font Size** drop-down list to display the list of available font sizes (Figure 1-29).

1-28 *Font* drop-down list

1-29 *Font Size* drop-down list

5. Select a font size to apply to selected text.
 - You can also click the **Font Size** area and type a size.
 - Click the **Increase Font Size** and **Decrease Font Size** buttons to increase or decrease the size of the font in small increments.

▶ **ANOTHER WAY**

Press **Ctrl+>** (Ctrl+Shift+.) to *Increase Font Size*.
Press **Ctrl+<** (Ctrl+Shift+,) to *Decrease Font Size*.

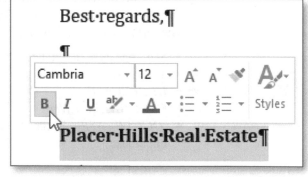

1-30 **Select or right-click text to display the mini toolbar**

The ***mini toolbar*** displays when you select or right-click text (Figure 1-30). You can use the mini toolbar to apply text formatting. Like the content menu, the mini toolbar is context-sensitive and displays different options depending on the selection you right-click.

Bold, Italic, and Underline Font Styles

You can add font styles such as ***Bold***, ***Italic***, and ***Underline*** to fonts to improve their appearance or call attention to specific text. The font style buttons for *Bold*, *Italic*, and *Underline* are available in the *Font* group on the *Home* tab.

To apply a font style, select the desired text and click the **Bold**, **Italic**, or **Underline** button in the *Font* group on the *Home* tab (Figure 1-31). You can also click a font style button to turn on a style, type the text, and click the font style button again to turn off the style.

1-31 *Font* group on the *Home* tab

> **ANOTHER WAY**
>
> **Ctrl+B** applies *Bold* formatting.
> **Ctrl+I** applies *Italic* formatting.
> **Ctrl+U** applies *Underline* formatting.

Other Font Style Buttons

The following are other font styles and effects in the *Font* group on the *Home* tab. Some of these style and effect features are available on the mini toolbar when you select or right-click text:

- *Strikethrough*
- *Subscript*
- *Superscript*
- *Text Effects and Typography*, which includes *Outline, Shadow, Reflection, Glow, Number Styles, Ligatures*, and *Stylistic Sets*
- *Text Highlight Color*
- *Font Color*

Change Case

The ***Change Case*** feature provides a quick and easy way to change the case of a single word or group of words. The *Change Case* button is in the *Font* group on the *Home* tab (Figure 1-32). The different case options are:

- *Sentence case* (capitalizes the first letter of the sentence)
- *lowercase*
- *UPPERCASE*
- *Capitalize Each Word*
- *tOGGLE cASE* (changes letters that are uppercase to lowercase and lowercase letters to uppercase)

1-32 *Change Case* options

Font Dialog Box

The **Font dialog box** combines many of the font *style* and *effect options* in one location for easy access. You can open the *Font* dialog box (Figure 1-33) by clicking the **Font** launcher in the bottom right corner of the *Font* group.

In addition to the *Font*, *Font Style*, and *Size* commands on the *Font* tab, use the *Font* dialog box to change *Font Color*, *Underline Style*, *Underline Color*, and *Effects*. The *Preview* area displays a preview of selected changes, styles, and effects.

The *Advanced* tab lists *Character Spacing* options such as *Scale*, *Spacing*, *Position*, and *Kerning*. From this tab, you can also open the *Format Text Effects* dialog box.

1-33 *Font* dialog box

 ANOTHER WAY

Ctrl+D opens the *Font* dialog box.

Font Color

By default, the font color in a Word document is black. You can change the font color of selected text to add emphasis. The **Font Color** drop-down list in the *Font* dialog box displays a list of available font colors.

▶ **HOW TO: Change Font Color**

1. Select the text you want to be a different color.
2. Click the **Font** launcher [*Home* tab, *Font* group]. The *Font* dialog box opens (Figure 1-34).
3. Click the **Font Color** drop-down arrow to display the list of font colors.
 - The drop-down list of font color options includes *Theme Colors*, *Standard Colors*, and *More Colors*. Theme colors are those colors associated with the theme of the document. For more on themes, see *SLO 2.7: Using Styles and Themes*.
4. Choose **OK** to close the *Font* dialog box.

1-34 Change font color in the *Font* dialog box

 ANOTHER WAY

Change the font color by clicking the **Font Color** button [*Home* tab, *Font* group].

Underline Style and Color

When you underline selected text, the default underline style is a solid black underline. Word provides a variety of additional underline styles. You can also change the color of the underline.

The **_Underline style_** and **_Underline color_** drop-down lists are available in the _Font_ dialog box (Figure 1-35). A preview of how the formatted text will appear in your document is displayed in the _Preview_ area of the _Font_ dialog box.

Font Effects

In the _Font_ dialog box you can choose a variety of font effects from the **_Effects_** section. Some of these font effects are available in the _Font_ group on the _Home_ tab. The following table lists the different font styles and effects.

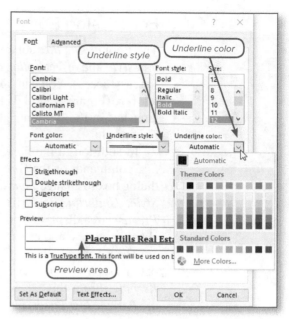

1-35 Change underline style and color

Font Styles and Effects

Style/Effect	Example
Bold	This **word** is in bold.
Italic	This _word_ is in italic.
Bold and Italic	This **_word_** is in bold and italic.
Underline	<u>This sentence is underlined.</u>
Double underline	This word is double underlined.
Underline Words only	This sentence is words only underlined.
Thick underline with color	This word has a thick, colored underline.
Strikethrough	This ~~word~~ has a strikethrough.
Double strikethrough	~~This sentence has a double strikethrough.~~
Subscript	H_2O uses a subscript number.
Superscript	Footnotes and endnotes use superscript numbers or letters.[1]
Small caps	MICROSOFT WORD 2016 is in small caps.
All caps	THIS SENTENCE IS IN ALL CAPS.
Hidden	
Text Highlight Color	This word has a highlight color.
Font Color	This sentence has a font color applied.

▶ MORE INFO

Hidden text appears in your on-screen document, but it does not print or display in print preview.

Character Spacing

The **Character Spacing** options allow you to add more or less space between letters and words. You can also vertically raise and lower letters and words (Figure 1-36).

The **Scale** option allows you to change the horizontal spacing of a word or group of words by a percentage. You can choose from preset percentages, or you can type a custom percentage for scaling.

Spacing has three options: *Normal*, *Expanded*, and *Condensed*. For *Expanded* and *Condensed*, you can choose the amount of points by which to expand the selected text.

The **Position** option vertically raises or lowers text by a selected number of points.

Kerning adjusts the space between letters in a proportional font.

1-36 *Font* dialog box *Advanced* tab

Text Effects

Text Effects add special formatting features to selected text, such as *Outline*, *Shadow*, *Reflection*, and *Glow* (Figure 1-37). The *Text Effects* button is located in the *Font* group on the *Home* tab. There are many preset options for each of the different text effects, and there are more custom text effect options available in the *Format Text Effects* dialog box.

1-37 *Text Effects* button in the *Font* group

1. Select the text you want to format.

2. Click the **Font** launcher [*Home* tab, *Font* group]. The *Font* dialog box opens.

3. Click the **Text Effects** button at the bottom. The *Format Text Effects* dialog box opens (Figure 1-38).

4. Click the **Text Fill & Outline** button to display fill and outline options.

 • Select **Text Fill** or **Text Outline** to expand and display options.

5. Click the **Text Effects** button to display text effect options.

 • Select **Shadow**, **Reflection**, **Glow**, **Soft Edges**, or **3-D Format** to expand and display options.
 • Each of these categories has *Presets* you can choose, or you can customize the effect.

6. Select the text effect of your choice. To the right of each option, you can choose a preset option from the drop-down list or customize the text effect as desired.

7. Click **OK** to close the *Format Text Effects* dialog box and click **OK** to close the *Font* dialog box.

1-38 *Format Text Effects* dialog box

Format Painter

The ***Format Painter*** copies text formatting from selected text and applies the same formatting to other text in the same document or a different document. The *Format Painter* copies font, font size, line spacing, indents, bullets, numbering, styles, and other formatting features in Word. This feature saves time in applying formats and ensures consistency in document format.

1. Select the text that has the formatting you want to copy.

2. Click the **Format Painter** button [*Home* tab, *Clipboard* group] (Figure 1-39). The *Format Painter* icon appears as your pointer (Figure 1-40).

3. Select the text you want to format, and Word applies the formatting to the selected text.

 • To apply formatting to multiple non-adjacent selections, double-click the **Format Painter** button and select the text you want to format. The *Format Painter* remains active until you turn off the feature.
 • Click the **Format Painter** button again or press the **Esc** key to turn off the *Format Painter*.

1-39 *Format Painter* button

1-40 *Format Painter* icon

Clear All Formatting

The **Clear All Formatting** feature allows you to remove all formatting for the selected text and change it back to plain text (Figure 1-41). For example, if you have applied multiple formatting styles and effects to text, you can use the *Clear Formatting* feature rather than individually deselecting all of the formatting options previously selected.

1-41 *Clear All Formatting* button in the *Font* group

> **MORE INFO**
>
> Be careful when using the *Clear Formatting* feature. It not only clears all text formatting but also clears line and paragraph spacing, numbering, bullets, and style formatting.

Change Default Font and Font Size

Recall that the default font in Microsoft Word is *Calibri* and the default font size is *11 pt*. This **default** setting is used on each new blank document you create. Each new document is based on the *Normal.dotm* template. This template stores the default settings for documents and controls document elements such as font, font size, line spacing, paragraph spacing, alignment, and styles.

You can change the default settings on the current document only or change the default settings in the *Normal* template. If you change the default settings for the *Normal* template, each new blank document you create uses this new default font and font size.

> ▶ **HOW TO:** Change the Default Font and Font Size

1. Select the text you want to format.
2. Click the **Font** launcher [*Home* tab, *Font* group]. The *Font* dialog box opens (Figure 1-42).
3. Click the **Font** tab if it is not already selected.
4. Select the font and font size to set as the default.
5. Click the **Set As Default** button on the bottom left. A confirmation dialog box opens giving you two options (Figure 1-43):
 - *This document only?*
 - *All documents based on the Normal template?*
6. Select an option and click **OK** to close the dialog box.
7. Click **OK** to close the *Font* dialog box.

1-42 *Set As Default* button in the *Font* dialog box

> **MORE INFO**
>
> Be careful about changing the default settings in the *Normal* template. Do this only when you are sure you want to make this global default settings change.

1-43 Change default setting confirmation options

In this Pause & Practice project, you customize the content of the block format letter Emma created for Placer Hills Real Estate using cut, copy, paste, and the *Clipboard*. You also enhance your document by changing the font and applying font attributes.

Files Needed: **[your initials] PP W1-1.docx** and **DisclosureStatement-01.docx** (Student data files are available in the Library of your SIMnet account)
Completed Project File Name: **[your initials] PP W1-2.docx**

1. Open the **[your initials] PP W1-1** document completed in *Pause & Practice 1-1*.
 a. Click the **File** tab to open the *Backstage* view and click **Open** on the left.
 b. Click **Browse** to open the *Open* dialog box.
 c. Browse to locate the **[your initials] PP W1-1** document, select the document, and click **Open**.

2. Save this document as **[your initials] PP W1-2**.
 a. Click the **File** tab to open the *Backstage* view and select **Save As** on the left.
 b. Click **Browse** to open the *Save As* dialog box and select the desired location to save the file.
 c. Change the file name to [your initials] PP W1-2.
 d. Click **Save** to rename the document and close the *Save As* dialog box.

3. Open the **DisclosureStatement-01** document from your student date files. Ignore any spelling and grammar errors in this document; you will fix these in *Pause & Practice 1-3*. If the document opens in *Protected View*, click the **Enable Editing** button.

4. In the **DisclosureStatement_01** document, copy both paragraphs of text to the *Clipboard*.
 a. Press **Ctrl+A** to select the text.
 b. Press **Ctrl+C** or click the **Copy** button [*Home* tab, *Clipboard* group].
 c. Close the document without saving.

5. Paste the contents of the *Clipboard* into the document.
 a. In the **[your initials] PP W1-2** document, place your insertion point to the left of "Best regards,".
 b. Click the **Clipboard** launcher [*Home* tab, *Clipboard* group] to display the *Clipboard* pane.
 c. Click the **drop-down arrow** to the right of the copied text in the *Clipboard*.
 d. Select **Paste** (Figure 1-44). The paragraphs of text are pasted in the document at the insertion point.
 e. Close the *Clipboard* pane by clicking the **X** in the upper right corner.

1-44 Paste text from the *Clipboard*

6. Copy the formatting of the first paragraph to the two new paragraphs.
 a. Place your insertion point in the first body paragraph of the letter.
 b. Click the **Format Painter** button [*Home* tab, *Clipboard* group].
 c. Select the last two paragraphs in the body of the letter. Be sure to include the paragraph mark at the end of the last body paragraph (Figure 1-45).

Make note on the disclosure statement if you have had any work done with or without permits. Some examples include a gas spa, a new water heater, or a wholehouse fan where a trus may have been cut. If you had granate counters installed, that does not require a permit.¶
Please complete the enclosed statement by [date] and return it to me. As always, if you have any questions or concerns, please call me at 916-450-3334 or email me at ecavalli@phre.com. Best wishes and thank you for you're business.¶ ⬛ ← *Format Painter* pointer
Best regards,¶

1-45 Use the *Format Painter* to apply formatting to selected text

7. Copy text using the drag-and-drop method.
 a. Click the **Show/Hide** button [*Home* tab, *Paragraph* group] to display formatting symbols.
 b. Select the word **"disclosure"** in the first sentence of the third body paragraph. Double-click a word to select it.
 c. Press the **Ctrl** key and click and hold the selected text with your pointer.
 d. Drag and drop the text between the words "enclosed" and "statement" in the last body paragraph (Figure 1-46). Make sure there is one space before and after the copied word.

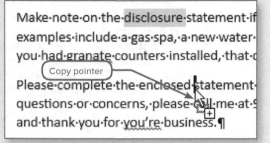

1-46 Copy text using drag and drop

8. Move a paragraph in the body of the letter.
 a. Select the entire third paragraph in the body of the letter (**"Make note . . ."**), including the paragraph mark at the end of the paragraph.
 b. Click the **Cut** button [*Home* tab, *Clipboard* group] or press **Ctrl+X**. The selected paragraph is cut from the document and stored in the *Clipboard*.
 c. Place your insertion point at the beginning of the second body paragraph.
 d. Click the top half of the **Paste** button [*Home* tab, *Clipboard* group] or press **Ctrl+V**.

9. Insert and format a date.
 a. Delete the placeholder "[date]" (including the brackets) in the last paragraph and type the date that is one week from today.
 b. Use month, day, year format (e.g., September 8, 2018).
 c. Select the date you just typed.
 d. Click the **Text Highlight Color** drop-down list button [*Home* tab, *Font* group] and choose the **Yellow** text highlight color (Figure 1-47).

1-47 Apply text highlight color

10. Change the font and font size of the entire document.
 a. Press **Ctrl+A** to select all of the text in the document.
 b. Click the **Font** drop-down list button [*Home* tab, *Font* group] and select **Cambria**.
 c. Click the **Font Size** drop-down list button [*Home* tab, *Font* group] and select **12**.

11. Change the case and spacing of selected text.
 a. Select the word **"Subject"** in the subject line of the document.
 b. Click the **Change Case** button [*Home* tab, *Font* group] and select **UPPERCASE**. Do not use the *Font* dialog box to change the case.
 c. Select the entire subject line.
 d. Click the **Font** launcher [*Home* tab, *Font* group] to open the *Font* dialog box. **Ctrl+D** also opens the *Font* dialog box.
 e. Click the **Advanced** tab.
 f. In the *Character Spacing* area, click the **Spacing** drop-down list and select **Expanded**.
 g. In the *By* area to the right of *Spacing*, click the up arrow to change the character spacing to expanded by **1.5 pt** (Figure 1-48).
 h. Click **OK** to close the *Font* dialog box.

1-48 Change character spacing

12. Apply font styles to selected text.
 a. Select the email address **"ecavalli@phre.com"** in the last body paragraph.
 b. Click the **Font Color** drop-down list button [*Home* tab, *Font* group] and select **Dark Blue** in the *Standard Colors* area.
 c. Click the **Underline** button or press **Ctrl+U** to apply an underline to the selected email address.
 d. Select the writer's name **"Emma Cavalli"** (below "Best regards,").
 e. Click the **Font** launcher in the bottom right corner of the *Font* group to open the *Font* dialog box.
 f. Click the **Font** tab and check the **Small caps** box in the *Effects* area.
 g. Click **OK** to close the *Font* dialog box.
 h. Select the writer's title **"Realtor Consultant"** and click the **Italic** button or press **Ctrl+I**.
 i. Select the company name **"Placer Hills Real Estate"** and click the **Bold** button or press **Ctrl+B**.

13. Save and close the document (Figure 1-49).

September·1,·2018¶

¶

David·and·Sharon·Wing↵
4685·Orange·Grove·Road↵
Rocklin,·CA·97725¶

Dear·Mr.·and·Mrs.·Wing:¶

SUBJECT:·Disclosure·Statement¶

Please·read·each·paragraph·before·signing·the·disclosure·statement·documents.·As·you·fill·out·the·required·disclosure·packet,·it·is·critical·to·the·transmission·of·sale·that·you·give·as·much·information·as·possible·about·your·residence,·no·matter·how·small·or·insignificant.·Please·use·additional·paper·if·necessary·and·make·a·notation·to·that·fact.¶

Make·note·on·the·disclosure·statement·if·you·have·had·any·work·done·with·or·without·permits.·Some·examples·include·a·gas·spa,·a·new·water·heater,·or·a·wholehouse·fan·where·a·trus·may·have·been·cut.·If·you·had·granate·counters·installed,·that·does·not·require·a·permit.¶

If·there·is·information·about·the·neighborhood·or·neighbors·that·you·as·a·buyer·would·want·to·know·about,·be·sure·to·reveal·that·information.·Be·sure·to·address·those·types·of·questions·on·the·Real·Estate·Transfer·Disclosure·Statement,·item·#11·on·page·2.¶

Please·complete·the·enclosed·disclosure·statement·by·September·8,·2018·and·return·it·to·me.·As·always,·if·you·have·any·questions·or·concerns,·please·call·me·at·916-450-3334·or·email·me·at·ecavalli@phre.com.·Best·wishes·and·thank·you·for·you're·business.¶

Best·regards,¶

¶

Emma·Cavalli↵
Realtor·Consultant↵
Placer·Hills·Real·Estate¶

rn↵
Enclosure¶

1-49 PP W1-2 completed

Changing Text Alignment, Line Spacing, and Paragraph Spacing

In addition to word wrap, line breaks, and paragraphs breaks, you can use text alignment, line spacing, and paragraph spacing to control the layout and the white space between parts of your document.

Default Settings

Just as there are default settings for font and font size, there are default settings for paragraph alignment, line spacing, and paragraph spacing. These default settings are stored in the *Normal* template on which all new blank documents are based. The following table summarizes font, line spacing, and paragraph default settings:

Normal Template Default Settings

Setting	Default Setting
Font	Calibri
Font Size	11 pt.
Horizontal Paragraph Alignment	Left
Line Spacing	1.08 lines
Paragraph Spacing—Before	0 pt.
Paragraph Spacing—After	8 pt.

Paragraph Alignment

Paragraph alignment controls how a paragraph is aligned horizontally on the page. A paragraph can be a single word, a group of words, a sentence, or multiple sentences. Paragraphs are separated by paragraph breaks. A group of words using word wrap and line breaks is considered one paragraph.

The four different paragraph alignment options are:

- ***Left*** (default): The paragraph is aligned on the left margin.
- ***Center***: The paragraph is centered between the left and right margins.
- ***Right***: The paragraph begins and is aligned on the right margin.
- ***Justify***: The paragraph is aligned flush with both the left and right margins.

Change the alignment of a paragraph by clicking a paragraph alignment button in the *Paragraph* group on the *Home* tab (Figure 1-50). When changing the alignment of a single paragraph, the entire paragraph need not be selected; the insertion point only needs to be within the paragraph for the alignment to be applied. Text alignment can also be changed in the *Paragraph* dialog box, which we discuss later.

> **ANOTHER WAY**
>
> Press **Ctrl+L** to *Align Text Left*.
> Press **Ctrl+E** to *Center* text.
> Press **Ctrl+R** to *Align Text Right*.
> Press **Ctrl+J** to *Justify* text.

1-50 Paragraph alignment options in the *Paragraph* group

Line Spacing

Line spacing refers to the amount of blank space between lines of text within a paragraph. The default setting in Word is 1.08 lines, which is slightly more than single spacing. Most documents you type are single-spaced or 1.08 line spacing, but there are times you may want to use double-spacing (two lines), such as when typing an academic report.

As with paragraph alignment, you can apply line spacing to an individual paragraph, multiple paragraphs, or an entire document.

You change line spacing using the *Line and Paragraph Spacing* button in the *Paragraph* group on the *Home* tab (Figure 1-51). You can choose from the preset line spacing options, or you can select *Line Spacing Options* and set custom line spacing in the *Paragraph* dialog box.

1-51 *Line and Paragraph Spacing* button in the *Paragraph* group

In the *Paragraph* dialog box, you see different line spacing options (Figure 1-52). The *At Least* and *Exactly* options allow you to specify points of spacing, rather than lines of spacing, between lines of text. The *Multiple* option allows you to set a line spacing option that is not a whole number, such as 1.3 or 2.25 line spacing.

1-52 *Line spacing* options in the *Paragraph* dialog box

Paragraph Spacing

While line spacing controls the amount of space between lines of text in a paragraph, **paragraph spacing** controls the amount of spacing before and after paragraphs. For example, you might want the text of a document to be single-spaced, but you prefer to have more blank space before and after paragraphs. You can use paragraph spacing to accomplish this task.

Before and **After** paragraph spacing is set in points. The default *After* paragraph spacing is 8 pt., which is a little less than one blank line. The default *Before* paragraph spacing is 0 pt.

Change *Before* and *After* paragraph spacing from the *Paragraph* group on the *Layout* tab (Figure 1-53). You can also change *Before* and *After* paragraph spacing in the *Paragraph* dialog box and from the *Line and Paragraph Spacing* button in the *Paragraph* group on the *Home* tab.

From the *Line and Paragraph Spacing* button in the *Paragraph* group on the *Home* tab, you can **Add/Remove Space Before Paragraph** or **Add/Remove Space After Paragraph** (Figure 1-54). These options are context sensitive, depending on whether there is already *Before* or *After* paragraph spacing.

1-53 *Paragraph* group on the *Layout* tab

> ### MORE INFO
>
> Use line breaks to keep lines of text as a single paragraph. *Before* and *After* paragraph spacing is not applied to lines of text where line breaks are used.

1-54 *Add/Remove* paragraph spacing options

Paragraph Dialog Box

The **Paragraph dialog box** combines many of the alignment and spacing options included in the *Paragraph* groups on the *Home* and *Layout* tabs.

▶HOW TO: Change Alignment and Spacing in the Paragraph Dialog Box

1. Select the text you want to format.
2. Click the **Paragraph** launcher [*Home* or *Layout* tab, *Paragraph* group] to open the *Paragraph* dialog box (Figure 1-55).
3. Click the **Alignment** drop-down list in the *General* area and select **Left**, **Centered**, **Right**, or **Justified**.
 - The *Indentation* section of this dialog box lets you control indents. Indents are covered in *SLO 2.3: Using Indents*.
4. In the *Spacing* section, you can change paragraph spacing and line spacing.
 - Type the number of points of spacing or use the up and down arrows.
 - The *Don't add space between paragraphs of the same style* check box controls paragraph spacing between paragraphs of the same style, which is primarily used with numbered and bulleted lists and outlines.
5. Click the **Line spacing** drop-down list to select a line spacing option.
 - You can select **Multiple** and type in a specific line spacing in the *At* area.
6. Notice the *Preview* area displays how your document will look with changes.
7. Click **OK** to close the *Paragraph* dialog box.

1-55 *Paragraph* dialog box

Change Default Line and Paragraph Spacing

You can set default paragraph alignment and spacing in the *Paragraph* dialog box. This process is similar to changing the font and font size default settings.

▶**HOW TO:** Change the Default Paragraph Alignment and Spacing

1. Click the **Paragraph** launcher [*Home* or *Layout* tab, *Paragraph* group] to open the *Paragraph* dialog box.

2. Click the **Indents and Spacing** tab if it is not already selected.

3. Make the desired changes to paragraph and line spacing.

4. Click the **Set As Default** button on the bottom left of the dialog box. Select one of the two options in the confirmation dialog box that opens (Figure 1-56):

 - *This document only?*
 - *All documents based on the Normal template?*

5. Click **OK**.

1-56 Change default setting confirmation options

SLO 1.7

Using Smart Lookup and Proofreading Tools

The words and grammar you use in a document reflect your professionalism and the reputation of your organization. Word provides you with many proofing and editing tools to improve the quality of the documents you produce. The *Smart Lookup* feature allows you to search for information on the Internet without leaving Word. The spelling, grammar, and thesaurus features help you to produce high-quality and professional-looking documents.

Smart Lookup and the Smart Lookup Pane

Smart Lookup is a new research feature in Word 2016. This feature uses Bing, an Internet search engine, to find information about a selected word or words in a Word document without leaving the application. The ***Smart Lookup pane*** displays information from the Internet about the words you select. You have the option to find additional information by clicking a hyperlink in the *Smart Lookup* pane, which opens an Internet browser displaying additional Internet content.

▶**HOW TO:** Use Smart Lookup and the Smart Lookup Pane

1. Select the word or words to research.

2. Click the **Smart Lookup** button [*Review* tab, *Insights* group] (Figure 1-57) to open the *Smart Lookup* pane on the right side of the Word window (Figure 1-58).

 - By default, the *Explore* area is displayed in the *Smart Lookup* pane.
 - Click the **Define** button at the top of the *Smart Lookup* pane to display a definition of the selected word(s).
 - A privacy notice appears in the Smart Lookup pane upon first use.

1-57 *Smart Lookup* button

3. View the research results in the *Smart Lookup* pane.

- To view additional information about a research result, click the result title, which is a hyperlink that will open an Internet browser window displaying additional information about the topic.
- To perform additional research on a different word, select the word in the document and click the **Smart Lookup** button again. The new results appear in the *Smart Lookup* pane.

4. Click the **X** in the upper right corner of the *Smart Lookup* pane to close the pane.

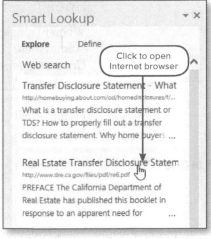

1-58 *Smart Lookup* pane

> ▶ **ANOTHER WAY**
>
> Right-click a word or selected word and select **Smart Lookup** from the context menu.

Automatic Spelling and Grammar Notifications

Recall that Word uses *AutoCorrect* to automatically correct many commonly misspelled words. But there are many ***spelling errors*** that Word does not automatically correct. When you are typing a document, Word is constantly checking the words you type against the words in its dictionary. When Word doesn't recognize a word, it marks it with a -Dot-dash ***red wavy underline***.

Word also checks the grammar of your document and marks potential word choice or ***grammatical errors*** with a ***blue wavy underline***.

> ▶ **MORE INFO**
>
> When Word marks a word as a possible spelling or grammatical error, it does not necessarily mean that the word is misspelled. Many proper nouns are not included in the dictionary.

▶**HOW TO:** Correct Spelling and Grammatical Errors

1. Right-click a word that has a red or blue wavy underline. A context menu opens that provides different editing options (Figure 1-59).

2. Select the correct word from the list to replace the misspelled word. You can also choose from the following editing options:

 - Select **Ignore All** to ignore all instances of this spelling throughout the document.
 - Select **Ignore Once** to ignore a potential grammar error.
 - Select **Add to Dictionary** to add the word to the Word dictionary.

3. Right-click the next item with a wavy red or blue underline to repeat the editing process.

1-59 Correct a spelling error

Spelling and Grammar Panes

When finalizing a document, it is important to proofread it one last time and use the spelling and grammar check. This is especially true with longer documents. You can use the *Spelling and Grammar panes* to check your entire document for potential spelling and grammatical errors.

The *Spelling* and *Grammar* panes are context sensitive. The name of the pane (*Spelling* or *Grammar*) and the available options change depending on whether a potential spelling or grammatical error is detected.

> **HOW TO:** Use the Spelling and Grammar Panes

1. Click the **Spelling & Grammar** button [*Review* tab, *Proofing* group] to open the *Spelling* pane (Figure 1-60).
 - The first potential spelling or grammatical error is displayed in the *Spelling* or *Grammar* pane.
2. If the word does not need to be changed, select **Ignore**, **Ignore All**, or **Add**.
 - If you select *Add*, the selected word is added to the dictionary so it is not detected as a potential error in the future.
3. If the word needs to be changed, select the correct word and select **Change** or **Change All**.
 - *Change* changes the word and *Change All* changes all instances of the misspelled word.
 - A definition of the selected word is displayed below the list of word options.
 - If no word options are available, retype the word in the body of the document.
4. Click **OK** to finish when the dialog box opens indicating the spell and grammar check is complete.

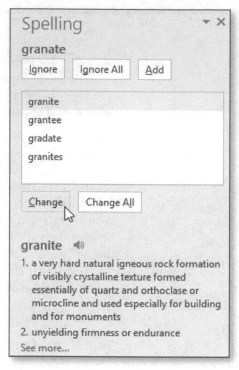

1-60 *Spelling* pane

> **ANOTHER WAY**
>
> **F7** opens the *Spelling and Grammar* pane.

Customize the Dictionary

When you spell check a document, you can easily add a word to the ***Word Dictionary***. When you add a word to the dictionary, Word actually creates a custom dictionary for you. You can manually add or delete words from the custom dictionary. Many proper nouns are marked as a misspelled word. You can add proper nouns you commonly use to the dictionary so they won't be marked as a misspelled word.

> **HOW TO:** Add Words to the Custom Dictionary

1. Click the **File** tab to open the *Backstage* view.
2. Click the **Options** button to open the *Word Options* dialog box.

3. Click the **Proofing** button.

4. Click the **Custom Dictionaries** button. The *Custom Dictionaries* dialog box opens (Figure 1-61).

5. Select the dictionary to edit in the *Dictionary List*.
 - The *RoamingCustom.dic* is typically the default custom dictionary.

6. Click the **Edit Word List** button. Your custom dictionary dialog box opens (Figure 1-62). The words that have been previously added to your dictionary are displayed in the *Dictionary* area.

7. Click in the **Word(s)** area, type a word to add to your dictionary, and click the **Add** button to add the word to your dictionary.
 - To delete a word from the dictionary, select the word and click the **Delete** button.

8. Click **OK** when finished to close the *RoamingCustom.dic* dialog box.

9. Click **OK** to close the *Custom Dictionaries* dialog box.

10. Click **OK** to close the *Word Options* dialog box.

1-61 *Custom Dictionaries* dialog box

1-62 Add word to custom dictionary

The Thesaurus

Word provides a ***Thesaurus*** feature that you can use to find ***synonyms*** of words to add variety to your writing. A varied vocabulary indicates a more educated and professional writer.

There are two ways to use the *Thesaurus* to find synonyms. The first and quickest way is to select a word in the document and use the context menu (right-click) to replace a selected word with an appropriate synonym.

▶HOW TO: Find Synonyms Using the Context Menu

1. Right-click the word you want to replace with an appropriate synonym. The context menu displays.

2. Place your pointer on **Synonyms**. Another context menu appears with a list of synonym choices.

3. Select the synonym you prefer (Figure 1-63). The selected synonym replaces the selected word in the text and the menus close.

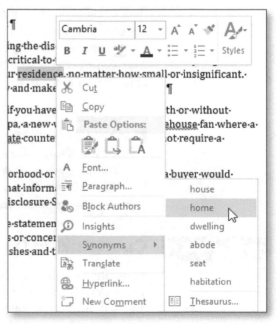

1-63 Use *Thesaurus* to find synonyms

You can also use the *Thesaurus* feature in the *Thesaurus* pane. This method allows you to search for synonyms of any word, not just a selected word in your document.

1-64 *Thesaurus* pane

▶HOW TO: Use the Thesaurus

1. Click the **Thesaurus** button [*Review* tab, *Proofing* group]. The *Thesaurus* pane opens on the right side of the Word window (Figure 1-64).

2. Type a word in the *Search* text box and press **Enter** or click the **Search** button (magnifying glass icon). A list of synonyms appears in the *Thesaurus* area.

3. Choose from the synonyms listed.
 - Click the **arrow** to the right of the word to display the drop-down list. You have options to *Insert* or *Copy* the synonym.
 - You can also click a synonym in the list to look up synonyms for that word. Click the **Back** arrow to return to the previous synonym list.

4. Click the **X** in the upper right corner of the *Thesaurus* pane to close this pane.

> **ANOTHER WAY**
>
> **Shift+F7** opens the *Thesaurus* pane.

Word Count

Word provides a running **word count** in each document, which is displayed on the *Status* bar in the bottom left corner of the Word window (Figure 1-65). Click the **Word Count** area to open the *Word Count* dialog box to display more detailed information: number of pages, words, characters (no spaces), characters (with spaces), paragraphs, and lines (Figure 1-66). You can also choose whether or not to have Word count words in textboxes, footnotes, and endnotes.

1-65 *Word Count* area on the *Status* bar

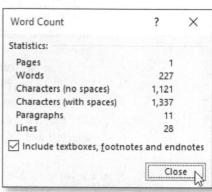

1-66 *Word Count* dialog box

> **ANOTHER WAY**
>
> Click the **Word Count** button in the *Proofing* group *on the Review* tab to open the *Word Count* dialog box.

SLO 1.8 Customizing Document Properties

Word allows you to include details about a document, which are called ***document properties***. These details are not visible in the text of the document but are included as hidden information within the document. These include fields such as *Title, Author, Comments, Subject, Company, Created,* and *Last Modified.* Some of the document properties are automatically

generated, such as *Words*, *Total Editing Time*, and *Last Modified*, whereas other document property details can be edited individually.

Document Properties

The document properties can be viewed and edited in the *Info* area on the *Backstage* view. Document properties are saved within the document and can be viewed by others who view or use the document.

▶**HOW TO:** Add Document Properties

1. Click the **File** tab to display the *Backstage* view.
2. Click the **Info** button if it is not already selected.
3. Review the document properties on the right side of the window (Figure 1-67).
 - Document property field names are listed on the left, and the information in these fields is listed on the right.
4. Click in a field and type information to edit the document property.
 - Some properties cannot be changed. These properties are automatically generated by Word.
5. Click the **Show All/Fewer Properties** link at the bottom to display more or fewer document property fields.
6. After entering and reviewing document properties, click the **Back** arrow in the upper left corner of the *Backstage* view to return to the document.

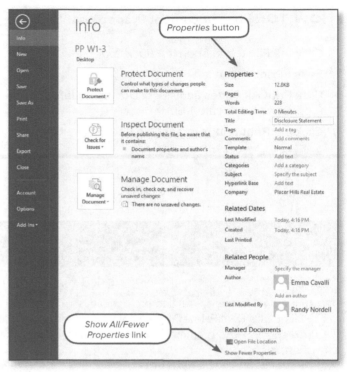

1-67 Document properties on the *Backstage* view

Advanced Properties

In addition to viewing and editing the document properties on the *Backstage* view, you can also display document properties in the ***Properties dialog box*** (Figure 1-68). In the *Info* area on the *Backstage* view, click the **Properties** button and select **Advanced Properties** to open the *Properties* dialog box.

You can modify the document properties on the *Summary* tab. The title of the *Properties* dialog box is context sensitive. The file name is displayed before *Properties* in the title bar of the dialog box.

1-68 *Properties* dialog box

Print Document Properties

After customizing document properties, you can print the document properties included in a document. When you print document properties, only a page listing the document properties prints, not the document itself.

▶HOW TO: Print Document Properties

1. Click the **File** tab to open the *Backstage* view.
2. Select **Print** on the left.
3. Click **Print All Pages** and select **Document Info** from the drop-down list (Figure 1-69).
4. Click the **Print** button to print the document properties.

1-69 Print document properties

PAUSE & PRACTICE: WORD 1-3

In the final Pause & Practice project in this chapter, you add the finishing touches on a document for Placer Hills Real Estate. You customize paragraph and line spacing, change paragraph alignment, and use spelling and grammar checkers to produce an error-free document. You also modify the document properties.

File Needed: *[your initials] PP W1-2.docx*
Completed Project File Name: *[your initials] PP W1-3.docx*

1. Open the *[your initials] PP W1-2* document completed in *Pause & Practice 1-2*.
 a. Click the **File** tab to open the *Backstage* view and click **Open** on the left.
 b. Click **Browse** to open the *Open* dialog box.
 c. Browse to locate the *[your initials] PP W1-2* document, select the document, and click **Open**.

2. Save this document with a different file name.
 a. Click the **File** tab to open the *Backstage* view and select **Save As** on the left.
 b. Click **Browse** to open the *Save As* dialog box and select the desired location to save the file.
 c. Change the file name to [your initials] PP W1-3.
 d. Click **Save** to save the document with a different file name and close the *Save As* dialog box.

3. Change the line and paragraph spacing on the entire document.
 a. Press **Ctrl+A** to select the entire document.
 b. Click the **Paragraph** launcher [*Home* or *Layout* tab, *Paragraph* group] to open the *Paragraph* dialog box (Figure 1-70).

c. Change the *Line spacing* to **Single**.
d. Change the *After* spacing to **12 pt**. Use the up arrow or type in the amount of spacing.
e. Click **OK** to close the dialog box.

ANOTHER WAY

Change line spacing in the *Paragraph* group on the *Home* tab. Change *Before* and *After* paragraph spacing in the *Paragraph* group on the *Layout* tab.

4. Add paragraph spacing before the date line of the business letter.
 a. Select or place your insertion point in the first line (date line) of the business letter.
 b. Click the **Layout** tab.
 c. Change the *Before* spacing to **72 pt**. (Figure 1-71). *Note: 72 pt. is approximately 1", which is commonly used as the spacing before the date line on business letters.*

5. Change the paragraph alignment of selected text.
 a. Select or place your insertion point in the subject line of the business letter.
 b. Click the **Center** button [*Home* tab, *Paragraph* group] or press **Ctrl+E**.

6. Use the *Thesaurus* to find synonyms for selected words.
 a. Select the word **"reveal"** in the third body paragraph.
 b. Click the **Thesaurus** button [*Review* tab, *Proofing* group]. The *Thesaurus* pane opens on the right with a list of synonyms for the selected word (Figure 1-72).
 c. Click the **drop-down arrow** to the right of the word "divulge" and choose **Insert**. The word "reveal" is replaced with "divulge."
 d. Click the **X** in the upper right corner of the *Thesaurus* pane to close the pane.
 e. Right-click the word **"residence"** in the first body paragraph. A context menu opens.
 f. Point to **Synonyms** and a list of synonyms appears.
 g. Select **"home"** from the list of synonyms. The word "residence" is replaced with "home."

7. Add a word to the custom dictionary.
 a. Click the **File** tab to open the *Backstage* view.
 b. Click the **Options** button to open the *Word Options* dialog box.
 c. Click **Proofing** on the left.
 d. Click the **Custom Dictionaries** button in the *When correcting spelling in Microsoft Office programs* area. The *Custom Dictionaries* dialog box opens.

1-70 Change *Line spacing* and *After* paragraph spacing in the *Paragraph* dialog box

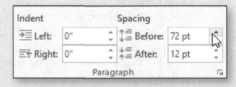

1-71 Change *Before* paragraph spacing in the *Paragraph* group

1-72 Insert a synonym from the *Thesaurus* pane

e. Select **RoamingCustom.dic** in the *Dictionary List*. If this dictionary is not available, select the available custom dictionary.

f. Click the **Edit Word List** button. The *RoamingCustom.dic* dialog box opens (Figure 1-73)

g. Type your last name in the *Word(s)* area and click the **Add** button. If your last name is already in the dictionary, the *Add* button is shaded gray.

h. Click **OK** to close the *RoamingCustom.dic* dialog box.

i. Click **OK** to close the *Custom Dictionaries* dialog box.

j. Click **OK** to close the *Word Options* dialog box.

1-73 Add a word to the custom dictionary

8. Spell and grammar check the document.

a. Right-click the word **"wholehouse"** in the second paragraph. A context list of words appears (Figure 1-74).

b. Select **"whole house."** The correctly spelled word replaces the incorrectly spelled word.

c. Click the **Spelling & Grammar** button [*Review* tab, *Proofing* group] or press **F7** to open the *Spelling* pane on the right (Figure 1-75).

d. Select **"truss"** in the *Spelling* pane and click the **Change** button.

e. Continue spell checking the remainder of the document. Change "granate" to **"granite"** and "you're" to **"your."**

f. Click **Add** for "Cavalli" if it is marked as incorrect.

g. Click **Ignore** for your reference initials if it is marked as incorrect.

h. Click **Ignore** for the capitalization grammar error (lowercase reference initials).

i. Click **OK** to close the dialog box that opens and informs you that the spelling and grammar check is complete. The *Spelling* pane closes.

1-74 Correct spelling using the context menu

9. Use *Smart Lookup* to research selected words.

a. Select **"Transfer Disclosure Statement"** in the third body paragraph.

b. Click the **Smart Lookup** button [*Review* tab, *Insights* group]. The *Smart Lookup* pane opens on the right. If you are using this feature for the first time, you might receive a message about privacy and have to click the **Got it** button before data is displayed.

c. Review the research results on the *Smart Lookup* pane.

d. Click the **X** in the upper right of the *Smart Lookup* pane to close the pane.

1-75 *Spelling* pane

10. Add document properties to your letter.
 a. Click the **File** tab to open the *Backstage* view.
 b. Click **Info** on the left if it is not already selected. The document properties are displayed on the right side of the *Backstage* view (Figure 1-76).
 c. Click in the *Title* field and type Disclosure Statement.
 d. In the *Author* area, right-click the existing author and select **Remove Person**.
 e. In the *Author* area, click **Add an author**, type Emma Cavalli, and press **Tab**.
 f. Click the **Show All Properties** link at the bottom. More document properties are displayed.
 g. Click in the *Company* area and type Placer Hills Real Estate.
 h. Click the **Properties** drop-down list at the top of the *Properties* area and choose **Advanced Properties**. The document properties display in the *Summary* tab of the *Properties* dialog box.
 i. Click **OK** to close the *Properties* dialog box and click the **Back** arrow to return to the document.

11. Save and close the document (Figure 1-77).

Properties *

Size	12.6KB
Pages	1
Words	228
Total Editing Time	21 Minutes
Title	Disclosure Statement
Tags	Add a tag
Comments	Add comments
Template	Normal
Status	Add text
Categories	Add a category
Subject	Specify the subject
Hyperlink Base	Add text
Company	Placer Hills Real Estate

Related Dates

Last Modified	Yesterday, 4:56 PM
Created	Yesterday, 4:36 PM
Last Printed	

Related People

Manager	Specify the manager
Author	Emma Cavalli
	Add an author

1-76 Document properties on the *Backstage* view

September·1,·2018¶

¶

David·and·Sharon·Wing↵
4685·Orange·Grove·Road↵
Rocklin,·CA·97725¶

Dear·Mr.·and·Mrs.·Wing:¶

SUBJECT:··Disclosure·Statement¶

Please·read·each·paragraph·before·signing·the·disclosure·statement·documents.·As·you·fill·out·the·required·disclosure·packet,·it·is·critical·to·the·transmission·of·sale·that·you·give·as·much·information·as·possible·about·your·home,·no·matter·how·small·or·insignificant.··Please·use·additional·paper·if·necessary·and·make·a·notation·to·that·fact.¶

Make·note·on·the·disclosure·statement·if·you·have·had·any·work·done·with·or·without·permits.·Some·examples·include·a·gas·spa,·a·new·water·heater,·or·a·whole·house·fan·where·a·truss·may·have·been·cut.·If·you·had·granite·counters·installed,·that·does·not·require·a·permit.¶

If·there·is·information·about·the·neighborhood·or·neighbors·that·you·as·a·buyer·would·want·to·know·about,·be·sure·to·divulge·that·information.·Be·sure·to·address·those·types·of·questions·on·the·Real·Estate·Transfer·Disclosure·Statement,·item·#11·on·page·2.¶

Please·complete·the·enclosed·disclosure·statement·by·September·8,·2018·and·return·it·to·me.·As·always,·if·you·have·any·questions·or·concerns,·please·call·me·at·916-450-3334·or·email·me·at·ecavalli@phre.com.··Best·wishes·and·thank·you·for·your·business.¶

Best·regards,¶

¶

EMMA·CAVALLI↵
Realtor·Consultant↵
Placer·Hills·Real·Estate¶

rn↵
Enclosure¶

1-77 PP W1-3 completed

Chapter Summary

1.1 Create, save, and open a Word document (p. 277).

- New Word documents are based on the **Normal template** (*Normal.dotx*).
- You can save documents with the existing file name or with a different file name.
- A **Word document** (*.docx*) is the standard file format. There are a variety of Word file formats in which to save a document.
- You can open, edit, and save existing Word documents.

1.2 Customize a document by entering and selecting text, using word wrap, and using *AutoComplete*, *AutoCorrect*, and *AutoFormat* features (p. 281).

- **Word wrap** automatically wraps text to the next line as you reach the right margin of the document.
- The **Show/Hide** button displays formatting symbols in the document to properly and consistently format documents.
- You can select text in a variety of ways, and you can select individual words, an entire line, multiple lines of text, a sentence, a paragraph, multiple paragraphs, or the entire document.
- **AutoComplete** automatically completes a day, month, or date for you.
- **AutoCorrect** automatically corrects commonly misspelled words and capitalization errors.
- **AutoFormat** automatically controls the formatting of items such as numbered and bulleted lists.
- You can add, delete, and edit *AutoCorrect* entries and customize *AutoCorrect* options in Word.

1.3 Enhance a document using paragraph breaks, line breaks, spaces, and non-breaking spaces (p. 284).

- The **Enter** key on the keyboard inserts a **paragraph break**. The **paragraph symbol** is visible when *Show/Hide* is turned on.
- **Line breaks** control breaks between lines or sentences to retain paragraph formatting between lines.
- **Non-breaking spaces** keep related words together.

1.4 Edit a document using cut, copy, paste, the *Clipboard*, and the undo, redo, and repeat features (p. 289).

- You can move or copy selected text within a document. There are a variety of methods to **cut**, **copy**, and **paste** text in a document.
- The **Clipboard** stores text that you have cut or copied. You can use the *Clipboard* to paste text into your document.
- You can **Undo**, **Redo**, and **Repeat** previous actions when working on a document. These features are available on the **Quick Access toolbar**.

1.5 Customize a document using different fonts, font sizes, and attributes (p. 292).

- **Serif** and **sans serif** are the two main categories of **fonts**.
- Fonts are measured in **points** (pt.). Most documents use between 10 and 12 pt. font size.
- You can change fonts and font size for specific text or the entire document.
- **Bold**, **Italic**, and **Underline** are font styles that you can apply quickly to text.
- Other font effects include **Strikethrough**, **Subscript**, **Superscript**, **Small caps**, and **All caps**.
- You can change the case of text in Word.
- The **Font dialog box** provides many **font**, **size**, **style**, and **effect options**.
- You can modify the **scale**, **spacing**, **position**, and **kerning** of selected text.
- The **Format Painter** applies formatting from selected text to other text.
- The **Clear Formatting** feature removes all formatting applied to selected text.
- You can change the **default** font and font size in Word.

1.6 Enhance a document using text alignment and line and paragraph spacing (p. 302).

- **Paragraph alignment** describes how text is aligned horizontally between the margins of a document: **Left**, **Center**, **Right**, or **Justified**.
- **Line spacing** refers to the amount of blank space between lines of text in a paragraph.
- **Paragraph spacing** is the amount of space between paragraphs. Paragraph spacing is measured in points.

- You can modify alignment, line spacing, and paragraph spacing on the *Home* or *Layout* tab or in the **Paragraph dialog box**.
- You can change the default line and paragraph spacing in Word.

1.7 Finalize a document using Word's research and proofing tools (p. 306).

- **Smart Lookup** is used to research selected word(s) without leaving Word. Research results display in the **Smart Lookup pane**.
- By default, Word automatically checks documents for **spelling** and **grammatical errors**.
- Word marks potential spelling, incorrect word, or grammatical errors with a colored wavy line under the words. You can correct errors by selecting from options in the context menu.

- You can manually spell and grammar check a document using the *Spelling and Grammar* pane.
- You can customize the **Word dictionary** by adding, deleting, or modifying words in the word list.
- The **Thesaurus** finds synonyms for words in your document.
- Word also provides you with a **Word Count**.

1.8 Apply custom document properties to a document (p. 310).

- You can add **document properties**, such as *Title, Author, Company, Subject, Created*, and *Last Modified*, into a document.
- You can add document properties on the *Backstage* view or in the *Properties* dialog box.

Check for Understanding

The SIMbook for this text (within your SIMnet account) provides the following resources for concept review:

- Multiple choice questions
- Matching exercises
- Short answer questions

Guided Project 1-1

In this project, Jennie Owings at Central Sierra Insurance is writing a business letter to Hartford Specialty regarding the renewal of the insurance policy for Valley Custom Manufacturing. This business letter is typed in block format and uses open punctuation. See *Appendix B* (online resource) for examples of business document formats and mixed and open punctuation.
[Student Learning Outcomes 1.1, 1.2, 1.3, 1.4, 1.5, 1.6, 1.7, 1.8]

File Needed: ***ValleyCustomManufacturing-01.docx*** *(Student data files are available in the* **Library** *of your SIMnet account)*
Completed Project File Name: *[your initials] Word 1-1.docx*

Skills Covered in This Project

- Add document properties.
- Use block business letter format using open punctuation.
- Change line spacing.
- Change paragraph spacing.
- Use *AutoComplete*.
- Use paragraph breaks for proper spacing between the parts of a business letter.

- Copy and paste text from another document using the *Clipboard*.
- Use *Show/Hide*.
- Undo automatic capitalization.
- Change font size.
- Apply font styles.
- Use *Smart Lookup*.
- Use spelling and grammar checker.
- Add words to the dictionary.

1. Open a new Word document.
 a. Click the **File** tab to open the *Backstage* view.
 b. Click **New** on the left and click **Blank document**. You can also click **Blank document** from the *Start* page when you first open Word.

2. Save the document as *[your initials] Word 1-1*.
 a. Click the **File** tab to open the *Backstage* view and select **Save As** on the left.
 b. Click **Browse** to open the *Save As* dialog box and select the desired location to save the file.
 c. Change the file name to [your initials] Word 1-1.
 d. Click **Save** to rename the document and close the *Save As* dialog box.

3. Add document properties.
 a. Click the **File** tab to open the *Info* area on the *Backstage* view and click the **Show All Properties** link.
 b. Type Valley Custom Manufacturing in the *Title* field.
 c. Type Central Sierra Insurance in the *Company* field.
 d. Click the **Back** arrow in the upper left of the *Backstage* view to return to the document.

4. Change the line and paragraph spacing of the document.
 a. Click the **Paragraph** launcher [*Home* or *Layout* tab, *Paragraph* group] to open the *Paragraph* dialog box (Figure 1-78).
 b. Change the *Line spacing* to **Single**.

c. Change the *After* paragraph spacing to **0 pt**.

d. Choose **OK** to close the *Paragraph* dialog box.

5. Use *AutoComplete* to type a date.

a. Turn on **Show/Hide** [*Home* tab, *Paragraph* group] if it is not already turned on.

b. Type the current date using month, day, year format (e.g., September 1, 2018). As you begin typing the date, *AutoComplete* completes the month and current date. Press **Enter** to accept the *AutoComplete* date.

c. Press **Enter** four times (quadruple space) after the date.

6. Type the inside address, salutation, and subject line.

a. Type Mrs. Cammie Speckler and press **Enter** once at the end of the line.

b. Type Hartford Specialty and press **Enter** once.

c. Type 4788 Market Street, Suite A205 and press **Enter** once.

d. Type San Francisco, CA 95644 and press **Enter** two times.

e. Type Dear Mrs. Speckler as the salutation and press **Enter** two times. No colon is used after the salutation when using open punctuation.

f. Type RE: Valley Custom Manufacturing as the subject line and press **Enter** two times.

1-78 *Paragraph* dialog box

7. Copy text from another document and paste it into the current document.

a. Open the ***ValleyCustomManufacturing-01*** document from your student data files. If the document opens in *Protected View*, click the **Enable Editing** button.

b. Press **Ctrl+A** to select the entire document.

c. Click the **Copy** button [*Home* tab, *Clipboard* group] or press **Ctrl+C**.

d. Close ***ValleyCustomManufacturing-01*** without saving the document.

e. In the ***[your initials] Word 1-1*** document, place your insertion point on the last blank line of the document.

f. Click the **Clipboard** launcher [*Home* tab, *Clipboard* group] to open the *Clipboard* pane (Figure 1-79).

g. Click the **drop-down arrow** to the right of the copied text in the *Clipboard* and click **Paste**. The paragraphs of text are pasted in the body of the document.

h. Click the **X** in the upper right corner of the *Clipboard* pane to close it.

1-79 Paste from the *Clipboard*

8. Use the *Format Painter* to format the inserted paragraphs.

a. Place your insertion point on the first line of the document (date line).

b. Click the **Format Painter** button [*Home* tab, *Clipboard* group] to turn on the *Format Painter*.

319

c. Select the five body paragraphs of the letter to apply the formatting (Figure 1-80).

9. Insert a blank line between each of the body paragraphs so there is a double space after each body paragraph (one blank line between paragraphs).
 a. Place your insertion point at the end of the first body paragraph and press **Enter**. A paragraph symbol marks the end of each paragraph.
 b. Repeat for each of the remaining body paragraphs including the last body paragraph.

RE:·Valley·Custom·Manufacturing¶
¶
Central·Sierra·Insurance·has·insured·Valley·Custom·Manufacturing·(VCM)·since·1992.·We·changed· companys·twice·only·because·the·original·underwriters·and/or·branch·managers·left·and·the·new· personnel·did·not·take·the·time·to·study·the·risk.·In·both·cases,·renewal·numbers·were·offered·but·were· not·competitive.·In·all·cases,·in·every·year·with·all·three·companies,·this·risk·has·been·very·profitible.¶

Valley·Custom·Manufacturing·are·best·known·as·a·manufacterer·of·nut·harvesting·equipment.·Since· 1946·the·Sanchez·family·has·been·developing·new·and·innovative·machines·to·help·the·nut·growers· more·efficintly,·quickly,·and·safely·harvest·their·product.·Over·the·years,·VCM·has·earned·an·unsurpassed· reputation.·There·are·very·few·almond,·walnut,·pecan,·fillbert·macadamia·and·pistachio·growers·who· don't·identify·VCM·equipment·with·quality·and·value.¶

Valley·Custom·Manufacturing·is·a·family·owned·and·closely·held·corporation.·All·owners·are·full·time· employees·of·VCM.·This·organization·is·a·model·for·professionalism·and·quality.·They·take·great·care·in· designing·and·building·their·products·and·servicing·their·costomers.·They·encourage·loss·control· recommendations·and·are·highly·reciptive·to·all·forms·of·improvement.¶

Your·loss·control·people·hvae·visited·VCM·several·times,·and·I'm·told·the·reports·are·very·good.·Expiring· combined·premiums·are·around·$525,000.·I·expect·well·see·some·inflation·for·the·June·renewal.¶

Thank·you·for·your·careful·consederation.·Please·note·that·I·am·encouraging·a·joint·meeting·to·discuss· this·renewal.·Please·review·the·enclosed·information,·and·feel·free·to·call·if·I·may·be·of·any·asistance.¶
¶

1-80 Use the *Format Painter* to copy formatting

10. Enter the closing lines of the document.
 a. Place your insertion point on the last blank line below the body of the letter.
 b. Type Sincerely and press **Enter** four times.
 c. Type Jennie Owings, Vice President and press **Enter**.
 d. Type Central Sierra Insurance and press **Enter** two times.
 e. Type your reference initials (your first and last initials in lowercase letters with no punctuation).
 f. Press **Enter**. *AutoCorrect* automatically capitalizes the first letter of your reference initials.
 g. Click the **AutoCorrect Options** smart tag (Figure 1-81). The *AutoCorrect Options* smart tag appears when you place your pointer below your reference initials.
 h. Select **Undo Automatic Capitalization** to undo the automatic capitalization of your reference initials.
 i. Place your insertion point on the blank line below your reference initials and type Enclosure as an enclosure notation.

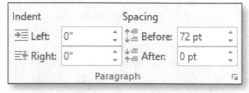

Thank·you·for·your·careful·consederation.·Pl
this·renewal.·Please·review·the·enclosed·info
¶
Sincerely¶
¶
¶
¶
Jennie·Owings,·Vice·President¶
Central·Sierra·Insurance¶
¶
Rh¶

↩ Undo Automatic Capitalization
 Stop Auto-capitalizing First Letter of Sentences
⚡ Control AutoCorrect Options...

1-81 *AutoCorrect Options* smart tag

11. Select the entire document (**Ctrl+A**) and change the font size to **10 pt**. [*Home* tab, *Font* group].

12. Add *Before* paragraph spacing to the date line.
 a. Select or place your insertion point in the date line.
 b. Change the *Before* spacing to **72 pt**. [*Layout* tab, *Paragraph* group] (Figure 1-82).

Indent			Spacing		
≡ Left:	0"	▲▼	↕≡ Before:	72 pt	▲▼
≡ Right:	0"	▲▼	↓≡ After:	0 pt	▲▼
			Paragraph		⬐

1-82 Change *Before* paragraph spacing on the date line

13. Apply a font style to selected text.
 a. Select the words **"Central Sierra Insurance"** in the first paragraph.
 b. Click the **Underline** button [*Home* tab, *Font* group] or press **Ctrl+U**.
 c. Select the words **"Valley Custom Manufacturing (VCM)"** in the first paragraph.
 d. Click the **Bold** button [*Home* tab, *Font* group] or press **Ctrl+B**.

14. Use *Smart Lookup* to research selected words.
 a. Select **"harvesting equipment"** in the second body paragraph.
 b. Click the **Smart Lookup** button [*Review* tab, *Insights* group]. The *Smart Lookup* pane opens on the right.

c. Review the research results on the *Smart Lookup* pane.
d. Click the **X** in the upper right of the *Smart Lookup* pane to close the pane.

15. Spell and grammar check the entire document.
 a. Press **Ctrl+Home** to move to the top of the document.
 b. Click the **Spelling & Grammar** button [*Review* tab, *Proofing* group]. The *Spelling* pane opens (Figure 1-83).
 c. If "Cammie" and "Speckler" are marked as potential spelling errors, click **Add** to add each of these names to the dictionary.
 d. For the remaining spelling and grammatical errors, select the correct word in the *Spelling* (or *Grammar*) pane and click **Change**.
 e. If prompted to continue checking the document from the beginning, choose **Yes**.
 f. Click **Ignore** if your reference initials are marked as a potential spelling or grammatical error.
 g. Click **OK** to close the dialog box that informs you the spelling and grammar check is complete.

16. Save and close the document (Figure 1-84).

1-83 Add word to the dictionary

1-84 Word 1-1 completed

Guided Project 1-2

Sierra Pacific Community College District is a multi-campus community college district. In this project, you format an informational handout regarding online learning.
[**Student Learning Outcomes 1.1, 1.2, 1.3, 1.4, 1.5, 1.6, 1.7, 1.8**]

File Needed: ***OnlineLearning-01.docx*** *(Student data files are available in the* Library *of your SIMnet account)*
Completed Project File Name: *[your initials] Word 1-2.docx*

Skills Covered in This Project

- Open and edit an existing document.
- Change line spacing.
- Change paragraph spacing.
- Use *Show/Hide*.
- Change font size and apply color, styles, and effects.

- Cut and paste to move a paragraph.
- Use drag and drop to move a paragraph.
- Apply a shadow text effect.
- Use the *Format Painter*.
- Use spelling and grammar checker.
- Add document properties.

1. Open the ***OnlineLearning-01*** document from your student data files.
 a. Click the **File** tab to open the *Backstage* view and click **Open** at the left.
 b. Click **Browse** to open the *Open* dialog box.
 c. Browse to locate the ***OnlineLearning-01*** document, select the document, and click **Open**. If the document opens in *Protected View*, click the **Enable Editing** button.

2. Save the document as *[your initials] Word 1-2*.
 a. Click the **File** tab to open the *Backstage* view and select **Save As** on the left.
 b. Click **Browse** to open the *Save As* dialog box and select the desired location to save the file.
 c. Change the file name to [your initials] Word 1-2.
 d. Click **Save** to rename the document and close the *Save As* dialog box.

3. Change the line and paragraph spacing of the entire document.
 a. Press **Ctrl+A** to select the entire document.
 b. Click the **Paragraph** launcher [*Home* or *Layout* tab, *Paragraph* group] to open the *Paragraph* dialog box (Figure 1-85).
 c. In the *Line spacing* area, select **Multiple** from the drop-down list.
 d. In the *At* area, type 1.2.
 e. Change the *After* paragraph spacing to **12 pt**.
 f. Click **OK** to close the *Paragraph* dialog box.

4. Turn on **Show/Hide** [*Home* tab, *Paragraph* group] and delete the one extra blank line between each paragraph including after the title.

5. Change the font and font size of the entire document.
 a. Select the entire document (**Ctrl+A**).
 b. Change the font to **Cambria** [*Home* tab, *Font* group].

1-85 Change *Line spacing* and *After* paragraph spacing

6. Change the paragraph spacing, alignment, font size, styles, effects, and color of the title.
 a. Select the title of the document (**Online Learning Information**).
 b. Click the **Layout** tab.
 c. Change the *Before* spacing to **36 pt**. and the *After* spacing to **18 pt**. [*Paragraph* group].
 d. Click the **Center** button [*Home* tab, *Paragraph* group].
 e. Click the **Font** launcher [*Home* tab, *Font* group]. The *Font* dialog box opens (Figure 1-86).
 f. Change the *Font* style to **Bold** and change the *Font Size* to **24**.
 g. In the *Effects* area, click the **Small caps** check box.
 h. Click the **Font color** drop-down list and choose **Blue-Gray, Text 2** from the *Theme Colors*.
 i. Click the **Advanced** tab.
 j. Click the **Spacing** drop-down list and select **Expanded**. Change the *By* to **1.2 pt**.
 k. Click **OK** to close the *Font* dialog box.

1-86 Change font style, size, effects, and color

7. Move paragraphs in the document and insert a heading.
 a. Select the last paragraph in the document, including the paragraph mark at the end of the document.
 b. Click the **Cut** button [*Home* tab, *Clipboard* group] or press **Ctrl+X**.
 c. Place your insertion point before the second line of the document ("Definition of Online Learning Modalities").
 d. Click the top half of the **Paste** button [*Home* tab, *Clipboard* group] or press **Ctrl+V**.
 e. Click at the beginning of the pasted paragraph and type Where are we now with Online Learning? and press **Enter**.
 f. Select the paragraph that begins "Hybrid Course:," including the paragraph mark at the end of the paragraph.
 g. Move this paragraph using the drag-and-drop method (click, hold, and drag) so it appears before the paragraph that begins with "Television or Tele-Web Course:" (Figure 1-87).

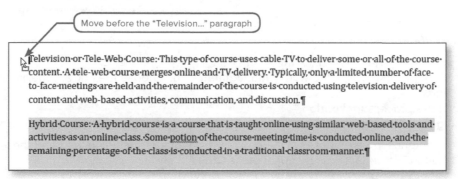

1-87 Move paragraph using drag and drop

8. Format section headings in the document and use the *Format Painter*.
 a. Select the first section heading ("**Where are we now with Online Learning?**").

b. Click the **Font** launcher [*Home* tab, *Font* group] to open the *Font* dialog box and click the **Font** tab (Figure 1-88).

c. Change the font *Size* to **12 pt**.

d. Change the *Font color* to **Blue-Gray, Text 2**.

e. Change the *Underline style* to **Double underline**.

f. Change the *Underline color* to **Blue-Gray, Text 2**.

g. In the *Effects* area, click the **All caps** check box.

h. Click **OK** to close the *Font* dialog box.

i. Click the **Text Effects and Typography** button [*Home* tab, *Font* group].

j. Place your pointer on **Shadow** and select **Offset Diagonal Bottom Right** (Figure 1-89).

k. With the formatted heading still selected, click the **Format Painter** button [*Home* tab, *Clipboard* group].

l. Select the next heading (**"Definition of Online Learning Modalities"**) to apply formatting.

9. Format paragraph headings in the document.

a. Select the first paragraph heading (**"Online Course:"**), including the colon.

b. Click the **Font** launcher [*Home* tab, *Font* group] to open the *Font* dialog box.

c. Change the *Font style* to **Bold**.

d. Change the *Font color* to **Blue-Gray, Text 2**.

e. In the *Effects* area, click the **Small caps** check box.

f. Click **OK** to close the *Font* dialog box.

10. Use the *Format Painter* to copy formatting to the other paragraph headings.

a. With the **"Online Course:"** heading still selected, double click the **Format Painter** button.

b. Select the other paragraph headings (**"Hybrid Course:", "Television or Tele-Web Course:",** and **"Web-Enhanced Course:"**) to apply the formatting.

c. Click the **Format Painter** button again to turn off the *Format Painter*.

11. Correct spelling and grammar in the document using the context menu.

a. Right-click the first misspelled word (**"managment"**) and choose the correct spelling from the list of options.

b. Repeat this process for **"potion."**

c. Click **Ignore All** or **Ignore Once** if there are other words that are marked as potentially incorrect.

12. Select the sentence in parentheses at the end of the document, including the parentheses, and click the **Italic** button [*Home* tab, *Font* group] or press **Ctrl+I**.

13. Add document properties using the *Properties* dialog box.

a. Click the **File** tab to open the *Backstage* view and click the **Info** button if it is not already selected.

b. Click the **Properties** button on the right and choose **Advanced Properties**. The *Properties* dialog box opens.

1-88 Format heading using the *Font* dialog box

1-89 Apply *Shadow* text effect

c. In the *Title* area, type **Online Learning Information**.

d. In the *Subject* area, type **Online Learning**.

e. In the *Author* area, delete the existing author name and type **Tanesha Morris** as the author.

f. Click **OK** to accept changes and close the *Properties* dialog box.

g. Click the **Back** arrow in the upper left of the *Backstage* view to return to the document.

14. Save and close the document (Figure 1-90).

ONLINE·LEARNING·INFORMATION¶

WHERE·ARE·WE·NOW·WITH·ONLINE·LEARNING?¶

SPCCD·was·a·pioneer·in·online·education·and·was·one·of·the·first·community·colleges·in·California· to·offer·fully·online·courses·in·1998.·However,·over·the·next·few·years·there·was·limited·growth·in· online·offerings·and·only·15·course·sections·were·taught·online·during·Fall·2000.·The·adoption·of·a· learning·management·system·in·Spring·2001,·and·the·availability·of·training·to·teach·online,·and· recruitment·of·new·faculty·interested·in·teaching·online·resulted·in·a·rapid·increase·in·online· offerings.¶

DEFINITION·OF·ONLINE·LEARNING·MODALITIES¶

All·online·learning·modes·offered·at·SPCCD·will·be·considered·in·the·plan.·Currently,·these·include· the·following:·online,·hybrid,·television,·and·tele-web.¶

ONLINE·COURSE:·An·online·course·is·a·course·that·is·offered·over·the·Internet.·Typically,·content·is· presented·through·web·pages·and·class·discussions·using·a·combination·of·email,·mailing·lists,· bulletin·boards,·chat·rooms,·or·newsgroups.·All·class·meetings,·assignments,·lectures,·and· assessments·are·online·(with·the·exception·of·orientation·meetings·or·other·face-to-face· examinations·as·determined·by·the·professor).¶

HYBRID·COURSE:·A·hybrid·course·is·a·course·that·is·taught·online·using·similar·web-based·tools·and· activities·as·an·online·class.·Some·portion·of·the·course·meeting·time·is·conducted·online,·and·the· remaining·percentage·of·the·class·is·conducted·in·a·traditional·classroom·manner.¶

TELEVISION·OR·TELE-WEB·COURSE:·This·type·of·course·uses·cable·TV·to·deliver·some·or·all·of·the· course·content.·A·tele-web·course·merges·online·and·TV·delivery.·Typically,·only·a·limited·number· of·face-to-face·meetings·are·held·and·the·remainder·of·the·course·is·conducted·using·television· delivery·of·content·and·web-based·activities,·communication,·and·discussion.¶

WEB-ENHANCED·COURSE:·This·type·of·course·is·taught·face-to-face·for·100%·of·the·course·meeting· time,·but·classroom·assignments·and·materials·are·supplemented·with·web-based·activities.· Examples·are:·online·projects,·handouts·and·materials,·online·discussion,·or·online·testing·(Note:· this·is·a·definition·of·a·non-online·learning·course·which·uses·online·learning·tools).¶

1-90 Word 1-2 completed

Guided Project 1-3

In this project, you create a memo for American River Cycling Club about using heart rate to increase the effectiveness of training. See *Appendix B* (online resource) for examples of business document formats. **[Student Learning Outcomes 1.1, 1.2, 1.3, 1.5, 1.6, 1.7, 1.8]**

File Needed: ***HeartRate-01.docx*** *(Student data files are available in the* Library *of your SIMnet account)*
Completed Project File Name: *[your initials]* **Word 1-3.docx**

Skills Covered in This Project

- Open and edit an existing document.
- Change line spacing.
- Change paragraph spacing.
- Use *Show/Hide*.
- Add a memo heading to a document.
- Change paragraph alignment.

- Change font size and apply styles and effects.
- Use the *Format Painter*.
- Add text highlight color.
- Use non-breaking space.
- Use *Thesaurus*.
- Add words to the dictionary.
- Add document properties.

1. Open the *HeartRate-01* document from your student data files.
 a. Click the **File** tab to open the *Backstage* view and click **Open** on the left.
 b. Click **Browse** to open the *Open* dialog box.
 c. Browse to locate the *HeartRate-01* document, select the document, and click **Open**. If the document opens in *Protected View*, click the **Enable Editing** button.

2. Save the document as *[your initials] Word 1-3*.
 a. Click the **File** tab to open the *Backstage* view and select **Save As** on the left.
 b. Click **Browse** to open the *Save As* dialog box and select the desired location to save the file.
 c. Change the file name to [your initials] Word 1-3.
 d. Click **Save** to rename the document and close the *Save As* dialog box.

3. Change the line and paragraph spacing of the entire document and insert a paragraph break between each paragraph.
 a. Press **Ctrl+A** to select the entire document.
 b. Click the **Paragraph** launcher [*Home* or *Layout* tab, *Paragraph* group]. The *Paragraph* dialog box opens.
 c. In the *Line spacing* area, select **Single** from the drop-down list.
 d. Change the *After* paragraph spacing to **0 pt**.
 e. Click **OK** to close the *Paragraph* dialog box.
 f. Turn on **Show/Hide** [*Home* tab, *Paragraph* group] if it is not already on.
 g. Click at the end of each paragraph and press **Enter** once to add a blank line between each of the paragraphs. Don't press *Enter* after the last body paragraph. A paragraph symbol marks the end of each paragraph.

4. Add a memo heading to the document.
 a. Place your insertion point at the beginning of the first paragraph and press **Enter**.
 b. Place the insertion point on the blank line above the first paragraph.
 c. Type TO: and press **Tab** two times.
 d. Type All ARCC Club Members and press **Enter** two times.
 e. Type FROM: and press **Tab** two times.
 f. Type Taylor Mathos, ARCC Coach and press **Enter** two times.
 g. Type DATE: and press **Tab** two times.
 h. Type the current date in month, day, year format (e.g., October 1, 2018) and press **Enter** two times.
 i. Type SUBJECT: and press **Tab** once.
 j. Type Heart Rate Training and press **Enter** two times.

5. Change the paragraph alignment and font styles of selected text.
 a. Select the second and third paragraphs in the body of the memo (beginning with **"220 – Your Age . . ."** and ending with **". . . heart rate is 180.)"**), including the paragraph mark at the end of the third paragraph.
 b. Click the **Center** button [*Home* tab, *Paragraph* group] or press **Ctrl+E**.
 c. Select the paragraph beginning **"220 – Your Age . . ."** and click the **Bold** button [*Home* tab, *Font* group] or press **Ctrl+B**.
 d. Select the next paragraph and click the **Italic** button [*Home* tab, *Font* group] or press **Ctrl+I**.
 e. Delete the blank line between the second and third paragraphs (Figure 1-91).

6. Change the font and style of selected text.
 a. Press **Ctrl+A** to select the entire document.

TO: → → All·ARCC·Club·Members¶
¶
FROM:→ → Taylor·Mathos,·ARCC·Coach¶
¶
DATE:→ → [Current·Date]¶
¶
SUBJECT: → Heart·Rate·Training¶
¶
¶
What·is·Maximum·Heart·Rate?·The·maximum·heart·rate·is·the·highest·your·pulse·rate·can·get.·To·calculate·your·predicted·maximum·heart·rate,·use·this·formula:¶
¶
 220·-·Your·Age·=·Predicted·Maximum·Heart·Rate¶
 (Example:·a·40-year-old's·predicted·maximum·heart·rate·is·180.)¶
¶

1-91 Memo heading added and paragraphs formatted

1-92 *Increase Font Size* button

1-93 *Change font style and effects*

b. Click the **Increase Font Size** button [*Home* tab, *Font* group] to increase the font size to 12 pt. (Figure 1-92).

c. Select the words **"Maximum Heart Rate?"** in the first sentence of the first body paragraph.

d. Click the **Font** launcher [*Home* tab, *Font* group] to open the *Font* dialog box (Figure 1-93).

e. Change the *Font style* to **Bold**.

f. Change the *Underline style* to **Words only** and change the *Underline color* to **Green, Accent 6**.

g. In the *Effects* area, select the **Small caps** check box.

h. Click **OK** to close the *Font* dialog box.

i. With the words still selected, click the **Format Painter** button [*Home* tab, *Clipboard* group].

j. Select the words **"Target Heart Rate Zone"** in the first sentence of the fifth paragraph in the body ("You gain the most benefits . . ."). The *Format Painter* applies the formatting to the selected words.

k. Select the last two sentences of the fifth body paragraph (**"Do not exercise above 85 percent . . ."**) including the period at the end of the second sentence.

l. Click the **Text Highlight Color** drop-down arrow [*Home* tab, *Font* group] (Figure 1-94) and select **Gray-25%** text highlighting.

1-94 *Text Highlight Color* drop-down list

7. Use a non-breaking space to keep words together.
 a. In the first sentence of the fifth paragraph in the body ("You gain the most benefits . . ."), delete the space between the words "Target" and "Heart."
 b. Place your insertion point between these two words and press **Ctrl+Shift+Spacebar** to insert a non-breaking space. "Target" is wrapped to the next line so the words do not break between lines.

8. Add *Before* paragraph spacing to the first line of the memo heading.
 a. Place the insertion point in the first line of the memo heading (**"TO: . . ."**).
 b. Change the *Before* spacing to **72 pt**. [*Layout* tab, *Paragraph* group].

9. Use the *Thesaurus* to find synonyms for selected words.
 a. Right-click the word **"medicines"** in the third sentence of the fourth body paragraph ("Your actual maximum . . .").
 b. Point to **Synonyms** to display a list of synonyms.
 c. Select **"medications"** as the synonym (Figure 1-95).

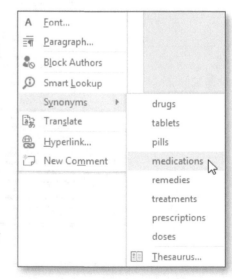

1-95 *Select synonym from context menu*

d. In the last sentence of the fifth paragraph ("You gain the most benefits . . ."), right-click the word **"added."**

e. Point to **Synonyms** and select **"additional."**

10. Add reference initials to the document.

 a. Click at the end of the last paragraph and press **Enter** two times.

 b. Type your reference initials in lowercase letters.

11. Add document properties.

 a. Click the **File** tab to open the *Backstage* view.

 b. Click the **Info** button, if it is not already selected, to display the document properties on the right.

 c. In the *Title* area, type Heart Rate Training.

 d. In the *Author* area, right-click the existing author and select **Remove Person**.

 e. In the *Author* area, type Taylor Mathos.

 f. Click the **Show All Properties** link at the bottom of the document properties.

 g. In the *Company* area, type ARCC.

 h. Click the **Back** arrow in the upper left of the *Backstage* view to return to the document.

12. Add words to the dictionary.

 a. Right-click the word **"Mathos"** in the second line of the memo heading.

 b. Choose **Add to Dictionary** from the context menu.

 c. If your reference initials are marked as incorrectly spelled (red wavy underline), right-click them and choose **Add to Dictionary**.

13. Save and close the document (Figure 1-96).

1-96 Word 1-3 completed

Independent Project 1-4

In this project, you format a business letter for Emma Cavalli to send to clients whose current home listings are expiring. See *Appendix B* (online resource) for examples of business document formats and mixed and open punctuation.
[Student Learning Outcomes 1.1, 1.2, 1.3, 1.4, 1.5, 1.6, 1.7, 1.8]

File Needed: ***ExpiredLetter-01.docx*** *(Student data files are available in the* Library *of your SIMnet account)*
Completed Project File Name: ***[your initials] Word 1-4.docx***

Skills Covered in This Project

- Open and edit an existing document.
- Change line spacing.
- Change paragraph alignment and spacing.
- Change font and font size.
- Use *Show/Hide*.
- Format document as a block format business letter with mixed punctuation.
- Move text.
- Change font styles and effects.
- Use *Smart Lookup*.
- Add document properties.
- Use spelling and grammar checker.

1. Open the ***ExpiredLetter-01*** document from your student data files.

2. Save this document as ***[your initials] Word 1-4***.

3. Apply the following formatting changes to the entire document:
 a. Select the entire document.
 b. Change the *Before* and *After* paragraph spacing to **0 pt**.
 c. Change the line spacing to **Single**.
 d. Change the paragraph alignment to **Left**.
 e. Change the font and font size to **Calibri** and **11 pt**.

4. Turn on **Show/Hide** and press **Enter** at the end of each paragraph to add a blank line after each paragraph (including the last paragraph).

5. Type and format the opening lines of the business letter.
 a. Press **Ctrl+Home** to move your insertion point to the top of the document.
 b. Type the current date (use August 15, 2018 format) and press **Enter** four times.
 c. Type the following inside address and press **Enter** two times after the last line:

 Mr. Rick Hermann
 9035 Masi Drive
 Fair Oaks, CA 95528

 d. Type Dear Mr. Hermann: as the salutation and press **Enter** two times after the salutation. There should be one blank line between the salutation and the body of the letter.
 e. Add **72 pt**. *Before* paragraph spacing to the date line.

6. Type the closing lines of the business letter.
 a. Place your insertion point on the blank line below the last body paragraph and press **Enter**.
 b. Type Best regards, and press **Enter** four times.
 c. Type the following closing lines:

 Emma Cavalli
 Realtor Consultant
 Placer Hills Real Estate

 d. Press **Enter** two times after the company name and type your reference initials in lowercase letters.

7. Move a paragraph and sentence.
 a. Move the third body paragraph so it appears before the second body paragraph. Make sure there is one blank line between each of the body paragraphs. If there is a blank space in front of the first word in the third paragraph, delete it.
 b. In the new second body paragraph ("There was a lot of detail . . ."), move the last two sentences to the beginning of the paragraph. Make sure there is proper spacing between sentences.

8. Apply formatting to text in the business letter.
 a. Select **"Placer Hills Real Estate"** in the first body paragraph and make the company name **Bold, Underline** (single line), and **Small caps**.
 b. Select the first sentence in the third paragraph including the period ("The service and experience . . .") and apply **Italic** formatting.
 c. Select the writer's name at the bottom and apply **Small caps** formatting.
 d. Select the writer's title and apply **Italic** formatting.
 e. Select the company name below the writer's title and apply **Bold** formatting.

9. Use *Smart Lookup* to research selected words.
 a. Select **"Placer Hills Real Estate"** in the first body paragraph.
 b. Click the **Smart Lookup** button [*Review* tab, *Insights* group]. The *Smart Lookup* pane opens on the right.
 c. Review the research results in the *Smart Lookup* pane.
 d. Click the **X** in the upper right of the *Smart Lookup* pane to close the pane.

10. Add the following document properties:
 a. *Title*: Expired Letter
 b. *Company*: Placer Hills Real Estate
 c. *Manager*: Kelsey Kroll
 d. *Author*: Emma Cavalli (right-click and choose **Remove Person** to remove existing author)

11. Spell and grammar check the entire document, make changes where necessary, and ignore proper nouns.

12. Save and close the document (Figure 1-97).

1-97 Word 1-4 completed

Independent Project 1-5

In this project, you combine information from different documents to create a memo for Sierra Pacific Community College District. This memo is a draft of the values statement for the district. See *Appendix B* (online resource) for examples of business document formats.
[Student Learning Outcomes 1.1, 1.2, 1.3, 1.4, 1.5, 1.6, 1.7, 1.8]

File Needed: ***ValuesStatement-01a.docx*** and ***ValuesStatement-01b.docx*** *(Student data files are available in the* Library *of your SIMnet account)*
Completed Project File Name: *[your initials] Word 1-5.docx*

Skills Covered in This Project	
• Open and edit an existing document.	• Format document as a memo.
• Change line spacing.	• Use spelling and grammar checker.
• Change paragraph spacing.	• Change font styles and effects.
• Change font and font size.	• Use the *Format Painter*.
• Use *Show/Hide*.	• Move text.
	• Add document properties.

1. Open the ***ValuesStatement-01a*** document from your student data files.

2. Save this document as *[your initials] Word 1-5*.

3. Copy text from another document and paste it into the current document.
 a. Open the ***ValuesStatement-01b*** document from your student data files.
 b. Select all of the text in this document and copy to the *Clipboard*.
 c. Close the ***ValuesStatement-01b*** document without saving.
 d. In the *[your initials] Word 1-5* document, press **Enter** at the end of the document and paste the copied text from the *Clipboard*.
 e. **Delete** the extra paragraph breaks between the first four paragraphs and at the end of the document.

4. Select the entire document and apply the following formatting changes:
 a. Change *After* paragraph spacing to **12 pt**.
 b. Change the line spacing to **1.15**.
 c. Change the font and font size to **Calibri** and **10 pt**.

5. Type and format the heading lines in the memorandum.
 a. Turn on **Show/Hide**.
 b. Place your insertion point at the beginning of the document and press **Enter**.
 c. Place your insertion point on the blank line at the beginning of the document and type the following memo information. Press **Tab** (once or twice) after the guidewords to line up information at 1" and press **Enter** once at the end of the first three lines of the memo heading.

 TO: All SPCCD Faculty, Staff, and Managers
 FROM: Lanita Morrow, Chancellor
 DATE: type current date (use November 1, 2018 format)
 SUBJECT: Draft of SPCCD Values Statement

 d. On the first line of the memo heading, change the *Before* paragraph spacing to **24 pt**.
 e. On the "SUBJECT" line of the memo heading, change the *After* paragraph spacing to **18 pt**.

6. Spell and grammar check the entire document.
 a. Add the chancellor's first and last names to the dictionary if they are marked as potential spelling errors.
 b. Correct other spelling and grammar errors as necessary.

7. Apply formatting to a paragraph heading and use the *Format Painter* to copy formatting.
 a. Select the first paragraph heading (**"Access"**) in the body of the memo and apply the following formatting:

 Font style: **Bold**
 Font color: **Blue-Gray, Text 2**
 Underline: **Double Underline**
 Underline color: **Blue-Gray, Text 2**
 Effects: **Small caps**

 b. Use the *Format Painter* to apply these styles to each of the other paragraph headings in the body of the memo.

8. Move body paragraphs.
 a. Use cut and paste or drag and drop to move the body paragraphs so they are ordered alphabetically by paragraph heading. Exclude the first body paragraph. Be sure to include the paragraph symbol at the end of each paragraph when cutting or dragging.
 b. Verify there are not extra *Enters* (paragraph marks) between paragraphs at the end of the document. This document will fit on one page.
 c. Verify there are not extra spaces before the first word in each of the paragraphs.

9. Delete any extra blank lines at the end of the document so this document fits on one page.

10. Add the following document properties:
 a. *Title*: SPCCD Values Statement
 b. *Company*: Sierra Pacific Community College District
 c. *Author*: Yoon Soo Park (right-click and choose **Remove Person** to remove existing author)

11. Save and close the document (Figure 1-98).

1-98 Word 1-5 completed

Independent Project 1-6

In this project, you use formatting features in Word to create a professional and appealing brochure for Emma Cavalli at Placer Hills Real Estate.
[Student Learning Outcomes 1.1, 1.2, 1.3, 1.4, 1.5, 1.6, 1.7, 1.8]

File Needed: ***Brochure-01.docx*** *(Student data files are available in the* Library *of your SIMnet account)*
Completed Project File Name: *[your initials] **Word 1-6.docx***

Skills Covered in This Project

- Open and edit an existing document.
- Change font and font size.
- Change paragraph spacing.
- Change line spacing.
- Use *Show/Hide*.
- Change paragraph alignment.
- Change font styles and effects.
- Use the *Format Painter*.
- Move text.
- Use the thesaurus to find synonyms.
- Use *Smart Lookup*.
- Add document properties.

1. Open the ***Brochure-01*** document from your student data files.

2. Save this document as *[your initials] **Word 1-6***.

3. Select the entire document and apply the following formatting changes:
 a. Change the font and font size to **Cambria** and **10 pt**.
 b. Change the *After* paragraph spacing to **6 pt**.
 c. Change the line spacing to **Single**.

4. Apply formatting to the opening lines of the document.
 a. Select the first five lines of the document (**"Emma Cavalli"** to **"Email: ecavalli@phre.com"**) and change the *After* paragraph spacing to **2 pt**.
 b. Select the first six lines of the document (**"Emma Cavalli"** to **"Web: www.phre.com/ecavalli"**) and **Center** these lines.
 c. Select the first line of the document (**"Emma Cavalli"**) and apply the following changes:
 Font size: **12 pt**.
 Font style: **Bold**
 Font color: **Green, Accent 6, Darker 50%**
 d. Select the second line of the document ("**Realtor Consultant**") and apply **Bold** formatting.
 e. Select the third line of the document (**"Putting Your Needs First"**) and apply **Italic** formatting.

5. Apply formatting to a section heading and use the *Format Painter*.
 a. Select the first section heading, **"Personal Statement,"** and apply **Bold**, **Underline**, and **Small Caps** formatting.
 b. On the first section heading, change the *Before* paragraph spacing to **12 pt**. and the *After* paragraph spacing to **3 pt**.
 c. Use the *Format Painter* to copy this formatting to the other section headings:

 "Real Estate Experience"
 "Why I am a Real Estate Agent"
 "What Clients are Saying"
 "Professional Credentials"
 "Education & Training"

6. In the "Why I Am a Real Estate Agent" section, combine the four sentences into one paragraph, deleting paragraph marks and inserting spaces as needed. Turn on **Show/Hide**.

7. In the "What Clients are Saying" section, make the following changes:
 a. Select the second paragraph ("It was a pleasure . . ."), make it **Italic**, and change the *After* spacing to **0 pt**.
 b. Select the source of the quote (**"-Rod & Luisa Ellisor, Rocklin, CA"**) and right-align this text.
 c. Repeat the above two steps for the second quote ("Emma is conscientious . . .") and the source of the quote ("-Jon & Robin Anderson . . .").

8. Move the third section heading and the paragraph below it ("Why I Am a Real Estate Agent") so it appears before the second section ("Real Estate Experience").

9. Select the lines of text in the "Professional Credentials" section (don't include the heading) and change the *After* paragraph spacing to **3 pt**.

10. Use the *Format Painter* to repeat the above formatting to the lines of text (excluding the heading) in the "Education & Training" section.

11. Use the thesaurus to find an appropriate synonym for the following words:
 a. Replace "surpass" (in the "Personal Statement" section) with **"exceed."**
 b. Replace "emotions" (in the "Why I Am a Real Estate Agent" section) with **"sentiments."**

12. Use *Smart Lookup* to research selected words.
 a. Select **"University Nevada, Reno"** in the "Education & Training" section.
 b. Click the **Smart Lookup** button [*Review* tab, *Insights* group]. The *Smart Lookup* pane opens on the right.
 c. Review the research results in the *Smart Lookup* pane.
 d. Click the **X** in the upper right of the *Smart Lookup* pane to close the pane.

13. Add the following document properties:
 a. *Title*: Brochure
 b. *Company*: Placer Hills Real Estate
 c. *Author*: Emma Cavalli (right-click and choose **Remove Person** to remove existing author)

14. Save and close the document (Figure 1-99).

1-99 Word 1-6 completed

Improve It Project 1-7

In this project, you create a block format business letter for Margaret Jepson, an insurance agent at Central Sierra Insurance. You improve the formatting and text in this document and add opening and closing lines to create a properly formatted business letter. For more information on creating a correctly formatted block format business letter, see *Appendix B*.
[**Student Learning Outcomes 1.1, 1.2, 1.3, 1.5, 1.6, 1.7, 1.8**]

File Needed: ***RenewalLetter-01.docx*** *(Student data files are available in the* Library *of your SIMnet account)*
Completed Project File Name: ***[your initials] Word 1-7.docx***

Skills Covered in This Project

- Open and edit an existing document.
- Change font and font size.
- Change paragraph spacing.
- Change line spacing.
- Use spelling and grammar checker.

- Format a business letter.
- Change paragraph alignment.
- Change font styles and effects.
- Use the *Format Painter*.
- Add document properties.

1. Open the ***RenewalLetter-01*** document from your student data files.

2. Save this document as ***[your initials] Word 1-7***.

3. Select the entire document and apply the following formatting:
 a. *Line spacing*: **Single**
 b. *Before* and *After paragraph spacing*: **0 pt**.
 c. *Font*: **Calibri**
 d. *Font size*: **11 pt**.

4. Correct spelling and grammar as needed.

5. Type the opening lines of the business letter.
 a. Turn on **Show/Hide** if it is not already on.
 b. Place your insertion point at the top of the document and press **Enter**.
 c. On the blank line at the beginning of the document, type the current date (e.g., September 1, 2018) and press **Enter** four times.
 d. Type the following inside address and press **Enter** two times after the last line:

 Mr. Rick DePonte
 8364 Marshall Street
 Granite Bay, CA 95863

 e. Type Dear Mr. DePonte: as the salutation press **Enter** two times.
 f. Type Subject: Policy HO-2887-5546-B as the subject line and press **Enter** once.
 g. Apply **72 pt**. *Before* paragraph spacing on the date line.

6. Type the closing lines of the business letter.
 a. On the last blank line of the document, type Best regards, as the complimentary close and press **Enter** four times.
 b. Type the following information below as the writer's name, title, and company and press **Enter** two times after the last line:

Margaret Jepson, ARM, CIC, CRM
Insurance Agent
Central Sierra Insurance

 c. Type your initials in lowercase letters as the reference initials and press **Enter** once. Undo the automatic capitalization of your reference initials.

 d. Type Enclosure as the enclosure notation at the end of the business letter.

7. Apply formatting to the renewal premium information.

 a. **Center** the four lines of renewal premium information in the body of the letter.

 b. Apply **Bold** and **Small caps** formatting to the headings (not including the colons) for each of these four lines of renewal premium information.

 c. Format the "Total Premium" dollar amount as **Bold**, *Italic*, and **Double Underline**.

8. In the second body paragraph, type Hartford Specialty to replace the "*[Company Name]*" placeholder.

9. In the last body paragraph, type Rick to replace the "*[First Name]*" placeholder.

10. Add the following document properties:

 a. *Title*: Renewal Letter

 b. *Company*: Central Sierra Insurance

 c. *Author*: Margaret Jepson (right-click and choose **Remove Person** to remove existing author)

11. Save and close the letter (Figure 1-100).

1-100 Word 1-7 completed

Challenge Project 1-8

Create a cover letter for a job application. A cover letter typically accompanies a resume to introduce an applicant to a prospective employer. You can use and modify an existing cover letter, or you can create a new one. It is important to customize each cover letter for each job for which you are applying.

There are many online resources available to help you with both content and format. One of the best online resources for writing is the Online Writing Lab (OWL) from Purdue University (http://owl.english .purdue.edu/owl/). You can search this site for helpful information about cover letters.
[Student Learning Outcomes 1.1, 1.2, 1.3, 1.4, 1.5, 1.6, 1.7, 1.8]

File Needed: None
Completed Project File Name: *[your initials] Word 1-8.docx*

Open a new document and save this document as *[your initials] Word 1-8*.

Type this document as a personal business letter in block format. For more information on formatting a personal business letter, see *Appendix B*. Modify your document according to the following guidelines:

- Move sentences and paragraphs as needed to produce a well-organized cover letter.
- Add words to the dictionary as needed.
- Use the *Thesaurus* to find synonyms as needed.
- Include document properties, and spell and grammar check the document.

Challenge Project 1-9

Create a list of five places you would like to visit in the next five years. For each of the places you list, compose a short paragraph about that place and why it is interesting to you. Research each of the places you choose on the Internet. Use your own words when composing the paragraphs about each place.
[Student Learning Outcomes 1.1, 1.2, 1.3, 1.4, 1.5, 1.6, 1.7, 1.8]

File Needed: None
Completed Project File Name: *[your initials] Word 1-9.docx*

Open a new document and save it as *[your initials] Word 1-9*. Modify your document according to the following guidelines:

- Create and format a title for the document.
- Format each of the headings by modifying the font, style, and attributes.
- Change line and paragraph spacing as needed to create an attractive and readable document.
- Use consistent line and paragraph spacing throughout the document.
- Use the *Format Painter* to keep formatting consistent throughout the document.
- Move the paragraphs so the places are listed in order of your preference.
- Include document properties, and spell and grammar check the document.

Challenge Project 1-10

Create a flyer for an upcoming event for an organization to which you belong. Be sure to include all the relevant information for this event and arrange it attractively and professionally on the page.
[**Student Learning Outcomes 1.1, 1.2, 1.3, 1.5, 1.6, 1.7, 1.8**]

File Needed: None
Completed Project File Name: *[your initials] Word 1-10.docx*

Open a new document and save it as *[your initials] Word 1-10*. Modify your document according to the following guidelines:

- Create and format a title for the document.
- Format the information by modifying the fonts, styles, and attributes.
- Change line and paragraph spacing as needed to create an attractive and readable document.
- Change the text alignment as desired.
- Use the *Format Painter* to keep formatting consistent throughout the document.
- Include document properties, and spell and grammar check the document.

Formatting and Customizing Documents

CHAPTER OVERVIEW

In addition to giving you the ability to create common business documents, Microsoft Word 2016 provides formatting and editing tools you can use to customize a variety of documents. Formatting features such as custom margins, tab stops, indents, page numbering, headers, footers, breaks, lists, styles, themes, borders, and shading help you to produce readable and attractive professional and personal documents.

STUDENT LEARNING OUTCOMES (SLOs)

After completing this chapter, you will be able to:

SLO 2.1 Format a document by customizing margins, page orientation, paper size, and vertical alignment (p. 340).

SLO 2.2 Improve alignment and page layout by setting, using, and editing tab stops in a document (p. 343).

SLO 2.3 Apply indents to control text alignment (p. 348).

SLO 2.4 Enhance document layout by inserting page numbers, headers, and footers (p. 353).

SLO 2.5 Control pagination with page and section breaks (p. 360).

SLO 2.6 Use customized bulleted and numbered lists to effectively present information (p. 362).

SLO 2.7 Apply styles and themes to improve consistency in document format (p. 366).

SLO 2.8 Use find and replace to edit a document (p. 371).

SLO 2.9 Improve overall document design and format with borders, shading, horizontal lines, and hyperlinks (p. 374).

CASE STUDY

Courtyard Medical Plaza has a preschool for its employees' children. The preschool is currently looking for qualified applicants to fill a vacant teacher position. In the Pause & Practice projects, you modify a résumé for Richelle Wilkinson. You apply features covered in this chapter to create an attractive and informative résumé.

Pause & Practice 2-1: Edit the résumé to change margins and set tab stops and indents.

Pause & Practice 2-2: Modify the résumé to include a header with text and a page number.

Pause & Practice 2-3: Enhance the résumé by using bulleted lists, a page break, and a theme.

Pause & Practice 2-4: Finalize the résumé by using find and replace, borders, shading, horizontal line, and hyperlinks.

WORD

339

Customizing Margins and Page Layout

You can use margins to create *white space* around the edges of a document. White space improves the readability of a document and prevents the document from appearing cluttered. The document type and content influence the margins you use. You can also customize a document by changing the page orientation, page size, or vertical alignment.

Page Layout Settings

When you open a new Word document, the default settings control margins, page orientation, paper size, and vertical alignment. The following table lists the default page layout settings for a new document:

Default Page Layout Settings

Page Layout Option	Default Setting
Margins	1" top, bottom, left, and right
Page Orientation	Portrait
Paper Size	8.5" × 11" (Letter)
Vertical Alignment	Top

These settings are applied to the entire Word document, and you can easily change all of these settings in Word.

Margin Settings

Margin settings are measured in inches; the default margin settings for a new Word document are 1". Word provides you with a variety of *preset margin settings*. You can choose and change margins from the *Margins* drop-down list.

2-1 *Margins* drop-down list

▶HOW TO: Change Margin Settings

1. With a document open in Word, click the **Layout** tab.
2. Click the **Margins** button [*Page Setup* group]. Preset margin options appear in the *Margins* drop-down list (Figure 2-1).
3. Select the desired margin settings from the drop-down list of options.

The *Margins* drop-down list provides preset margin options. You are not limited to these preset options; you can also create your own custom margin settings in the *Page Setup* dialog box.

▶ MORE INFO

At the top of this *Margins* list, the **Last Custom Setting** option displays the most recent custom margin settings you have used.

Page Setup Dialog Box

If you want margin settings that are not listed in the preset margin settings in the *Margins* drop-down list, use the ***Page Setup dialog box*** (Figure 2-2) to change one or more of the margin settings and to create custom margins.

▶ HOW TO: Set Custom Margins

1. Click the **Layout** tab.
2. Click the **Margins** button [*Page Setup* group] and select **Custom Margins**. The *Page Setup* dialog box opens (see Figure 2-2).
3. Click the **Margins** tab if it is not already selected.
4. Change the *Top*, *Bottom*, *Left*, and *Right* margin settings as desired. You can do this the following ways:
 - Click the **Top**, **Bottom**, **Left**, or **Right** margin box and type your desired margin setting.
 - Click the **up** or **down arrow** to increase or decrease the margin size. Each click of the up or down arrow increases or decreases the margins by 0.1".
 - Press **Tab** to move from one box to another in the *Margins* area.
5. View the *Preview* area to see how the margin settings appear when applied to the document.
6. Click the **Apply to** drop-down list and select the area to apply margin settings: **Whole document**, **This point forward**, or **This section**.
7. Click **OK** to apply the custom margin settings.

2-2 *Page Setup* dialog box

> ### MORE INFO
>
> Margin settings apply to the entire document by default. However, you can apply different margin settings to different sections of a document. Sections and section breaks are covered later in this chapter.

Page Orientation

Page orientation refers to the direction of the page. The two different orientation options in Word are ***Portrait*** and ***Landscape***. Portrait is the tall orientation (8.5" × 11"), which is the default page orientation in Word. Landscape is the wide orientation (11" × 8.5"). You can change page orientation by clicking the **Orientation** button in the *Page Setup* group on the *Layout* tab (Figure 2-3).

> ### ANOTHER WAY
> You can also change page orientation in the *Page Setup* dialog box.

2-3 Page orientation settings

Paper Size

Paper size refers to the actual size of the paper of your final printed document. A new document in Word is standard letter size, which is 8.5" × 11" by default. Word also provides other preset paper size settings, some of which are displayed in Figure 2-4.

You can change paper size by clicking the **Size** button in the *Page Setup* group on the *Layout* tab. When a different paper size is set, the margins of the document do not change. You may need to adjust the margin setting when you change the paper size. You can also set a custom paper size in the *Page Setup* dialog box.

2-4 Paper size preset options

Vertical Alignment

If you are creating a flyer or a title page for a report, you might want to vertically center the information on the page. **Vertical alignment** controls the position of text between the top and bottom margins. Changing the vertical alignment of a page, section, or document is a much more effective method than using paragraph breaks (pressing *Enter* multiple times) to align information vertically. Word has four different vertical alignment options.

- *Top*: Text begins at the top margin of the document.
- *Center*: Text is centered vertically between the top and bottom margins.
- *Justified*: Space is automatically added between lines to fill the entire vertical space between the top and bottom margins.
- *Bottom*: Text begins at the bottom margin of the document.

▶ **HOW TO:** Change Vertical Alignment

1. Click the **Layout** tab.
2. Click the **Page Setup** launcher [*Page Setup* group]. The *Page Setup* dialog box opens.
3. Click the **Layout** tab.
4. In the *Page* area, click the **Vertical alignment** drop-down list (Figure 2-5).
5. Select the vertical alignment option of your choice.

2-5 Change vertical alignment

Use the Ruler

Microsoft Word provides horizontal and vertical ***rulers*** that display both the typing line length and the vertical typing space available in a document. The rulers are broken into 1/8" increments. Half-inch markers are longer vertical or horizontal lines (depending on the ruler) and inch markers are numerical. On the rulers, the typing area is displayed in white, while the margin area is shaded (Figure 2-6). To display the rulers, check the **Ruler** box on the *View* tab in the *Show* group. This check box toggles on and off the display of the rulers.

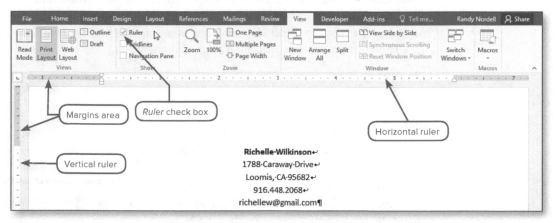

2-6 Horizontal and vertical rulers displayed

> **MORE INFO**
>
> The rulers are increasingly important and useful as you begin using tab stops, indents, columns, tables, and section breaks.

SLO 2.2

Setting, Using, and Editing Tab Stops

Tabs are useful tools to control the alignment of text. A tab is often used to indent the first line of a paragraph. A ***tab stop*** is where your insertion point stops when you press the *Tab* key. Tabs can also be used, for example, to align text in columns, or to begin the date at the horizontal midpoint on a modified block business letter.

The five different types of tabs stops that you can set and use in your documents are described in the following table:

Types of Tab Stops

Type of Tab Stop	Description	Tab Stop Indicator	Tab Stop in Use
Left	Text is left aligned at the tab stop	└	Left tab
Center	Text is centered on the tab stop	┴	Center tab
Right	Text is right aligned at the tab stop	┘	Right tab
Decimal	Decimal point is aligned at the tab stop	┴	Decimal tab 620.50 / 8.375
Bar	A vertical bar (line) is inserted at the tab stop	│	There is a bar \| tab between these words

Set a Tab Stop

Tabs are different from margins because tab stops apply to a paragraph or selected paragraphs rather than an entire document or sections of a document. This is important to keep in mind when setting, using, and editing tab stops.

By default in a Word document, there is left tab stop every 0.5". You can set tab custom stops in a new document before text is typed, or you can set tab stops in existing text. If you open a new blank document and set a left tab stop at 3.25", that tab stop applies to the entire document. On the other hand, if you open an existing document and set a tab stop on the first line, the tab stop is only set for that paragraph. When setting a tab stop in existing documents or text, remember to select all the text or paragraphs where you want the tab settings to apply.

There are two ways to set a tab stop in Word.

- *Tabs* dialog box
- Ruler

Set a Tab Stop Using the Tabs Dialog Box

The ***Tabs dialog box*** is an effective and easy method to set single or multiple tab stops. The *Tabs* dialog box is available from the *Paragraph* dialog box, which you can open from the *Paragraph* group on either the *Home* or *Layout* tabs.

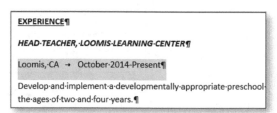

2-7 Select text before setting tab stops

2-8 *Tabs* button in the *Paragraph* dialog box

▶ HOW TO: Set a Tab Stop Using the Tabs Dialog Box

1. Select the text where you want to set a tab stop (Figure 2-7).
2. Click the **Home** tab.
3. Click the **Paragraph** launcher to open the *Paragraph* dialog box.
4. Click the **Tabs** button (Figure 2-8) to open the *Tabs* dialog box.
5. Click in the **Tab stop position** area and type the desired tab stop position.
6. In the *Alignment* area, select the type of tab stop radio button you want to set.
7. Click the **Set** button (Figure 2-9). The tab stop appears in the list of tab stops below the *Tab stop position* area.
8. Click **OK** to close the *Tabs* dialog box.
 - The tab stop is applied to the selected text.
 - The tab stop is visible on the ruler.

> ▶ MORE INFO
>
> Set and use tab stops to align and balance columns of text rather than pressing *Tab* multiple times between columns.

2-9 Set a right tab stop in the *Tabs* dialog box

Set a Tab Stop Using the Ruler

Using the ruler to set tab stops is a quick way to add them to a document. You can also easily move or remove tab stops using the ruler. Use the **Tab selector** to select the type of tab stop you want to insert. The *Tab* selector is located at the top of the vertical ruler on the left side of the Word window. When setting tab stops in an existing document, it is very important to select the text or paragraphs where you want the tab stop to apply before setting the tab stop.

> ### ▶HOW TO: Set a Tab Stop Using the Ruler
>
> 1. Select the text where you want to set the new tab stop(s).
> - If the rulers are not displayed, check the **Ruler** box [*View* tab, *Show* group].
> 2. Click the **Tab** selector to select the type of tab stop to set (Figure 2-10).
> 3. Click the ruler to set a tab stop.
> - When setting tab stops using the ruler, click the bottom edge of the ruler to set a tab stop (Figure 2-11).

2-10 *Tab* selector

> ### ▶ MORE INFO
>
> Use the *Format Painter* to copy tab stops from one area of your document to another area.

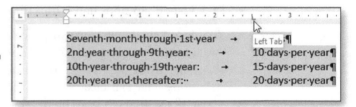

2-11 Set a left tab stop at 2.5″ on the ruler

Move a Tab Stop

It can be challenging to align text correctly and balance space between columns. But as you set and use tab stops more regularly, you become more comfortable selecting the correct type of tab stop to use, adjusting the settings of existing tab stops, and removing tab stops. When using multiple columns, adjust tab stops so you have about the same amount of white space between columns.

The easiest way to move tab stops is by using the ruler. When using the ruler to adjust a tab stop, be sure to select the appropriate text before moving a tab stop.

▶HOW TO: Move a Tab Stop

1. Select the text or paragraphs where the tab stops you want to edit are set.
2. Left-click the **tab stop** on the ruler and drag it to the new location (Figure 2-12).
 - As you click the tab stop to be moved, a vertical alignment guide appears on your document. This alignment guide displays where your text aligns.

2-12 Move a tab stop using the ruler

- Press the **Alt** key when you are moving a tab stop to display a vertical guide that allows you to place the tab stop at a specific measurement (Figure 2-13).

3. Release the pointer to set the tab stop in the new location.

4. Repeat this process until you are satisfied with the placement of your tab stops.

2-13 Use the *Alt* key to adjust a tab stop

Remove a Tab Stop

Occasionally, when setting tab stops using the ruler, you unintentionally add an unwanted tab stop. Or sometimes you might just want to remove unwanted tab stops. To remove tab stops from existing text, it is very important to select the text or paragraphs before deleting the tabs. When you remove or clear a tab stop, the tabbed text realigns to the default 0.5" tab stop or nearest remaining custom tab stop. Following are three different ways to remove tab stops:

- Drag a tab stop off (below) the ruler.
- Clear a single tab stop in the *Tabs* dialog box.
- Clear all tab stops in the *Tabs* dialog box.

To clear a single tab stop using the ruler, select the text or paragraphs, select the tab stop you want to remove, drag the tab stop down below the ruler, and release the pointer.

When using the *Tabs* dialog box to remove tab stops, you can clear a single tab stop or clear all existing tab stops on the selected text or paragraphs.

▶ HOW TO: Clear a Tab Stop Using the Tabs Dialog Box

1. Select the text or paragraphs that contain the tab stops you want to remove.

2. Click the **Paragraph** launcher [*Home* or *Layout* tab] to open the *Paragraph* dialog box.

3. Click the **Tabs** button to open the *Tabs* dialog box.

4. To remove a single tab stop, select the tab stop to remove in the list of existing tab stops and click the **Clear** button (Figure 2-14). Repeat on any other tab stops you want to remove.

5. To clear all tab stops, click the **Clear All** button.

6. Click **OK** to close the *Tabs* dialog box.

2-14 Clear a tab stop in the *Tabs* dialog box

Add a Tab Leader

You can use **leaders** to insert dots or a line between text when using tab stops. The most common type of leader is the dot leader, which is regularly used in a table of contents. In a table of contents, a dot leader is inserted between the text and the right aligned page number. You can also use leaders to insert a dashed line in the blank space between columns or to create a solid underline when creating a printed form.

Word has three different types of leaders. Examples of each of these are in the following table:

Types of Leaders

Leader	Example of Use
Dot	Chapter 1 .. 4
Dash	Vacation Days -------- 10 days per year
Solid underline	Name _____

You can add leaders to existing or new tab stops, but they can only be added in the *Tabs* dialog box.

▶ HOW TO: Add a Tab Leader

1. Select the text or paragraphs where you want to add a tab leader.

2. Click the **Paragraph** launcher [*Home* or *Layout* tab] to open the *Paragraph* dialog box.

3. Click the **Tabs** button to open the *Tabs* dialog box.

4. Select an existing tab stop or type a number in the *Tab stop position* text box to set a new tab stop.

5. Select the type of leader to apply in the *Leader* area.

6. Click **Set**. Figure 2-15 is an example of a dash leader.

7. Click **OK** to close the *Tabs* dialog box.

Dash tab leader

1. As indicated in the Employee Handbook, paid vacation accrues as per the following schedule:

Seventh month through 1st year:----- 5 days
2nd year through 9th year: ----------- 10 days per year
10th year through 19th year:---------- 15 days per year
20th year and thereafter: ------------ 20 days per year

2-15 Tab stop with a dash leader

Change Default Tab Stops

By default, Word has a left tab stop every 0.5". When you set a tab stop in Word, this custom tab stop overrides all preceding default tab stops. The default tab stops after your custom tab stop still remain. For example, if you set a left tab stop at the horizontal midpoint (typically 3.25") and press **Tab** to move to the horizontal midpoint, your insertion point will move to the midpoint, not 0.5". But if you press **Tab** again, your insertion point will stop at the next default tab stop, which would be 3.5".

You can customize the interval for default tab stops. If you change the default tab stop setting, this change affects only the current document, not all new documents.

▶ HOW TO: Change Default Tab Stops

1. Click the **Paragraph** launcher [*Home* or *Layout* tab] to open the *Paragraph* dialog box.

2. Click the **Tabs** button to open the *Tabs* dialog box.

3. In the *Default tab stops* area, use the up or down arrow to change the default tab stops (Figure 2-16).

4. Click **OK** to close the *Tabs* dialog box.

2-16 Change default tab stops

Using Indents

Indents are another powerful tool to help you control how text aligns between the left and right margins. Indents can be thought of as temporary margins, which apply to selected paragraphs. You can use indents to indent the first line of each paragraph, set off a long quote in a report, or indent the carry-over lines when creating bulleted or numbered lists.

Similar to setting tab stops, it is important to select the text where you want to apply indent settings. You can set indents using the ruler, the *Paragraph* group on the *Layout* tab, or the *Paragraph* dialog box. The four different types of indents that you can set and use in your document are described in the following table:

Types of Indents

Indent	Example of Use	Ruler Indent Marker
Left Indent	This line has a left indent.	Left Indent
Right Indent	This line has a right indent.	Right Indent
First Line Indent	This line has a first line indent.	First Line Indent
Hanging Indent	This line has a hanging indent.	Hanging Indent

Left and Right Indents

Indents apply to an entire paragraph or multiple paragraphs, not just lines of text within a paragraph. When setting an indent, select the paragraph(s) on which to apply the indent. If your insertion point is in a paragraph, the indent you set applies to that paragraph only.

▶HOW TO: Set a Left and Right Indent Using the Ribbon

1. Select the text or paragraph where you want to apply the indent. If it is just one paragraph, place your insertion point in that paragraph.

2. Click the **Layout** tab.

3. Change the *Left* and *Right* indent settings [*Paragraph* group]. This change is applied to the selected text (Figure 2-17).

 • When an indent is set on a paragraph and you press *Enter* at the end of the paragraph, the indent carries over to the next paragraph.

2-17 Change left and right indents

Indents can also be set using the ruler by dragging the indent marker to the desired location after you select the text you want to indent. As you drag the indent marker, an alignment guide displays the location where your text aligns.

2-18 Change left indent using the ruler

▶HOW TO: Set Indents Using the Ruler

1. Select the text or paragraph you want to indent. If it is just one paragraph, place your insertion point in that paragraph.
2. Left click the **left indent marker** (bottom square), drag to the desired location, and release the pointer. The left indent is applied to the text (Figure 2-18).
3. Left click the **right indent marker**, drag to the desired location, and release the pointer. The right indent is applied to the text (Figure 2-19).

2-19 Change right indent using the ruler

> **ANOTHER WAY**
>
> Set left and right indents using the *Paragraph* dialog box. Click the **Paragraph** launcher to open the *Paragraph* dialog box.

The **Decrease Indent** and **Increase Indent** buttons in the *Paragraph* group on the *Home* tab increase or decrease the left indent in increments of 0.5" (Figure 2-20). Remove a left indent by clicking at the beginning of the paragraph and pressing **Backspace** or clicking the **Decrease Indent** button.

2-20 *Decrease Indent* and *Increase Indent* buttons

First Line and Hanging Indents

You can use a **First line indent** to indent the first line of a paragraph instead of using a tab. A **Hanging indent** is typically used with bulleted and numbered lists but can be used effectively to indent text that wraps to a second or more lines, such as a references page. You can use the *Paragraph* dialog box to set first line and hanging indents.

▶HOW TO: Set a First Line or a Hanging Indent Using the Paragraph Dialog box

1. Select the paragraph(s) you want to indent.
2. Click the **Paragraph** launcher [*Home* or *Layout* tab] to open the *Paragraph* dialog box.
3. Click the **Special** drop-down list in the *Indentation* area and choose the type of indent: **First line** or **Hanging** (Figure 2-21).
4. In the *By* area, type the indent amount or use the up or down buttons to increase or decrease the amount of the indent.
 - The *Preview* area displays the text with the indent applied.
5. Click **OK** to close the *Paragraph* dialog box.

You can also use the ruler to set a first line indent. Select the paragraph(s) you want to indent and drag the first line indent marker (top triangle) to the desired location (Figure 2-22). The alignment guide displays where the first line of each paragraph align.

To set a hanging indent using the ruler, select the paragraph(s) you want to indent and drag the hanging indent marker (bottom triangle) to the desired location (Figure 2-23). The alignment guide displays where the carryover lines of the paragraph align.

2-21 Set first line or hanging indent using the *Paragraph* dialog box

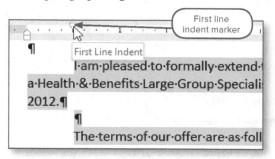

2-22 Set a first line indent using the ruler

2-23 Set a hanging indent using the ruler

An ***outdent*** aligns text outside the left or right margins. Outdents are sometimes used to emphasize section headings so they are slightly to the left of the left margin. To apply an outdent, set a ***negative value*** (−0.25") in the indents area in the *Paragraph* dialog box or *Paragraph* group on the *Layout* tab or by dragging the indent marker outside of the left or right margins.

Remove Indents

Removing indents moves the indent markers back to either the left or right margin, so the margins control the alignment of text rather than the indents. Remember to select the paragraph or paragraphs before removing the indents. You can remove indents using the *Paragraph* dialog box or the *Paragraph* group on the *Layout* tab. When using either of these methods, set the indent value to 0" (Figure 2-24).

The ruler can also be used to remove indents. When using this method, select the text or paragraphs on which to remove the indents, and drag the indent marker(s) to the margin.

2-24 Remove indents using the *Paragraph* dialog box

In this Pause & Practice project, you format a résumé for Richelle Wilkinson. This résumé is a two-page document, and you change the margins, set tab stops and leaders, and use indents.

File Needed: ***Resume-02.docx*** *(Student data files are available in the Library of your SIMnet account)*
Completed Project File Name: ***[your initials] PP W2-1.docx***

1. Open the ***Resume-02*** document from your student data files.
2. Save this document as [your initials] PP W2-1.
3. Change the margins of the résumé.
 a. Click the **Layout** tab.
 b. Click the **Margins** button [*Page Setup* group] and select **Custom Margins** from the drop-down list. The *Page Setup* dialog box opens.
 c. In the *Margins* area (Figure 2-25), click in the **Top** box, delete the existing margin, and type .75.
 d. Click in the **Bottom** box, delete the existing margin, and type .75.
 e. Click the **down arrow** to the right of the *Left* box to change the left margin to **1"**.
 f. Click the **down arrow** to the right of the *Right* box to change the right margin to **1"**.
 g. Click the **Apply to** drop-down list at the bottom of the dialog box and select **Whole document** if it is not already selected.
 h. Click **OK** to apply the new margin settings and close the dialog box.

2-25 Change margins in the *Page Setup* dialog box

4. Set a right tab stop with a dash leader.
 a. Select the **"Loomis, CA October 2014 Present"** text below "*HEAD TEACHER, LOOMIS LEARNING CENTER.*"
 b. Click the **Paragraph** launcher [*Layout* or *Home* tab] to open the *Paragraph* dialog box.
 c. Click the **Tabs** button in the bottom left of the *Paragraph* dialog box to open the *Tabs* dialog box (Figure 2-26).
 d. Type 6.5 in the *Tab stop position* area.
 e. Select the **Right** radio button in the *Alignment* area.
 f. Select the **3** (dash leader) radio button in the *Leader* area.
 g. Click the **Set** button to set this tab stop and leader.
 h. Click the **OK** button to close the dialog box.
5. Use the *Format Painter* to apply the tab setting to multiple areas of the résumé.
 a. Place the insertion point in the line you just formatted.
 b. Double-click the **Format Painter** button [*Home* tab, *Clipboard* group].

2-26 Set a right tab stop with a dash leader

c. Click each of the city, state, and date lines in the "EXPERIENCE" and "EDUCATION" sections to apply the tab settings as shown in Figure 2-27.

d. Click the **Format Painter** button to turn off copy format.

6. Remove an existing tab stop and set a left tab stop.

a. On the second page, select the lines of text below the "REFERENCES" heading.

b. Click the **Paragraph** launcher [*Layout* or *Home* tab] to open the *Paragraph* dialog box.

c. Click the **Tabs** button in the bottom left of the *Paragraph* dialog box to open the *Tabs* dialog box.

d. In the *Tab stop position* area, select the existing tab stop (**2.5"**) and click the **Clear** button to remove the existing tab.

e. Type 3.75 in the *Tab stop position* area.

f. Select the **Left** radio button in the *Alignment* area if it is not already selected.

g. Select the **1 None** radio button in the *Leader* area if it is not already selected.

h. Click the **Set** button to set this left tab stop (Figure 2-28).

i. Click the **OK** button to close the dialog box.

7. Apply a left and right indent to selected text.

a. Place the insertion point in the paragraph below the "PROFILE" heading on the first page.

b. Click the **Layout** tab.

c. Click the **Left** indent area [*Paragraph* group], type .25 to replace the existing setting, and press **Enter**.

d. Click the **Right** indent area, type .25 to replace the existing setting, and press **Enter**.

8. Save and close this document (Figure 2-29).

2-27 Use the *Format Painter* to apply tab settings

2-28 Set a left tab stop on selected text

2-29 PP W2-1 completed

Inserting Page Numbers, Headers, and Footers

Page numbering, *headers*, and *footers* are regularly used in multiple-page documents. You can set the header, footer, or page number to appear on each page of the document, which means you only have to type the information once, and Word repeats that information on each subsequent page. The header area of a document is above the top margin, and the footer area is below the bottom margin.

Page Numbering

When you use Word to insert page numbers, a *page number field* is inserted in the header or footer of the document. This page number field automatically displays the current page number. You can control the page number location and the page number format.

Insert Page Number

Word gives you a variety of page number locations, horizontal alignment options, and number format options. The following is a list of the basic page number placement options:

- *Top of Page*
- *Bottom of Page*
- *Page Margins*
- *Current Position*

▶ **HOW TO: Insert a Page Number**

1. Click the **Insert** tab.
2. Click the **Page Number** button [*Header & Footer* group]. A drop-down list of options appears (Figure 2-30).
3. Click either **Top of Page** or **Bottom of Page**. Another drop-down list of page number options appears.
 - The top three options in this list are simple page numbers aligned at the left, center, or right.
 - Further down this list there are custom page number options.
4. Click one of the page number options to insert the current page number. The header or footer area opens with the page number inserted, and the *Header & Footer Tools Design* tab opens (Figure 2-31).
5. Click the **Close Header and Footer** button [*Close* group].

2-30 Insert page number

2-31 Page number inserted in the header on the left

> ▶ **ANOTHER WAY**
>
> Close the header and footer by pressing the **Esc** key or double-clicking in the body of the document.

Edit Page Number in Header or Footer

When you close the header or footer, the page number appears in gray rather than black like the text of the document. The header and footer areas are outside the boundaries of the

margins. If you want to edit the page number or contents of the header or footer, you have to open the header or footer. There are three ways to do this:

- Right-click the header or footer and select **Edit Header** or **Edit Footer**.
- Click the **Insert** tab, click the **Header** or **Footer** button in the *Header & Footer* group, and choose **Edit Header** or **Edit Footer**.
- Double-click the header or footer area of the document.

Different First Page

There are times when you might not want the page number and header or footer to print on the first page, but you want it to appear on the second and continuing pages. For example, on both multiple-page business letters and reports, the page number is typically not on the first page but is on the second and subsequent pages. Word gives you the option to set a *different first page*.

▶**HOW TO:** Set a Different First Page Header and Footer

1. Go to the first page of the document.

2. Open the header or footer if it is not already open. Use one of the following methods to open the header or footer if it is not already open:

 - Right-click the header or footer and select **Edit Header** or **Edit Footer**.
 - Click the **Insert** tab, click the **Header** or **Footer** button in the *Header & Footer* group, and choose **Edit Header** or **Edit Footer**.
 - Double-click in the header or footer area of the document.

3. Click the **Different First Page** check box [*Header & Footer Tools Design* tab, *Options* group] (Figure 2-32).

4. Click the **Close Header and Footer** button [*Close* group]. The page number, header, and footer no longer appear on the first page but do appear on the second and continuing pages.

2-32 *Different First Page* check box

> ▶ MORE INFO
>
> When inserting a page number, header, or footer, it is best to insert it on the first page of the document. This becomes increasingly important as you add section breaks to a document.

Page Number Format

When using page numbering, you might want a different type of page number format, numbering to begin with a different page number, or a chapter number before the page number. The *Page Number Format* dialog box provides you with page numbering options (Figure 2-33).

2-33 *Page Number Format* dialog box

1. After inserting a page number, click the **Page Number** button [*Header & Footer Tools Design* or *Insert* tab, *Header & Footer* group] and select **Format Page Numbers**. The *Page Number Format* dialog box opens (see Figure 2-33).
2. Click the *Number format* **drop-down list** and select a page number format. There are six preset page numbering options from which to choose.
3. Select an option in the *Page numbering* section to *Continue from previous section* (default setting) or *Start at* a different page number.
 - Click the **Start at** radio button to set a different starting page number.
 - Type in the starting page number or use the up or down arrow to set the starting page number.
4. Click **OK** to close the *Page Number Format* dialog box.
5. Click the **Close Header and Footer** button [*Close* group].

Remove Page Number

If you want to remove the page numbering from a document, there are two different ways to do this.

- Select **Remove Page Numbers** from the *Page Number* drop-down list (Figure 2-34).
- Open the header or footer and manually delete the page number.

2-34 Remove page numbers

Insert Header and Footer Content

In addition to inserting page numbers into the header or footer of a document, you might want to include the number of pages in the document, date or time, title of the document, company name, or other custom content. You can enter information manually into the header or footer, or you can have Word insert document property fields.

1. Click the **Insert** tab.
2. Click the **Header** button and choose **Edit Header** in the drop-down list, or double-click in the *Header* area of the document (above the top margin). The header of the document opens and the *Header & Footer Tools Design* tab displays.
 - When you edit a header or footer, both the header and footer open and the *Header & Footer Tools Design* tab displays.
 - On this tab, there is a *Navigation* group to help you move between the header and footer and move through the different headers and footers in the document (Figure 2-35).
3. Type your information in the *Header* area (Figure 2-36).
 - You can change the formatting and alignment as desired.
 - You can insert a page number with the header or footer open.
4. Click the **Close Header and Footer** button [*Close* group].

2-35 *Navigation* group on the *Header & Footer Tools Design* tab

2-36 Enter custom information in the header

Number of Pages Field

In addition to inserting the current page number in a document, you can add a field code to automatically insert the total number of pages in a document (*NumPages* field).

▶HOW TO: Insert the Number of Pages Field

1. Open the header or footer. The page number should already be inserted in the document.
2. Click before the page number, type Page, and press the **spacebar**.
3. Click after the page number and press the **spacebar**, type of, and press the **spacebar**.
4. Click the **Document Info** button [*Header & Footer Tools Design* tab, *Insert* group] (Figure 2-37).
 - You can also click the **Quick Parts** button.
5. Select **Field** from the drop-down list. The *Field* dialog box opens (Figure 2-38).
6. In the *Field names* area, scroll down and select **NumPages**. The description of the field is displayed in the *Description* area.
7. In the *Format* area, select a page number format.
8. Click **OK** to close the *Field* dialog box. The number of pages in the document displays (Figure 2-39).
9. Click the **Close Header and Footer** button [*Close* group].

2-37 Insert field code

2-38 Insert *NumPages* field from the *Field* dialog box

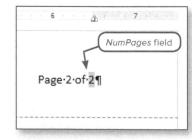

2-39 Page number and number of pages field inserted into the header

Date and Time

You can type a date or the time in the header or footer of a document, or you can have Word insert this information. The advantages of inserting the date and time are that you have a variety of date and time formats from which to choose, and you can choose to have the date and time update automatically each time you open the document.

▶ HOW TO: Insert the Date and Time

1. Open the header or footer area and position the insertion point at the position where you want the date inserted.

2. Click the **Date & Time** button [*Header & Footer Tools Design* tab, *Insert* group]. The *Date and Time* dialog box opens (Figure 2-40).

3. Select the date or time format to use in the *Available formats* area.

4. Check the **Update automatically** check box if you want the date to update automatically.

 - Do not check *Update automatically* on time-sensitive documents where the date should remain constant.

5. Click **OK** to close the *Date and Time* dialog box. The date displays the header.

6. Click the **Close Header and Footer** button [*Close* group].

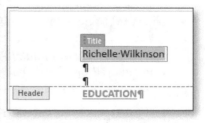

2-40 *Date and Time* dialog box

Document Properties

When you have entered document properties in a Word document, you can automatically insert this information in the header or footer. For example, you might want to include the title of the document, name of the author, or date last modified. One of the advantages of inserting document properties rather than typing this information is that when you update the document properties, these fields automatically update in the header or footer and throughout the document.

▶ HOW TO: Insert Document Properties

1. Open the header or footer and place the insertion point at the location where you want the document property inserted.

2. Click the **Document Info** button [*Header & Footer Tools Design* tab, *Insert* group] (Figure 2-41).

3. Select the document property field or click **Document Property** and select the document property of your choice from the drop-down list. The document property displays in the document (Figure 2-42).

 - You can also click the **Quick Parts** button [*Header & Footer Tools Design* tab, *Insert* group] and select **Document Property**.
 - Press the **right arrow** key on your keyboard to deselect a document property field.

4. Click the **Close Header and Footer** button [*Close* group].

2-41 Insert document property field

2-42 *Title* document property field inserted in the header

Built-In Headers, Footers, and Page Numbers

In addition to inserting basic page numbers, manually adding header or footer content, and inserting date and time, Word provides you with a variety of built-in custom header, footer, and page number format options. Many of the header and footer options include document properties that are automatically inserted and updated.

▶ HOW TO: Insert a Built-In Header, Footer, or Page Number

2-43 List of built-in headers

1. Click the **Insert** tab.
2. Click the **Header**, **Footer**, or **Page Number** button [*Header & Footer* group] and select a built-in header, footer, or page number from the choices in the drop-down list (Figure 2-43). The selected content displays into the document.
 - Document property fields update automatically with document property information.
 - Some fields, such as *Pick the date*, require you to input or select information.
3. Click the **Close Header and Footer** button [*Close* group].

Keep in mind when you are using built-in headers, footers, and page numbers that many of these use tables, graphics, and advanced formatting, which makes editing more challenging without a thorough understanding of this type of content.

PAUSE & PRACTICE: WORD 2-2

In this Pause & Practice project, you modify the résumé from *Pause & Practice 2-1*. You add a header that appears only on the second page of this document and insert a document property field, page number, and Word field into the header.

File Needed: *[your initials] PP W2-1.docx*
Completed Project File Name: *[your initials] PP W2-2.docx*

1. Open the *[your initials] PP W2-1* document completed in *Pause & Practice 2-1*.
2. Save this document as [your initials] PP W2-2.

3. Edit the document properties.
 a. Click the **File** tab to open the *Backstage* view.
 b. In the *Info* area, click in the **Title** document property text box and type Richelle Wilkinson.
 c. Click the **Back** arrow to return to the résumé.

4. Insert a document property field in the header of the résumé.
 a. Place the insertion point at the beginning of the first page.
 b. Click the **Insert** tab.
 c. Click the **Header** button [*Header & Footer* group] and select **Edit Header** from the drop-down list. The header on the first page opens.
 d. Click the **Document Info** button [*Header & Footer Tools Design* tab, *Insert* group] and select **Document Title** from the drop-down list. The *Title* document property displays in the header.
 e. Leave the header open for the next instructions.

5. Insert a page number and number of pages field in the header and set it to display only on the second page.
 a. With the header still open, press the **right arrow** key once to deselect the document property field you just inserted.
 b. Press **Tab** two times to move to the right margin, type Page and **space** once.
 c. Click the **Page Number** button [*Header & Footer* group], select **Current Position** from the drop-down list, and select **Plain Number**. The page number displays in the header.
 d. **Space** once, type of, and **space** once.
 e. Click the **Document Info** (or **Quick Parts**) button [*Header & Footer Tools Design* tab, *Insert* group] and select **Field** from the drop-down list. The *Field* dialog box opens.
 f. Select **NumPages** in the *Field names* area (this is the field code to insert the total number of pages in the document) (Figure 2-44).
 g. Select **1**, **2**, **3** in the *Format* area and click **OK** to insert the number of pages in the header.
 h. Press **Enter** two times to insert two blank lines after the header.
 i. Check to ensure that there are spaces between each of the words and page numbers.
 j. Check the **Different First Page** check box [*Header & Footer Tools Design* tab, *Options* group]. This removes the header content from the first page, but the header content displays on the second page (Figure 2-45).

2-44 Insert *NumPages* field

2-45 Header with document property field, page number, and number of pages field

 k. Click the **Close Header and Footer** button [*Close* group] to close the header and return to the document.

6. Save and close the document (Figure 2-46).

Using Page and Section Breaks

As you're typing a document and you get to the bottom of the page, Word automatically moves to the top of the next page so you can continue typing; this is referred to as a *soft page break*. The document's content and margins determine how much information fits on a page and what information flows to a new page.

There may be times when you want to start a new page before you get to the bottom margin or you might want different margins or page orientation in a different section of your document. Word provides options for page and section breaks to control page endings and formatting (Figure 2-47).

2-47 Page and section breaks

> MORE INFO
>
> Turn **Show/Hide** [*Home* tab, *Paragraph* group] on when working with page and section breaks, so you can view the placement of these breaks.

Page Breaks

Page breaks end one page and begin a new page. When you insert a *Page* break, you control where one page ends and a new page begins. There are three different types of page breaks: *Page*, *Column*, and *Text Wrapping*.

▶ HOW TO: Insert a Page Break

1. Position the insertion point at the point in your document where you want to end one page and begin a new page.
2. Click the **Layout** tab.
3. Click the **Breaks** button [*Page Setup* group]. A drop-down list appears.
4. Select **Page** from the drop-down list. A page break displays in the document (Figure 2-48).
 - Turn on **Show/Hide** [*Home* tab, *Paragraph* group].
 - The *Page Break* indicator is visible and displays where the page breaks (Figure 2-49).

2-48 Insert *Page* break

ANOTHER WAY

Press **Ctrl+Enter** to insert a page break at the insertion point.

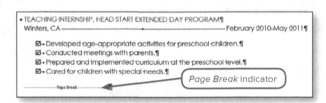

2-49 *Page* break inserted in a document

Section Breaks

Section breaks allow you even more formatting control over your document than page breaks. Section breaks can be used to format different headers, footers, and page numbering in different sections of your document. For example, if you want one page in your document to be landscape orientation, you can use a section break to control the format of an individual section. There are four different types of section breaks:

- *Next Page*: Insert a section break and start the new section on the next page.
- *Continuous*: Insert a section break and start the new section on the same page.
- *Even Page*: Insert a section break and start the new section on the next even-numbered page.
- *Odd Page*: Insert a section break and start the new section on the next odd-numbered page.

▶ HOW TO: Insert a Next Page Section Break

1. Position the insertion point at the point in your document where you want to end one page and begin new section on a new page.
2. Click the **Layout** tab.
3. Click the **Breaks** button [*Page Setup* group]. A drop-down list appears.
4. Select **Next Page** from the drop-down list. A next page section break displays in the document.
 - Turn on **Show/Hide** [*Home* tab, *Paragraph* group].
 - The *Section Break (Next Page)* indicator is visible and displays where the next page section break occurs (Figure 2-50).

2-50 *Next Page* section break inserted in a document

Edit Page and Section Breaks

When finalizing a document, you might need to change the placement of a page or section break or remove a page or section break from the document. You can delete and move breaks in the same way you delete and move text from a document.

To delete a page or section break, select the break and press **Delete**.

There are two different ways to move a section or page break to a new location. First select the **Page Break** or **Section Break**, and then use one of the move options below:

- Cut and paste
- Drag and drop (Figure 2-51)

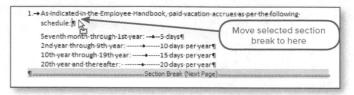

2-51 Move section break using drag and drop

Using Bulleted, Numbered, and Multilevel Lists

Bulleted and *numbered lists* highlight important information. Generally, use bulleted lists when the order of information is not important, and use numbered lists for sequential information. A *Multilevel list* can combine a variety of numbers, letters, and bullets. Word provides you with built-in bulleted, numbered, and multilevel lists, but you can also customize how the information in the list displays and aligns.

 MORE INFO

When using bulleted and numbered lists, do not use a period at the end of lists containing only words or short phrases. If you are using complete sentences in your list, use a period at the end of each sentence.

Create a Bulleted List

You can create a bulleted list from existing text or you can create a new bulleted list. You choose the type of bullet to use from the *Bullet Library* in the *Bullets* drop-down list.

▶HOW TO: Create a Bulleted List

1. Select the text to be converted to a bulleted list, or, if you are beginning a new bulleted list, place the insertion point at the location where you want to begin the list.

2. Click the **Bullets** drop-down arrow [*Home* tab, *Paragraph* group] to open the library of bullet options (Figure 2-52).
 - If you click the *Bullets* button (not the *Bullets* drop-down arrow), the most recently used bullet is used for the bulleted list.

3. Select a bullet from the list of options.

4. Type your information after the bullet if you are typing a new bulleted list.

5. Press **Enter** after a bulleted item to add another bullet.

6. Press **Enter** two times after the last bullet, or click the **Bullets** button to turn off bullets.

2-52 *Bullets* drop-down list

By default, bulleted lists are formatted using a hanging indent. The first line is indented 0.25" and the hanging indent is set at 0.5". You can adjust the indent using the *Decrease Indent* or *Increase Indent* buttons, ruler, or *Paragraph* dialog box.

You can add new bulleted items in the middle or at the end of the list by pressing **Enter** in front of or at the end of an existing bulleted item. To add a bulleted item before the first item in the list, click at the beginning of the first item and press **Enter**.

> **MORE INFO**
>
> You can use a line break (**Shift+Enter**) at the end of a bulleted sentence to add a blank line between bulleted items.

Customize a Bulleted List

In addition to using the bullets listed in the *Bullets Library*, you can select and use a custom bullet. You have the option of using a symbol from one of the font groups, or you can use a picture. If you use a picture, you can select one from the Bing Image Search or import a graphic of your own to use as a bullet.

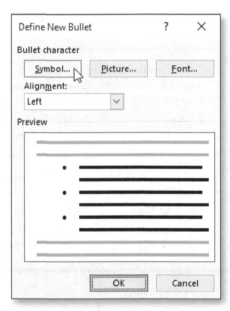

▶**HOW TO:** Customize a Bulleted List

1. Select the bulleted list.
2. Click the **Bullets** drop-down arrow [*Home* tab, *Paragraph* group] and select **Define New Bullet**. The *Define New Bullet* dialog box opens (Figure 2-53).
3. Click the **Symbol** or **Picture** button to open the *Symbol* or *Picture* dialog box.
 - If you click the **Symbol** button, the *Symbol* dialog box opens (Figure 2-54). From the *Font* drop-down list, you can select a symbol from any of the font sets (the most common are *Symbol*, *Wingdings*, and *Webdings*) or from *Recently used symbols*.
 - Each symbol has a character code to identify the symbol (see Figure 2-54).
 - If you click the **Picture** button, the *Insert Pictures* dialog box opens. You can import your own picture bullet from a file or use Bing Image Search to locate a picture to use as a bullet.
4. Select the bullet to use and click **OK** (or **Insert** or **Open** depending on the open dialog box) to close the dialog box.
5. Click **OK** to close the *Define New Bullet* dialog box.

2-53 *Define New Bullet* dialog box

You also have the option of having multiple levels of bullets with a different bullet for each level. Each subsequent bullet level is indented to distinguish it from the previous level. There are a few ways to increase or decrease the bullet level.

2-54 *Symbol* dialog box

- Click the **Bullets** drop-down arrow [*Home* tab, *Paragraph* group] and select a bullet list level from the **Change List Level** drop-down list (Figure 2-55).
- Select or click at the beginning of a bulleted item and press **Tab** to increase bullet level.
- Select or click at the beginning of a bulleted item and click the **Increase Indent** button [*Home* tab, *Paragraph* group] to increase bullet level.
- Press **Shift+Tab** or click the **Decrease Indent** button to decrease the bullet level.

2-55 Change bulleted list level

Create a Numbered List

Creating a numbered list is similar to creating a bulleted list. The **Numbering Library** in the *Numbering* drop-down list contains number format options.

▶ HOW TO: Create a Numbered List

1. Select the text you want to convert to a numbered list, or, if you are beginning a new numbered list, place the insertion point at the location where you want to begin the list.

2. Click the **Numbering** drop-down arrow [*Home* tab, *Paragraph* group] to open the *Numbering Library* of number format options (Figure 2-56).
 - If you click the *Numbering* button, the most recently used number format is used for the numbered list.

3. Select a number style from the list of options.

4. Type your information after the number if you are typing a new numbered list.

5. Press **Enter** after a numbered item to add another numbered item.

6. Press **Enter** two times after the last numbered item, or click the **Numbering** button to turn off numbering.

2-56 Numbering format options

> **ANOTHER WAY**
> Both the *Numbering* and *Bullets* drop-down lists are available from the mini toolbar when you select or right-click text.

Customize a Numbered List

In addition to being able to select a format from the *Numbering Library*, you also have the options to *Change List Level*, *Define New Number Format*, and *Set Numbering Value*.

The **Change List Level** option in the *Numbering* drop-down list allows you to select the level of the list. The numbering of each subsequent level of the list is dependent upon the number format you select.

You are not limited to the numbering formats available in the *Numbering* drop-down list. The **Define New Number Format** option allows you to customize how the numbered list displays.

1. Select the text where you want to change the number format, or, if you are beginning a new numbered list, place the insertion point at the location where you want to begin the list.

2. Click the **Numbering** drop-down arrow [*Home* tab, *Paragraph* group], and select **Define New Number Format**. The *Define New Number Format* dialog box opens (Figure 2-57).

3. Click the **Number style** drop-down arrow to select a number format from the list of options.
 - You can also change the numbering font by clicking the **Font** button and selecting a font, size, and style to apply to the numbered list.

4. In the *Number format* area, customize how the numbers display.
 - Typically, a period follows the numbers, but you can change this to an ending parenthesis, hyphen, other character, or no punctuation.

5. Click the **Alignment** drop-down arrow to change number alignment.
 - Numbers align on the left by default, but you can change the number alignment to center or right.

6. The *Preview* area displays how your number format will appear in your document.

7. Click **OK** to apply the number format and close the dialog box.

2-57 *Define New Number Format* dialog box

The ***Set Numbering Value*** dialog box includes options to *Start new list* or *Continue from previous list*. You can also set the number value to begin a new list. Open the *Set Numbering Value* dialog box from the *Numbering* drop-down list or right-click a numbered list and select *Set Numbering Value* from the context menu (Figure 2-58).

When using numbering, the context menu lists options to *Adjust List Indents*, *Restart at 1*, *Continue Numbering*, and *Set Numbering Value* (Figure 2-59).

2-58 *Set Numbering Value* dialog box

> ▌ MORE INFO
>
> Use the *Format Painter* to copy numbered or bulleted list formatting to other areas in a document.

2-59 Context menu numbering options

Multilevel Lists

Multilevel lists allow you to customize a list using a combination of numbers, letters, or bullets. Word provides you with a *List Library* from which to select a multilevel list. You can customize an existing multilevel list or define your own list.

As you define a new multilevel list, you have the following options to customize each level of the list:

- Number format including font and starting number
- Number style, which can be a number, letter, Roman numeral, or bullet
- Position of the number and the text that follows

▶ **HOW TO:** Define a New Multilevel List

1. Select the text or the beginning point on which to apply a multilevel list.

2. Click the **Multilevel List** drop-down arrow [*Home* tab, *Paragraph* group].

3. Select **Define New Multilevel list** from the drop-down list. The *Define new Multilevel list* dialog box opens (Figure 2-60).

4. Click the **More** button in the bottom left of the dialog box to display all formatting options.

5. In the *Click level to modify* area, select the level you want to modify.

6. In the *Number format* area, select the number format, starting number, and number style for the selected level.

7. In the *Position* area, set the *Number alignment*, the *Aligned at* measurement (which is the first line indent), *Text indent at* measurement (which is the hanging indent).

8. Click the **Set for All Levels** button to open the *Set for All Levels* dialog box where you to set the indents for all levels (Figure 2-61).

9. Click **OK** to apply the multilevel list settings.

2-60 *Define new Multilevel list* dialog box

2-61 *Set for All Levels* dialog box

SLO 2.7

Using Styles and Themes

Styles are a collection of preset formatting that you can apply to a paragraph or selected text. A style can control the font, font size, style, color, effects, indents, line spacing, paragraph spacing, and borders applied to text. You can use styles to apply this preset formatting to titles, section headings, paragraph headings, text, lists, and tables. *Themes* are a collection of fonts, colors, and effects that you can apply to an entire document. Both styles and themes keep the formatting consistent throughout a single document or multiple documents.

Style Gallery

The *Style gallery* in the *Styles* group on the *Home* tab provides you with numerous built-in styles to apply to selected text in a document (Figure 2-62). The *Style* gallery does not display all of the available styles but rather displays the more commonly used styles.

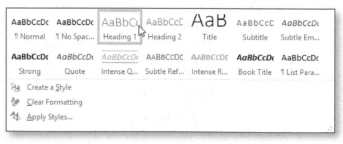

2-62 *Style* gallery

Apply a Built-In Style

You can quickly preview or apply styles to selected text or paragraphs. To preview a style, place the pointer on a style in the *Style* gallery. A live preview of the style displays on the selected text or paragraph. You can apply a style to the text by clicking a style in the *Style* gallery.

> ▶**HOW TO:** Apply a Built-In Style from the Style Gallery

1. Select the text or paragraph where you want to apply the style.
2. Select a style from the *Style* gallery [*Home* tab, *Styles* group].
 - To see all of the styles in the *Style* gallery, click the **More** button (Figure 2-63).
 - To see the next row of styles available in the *Style* gallery, click the **down arrow** at the right side of the gallery.

2-63 Click the *More* button to display more styles

> ▶
> ## ANOTHER WAY
> Apply a style to selected text by selecting or right-clicking text, choosing **Styles** from the mini tool-bar, and selecting the style to apply.

Modify a Style

Once a style has been applied to the text, you can change the formatting of this text. One way to do this is to make changes to font, font size, color, style, effects, etc., to the selected text without actually changing the style.

The other option is to modify the style. The advantage of modifying a style when you make a change is that the style will be consistent when applied to other text in a document. When you modify a style, text formatted with the modified style automatically updates to match the modified style. There are two ways to modify a style:

- *Update [style name] to Match Selection*
- *Modify* style

> ▶**HOW TO:** Update Style to Match Selection

1. Apply a style to selected text.
2. Make formatting changes on the text where the style was applied.
3. Select the text you changed.
4. Right-click the style in the *Style* gallery and choose **Update [style name] to Match Selection** (Figure 2-64).
 - The style updates to match the selected text.
 - All other text with this style applied updates automatically.

2-64 Update style to match selected text

You can also modify a style using the *Modify Style* dialog box.

> **HOW TO:** Modify an Existing Style

1. Right-click the style to modify in the *Style* gallery and select **Modify**. The *Modify Style* dialog box opens (Figure 2-65).
2. Make desired changes to the style. You can make basic formatting changes in the *Formatting* area of this dialog box.
3. Click the **Format** button at the bottom left to open other dialog boxes, such as *Font*, *Paragraph*, *Tabs*, *Borders*, etc.
 - Make desired formatting changes to the style and click **OK** to apply changes.
 - The formatting changes display in the *Preview* area.
4. Click **OK** to apply the style change and to close the *Modify Style* dialog box.

2-65 *Modify Style* dialog box

Apply a Theme

A theme is a collection of fonts, colors, and effects. Themes are similar to styles, but instead of just applying format to selected text, themes apply to an entire document. All documents have a theme; the default theme for a new document is *Office*. You can change the theme of a document or you can individually change the *Theme Colors*, *Theme Fonts*, or *Theme Effects* set in a document.

> **HOW TO:** Apply a Document Theme

1. Click the **Design** tab.
2. Click the **Themes** button [*Document Formatting* group].
3. Select the theme to apply from the *Themes* gallery (Figure 2-66).
4. Click the **Colors**, **Fonts**, or **Effects** buttons [*Design* tab, *Document Formatting* group] to change each of these individually within the existing theme.

2-66 Change the *Theme* of a document

In this Pause & Practice project, you modify the résumé you edited in *Pause & Practice 2-2*. You add a bulleted list, customize the bulleted list, insert a page break, apply and modify styles, and apply a document theme.

File Needed: *[your initials] PP W2-2.docx*
Completed Project File Name: *[your initials] PP W2-3.docx*

1. Open the *[your initials] PP W2-2* document completed in *Pause & Practice 2-2*.

2. Save this document as [your initials] PP W2-3.

3. Convert text to a bulleted list and customize the bullet.
 a. Select the four paragraphs of text below the "EXPERIENCE" heading and the city, state, and date line.
 b. Click the **Bullets** button [*Home* tab, *Paragraph* group]. The selected text converts to a bulleted list (Figure 2-67).
 c. With the bulleted paragraphs still selected, click the **Bullets** drop-down arrow and select **Define New Bullet**. The *Define New Bullet* dialog box opens.
 d. Click the **Symbol** button. The *Symbol* dialog box opens (Figure 2-68).
 e. Click the **Font** drop-down list and scroll down to select **Wingdings**.
 f. Scroll down the list of symbols and select the **check box** symbol (*Character code* 254).
 g. Click **OK** to close the *Symbol* dialog box.
 h. Click **OK** to close the *Define New Bullet* dialog box.

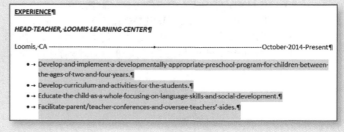

EXPERIENCE¶

HEAD·TEACHER,·LOOMIS·LEARNING·CENTER¶

Loomis,·CA --→--October·2014·Present¶

 ●→ Develop·and·implement·a·developmentally·appropriate·preschool·program·for·children·between·the·ages·of·two·and·four·years.¶
 ●→ Develop·curriculum·and·activities·for·the·students.¶
 ●→ Educate·the·child·as·a·whole·focusing·on·language·skills·and·social·development.¶
 ●→ Facilitate·parent/teacher·conferences·and·oversee·teachers'·aides.¶

2-67 Apply bullets to selected text

2-68 *Symbol* dialog box

4. Use the *Format Painter* to apply this bullet format to lines of text in the other "EXPERIENCE" sections and the "EDUCATION" section. Don't apply bullet formatting to the city, state, and date lines where the tab stops and leaders are applied.

5. Insert a page break in the document.
 a. Turn on **Show/Hide** [*Home* tab, *Paragraph* group].
 b. Place the insertion point in front of the "EDUCATION" heading.
 c. Select the **Layout** tab and click the **Breaks** button [*Page Setup* group].
 d. Select **Page** from the drop-down list. A page break displays at the bottom of the first page, and the "EDUCATION" section moves to the next page.

6. Change the theme and theme color of the document.
 a. Click the **Design** tab.
 b. Click the **Themes** button [*Document Formatting* group] and select **Ion** from the *Themes* gallery.
 c. Click the **Colors** button [*Document Formatting* group] and select **Red** from the *Theme Colors* drop-down list.

7. Apply styles from the *Style* gallery to selected text.
 a. On the first page of the résumé, select **"Richelle Wilkinson"** and click the **Title** style from the *Style* gallery [*Home* tab].
 b. With this text still selected, change the font size to **20 pt**.
 c. Apply the **Heading 1** style to each of the main headings ("PROFILE," "EXPERIENCE," "EDUCATION," "SKILLS," and "REFERENCES").
 d. Apply the **Heading 2** style to each of the bold and italicized subheadings in the "EXPERIENCE" and "EDUCATION" sections.

8. Modify a style.
 a. Select the **"PROFILE"** heading.
 b. Change the *Before* paragraph spacing to **16 pt**.
 c. Right-click the **Heading 1** style in the *Style* gallery and select **Update Heading 1 to Match Selection** (Figure 2-69). This style change is applied to all text with *Heading 1* style.
 d. On the second page, select **"CALIFORNIA STATE UNIVERSITY CHICO, BACHELOR OF ARTS IN CHILD DEVELOPMENT"** in the "EDUCATION" section and change the font size to **11 pt**.
 e. Right-click the **Heading 2** style in the *Style* gallery and select **Update Heading 2 to Match Selection**.

2-69 Update style to match selection

9. Save and close the document (Figure 2-70).

2-70 PP W2-3 completed

Using Find and Replace

Find and *Replace* are two extremely useful and powerful tools in Word. The *Find* feature allows you to search for and locate words and phrases in a document. The *Replace* feature allows you to search for a word or phrase and replace it with other text. You can also use *Find* and *Replace* to search for a specific type of formatting in a document and replace it with different formatting. These features are particularly useful in longer documents. When using *Find* or *Replace*, it is best to position your insertion point at the top of the document so Word searches from the beginning of your document.

Find

You can use the ***Navigation pane*** in Word to search for text and display all instances of the matching text. Word also highlights in yellow each instance of the matching text in the document. You are able to navigate through the document, see each instance, and edit as desired.

▶HOW TO: Use Find in the Navigation Pane

1. Place your insertion point at the beginning of the document.
2. Click the **Find** button [*Home* tab, *Editing* group]. The *Navigation* pane opens on the left side of the Word window.
3. Click the **Search document** text box at the top of the *Navigation* pane and type the text you want to search.
 - The matching results display below the text box.
 - Word highlights the matching text in the document.
4. Click the **Next** or **Previous** search result buttons to move through each matching instance in the document (Figure 2-71).
 - You can also click the matching instances below the *Search document* text box to go to a specific occurrence of the matching text.

2-71 Use *Find* in the *Navigation* pane

5. Edit the highlighted text in the document if you want to make changes.
6. Click the **X** to the right of the *Search Document* text box to clear the current search.
7. Click the **X** in the upper right of the *Navigation* pane to close the pane.

Find and Replace

The ***Find and Replace*** dialog box provides you three different advanced options for searching your document:

- *Find*
- *Replace*
- *Go To*

The *Find* tab of the *Find and Replace* dialog box not only searches for text in your document but also searches for specific formatting (such as font styles, line spacing, or paragraph spacing). For example, you can search for all text that is bold or italic, or that has 6 pt. *After* paragraph spacing.

Use the *Replace* feature to search for text, formatting, or a combination of text and formatting and to replace the matching text with other text, formatting, or formatted text. This feature is a quick and efficient way to find and replace text in a document.

▶HOW TO: Use Replace

1. Place your insertion point at the beginning of the document.
2. Click the **Replace** button [*Home* tab, *Editing* group] or press **Ctrl+H**. The *Find and Replace* dialog box opens with the *Replace* tab displayed (Figure 2-72).
3. Click the **Find what** text box and type the text for which you are searching.
4. Click the **Replace with** text box and type the text you want to replace the found text.
5. Click the **More** button to display advanced find options. The *Less* button hides the advanced find options.
6. Click the **Format** or **Special** button to add formatting options or special characters to either the text for which you are searching or the replacement text.
 - Put the insertion point in the **Find what** or **Replace with** text box before selecting a format or special character.
7. Click the **Find Next** button to locate the first occurrence of the text (and formatting) for which you are searching.
 - It is best to click the **Less** button to collapse this dialog box when finding and replacing content in your document.
8. When the first occurrence is found, select **Replace** (this occurrence), **Replace All** (all occurrences), or **Find Next** (skip this occurrence without replacing and move to the next).
9. Click the **Find Next** button to move to the next occurrence of the matching text and formatting.
10. When you finish finding and replacing text in the document, a dialog box opens informing you that Word has finished searching the document. Click **OK** to close this dialog box.
11. Click the **X** in the upper right corner to close the *Find and Replace* dialog box.

2-72 Replace text

When using *Find* or *Replace*, wildcards can be used to help find information. You can use wildcards before, after, or between words.

- **Question mark (?)**: A wildcard for a single character. For example, *w???* finds any words that begins with "w" and contains four letters (e.g., when, with, warm, or wish).
- **Asterisk (*)**: A wildcard for a string of characters. For example, **search*** finds any form of the word "search" (e.g., searches, searching, or searched).

> **ANOTHER WAY**
>
> **Ctrl+H** opens the *Find and Replace* dialog box with the *Replace* tab selected.

> **MORE INFO**
>
> It is a good idea to use *Match Case* when replacing acronyms (capital letters) with words so the replaced words will not be all upper case. Also, use *Find whole words only* to refine your search.

Go To

The *Go To* feature allows you to go quickly to specific items or locations in your document. This feature is different from *Find* in that *Go To* moves you to specific objects or locations in your document such as a page, section, or bookmark. This feature is available in the *Find and Replace* dialog box.

▶ HOW TO: Use the Go To Feature

1. Click the **Find** drop-down arrow [*Home* tab, *Editing* group].
2. Select **Go To**. The *Find and Replace* dialog box opens with the *Go To* tab displayed (Figure 2-73).
3. In the *Go to what* area, select the item to go to from the list of options: *Page, Section, Line, Bookmark, Comment, Footnote*, etc.
 - The text box to the right is context sensitive and changes depending on the item chosen.
4. In the text box to the right, type in a page number, section, line, bookmark, etc.
5. Click the **Go To** button.
6. Click **Close** to close this dialog box.

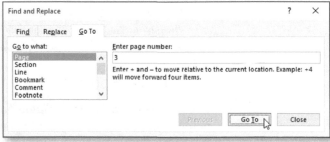

2-73 *Go To* in the *Find and Replace* dialog box

> **ANOTHER WAY**
>
> **Ctrl+G** or **F5** opens the *Find and Replace* dialog box with the *Go To* tab selected.

Using Borders, Shading, and Hyperlinks

Borders and *shading* are excellent ways to highlight or emphasize important information in a document. In Word, there are many different border and shading options including preset border options. You also have the option of applying custom borders and shading to selected text or paragraphs of your document.

A *hyperlink* functions like a button and is used to take a reader to a web page, open an existing or new document, open an email message, or move to another location in the current document. You can add a hyperlink to text or a graphic in a document.

Apply Built-In Borders

You can use the **Borders drop-down list** in the *Paragraph* group on the *Home* tab to quickly apply borders to selected text. Borders are typically applied to paragraphs, but they can also be applied to other selected text. Borders, by default, apply to the paragraph where your insertion point is unless you select specific text. Figure 2-74 shows the different types of built-in borders.

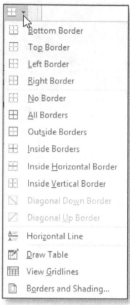

2-74 *Borders drop-down list*

▶ HOW TO: Apply Built-In Borders

1. Select the paragraph or place the insertion point in the paragraph where you want to apply the border.
2. Click the **Home** tab.
3. Click the **Borders** drop-down arrow [*Paragraph* group] (see Figure 2-74).
4. Click the border option to apply to the selected paragraph.

> **MORE INFO**
>
> You can remove borders by selecting the paragraph or text on which the borders are applied and clicking the **No Border** option in the *Borders* drop-down list.

Customize Borders

The **Borders and Shading dialog box** provides many more options to customize the type of borders you use. Not only can you customize the style, width, and color of border line, but also you can customize where the border is placed in relation to the selected text. The *Borders and Shading* dialog box is available from the *Borders* drop-down list in the *Paragraph* group on the *Home* tab.

▶ HOW TO: Apply Custom Borders

1. Select the paragraph(s) where you want to apply a border.
2. Click the **Borders** drop-down arrow [*Home* tab, *Paragraph* group] and choose the **Borders and Shading** option at the bottom of the list. The *Borders and Shading* dialog box opens (Figure 2-75).
 - In the *Apply to* area, select where you want to apply the borders. Your options are *Text* and *Paragraph*.

3. In the *Setting* area, select the type of border to use. Your options are *None, Box, Shadow, 3-D,* and *Custom.*

4. In the *Style* area, select a style of the line from the list of options.

5. Click the **Color** drop-down arrow and select line color.

6. Click the **Width** drop-down arrow and select the width of the border line. The width of the line is measured in points.

7. View the *Preview* area to see how the border will appear in your document.

 - In the *Preview* area, you can customize how the borders appear by clicking the *Top, Bottom, Left,* or *Right* border buttons to turn on or off a border (see Figure 2-75).

8. Click the **Options** button to open the *Border and Shading Options* dialog box (Figure 2-76).

 - This dialog box includes the option to add in additional space (padding) between the border and the text at the *Top, Bottom, Left,* and *Right.*
 - The spacing is measured in points.
 - Click **OK** to close the *Border and Shading Options* dialog box.

9. Click **OK** to close the *Borders and Shading* dialog box.

2-75 *Borders and Shading* dialog box

2-76 *Border and Shading Options* dialog box

> ### MORE INFO
>
> When you use the *Borders* button [*Paragraph* group], the last border selected becomes the function of the *Borders* button. For example, if you last applied a bottom border, you can apply a bottom border again by clicking the **Borders** button.

Apply Shading

Applying shading to a paragraph or text is very similar to applying borders. **Shading** applies a background color to selected text. *Shading* color options are available from the *Shading* drop-down list in the *Paragraph* group on the *Home* tab or in the *Borders and Shading* dialog box on the *Shading* tab.

The shading colors available are dependent upon the theme of the document. In the *Shading* drop-down list, you can select from *Theme Colors* or *Standard Colors* (Figure 2-77). If you want a color that is not available in the menu, you can click *More Colors* to select from a color palette.

2-77 Shading color options from the *Shading* drop-down list

> ▶**HOW TO:** Apply Shading from the Borders and Shading Dialog Box

1. Select the paragraph(s) you want to shade.
2. Click the **Borders** drop-down arrow [*Home* tab, *Paragraph* group] and choose the **Borders and Shading** option at the bottom of the list. The *Borders and Shading* dialog box opens (Figure 2-78).
3. Click the **Shading** tab.
4. Click the **Fill** drop-down arrow and select a shading fill color.
 - Alternatively, select a shading *Style* and *Color* in the *Patterns* area.
 - From the *Style* drop-down list, you can select a gradient percent or a fill pattern as the shading style.
 - From the *Color* drop-down list, you can select a fill color for the gradient or pattern you selected.
 - You do not have to use a pattern style or color for shading. Usually just a fill color is sufficient.
5. Click **OK** to close the *Borders and Shading* dialog box.

2-78 Shading options in the *Borders and Shading* dialog box

Apply a Page Border

Page borders are different from paragraph or text borders. A page border is around the entire page rather than selected paragraphs or text. Page borders are useful and attractive when creating flyers or handouts. A page border can be a line with varying styles, widths, and colors, or you can use art graphics as a page border.

> ▶**HOW TO:** Apply a Page Border

1. Click the **Design** tab.
2. Click the **Page Borders** button [*Page Background* group]. The *Borders and Shading* dialog box opens with the *Page Border* tab displayed (Figure 2-79).

3. In the *Setting* area, select the type of page border you want to apply.

4. From the *Style* list, select a border style.
 - Alternatively, you can select an art to apply as the border from the **Art** drop-down list.

5. Select a border color and width from the **Color** and **Width** drop-down lists.

6. In the *Preview* area, customize how the page border appears by clicking the **Top**, **Bottom**, **Left**, or **Right** border buttons to turn on or off borders.

2-79 Apply a page border

7. In the *Apply to* area, select the page(s) where you want to apply the page border. Your options are:
 - *Whole document*
 - *This section*
 - *This section—First page only*
 - *This section—All except first page*

8. Click **OK** to close the *Borders and Shading* dialog box.

> **MORE INFO**
>
> When you apply a page border, the text in the document is not affected because the page border is placed outside the margin boundaries.

Insert a Horizontal Line

In addition to being able to insert top and bottom borders on selected text, you can also insert a ***horizontal line*** to use as a border to separate information on a page. A horizontal line is actually a graphic object that is inserted into the document. When you insert a horizontal line, the line is the width of the page. More information about using and customizing graphics is covered in *SLO 4.5: Working with Graphics*.

▶**HOW TO:** Insert a Horizontal Line

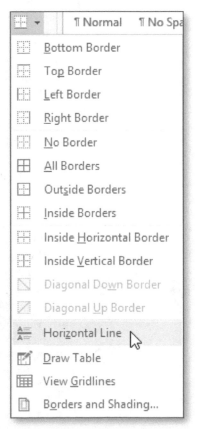

1. Place your insertion point in the document where you want a horizontal line.

2. Click the **Borders** drop-down arrow [*Home* tab, *Paragraph* group].

3. Select **Horizontal Line** from the drop-down list (Figure 2-80).
 - The horizontal line is treated as a separate paragraph and has a paragraph mark to the right.

2-80 Insert a horizontal line

Create a Hyperlink

A hyperlink is an excellent way to direct users to information on a web site, another document, or a location in the same document. You can also create a hyperlink for an email address, which automatically opens a new Microsoft Outlook email message addressed to the recipient. You can create a hyperlink by selecting the text or figure you want to turn into a hyperlink and then providing the information about the location where the user will be directed. You can also customize the *ScreenTip* and the target frame.

> **MORE INFO**
>
> Typically, hyperlinks are underlined and a different color to distinguish them from regular text in a document. In a Word document, Press **Ctrl+Click** to follow a hyperlink.

The **ScreenTip** is the text that displays when you place your pointer over the hyperlink in the document. The **target frame** is the window where the hyperlink document or web site opens. There are many different target frame options from which to choose. Usually it is best to choose **New window** if the link is to a different document or a web page. An email hyperlink always opens in a new window.

▶HOW TO: Create a Hyperlink

1. Select the text or graphic where you want to create a hyperlink.
2. Click the **Insert** tab.
3. Click the **Hyperlink** button [*Links* group]. The *Insert Hyperlink* dialog box opens (Figure 2-81).
 - The text you selected in the document as the hyperlink is displayed in the *Text to display* area. If you type other text in this text box, it will replace the text you selected in the document.

2-81 *Insert Hyperlink* dialog box

4. In the *Link to* area, select the type of hyperlink you want to create. Your options are *Existing File or Web Page*, *Place in This Document*, *Create New Document*, or *E-mail Address*.
 - If you are linking to a file, browse your computer in the *Look in* area to locate and select the file.
 - If you are linking to a web page, or type or paste (**Ctrl+V**) a web address in the *Address* area
 - If you are linking to a place in the document, a list of headings from which to choose displays.
 - If you are inserting a link to create a new document, options for the new document display.
 - If you are linking to an email address, you type in the email address and have the option to create a subject line for the email.

5. Click the **ScreenTip** button to insert text that displays when you place pointer over the hyperlink (Figure 2-82).

6. Type the *ScreenTip* text and click **OK** to close the *Set Hyperlink ScreenTip* dialog box.

7. Click the **Target Frame** button to open the *Set Target Frame* dialog box (Figure 2-83).
 - From the drop-down list of options, select where the hyperlink destination will be opened.
 - The *Set as default for all hyperlinks* check box allows you to make your target frame selection the default for all hyperlinks in your document.

8. Click **OK** to close the *Set Target Frame* dialog box.

9. Click **OK** to insert the hyperlink and close the *Insert Hyperlink* dialog box.

2-82 *Set Hyperlink ScreenTip* dialog box

2-83 *Set Target Frame* dialog box

> ## ANOTHER WAY
> **Ctrl+K** opens the *Insert Hyperlink* dialog box.

Edit or Remove a Hyperlink

There might be times when you have incorporated text from a web site or another document that includes hyperlinks to a document, or you might want to edit a hyperlink in an existing document. Word allows you to quickly edit hyperlinks to change hyperlink information, add a *ScreenTip*, or change the target frame.

You can quickly remove a hyperlink from a document without deleting the text in the document. When you remove a hyperlink from existing text, the text in your document is not deleted. Only the hyperlink attached to the text is removed.

▶ HOW TO: Edit or Remove a Hyperlink

1. Select or click the hyperlink to edit.

2. Click the **Hyperlink** button [*Insert* tab, *Links* group]. The *Edit Hyperlink* dialog box opens.
 - You can also press **Ctrl+K** or right-click the selected hyperlink and select **Edit Hyperlink**.

3. Change hyperlink information or options as needed.

4. Click the **Remove Link** button to remove an existing hyperlink (Figure 2-84).
 - When you remove a hyperlink, the *Edit Hyperlink* dialog box closes automatically.

5. Click **OK** to close the *Edit Hyperlink* dialog box if necessary.

2-84 Edit or remove a hyperlink

PAUSE & PRACTICE: WORD 2-4

In this Pause & Practice project, you finalize the résumé you worked on in *Pause & Practice 2-3*. You use *Find and Replace*, apply borders and shading to selected text, and add hyperlinks to the document.

File Needed: *[your initials] PP W2-3.docx*
Completed Project File Name: *[your initials] PP W2-4.docx*

1. Open the *[your initials] PP W2-3* document completed in *Pause & Practice 2-3*.

2. Save this document as [your initials] PP W2-4.

3. Use *Find and Replace* to replace the hyphen between dates with an en dash.
 a. Press **Ctrl+Home** to move to the top of the document.
 b. Click the **Replace** button [*Home* tab, *Editing* group] or press **Ctrl+H** to open the *Find and Replace* dialog box.
 c. In the *Find what* text box, type – (hyphen).
 d. Place the insertion point in the *Replace with* text box.
 e. Click the **More** button if the *Search Options* are not already displayed.
 f. Click the **Special** button and select **En Dash** (Figure 2-85).
 g. Click the **Less** button to collapse the **Find and Replace** dialog box (Figure 2-86).
 h. Click the **Find Next** button to locate the first instance of a hyphen.
 i. Choose **Find Next** to skip the hyphenated word in the first paragraph.
 j. Click the **Replace** button to replace each occurrence of a hyphen between the dates with an en dash; choose **Find Next** to skip and not replace each occurrence of a hyphenated word.

2-85 Select *En Dash* as the special character to replace a hyphen

2-86 Use *Find and Replace*

 k. Click **OK** when Word has finished searching the document.
 l. Click **Close** to close the *Find and Replace* dialog box.

4. Add borders and shading to a paragraph.
 a. Select the paragraph after the "PROFILE" heading on the first page. Be sure to include the paragraph mark at the end of the paragraph.

> **MORE INFO**
>
> Word highlights each found occurrence. If you need to, you can move the *Find and Replace* dialog box to view highlighted text.

Word 2016 Chapter 2 Formatting and Customizing Documents

b. Click the **Borders** drop-down arrow [*Home* tab, *Paragraph* group] and select **Borders and Shading** to open the *Borders and Shading* dialog box.

c. Select **Shadow** in the *Setting* area.

d. Select the **solid line** in the *Style* area.

e. Click the **Color** drop-down list and select **Dark Red, Accent 1** (Figure 2-87).

f. Select **½ pt** in the *Width* area.

g. Select **Paragraph** in the *Apply to* area.

h. Click the **Options** button to open the *Border and Shading Options* dialog box and change *Top* and *Bottom* to **2 pt**.

i. Click **OK** to close the *Border and Shading Options* dialog box.

j. Click the **Shading** tab.

k. Click the **Fill** drop-down list and select **White, Background 1, Darker 5%** (Figure 2-88).

l. Click **OK** to close the *Borders and Shading* dialog box.

2-87 Select border color in the *Borders and Shading* dialog box

5. Add a bottom border to the header.

a. Right-click the header on the second page and select **Edit Header** to open the header area on the second page.

b. Place the insertion point in the first line of the header.

c. Click the **Borders** drop-down arrow [*Home* tab, *Paragraph* group].

d. Select **Bottom Border**. A bottom border displays below the header text.

e. Click the **Close Header and Footer** button [*Header & Footer Tools Design* tab, *Close* group].

2-88 Apply shading to selected text

6. Insert a hyperlink to an email address.

a. Select the email address in the heading information on the first page.

b. Click the **Hyperlink** button [*Insert* tab, *Links* group] or press **Ctrl+K** to open the *Insert Hyperlink* dialog box (Figure 2-89).

c. Click the **E-mail Address** button in the *Link to* area.

d. Type richellew@gmail.com in the *Text to display* area.

e. Type richellew@gmail.com in the *E-mail address* area. Word automatically inserts "mailto:" before the email address.

f. Click the **ScreenTip** button. The *Set Hyperlink ScreenTip* dialog box opens (Figure 2-90).

g. Type Email Richelle in the *ScreenTip text* area and click **OK** to close the *Set Hyperlink ScreenTip* dialog box.

h. Click **OK** to close the *Insert Hyperlink* dialog box.

2-89 Insert hyperlink to an email address

2-90 *Set Hyperlink ScreenTip* dialog box

7. Insert a hyperlink to a web site.

a. In the "REFERENCES" section on the second page, select **"California State University, Chico."** Don't select this text in the "EDUCATION" section.

b. Click the **Hyperlink** button or press **Ctrl+K** to open the *Insert Hyperlink* dialog box (Figure 2-91).

c. Select **Existing File or Web Page** in the *Link to* area. The *Text to display* area has *California State University, Chico* already filled in.

d. In the *Address* area, type www.csuchico.edu. Word automatically inserts "http://" before the web address.

e. Click the **ScreenTip** button. The *Set Hyperlink ScreenTip* dialog box opens.

f. Type CSU Chico web site in the *ScreenTip text* area and click **OK** to close the *Set Hyperlink ScreenTip* dialog box.

g. Click the **Target Frame** button in the *Insert Hyperlink* dialog box to open the *Set Target Frame* dialog box.

h. Select **New window** from the drop-down list and check the **Set as default for all hyperlinks** check box (Figure 2-92).

i. Click **OK** to close the *Set Target Frame* dialog box and click **OK** to close the *Insert Hyperlink* dialog box.

2-91 Insert hyperlink to a web page

2-92 *Set Target Frame* dialog box

8. Automatically add hyperlinks to email addresses.

a. Place the insertion point after "rsanchez @chico. edu" in the "REFERENCES" section on the second page.

b. Press the **spacebar** once to automatically add a hyperlink to the email address.

c. Place the insertion point after "diana.samuels@loomislearning.com" in the "REFERENCES" section on the second page and press the **spacebar** once to automatically add a hyperlink to the email address.

9. Save and close the document (Figure 2-93).

2-93 PP W2-4 completed

Chapter Summary

2.1 Format a document by customizing margins, page orientation, paper size, and vertical alignment (p. 340).

- Adjust the *margins* of a document to increase or decrease the *white space* surrounding the text. You can adjust the top, bottom, left, and right margins of a document.
- *Landscape* and *Portrait* are the two *page orientation* options.
- A standard sheet of paper is 8½" × 11". Select other paper sizes or create a custom paper size.
- *Vertical alignment* controls how text aligns between the top and bottom margins. By default, text aligns vertically at the top of the document. You can also use center, justified, or bottom vertical alignment.
- Use horizontal and vertical *rulers* to display the typing area on a document.
- You can change default page settings in the *Page Setup dialog box*.

2.2 Improve alignment and page layout by setting, using, and editing tab stops in a document (p. 343).

- There are five different types of *tab stops: Left, Center, Right, Decimal,* and *Bar*.
- Set, modify, or remove tab stops using the ruler or the *Tabs dialog box*.
- Use the *Tab selector* on the left side of the ruler to select a type of tab stop to set.
- *Leaders* can be used with tab stops. There are three different types of leaders: *Dot, Dash,* and *Solid underline*.
- In a Word document, default tab stops are set every 0.5". You can change the default tab stops.

2.3 Apply indents to control text alignment (p. 348).

- *Indents* can function as temporary margins and allow you to arrange paragraphs horizontally between the margins.
- There are four different types of indents: *left, right, first line,* and *hanging*.
- You can apply, modify, and remove indents with the ruler, *Layout* tab, or *Paragraph* dialog box.

2.4 Enhance document layout by inserting page numbers, headers, and footers (p. 353).

- You can insert a *page number* into the header or footer in various locations.

- *Headers* and *footers* are areas above and below a document's top and bottom margins.
- The *Different First Page* option allows you to remove or have different first page content in the header or footer.
- You type header and footer content once and it appears on subsequent pages.
- You can customize headers and footers with text, page numbers, the date, and other document property fields.
- You have a variety of built-in header, footer, and page numbering options.

2.5 Control pagination with page and section breaks (p. 360).

- Use *page breaks* to control the ending and beginning of pages in a document.
- Use *section breaks* to allow for different page setup formatting on different sections of a document.
- There are four different options for section breaks: *Next Page, Continuous, Even Page,* and *Odd Page*.
- Section breaks are visible in a document when the *Show/Hide* feature is turned on.

2.6 Use customized bulleted and numbered lists to effectively present information (p. 362).

- Use *bulleted* and *numbered lists* to emphasize important information.
- You can customize lists by using different symbols or pictures as bullets.
- Use numbering to display an ordered list.
- You can customize number format and levels.
- *Multilevel lists* allow you to customize a list using a combination of numbers, letters, or bullets.

2.7 Apply styles and themes to improve consistency in document format (p. 366).

- A *style* is a collection of preset formatting that you can apply to selected text.
- The *Style gallery* is a collection of built-in styles available in a document.
- You can modify existing styles.
- A *theme* is a collection of fonts, colors, and effects that you can apply to a document.

2.8 Use find and replace to edit a document (p. 371).

- The *Find* feature in Word allows you to search for specific text or format in a document.

- The **Navigation pane** displays all occurrences of the text for which you are searching.
- The **Replace** feature allows you to search for specific text in a document and replace it with other text.
- Both *Find* and *Replace* allow you to search for and replace formatting in a document.
- Use the **Go To** feature to go directly to a page, section, line, or other area in your document.

2.9 Improve overall document design and format by using borders, shading, horizontal lines, and hyperlinks (p. 374).

- *You can apply* **borders** *and* **shading** *to text and paragraphs in a document.*

- Word provides a variety of built-in border and shading options that you can apply to text, or you can customize borders and shading using the **Borders and Shading dialog box**.
- You can apply **page borders** to an individual page or all pages in a document.
- A **horizontal line** is a graphic that you can insert into a document.
- A **hyperlink** takes readers to a web page, a different document, a different location in a document, or an email address. An email hyperlink opens Microsoft Outlook and places the recipient's email address in the email message.

Check for Understanding

The SIMbook for this text (within your SIMnet account) provides the following resources for concept review:

- Multiple choice questions
- Matching exercises
- Short answer questions

Guided Project 2-1

In this project, you create a form for contractors seeking insurance coverage at Central Sierra Insurance. You apply a theme, styles, a multilevel list, tab stops, leaders, indents, borders and shading, a page break, and page numbering.
[Student Learning Outcomes 2.1, 2.2, 2.3, 2.4, 2.5, 2.6, 2.7, 2.9]

File Needed: ***InsuranceQuestionnaire-02.docx*** *(Student data files are available in the* Library *of your* SIMnet account)
Completed Project File Name: ***[your initials] Word 2-1.docx***

Skills Covered in this Project

- Modify an existing document.
- Change margins.
- Apply a document theme and theme color.
- Change font size, line spacing, and paragraph spacing.
- Apply a style to selected text.

- Modify an existing style.
- Apply borders and shading to selected text.
- Set and use a tab stop with an underline leader.
- Apply and modify a multilevel list.
- Insert a page break.
- Insert a built-in page number in the footer.

1. Open the ***InsuranceQuestionnaire-02*** document from your student data files.

2. Save this document as [your initials] Word 2-1.

3. Change the margins of the document.
 a. Click the **Margins** button [*Layout* tab, *Page Setup* group] and select **Custom Margins**. The *Page Setup* dialog box opens.
 b. Change the *Left* and *Right* margins to **0.75"**.
 c. Click **OK** to close the *Page Setup* dialog box.

4. Change the theme and theme color of the document.
 a. Click the **Themes** button [*Design* tab, *Document Formatting* group].
 b. Select **Integral** from the drop-down list.
 c. Click the **Colors** button [*Document Formatting* group] (Figure 2-94).
 d. Select **Aspect** from the drop-down list.

5. Change the font size, paragraph spacing, and line spacing of the entire document.
 a. Press **Ctrl+A** to select the entire document.
 b. Change the font size to **11 pt**.
 c. Change the line spacing to **Single (1.0)**.
 d. Change the *After* paragraph spacing to **6 pt**.

6. Apply styles to selected text.
 a. Place the insertion point in the first line of text ("Contractor's Insurance Questionnaire").

2-94 *Theme Colors drop-down list*

b. Click the **Title** style [*Home* tab, *Styles* group] in the *Style* gallery.

c. Select the second line of the document (**"Please carefully . . . "**).

d. Right-click the selected text, click **Styles** on the mini toolbar, and select **Book Title** from the *Style* gallery.

e. With this text still selected, click the **Change Case** button [*Home* tab, *Font* group] and select **UPPERCASE**.

f. Select **"Applicant's Instructions"** and apply the **Intense Quote** style from the *Style* gallery.

g. In the next paragraph ("Please answer ALL questions . . ."), apply the **Strong** style to the three words in all caps (**"ALL," "NONE,"** and **"NONE"**).

h. On the second page of the document, select **"Insurance Application Disclaimer"** and apply the **Intense Quote** style.

7. Modify an existing style.

a. Click the **More** button [*Home* tab, *Styles* group] to display all of the styles in the *Style* gallery.

b. Right-click the **Intense Quote** style in the *Style* gallery and select **Modify** (Figure 2-95). The *Modify Style* dialog box opens.

2-95 Modify an existing style

c. In the *Formatting* area, change the font size to **12 pt**.

d. Click the **Format** button on the bottom left and select **Paragraph**. The *Paragraph* dialog box opens.

e. Change the *Left* and *Right* indent to **0**.

f. Click **OK** to close the *Paragraph* dialog box.

g. Click the **Only in this document** radio button if it is not already selected to apply the style changes to only this document.

h. Click **OK** to close the *Modify Style* dialog box. The style changes apply to all text formatted with the *Intense Quote* style on both the first and second pages.

2-96 Apply a left and right border

8. Add borders and shading to selected text.

a. On the second page, select the first three paragraphs below "Insurance Application Disclaimer."

b. Click the **Borders** drop-down arrow [*Home* tab, *Paragraph* group] and select **Borders and Shading** to open the *Borders and Shading* dialog box (Figure 2-96).

c. In the *Setting* area, select **Custom**.

d. In the *Style* area, select the **solid line** border.

e. In the *Color* area, select **Orange, Accent 1**.

f. In the *Width* area, select **1 pt**.

g. In the *Preview* area, click the **Left** and **Right** border buttons (see Figure 2-96).

h. In the *Apply to* area, select **Paragraph**.

i. Click the **Options** button to open the *Border and Shading Options* dialog box.

j. Change the *Left* and *Right* settings to **5 pt**. and click **OK** to close the *Border and Shading Options* dialog box.

k. Click the **Shading** tab (Figure 2-97), and from the *Fill* drop-down list, select **Orange, Accent 1, Lighter 80%**.

l. Click **OK** to close the *Borders and Shading* dialog box.

2-97 Select shading *Fill* color

9. Change the paragraph spacing and add a tab stop with an underline leader to selected text.
 a. On the second page, select the last three lines of text.
 b. Click the **Paragraph** launcher [*Home* or *Layout* tab] to open the *Paragraph* dialog box.
 c. Change the *Before* paragraph spacing to **12 pt**.
 d. Click the **Tabs** button to open the *Tabs* dialog box (Figure 2-98).
 e. Type 7 in the *Tab stop position* area.
 f. Click the **Right** radio button in the *Alignment* area.
 g. Click the **4** (solid underline) radio button in the *Leader* area.
 h. Click the **Set** button to set this tab stop and click **OK** to close the *Tabs* dialog box.
 i. Click at the end of the "Name and Title of the Insured" line and press **Tab**. A solid underline displays across the page to the right margin.
 j. Repeat step i on the next two lines.

2-98 Set a right tab stop with an underline leader

10. Add a multilevel list to selected text and modify lists settings.
 a. Select the lines of text beginning with **"Applicant"** on the first page and ending with the last **"If yes, please explain:"** on the second page.
 b. Click the **Multilevel List** button [*Home* tab, *Paragraph* group] and select the **1), a), i)** option.
 c. With the text still selected, click the **Multilevel List** button again and select **Define New Multilevel List**. The *Define new Multilevel list* dialog box opens.
 d. Click the **Set for All Levels** button to open the *Set for All Levels* dialog box (Figure 2-99).
 e. Set the *Bullet/Number position for first level* to **0"**.
 f. Set the *Text position for first level* to **0.3"**.
 g. Set the *Additional indent for each level* to **0.3"**.
 h. Click **OK** to close the *Set for All Levels* dialog box and click **OK** to close the *Define new Multilevel list* dialog box.

2-99 Change settings for a multilevel list

11. Increase indent on selected lines.
 a. Click anywhere on the list to deselect it.
 b. Place your insertion point in 13 in the numbered list ("If yes, . . .") and click **Increase Indent** [*Home* tab, *Paragraph* group]. This line is now letter *a)*.
 c. Repeat step b on each of the lines in the list that begin with "If yes, . . ." There should be 28 numbered items in the list when you finish this process.

12. Change paragraph spacing on the multilevel list and add a right tab stop with an underline leader.
 a. Select the entire multilevel list.
 b. Click the **Paragraph** launcher [*Home* or *Layout* tab] to open the *Paragraph* dialog box.
 c. Deselect the **Don't add space between paragraphs of the same style** check box (Figure 2-100).
 d. Click the **Tabs** button to open the *Tabs* dialog box.
 e. In the *Tab stop position* area, type 7.

f. Click the **Right** radio button in the *Alignment* area.

g. Click the **4** (solid underline) radio button in the *Leader* area.

h. Click the **Set** button to set this tab stop and click **OK** to close the *Tabs* dialog box.

i. Click at the end of the first numbered item ("Applicant:") and press **Tab**. A solid underline displays across the page to the right margin.

j. Repeat step i on each of the numbered and lettered paragraphs.

13. Save the document.

14. Insert a page break in the document.
 a. Place the insertion point before the text in number 22 in the multilevel list.
 b. Press **Ctrl+Enter** to insert a page break.

15. Add a page number in the footer of the document.
 a. Press **Ctrl+Home** to move to the top of the document.
 b. Click the **Page Number** button [*Insert* tab, *Header & Footer* group].
 c. Place your pointer on **Bottom of Page** to display the drop-down list.
 d. Scroll down and choose **Bold Numbers 3** in the *Page X of Y* section. The page numbers display at the right of the footer.
 e. Click the blank line below the page numbers in the footer and press **Backspace** to delete the blank line.
 f. Click the **Close Header and Footer** button [*Header & Footer Tools Design* tab, *Close* group].

16. Save and close the document (Figure 2-101).

2-100 Add spacing between lines of text with the same style

2-101 Word 2-1 completed

Guided Project 2-2

In this project, you create a checklist for employees at Placer Hills Real Estate to track the tasks they need to complete when a house enters escrow. You create a bulleted list, modify a bullet in a list, set and modify tab stops, apply and modify styles, and insert document properties in the footer.
[Student Learning Outcomes 2.1, 2.2, 2.3, 2.4, 2.6, 2.7, 2.9]

File Needed: **SellerEscrowChecklist-02.docx** *(Student data files are available in the* Library *of your SIMnet account)*
Completed Project File Name: *[your initials]* **Word 2-2.docx**

Skills Covered in this Project

- Modify an existing document.
- Change margins, line spacing, font, and font size.
- Set a tab stop using the ruler.
- Set a tab stop with leader.
- Apply a style to selected text.
- Modify an existing style.
- Apply and customize a bulleted list.
- Use the *Format Painter*.
- Insert a document property field and date in the footer.
- Apply a border in the footer.

1. Open the **SellerEscrowChecklist-02** document from your student data files.
2. Save this document as [your initials] Word 2-2.
3. Change margins, vertical alignment, line spacing, and font and font size, and delete blank lines.
 a. Click the **Margins** button [*Layout* tab, *Page Setup* group] and select **Normal** from the drop-down list.
 b. Click the **Page Setup** launcher to open the *Page Setup* dialog box and click the **Layout** tab.
 c. In the *Page* area, change *Vertical alignment* to **Center** and click **OK** to close the *Page Setup* dialog box.
 d. Press **Ctrl+A** to select the entire document.
 e. Change the font to **Calibri** and change the font size to **12 pt**.
 f. Change the line spacing to **2.0** (Double).
 g. Turn on **Show/Hide**.
 h. Delete all of the blank lines between the lines of text.

4. Add text to the document.
 a. In the second line of the document, place the insertion point after "Seller" and press **Tab** once.
 b. Type Property Address.
 c. Place the insertion point after "Escrow Company" and press **Tab** once.
 d. Type Escrow #.
 e. Place the insertion point after "Tasks to be Completed" and press **Tab** once.
 f. Type Date Completed.

5. Set tab stops using the ruler to align information. If the ruler is not displayed, check the **Ruler** box [*View* tab, *Show* group].
 a. Select the second and third lines of text (beginning with **"Seller"** and ending with **"Escrow #"**).
 b. Verify that the **Left Tab** is selected in the *Tab* selector area to the left of the horizontal ruler.
 c. Click the ruler at **3.5"** to set a left tab stop. If you click the wrong location on the ruler, drag the tab stop to the correct location (Figure 2-102).

Tab selector

2-102 Set left tab stop using the ruler

 d. Select the fourth line of text (beginning with "Tasks").

 e. Click the **Tab** selector to change to a **Center Tab** stop (Figure 2-103).

 f. Click the ruler at **5.5"** to set a center tab stop.

6. Set tab stops and add leaders to create lines for users to fill in information.

 a. Select the second and third lines of text (beginning with "Seller").

 b. Click the **Paragraph** launcher to open the *Paragraph* dialog box.

 c. Click the **Tabs** button to open the *Tabs* dialog box.

 d. Type 3 in the *Tab stop position* area.

 e. Click the **Right** radio button in the *Alignment* area.

 f. Click the **4** (solid underline) radio button in the *Leader* area.

 g. Click the **Set** button to set this tab stop.

 h. Type 6.5 in the *Tab stop position* area.

 i. Click the **Right** radio button in the *Alignment* area.

 j. Click the **4** (solid underline) radio button in the *Leader* area.

 k. Click the **Set** button to set this tab stop and click **OK** to close the *Tabs* dialog box.

7. Use tab stops to align text and insert underline leader.

 a. Place the insertion point before "Property Address" and press **Tab** once.

 b. Place the insertion point to the right of "Property Address" and press **Tab** once.

 c. Place the insertion point before "Escrow #" and press **Tab** once.

 d. Place the insertion point to the right of "Escrow #" and press **Tab** once.

8. Apply styles to selected text and update a style.

 a. Place the insertion point in the first line of text ("Seller Escrow Checklist").

 b. Select **Title** style in the *Style* gallery [*Home* tab, *Styles* group].

 c. Change the *After* paragraph spacing to **24 pt**. [*Layout* tab, *Paragraph* group].

 d. Click the **Center** alignment button [*Home* tab, *Paragraph* group] to center the title.

 e. Select **"Tasks to be Completed"** and apply the **Book Title** style from the *Style* gallery.

 f. Change the font size of the selected text to **14 pt**. and apply a **Double underline**.

 g. Right-click the **Book Title** style in the *Style* gallery and select **Update Book Title to Match Selection**. The *Book Title* style is updated.

 h. Select "**Date Completed**" and apply the **Book Title** style.

9. Create a bulleted list to selected text and apply a custom bullet.

 a. Select the lines of text beginning with **"Open Escrow . . . "** and ending with **"Disclosures Sent to Agent."**

 b. Click the **Bullets** drop-down arrow [*Home* tab, *Paragraph* group] and select **Define New Bullet**. The *Define New Bullet* dialog box opens.

 c. Click the **Symbol** button to open the *Symbol* dialog box (Figure 2-104).

 d. Click the **Font** drop-down arrow and select **Wingdings**.

 e. Scroll down the list and select the **open square** bullet (Character code 113).

 f. Click **OK** to close the *Symbol* dialog box.

 g. Click the **Font** button in the *Define New Bullet* dialog box. The *Font* dialog box opens.

 h. Change the *Size* to **14 pt**.

 i. Click **OK** to close the *Font* dialog box and click **OK** to close the *Define New Bullet* dialog box.

 j. With the bulleted list still selected, click the **Decrease Indent** button to align the bulleted list at the left margin.

2-104 Select a symbol for a custom bullet

10. Change the hanging indent and add tab stops.

 a. Select the bulleted list.

 b. Click the **Paragraph** launcher to open the *Paragraph* dialog box.

c. Change the *Hanging* indent to **0.3"**.
d. Click the **Tabs** button to open the *Tabs* dialog box (Figure 2-105).
e. Type 4.5 in the *Tab stop position* area.
f. Click the **Left** radio button in the *Alignment* area, click the **1 None** radio button in the *Leader* area, and click the **Set** button to set this tab stop.
g. Type 6.5 in the *Tab stop position* area.
h. Click the **Right** radio button in the *Alignment* area, click the **4** (solid underline) radio button in the *Leader* area, and click the **Set** button to set this tab stop, and click **OK** to close the *Tabs* dialog box.
i. Place the insertion point after "Open Escrow with Escrow Company" and press **Tab** two times. A solid underline displays between 4.5" and 6.5".
j. Repeat step i on the remaining lines in the bulleted list.

2-105 *Tabs* dialog box

11. Add text to the document.
 a. Press **Enter** after the solid underline in the last line of text in the document.
 b. Click the **Bullets** button [*Home* tab, *Paragraph* group] to turn off the bullet on this line.
 c. Type Fax/Email Clear Pest Report and press **Enter**.
 d. Type Title and press **Enter**.
 e. Type Lender and press **Enter**.
 f. Type Buyer's Agent.

12. Apply a style to selected text and use the *Format Painter*.
 a. Select **"Fax/Email Clear Pest Report"** and apply the **Subtle Reference** style.
 b. Place the insertion point in one of the bulleted items.
 c. Click the **Format Painter** button [*Home* tab, *Clipboard* group] to copy the formatting of this bulleted item.
 d. Select the last three lines of text (beginning with **"Title . . ."**). The *Format Painter* copies the bullet formatting and tab settings to these lines of text.
 e. Press **Tab** two times after each of these last three lines to insert the tabs and leaders.

13. Insert a document property field, the date, and a border in the footer of the document.
 a. Click the **Footer** button [*Insert* tab, *Header & Footer* group] and select **Edit Footer** from the drop-down list to open the footer.
 b. Click the **Document Info** button [*Header & Footer Tools Design* tab, *Insert* group], click **Document Property**, and select **Company**. The *Company* document property field displays in the footer.
 c. Press the **right arrow** key once to deselect the *Company* field.
 d. Press **Tab** two times, type Last updated:, and **space** once. The text aligns at the right side of the footer.
 e. Click the **Date & Time** button [*Header & Footer Tools Design* tab, *Insert* group] to open the *Date and Time* dialog box.
 f. Select the spelled out month, day, year option (e.g., January 1, 2018), check the **Update automatically** box, and click **OK** to insert the date and close the dialog box.
 g. Select all of the text in the footer and change the font to **Calibri** and the font size to **10 pt**.
 h. Click the **Borders** drop-down arrow [*Home* tab, *Paragraph* group] and select **Borders and Shading** to open the *Borders and Shading* dialog box.
 i. Click the **Color** drop-down list and select **Black**, **Text 1**.
 j. Click the **Width** drop-down list and select **1 pt**.
 k. In the *Preview* area, click the **Top** border button to apply a top border to the footer.

l. Click **OK** to close the *Borders and Shading* dialog box.

m. Click the **Close Header and Footer** button [*Header & Footer Tools Design* tab, *Close* group].

14. Save and close the document (Figure 2-106).

2-106 Word 2-2 completed

Guided Project 2-3

In this project, you edit and format the personal training guide for the American River Cycling Club to improve readability and effectiveness. You use find and replace, apply a document theme, modify styles, customize numbered and bulleted lists, apply borders and shading, and insert headers, footers, and document properties.

[Student Learning Outcomes 2.1, 2.3, 2.4, 2.6, 2.7, 2.8, 2.9]

File Needed: ***PersonalTrainingProgram-02.docx*** *(Student data files are available in the* Library *of your SIMnet account)*

Completed Project File Name: *[your initials] Word 2-3.docx*

Skills Covered in this Project

- Modify an existing document.
- Apply a document theme.
- Change margins.
- Change line spacing and paragraph spacing.
- Apply a style to selected text.
- Apply borders and shading to selected text.
- Update an existing style.
- Customize a multilevel bulleted list.
- Use *Find*.
- Use *Find* and *Replace*.
- Insert a hyperlink.
- Insert header, footer, page number, and document properties.

1. Open the *PersonalTrainingProgram-02* document from your student data files.

2. Save this document as [your initials] Word 2-3.

3. Apply a document theme and change the line and paragraph spacing.
 a. Click the **Themes** button [*Design* tab, *Document Formatting* group] and select **Slice** from the drop-down list of theme options.
 b. Click the **Margins** button [*Layout* tab, *Page Setup* group] and select **Custom Margins** to open the *Page Setup* dialog box.
 c. Change the *Left* and *Right* margins to **1"** and click **OK** to close the *Page Setup* dialog box.
 d. Press **Ctrl+A** to select the entire document.
 e. Change the line spacing to **1.15** and change the *After* paragraph spacing to **10 pt**.
 f. Turn on **Show/Hide**.

4. Apply styles to the title, subtitle, and section headings.
 a. Select the title (first line) of the document.
 b. Apply the **Title** style from the *Style* gallery [*Home* tab, *Styles* group].
 c. Change the font size to **20 pt**. and apply **bold** and **center** alignment.
 d. Select the subtitle (second line) of the document.
 e. Apply the **Subtitle** style from the *Style* gallery.
 f. Change the font size to **16 pt**. and **center** it.
 g. Select the first section heading (**"General Guidelines"**).
 h. Apply the **Heading 1** style from the *Style* gallery.
 i. Apply the **Heading 1** style to the remaining section headings in the document (**"Personal Training Program Guidelines," "More About Long Rides," "Training Intensity and Heart Rate," "Tracking Training Miles versus Hours,"** and **"Using a Training Log"**).

5. Update a style in the document.
 a. Select the first section heading (**"General Guidelines"**) including the paragraph mark at the end of the line.
 b. Change the *Before* paragraph spacing to **12 pt**. and the *After* paragraph spacing to **6 pt**.
 c. Click the **Borders** drop-down arrow [*Home* tab, *Paragraph* group] and select **Borders and Shading**. The *Borders and Shading* dialog box opens.
 d. In the *Setting* area, select **Shadow**.
 e. In the *Style* area, select the **solid line**.
 f. In the *Color* area, select **Dark Blue, Accent 1, Darker 50%** (Figure 2-107).
 g. In the *Width* area, select **1 pt**.
 h. In the *Apply to* area, select **Paragraph**.
 i. Click the **Shading** tab, and in the *Fill* area, select **Dark Blue, Accent 1, Lighter 80%**.
 j. In the *Apply to* area, select **Paragraph**, and click **OK** to close the *Borders and Shading* dialog box.
 k. With the heading still selected, right-click the **Heading 1** style in the *Style gallery* and select **Update Heading 1 to Match Selection**. All of the headings in the document with the *Heading 1* style applied update automatically.

6. Customize the bullets and indents for the bulleted list.
 a. Right-click the first bulleted item on the first page and select **Adjust List Indents**. The *Define new Multilevel list* dialog box opens.
 b. Click **1** in the *Click level to modify* area.
 c. In the *Number style for this level* area, select **New Bullet** from the drop-down list (Figure 2-108). The *Symbol* dialog box opens.

2-107 Select border line color

2-108 Customize bulleted list

393

d. In the *Font* area, select **Webdings** from the drop-down list, click the **right pointing triangle** (Character code 52), and click **OK** to close the *Symbol* dialog box (Figure 2-109).

e. Click **2** in the *Click level to modify* area in the *Define new Multilevel list* dialog box.

f. In the *Number style for this level* area, select **New Bullet** from the drop-down list. The *Symbol* dialog box opens.

g. In the *Font* area, select **Webdings** from the drop-down list, click the **double right pointing triangle** (Character code 56), and click **OK** to close the *Symbol* dialog box.

h. Click the **Set for All Levels** button in the *Define new Multilevel list* dialog box. The *Set for All Levels* dialog box opens (Figure 2-110).

i. Change the *Bullet/Number position for first level* to **0.25"**, change the *Text position for first level* to **0.5"**, and change *Additional indent for each level* to **0.25"**.

j. Click **OK** to close the *Set for All Levels* dialog box and click **OK** to close the *Define new Multilevel list* dialog box. All of the first and second level bullets and indents in the entire document are changed.

2-109 Select bullet from *Webdings* font set

2-110 Set indents for all levels

7. Use the *Find* feature to find text in the document.

a. Press **Ctrl+Home** to go to the beginning of the document.

b. Click the **Find** button [*Home* tab, *Editing* group] or press **Ctrl+F** to open *Find* in the *Navigation* pane.

c. Type personal training program in the *Search Document* area. All instances of this text appear in the *Navigation* pane.

d. Click after "personal training program" in the first body paragraph on the first page and type (PTP). Make sure there is one space before and after "(PTP)".

e. Select **"PTP"** (not the parentheses) and apply **italic** format.

f. Click the **X** in the upper right of the *Navigation* pane to close this pane.

8. Use the replace feature to find and replace text in the document.

a. Press **Ctrl+Home** to go to the beginning of the document.

b. Click the **Replace** button [*Home* tab, *Editing* group] to open the *Find and Replace* dialog box with the *Replace* tab selected (Figure 2-111).

c. In the *Find what* area, type personal training program.

d. In the *Replace with* area, type PTP.

e. Click the **More** button to display more search options.

f. Click the **Format** button and select **Font** to open the *Replace Font* dialog box.

g. Click **Italic** in the *Font style* area and click **OK** to close the *Replace Font* dialog box.

2-111 Replace text with text and formatting

h. Click the **Less** button to collapse the *Find and Replace* dialog box.

i. Click the **Find Next** button to find the first occurrence of "personal training program" in the document.

j. Do not replace this text in the title, first body paragraph, or section heading. Replace all other occurrences of "personal training program" with "*PTP*". Click the **Replace** button to replace the highlighted occurrence or click the **Find Next** button to skip and not replace an occurrence.

k. Click **OK** when you are finished searching the document and click **Close** to close the *Find and Replace* dialog box.

9. Add a hyperlink to the document.

a. Select the subtitle of the document (**"American River Cycling Club"**).

b. Click the **Hyperlink** button [*Insert* tab, *Links* group] or press **Ctrl+K** to open the *Insert Hyperlink* dialog box.

c. Click the **Existing File or Web Page** button in the *Link to* area.

d. Type www.arcc.org in the *Address* area. Word automatically inserts "http://" before the web address.

e. Click the **ScreenTip** button to open the *Set Hyperlink ScreenTip* dialog box.

f. Type American River Cycling Club in the *ScreenTip text* area and click **OK** to close the *Set Hyperlink ScreenTip* dialog box.

g. Click the **Target Frame** button to open the *Set Target Frame* dialog box.

h. Select **New window** from the drop-down list.

i. Click **OK** to close the *Set Target Frame* dialog box and click **OK** to close the *Insert Hyperlink* dialog box.

10. Insert header and footer on the second and continuing pages.

a. Press **Ctrl+Home** to move to the beginning of the document.

b. Click the **Page Number** button [*Insert* tab, *Header & Footer* group].

c. Click **Top of Page** and select **Accent Bar 2** from the drop-down list. The page number displays in the header area.

d. Check the **Different First Page** check box [*Header & Footer Tools Design* tab, *Options* group] to remove the header from the first page so it only displays on the second and continuing pages.

11. Insert document property fields in the footer.

a. With the header still open, click the **Go to Footer** button [*Navigation* group].

b. Click the **Next** button [*Navigation* group] to move to the footer on the second page.

c. Click the **Document Info** button [*Insert* group], click **Document Property**, and select **Company** to insert the company document property field.

d. Press the **right arrow** key once to deselect the property field.

e. Press **Tab** two times to move the insertion point to the right margin in the footer.

f. Click the **Document Info** button [*Insert* group] and select **Document Title** to insert the title document property field.

g. Press **Ctrl+A** to select all of the text in the footer.

h. Apply **bold** and *italic* formatting and change the font size to **10 pt**.

i. Click the **Go to Header** button [*Header & Footer Tools Design* tab, *Navigation* group] to move to the header on the second page.

j. Press **Ctrl+A** to select all of the text in the header and change the font size to **10 pt**.

k. Click the **Close Header and Footer** button [*Header & Footer Tools Design* tab, *Close* group]. The header and footer information should appear on the second and continuing pages in the document.

12. Save and close the document (Figure 2-112).

2-112 Word 2-3 completed (pages 1 and 2 of 5)

Independent Project 2-4

In this project, you use styles, indents, lists, tab stops, the replace feature, footers, and document properties to customize the Emergency Procedures document for Sierra Pacific Community College District. **[Student Learning Outcomes 2.1, 2.2, 2.3, 2.4, 2.6, 2.7, 2.8, 2.9]**

File Needed: ***EmergencyProcedures-02.docx*** *(Student data files are available in the* **Library** *of your SIMnet account)*
Completed Project File Name: *[your initials]* **Word 2-4.docx**

Skills Covered in this Project

- Modify an existing document.
- Apply a document theme and theme color.
- Change margins and font size.
- Apply and modify a style.
- Apply a border to selected text.
- Apply and customize a numbered and bulleted list.
- Use the *Format Painter*.
- Set and modify tab stops.
- Use *Replace*.
- Insert a footer with document properties and current date.
- Insert a page border.
- Center text vertically.

1. Open the *EmergencyProcedures-02* document from your student data files.

2. Save this document as [your initials] Word 2-4.

3. Change the theme to **Integral** and the theme color to **Red**.

4. Change the top, bottom, left, and right margins to **0.75"**.

5. Select the entire document and change the font size to **12 pt**.

6. Format the title of the document.
 a. Select the title of the document and apply **Heading 1** style.
 b. Open the *Font* dialog box, apply **All caps** effect, and change the font size to **16 pt**.
 c. Change the *Before* paragraph spacing to **0 pt**.
 d. Add a **bottom border** to the title using the **Borders** drop-down list.

7. Select each of the bold section headings and apply the **Heading 2** style.

8. Modify the *Heading 2* style.
 a. Select the first section heading (**"Emergency Telephones [Blue Phones]"**).
 b. Change *Before* paragraph spacing to **12 pt**. and *After* paragraph spacing to **3 pt**.
 c. Apply **small caps** effect and **underline**.
 d. Update **Heading 2** style to match this heading. All of the section headings are updated.

9. Turn on **Show/Hide** and delete all of the blank lines in the document.

10. Select the bulleted list in the first section and change it to a numbered list.

11. Apply numbering format, make formatting changes, and use the *Format Painter*.
 a. Apply numbering to the text in the following sections: "*Assaults, Fights, or Emotional Disturbances*"; "*Power Failure*"; "*Fire*"; "*Earthquake*"; and "*Bomb Threat.*"
 b. Select the numbered list in the "Bomb Threat" section.
 c. Open the *Paragraph* dialog box, set before and after paragraph spacing to **2 pt**., and deselect the **Don't add space between paragraphs of the same style** check box.
 d. Use the *Format Painter* to copy this numbering format to each of the other numbered lists.
 e. Reset each numbered list so it begins with **1** (right-click the first item in each numbered list and select **Restart at 1** from the context menu).

12. Customize a bulleted list and use the *Format Painter*.
 a. Select the text in the "Accident or Medical Emergency" section.
 b. Use a **solid square bullet** (*Wingdings*, Character code 110).
 c. Confirm the left indent is **0.25"** and hanging indent is **0.25"**. If they are not, make these changes.
 d. Set *Before* and *After* paragraph spacing to **2 pt**.
 e. Deselect the **Don't add space between paragraphs of the same style** check box (*Paragraph* dialog box).
 f. Use the *Format Painter* to apply this bulleted list format to the following text in the following sections: "*Tips to Professors and Staff*" and "*Response to Students.*"

13. Change indent and paragraph spacing and apply a style.
 a. Select the text below the "Emergency Telephone Locations" heading.
 b. Set a **0.25"** left indent.
 c. Set *Before* and *After* paragraph spacing to **2 pt**.
 d. Confirm the **Don't add space between paragraphs of the same style** box is unchecked.
 e. In the "Emergency Telephone Locations" section, apply **Book Title** style to each of the telephone locations. Select only the location, not the text in parentheses or following text.

14. Change left indent and paragraph spacing and set a tab stop with a dot leader.
 a. Select the text below the "Emergency Phone Numbers" heading.
 b. Set a **0.25"** left indent for this text.
 c. Set *Before* and *After* paragraph spacing to **2 pt**.

d. Confirm the **Don't add space between paragraphs of the same style** box is unchecked.

e. With the text still selected, set a right tab stop at **7"** and use a **dot leader (2)**.

f. Press **Tab** before the phone number on each of these lines. The phone numbers align at the right margin with a dot leader between the text and phone number.

15. Apply the **Intense Reference** style to the paragraph headings in the "Accident or Medical Emergency" section (*"Life-Threating Emergencies"* and *"Minor Emergencies"*). Don't include the colon when selecting the paragraph headings.

16. Use the *Replace* feature to replace all instances of "Phone 911" with "PHONE 911" with **bold** font style.

17. Insert a footer with document property fields and the current date that appears on every page.
 a. Edit the footer and use the ruler to move the center tab stop to **3.5"** and the right tab stop to **7"**.
 b. Insert the **Title** document property field on the left. Use the **right arrow** key to deselect the document property field.
 c. Insert the **Company** document property field at center. Use the center tab stop for alignment. Use the **right arrow** key to deselect the document property field.
 d. Insert a date (use January 1, 2018 format) that updates automatically on the right. Use the right tab stop for alignment.
 e. Change the font size of all the text in the footer to **10 pt**.
 f. Add a **top border** to the text in the footer using the **Borders** drop-down list.

18. Insert a page border on the entire document. Use **Shadow** setting, **solid line** style, **Dark Red**, **Accent 1** color, and **1 pt**. line width.

19. Center the entire document vertically.

20. Save and close the document (Figure 2-113).

2-113 Word 2-4 completed

Independent Project 2-5

In this project, you format a bank authorization letter for Placer Hills Real Estate. You modify the formatting of an existing document, apply a theme, apply and modify styles, set tab stops, apply borders, and insert and edit hyperlinks.
[**Student Learning Outcomes 2.1, 2.2, 2.7, 2.9**]

File Needed: ***BankAuthorization-02.docx*** *(Student data files are available in the* Library *of your SIMnet account)*
Completed Project File Name: ***[your initials] Word 2-5.docx***

Skills Covered in this Project

- Modify an existing document.
- Apply a document theme.
- Change margins.
- Insert an automatically updated date.
- Apply and modify a style.
- Expand font spacing.
- Change paragraph spacing.
- Use the *Format Painter.*
- Set and use tab stops.
- Apply borders and shading to selected text.
- Insert a hyperlink.
- Edit a hyperlink.

1. Open the ***BankAuthorization-02*** document from your student data files.

2. Save this document as [your initials] Word 2-5.

3. Change the theme to **Wisp**.

4. Change the margins to **Normal**.

5. Select the entire document and change the *After* paragraph spacing to **18 pt**.

6. Press **Enter** after the first line of the document, insert (don't type) the current date (use January 1, 2018 format), and set it to update automatically.

7. Click at the end of the document, press **Enter**, and type the following information. Use line breaks (**Shift+Enter**) after the first three lines. (*Note: The email address is automatically converted to a hyperlink; you will edit this later.*)

 Emma Cavalli
 Placer Hills Real Estate
 ecavalli@phre.com
 916-450-3334

8. Select the date line and change the *After* paragraph spacing to **30 pt**.

9. Use the *Format Painter* to copy the date line format to the **"Sincerely,"** line.

10. Apply styles and use the *Format Painter*.
 a. Apply the **Title** style to the first line of the document and change the *Before* paragraph spacing to **36 pt**.
 b. Select **"Authorization Letter to Lender,"** apply the **Intense Reference** style, and expand the font *Spacing* to **1 pt**.
 c. Select the five lines of text beginning with **"Bank/Financial Institution:"** and ending with **"Borrower Name(s):"** and apply the **Book Title** style.
 d. Use the *Format Painter* to copy the "Bank/Financial Institution" format to **"Seller/Borrower Signature(s)"**.

11. Set a tab stop with a leader.
 a. Select the five lines of text beginning with **"Bank/Financial Institution:"** and ending with **"Borrower Name(s):."**

 b. Set a right tab stop at **6.5"** with a **solid underline leader**.

 c. Press **Tab** after each of these five lines to insert the solid underline leader to the right margin.

12. Apply a border and shading to the paragraph.

 a. Select the paragraph beginning **"Please consider . . . "**.

 b. Apply a border with **Shadow** setting, **solid line** style, **Black**, **Text 1**, **Lighter 50%** color, and **1½ pt.** line width.

 c. Change the border options so there is **4 pt.** from text on the top, bottom, left, and right.

 d. Set the shading fill color to **White**, **Background 1**, **Darker 5%**.

13. Select the "**Seller/Borrower Signature(s)**" line and apply a custom border that is **solid line**, **Black**, **Text 1**, and **2¼ pt.** width, and apply it to the **top** of the selected paragraph.

14. Insert and customize a hyperlink.

 a. Select "**Placer Hills Real Estate**" in the closing lines and insert a hyperlink.

 b. Type www.phre.com as the web page address.

 c. Type Placer Hills Real Estate as the *ScreenTip*.

 d. Set the target frame to **New window** and make this the default for all hyperlinks.

15. Edit the "ecavalli@phre.com" email hyperlink and type Email Emma Cavalli as the *ScreenTip*.

16. Save and close the document (Figure 2-114).

2-114 Word 2-5 completed

Independent Project 2-6

In this project, you edit, format, and customize the conference registration form for Central Sierra Insurance's Agriculture Insurance Conference. You use a continuous section break, find and replace, tab stops and leaders, styles, bullets, indents, borders, shading, and hyperlinks.
[Student Learning Outcomes 2.1, 2.2, 2.3, 2.4, 2.5, 2.6, 2.7, 2.8, 2.9]

File Needed: ***ConferenceRegistrationForm-02.docx*** *(Student data files are available in the* Library *of your SIMnet account)*
Completed Project File Name: ***[your initials] Word 2-6.docx***

Skills Covered in this Project

- Modify an existing document.
- Change margins, font, font size, line spacing, and paragraph spacing.
- Insert a header.
- Apply a style.
- Use *Find and Replace*.
- Insert a continuous section break.
- Insert a horizontal line.
- Set different margins for different sections.
- Customize a bulleted list and indents.
- Set and use tab stops and leaders.
- Apply borders and shading to selected text.
- Insert hyperlinks.

1. Open the ***ConferenceRegistrationForm-02*** document from your student data files.

2. Save this document as [your initials] Word 2-6.

3. Change the top and bottom margins to **0.5"**.

4. Select all of the text in the document and change the font size to **10 pt.**, line spacing to **1** (Single), and *After* paragraph spacing to **6 pt**.

5. Apply styles to title and subtitle.
 a. Select and cut the first line of the document and paste it in the header.
 b. Delete the blank line below the text in the header.
 c. Select the text in the header, apply **Title** style, align **center**, change the *After* paragraph spacing to **6 pt.**, and close the header.
 d. In the body of the document, select the first two lines beginning with "Central Sierra Insurance," apply **Subtitle** style, align **center**, and change the *After* paragraph spacing to **6 pt**.

6. Use *Find* and *Replace*.
 a. Use *Find* to locate all occurrences of "Agriculture Insurance Conference."
 b. Apply **italic** formatting to each occurrence except in the header.
 c. Use *Replace* to find all occurrences of "Oct." (include the period) and replace with **"May"**.
 d. Use *Replace* to find all occurrences of "Westfield Hotel & Spa" and replace with **"Northgate Resort"** with **Bold Italic** font style.

7. Click at the end of the second body paragraph ("Please help us to determine . . .") and insert a **continuous** section break.

8. On the blank line below the section break, insert a **Horizontal Line** from the **Borders** drop-down list (see "Insert a Horizontal Line" in *SLO 2.9: Using Borders, Shading, and Hyperlinks*).

9. Click in the document below the section break and change the left and right margins to **1.25"** and apply to **This section**.

10. Set a tab stop with a leader.
 a. Select the first two lines of text below the horizontal line.
 b. Set a right tab stop at **6"** with a **solid underline leader**.
 c. Press **Tab** after each of these lines to insert the solid underline leader to the right margin.

11. Define a new multilevel list and customize bullets and indents.
 a. Press the **Ctrl** key and select the four different bulleted lists in the document. The *Ctrl* key allows you to select non-adjacent text in the document. Don't select the text between each of the bulleted lists, and make sure all bulleted items are selected.
 b. Open the *Define new Multilevel list* dialog box (in the *Multilevel List* drop-down list).
 c. On the first, second, and third levels, change the bullet to a shaded open square bullet (*Wingdings*, Character code 113).
 d. Change the font size of the bullets on each of the first three levels to **12 pt**.
 e. Set the indents for all levels so that the first level begins at **0"**, the text for the first level begins at **0.25"**, and additional indent for each level is **0.25"**.

12. Set tab stops with a leader.
 a. Select the **"Flying—Arrival time:"** line.
 b. Set a **right** tab stop at **3"** with a **solid underline leader**.
 c. Press **Tab** after this line to insert the leader.
 d. Select the **"I need directions to *Northgate Resort* from:"** line.
 e. Set a **right** tab stop at **5"** with a **solid underline leader**.
 f. Press **Tab** after this line to insert the leader.

13. Change indents and apply custom borders and shading to selected text.
 a. Select the last two lines of the document, align **center**, and change the left and right indents to **1"**.
 b. With these two lines selected, apply a top and bottom **double line** border, **¾ pt.** width, and **Dark Blue**, **Text 2** color.
 c. Apply **Dark Blue**, **Text 2**, **Lighter 80%** shading to the selected text.

14. Insert and customize hyperlinks to email addresses.
 a. Use *Find* to locate the first occurrence of "apelandale@ centralsierra.com."
 b. Select this email address and insert a hyperlink.
 c. Type apelandale@centralsierra.com as the *Text to display* and *E-mail address*. In the *E-mail address* text box, "mailto:" is automatically inserted in front of the email address.
 d. Type Email Asia Pelandale as the *ScreenTip*.
 e. Repeat steps b–d above on the second occurrence of this email address.

15. Save and close the document (Figure 2-115).

2-115 Word 2-6 completed

Improve It Project 2-7

In this project, you clean up a document that contains shortcuts for Microsoft Outlook. Courtyard Medical Plaza wants to make this document available to all of its employees. You use tab stops, styles, and many other page layout features that you have learned in this chapter to create a professional and attractive reference document.
[Student Learning Outcomes 2.1, 2.2, 2.4, 2.5, 2.7, 2.9]

File Needed: ***OutlookShortcuts-02.docx*** *(Student data files are available in the* Library *of your SIMnet account)*
Completed Project File Name: *[your initials]* **Word 2-7.docx**

Skills Covered in this Project

- Modify an existing document.
- Change margins, line spacing, and paragraph spacing.
- Apply and modify a style.
- Apply borders and shading to selected text.
- Set and modify tab stops and leaders.
- Use the *Format Painter.*
- Insert a page break.
- Edit footer content and tab stops.

1. Open the ***OutlookShortcuts-02*** document from your student data files.

2. Save this document as [your initials] Word 2-7.

3. Change the page orientation to **Landscape**.

4. Change the top margin to **0.5**" and the bottom, left, and right margins to **0.75**".

5. Select the entire document and change the line spacing to **1.0** (or **Single**) and the *After* paragraph spacing to **4 pt**.

6. Remove the bottom border from the title and change the *After* paragraph spacing to **0 pt**.

7. Apply custom borders and shading, change paragraph spacing, and modify the *Heading 1* style.
 a. Select "**Global Outlook Commands**."
 b. Apply a custom **single line** top and bottom border with **1 pt**. width and **Dark Blue, Text 2** color, and apply **White, Background 1, Darker 5%** shading.
 c. Change the *Before* paragraph spacing to **12 pt**. and the *After* spacing to **0 pt**.
 d. Update **Heading 1** to match selected text.
 e. Apply the **Heading 1** style to each of the remaining section headings ("*Mail,*" "*Calendar,*" "*Contacts,*" "*Tasks,*" "*Notes,*" "*Journal,*" and "*Formatting*").

8. Change paragraph spacing, set tab stops, and modify the *Heading 2* style.
 a. Select the third line of text on the first page ("Activity Shortcut . . .") and change the *Before* paragraph spacing to **6 pt**. and the *After* spacing to **3 pt**.
 b. Apply **Small caps** formatting to the selected text.
 c. Set **left** tab stops on the selected text at **3**", **5**", and **8.25**".
 d. Update **Heading 2** to match selected text.
 e. Apply the **Heading 2** style to the first line of text ("Activity Shortcut . . .") after each section heading to create column headings.

9. Set tab stops and leaders to align text under the column headings and use the *Format Painter* to copy formatting.
 a. In the first section ("Global Outlook Commands") below the column headings ("ACTIVITY SHORTCUT . . ."), select all of the tabbed text beginning with "**Go to Mail**" and ending with "**Delete selected item**."

 b. Set the following tabs stops:
 3" left tab stop with **dot leader (2)**
 5" left tab stop with **no leader (1)**
 8.25" left tab stop with **dot leader (2)**
 c. Use the *Format Painter* to apply the tab settings to the remaining text below the column headings ("ACTIVITY SHORTCUT . . .") in the other sections.
 d. Turn on **Show/Hide** and delete any blank lines in the document.

10. Remove the existing footer and insert a custom footer.
 a. Place your insertion point at the beginning of the document.
 b. Edit the footer and remove all content.
 c. Open the *Tabs* dialog box and **Clear All** existing tab stops.
 d. Set a center tab stop at **4.75"** and the right tab stop at **9.5"**.
 e. Insert the **Company** document property field on the left side of the footer.
 f. Press the **right arrow** key to deselect the document property field, **tab** to the center tab stop, and insert the **Title** (or **Document Title**) document property field.
 g. Press the **right arrow** key to deselect the document property field, **tab** to the right tab stop.
 h. Type Page, **space** once, insert a plain page number in the current position.
 i. **Space** once, type of, **space** once, and insert the *NumPages* field (use **1,2,3**. . . format).
 j. Apply a **single line** top border in the footer with **1 pt.** width, **Dark Blue**, **Text 2** color.
 k. Change the font size of all of the text in the footer to **10 pt**.
 l. Set the footer so it does not appear on the first page.

11. On the third page, insert a **page break** before the "Formatting" heading. This document fits on four pages.

12. Save and close the document (Figure 2-116).

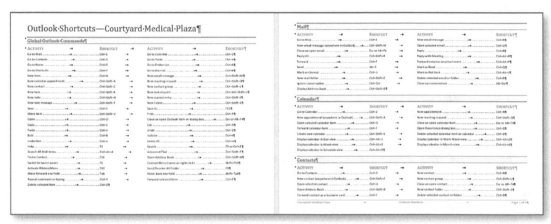

2-116 Word 2-7 completed (pages 1 and 2 of 4)

Challenge Project 2-8

Create an agenda for an upcoming meeting for an organization you are a member of, such as a club, church, volunteer organization, student group, or neighborhood association. Research online to find the common components of agendas. Robert's Rules of Order is a good source of information about meetings and guidelines for meeting protocol.
[**Student Learning Outcomes 2.1, 2.2, 2.3, 2.6, 2.7, 2.9**]

File Needed: None
Completed Project File Name: *[your initials] Word 2-8.docx*

Create a new document and save it as [your initials] Word 2-8. An agenda can include, but is not limited to, the following items:

- Organization name as the title
- Meeting date, start time, and end time
- Meeting location
- Meeting attendees
- Topic headings
- Topic subheadings (include details for each topic heading)
- The time each topic is expected to last

Modify your document according to the following guidelines:

- Apply styles.
- Use a multilevel list for the agenda items and subheadings.
- Customize number or bullet format and indents as needed.
- Use a right tab stop with a leader to line up the amount of time allocated for each main topic heading.
- Apply borders, shading, and/or a horizontal line to create an attractive agenda.
- Adjust margins as needed.
- Include an appropriate header and/or footer.

Challenge Project 2-9

Update your résumé using some of the document formatting features learned in this chapter. Edit your résumé so it is consistently formatted, easy to read, and professional looking. Research résumés online to get ideas about formatting and content.
[Student Learning Outcomes 2.1, 2.2, 2.3, 2.4, 2.5, 2.6, 2.7, 2.8, 2.9]

File Needed: None
Completed Project File Name: *[your initials] Word 2-9.docx*

Open your existing résumé or create a new document and save it as [your initials] Word 2-9. Modify your document according to the following guidelines:

- Apply a document theme.
- Apply styles to headings and subheadings to improve consistency in format.
- Adjust margins as needed.
- Use bulleted lists with customized bullets and indents to attractively arrange information.
- Set and use tab stops and indents as necessary to align information.
- Apply borders, shading, and/or a horizontal line to emphasize information in your résumé.
- Use page or section breaks as needed.
- Use *Find and Replace* as needed.
- Insert hyperlinks for appropriate information (e.g., email address and company names).
- If your résumé is more than one page, include a header and/or footer on the second and continuing pages.

Challenge Project 2-10

Format your favorite recipe using some of the formatting features learned in this chapter. You can look up recipes online on the Food Network, Epicurious, Simply Recipes, or other food web sites.
[Student Learning Outcomes 2.1, 2.2, 2.3, 2.6, 2.7, 2.9]

File Needed: None
Completed Project File Name: *[your initials] Word 2-10.docx*

Create a new document and save it as [your initials] Word 2-10. Your recipe should include, but is not limited to, the following:

- Recipe title
- Descriptive paragraph about the recipe
- Tab stops to arrange quantity and ingredients (and special instructions if needed)
- Numbered, step-by-step instructions
- Recipe source and/or additional information

Modify your document according to the following guidelines:

- Apply a document theme.
- Apply styles.
- Adjust margins as needed.
- Set and use a combination of tab stops (e.g., left, right, center, decimal, bar, and leaders) as necessary to attractively line up information.
- Use a numbered list for instructions.
- Use left, right, first line, and/or hanging indents as necessary.
- Apply borders, shading, page border, and/or a horizontal line to set off information in your recipe.
- Insert hyperlinks to appropriate information (e.g., link to online recipe).

EXCEL

Microsoft® Office

IN PRACTICE

excel

Creating and Editing Workbooks

CHAPTER OVERVIEW

Microsoft Excel (Excel) is spreadsheet software for creating an electronic workbook. A workbook consists of rows and columns used to organize data, perform calculations, print reports, and build charts. With Excel, you can create simple to complex personal or business workbooks. This chapter presents basic procedures for creating and editing an Excel workbook.

STUDENT LEARNING OUTCOMES (SLOs)

After completing this chapter, you will be able to:

SLO 1.1 Create, save, and open an Excel workbook (p. 411).

SLO 1.2 Enter and edit labels and values in a worksheet (p. 414).

SLO 1.3 Use the *SUM* function to build a simple formula (p. 427).

SLO 1.4 Format a worksheet with font attributes, borders, fill, cell styles, and themes (p. 429).

SLO 1.5 Modify columns and rows in a worksheet (p. 439).

SLO 1.6 Insert, delete, and move worksheets in a workbook (p. 445).

SLO 1.7 Modify the appearance of a workbook by adjusting zoom size, changing views, and freezing panes (p. 450).

SLO 1.8 Review and prepare a workbook for final distribution by spell checking, setting properties, and adjusting page setup options (p. 455).

CASE STUDY

Throughout this book you have the opportunity to put into practice the application features that you are learning. Each chapter begins with a case study that introduces you to the Pause & Practice projects in the chapter. These Pause & Practice projects give you a chance to apply and practice key skills in a realistic and practical context. Each chapter contains three to five Pause & Practice projects.

Paradise Lakes Resort (PLR) is a vacation company with properties located throughout northern Minnesota. PLR staff use Excel to track revenue, to monitor expenses, to maintain employee records, and similar tasks. In the Pause & Practice projects for Chapter 1, you create, edit, and format a workbook that displays categories of revenue for one week.

Pause & Practice 1-1: Open, edit, and save a workbook.

Pause & Practice 1-2: Use *SUM* and format data in a worksheet.

Pause & Practice 1-3: Edit columns, rows, and sheets in a workbook.

Pause & Practice 1-4: Finalize a workbook for distribution.

Creating, Saving, and Opening a Workbook

In Microsoft Excel, the file that you open, edit, and save is a *workbook*. Each workbook contains *worksheets*, which are comparable to individual pages in a Word document. A worksheet is also referred to as a *spreadsheet* or a *sheet*, and you can use these terms interchangeably. This text also uses the terms "workbook" and "file" interchangeably.

Create a New Workbook

By default, a new workbook includes one worksheet, but a workbook can include multiple sheets. The worksheet *tab* is located near the bottom left of the workbook window and is labeled *Sheet1*.

When you first open Excel, the *Excel Start page* displays. From the *Start* page, you can create a new blank workbook, open a recently saved workbook, or create a workbook from an Excel template (a model workbook). Click **Blank workbook** to start a new blank workbook. You can also select *Blank workbook* from the *New* area in the *Backstage* view.

> **ANOTHER WAY**
>
> Press **Esc** to leave the Excel *Start* page and open a blank workbook.

▶HOW TO: Create a New Workbook

1. Click the **File** tab to display the *Backstage* view.
2. Select **New** on the left to display the *New* area in the *Backstage* view (Figure 1-1).

1-1 *Backstage* view for creating new workbooks

3. Click **Blank workbook** to create a new blank workbook.

> **ANOTHER WAY**
>
> Press **Ctrl+N** to open a new workbook.

Save and Close a Workbook

When you open a blank workbook, Excel automatically assigns a file name, such as *Book1*. The first time you save a workbook, you should type a descriptive file name for the workbook in the *Save As* dialog box. You can save a workbook on your computer, in a *OneDrive* folder, or on external media.

▶HOW TO: Save a New Workbook

1. Click the **File** tab to display the *Backstage* view.

2. Select **Save As** on the left to display the *Save As* area.

 - You can press **Ctrl+S** to open the *Save As* area in the *Backstage* view for a workbook that has not yet been saved.

3. Select the location to save your workbook.

 - Click **This PC** to see recently used folders.
 - Click **Browse** to open the *Save As* dialog box for further navigation.
 - Click **OneDrive** to see your cloud folder names.

4. Click the folder name to open the *Save As* dialog box (Figure 1-2).

5. Type the file name in the *File name* area.

6. Click **Save** to close the *Save As* dialog box.

1-2 *Save As* dialog box

▶ ANOTHER WAY
Press **F12** (**FN+F12**) to open the *Save As* dialog box.

Once a workbook has been saved, you can re-save it with the same file name by pressing **Ctrl+S** or by clicking the **Save** button in the *Quick Access toolbar*.

To close a workbook, click the **File** tab and choose **Close**. You can press **Ctrl+W** or **Ctrl+F4** to close a workbook, too. These commands leave Excel running with a blank screen so that you can open another file or start a new workbook.

You can also click the **X** (**Close** button) in the upper right corner of the window. If the workbook is the only one open, this command closes the file and exits Excel. If multiple workbooks are open, clicking the *Close* button closes only the active workbook.

Open a Workbook

A workbook can be opened from the *Start* page, the *Open* area in the *Backstage* view, or the *Open* dialog box. When a workbook is opened from an Internet or unrecognized source, it opens in ***Protected View***. Click **Enable Editing** when you know that it is safe to work with the file.

▶HOW TO: Open a Workbook

1. Click the **File** tab to open the *Backstage* view.

2. Click **Open** to display the *Open* area.

3. Select the location where the workbook is stored.

- The *Recent* list displays workbook file names on the right.
- The *This PC* option lists recently used folder names.
- Click **Browse** to locate a folder.

4. Click the folder name that stores the file.

5. Select the workbook name and click **Open** (Figure 1-3).

1-3 *Open* dialog box

> **ANOTHER WAY**
>
> **Ctrl+O** displays the *Open* area in the *Backstage* view. **Ctrl+F12** displays the *Open* dialog box.

> **MORE INFO**
>
> From an Explorer window, you can double-click a workbook file name to launch Excel and open the workbook.

Save a Workbook with a Different File Name

To preserve an existing workbook, you can open and save it with a different file name, creating a copy of the original file with a new name. Follow the same steps that you would when saving a new workbook.

> **HOW TO:** Save a Workbook with a Different File Name

1. Click the **File** tab to open the *Backstage* view.
2. Click **Save As** to display the *Save As* area.
3. Navigate to and select the folder name to open the *Save As* dialog box.
 - You can press **F12** (**FN+F12**) to open the *Save As* dialog box.
4. Type the name in the *File name* area.
5. Click **Save** to close the *Save As* dialog box and save the file.

Workbook File Formats

Excel workbooks are saved as *.xlsx* files, indicated as *Excel Workbook* in the *Save As* dialog box. You can save a workbook in other formats for ease in sharing data. For example, you can save a workbook in *Excel 97-2003* format so that a coworker with an earlier version of Excel can use the data. Or you can create a PDF file of a workbook to provide data to users who do not have Excel.

The *Save as type* area of the *Save As* dialog box lists available formats (Figure 1-4). The following table lists common formats for saving an Excel workbook.

1-4 Workbook file formats

Save Formats

Type of Document	File Name Extension	Uses of This Format
Excel Workbook	.xlsx	Excel workbook compatible with versions 2010 and later
Excel Macro-Enabled Workbook	.xlsm	Excel workbook with embedded macros
Excel 97-2003 Workbook	.xls	Excel workbook compatible with older versions of Microsoft Excel
Excel Template	.xltx	Model or sample Excel workbook stored in the Custom Office Templates folder
Excel Macro-Enabled Template	.xltm	Model or sample Excel workbook with embedded macros stored in the Custom Office Templates folder
Portable Document Format (PDF)	.pdf	An uneditable image of the workbook for viewing that can be opened with free software
Text (tab-delimited)	.txt	Data only with columns separated by a tab character. File can be opened by many applications.
Comma Separated Values (CSV)	.csv	Data only with columns separated by a comma. File can be opened by many applications.
OpenDocument Spreadsheet	.ods	Workbook for the Open Office suite as well as Google Docs
Web Page	.htm, .html	Excel workbook formatted for posting on a web site that includes data, graphics, and linked objects

<table>
<tr><td>SLO 1.2</td></tr>
</table>

Entering and Editing Data

A worksheet consists of columns and rows. Columns are labeled with letters and rows are labeled with numbers. You enter data in a *cell*, which is the intersection of a column and a row. Each cell is identified with a *cell reference* (or *cell address*), the column letter and row number that represents the location of the cell. Cell A1 is the intersection of column A and

414

row 1. A rectangular group of cells is a *range*. The range address **A1:B3** identifies six cells in two columns and three rows.

You see column and row headings as well as gridlines on the worksheet to help you identify the location of data. You can change these options from the *View* tab if you prefer to see a cleaner background for your work. The *Gridlines* and *Headings* settings in the *Show* group are toggles that display or hide these features.

> **MORE INFO**
>
> From the *View* tab, you can also display or hide the formula bar and the ruler.

Enter Labels and Values

Data in a worksheet cell is text, a number, or a formula. A *label* is text that displays a name, a main title, row or column titles, and similar descriptive information. Labels are not included in calculations. A *value* is a number that can be used in a calculation or is the result of a calculation. A *formula* is a calculation or expression that displays a result.

When you type data that includes alphabetic characters and numbers, Excel treats that data as a label. Examples include a street address or an ID such as ABC123. When you type data with numbers that are not used in calculations, enter the data as a label by typing an apostrophe (') before the data. Examples of this type of data include a telephone or Social Security number without hyphens.

> **MORE INFO**
>
> If you type a Social Security number *with* hyphens, Excel will identify it as a label.

When a label in a cell is longer or wider than the cell, the label spills into an empty adjacent cell. If adjacent cells are not empty, the label is truncated or cut off in the cell, but the entire entry is visible in the *Formula bar*. The *Formula* bar appears below the *Ribbon* and displays the contents of the selected cell. When a value is too large for the width of the cell, the cell displays a series of # symbols or shows the value in exponential notation (part of the number with E+n as in 1235E+4). You can simply widen the column to see all cell contents.

To enter data, click the cell with the pointer to select and activate the cell. The pointer appears as a solid, white cross (a thick plus sign) when selecting data in the worksheet. The *active cell* displays a solid border, and its address appears in the *Name box* (Figure 1-5).

1-5 Entering data

1. Select the cell and type the data.
 - The label or value appears in the cell with an insertion point and in the *Formula* bar.
2. Press **Enter** to complete the entry and activate the cell below.
 - Press **Tab** to complete the entry and activate the cell to the right.
 - Press any keyboard directional arrow key to complete the entry and activate the cell in the direction of the arrow.
 - Press **Ctrl+Enter** to complete the entry and keep the current cell active.
 - Click the **Enter** button in the *Formula* bar to complete the entry and keep the cell active.

Edit Cell Contents

You can edit cell data as you type or after the entry is complete. To edit as you type, press the **Backspace** key to delete characters to the left of the insertion point. Or use arrow keys to move the insertion point and press the **Delete** key to erase characters to the right of the insertion point. To edit a completed entry, start *Edit* mode by double-clicking the cell or by pressing **F2 (FN+F2)**. The word "Edit" appears in the *Status* bar to alert you that data entry is in progress. Position the insertion point either in the cell or in the *Formula* bar, make the change, and press any completion key.

When using some keyboard function keys, you may need to press the **FN** key with the function key to access the command. This depends on the type of computer as well as the keyboard. This text will show a shortcut like this **F2 (FN+F2)** as a reminder to note your keyboard layout.

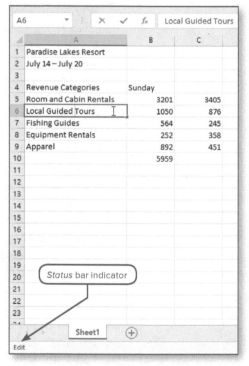

1-6 *Edit* mode

▶ **HOW TO:** Edit Cell Contents

1. Double-click the cell to be edited.
 - You can also click the cell and press **F2 (FN+F2)** to start *Edit* mode.
2. Position the insertion point in the cell or the *Formula* bar (Figure 1-6).
3. Edit the data.
4. Press **Enter**.

Replace or Clear Cell Contents

To replace data in a cell, select the cell and type the new data. Then press **Enter**, click the **Enter** button in the *Formula* bar, or press any completion key. The new data displays in the cell. To delete data from a cell, select the cell and press **Delete** or click the **Clear** button [*Home* tab, *Editing* group]. From the **Clear** button options, you can choose *Clear All*, *Clear Formats*, or *Clear Contents* (Figure 1-7). Pressing the **Delete** key removes the contents and preserves formatting.

▶ HOW TO: Clear Cell Contents

1. Select the cell or cells.
2. Press **Delete** on the keyboard.
 - Click the **Clear** button [*Home* tab, *Editing* group] and choose an option.
 - *Clear All* removes formatting and content.
 - *Clear Formats* only clears formatting and keeps data.
 - *Clear Contents* deletes content but keeps formatting.

1-7 *Clear* button options

Align and Indent Cell Contents

Excel recognizes a combination of letters, numbers, spaces, and other characters as a label. Labels are aligned on the left and bottom of the cell. When you type only numbers into a cell, Excel identifies the entry as a value. Values are aligned on the right and bottom of the cell.

You can change the vertical and horizontal *alignment* of data in a cell from the *Alignment* group on the *Home* tab (Figure 1-8). Horizontal alignment choices are *Align Left*, *Center*, and *Align Right*. Vertical alignment options are *Top Align*, *Middle Align*, and *Bottom Align*.

An **indent** moves cell contents away from the left edge of the cell. In Figure 1-8, labels in rows 5:9 are offset from the label in row 4. The **Increase Indent** button [*Home* tab, *Alignment* group] moves cell contents one space to the right if the data is left-aligned. You can remove an indent by clicking the **Decrease Indent** button [*Home* tab, *Alignment* group].

▶ HOW TO: Align and Indent Text

1. Select the cell.
2. Click a horizontal text alignment button [*Home* tab, *Alignment* group].
 - *Center* positions a label midway between the left and right boundaries of the cell.
 - *Align Left* starts a label at the left boundary of the cell.
 - *Right Align* sets a label to end at the right cell boundary.
3. Click a vertical text alignment button [*Home* tab, *Alignment* group].
 - *Middle Align* positions data midway between the top and bottom cell boundaries.
 - *Top Align* places data at the top cell boundary.
 - *Bottom Align* aligns data at the bottom boundary of the cell.
4. Click an indent button [*Home* tab, *Alignment* group].
 - The *Increase Indent* button moves data toward the right cell boundary.
 - The *Decrease Indent* button moves data toward the left cell boundary.

1-8 Alignment and indent options

In addition to horizontal and vertical settings, the *Alignment* group on the *Home* tab includes the *Orientation* button to display data vertically or at an angle. These settings are also available in the *Format Cells* dialog box on the *Alignment* tab (Figure 1-9).

1-9 *Alignment* tab, *Format Cells* dialog box

> **MORE INFO**
>
> Click the **Alignment** launcher [*Home* tab, *Alignment* group] or press **Ctrl+1** to open the *Format Cells* dialog box.

Select Cells

As you format or edit a worksheet, the first step is to select the cell or cells to be edited. Select a single cell by clicking it. Select a range by clicking the first cell and dragging the pointer in any direction to select adjacent cells. The following table outlines basic selection methods.

Selection Methods

Selection	Instructions
Entire Column or Row	Point to and click the column heading. Point to and click the row heading.
All Worksheet Cells	Press **Ctrl+A** or click the **Select All** button (above the row 1 heading and to the left of the column A heading).
Adjacent Cells by Dragging the Pointer	Click the first cell and drag the selection pointer over the cells to be included. Release the pointer button.
Adjacent Cells Using the Shift Key and the Pointer	Click the first cell, press **Shift**, and click the last cell in the range.
Adjacent Cells Using the Shift and Arrow Keys	Click the first cell, press **Shift**, and press any **Arrow** key.
Nonadjacent Cells	Click a cell or select the first range, press **Ctrl**, and select the next cell or range. Release the pointer button first; then release the **Ctrl** key.
Single Cell or Range Using the *Name Box*	Type a cell or range address in the *Name* box and press **Enter**.

You can see selected cell ranges in Figure 1-10.

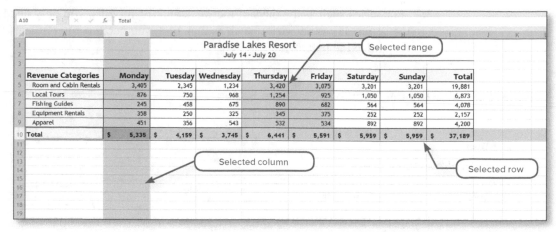

1-10 Selected cells in a worksheet

> **MORE INFO**
>
> To enter data column by column, select the entire cell range, type the first entry, and press **Enter**. Continue to type each entry and press **Enter**. The insertion point moves down each column and to the top of the next column based on the selected range.

The pointer changes shape depending on the current task or mode. The following table describes the shapes and indicates when they appear.

Pointer Shapes

Pointer Icon	Pointer Use
✚	**Selection pointer** (thick, white cross or plus sign) selects a cell or range; the selection pointer appears when you move the pointer over a cell.
➕	**Fill pointer** (crosshair or thin, black plus sign) copies cell contents or completes a series; it appears when you place the pointer on the *Fill Handle*, the tiny, black square in the bottom right corner of a selected cell or range.
✛	**Move pointer** (solid, white arrow with a black four-pointed arrow) moves data; it appears when you place the pointer on the border of a selected cell or range.
22↘	**Resize pointer** (two-pointed arrow) adjusts a formula cell range or an object; it appears when you place the pointer on a selection handle in a formula range or on a sizing handle for a selected object.

The Fill Handle

A *series* is a list of labels or values that follows a pattern. An example of a label series is the days of the week or the months of the year. A series of values is 1, 3, 5, 7, 9. Excel recognizes patterns and can complete most series with the **Fill Handle**. If there is no recognizable series, the *Fill Handle* copies the data.

The *Fill Handle* is a small, black square in the lower right corner of the cell or selected range. You drag this handle across the cell range for the series or to copy data. When you release the pointer button, the data is completed, and the *Auto Fill Options* button displays near the end of the series. This button provides choices for how to complete the series, but you usually need not make any changes.

For series such as the days of the week and the months, you only need enter the first item in the series. For other series, such as 2, 4, 6, 8, you need to enter at least two items for Excel to recognize the pattern.

▶ HOW TO: Use the Fill Handle to Create a Series

1. Type the first item in the series and press **Enter**.
 - Press **Ctrl+Enter** to keep the cell active.
 - Type two or three entries to identify a custom series.
2. Select the cell with the entry.
 - Select all cells with data that identify the series.
3. Point to the *Fill Handle* to display the *Fill* pointer (thin, black plus sign) (Figure 1-11).
4. Click and drag the *Fill* pointer through the last cell for the series.
 - A series can be horizontal or vertical.
 - You can double-click the *Fill* pointer to complete data down a column if other columns are already completed to the last row.
5. Release the pointer button.
 - The series is complete and the *Auto Fill Options* button appears.
6. Click the **Auto Fill Options** button.
 - Choose an option as desired (Figure 1-12).
7. Press **Esc** to remove the *Auto Fill Options* button or continue to the next task.

1-11 Use the *Fill Handle* to complete a series

1-12 Completed series with *Auto Fill Options* button

AutoComplete

AutoComplete is an Excel feature that displays a suggested label in a column when the first character or two that you type matches a label already in the column. *AutoComplete* enables you to quickly and accurately complete repetitive data. It works only for data that is alphanumeric, not for a column of values.

In a column that lists city names, for example, a particular city name might be repeated many times. The first time it appears, you type it as usual. On the second and succeeding occurrences of the name, as soon as you type the first character, Excel completes the label but waits for you to accept it. If the *AutoComplete* suggestion is correct, press **Enter**. If the suggestion is not correct, continue typing the label as needed.

Excel usually makes a suggestion after you type a single character in a cell in the column. If the column has more than one entry that begins with that character, type a second character and *AutoComplete* makes another or a better suggestion.

▶HOW TO: Use AutoComplete

1. Type the first character in a label.
 - A suggested label appears in the cell.
 - Type a second and third character when there are many labels that begin with the same letter.
 - You can type uppercase or lowercase characters to display an *AutoComplete* suggestion.
2. Press **Enter** to accept the *AutoComplete* suggestion (Figure 1-13).
 - Continue typing to ignore an *AutoComplete* suggestion.
 - Press **Enter** to complete a new label.

1-13 *AutoComplete* suggestion

Cut, Copy, and Paste Cell Contents

Excel has the same *Cut*, *Copy*, and *Paste* commands as other Windows applications. Use the *Cut* command to move data from one location to another. The *Copy* command duplicates cell contents to a different location. The *Paste* command places cut or copied data in the selected location. Data is cut or copied from a *source cell* or range and is pasted in a *destination cell* or range. When you cut or copy data, it is usually stored on the Windows *Clipboard* as well as the *Office Clipboard*.

Move or Cut Cell Contents

You can move data using drag and drop, keyboard shortcuts, or *Cut* and *Paste* in the *Clipboard* group on the *Home* tab. Drag and drop is quick when you want to move or copy cells within a visible range on the worksheet. When you use the drag-and-drop method, the source data is not stored on either clipboard.

▶HOW TO: Move Data Using Drag and Drop

1. Select the cell(s) to be moved.
2. Point to a border of the selection to display a move pointer (white arrow with four-pointed arrow).
3. Click and drag the selection to the new location (Figure 1-14).
 - A preview selection shows the destination address.
4. Release the pointer button.

1-14 Drag and drop to move data

When you use the *Cut* command from the *Ribbon* or the keyboard, the selected data is placed on both clipboards. You can paste once from the Windows *Clipboard*. You can paste multiple times from the *Office Clipboard*. There are three methods to cut data:

- *Ribbon* buttons: **Cut** and **Paste** buttons [*Home* tab, *Clipboard* group]
- Shortcut commands: **Ctrl+X** to cut and **Ctrl+V** to paste
- Context menu: Right-click and select **Cut**; right-click and select **Paste**

▶ HOW TO: Move Data Using Cut and Paste

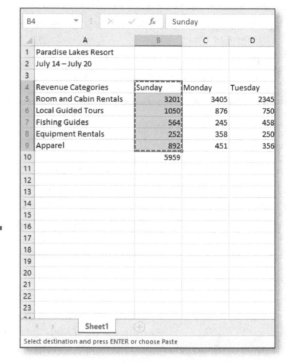

1-15 Cut data has moving border

1. Select the cell or range to be moved.
2. Click the **Cut** button [*Home* tab, *Clipboard* group].
 - A moving border surrounds the source cell(s) (Figure 1-15).
3. Select the destination cell.
 - Select the top-left cell in a destination range.
4. Click the **Paste** button [*Home* tab, *Clipboard* group].
 - If the destination cell(s) are not empty, pasted data overwrites existing data.

> **MORE INFO**
>
> After cutting data, right-click the destination cell and select **Insert Cut Cells** to avoid overwriting existing data.

The Office Clipboard

The *Office Clipboard* stores cut or copied data from Office applications and makes the data available for pasting in any application. The *Office Clipboard* can hold up to 24 items with each cut or copied item appearing, in turn, at the top of the pane. Click the **Clipboard** launcher to open the *Clipboard* task pane.

▶ HOW TO: Use the Office Clipboard

1. Click the **Home** tab.
2. Click the **Clipboard** launcher to open the *Clipboard* pane (Figure 1-16).
3. Click **Clear All** to empty the *Clipboard*.
 - The button is grayed out if there is no data on the clipboard.

4. Select data to be cut or copied.

5. Click the **Copy** button [*Home* tab, *Clipboard* group].

 - Use any *Cut* or *Copy* command from the *Ribbon* or keyboard.
 - Each item rotates into the first position in the *Clipboard* pane.

6. Select a destination cell.

7. Click the item icon in the *Clipboard* to paste it.

 - You can paste an item multiple times in different locations.

8. Click the **Close** button (X) to hide the *Clipboard*.

1-16 *Clipboard* pane

> **MORE INFO**
>
> To remove an item from the *Clipboard* task pane, click its drop-down arrow and choose **Delete**.

Copy Cell Contents

Copying data places a duplicate on the *Clipboard* so that it can be pasted in another location. When you use a *Ribbon*, keyboard, or context menu command, you can paste the data multiple times. You can copy data using the drag-and-drop method and paste it multiple times, even though the copied data is not placed on the *Clipboard*.

The *Copy* command stores data on the *Clipboard*, and the *Paste* command duplicates *Clipboard* contents in the worksheet.

- *Ribbon* buttons: **Copy** and **Paste** buttons [*Home* tab, *Clipboard* group]
- Shortcut commands: **Ctrl+C** to copy and **Ctrl+V** to paste
- Context menu: Right-click and choose **Copy**; right-click and choose **Paste**

▶ HOW TO: Copy Data Using Drag and Drop

1. Select the cell(s) to be copied.

2. Point to a border of the selection to display the move pointer.

3. Press **Ctrl** to display the copy pointer.

 - The copy pointer is a white arrow with a tiny plus sign.

4. Drag the selection to the desired location (Figure 1-17).

 - A preview selection shows where the copy will be pasted.

5. Continue to press **Ctrl** and drag to the next location for another copy.

6. Release the pointer button first and then release **Ctrl**.

1-17 Copy data using drag and drop

Paste Options

When you paste data, you can choose how it is copied in the new location. You can paste data and formatting, only the data, only the formatting, and so on. To see the options, click the lower half of the **Paste** button [*Home* tab, *Clipboard* group] to open the **Paste Options** gallery. The gallery also displays when you right-click a destination cell.

The table describes the icons in the *Paste Options* gallery:

Paste Options

Group	Paste Icon	Paste Option	Description
Paste		*Paste*	Copies all data and formatting; this is the default option.
		Formulas	Copies all data and formulas, but no formatting
		Formulas & Number Formatting	Copies all data and formulas with formatting
		Keep Source Formatting	Copies all data and formatting; same as *Paste*
		Match Destination Formatting	Copies data and applies formatting used in the destination
		No Borders	Copies all data, formulas, and formatting except for borders
		Keep Source Column Widths	Copies all data, formulas, and formatting and sets destination column widths to the same width as the source columns
		Transpose	Copies data and formatting and reverses data orientation so that rows are pasted as columns and columns are pasted as rows
		Merge Conditional Formatting	Copies data and *Conditional Formatting* rules. This option is available only if the copied data has conditional formatting.
Paste Values		*Values*	Copies only formula results (not the formulas) without formatting
		Values & Number Formatting	Copies only formula results (not the formulas) with formatting
		Values & Source Formatting	Copies only formula results (not the formulas) with all source formatting
Other Paste Options		*Formatting*	Copies only formatting, no data
		Paste Link	Pastes a 3-D reference to data or a formula
		Picture	Pastes a selectable picture object of the data. Data is static, but the object can be formatted like any object.
		Linked Picture	Pastes a selectable picture object of the data. The copied data is dynamic and reflects edits made in the source data. The picture can be formatted like any object.

> **MORE INFO**
> The *Paste Special* command opens a dialog box with additional options to paste comments, data validation, themes, and arithmetic operations.

PAUSE & PRACTICE: EXCEL 1-1

In this project, you open an Excel workbook that tracks revenue for one week at Paradise Lakes Resort. You add labels and values to complete the report; align labels; and edit, cut, and paste data. Your worksheet will have deliberate spelling errors for checking in a later Pause & Practice exercise.

File Needed: ***ParadiseLakes-01**.xlsx*
Completed Project File Name: ***[your initials] PP E1-1**.xlsx*

1. Open a workbook.
 a. Click the **File** tab and click **Open**.
 b. Navigate to the folder where your data files are stored.
 c. Double-click the name of the folder to open it.
 d. Locate the file name ***ParadiseLakes-01*** and click to select it.
 e. Click **Open**.
 f. Click **Enable Editing** if the workbook has opened in *Protected View* (Figure 1-18).

1-18 Worksheet opened in *Protected View*

2. Save the workbook with a different name.
 a. Press **F12** (**FN+F12**) to open the *Save As* dialog box.
 b. Select a location to save the workbook.
 c. Change the file name to [your initials] PP E1-1 in the *File name* area.
 d. Click **Save** to save the file and close the *Save As* dialog box.

3. Enter data.
 a. Click cell **A1** and type Paradise Lakes Resort.
 b. Press **Enter**.
 c. Click cell **A10**, type Total, and press **Enter**.
 d. Type the values shown below in cells **G5:H9**.

	G	H
5	3075	3201
6	925	1050
7	682	564
8	375	252
9	534	892

4. Use the *Fill Handle* to complete a series.
 a. Click **B4**.
 b. Point to the *Fill Handle* (small, black square in the lower right corner) until the *Fill* pointer (thin, black plus sign) appears.
 c. Click and drag the *Fill* pointer to reach cell **H4**.
 d. Release the pointer button.

5. Edit worksheet data.
 a. Click cell **B10**.
 b. Press **Delete** to remove the contents.
 c. Double-click cell **A4** to start *Edit* mode.
 d. Click to position the insertion point and delete the "i" in "Categories" to create a deliberate spelling error.
 e. Press **Enter** to accept the edit.
 f. Click cell **A9** and type **Aparel** with the error. You will correct errors in Pause & Practice 1-4.
 g. Press **Enter** to replace the entry.

6. Indent and align text.
 a. Select cells **A5:A9**.
 b. Click the **Increase Indent** button twice [*Home* tab, *Alignment* group].
 c. Select cells **B4:H4**.
 d. Click the **Center** button [*Home* tab, *Alignment* group].

7. Cut and paste data.
 a. Select cells **B4:B9**.
 b. Click the **Cut** button [*Home* tab, *Clipboard* group].
 c. Click cell **I4**.
 d. Click the **Paste** button [*Home* tab, *Clipboard* group].
 e. Select cells **C4:I9**.
 f. Point to any border of the selected range to display a four-pointed arrow with a white arrow.
 g. Drag the range to start in cell **B4** and release the pointer button.
 h. Click cell **A1**.

8. Save and close the workbook (Figure 1-19).
 a. Press **Ctrl+S** to save the workbook with the same file name.
 b. Click the **Close** button in the upper right corner to exit Excel.

◢	A	B	C	D	E	F	G	H
1	Paradise Lakes Resort							
2	July 14 – July 20							
3								
4	Revenue Categores	Monday	Tuesday	Wednesday	Thursday	Friday	Saturday	Sunday
5	Room and Cabin Rentals	3405	2345	1234	3420	3075	3201	3201
6	Local Tours	876	750	968	1254	925	1050	1050
7	Fishing Guides	245	458	675	890	682	564	564
8	Equipment Rentals	358	250	325	345	375	252	252
9	Aparel	451	356	543	532	534	892	892
10	Total							
11								

1-19 PP E1-1 completed

SLO 1.3

Using the SUM Function

A **formula** calculates a result for numeric data in a cell. A **function** is a built-in formula. **SUM** is a function that adds the values in a cell range. The terms "formula" and "function" are used interchangeably.

To use the *SUM* function, click the cell where you want to show a total. Then click the **AutoSum** button [*Home* tab, *Editing* group]. Excel inserts the function =SUM() with a suggested range of cells to be added between the parentheses. If that range is correct, press **Enter**, **Ctrl+Enter**, or click the **Enter** button in the *Formula* bar to complete the function. If the suggested range is not correct, you can select a different range or choose cells individually and then press a completion key. The sum is shown in the cell, and the function is visible in the *Formula* bar.

> **ANOTHER WAY**
>
> The *Function Library* group on the *Formulas* tab has an *AutoSum* button. You can also enter = SUM() in a cell by pressing **Alt** and the **+/=** key on the top keyboard row.

HOW TO: Use the SUM Function

1. Click the cell for the total.
2. Click the **AutoSum** button [*Home* tab, *Editing* group] (Figure 1-20).
3. Press **Enter** to accept the range and complete the function.
 - Drag the pointer to select a different range before pressing **Enter**.
 - If the row or column of values to be added is adjacent to the formula cell as shown in Figure 1-20, you can double-click the **AutoSum** button to insert and accept the function.

1-20 *SUM* function

> **MORE INFO**
>
> You can display formulas instead of results by clicking the **Show Formulas** button on the *Formulas* tab or by pressing **Ctrl+~**.

Function Syntax

An Excel function has **syntax**, the required elements and the order of those elements for the function to work. Every function starts with the equals sign [=] followed by the name of the function and a set of parentheses. Within the parentheses, you enter the argument(s). An

argument is the cell reference or value required to complete the function. A function can have a single or multiple arguments. In = SUM(B5:B9), the argument is the range B5:B9. Multiple arguments in a function are separated by commas. There are three arguments in this function: =SUM(B5, B10, B15).

<div style="border:1px solid #000; text-align:center; padding:20px;">

SUM(B5:B9)

SUM(B5, B10, B15)

</div>

Copy the SUM Function

The *SUM* function can be copied using regular copy and paste commands as well as the *Fill Handle*. When *SUM* is used to total data in rows or columns, you can enter the formula in the first column or row and copy it to the other locations. In Figure 1-21, for example, the same function is used in cells B10 through H10, each with its own argument. The formula in cell B10 is =SUM(B5:B9), the formula for cell C10 is =SUM(C5:C9) and so on. When a function is copied into adjacent cells, use the *Fill Handle*. Excel copies the formula and adjusts each argument based on the location in the worksheet.

> ▶ **HOW TO: Use the Fill Handle to Copy a Function**
>
> 1. Click the cell with the function to be copied.
> 2. Point to the *Fill Handle* in the lower right corner.

1-21 Use the *Fill Handle* to copy a function

> 3. Click and drag the *Fill* pointer across the cells where the function should be pasted (Figure 1-21).

> ▶ **ANOTHER WAY**
>
> You can use regular copy and paste commands to copy a function or formula to any location on the worksheet.

Edit the Function Argument

If you edit a value in a cell that is referenced in a formula or function, the results are automatically recalculated. If you must change a cell or range argument in a function, however, you use *Edit* mode to enter new references. In *Edit* mode, you can make a change in the *Formula* bar or in the cell. You can often use the ***Range Finder*** to drag or select a new range, too. The *Range Finder* is an Excel feature that highlights and color-codes formula cells as you enter or edit a formula or function.

▶ **HOW TO:** Edit an Argument Range in the Formula Bar

1. Select the cell with the function.
2. Click the argument cell range in the *Formula* bar.
 - The *Range Finder* highlights the argument range in the worksheet.
 - The range is color-coded in the *Formula* bar to match the highlighted range (Figure 1-22)
3. Type the new cell references in the *Formula* bar.
4. Press **Enter**.
 - You can click the **Enter** button in the *Formula* bar to complete the edit.

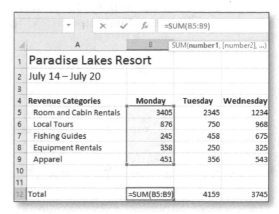

1-22 Argument range is color-coded

You can drag a *Range Finder* handle to select a different argument range, expanding or shrinking the number of included cells. This is easy to do when the formula cell is not adjacent to the range.

> **ANOTHER WAY**
>
> Double-click the cell with the function and edit the argument in the cell.

▶ **HOW TO:** Edit an Argument Range by Dragging

1. Double-click the cell with the function.
 - *Edit* mode starts (Figure 1-23).
2. Drag the selection handle down to expand the argument range.
 - Drag the selection handle up to shrink the argument range.
3. Press **Enter** to complete the change.
 - Click the **Enter** button in the *Formula* bar.

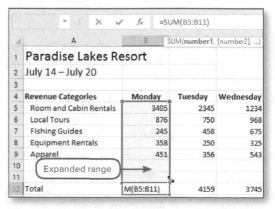

1-23 Edit a cell reference range by dragging

SLO 1.4

Formatting a Worksheet

A new workbook uses a default ***theme*** named *Office* which is a collection of fonts, colors, and special effects. The default theme applies the 11 point Calibri font and the *General* number format to all cells. You can change the theme as well as individual font attributes, or you can add fill and borders to highlight or emphasize data.

Font Face, Size, Style, and Color

A *font* is a type design for alphanumeric characters, punctuation, and keyboard symbols. *Font size* specifies the size of the character, measured in *points* (pt.). A point is equal to 1/72 of an inch. The *font style* refers to the thickness or angle of the characters and includes settings such as **bold**, <u>underline</u> or *italic*. *Font color* is the hue of the characters in the cell. You can apply any of these font attributes to a single cell or a range of cells.

Default font attributes for Excel 2016 workbooks are:

- Font: Calibri
- Font size: 11 point
- Font color: Black, Text 1

> **MORE INFO**
>
> The font list displayed on your computer depends on your Windows installation and other applications that are installed.

HOW TO: Customize Font, Style, Font Size, and Font Color

1. Select the cell or range to be formatted.
 - You can format cells before any data is entered if you prefer.
2. Click the **Font** drop-down list [*Home* tab, *Font* group].
 - A list of available fonts is displayed.
3. Point to a font name.
 - *Live Preview* shows the selected data with the new font applied (Figure 1-24).
4. Click the **Font Size** drop-down list [*Home* tab, *Font* group] and select a size.
 - *Live Preview* shows the selected data in the new size.
 - You can type a custom size in the *Font Size* area.
 - You can also click the **Increase Font Size** or **Decrease Font Size** button [*Home* tab, *Font* group] to adjust the font size in 1-point increments.
5. Click the **Bold**, **Italic**, or **Underline** button [*Home* tab, *Font* group] to apply a style.
 - You can apply multiple styles.
6. Click the **Font Color** drop-down list [*Home* tab, *Font* group] and select a color.
 - Click the **Font Color** button (not the arrow) to apply the most recent font color shown on the button.

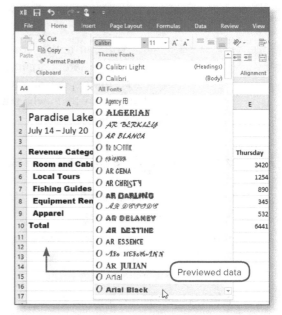

1-24 *Live Preview* when selecting a font name

The *mini toolbar* includes common commands from the *Font*, *Alignment*, and *Number* groups. It appears when you right-click a cell or selected range (Figure 1-25).

1-25 Mini toolbar

The *Format Cells* dialog box includes basic format settings and more. It has six tabs: *Number*, *Alignment*, *Font*, *Border*, *Fill*, and *Protection*.

- Mini toolbar: Right-click a cell or selected range.
- *Format Cells* dialog box: Click the **Font** launcher in the *Font* group, press **Ctrl+1** or right-click a selected cell and choose **Format Cells** (Figure 1-26).

The Format Painter

The *Format Painter* copies formatting attributes and styles from one cell to another cell or range. You can apply your custom formats without having to redefine each attribute, saving time and ensuring an exact duplicate.

1-26 *Format Cells* dialog box

▶ **HOW TO:** Use the Format Painter

1. Select a cell that contains the formatting you want to copy.
2. Click the **Format Painter** button [*Home* tab, *Clipboard* group].
 - The pointer changes to a thick, white cross with a tiny paint brush.
 - Double-click the **Format Painter** button to lock it for painting formats to multiple areas in the worksheet.
3. Click the cell or drag across the range to be formatted (Figure 1-27).
4. Release the pointer button.
 - The *Format Painter* is canceled.
 - If the *Format Painter* command is locked, click the **Format Painter** button or press **Esc** to turn it off.

1-27 Copy formats to a range using *Format Painter*

Number Formats

You can format values with currency symbols, decimal points, commas, percent signs, and more so that data is quickly recognized and understood. The *Number* group on the *Home* tab includes command buttons for *Accounting*, *Percent*, and *Comma* styles as well as command buttons to *Increase Decimal* or *Decrease Decimal*. Dates and times are values, and *Date* and *Time* formats are included in the *Number* group. From the *Format Cells* dialog box, you can apply and customize these number formats or create your own format.

▶ **HOW TO:** Format Numbers

1. Select the cell or range of values.
2. Click a command button [*Home* tab, *Number* group] (Figure 1-28).

- Click the **Number Format** drop-down list to choose a format.
- Press **Ctrl+1** to open the *Format Cells* dialog box and click the **Number** tab to select a format.

3. Click the **Increase Decimal** or **Decrease Decimal** button to control the number of decimal places.

 - When a cell displays a series of pound or number symbols (#####), you can widen the column to see the value.

1-28 *Number* group on the *Home* tab

ANOTHER WAY

Click the **Number** launcher [*Home* tab] to open the *Format Cells* dialog box.

Borders and Fill

A *border* is an outline for a cell or a range. You can design a border to separate main or column headings, to emphasize totals, or to group data. *Fill* is a background color or pattern and is used to highlight or draw attention to data. You can use the *Ribbon* or the *Format Cells* dialog box to apply borders and fill color.

▶ HOW TO: Add Borders and Fill Using the Ribbon

1. Select the cell or range.
2. Click the arrow next to the **Borders** button [*Home* tab, *Font* group].

 - The **Borders** button shows the most recently used border style.

3. Select a border option from the list (Figure 1-29).

 - To remove a border, choose **No Border**.

4. Click the arrow for the **Fill Color** button [*Home* tab, *Font* group].

 - Click the **Fill Color** button to apply the most recently selected color.
 - To remove a fill, choose **No Fill**.

1-29 *Borders* drop-down list

5. Select a color tile in the palette (Figure 1-30).

- *Live Preview* displays the cell or range with the color applied.
- Click **More Colors** to build a custom color.

1-30 *Fill Color* palette

The *Format Cells* dialog box has a *Border* tab and a *Fill* tab. From the *Border* tab, you can choose a different line style, a different color, or different positions for the border. From the *Fill* tab, you can design patterned or gradient fills. A **pattern** fill uses crosshatches, dots, or stripes. A **gradient** is a blend of two or more colors. Use fill choices carefully, because they affect the readability of your data.

1-31 Build a custom border in the *Format Cells* dialog box

▶ HOW TO: Add Borders and Fill Using the Format Cells Dialog Box

1. Select the cell or range.
2. Click the **Font** launcher [*Home* tab, *Font* group] to open the *Format Cells* dialog box.
 - Press **Ctrl+1** to open the *Format Cells* dialog box.
 - Right-click a cell in the range and select **Format Cells**.
3. Click the **Border** tab (Figure 1-31).
 - Click **None** to remove all borders.
4. Choose a color from the *Color* drop-down list.
 - Select the color before choosing a line style or location.
5. Select a line style in the *Style* area.
6. Click **Outline** in the *Presets* area to apply an outside border.
 - The *Preview* area shows the border.
 - Build a custom border by clicking the desired icons in the *Border* area or by clicking the desired position in the *Preview* area.
7. Click the **Fill** tab (Figure 1-32).

1-32 *Fill* tab in the *Format Cells* dialog box and *Fill Effects* dialog box

8. Select a color tile in the *Background Color* area.
 - Select a color from the *Pattern Color* list and select a pattern from the *Pattern Style* list.
 - Click **Fill Effects** to apply a gradient. Choose two colors, a shading style, and a variant.
9. Click **OK** to close the *Format Cells* dialog box.

Cell Styles

A *cell style* is a set of formatting elements that includes font style, size, color, alignment, borders, and fill as well as number formats. Like other formatting, you select the cell or range and then apply a cell style. When you apply a cell style, the style format overwrites individual formatting already applied. After a cell style is applied, however, you can individually change any of the attributes. The *Cell Styles* gallery is located in the *Styles* group on the *Home* tab.

> **MORE INFO**
>
> Your screen size and settings determine if you see part of the *Cell Styles* gallery in the *Ribbon* or only the *Cell Styles* button.

 HOW TO: Apply Cell Styles

1. Select the cell or range.
2. Click the **More** button in the *Cell Styles* gallery.
 - Click the **Cell Styles** button [*Home* tab, *Styles* group] to open the gallery (Figure 1-33).

1-33 *Cell Styles* gallery and *Live Preview* for selected cell

3. Point to a style name to see a *Live Preview* in the worksheet.
4. Click a style name to apply it.

Workbook Themes

A workbook *theme* is a professionally designed set of fonts, colors, and effects. When you change the workbook theme, data formatted with theme settings are reformatted with the new

theme fonts, colors, and effects. You can change the theme to quickly restyle a worksheet without having to individually edit cell formats throughout the sheet.

A theme includes a font name for headings and one for body text, and some themes use the same font for both. You can see the names of *Theme Fonts* at the top of the *Font* list. *Theme Colors* are identified in the color palettes for the **Fill** and **Font Color** buttons [*Home* tab, *Font* group]. Cell styles use font and color settings from the theme.

The *Themes* gallery lists built-in themes, and there are additional themes available online. You can also create and save your own theme.

▶HOW TO: Change the Workbook Theme

1. Click the **Theme** button [*Page Layout* tab, *Themes* group]
 - The *Themes* gallery opens.
2. Point to a theme name.
 - *Live Preview* displays the worksheet with new format settings (Figure 1-34).

1-34 *Themes* gallery and a *Live Preview* in the worksheet

3. Click a theme icon to apply a different theme.
 - Display the **Font** button list [*Home* tab, *Font* group] to see the new theme font names at the top of the list.
 - Display the **Font Color** and **Fill Color** button galleries [*Home* tab, *Font* group] to see new theme colors.

▶ MORE INFO

Rest the pointer on the **Themes** button [*Page Layout* tab, *Themes* group] to see the name of the current theme.

In this project, you open the workbook you created in *Pause & Practice Excel 1-1*. You add totals using *SUM* and copy the function using *AutoFill*. Your format changes result in truncated or cutoff data; you learn how to adjust column widths in the next learning objective and will fix this problem in the next Pause & Practice project.

File Needed: ***[your initials] PP E1-1**.xlsx*
Completed Project File Name: ***[your initials] PP E1-2**.xlsx*

1. Open a workbook and save it as a different name.
 a. Click the **File** tab and choose **Open**. If you have just started Excel and the file name appears in the *Recent* list in the Excel *Start* page, click the name to open it. Otherwise, click **Open Other Workbooks** at the bottom of the *Start* page.
 b. Locate the folder where your file is stored.
 c. Open ***[your initials] PP E1-1**. (Click **Enable Editing** if the workbook has opened in *Protected View*).
 c. Press **F12** (**FN+F12**) to open the *Save As* dialog box.
 d. Locate the folder where your files are saved.
 e. Edit the file name to [your initials] PP E1-2 and click **Save**.

2. Calculate daily totals using *SUM*.
 a. Click cell **B10**.
 b. Click the **AutoSum** button [*Home* tab, *Editing* group].
 c. Press **Enter** to accept the suggested range and to complete the formula.

3. Copy a function using the *Fill Handle*.
 a. Click cell **B10**.
 b. Point to the *Fill Handle* in the lower right corner of the cell.
 c. Click and drag the *Fill* pointer to cell **H10** (Figure 1-35). Release the pointer button.

1-35 Copy a function with the *Fill* pointer

4. Calculate sales category totals.
 a. Click cell **J5**.
 b. Double-click the **AutoSum** button [*Home* tab, *Editing* group] to accept and complete the formula.

5. Edit the argument cell range.
 a. Click cell **J5**.
 b. Click the *Formula* bar within the range **B5:I5**.
 c. Position the insertion point and edit the range to **B5:h5**. When you type the "h," you will see a *Formula AutoComplete* list which you can ignore (Figure 1-36).
 d. Press **Enter** to accept the new range.

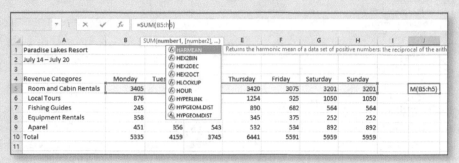

1-36 Edit the cell reference in the *Formula* bar

6. Copy a function using the *Fill Handle*.
 a. Select cell **J5** and point to the *Fill Handle*.
 b. Click and drag the *Fill* pointer to cell **J10**. Release the pointer button.

7. Drag and drop to move a cell range.
 a. Select cells **J5:J10**.
 b. Point to any border of the selected range to display the move pointer.
 c. Drag the range to cells **I5:I10**.
 d. In cell **I4**, type Total.

8. Apply cell styles.
 a. Select cell **A1** and click the **Cell Styles** button or the **More** button [*Home* tab, *Styles* group] to open the *Cell Styles* gallery.
 b. Click **Title** in the *Titles and Headings* group.
 c. Select cell **A2** and click the **Cell Styles** button or the **More** button [*Home* tab, *Styles* group].
 d. Select **Heading 2** in the *Titles and Headings* group.
 e. Select cells **A10:I10** and open the *Cell Styles* gallery [*Home* tab, *Styles* group].
 f. Select **Total** in the *Titles and Headings* group.
 g. Select cells **A4:A10**, press **Ctrl**, and select cells **B4:I4** to add them to the selection.
 h. Open the *Cells Style* gallery and select **20%, Accent1** in the *Themed Cell Styles* category.
 i. Click cell **F1** to deselect cells and view the styles.

9. Change the theme and apply font attributes.
 a. Click the **Themes** button [*Page Layout* tab, *Themes* group] and choose **Facet** from the gallery.
 b. Select cell **A4** and click the **Home** tab.
 c. Click the **Font** drop-down list [*Font* group] and select **Candara** in the *All Fonts* section.
 d. Click the **Font Size** drop-down list and select **16 pt**.
 e. Click the **Bold** button [*Font* group].
 f. Select cells **A5:I10**.
 g. Click the **Font Size** drop-down list and choose **12 pt**.

10. Use the *Format Painter*.
 a. Click cell **A4**.
 b. Click the **Format Painter** button [*Home* tab, *Clipboard* group].
 c. Drag to paint cells **B4:I4** and release the pointer button (Figure 1-37).

Revenue Categores	Monday	Tuesday	Wednesd	Thursday	Friday		Saturday	Sunday	Total
Room and Cabin Rentals	3405	2345	1234	3420	3075		3201	3201	19881
Local Tours	876	750	968	1254	925		1050	1050	6873
Fishing Guides	245	458	675	890	682		564	564	4078
Equipment Rentals	358	250	325	345	375		252	252	2157
Aparel	451	356	543	532	534		892	892	4200
Total	5335	4159	3745	6441	5591		5959	5959	37189

1-37 Paint the format from cell A4

11. Apply number formats and align text.
 a. Select cells **B5:I9**.
 b. Click the **Comma Style** button [*Home* tab, *Number* group] and leave cells B5:I9 selected.
 c. Click the **Decrease Decimal** button [*Home* tab, *Number* group] two times while cells B5:I9 are selected.
 d. Select cells **B10:I10**.
 e. Click the **Accounting Number Format** button [*Home* tab, *Number* group]. You may see a series of # symbols in the cells.
 f. Click the **Decrease Decimal** button [*Home* tab, *Number* group] two times.
 g. Select cells **B4:I4**.
 h. Click the **Align Right** button [*Home* tab, *Alignment* group]. Not all labels are visible with this alignment setting.
 i. Apply **Bold** to cell **A10**.

1-38 Remove the bottom border

12. Add borders.
 a. Select cells **A4:I10** and click the **Border** button arrow [*Home* tab, *Font* group].
 b. Select **All Borders**. The border format from the *Total* cell style in row 10 is overwritten with the *All Borders* format.
 c. Select cells **A10:I10** and press **Ctrl+1** to open the *Format Cells* dialog box.
 d. Click the **Border** tab.
 e. Click the bottom border icon In the *Border* preview area to remove the border (Figure 1-38).
 f. Click the double solid line style (second column, seventh style).
 g. In the preview area, click the bottom border position to reset the border (Figure 1-39).
 h. Click **OK** to close the *Format Cells* dialog box and to apply the new border.
 i. Select cells **A2:I2** and open the *Format Cells* dialog box.
 j. Click the **Border** tab and click the bottom border position two times to remove the bottom border.
 k. Click the **Color** drop-down list, and select **Dark Green, Accent 2, Darker 25%**.

1-39 Reset the bottom border

Excel 2016 Chapter 1 Creating and Editing Workbooks

l. Select the thick, solid line style (second column, fifth style).

m. In the preview area, click the bottom border location to reset the border.

n. Click **OK** and then click cell **A1**.

13. Click the **Save** button in the *Quick Access* toolbar.

14. Click the **File** tab and click **Close**, or press **Ctrl+W** to close the workbook (Figure 1-40).

	A	B	C	D	E	F	G	H	I
1	Paradise Lakes Resort								
2	July 14 - July 20								
3									
4	**Revenue Categores**	**Monday**	**Tuesday**	**ednesday**	**Thursday**	**Friday**	**Saturday**	**Sunday**	**Total**
5	Room and Cabin Rentals	3,405	2,345	1,234	3,420	3,075	3,201	3,201	19,881
6	Local Tours	876	750	968	1,254	925	1,050	1,050	6,873
7	Fishing Guides	245	458	675	890	682	564	564	4,078
8	Equipment Rentals	358	250	325	345	375	252	252	2,157
9	Aparel	451	356	543	532	534	892	892	4,200
10	**Total**	$ 5,335	$ 4,159	$ 3,745	$ 6,441	$ 5,591	$ 5,959	$ 5,959	$ 37,189
11									

1-40 PP E1-2 completed

Modifying Columns and Rows

A worksheet has a default number of rows and columns, each in the default width and height for the workbook theme. There are over 1 million rows and more than 16,000 columns available for use. You can modify the width of a column, insert columns, change the height of a row, delete a column, and more.

> **MORE INFO**
>
> Unused rows and columns are ignored when you print a worksheet with default print settings.

Adjust Column Width and Row Height

The default width for a column in a worksheet using the Office theme is 8.43 characters (64 pixels) in the default font. Column width can be set to any value between 0 and 255 characters. The default height of each row is 15 points (20 pixels). A *pixel* measures one screen dot. You can change *column width* or *row height* by dragging the border between column or row headings, by using the context menu, or by selecting a command from the **Format** button list [*Home* tab, *Cells* group]. You can adjust one or more columns or rows at the same time.

▶**HOW TO:** Change Column Width or Row Height

1. Select one or more cells in the same column.
 - The cells need not be in adjacent rows.
2. Click the **Format** button [*Home* tab, *Cells* group].
3. Select **Row Height**.
 - The *Row Height* dialog box opens.

4. Enter a height in points and click **OK**.

 - The row height is adjusted for the rows in which you selected cells.

5. Select one or more cells in the same row.

 - The cells need not be in adjacent columns.

6. Click the **Format** button [*Home* tab, *Cells* group].

7. Select **Column Width**.

 - The *Column Width* dialog box opens.

8. Enter a new width in characters and click **OK** (Figure 1-41).

1-41 Change the column width for several columns

> **MORE INFO**
>
> Click the **Format** button [*Home* tab, *Cells* group] and select **Default Width** to change the default column width for the entire worksheet.

You can quickly change column widths and row heights using the worksheet headings. Point to the border between two column or row headings and click and drag to set a new width or height. When you point to a border, the pointer changes to a resize arrow, and you will see a *ScreenTip* with the setting as you drag. You can use this method with multiple columns or rows, too. Drag across the headings to select the number of columns or rows to be adjusted, and then click and drag any border in the selected group.

AutoFit Columns and Rows

The *AutoFit* feature resizes column width or row height to fit the width or height of the longest or tallest entry. The quickest way to *AutoFit* a column is to double-click the right border of the column heading (Figure 1-42). To *AutoFit* a row, double-click the bottom border of the row heading. You can *AutoFit* multiple columns or rows by first selecting them and double-clicking any border within the selection. You can also use the *AutoFit Column Width* or the *AutoFit Row Height* commands on the **Format** button in the *Cells* group on the *Home* tab.

▶ **HOW TO: AutoFit Column Width or Row Height**

1. Point to the border to the right of the column heading or below the row heading.

 - Drag to select more than one column or row.

2. Double-click the resize arrow.

 - All selected columns and rows are set to fit the longest or tallest entry.

1-42 Double-click a column border to *AutoFit* its width to the longest item

Wrap Text, Merge Cells, and Center Across Selection

When a label is too long for the column width, it spills into an empty adjacent cell. If that adjacent cell is not empty, a long label may be cut off within the cell. You can widen the column, or you can wrap text. Wrapped text is often used to show lengthy column titles on more than one line (Figure 1-43).

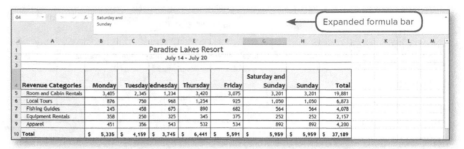

	A	B	C	D	E	F	G	H	I	J	K	L	M
1					Paradise Lakes Resort								
2					July 14 - July 20								
3													
4	Revenue Categories	Monday	Tuesday	ednesday	Thursday	Friday	Saturday and Sunday	Sunday	Total				
5	Room and Cabin Rentals	3,405	2,345	1,234	3,420	3,075	3,201	3,201	19,881				
6	Local Tours	876	750	968	1,254	925	1,050	1,050	6,873				
7	Fishing Guides	245	458	675	890	682	564	564	4,078				
8	Equipment Rentals	358	250	325	345	375	252	252	2,157				
9	Apparel	451	356	543	532	534	892	892	4,200				
10	Total	$ 5,335	$ 4,159	$ 3,745	$ 6,441	$ 5,591	$ 5,959	$ 5,959	$ 37,189				

1-43 Label in cell G4 is wrapped to two lines; *Formula* bar is expanded

The ***Wrap Text*** command displays a label on multiple lines within the cell, splitting the label between words to fit the width of the column. You can control where the label splits by inserting a manual ***line break***. Press **Alt+Enter** after the word where you want a new line to start. When using multi-line labels, you can expand the *Formula* bar by clicking the **Formula Bar** expand or collapse button at the right edge of the *Formula* bar.

> **MORE INFO**
>
> After using the *Wrap Text* command, you may need to adjust the column width or row height to better display the label.

▶HOW TO: Wrap Text in a Cell

1. Select the cell with the label.
2. Click the **Home** tab.
3. Click the **Wrap Text** button in the *Alignment* group.
 - To control the split, edit the cell and click at the desired location. Press **Alt+Enter** to insert a manual line break and then press **Enter** to finish.
4. Adjust the column width and row height as desired.

> **ANOTHER WAY**
>
> As you type a label, press **Alt+Enter** at the point where a new line should start, finish the label, and press **Enter**. The *Wrap Text* command is automatically enabled.

The ***Merge & Center*** command combines two or more cells into one cell and centers the data within the combined cell. This command is a quick way to center a main label over multiple columns. Because the result is one large cell, you can format the area with special fill effects. When you use *Merge & Center*, the data must be in the upper left cell of the selection.

The *Merge & Center* button [*Home* tab, *Alignment* group] includes options to merge cells without centering and to unmerge cells.

▶**HOW TO:** Merge and Center

1. Select the cells to be merged and centered.

 - You can merge and center the cells first and then enter the data.

2. Click the **Home** tab.

3. Click the **Merge & Center** button [*Alignment* group] (Figure 1-44).

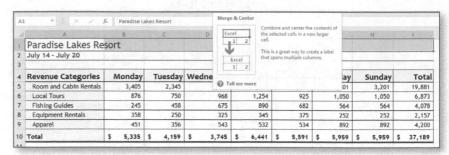

1-44 Select cells to merge and center

The ***Center Across Selection*** command horizontally centers multiple rows across multiple columns. When you have two or three rows of labels to center, you can select the entire range and center them with one command. This command does not merge cells, and you can still insert and delete rows and columns in the centered area.

The *Center Across Selection* command is on the *Alignment* tab in the *Format Cells* dialog box.

▶**HOW TO:** Center Across a Selection

1. Select the cell range that includes the data to be centered.

 - Select all rows with data to be centered.
 - Select columns to identify the range over which the labels should be centered.

2. Click the **Alignment** launcher [*Home* tab, *Alignment* group].

3. Click the **Horizontal** drop-down arrow and choose **Center Across Selection** (Figure 1-45).

4. Click **OK**.

1-45 Selection identifies area for centering

Insert and Delete Columns and Rows

You can insert or delete rows or columns in a worksheet. When you do, Excel moves existing data to make room for new data or to fill the gap left by deleted data. Functions or formulas are automatically updated to include an inserted row or column, and they reflect deleted rows or columns in the argument or range.

You can insert rows and columns from options on the **Insert** button [*Home* tab, *Cells* group]. You can also right-click a column or row heading and choose **Insert** from the context menu. To insert multiple columns or rows, first select the number of columns or rows that you want to insert. For example, if you want to insert two columns to the left of column A, select columns A:B. Then use any **Insert** command to insert two new columns.

▶ HOW TO: Insert a Column or a Row

1. Select a cell in the column to the right of where a new column is to be inserted.
2. Click the arrow on the **Insert** button [*Home* tab, *Cells* group].
3. Select **Insert Sheet Columns**.
 - A column is inserted to the left of the current column.
4. Right-click the row heading below the row where a new row should appear.
5. Choose **Insert** from the context menu (Figure 1-46).
 - A row is inserted above the selected row.

1-46 Insert a row above row 9

When you delete a column or row, data is deleted and remaining columns and rows shift to the left or up. Most functions or formulas are updated if you delete a row or column that is within the argument range.

You can delete rows and columns from the **Delete** button [*Home* tab, *Cells* group] or from the context menu. To delete multiple columns or rows, select them and use the **Delete** command.

> ▶ **ANOTHER WAY**
>
> Select a cell and press **Ctrl+plus sign (+)** in the numeric keypad. Choose **Entire Column** or **Entire Row** and press **Enter**. Press **Ctrl+minus sign (−)** in the numeric keypad to delete a column or row.

▶ HOW TO: Delete Columns or Rows

1. Select a cell in the column to be deleted.
2. Click the arrow on the **Delete** button [*Home* tab, *Cells* group].
3. Select **Delete Sheet Columns**.
 - The entire column is deleted.
 - Remaining columns shift to the left.
4. Right-click the row heading for the row to be deleted.
 - The context menu opens.
5. Choose **Delete**.
 - The entire row is deleted.
 - Remaining rows shift up.

Hide and Unhide Columns and Rows

If a worksheet has more data than necessary for your current task, you can hide data to optimize screen space. In a checkbook register with data for several years, you might want to hide rows from two years ago so that you only see the current year's data. You should not delete the old data because it is necessary for record-keeping.

Hidden rows and columns are available and included in calculations and can be shown whenever necessary. The *Hide* and *Unhide* commands apply to columns or rows; you cannot hide cells. When a column or row is hidden, there is a tiny gap between the column or row headings. In addition, column or row headings are not consecutive, so you can quickly identify what is hidden.

 HOW TO: Hide and Unhide Columns or Rows

1. Click the row or column heading of the row or column to be hidden.
 - Select multiple row or column headings as desired.
 - Rows or columns need not be adjacent.
2. Right-click one of the selected row or column headings.
 - The context menu opens.
3. Select **Hide** (Figure 1-47).
 - The entire row or column is hidden.
 - Formula references to hidden cells are maintained.
4. Drag across the column or row headings where there are hidden columns or rows.
 - Drag from the column to the left of a hidden column to one column to the right of a hidden column.
 - Drag from the row above hidden rows to one row below hidden rows.
5. Right-click one of the selected row or column headings.
 - The context menu opens.
6. Select **Unhide**.

1-47 Hide two columns

Modifying Worksheets

Each worksheet in an Excel workbook has a worksheet tab near the bottom left of the Excel window that displays the name of the sheet. A new workbook starts with one sheet, but the number of worksheets is limited only by the size of memory on the computer. You can insert and delete sheets, rename them, and change the tab color. You can also hide, copy, or move sheets.

Insert and Delete Worksheets

You can keep related worksheets in a single workbook for ease in managing your files and tasks. For example, a monthly workbook could include revenue and expense, payroll, and customer data sheets. When there are multiple worksheets in a workbook, activate a sheet by clicking its tab name.

You can insert worksheets from the **Insert** button [*Home* tab, *Cells* group] or by simply clicking the **New Sheet** button to the right of the tab names. You can also right-click an existing sheet tab and choose **Insert** to open an *Insert* dialog box. Inserted worksheets are named *SheetN*, where *N* is the next available number.

To delete the active worksheet, right-click the sheet tab and select **Delete**. You can also click the arrow on the **Delete** button [*Home* tab, *Cells* group] and select **Delete Sheet**.

>
>
> **MORE INFO**
>
> Press **Ctrl+Page Down** to move to the next worksheet in the tab order. Press **Ctrl+Page Up** to move to the previous sheet.

▶**HOW TO:** Insert and Delete Worksheets

1. Click the **New Sheet** button (plus sign) to the right of the worksheet tabs (Figure 1-48).
 - A new sheet is inserted to the right of the active sheet.
2. Click the arrow on the **Insert** button [*Home* tab, *Cells* group].
3. Select **Insert Sheet**.
 - A new sheet is inserted to the left of the active sheet.
4. Right-click a tab and select **Insert**.
 - The *Insert* dialog box opens.
5. Select **Worksheet** and click **OK**.
 - The new sheet is inserted to the left of the active sheet.
6. Right-click a sheet tab and choose **Delete**.
 - The sheet is deleted.
7. Click the arrow on the **Delete** button [*Home* tab, *Cells* group] and select **Delete Sheet**.
 - The sheet is deleted.

1-48 *New Sheet* button

> **ANOTHER WAY**
>
> Press **Shift+F11** to insert a worksheet to the left of the active sheet.

Rename Worksheets and Change Tab Color

New worksheets are named *Sheet1*, *Sheet2*, and so on, but you can rename a worksheet to identify its contents and purpose. The tab width adjusts to display the name, so if you use lengthy names, you limit the number of tabs visible at the same time. When you cannot see all the tabs, use the ***tab scrolling buttons*** located to the left of the leftmost tab name. Move forward and backward through the tabs, or you can right-click a tab scrolling button to display the *Activate* dialog box with a list of existing worksheet names (Figure 1-49). The tab scrolling buttons are enabled when needed.

1-49 *Activate dialog box and tab scrolling buttons*

You can apply a ***tab color*** to further distinguish a particular sheet. The color palette includes tiles for theme and standard colors as well as an option to build a custom color.

▶ HOW TO: Rename a Worksheet and Apply a Tab Color

1. Double-click the worksheet tab.
 - You can right-click the tab and select **Rename**.
2. Type the new name on the tab and press **Enter**.
 - You can click the **Format** button [*Home* tab, *Cells* group] and select **Rename Sheet**.
3. Right-click the worksheet tab.
4. Choose **Tab Color** from the context menu to open the palette (Figure 1-50).
 - You can click the **Format** button [*Home* tab, *Cells* group] and select **Tab Color**.

1-50 Change the tab color

Excel 2016 Chapter 1 Creating and Editing Workbooks

5. Select a color.

6. Click another tab to better see the tab color.

Move and Copy Worksheets

You can rearrange (move) tabs to display the worksheets in your preferred left-to-right order. You can also move worksheets to another workbook.

You can copy a worksheet to make an exact duplicate of the data and formatting. When you copy a worksheet, the copy is named with the same name as the original followed by a number in parentheses (i.e., *January (2)*).

When moving sheets within a workbook, you simply drag the tab to the desired location. When moving or copying to another workbook, however, use the ***Move or Copy*** dialog box.

You can move or copy multiple sheets, too. Select sheet names using **Ctrl** or **Shift**. The word *[Group]* displays in the title bar. After you complete the move or copy command, right-click any tab in the group and choose **Ungroup**.

▶**HOW TO:** Move and Copy Worksheets

1. Point to the worksheet tab to be moved.

2. Drag the pointer to the desired location in the tab names.

 - A triangle and a worksheet icon preview where the worksheet will be moved (Figure 1-51).

3. Release the pointer button.

4. Right-click the worksheet tab to be copied.

5. Select **Move or Copy**.

 - The *Move or Copy* dialog box opens.
 - You can also click the **Format** button [*Home* tab, *Cells* group] to select **Move or Copy Sheet**.

6. Click the **To book** drop-down arrow and choose a workbook name.

 - To copy the sheet in the same workbook, choose its name.
 - To copy the worksheet into a different workbook, choose its name; the workbook must be open.

7. In the *Before sheet* list, choose a sheet name as desired.

 - Choose **(move to end)** to place the copied sheet as the last tab.

8. Select the **Create a copy** box (Figure 1-52).

9. Click **OK** to close the dialog box.

 - The copied worksheet has the same name as the original followed by *(2)*.

10. Rename the copied sheet as desired.

1-51 Drag a sheet tab to a position

1-52 *Move or Copy* dialog box

> **ANOTHER WAY**
>
> To copy a worksheet by dragging, press **Ctrl** and drag the tab to the desired location for the copy.

In this project, you open *[your initials] PP E1-2* and adjust column heights and row widths, insert a row, merge and center cells, and add borders. You also copy and rename sheets, apply tab colors, and delete worksheets.

File Needed: *[your initials] PP E1-2*.xlsx
Completed Project File Name: *[your initials] PP E1-3*.xlsx

1. Open the *[your initials] PP E1-2* workbook completed in *Pause & Practice 1-2.*

2. Save the file as [your initials] PP E1-3.

3. Change the width of columns B through I.
 a. Point to the column **B** heading to display a down-pointing arrow.
 b. Click and drag to reach column **I**.
 c. Click the **Format** button [*Home* tab, *Cells* group].
 d. Select **Column Width** from the menu.
 e. Enter 14 in the *Column Width* dialog box.
 f. Click **OK** to set the new width for the selected columns.

4. Change the row height for rows 4 and 10.
 a. Click the row **4** heading.
 b. Press **Ctrl** and click the row **10** heading. Two rows are selected.
 c. Right-click the row **4** heading.
 d. Choose **Row Height** from the menu.
 e. Enter 24 as the new height.
 f. Click **OK** to set the row height for both rows.

5. Insert a row.
 a. Right-click row heading **9**.
 b. Choose **Insert**. The inserted row is row 9, and the remaining rows have shifted down.
 c. In cell **A9**, type Food & Beverage. The new row uses the same format as the other rows (Figure 1-53).
 d. Press **Enter**.

A10	▼	× ✓ *fx*	Aparel						
	A	B	C	D	E	F	G	H	I
1	Paradise Lakes Resort								
2	July 14 - July 20								
3									
4	**Revenue Categores**	**Monday**	**Tuesday**	**Wednesday**	**Thursday**	**Friday**	**Saturday**	**Sunday**	**Total**
5	Room and Cabin Rentals	3,405	2,345	1,234	3,420	3,075	3,201	3,201	19,881
6	Local Tours	876	750	968	1,254	925	1,050	1,050	6,873
7	Fishing Guides	245	458	675	890	682	564	564	4,078
8	Equipment Rentals	358	250	325	345	375	252	252	2,157
9	Food & Beverage								
10	Aparel	451	356	543	532	534	892	892	4,200
11	Total	$ 5,335	$ 4,159	$ 3,745	$ 6,441	$ 5,591	$ 5,959	$ 5,959	$ 37,189
12									

1-53 New row and label inserted

6. Hide a row.
 a. Select cell **A9**.
 b. Click the **Format** button [*Home* tab, *Cells* group].
 c. Select **Hide & Unhide** in the *Visibility* category.
 d. Select **Hide Rows**. The selected row is hidden.

7. Center titles across a selection.
 a. Select cells **A1:I2**.
 b. Click the **Alignment** launcher [*Home* tab, *Alignment* group].

 c. Click the **Horizontal** drop-down arrow and choose **Center Across Selection**.

 d. Click **OK**.

8. Rename a worksheet and change the tab color.

 a. Double-click the **Sheet1** tab name.

 b. Type Cass Lake.

 c. Press **Enter**.

 d. Right-click the **Cass Lake** tab name and select **Tab Color**.

 e. Select **Green Accent 1, Darker 50%** (fifth column).

9. Copy and rename a worksheet.

 a. Right-click the **Cass Lake** tab.

 b. Choose **Move or Copy**. The *Move or Copy* dialog box opens.

 c. Choose **(move to end)** in the *Before Sheet* list.

 d. Select the **Create a copy** box.

 e. Click **OK**. The copied sheet is named *Cass Lake (2)*.

 f. Double-click the **Cass Lake (2)** tab, type Breezy Point, and press **Enter**.

 g. Right-click the **Breezy Point** tab and choose **Tab Color**.

 h. Format the tab color to **Orange, Accent 4, Darker 25%**.

 i. Select cells **B5:H10** and press **Delete** (Figure 1-54).

 j. Press **Ctrl+Home**.

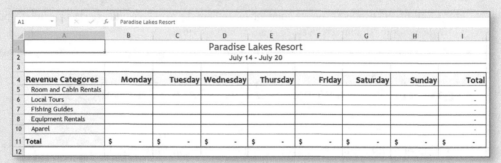

1-54 Data deleted on copied sheet

10. Click the **Cass Lake** tab and press **Ctrl+Home**.

11. Press **Ctrl+S** to save the workbook.

12. Click the **File** tab and click **Close** to close the workbook (Figure 1-55).

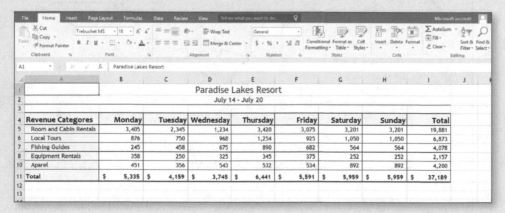

1-55 PP E1-3 completed worksheet

Modifying the Appearance of the Workbook

You can adjust how you see data in a worksheet to make your work as easy as possible. You can select a view, zoom in or out on the data, freeze parts of the screen, split the worksheet into two panes, and switch between multiple open windows.

Workbook Views

The *View* tab has a *Workbook Views* group with three main views or layouts for working in an Excel worksheet. The views are **Normal**, **Page Layout**, and **Page Break Preview**.

- *Normal* view is the default and is used to create and modify a worksheet.
- *Page Layout* view opens the header and footer areas, indicates margin areas, and shows rulers.
- *Page Break Preview* displays printed pages with dashed or dotted lines to mark where new pages start.

There are buttons for *Normal* view, *Page Layout* view, and *Page Break Preview* on the right side of the *Status* bar.

> **MORE INFO**
>
> The **Ribbon Display Options** button (on the right of the workbook title bar) can be used to hide the *Ribbon* for maximum screen space in any workbook view.

▶ HOW TO: Switch Workbook Views Using the Status Bar

1. Click the **View** tab.
 - The *Normal* button is activated in the *Workbook Views* group.
2. Click the **Page Layout** button in the *Status* bar.
 - This view displays the header, the footer, and margin areas (Figure 1-56).

1-56 *Page Layout* view

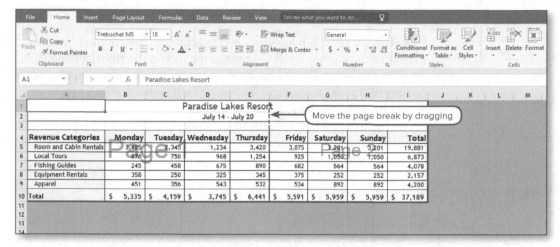

1-57 *Page Break Preview*

3. Click the **Page Break Preview** button in the *Status* bar.

 • If the data does not fit on a single page, a dashed line indicates where the second page will start (Figure 1-57).

4. Click the **Normal** button in the *Status* bar.

Zoom Options

You can change a sheet's magnification to see more of the data at once (zoom out) or to scrutinize content more carefully (zoom in). There is a *Zoom* group on the *View* tab as well as *Zoom* controls in the *Status* bar.

The *Status* bar controls include a **Zoom In** button, a **Zoom Out** button, and the **Zoom** slider. The slider is the vertical bar in the middle of the horizontal line which you can drag to change the magnification level.

▶HOW TO: Change Zoom Levels

1. Click the **Zoom In** button in the *Status* bar.

 • The magnification is increased in 10% increments with each click.

2. Click the **Zoom Out** button in the *Status* bar.

 • The magnification is decreased in 10% increments with each click.

3. Drag the **Zoom** slider in the middle of the horizontal line to the left or right to set a value (Figure 1-58).

 • The magnification percentage is displayed to the right of the line.

4. Click the **Zoom** button [*View* tab, *Zoom* group].

 • The *Zoom* dialog box includes preset values.

5. Click a radio button to choose a *Magnification* level.

 • Select **Fit selection** for a selected range to fill the screen.
 • Choose **Custom** to enter any magnification value.

6. Click **OK**.

1-58 *Zoom* slider

> **ANOTHER WAY**
>
> The *Zoom* group [*View* tab] has *100%* and *Zoom to Selection* buttons.

Freeze Panes

In a worksheet with many rows and columns of information, it is not possible to see all the data at once. As you scroll to see information on the right, related labels or values on the left scroll out of view. The **Freeze Panes** command locks rows or columns in view so that you can position data for easy review. The worksheet is divided into two or four panes (sections) with a thin, black border to indicate the divisions.

The active cell becomes the top left corner of the moving pane. For example, if you select cell B5 and select the *Freeze Panes* command, column A and rows 1:4 are stationary.

▶ HOW TO: Freeze and Unfreeze Panes

1. Select a cell in the worksheet.
 - Click a cell one row below the last row to be frozen.
 - Click a cell one column to the right of the last column to be locked.
2. Click the **Freeze Panes** button [*View* tab, *Window* group].
 - Select **Freeze Top Row** to lock row 1 in view, regardless of the active cell.
 - Choose **Freeze First Column** to keep the first column in view, regardless of the active cell.
3. Select **Freeze Panes**.
 - All rows above and all columns to the left of the active cell are locked in position.
 - A thin, black border identifies frozen rows and columns.
4. Scroll the data in any direction (Figure 1-59).
5. Click the **Freeze Panes** button [*View* tab, *Window* group].
6. Select **Unfreeze Panes**.
 - The black border is removed.

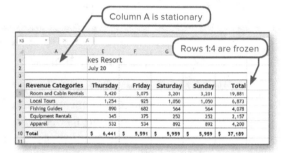

1-59 *Freeze Panes* results when cell B5 is selected and columns B:D are scrolled left

Split a Worksheet into Panes

The **Split** command divides a worksheet into two or four display panes. Each pane shows the same sheet, but you can arrange each pane to show different or the same rows and columns. There is only one active cell, and you may not see it in all the panes. Because it is one worksheet, an edit can be made in any pane.

The panes are split based on the position of the active cell when you give the command. A *splitter bar* is a light gray bar that spans the window, either horizontally, vertically, or both. You can drag a splitter bar to resize the panes.

▶ HOW TO: Split a Worksheet

1. Select the cell for the location of a split.
 - Click a cell in column A (except cell A1) to split the worksheet into two horizontal panes.
 - Click a cell in row 1 (but not cell A1) to split the worksheet into two vertical panes.
 - Click a cell to split the worksheet into four panes.
2. Click the **Split** button [*View* tab, *Window* group].

452

3. Drag a splitter bar to resize a pane (Figure 1-60).

4. Click the **Split** button [*View* tab, *Window* group] to remove the split.

1-60 Split worksheet

> **ANOTHER WAY**
>
> You can remove a window split by double-clicking the splitter bar.

Hide or Unhide Worksheets

A **hidden worksheet** is a worksheet whose tab is not displayed. It is part of the workbook and can be referenced in calculations. A worksheet might be hidden to prevent accidental changes to it, or it might hold data that should not be easily visible. You can hide a worksheet using the **Format** button [*Home* tab] or by right-clicking the sheet tab. You cannot hide a worksheet if it is the only sheet in the workbook.

> **MORE INFO**
>
> The command to print an *Entire Workbook* does not print a hidden worksheet.

▶ HOW TO: Hide and Unhide Worksheets

1. Right-click the sheet tab to hide.
 - Press **Ctrl** to select multiple sheets, then right-click any one of the selected tabs.
2. Select **Hide**.
 - The worksheet tab is hidden.
3. Right-click any worksheet tab.
4. Select **Unhide**.
 - The *Unhide sheet* dialog box opens.
5. Select the tab name to unhide (Figure 1-61).
6. Click **OK**.

1-61 *Unhide sheet* dialog box

> **MORE INFO**
>
> The *Hide* command on the *View* tab hides a workbook. A hidden workbook can be used to store programming routines such as macros or external reference data that should be protected from viewing or accidental editing.

Switch Windows Command

When more than one workbook is open, the *Switch Windows* command changes or cycles through open workbooks. You can switch windows from the *Ribbon*, from the Windows taskbar, or with the keyboard shortcut **Ctrl+F6**. When you click the **Switch Windows** button [*View* tab, *Window* group], a menu lists the names of open workbooks so that you can select one. To use the Windows taskbar, point to the Excel icon to see a thumbnail with the file name of each open workbook and click the one to be edited. The keyboard shortcut toggles between the last two viewed workbooks.

When only two workbooks are open, you can view them side by side. The *View Side by Side* button is grayed out when only one workbook is open. For side-by-side viewing, you can scroll the windows together or separately. *Synchronous Scrolling* moves both workbooks in the same direction at the same time. This is especially helpful when worksheets have the same types of data in the same locations. Synchronous scrolling is automatically enabled when you choose the *View Side by Side* command.

> **▶ HOW TO: Switch Windows Using the Ribbon**
>
> 1. Open two or more workbooks.
> 2. Click the **Switch Windows** button [*View* tab, *Window* group].
> - The names of open workbooks are listed.
> 3. Click the name of the workbook to view.

> **▶ MORE INFO**
>
> If three or more workbooks are open when you select the *View Side by Side* command, the *Compare Side by Side* dialog box opens with the names of open workbooks. The one you select is displayed side by side with the active workbook.

View Multiple Worksheets

The *New Window* command opens a new separate window with the same workbook. The new window displays the workbook name in the title bar followed by a colon and number. Combined with the *Arrange All* command, you can position different parts of the workbook to make comparisons or monitor changes as you work. Figure 1-62 shows different sheets in the same workbook.

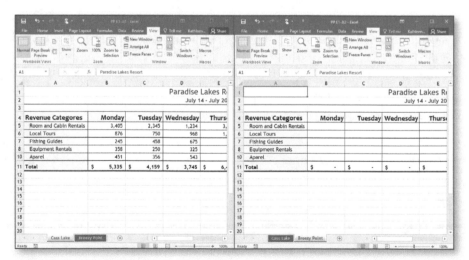

1-62 Two windows for a workbook

> **▶ MORE INFO**
>
> You can open as many windows as needed and arrange them all.

▶ HOW TO: View Multiple Worksheets at the Same Time

1. Click the **View** tab and click the **New Window** button [*Window* group].
 - A second window opens for the same workbook and is active.
 - Both windows are maximized.
2. Click the **Arrange All** button [*View* tab, *Window* group].
 - The *Arrange Windows* dialog box opens.
3. Choose an option for arranging the windows.
 - The active window is arranged on the left (vertically tiled) or at the top (horizontally tiled).
 - If several workbooks are open but only the active workbook has multiple windows, choose **Windows of active workbook** so that only those windows are arranged.
4. Click **OK**.
 - The active window is arranged on the left or at the top.
5. Click the **Maximize** button in either title bar.
 - The window is full size.
6. Click the **Close** button (**X**) in the title bar to close the window.
 - The other window is displayed at its tiled size.
7. Click the **Maximize** button.

SLO 1.8

Finalizing a Workbook

Before you distribute your work to others, make sure that it is ready for sharing. A quick spell check can help locate and correct misspelled labels. You can enter document properties or insert headers and footers to help identify your work. You can control how your worksheet prints by setting margins, changing the orientation, or adjusting page breaks.

Check Spelling

The *Spelling* command scans a worksheet and locates words that do not match entries in the main Office dictionary; it also finds duplicate words. The dictionary is shared among all Office applications, and you can add labels to it, such as unusual or technical words. You can spell check the entire worksheet or a selected range.

The *Spelling* dialog box includes options for handling an error as shown in the following table:

Spelling Dialog Box Options

Option	Action
Ignore Once	Skips the occurrence of the label
Ignore All	Skips all occurrences of the same spelling of the label
Add to Dictionary	Adds the label to the default dictionary
Change	Changes the label to the highlighted entry in the *Suggestions* box
Change All	Same as *Change*, but changes the same label throughout the worksheet
Delete	Appears for *Repeated Word*. Click to delete one occurrence of the label.
AutoCorrect	Adds the label to the *AutoCorrect* list
Options	Opens the *Excel Options* dialog box to the *Proofing* tab for changing default settings
Undo Last	Reverses the most recent correction
Cancel	Discontinues spell checking

▶ HOW TO: Spell Check a Worksheet

1. Press **Ctrl+Home** to move to cell **A1**.
 - Start at the beginning of the worksheet.
 - Select a range to limit spell checking to that group of cells.
2. Click the **Review** tab and click the **Spelling** button [*Proofing* group].
 - The first error is located.
 - A list of suggested corrections is displayed.
3. Select the correct spelling in the list.
 - If there is no acceptable suggestion, click the **Not in Dictionary** box and type the correct spelling of the label.
4. Click **Change** to replace the misspelled label (Figure 1-63).
5. Click **Close** when spelling is complete.

1-63 *Spelling* dialog box

Document Properties

A ***document property*** or ***metadata*** is a field of information. Metadata are settings and content including the author name, the date the file was created, the type and size of file, and more. Some properties are uneditable such as dates and file size; these settings are automatically updated. You can edit other document properties, including *Title*, *Author*, and *Subject*. A partial list of properties is available in the *Backstage* view on the right in the *Info* pane.

▶ HOW TO: Add Document Properties in Backstage View

1. Click the **File** tab to display the *Backstage* view.
2. Select **Info** if it is not already selected.
 - Property field names are listed.
 - An editable property has an entry box.
3. Click an entry box to enter or edit an item (Figure 1-64).
4. Return to the workbook and save the file.

1-64 Workbook properties

The Properties Dialog Box

You can review all properties in the *Properties* dialog box. The *General*, *Statistics*, and *Contents* tabs list uneditable metadata. The *Summary* tab has properties such as the title, subject, and keywords. Keywords are used in file search commands. On the *Custom* tab, you can choose an additional property and type a default value.

> ▶ **HOW TO:** Open the Properties Dialog Box

1. Display the *Backstage* view and click **Info**.
2. Click the **Properties** button.
3. Select **Advanced Properties**.
 - The *Properties* dialog box opens (Figure 1-65).
4. Click a tab to view or edit a property.
5. Click **OK** to close the dialog box.

1-65 *Properties* dialog box

The Page Setup Dialog Box

The *Page Setup* dialog box offers several command groups for controlling how a worksheet prints. The commands are from the *Sheet Options*, *Scale to Fit*, and *Page Setup* groups on the *Page Layout* tab as well as commands for setting headers and footers. The **Page Setup** launcher [*Page Layout* tab, *Page Setup* group] opens the dialog box.

> ▶ **ANOTHER WAY**
>
> Open the *Page Setup* dialog box by clicking the launcher in the *Scale to Fit* or the *Sheet Options* group on the *Page Layout* tab.

Each tab in the *Page Setup* dialog box has a *Print*, a *Print Preview*, and an *Options* button (Figure 1-66). The *Options* button opens the *Printer Properties* dialog box. The following table summarizes commands on each tab in the *Page Setup* dialog box:

1-66 *Page* tab in the *Page Setup* dialog box

Page Setup Dialog Box Options

Tab	Available Settings
Page	Set the *Orientation* to *Portrait* or *Landscape*. Use *Scaling* to shrink or enlarge the printed worksheet to the paper size. Choose a *Paper size* or set *Print quality*. Define the *First page number*.
Margins	Adjust *Top*, *Bottom*, *Left*, and *Right* worksheet margins. Set *Header* and *Footer* top and bottom margins. *Center on page* horizontally and/or vertically.
Header/Footer	Choose a preset header or footer layout. Create a custom header or footer. Specify first and other page headers. Set header and footers to scale with worksheet and to align with margins.
Sheet	Identify a *Print area* other than the entire worksheet. Identify *Print titles* to repeat on each page. Print *Gridlines*, *Row and column headings*, *Comments*, and *Error messages*.

> **MORE INFO**
>
> You can make changes to multiple worksheets at the same time from the *Page Setup* dialog box. Select the tabs first to group the worksheets.

> **ANOTHER WAY**
>
> Open the *Page Setup* dialog box by clicking the *Page Setup* link in the *Print* area on the *Backstage* view.

Margins, Page Orientation, and Paper Size

A new Excel workbook uses the following default settings:

- Top and bottom margins: 0.75"
- Left and right margins: 0.7"
- Header and footer margins: 0.3"
- Portrait orientation
- Letter size paper

The *Margins* button [*Page Layout* tab, *Page Setup* group] lists *Normal*, *Wide*, and *Narrow* for margin settings as well as *Custom Margins*. When you select **Custom Margins**, the *Page Setup* dialog box opens to the *Margins* tab. Here you can set any value for any margin area, including the header and the footer. You can also center the page horizontally or vertically from this tab.

The *Orientation* button [*Page Setup* group, *Page Layout* tab] has two choices, *Portrait* or *Landscape*. A portrait page is taller than it is wide. A landscape page is wider than it is tall. The *Size* button lists paper sizes, but your printer must be able to accommodate the size.

You can modify settings for one worksheet or for several worksheets at a time. To format multiple worksheets, you need to group the worksheet tabs. Do this by clicking the first tab name, holding down **Shift**, and clicking the last tab name to select all sheets between those two names. You can also click the first tab name, press **Ctrl**, and click nonadjacent sheet names to create a group.

> **HOW TO:** Set Margins, Page Orientation, and Paper Size

1. Click the **Margins** button [*Page Layout* tab, *Page Setup* group].
2. Select **Custom Margins** to open the *Page Setup* dialog box (Figure 1-67).
 - The dialog box opens to the *Margins* tab.
3. Type each margin setting as desired.
 - You can use the spinner buttons to change the margin value.
4. Select the **Horizontally** box in the *Center on page* area.
 - This command centers the data between the left and right margins.
 - You can also vertically center the data on the page.
5. Click the **Page** tab in the *Page Layout* dialog box.
6. Select the radio button for **Portrait** or **Landscape**.
7. Click the **Paper size** arrow and select a paper size.
 - The default paper size is 8½ × 11", which is called *Letter*.
8. Click **OK** to close the dialog box.

1-67 *Margins* tab in the *Page Setup* dialog box

> **MORE INFO**
>
> Top and bottom margins must be greater than header and footer margins. If they are not, worksheet data prints over header and footer text.

> **ANOTHER WAY**
>
> In *Page Layout* view, you can set margins using the ruler. Display the rulers by clicking the *View* tab and selecting the *Ruler* box [*Show* group]. Point to a margin boundary to display a two-pointed arrow and drag the pointer to a new setting.

Headers and Footers

A **header** is information that prints at the top of each page. A **footer** is data that prints at the bottom of each page. You can use a header or a footer to display identifying information such as a company name or logo, page numbers, the date, or the file name.

Each header or footer has left, middle, and right sections. Information in the left section is left aligned, data in the middle section is centered, and material in the right section is right aligned. You can select a predefined header and footer, or you can create your own.

> **MORE INFO**
>
> Predefined headers and footers include one, two, or three elements, separated by commas. One element prints in the center section. Two elements print in the center and right sections. Three elements use all three sections.

Headers and footers are not visible in *Normal* view, but you can see them in *Page Layout* view or *Print Preview*. Headers and footers are inserted and edited in *Page Layout* view at the top or bottom of the worksheet.

▶**HOW TO:** Insert a Header and Footer Using the Ribbon

1. Select the worksheet.
 - You can select more than one worksheet to apply the same header or footer.
2. Click the **Insert** tab.
3. Click the **Header & Footer** button [*Text* group].
 - The view changes to *Page Layout* view.
 - Three header sections are visible at the top of the worksheet.
 - The *Header & Footer Tools Design* tab is active.
4. Click a header section.
5. Click an element name in the *Header & Footer Elements* group [*Header & Footer Tools Design* tab].
 - A code is inserted with an ampersand (&) and the element name enclosed in square brackets (Figure 1-68).
 - You can type your own label in a section.
 - You can select and delete codes and text in a section.

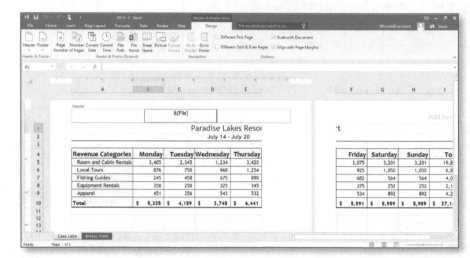

1-68 Header section in *Page Layout* view

6. Click the **Go To Footer** button [*Header & Footer Tools Design* tab, *Navigation* group].
7. Click a footer section.
8. Click an element name in the *Header & Footer Elements* group [*Header & Footer Tools Design* tab].
 - The related code is inserted.
 - You can type your own label in a footer section.
 - You can select and delete codes and text in a section.
9. Click any worksheet cell.
 - The header and footer appear as they will print.
 - The *Header & Footer Tools Design* tab is hidden.
10. Click the **Normal** button in the *Status* bar.
 - The header and footer are not visible in *Normal* view.

▶ ANOTHER WAY

To insert a built-in header or footer, click the **Header or Footer** button [*Header & Footer Tools Design* tab, *Header & Footer* group] and make a selection.

▶ MORE INFO

In a typed header or footer label such as "Research & Development," type two ampersands in the section like this: *Research && Development*. This distinguishes the required ampersand from the one used in an element code such as &[Date].

You can also use the *Page Setup* dialog box to insert a header or a footer. There is a *Header & Footer* tab which includes the preset headers and footers as well as a *Custom Header* or *Custom Footer* option.

▶ HOW TO: Insert Headers or Footers on Multiple Sheets

1. Select a single or multiple worksheet tabs.
 - Click the first worksheet tab for the group, press **Shift**, and click the last tab.
 - Click a worksheet tab, press **Ctrl**, and click a nonadjacent tab.
 - Right-click any tab and click **Select All Sheets**.
2. Click the **Page Setup** launcher [*Page Layout* tab, *Page Setup* group.
 - The *Page Setup* dialog box opens.
3. Click the **Header/Footer** tab.
4. Click the arrow for the *Header* or the *Footer* text box (Figure 1-69).
 - A list of built-in header or footer layouts opens.
 - Choose **(none)** to remove a header or footer.
5. Choose a predefined header or footer.
 - The header or footer is displayed in the preview area.
6. Click **Custom Header** or **Custom Footer** to open the *Header* or *Footer* dialog box (Figure 1-70).
7. Click a section.
8. Click a button to insert an element.
 - Point to a button to see its *ScreenTip*.
 - The text or code appears in the section.
9. Click **OK** to close the *Header* or *Footer* dialog box.
 - The custom header or footer is displayed in the preview area.
10. Click **OK** to close the *Page Setup* dialog box.
11. Right-click a sheet tab and choose **Ungroup Sheets**.

1-69 Select a built-in header or footer in the *Page Setup* dialog box

1-70 *Footer* dialog box

You can remove a header or footer in *Page Layout* view or from the *Page Setup* dialog box. To remove headers and footers from multiple worksheets, select the sheet tabs so that they are grouped. In *Page Layout* view, click the header or footer section and delete labels and codes. From the *Page Setup* dialog box, you can simply select **(none)** from the *Header* or *Footer* drop-down list.

▶ HOW TO: Remove Headers and Footers

1. Select the worksheet(s).
2. Click the **Page Setup** launcher [*Page Layout* tab, *Page Setup* group].
3. Click the **Header/Footer** tab.
4. Click the **Header** or **Footer** drop-down list and select **(none)**.
5. Click **OK** to close the *Page Setup* dialog box.
6. Ungroup sheets if needed.

Page Breaks

A *page break* is a printer code that starts a new page. When worksheet data spans more than one printed page, automatic page breaks are inserted based on the paper size, the margins, and scaling. Automatic page breaks readjust as you add or delete data. You can insert manual page breaks, too. Manual page breaks do not adjust as you make edits.

In *Page Break Preview*, an automatic page break displays as a dotted or dashed blue line. A manual page break appears as a solid, blue line.

▶ HOW TO: Insert a Page Break

1. Select the cell for the location of a page break.
 - Select a cell in column A below the row where you want to start a new page.
 - Select a cell in row 1 to the right of the column where you want to start a new page.
 - Select a cell below and to the right of where new pages should start.
2. Click the **Page Layout** tab.
3. Click the **Breaks** button.
4. Select **Insert Page Break** (Figure 1-71).
 - A manual page break is shown as a thin, solid line in the worksheet in *Normal* view.

1-71 Page break inserted after column D

Preview and Move a Page Break

In *Page Break Preview*, you can move an automatic or a manual page break by dragging its blue line. You can see how the data is affected and evaluate the new printed pages. Depending on the amount of data, as you move one page break, another automatic break may be inserted. When you move an automatic page break, it becomes a manual page break.

> ▶ MORE INFO
>
> To move a page break in *Normal* view, you must delete the existing break and insert a new one; you cannot drag the line.

▶ HOW TO: Preview and Move a Page Break

1. Click the **Page Break Preview** button in the *Status* bar.
 - You can adjust the zoom size in *Page Break Preview*.
2. Point to the page break (dashed or solid, blue line) to display a two-pointed arrow.
3. Drag the pointer to a new location (Figure 1-72).
 - You cannot drag an automatic page break to the right of its current location.

4. Release the pointer button.
 - A manual page break appears as a solid, blue line.
 - Another automatic page break may be inserted if the data requires it.
5. Click the **Normal** button in the *Status* bar.

1-72 Drag a page break line to a new position

Remove a Manual Page Break

You can remove a manual page break in *Normal* view or *Page Break Preview*. Click a cell immediately to the right of or below the break and then click the **Remove Page Break** button [*Page Layout* tab, *Page Setup* group]. When you delete a manual page break, Excel may insert a new automatic page break.

> **MORE INFO**
>
> An automatic page break can be "deleted" by inserting a manual page break before it.

▶HOW TO: Remove a Manual Page Break

1. Click the **Page Break Preview** button in the *Status* bar.
2. Click a cell immediately to the right of or below the page break to be removed.
3. Click the **Breaks** button [*Page Layout* tab, *Page Setup* group].
 - You can select **Reset All Page Breaks** to remove all manual page breaks.
4. Click **Remove Page Break** (Figure 1-73).
 - An automatic page break is inserted if required.

1-73 Remove a manual page break

> **ANOTHER WAY**
>
> In *Page Break Preview*, you can drag a manual page break off the page to the right. Excel will insert an automatic page break if required by the margins and other settings.

Customize Print Settings

You can print the entire workbook, the current worksheet, or a selected cell range by making a choice in the *Settings* area in the *Backstage view* for the *Print* command. The *Sheet Options* and *Page Setup* groups on the *Page Layout* command tab include additional options for repeating titles, displaying a background image, and printing gridlines, column letters, and row numbers.

Gridlines, the vertical and horizontal lines that form the columns and rows, are a visual guide to your working on the sheet. Row and column headings serve a similar purpose—to

help you navigate in a worksheet. By default, the gridlines and headings do not print but you can print them from an option on the *Page Layout* tab.

A ***print title*** is a row or column of data that is repeated on each printed page. For example, you can print main labels from rows 1:3 and from column A on each printed page of a 20-page worksheet.

▶ HOW TO: Print Gridlines, Print Titles, and Column and Row Headings

1. Click the **Page Layout** tab.
2. Select the **Print** box under *Gridlines* in the *Sheet Options* group.
3. Select the **Print** box under *Headings* in the *Sheet Options* group.
4. Click the **Print Titles** button *[Page Layout tab, Page Setup group]*.
 - The *Page Setup* dialog box opens to the *Sheet* tab.
5. Select the **Rows to repeat at top** box.
6. Drag to select the heading(s) for the row(s) to print on each page.
 - The dialog box collapses as you select row headings.
 - The dialog box expands when you release the pointer button.
 - You can type a reference such as $1:$3 to repeat data in the first three rows.
7. Select the **Columns to repeat at left** box (Figure 1-74).
8. Drag to select the heading(s) for the column(s) to print on each page.
 - The dialog box collapses as you select column headings.
 - You can type a reference such as $A:$A to repeat data in column A.
9. Click **OK**.

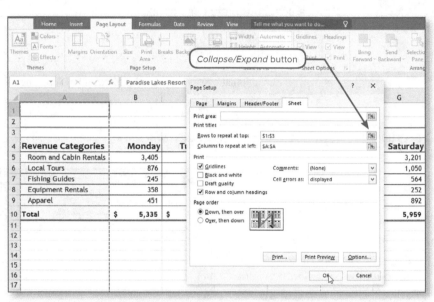

1-74 *Sheet* tab in the *Page Setup* dialog box

▶ ANOTHER WAY

You can print *Gridlines* and *Row and column headings* from an option in the *Page Setup* dialog box.

Scale to Fit

The ***Scale to Fit*** command enlarges or shrinks printed data to fit a specific number of pages or a particular paper size. You can scale printed data as a percentage of normal size or by setting the number of pages. Normal size is how the data would print in the current font size and is shown as *Automatic* in the *Scale to Fit* group *[Page Layout tab]*.

▶ HOW TO: Scale to Fit

1. Click the **Page Layout** tab.
2. Click the **Width** drop-down list *[Scale to Fit group]* and select an option.

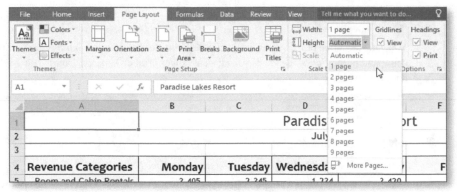

1-75 *Scale to Fit* options

3. Click the **Height** drop-down list [*Scale to Fit* group] and select an option (Figure 1-75).
 • You can click the **Scale** button spinner arrows to set a percentage of the normal size.

> **ANOTHER WAY**
>
> Click the **Scale to Fit** launcher [*Page Layout* tab, *Scale to Fit group*] to open the *Page Setup* dialog box and set options in the *Scaling* area.

Print Area

A *print area* is the data that prints when you give a *Print* command. The default is the entire worksheet, but you can identify any range of cells as a print area. You can add adjacent data to a print area, and you can clear a print area to return to the default.

HOW TO: Set and Clear a Print Area

1. Select the cells to print.
 • You can select nonadjacent ranges but they print on separate pages.
2. Click the **Page Layout** tab.
3. Click the **Print Area** button [*Page Setup* group] (Figure 1-76).
4. Select **Set Print Area**.
 • You can see the print area in the *Backstage view* for the *Print* command and in *Page Break Preview*.
 • A print area is saved with the workbook.
5. Click the **Print Area** button [*Page Layout* tab, *Page Setup* group].
6. Select **Clear Print Area**.
 • All print areas are cleared.
 • The default print area of the entire sheet is reset.

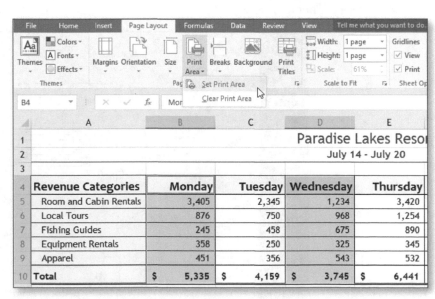

1-76 Nonadjacent print areas

Print a Worksheet or Workbook

The *Print* command in the *Backstage view* provides a preview so that you can make changes before actual printing. The *Show Margins* button toggles the display of margin and column markers which can be dragged to new settings. The *Zoom to Page* button toggles between two zoom settings for the preview.

▶HOW TO: Preview and Print a Worksheet

1. Click the **File** tab and select **Print**.
 - You can also click **Print Preview** in the *Page Setup* dialog box to open the *Print* command in the *Backstage* view.
2. Click **Show Margins** to display margin and column markers (Figure 1-77).
3. Click **Zoom to Page** to toggle between zoom sizes.
4. Set the number of *Copies*.
 - Type a number or use the spinner arrows.
5. Click the **Printer** arrow.
 - Choose the printer name.
 - Make sure the printer is ready.

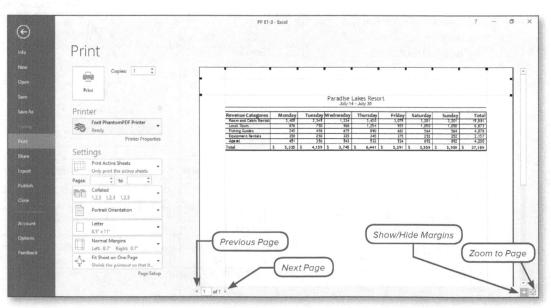

1-77 *Backstage* view for *Print*

6. Click the **Settings** arrow.
 - The active sheets are the default.
 - Cell ranges must be selected in order to print a selection.
 - The workbook setting prints all worksheets.
7. Specify which pages to print.
 - The default is all pages of the worksheet.
 - Click the **Next Page** or **Previous Page** arrow to navigate through multiple pages.
8. Verify orientation, paper size, margin settings, and scaling.
 - You can make changes from the *Page Setup* dialog box by clicking the **Page Setup** link at the bottom of the *Settings* area.
9. Click **Print**.
 - The data is sent to the printer.
 - The *Backstage view* closes.

> **ANOTHER WAY**
> Press **Ctrl+P** to open the *Print* command in the *Backstage view*.

PAUSE & PRACTICE: EXCEL 1-4

In this project, you open *[your initials] PP E1-3.xlsx* to unhide a row, add data, and hide a sheet. You also spell check a worksheet, set document properties, and finalize the workbook for distribution.

File Needed: *[your initials] PP E1-3.xlsx*
Completed Project File Name: *[your initials] PP E1-4.xlsx*

1. Open *[your initials] PP E1-3* completed in *Pause & Practice 1-3*.
2. Save the workbook as [your initials] PP E1-4.
3. Select the **Cass Lake** worksheet.
4. Unhide row 9.
 a. Click and drag to select row headings **8:10**.
 b. Right-click either of the selected row headings.
 c. Choose **Unhide** from the context menu.
5. Enter the following data in cells **B9:H9**. The data is formatted the same as row 8.

	B	C	D	E	F	G	H
Food & Beverage	254	209	198	402	519	677	399

6. Hide a worksheet.
 a. Right-click the **Breezy Point** tab.
 b. Choose **Hide**.

7. Check spelling.
 a. Press **Ctrl+Home**.
 b. Click the **Spelling** button [*Review* tab, *Proofing* group].
 c. Click **Change** to accept the suggested correction for "Categores."
 d. Click **Change** to accept the suggested correction for "Aparel."
 e. Click **OK** when spell checking is finished.
 f. Press **Ctrl+Home**.

8. Enter document properties.
 a. Click the **File** tab to display the *Backstage* view.
 b. Click the **Show All Properties** link at the bottom of the properties list.
 c. Click the *Title* text box and type PP Excel 1-4.
 d. Click the *Subject* text box and type Weekly Revenue.
 e. In the *Status* text box, type Draft (Figure 1-78).

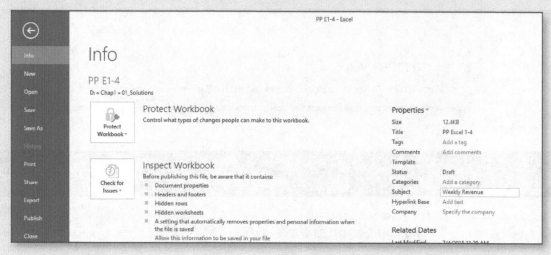

1-78 Properties in *Backstage* view

 f. Click the **Show Fewer Properties** link at the bottom of the properties list.
 g. Return to the worksheet.

9. Change page setup options.
 a. Click the **Page Layout** tab.
 b. Click the **Orientation** button and select **Landscape**.
 c. Click the **Page Setup** launcher to open the *Page Setup* dialog box.
 d. On the **Page** tab, click the **Fit to** button.
 e. Set **1** page wide and **1** page tall.
 f. Click the **Margins** tab.
 g. Select the **Horizontally** box in the *Center on page* area.
 h. Do not close the dialog box.

10. Add a header and footer.
 a. Click the **Header/Footer** tab.
 b. Click the **Header** drop-down list and select *[your initials] PP E1-4*. The file name displays in the preview center section.
 c. Click the **Footer** drop-down list and select **Cass Lake** to insert the sheet name in the center section of the footer.
 d. Click **OK** to close the *Page Setup* dialog box.

11. Preview and print the worksheet.
 a. Click the **File** tab and select **Print**. *Print Preview* displays how the worksheet will print.
 b. Select the printer.
 c. Click **Print** to print the worksheet.

12. Save and close the workbook (Figure 1-79).

PP E1-4

Paradise Lakes Resort
July 14 - July 20

Revenue Categories	Monday	Tuesday	Wednesday	Thursday	Friday	Saturday	Sunday	Total
Room and Cabin Rental	3,405	2,345	1,234	3,420	3,075	3,201	3,201	19,881
Local Tours	876	750	968	1,254	925	1,050	1,050	6,873
Fishing Guides	245	458	675	890	682	564	564	4,078
Equipment Rentals	388	250	325	346	375	282	282	2,157
Food & Beverage	254	209	198	402	519	677	399	2,658
Apparel	451	356	543	532	534	892	892	4,200
Total	$ 5,589	$ 4,368	$ 3,943	$ 6,843	$ 6,110	$ 6,636	$ 6,358	$ 39,847

Cass Lake

1-79 PP E1-4 completed

Chapter Summary

1.1 Create, save, and open an Excel workbook (p. 411).

- A new Excel workbook has one worksheet and is named *BookN*, with numbers assigned in order throughout a work session.
- Save a workbook with a descriptive name that identifies the contents and purpose.
- Create a new workbook from the *Excel Start* page or from the *New* command on the *File* tab.
- A workbook that is opened or copied from an online source will open in **Protected View**.
- An Excel workbook is an *.xlsx* file, but it can be saved in other formats for easy sharing of data.

1.2 Enter and edit labels and values in a worksheet (p. 414).

- Data is entered in a cell which is the intersection of a column and a row. Each cell has an address or reference.
- Data is recognized as a label or a value. Labels are not used in calculations. A label is left-aligned in the cell; a value is right-aligned.
- A **formula** is a calculation that displays a value as its result in the worksheet.
- Press **F2** (**FN+F2**) or double-click a cell to start *Edit* mode. After making the change, press **Enter** to complete the edit.
- Horizontal alignment options for cell data include *Align Left*, *Center*, and *Align Right*. Data can also be indented from the cell border. Vertical alignment choices are *Top Align*, *Middle Align*, and *Bottom Align*.
- A group or selection of cells is a **range**. You can use the pointer and keyboard shortcuts to select a range.
- Use the **Fill Handle** to create a series that follows a pattern. The *Fill Handle* copies data when there is no pattern.
- **AutoComplete** supplies a suggestion for a column entry that begins with the same character as a label already in the column.
- Cut, copy, and paste commands include drag and drop as well as regular Windows **Cut**, **Copy**, and **Paste** buttons on the *Home* tab, context menus, and keyboard shortcuts.

1.3 Use the *SUM* function to build a simple formula (p. 427).

- A **function** is a built-in formula. Results appear in the worksheet cell, but the function is displayed in the *Formula* bar.
- The *AutoSum* button [*Home* tab, *Editing* group] inserts the *SUM* function in a cell to add the values in a selected range.
- Each function has **syntax** which is its required parts in the required order. A function begins with an equals sign (=), followed by the name of the function. After the name, the function **argument** is shown in parentheses.
- You can change a function argument by entering new cell references in the *Formula* bar or by dragging the range border in the worksheet.
- When you copy a function, Excel adjusts cell references to match their locations in the worksheet.

1.4 Format a worksheet with font attributes, borders, fill, cell styles, and themes (p. 429).

- Apply font attributes from the *Font* group on the *Ribbon* or from the *Format Cells* dialog box.
- Font attributes include the **font** name or face, the **font size**, font styles such as bold, italic, and underline, and the **font color**.
- Number formats include decimals, commas, currency symbols, and percent signs. They also determine how negative values appear in the worksheet.
- Number formats are applied from the *Ribbon* or the *Format Cells* dialog box.
- The **Format Painter** copies formatting from one cell to another.
- Add borders or fill color to cells for easy identification, clarification, and emphasis.
- A **cell style** is a preset collection of font, font size, alignment, color, borders, and fill color and is based on the theme.
- A **theme** is a collection of fonts, colors, and special effects for a workbook.
- You can use themes and cell styles to quickly format a worksheet with consistent, professionally designed elements.

1.5 Modify columns and rows in a worksheet (p. 439).

- The default column width and row height depend on the font size defined by the workbook theme.
- You can change the width of a column or the height of a row by dragging the border between the headings.
- *AutoFit* a column or row by double-clicking the border between the headings.
- The *Format* button [*Home* tab, *Cells* group] includes commands to change *row height* and *column width*.
- Insert or delete a column or a row by right-clicking the column or row heading and choosing *Insert* or *Delete*.
- The *Insert* and *Delete* buttons include commands for inserting and deleting rows and columns.
- Display a label on multiple lines in a cell using the *Wrap Text* command to split the label.
- The *Merge & Center* command combines two or more cells into one and centers the data within that new cell.
- The *Center Across Selection* command can be used to center multiple rows of data across the same range.
- One or multiple rows or columns can be hidden, but they are still available for use in a formula.

1.6 Insert, delete, and move worksheets in a workbook (p. 445).

- The number of worksheets in a workbook is limited only by the amount of computer memory.
- You can click the *New Sheet* button next to the worksheet tabs to insert a new sheet in a workbook.
- The *Insert* and *Delete* buttons include options to insert and delete worksheets.
- You can double-click a worksheet tab, type a name, and press **Enter** to rename a sheet.
- You can apply a *tab color* to distinguish a particular sheet by changing the background color.

- Move a worksheet tab to another location in the list of tabs by dragging it to that location.
- You can create an exact duplicate of a worksheet in the same or another workbook with the *Move or Copy* command or the context menu.

1.7 Modify the appearance of a workbook by adjusting zoom size, changing views, and freezing panes (p. 450).

- A workbook can be viewed in three ways: *Normal*, *Page Layout*, and *Page Break Preview*.
- Switch views from the *Status* bar buttons or from the *Workbook Views* group on the *View* tab.
- Adjust the zoom size to display more or less data on screen. Zoom controls are available in the *Status* bar and from the *View* tab.
- Use the *Freeze Panes* command to lock selected rows or columns on screen so that you can scroll data while keeping important data in view.
- The *Split* command divides the screen into multiple sections so that you can see different areas of a large worksheet at once.
- You can hide a worksheet from view and unintended editing.
- When multiple workbooks are open, the *Switch Windows* command lists the open workbook names.
- You can switch among open workbooks from the Windows taskbar.
- The *New Window* command displays the same workbook in a second window. Use this command with the *Arrange All* command to view different areas or sheets of a workbook at the same time.

1.8 Review and prepare a workbook for final distribution by spell checking, setting properties, and adjusting page setup options (p. 455).

- Spell checking a workbook follows the same steps as other Office applications.
- A *document property* is *metadata* stored with the file.

- Some properties are supplied by Excel and cannot be edited. Other document properties are added or edited by the user.
- Several properties are visible and can be edited in the *Info* area in the *Backstage* view.
- You can open the *Properties* dialog box to build or edit properties.
- The *Page Layout* tab includes commands to set page margins and orientation.
- **Headers** and **footers** can be added to print at the top and bottom of each page.
- When a worksheet fills more than one printed page, Excel inserts automatic page breaks.
- You can insert manual **page breaks** to change where a new page starts.
- From commands on the *Page Layout* tab or in the *Page Setup* dialog box, you can print **gridlines** as well as row and column headings.

- You can make additional changes to the printed worksheet from the **Print** area in the *Backstage* view. These include choosing to print only a selection or the entire workbook.

Check for Understanding

The SIMbook for this text (within your SIMnet account) provides the following resources for concept review:

- Multiple choice questions
- Matching exercises
- Short answer questions

Guided Project 1-1

Life's Animal Shelter (LAS) maintains data in an Excel workbook that tracks daily expenses for categories that include supplies, animal food, and wages. You will create a new workbook for the current week, enter and format the data, and prepare the workbook for distribution.
[Student Learning Outcomes 1.1, 1.2, 1.3, 1.4, 1.5, 1.6, 1.7, 1.8]

File Needed: None
Completed Project File Name: *[your initials] Excel 1-1.xlsx*

Skills Covered in This Project

- Create and save a workbook.
- Enter labels and values.
- Use the *Fill Handle*.
- Set column widths and row heights.
- Merge and center labels.
- Apply a workbook theme and cell styles.

- Apply font attributes and insert borders.
- Use *SUM* and set number formatting.
- Copy and rename worksheets.
- Set worksheet tab color.
- Change page setup options.
- Use spell check.
- Adjust zoom size and freeze panes.

1. Create and save a workbook.
 a. Click the **File** tab to open the *Backstage* view.
 b. Select **New** and then click **Blank workbook**.
 c. Click the **Save** button on the *Quick Access* toolbar to open the *Save As* dialog box.
 d. Select the folder to save the workbook, or **Browse** to a location on *OneDrive*, your computer, or external media.
 e. Name the workbook [your initials] Excel 1-1 in the *File name* area.
 f. Click **Save**.

2. Enter data with deliberate errors.
 a. In cell **A1**, type Life's Aminal Shelter with the spelling error and press **Enter**.
 b. In cell **A2**, type Setember 1 through 7 with the spelling error and press **Enter**.
 c. In cell **A4**, type Expens Categories and press **Enter**.

3. Adjust column width.
 a. Point to the border between the column **A** and column **B** headings to display a two-pointed arrow.
 b. Double-click to *AutoFit* column **A**.

4. Enter labels and values as shown in Figure 1-80.

	A	B	C	D	E	F	G	H
1	Life's Aminal Shelter							
2	Setember 1 through 7							
3								
4	Expens Categories	Monday						
5	Pet nutrition	55.25	47.5	38.55	27.45	42.5	35.25	51.75
6	Veterinary supplies	27.85	32.35	35	25	28.5	38.75	44.85
7	Shelter supplies	78	56.45	65.35	55	70	60.25	45.35
8	Salaries and wages	475						
9	Utilities (prorated)	45						
10								

1-80 Labels and values to be entered with errors in cells A1:A2 and A4

5. Use the *Fill Handle* to fill a series and copy data.
 a. Select cell **B4**.
 b. Click and drag the *Fill* pointer to cell **H4**.
 c. Select cells **B8:B9**. There is one *Fill Handle* shown in cell B9.
 d. Click and drag the *Fill* pointer to cell **H9**. When there is no discernible pattern, the *Fill Handle* copies data.
 e. Point to the border between the column **D** and column **E** headings to display a two-pointed arrow.
 f. Double-click to *AutoFit* column **D**.

6. Merge and center labels.
 a. Select cells **A1:H1** and click the **Merge & Center** button [*Home* tab, *Alignment* group].
 b. Select cells **A2:H2** and click the **Merge & Center** button [*Home* tab, *Alignment* group].
 c. Select cells **B4:H4**.
 d. Click the **Center** button [*Home* tab, *Alignment* group].

7. Choose a workbook theme.
 a. Click the **Themes** button [*Page Layout* tab, *Themes* group].
 b. Choose **Integral** from the gallery.
 c. Click the **Home** tab. All labels and values are set in the **Tw Cen MT** font.

8. Apply cell styles.
 a. Select cell **A1** and click the **Cells Styles** button or the **More** button [*Home* tab, *Styles* group].
 b. Select **Title** in the *Titles and Headings* category. For the *Integral* theme, a title is format in the *Tw Cen MT Condensed* font, 18 points.
 c. Select cell **A2** and click the **Cells Styles** or the **More** button [*Home* tab, *Styles* group].
 d. Select **Heading 2** in the *Titles and Headings* category. The second level heading uses *Tw Cen MT* bold, 13 points. Both styles use a dark blue color.
 e. Select cells **A4:A9**.
 f. Press **Ctrl** and select cells **B4:H4**. Two ranges are selected.
 g. Click the **Cells Styles** or the **More** button [*Home* tab, *Styles* group].
 h. Select **40%, Accent 1** in the *Themed Cell Styles* category.
 i. Click the **Bold** button [*Home* tab, *Font* group].
 j. Select cell **A10**.
 k. Type Total and press **Enter**. The format from the column is automatically applied.

9. Apply font attributes.
 a. Select cells **A4:H10**.
 b. Click the **Font size** drop-down list [*Home* tab, *Font* group] and select **12**.
 c. Change the font size for cell **A2** to **14**.
 d. Select cells **A5:A9**.
 e. Click the **Increase Indent** button [*Home* tab, *Alignment* group] two times.
 f. Select cell **A10** and click the **Align Right** button [*Home* tab, *Alignment* group].

10. Use the *SUM* function and copy a formula.
 a. Select cell **B10**.
 b. Click the **AutoSum** button [*Home* tab, *Editing* group] and press **Enter** to accept the suggested range.
 c. Select cell **B10** and drag the *Fill* pointer to cell **H10**.

11. Apply number formatting.
 a. Select cells **B5:H10**.
 b. Click the **Accounting Number Format** button [*Home* tab, *Number* group]. Column widths are adjusted to accommodate the values.
 c. Click the **Decrease Decimal** button [*Home* tab, *Number* group] two times. Column widths do not adjust.

12. Change row heights.
 a. Click the heading for row **4**.
 b. Press **Ctrl** and click the row **10** heading. Two rows are selected.
 c. Right-click the row **4** heading.
 d. Choose **Row Height** and type 25 as the new height.
 e. Click **OK**.
 f. Click the heading for row **5** and drag down to select rows **5:9**.
 g. Point to the bottom border of the row **9** heading to display the resize arrow.
 h. Drag the pointer down to reach a height of **21.00** (**28 pixels**) and release the pointer button (Figure 1-81).

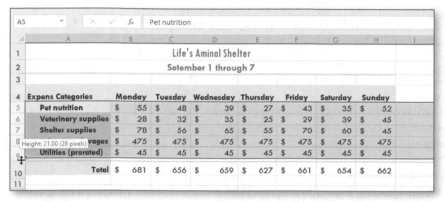

1-81 Change row heights for rows 5:9

13. Insert a row and change column width.
 a. Select cell **A9** and then right-click row heading **9**.
 b. Choose **Insert** from the context menu. The new row is located above the selected row; other rows shift down.
 c. In cell **A9**, type Cages and equipment.
 d. Point to the border between columns **A** and **B** to display the resize arrow.
 e. Drag the pointer to a width of **22.50** (**185 pixels**) and release the pointer button.

14. Enter the following data in row **9**. A zero (0) is displayed as a small dash.

	B	C	D	E	F	G	H
Cages and equipment	35	35	25	0	0	35	40

15. Insert borders and change the font size.
 a. Select cells **A4:H11**.
 b. Click the **Borders** button drop-down list and choose **All Borders**.
 c. Select cell **A2** and press **Ctrl+1** to open the *Format Cells* dialog box.
 d. Click the **Border** tab.
 e. Click the blue bottom border in the preview area to remove it.
 f. Click the **Color** drop-down arrow and select **Black, Text 1**.
 g. Click to select the solid, thick line (second column, sixth style) in the *Style* group,
 h. Click the bottom border In the preview area (Figure 1-82).
 i. Click **OK**.
 j. Select cell **A1** and change the font size to **24**.

1-82 Create a custom border

475

16. Rename the sheet and set the tab color.
 a. Double-click the **Sheet1** tab name.
 b. Type Week 1 and press **Enter**.
 c. Click the **Format** button [*Home* tab, *Cells* group].
 d. Select **Tab Color** in the *Organize Sheets* category.
 e. Select **Blue Accent 2, Darker 50%**.

17. Spell check a worksheet.
 a. Press **Ctrl+Home** to go to cell **A1**.
 b. Click the **Spelling** button [*Review* tab, *Proofing* group].
 c. Type Animal in the *Not in Dictionary* box and click **Change**.
 d. Choose "September" in the *Suggestions* list and click **Change**.
 e. Correct "Expens" when the error is located.
 f. Click **OK**.
 g. Press **Ctrl+Home**.

18. Change page setup options.
 a. Click the **Page Layout** tab and click the **Page Setup** launcher.
 b. On the **Page** tab, select the **Landscape** radio button.
 c. Click the **Margins** tab.
 d. Select the **Horizontally** box under *Center on page*.
 e. Click the **Header/Footer** tab.
 f. Click the **Header** drop-down list and choose *[your initials] Excel 1-1* to insert the file name in the center section.
 g. Click **OK**.
 h. Press **Ctrl+F2** to preview the worksheet.
 i. Press **Esc** to close the *Backstage* view.

19. Copy and edit a worksheet.
 a. Right-click the **Week 1** tab name.
 b. Select **Move or Copy** from the menu.
 c. Select **(move to end)** in the *Before sheet* list.
 d. Select the **Create a copy** box and click **OK**.
 e. On the copied worksheet, select cells **B5:H10** and delete the data.
 f. Double-click cell **A2** to start *Edit* mode.
 g. Change "September 1 through 7" to September 8 through 14.
 h. Double-click the **Week 1 (2)** tab name.
 i. Type Week 2 and press **Enter**.
 j. Right-click the **Week 2** tab name and choose **Tab Color**.
 k. Select **Green Accent 4, Darker 50%**.

20. Click the **Week 1** sheet tab.

21. Click the **File** tab and select **Print** to preview the **Week 1** worksheet.

22. Change the zoom size and freeze panes.
 a. Select cell **B5**.
 b. Click the **Zoom In** button in the *Status* bar five times.
 c. Click the **Freeze Panes** button [*View* tab, *Window* group].
 d. Choose **Freeze Panes**.
 e. Scroll the window on the right so that column **F** is immediately to the right of column **A** (Figure 1-83).
 f. Select cell **A1**.

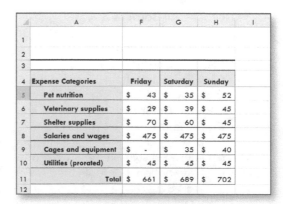

1-83 Panes frozen and positioned

23. Save and close the workbook (Figure 1-84).

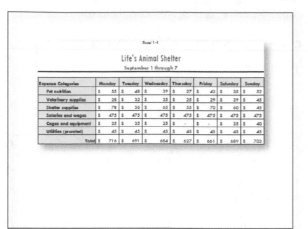

Guided Project 1-2

In this project, you edit a worksheet for Eller Software Services representative Adam White. He maintains client data with sales revenue and specific products or services. You plan to format the data, complete the calculation, and prepare the worksheet for sharing with management.
[Student Learning Outcomes 1.1, 1.2, 1.3, 1.4, 1.5, 1.6, 1.8]

File Needed: **EllerSoftwareServices-01.xlsx** [Student data files are available in the Library of your SIMnet account.]
Completed Project File Name: **[your initials] Excel 1-2**.xlsx

Skills Covered in This Project

- Open and save a workbook.
- Choose a workbook theme.
- Enter and copy labels using the *Fill Handle*.
- Set font attributes and number formats.
- Use *SUM*.
- Center labels across a selection.
- Change page orientation and scale a worksheet for printing.
- Design borders.
- Insert a row and hide a column.
- Rename and apply color to sheet tabs.
- Adjust page setup options.

1. Open the workbook **EllerSoftwareServices-01.xlsx** from your student data files. If the workbook has opened in *Protected View*, click **Enable Editing** in the security bar.

2. Save the workbook with a new file name.
 a. Press **F12** (**FN+F12**) to open the *Save As* dialog box.
 b. Navigate to the folder where your files are stored.
 c. Rename the file [your initials] Excel 1-2.
 d. Click **Save**.

3. Choose a workbook theme.
 a. Click the **Themes** button [*Page Layout* tab, *Themes* group].
 b. Choose **Ion** from the gallery. A different font, *Century Gothic*, is used for all data in the worksheet.
 c. Double-click the border between the column **C** and column **D** headings to *AutoFit* column **C**.

4. Enter and copy data.
 a. Select cell **F5**, type **MN**, and press **Enter**.
 b. Select cell **F5** and point to the *Fill Handle*.
 c. Click and drag the *Fill* pointer to cell **E13**.

5. Format data.
 a. Select cells **D5:D13**.
 b. Press **Ctrl+1** to open the *Format Cells* dialog box.
 c. Click the **Number** tab.
 d. In the *Category* list, click **Special**.
 e. Select **Phone Number** in the *Type* list and click **OK** (Figure 1-85).
 f. Select cells **I6:I13**.
 g. Click the **Comma Style** button [*Home* tab, *Number* group].
 h. Select cell **I5**.
 i. Click the **Accounting Number Format** button [*Home* tab, *Number* group]. A series of # symbols means the column is not wide enough to display the data (Figure 1-86).

1-85 Special number format

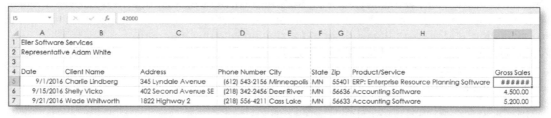

1-86 Column I is not wide enough

 j. Double-click the border between the column **I** and column **J** headings to *AutoFit* column **I**.

6. Enter and edit the reference range for the *SUM* function.
 a. Click cell **A15**, type Total, and press **Enter**.
 b. Select cell **I15**.
 c. Click the **AutoSum** button [*Home* tab, *Editing* group]. The suggested range includes an empty row.
 d. Click cell **I5** and drag to select cells **I5:I13**. Your selected range is highlighted and shown in the *Formula* bar and in the cell (Figure 1-87).
 e. Press **Enter** to accept the range. The *Accounting Number* format is applied.

7. Center labels across a selection.
 a. Select cells **A1:I2** and click the **Alignment** launcher [*Home* tab, *Alignment* group].
 b. Click the **Horizontal** arrow and select **Center Across Selection**.
 c. Click **OK**.

8. Apply font attributes and cell styles.
 a. Select cell **A1**, click the **Font Size** drop-down list [*Home* tab, *Font* group], and select **24**.
 b. Select cell **A2** and change the font size to **18**.
 c. Select cells **A4:A15**, press **Ctrl**, and then select cells **B4:I4**.
 d. Click the **Cell Styles** button or the **More** button and select **40% - Accent3** in the *Themed Cell Styles* category.
 e. While the cells are selected, click the **Bold** button [*Home* tab, *Font* group].
 f. Select cell **I15** and apply the **Total** cell style.
 g. Select cells **A4:I4**.
 h. Click the **Font Size** drop-down list [*Home* tab, *Font* group] and select **12**.
 i. Click the **Center** button [*Home* tab, *Alignment* group].
 j. *AutoFit* column **D**.
 k. Select cell **A15** and click the **Align Right** button [*Home* tab, *Alignment* group].

9. Edit a label.
 a. Double-click cell **H9** to start *Edit* mode.
 b. Press **Home** to position the insertion point before the word "Training".
 c. Type **ERP** and press **Spacebar**.
 d. Press **Enter**.

10. Insert a row.
 a. Right-click row heading **10**.
 b. Choose **Insert** from the context menu.
 c. In cell **A10**, type 10/10/16 and press **Tab**.
 d. Complete the data as shown here. For the phone number, do not type any spaces; it is automatically formatted when you press **Tab** to move to the next cell.

B10	Hillary Marschke
C10	245 West Third Avenue
D10	3203555443(press **Tab**)
E10	sa (press **Tab**)
F10	m (press **Tab**)
G10	56301
H10	t (press **Tab**)
I10	750

11. Apply borders.
 a. Select cells **A4:I14**.
 b. Click the **Border** drop-down arrow [*Home* tab, *Font* group] and choose **All Borders**.

c. Select cells **A16:I16**.

d. Press **Ctrl+1** to open the *Format Cells* dialog box and click the **Border** tab.

e. Select the solid, single line (first column, sixth option) in the *Style* list.

f. Click the top border In the *Border* preview area.

g. Select the solid, double line (second column, seventh option) in the *Style* list.

h. Click the bottom border In the *Border* preview area (Figure 1-88).

i. Click **OK**.

j. Select cells **A15:I16**.

k. Click the **Border** arrow [*Home* tab, *Font* group] and choose **Left Border**.

l. Click the **Border** arrow [*Home* tab, *Font* group] and choose **Right Border**.

1-88 Design a double border

12. Hide a column.

a. Right-click the column **F** heading.

b. Select **Hide**.

c. Press **Ctrl+Home**.

13. Rename and color a sheet tab.

a. Double-click the **Sheet1** tab.

b. Type MN Clients and press **Enter**.

c. Right-click the **MN Clients** tab.

d. Select **Tab Color** and choose **Gold, Accent 3**.

14. Change page setup options.

a. Click the **Page Layout** tab.

b. Click the **Orientation** button [*Page Setup* group] and choose **Landscape**.

c. In the *Scale to Fit* group, click the **Width** arrow and choose **1 page**.

d. Click the **Insert** tab.

e. Click the **Header & Footer** button In the *Text* group. The view switches to *Page Layout* with the insertion point in the center header section. The *Header & Footer Tools Design* toolbar displays.

f. Click the **Go to Footer** button in the *Navigation* group.

g. Click the **Footer** button in the *Header & Footer* group (Figure 1-89).

1-89 Select a built-in footer

h. Choose **MN Clients** to insert the sheet name in the footer. The *Header & Footer Tools Design* toolbar closes.

i. Click the **Normal** button in the *Status* bar. The footer is not visible in this view.

15. Preview and print the worksheet.
 a. Select **Print** from the *File* tab.
 b. Review the worksheet layout.
 c. Click **Print** or press **Esc** to return to the workbook.

16. Save and close the workbook (Figure 1-90).

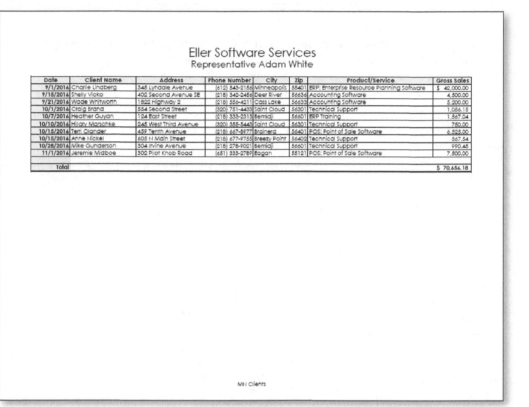

Guided Project 1-3

In this project, you edit a worksheet for Wear-Ever Shoes that tracks their product inventory. You change the zoom size, reset the panes, and format data. You copy an existing formula to calculate the value of the current stock and insert a column for new data. After adjusting print options, you set a print area for a specific product line.
[Student Learning Outcomes 1.1, 1.2, 1.4, 1.5, 1.6, 1.7, 1.8]

File Needed: ***WearEverShoes-01.xlsx*** [*Student data files are available in the Library of your SIMnet account.*]
Completed Project File Name: ***[your initials] Excel 1-3.xlsx***

Skills Covered in This Project

- Open and save a workbook.
- Change zoom size and remove a split.
- Freeze panes.
- Format labels and values.
- Use the *Fill Handle* to copy a formula and fill a series.
- Check spelling.
- Apply a workbook theme, cell styles, and font attributes.
- Merge and center labels.
- Insert a column and adjust column widths and row heights.
- Adjust alignment, indents, and borders.
- Rename the sheet tab.
- Use *Page Layout* view to insert a footer.

1. Open and rename a workbook.
 a. Open the workbook **WearEverShoes-01.xlsx** from your student data files. If the workbook has opened in *Protected View*, click **Enable Editing** in the security bar.
 b. Press **F12** (**FN+F12**) and locate the folder where your files are saved.
 c. Save the workbook as [your initials] Excel 1-3.

2. Remove a split and freeze panes.
 a. Click the **Split** button [*View* tab, *Window* group]. The split is removed.
 b. Click cell **A4** to freeze the column titles at this position.
 c. Click the **Freeze Panes** button [*View* tab, *Window* group].
 d. Choose **Freeze Panes**. There is a solid border between rows 3 and 4 to mark the pane.
 e. Scroll to row **31** and click cell **E31**. The column titles are frozen.
 f. Type 3 and press **Enter** (Figure 1-91).
 g. Press **Ctrl+Home**. The insertion point returns to cell **A4**.

E31	▾	:	×	✓	fx	3		
	A	B	C	D	E	F	G	H
1	Wear-Ever Shoes							
2	Current Stock							
3	Product ID	Product	Color	Size	Quantity	Men's or \	Cost	Value
16	WE013	Comfy Walking Shoes	Taupe	7.5	2	W	47.5	
17	WE014	Comfy Walking Shoes	Brown	8	3	W	47.5	
18	WE015	Lazy Flip-Flops	Pink	6	4	W	7.5	
19	WE016	Lazy Flip-Flops	Pink	7	0	W	7.5	
20	WE017	Lazy Flip-Flops	Pink	8	2	W	7.5	
21	WE018	Lazy Flip-Flops	White	6	3	W	7.5	
22	WE019	Lazy Flip-Flops	White	7	1	W	7.5	
23	WE020	Lazy Flip-Flops	White	8	2	W	7.5	
24	WE021	Lazy Flip-Flops	Brown	8	2	M	7.5	
25	WE022	Lazy Flip-Flops	Brown	9	4	M	7.5	
26	WE023	Lazy Flip-Flops	Brown	10	2	M	7.5	
27	WE024	Lazy Flip-Flops	Brown	11	2	M	7.5	
28	WE025	Seriously Tall Boots	Black	6	0	W	42.5	
29	WE026	Seriously Tall Boots	Black	6.5	0	W	42.5	
30	WE027	Seriously Tall Boots	Black	7	1	W	42.5	
31	WE028	Seriously Tall Boots	Black	7.5	3	W	42.5	

1-91 Panes frozen at cell A4

3. Change zoom size and unfreeze the pane.
 a. Click the **100%** button [*View* tab, *Window* group].
 b. Click the **Freeze Panes** button [*View* tab, *Window* group].
 c. Choose **Unfreeze Panes**.
 d. Click cell **A1**.

4. Check spelling in the worksheet.
 a. Click the **Spelling** button [*Review* tab, *Proofing* group]. The first occurrence of "Hikin" is found as misspelled.
 b. Select **Hiking** in the *Suggestions* list.
 c. Click **Change All** to correct all occurrences of the misspelled word (Figure 1-92).
 d. Click **OK**.

5. Use the *Fill Handle* to copy a formula.

 a. Click **H4**. The formula is visible in the *Formula* bar. The formula multiples the quantity by the cost to calculate the value of the current stock (Figure 1-93).

 b. Point to the *Fill Handle* for cell **H4**.

 c. Double-click the *Fill* pointer. The formula is copied down the entire column.

 d. Press **Ctrl+Home**.

1-92 Change all occurrences of a misspelled word

1-93 Formula to be copied

6. Click the **Themes** button [*Page Layout* tab, *Themes* group] and choose **Ion** from the gallery.

7. Merge and center the titles.

 a. Select cells **A1:J1** and click the **Merge & Center** button [*Home* tab, *Alignment* group].

 b. Merge and center cells **A2:J2**.

8. Apply cell styles and adjust row height.

 a. Select cell **A1**, click the **Cell Styles** button or the **More** button [*Home* tab, *Styles* group], and select **Title** in the *Titles and Headings* category.

 b. Select cell **A2** and apply the **Heading 4** style.

 c. Click the **Font Size** arrow [*Home* tab, *Font* group] and select **14 pt**. Your font size change overwrites the font size of the cell style.

 d. Point to the row **1** heading and drag to select row headings **1:2**.

 e. Click the **Format** button [*Home* tab, *Cells* group] and choose **Row Height**.

 f. Type 22 as the new row height and press **Enter**.

 g. Select cells **A3:J3**.

 h. From the *Cell Styles* gallery [*Home* tab], select **40% - Accent3**.

 i. Apply **bold** to the selected cells.

 j. Click the row **3** heading.

 k. Point to the bottom border of the row heading to display the resize arrow.

 l. Drag the resize arrow to **21.00 (28 pixels)** as the new row height and release the pointer button (Figure 1-94).

 m. Click the **Zoom Out** button in the *Status* bar if necessary so that you can see all rows (1:39).

1-94 Adjust row height from the row heading

9. Change alignment, format values, apply borders, and increase the indent.
 a. Select cells **D4:F39**.
 b. Click the **Center** button [*Home* tab, *Alignment* group].
 c. Select cells **G4:H39**.
 d. Click the **Accounting Number Format** button [*Home* tab, *Alignment* group].
 e. Click cells **A3:J39**.
 f. Click the **Borders** drop-down arrow [*Home* tab, *Font* group] and select **All Borders**.
 g. While the cells are selected, click the **Font size** drop-down arrow [*Home* tab, *Font* group] and choose **12**.
 h. Select cells **B4:C39** and click the **Increase Indent** button [*Home* tab, *Alignment* group] one time. This moves the label away from the border for easier reading.
 i. Click and drag to select columns **A:J**.
 j. Double-click the border between columns J and K to *AutoFit* the selected columns (Figure 1-95).
 k. Select and **center** align the labels in row **3**.

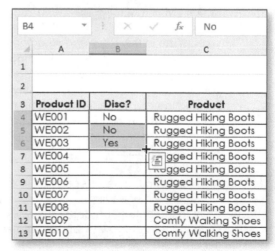

1-95 Select column headings to AutoFit

10. Insert a column and fill data.
 a. Right-click column heading **B**.
 b. Choose **Insert** from the context menu.
 c. In cell **B3**, type Disc? and press **Enter**.
 d. In cell **B4**, type No and press **Enter**.
 e. In cell **B5**, type No and press **Enter**.
 f. In cell **B6**, type Yes and press **Enter**.
 g. Select cells **B4:B6** and increase the indent twice.
 h. Select cells **B4:B6** and double-click the *Fill* pointer (Figure 1-96).
 i. Select cells **A4:A39** and increase the indent one time.
 j. Press **Ctrl+Home**.

11. Rename the sheet tab.
 a. Double-click the **Sheet1** tab.
 b. Type Inventory and press **Enter**.

1-96 Double-click the Fill pointer to complete a series

12. Use *Page Layout* view to insert a footer.
 a. Click the **Page Layout** button in the *Status* bar.
 b. Click the center header section. The *Header & Footer Tools Design* tab is active.
 c. Click the **Header & Footer Tools Design** tab.
 d. Click the **Go to Footer** button [*Header & Footer Tools Design* tab, *Navigation* group].
 e. Click the middle section if necessary.
 f. Click the **File Name** button in the *Header & Footer Elements* group. The code is *&[File]*.
 g. Click a worksheet cell to see the file name.
 h. Switch to *Normal* view and press **Ctrl+Home**.

13. Change page setup options.
 a. Click the **Page Layout** tab and click the **Page Setup** launcher.
 b. Display the *Page* tab and select the **Landscape** radio button under *Orientation*.
 c. Select the **Fit to** radio button and enter 1 page wide by 1 tall.
 d. Click **OK**.

14. Set a print area.
 a. Select cells **A1:K11**.
 b. Click the **Page Layout** tab.
 c. Click the **Print Area** button [*Page Setup* group] and select **Set Print Area**.
 d. Press **Ctrl+Home**.
 e. Click the **File** tab and select **Print** to preview the worksheet print area.
 f. Print the area and return to *Normal* view.

15. Click the **Save** button in the *Quick Access* toolbar to save the workbook changes. The print area is saved.

16. Close the workbook (Figure 1-97).

Product ID	Disc?	Product	Color	Size	Quantity	Men's or Women's	Cost	Value	Retail	Reorder
WE001	No	Rugged Hiking Boots	Brown	8	5	M	$ 46.50	$ 232.50	90	N
WE002	No	Rugged Hiking Boots	Brown	10	3	M	$ 46.50	$ 139.50	90	Y
WE003	Yes	Rugged Hiking Boots	Black	9.5	6	M	$ 46.50	$ 279.00	90	N
WE004	No	Rugged Hiking Boots	Black	10.5	4	M	$ 46.50	$ 186.00	90	N
WE005	No	Rugged Hiking Boots	Black	7.5	4	W	$ 53.50	$ 214.00	98	N
WE006	Yes	Rugged Hiking Boots	Black	8	2	W	$ 53.50	$ 107.00	98	Y
WE007	No	Rugged Hiking Boots	Brown	9	3	W	$ 53.50	$ 160.50	98	N
WE008	No	Rugged Hiking Boots	Brown	8.5	2	W	$ 53.50	$ 107.00	98	Y
WE009	Yes	Comfy Walking Shoes	Brown	8.5	4	M	$ 47.50	$ 190.00	65	N
WE010	No	Comfy Walking Shoes	Black	9	1	M	$ 47.50	$ 47.50	65	Y
WE011	No	Comfy Walking Shoes	Navy	7.5	4	W	$ 47.50	$ 190.00	65	N
WE012	Yes	Comfy Walking Shoes	Black	8	1	W	$ 47.50	$ 47.50	65	Y
WE013	No	Comfy Walking Shoes	Taupe	7.5	2	W	$ 47.50	$ 95.00	65	N
WE014	No	Comfy Walking Shoes	Brown	8	3	W	$ 47.50	$ 142.50	65	Y
WE015	Yes	Lazy Flip-Flops	Pink	6	4	W	$ 7.50	$ 30.00	14	N
WE016	No	Lazy Flip-Flops	Pink	7	0	W	$ 7.50	$ -	14	N
WE017	No	Lazy Flip-Flops	Pink	8	2	W	$ 7.50	$ 15.00	14	Y
WE018	Yes	Lazy Flip-Flops	White	6	3	W	$ 7.50	$ 22.50	14	N
WE019	No	Lazy Flip-Flops	White	7	1	W	$ 7.50	$ 7.50	14	N
WE020	No	Lazy Flip-Flops	White	8	2	W	$ 7.50	$ 15.00	14	Y
WE021	Yes	Lazy Flip-Flops	Brown	8	2	M	$ 7.50	$ 15.00	14	Y
WE022	No	Lazy Flip-Flops	Brown	9	4	M	$ 7.50	$ 30.00	14	N
WE023	No	Lazy Flip-Flops	Brown	10	2	M	$ 7.50	$ 15.00	14	Y
WE024	Yes	Lazy Flip-Flops	Brown	11	2	M	$ 7.50	$ 15.00	14	Y
WE025	No	Seriously Tall Boots	Black	6	0	W	$ 42.50	$ -	80	Y
WE026	No	Seriously Tall Boots	Black	6.5	0	W	$ 42.50	$ -	80	Y
WE027	Yes	Seriously Tall Boots	Black	7	1	W	$ 42.50	$ 42.50	80	Y
WE028	No	Seriously Tall Boots	Black	7.5	3	W	$ 42.50	$ 127.50	80	Y
WE029	No	Seriously Tall Boots	Black	8	2	W	$ 42.50	$ 85.00	80	Y
WE030	Yes	Seriously Tall Boots	Black	8.5	1	W	$ 42.50	$ 42.50	80	Y
WE031	No	Glide Running Shoes	White	8	6	M	$ 48.00	$ 288.00	75	N
WE032	No	Glide Running Shoes	White	9	6	M	$ 48.00	$ 288.00	75	N
WE033	Yes	Glide Running Shoes	White	10	6	M	$ 48.00	$ 288.00	75	N
WE034	No	Glide Running Shoes	Black	8	2	M	$ 48.00	$ 96.00	75	N
WE035	No	Glide Running Shoes	Black	9	3	M	$ 48.00	$ 144.00	75	N
WE036	Yes	Glide Running Shoes	Black	10	1	M	$ 48.00	$ 48.00	75	Y

Wear-Ever Shoes
Current Stock

Excel 1-3

1-97 Excel 1-3 completed

Independent Project 1-4

As staff at Blue Lake Sports Company, you are expected to prepare the monthly sales worksheet. You edit and format data, complete calculations, and prepare the workbook for distribution. You also copy the sheet for next month's data.
[Student Learning Outcomes 1.1, 1.2, 1.3, 1.4, 1.5, 1.6, 1.8]

File Needed: ***BlueLakeSports-01.xlsx*** [Student data files are available in the Library of your SIMnet account.]
Completed Project File Name: ***[your initials] Excel 1-4.xlsx***

Skills Covered in This Project

- Open and save a workbook.
- Choose a workbook theme.
- Edit and format data.
- Center labels across a selection.

- Use *SUM* and the *Fill Handle*.
- Adjust column width and row height.
- Insert a header and a footer.
- Adjust page layout options.
- Copy and rename a worksheet.

1. Open ***BlueLakeSports-01.xlsx*** from your student data files. If the workbook has opened in *Protected View*, click **Enable Editing** in the security bar.

2. Save the workbook as [your initials] Excel 1-4 in your usual location.

3. Apply the **Slice** theme to the worksheet.

4. Edit worksheet data.
 a. Edit the title in cell **A2** to display Monthly Sales by Department.
 b. Edit cell **D6** to 1950.

5. Select cells **A1:F2** and apply the *Center Across Selection* command.

6. Select and delete row **8**.

7. Use the *Fill Handle* to complete a series.
 a. Select cell **B3**.
 b. Use the *Fill Handle* to complete the series to **Week 4** in column **E**.
 c. *AutoFit* the columns to display the complete label.

8. Use *SUM* and the *Fill Handle* to calculate totals.
 a. Use the **AutoSum** button to build a *SUM* function in cell **F4**.
 b. Use the *Fill Handle* to copy the formula in cell **F4** to cells **F5:F16**.
 c. Delete the contents of cell **F17** if you copied the formula to that cell.
 d. Select cells **B17:F17** and click the **AutoSum** button. The *SUM* formula is inserted, and a **Quick Analysis** options button appears (Figure 1-98).
 e. Press **Esc** to ignore the *Quick Analysis* options.

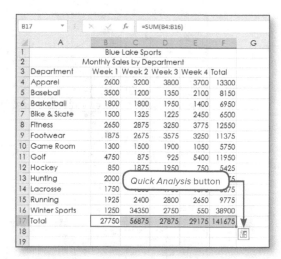

1-98 *AutoSum* complete with *Quick Analysis* button

9. Format labels and values.
 a. Select cells **A1:A2** and increase the font size to **18**.
 b. Increase the row height of rows **1:2** to **24 (32 pixels)**.
 c. Format cells **A3:F3** as **Bold** and increase the row height to **18 (24 pixels)**.
 d. Center the data in cells **B3:F3**.
 e. Format all values with **Comma Style** and decrease the decimal two times.
 f. Apply the **All Borders** format to cells **A3:F17**.
 g. Select cells **B17:F17** and apply the **Accounting Number Format** with no decimal places.
 h. *AutoFit* each column that does not display all data.

10. Finalize the worksheet.
 a. Click the **Insert** tab and click the **Header & Footer** button.
 b. In the right header section, insert the **Sheet Name** field.
 c. Go to the footer and click the right section.
 d. Type [your first and last name] (Figure 1-99).

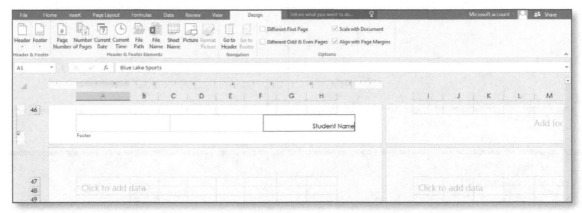

1-99 Add a footer in *Page Layout* view

 e. Click a cell in the worksheet and return to *Normal* view.
 f. Center the worksheet horizontally on the page.

11. Copy and rename a worksheet.
 a. Right-click the *January* sheet tab and choose **Move or Copy**.
 b. Make a copy of the sheet at the end.
 c. Rename the copied sheet February.
 d. Format the *February* sheet tab color to **Dark Blue, Accent 1**.
 e. Delete the values in cells **B4:E16** and press **Ctrl+Home**.
 f. Return to the *January* sheet.

12. Preview the *January* sheet.

13. Save and close the workbook (Figure 1-100).

Blue Lake Sports
Monthly Sales by Department

Department	Week 1	Week 2	Week 3	Week 4	Total
Apparel	2,600	3,200	3,800	3,700	13,300
Baseball	3,500	1,200	1,350	2,100	8,150
Basketball	1,800	1,800	1,950	1,400	6,950
Bike & Skate	1,500	1,325	1,225	2,450	6,500
Fitness	2,650	2,875	3,250	3,775	12,550
Footwear	1,875	2,675	3,575	3,250	11,375
Game Room	1,300	1,500	1,900	1,050	5,750
Golf	4,750	875	925	5,400	11,950
Hockey	850	1,875	1,950	750	5,425
Hunting	2,000	1,000	650	725	4,375
Lacrosse	1,750	1,800	1,750	1,375	6,675
Running	1,925	2,400	2,800	2,650	9,775
Winter Sports	1,250	34,350	2,750	550	38,900
Total	$27,750	$56,875	$27,875	$29,175	$141,875

Student Name

Blue Lake Sports
Monthly Sales by Department

Department	Week 1	Week 2	Week 3	Week 4	Total
Apparel					-
Baseball					-
Basketball					-
Bike & Skate					-
Fitness					-
Footwear					-
Game Room					-
Golf					-
Hockey					-
Hunting					-
Lacrosse					-
Running					-
Winter Sports					-
Total	$ -	$ -	$ -	$ -	$ -

Student Name

1-100 Excel 1-4 completed

Independent Project 1-5

Clemenson Imaging employs certified staff to perform mobile medical imaging at several hospitals state-wide. Your worksheet maintains a log of which hospitals were visited and what images were made. You need to format the data and finalize the worksheet.
[Student Learning Outcomes 1.1, 1.2, 1.3, 1.4, 1.5, 1.6, 1.7, 1.8]

File Needed: *ClemensonImaging-01.xlsx* [Student data files are available in the Library of your SIMnet account.]
Completed Project File Name: *[your initials] Excel 1-5.xlsx*

Skills Covered in This Project

- Open and save a workbook.
- Use *SUM*.
- Unfreeze panes and change the zoom size.
- Format data.
- Merge and center labels.
- Adjust column width and row height.
- Design borders.
- Copy a sheet and rename a tab.
- Add document properties.
- Change page layout options.

1. Open **ClemensonImaging-01.xlsx** from your student data files and save it as [your initials] Excel 1-5. If the workbook has opened in *Protected View*, click **Enable Editing** in the security bar.

2. Edit the label in cell **A1** to insert LLC after "Clemenson Imaging." Edit the label in cell **A2** to show "Second Quarter . . ." instead of "First Quarter."

3. Merge and center the label in cell **A1** across the worksheet data and then do the same for the label in cell **A2**.

4. Scroll to and select cell **A41**. Type Total. Right-align this label and apply bold format.

5. Use *SUM* in cell **F41** to add the values in cells **F5:F40**.

6. Unfreeze the panes and set a zoom size to display rows 1:30.

7. *AutoFit* columns **D** and **G**.

8. Format data.
 a. Click cell **A1** and set the font size to **18**.
 b. Change the label in cell **A2** to a font size of **14**.
 c. Select cells **A4:H4** and apply bold and center.
 d. Format cells **A4:H4** to use the **White, Background 1, Darker 15%** fill color.
 e. Format the row height for row **4** to **21.00 (28 pixels)**.
 f. Select cells **A4:H41** and apply **All Borders**.
 g. Select cells **A41:H41** and apply the fill color **White, Background 1, Darker 15%**.
 h. Make the value in cell **F41** bold.

9. Set page layout options.
 a. Change the page orientation to **Landscape**.
 b. Center the worksheet horizontally.
 c. Scale the sheet to fit on a single page.
 d. Add a footer that displays the current date in the left section and your first and last name in the right section.
 e. *Autofit* columns that do not display all the data.

10. Add document properties.
 a. Click the **File** tab and select **Info**.
 b. Click the **Properties** drop-down arrow and select **Advanced Properties**.
 c. Click the **Title** box and type Procedures.
 d. Click the **Author** box and type your first and last name (Figure 1-101).
 e. Return to the worksheet.

1-101 *Properties* dialog box

11. Rename *Sheet1* as Qtr 2.

12. Copy the *Qtr 2* sheet and place it at the end. Name the copy Qtr 3. Set this tab color to **Blue, Accent 1, Darker 50%**.

13. On the *Qtr 3* sheet, edit the label in cell **A2** to show "Third Quarter . . .".

14. Delete the contents of cells **A5:H40** on the *Qtr 3* sheet.

15. Select cell **A5** and return to the *Qtr 2* sheet.

16. Press **Ctrl+Home** and preview the entire workbook (Figure 1-102).

17. Save and close the workbook (Figure 1-103).

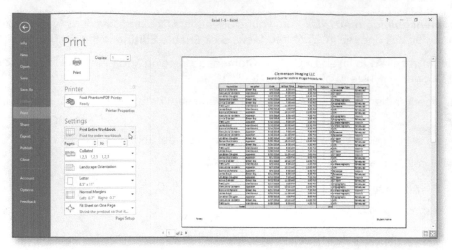

1-102 Entire workbook selected for preview and print

1-103 Excel 1-5 completed

Independent Project 1-6

As accounts receivable clerk for Livingood Income Tax & Accounting, you track daily payments from clients in an Excel worksheet. After entering the data, you format the worksheet and prepare it for distribution to coworkers.

[Student Learning Outcomes 1.1, 1.2, 1.3, 1.4, 1.5, 1.6, 1.8]

File Needed: None
Completed Project File Name: *[your initials] Excel 1-6.xlsx*

Skills Covered in This Project

- Create and save a workbook.
- Enter labels, dates, and values.
- Use the *Fill Handle* to build series.
- Use *SUM*.

- Change font size and attributes.
- Adjust column width and row height.
- Choose a theme and cell styles.
- Choose page layout options.
- Rename and apply color to sheet tabs.

1. Create a new workbook and save it as [your initials] Excel 1-6. If the workbook has opened in *Protected View*, click **Enable Editing** in the security bar.

2. Apply the **Organic** theme for the workbook.

3. In cell **A1**, type Livingood Income Tax and Accounting and press **Enter**

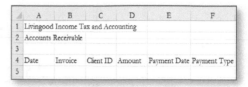

4. In cell **A2**, type Accounts Receivable and press **Enter**.

5. In row **4**, type the labels as shown here in Figure 1-104:

1-104 Data to be entered

6. *AutoFit* or widen the columns to display each label in row 4 in its cell.

7. In cell **A5**, type 8/18/17 to enter the date. In cell **A6**, type 8/20/17 to set a pattern for the dates.

8. Select cells **A5:A6** and use the *Fill Handle* to fill in dates to cell A15.

9. In cell **B5**, type 1001 for the first invoice number. In cell **B6**, type 1002 to set a pattern for the invoice numbers.

10. Select cells **B5:B6** and use the *Fill Handle* to fill in invoice numbers to reach cell B15.

11. In cell **C5**, type LITA001 as the first client ID. In cell **C6**, type LITA002 to set a pattern.

12. Use the *Fill Handle* to complete the client ID numbers.

13. Type 425 in cell **D5**. In cell **D6**, type 450 to set the pattern and fill in the amounts.

1-105 All columns filled

14. Type the first two payment dates in column **E** and fill the cells (Figure 1-105).

15. Type the first three payment types in cells **F5:F7** and then use the *Fill Handle* to complete the cells in column F.

16. Format data.
 a. Select cells **C5:C15**, increase the indent one time, and *AutoFit* the column. Do the same for the payment type data.
 b. Format the values in column **D** as **Accounting Number Format**.
 c. Select cells **A1:A2** and change the font size to **18**. Center the labels across cells **A1:F2**.
 d. Select the labels in row **4** and apply bold format center alignment.
 e. *AutoFit* columns that do not show all the data.
 f. Apply **All Borders** to cells **A4:F15**. Apply an **Outside Border** for cells **A1:F2**.
 g. Apply the **Green, Accent 1, Lighter 60%** fill color to cells **A1:F2** and **A4:F4**.
 h. Apply the **Green, Accent 1, Lighter 60%** fill color to cells **A6:F6**.
 i. Use the **Ctrl** key to select the data in rows **8**, **10**, **12**, and **14** and apply the same fill color.

17. Rename *Sheet1* as **AR** and set the tab color to **Green, Accent 1**.

18. Define page layout and add document properties.
 a. Center the worksheet horizontally on the page.
 b. Create a header with the sheet name in the left section and your name in the right section.
 c. Delete an existing author name and key your first and last name as *Author* in the *Properties* dialog box.
 d. Type Receivables in the *Title* box (Figure 1-106).
 e. Preview your worksheet.

1-106 Properties entered in dialog box

19. Save and close the workbook (Figure 1-107).

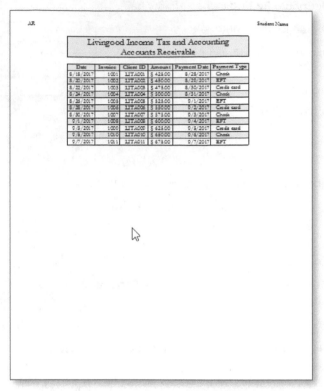

1-107 Excel 1-6 completed

Improve It Project 1-7

In this project, you complete a worksheet that maintains flight statistics for Boyd Air. The data has been imported from the reservation system, and you now need to add finishing touches.
[Student Learning Outcomes 1.1, 1.2, 1.3, 1.4, 1.5, 1.6, 1.7, 1.8]

File Needed: **BoydAir-01.xlsx** [Student data files are available in the Library of your SIMnet account.]
Completed Project File Name: **[your initials] Excel 1-7.xlsx**

Skills Covered in This Project

- Open and save a workbook.
- Change the zoom level and remove a split.
- Enter and merge and center labels.
- Insert a row and set column width.

- Format data.
- Use *SUM*.
- Apply cell styles.
- Rename and color the sheet tab.
- Adjust page layout options.
- Add document properties.

1. Open the workbook **BoydAir-01.xlsx** from your student data files. If the workbook has opened in *Protected View*, click **Enable Editing** in the security bar.

2. Save the workbook as [your initials] Excel 1-7.

3. Remove the split from the window.

4. Type **Boyd Air** in cell **A1** and **Flight Statistics** in cell **A2**.

5. Merge and center the labels in cells **A1** and **A2**. Change the font size for both labels to **16**.

6. Insert a row at row **3**.

7. Select the labels in row **4** and make them bold and centered. *AutoFit* columns to show each label in row 4.

8. Change the zoom size to **100%**.

9. Select cells **B5:D18**, press **Ctrl**, and select cells **G5:G18**. Increase the indent one time.

10. Apply **All Borders** for cells **A4:H19**.

11. Calculate the total number of passengers in cell **H19**.

12. Apply the **Accent2** cell style to cells **A3:H3** and cells **A20:H20**.

13. Select cells **A3:H3** and **A20:H20** and apply an **Outside Border**.

14. Modify page layout options.
 a. Change the orientation to **Landscape**.
 b. Center the worksheet horizontally on the page.
 c. Show the file name in the left header section.
 d. Type your first and last name in the right header section.

15. Name the sheet tab **Feb-Mar** and format the tab color as **Orange, Accent 2**.

16. Set the document properties to show your first and last name as the *Author*. In the *Title* field, type **Flight Stats**.

17. Preview your worksheet.

18. Save and close the workbook (Figure 1-108).

1-108 Excel 1-7 completed

Challenge Project 1-8

In this project, you create a workbook that lists and tracks candy and beverage sales at a gourmet chocolate store for selected holidays or special events. You enter and format the data and then finalize the workbook for distribution.
[Student Learning Outcomes 1.1, 1.2, 1.3, 1.4, 1.5, 1.6, 1.8]

File Needed: None
Completed Project File Name: *[your initials] Excel 1-8.xlsx*

Create a new workbook and save it as [your initials] Excel 1-8. Modify your workbook according to the following guidelines:

- Choose a workbook theme.
- Determine and type a name for the store in cell **A1**. In cell **A2**, type Sales by Holiday.
- Starting in cell **B3**, type names of four chocolate candies and one chocolate beverage (cells B3:F3).
- Type the names of five holidays, celebrations, or special events in cells **A4:A8**.
- Fill in values to reflect dollar or unit sales, and format these values appropriately.
- Calculate a total for each holiday and a total for each candy or beverage. Add labels for these values.
- Use cell styles, borders, fill color, or other formatting to design your worksheet.
- *AutoFit* columns and adjust row heights as needed.
- Insert a footer that includes your name in one section and the date in another section.
- Use portrait orientation and fit the worksheet to a single page. Center it horizontally.
- Name the sheet tab and set a tab color.
- Enter the company name in the *Title* field in the document properties.

Challenge Project 1-9

In this project, you create a worksheet for a photography club that rents retail space for selling used equipment. The equipment includes camera bodies, lenses, tripods, cases, accessories, books, and more. You are building the worksheet so that expected selling prices can be entered each month for each item.
[Student Learning Outcomes 1.1, 1.2, 1.4, 1.5, 1.6, 1.7, 1.8]

File Needed: None
Completed Project File Name: *[your initials] Excel 1-9.xlsx*

Create a new workbook and save it as [your initials] Excel 1-9. Modify your workbook according to the following guidelines:

- Create and type a name for the photography club as a main label. As a second label, type a label that specifies the purpose of the worksheet.
- In cell **B3**, type Jan. Fill the months to **Dec** in column **M**.
- Starting in cell **A4**, type the names of ten items related to any type of photography equipment in column **A**. Research a web site that sells similar items.

- As the January price for the first item, type a value that makes sense as a resale price. For the February price, type a value that is a few dollars more than the January price. Select these two cells and fill prices for the remaining months.
- Repeat the tasks in the previous step for each of the ten items to fill in values for all the items.
- Use cell styles, borders, fill color, or other formatting to design the worksheet.
- Adjust column widths and row heights.
- Insert a header that includes your name in the right section.
- Use landscape orientation and fit the worksheet to a single page.
- In the document properties, enter the club's name in the *Author* field.
- Name the worksheet tab and choose a tab color.
- Split the sheet at cell **G1**. Arrange the data so that you see cell **A1** in each window.

Challenge Project 1-10

In this project, you create a spreadsheet that details your expected monthly income and expenses. [**Student Learning Outcomes 1.1, 1.2, 1.3, 1.4, 1.5, 1.6, 1.8**]

File Needed: None
Completed Project File Name: *[your initials] Excel 1-10.xlsx*

Create a new workbook and save it as [your initials] Excel 1-10. Modify your workbook according to the following guidelines:

- Type the main label Expected Monthly Income and Estimated Expenses. Type your name as a second label.
- Type Income in cell **A3**. In cells **A4:A7**, enter labels for four categories of income. For example, you may have regular wages from one or more jobs, interest from a certificate of deposit, rent from property that you own, income from Internet sales, etc. Include descriptive labels, enter values in column **B**, and include a total income calculation using *SUM*.
- In cell **D3**, type Expenses. In cells **D4:D9**, enter labels for six categories of expenses. These include rent, a mortgage payment, insurance, loan payments, food, clothing, entertainment, transportation, and so on. Complete labels, enter values in column **E**, and use *SUM* to calculate total expenses.
- Format the data with borders, fill color, font styles, and number formats. Adjust page layout options so that the sheet fits on a single portrait page.
- Spell check the sheet.
- Name the sheet Jan and choose a tab color.
- Copy the sheet and name the copy Feb. Choose a different tab color.
- Delete the expense amounts on the *Feb* sheet.
- Make a copy of the *Feb* sheet to create a worksheet for March.
- Add document properties to identify the workbook.

Working with Formulas and Functions

CHAPTER OVERVIEW

With its capabilities in mathematical, scientific, engineering, and other calculations, Excel is a valuable tool for business, government, education, and you. You can use Excel to create a simple addition formula or a sophisticated calculation with layers of arithmetic. In this chapter, you learn how to build a basic formula and how to use mathematical rules. You also explore Excel function categories.

STUDENT LEARNING OUTCOMES (SLOs)

After completing this chapter, you will be able to:

SLO2.1 Build and edit basic formulas (p. 497).

SLO2.2 Set mathematical order of operations in a formula (p. 499).

SLO2.3 Use absolute, mixed, relative, and 3D references in a formula (p. 501).

SLO2.4 Use formula auditing tools in a worksheet (p. 507).

SLO2.5 Work with *Statistical* and *Date & Time* functions (p. 514).

SLO2.6 Work with functions from the *Financial*, *Logical*, and *Lookup & Reference* categories (p. 522).

SLO2.7 Build functions from the *Math & Trig* category (p. 530).

CASE STUDY

In the Pause & Practice projects in this chapter, you work with a multi-sheet workbook for Paradise Lakes Resort (PLR), the northern Minnesota chain of resorts. You build formulas to complete a simple income statement, to calculate data for the boutique division, and to track information about the youth camp.

Pause & Practice 2-1: Build and audit formulas in a worksheet.

Pause & Practice 2-2: Insert *Statistical* and *Date & Time* functions in a workbook.

Pause & Practice 2-3: Use *Financial*, *Logical*, *Lookup*, and *Math & Trig* functions in a workbook.

EXCEL

Building and Editing a Formula

An Excel *formula* is an expression or statement that uses common arithmetic operations to carry out a calculation. Basic arithmetic operations are addition, subtraction, multiplication, and division. The formula is entered in a cell and refers to other cells or ranges in the worksheet or workbook. The formula appears in the *Formula* bar, but the results appear in the cell.

You learned in Chapter 1 that a function is a built-in formula. Like a function, a formula begins with an equals sign (=). After the equals sign, you enter the address of the first cell, followed by the arithmetic operator, followed by the next cell in the calculation. An example of a simple addition formula is **=B5+B6** which adds the values in cells B5 and B6.

Basic arithmetic operators are listed in the table. Enter arithmetic operators using the numeric keypad or the symbols on the number keys at the top of the keyboard.

In the multiplication formula **=C5*C6**, the value in cell C5 is multiplied by the value in cell C6. You can use cell references in a formula or a value known as a *constant*. In the formula **=D5*85%**, the constant is 85%.

Character	Arithmetic Operator
+	Addition
–	Subtraction
*	Multiplication
/	Division

Type a Formula

For a simple formula, you can easily type it. Click the cell, type the equals sign, type the first cell address, type the operator, type the next cell address, and so on. Press any completion key when the formula is finished. Formulas are not case sensitive, so you can type cell addresses in lowercase letters. Excel automatically converts cell references to uppercase when the formula is completed. If you press **Esc** before completing a formula, it is canceled and nothing is entered in the cell.

As you type a cell address after the equals sign, ***Formula AutoComplete*** displays a list of functions and range names that match the character that you typed. You can ignore the list and continue typing. In addition, the ***Range Finder*** highlights and color codes each cell as you type its address.

▶ HOW TO: Type a Formula

1. Click the cell for the formula.
2. Type an equals sign (=) to begin the formula.
3. Type the column letter for the first cell reference (Figure 2-1).
 - *Formula AutoComplete* displays a list of functions and range names.
 - You can type a lowercase or uppercase character.
4. Type the row number for the cell reference.
 - The *Range Finder* color codes the cell and its reference.
5. Type the arithmetic operator.
6. Type the cell address for the next reference.

2-1 *Formula AutoComplete* while typing a formula

7. Press **Enter**.

- The result displays in the cell where the formula is located (Figure 2-2).
- The *Formula* bar displays the formula.
- You can click the **Enter** button (the check mark) on the *Formula* bar to complete a formula.
- You can press **Ctrl+Enter** to complete a formula.

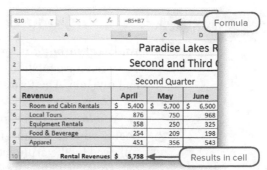

2-2 Formula and result

Point and Click to Build a Formula

Instead of typing a cell address, you point to and click the cell to enter its address in a formula. This method guards against your typing the wrong address. You will not see a *Formula AutoComplete* list, but the *Range Finder* will highlight and color code the cells.

> **▶ HOW TO: Point and Click to Build a Formula**

1. Click the cell for the formula.
2. Type an equals sign (=) to start the formula.
3. Point to and click the first cell for the formula.

 - The reference is entered in the cell and in the *Formula* bar.
 - The *Range Finder* highlights and color codes the reference.
 - If you click the wrong cell, click the correct cell to replace the address.

4. Type the arithmetic operator.
5. Point to and click the next cell for the formula (Figure 2-3).

 - The reference is entered in the cell and in the *Formula* bar.
 - The *Range Finder* highlights and color codes the reference.

6. Press **Enter**.

 - The result displays in the cell.
 - The *Formula* bar displays the formula.
 - Click the **Enter** button on the *Formula* bar or press **Ctrl+Enter** to complete a formula.

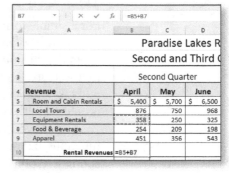

2-3 Point and click to build a formula

Edit a Formula

You edit a formula in *Edit* mode by double-clicking its cell or by clicking the *Formula* bar while the cell is active. The *Range Finder* highlights and color codes the formula cell as well as the cells used in the formula. You can add or remove cells and operators to build a new formula in the cell or in the *Formula* bar.

> **ANOTHER WAY**
>
> Click the cell and press **F2 (FN+F2)** to start *Edit* mode.

▶ HOW TO: Edit a Formula

1. Double-click the formula cell.
 - The *Range Finder* highlights and color codes the cells.
2. Edit the formula in the cell (Figure 2-4).
 - Edit the cell address or type a different operator.
 - Select a cell address and click a different cell to replace the reference.
 - You can make the same edits in the *Formula* bar.
3. Press **Enter**.
 - Click the **Enter** button on the *Formula* bar or press **Ctrl+Enter** to complete a formula.

2-4 Edit a formula in the cell

Setting Mathematical Order of Operations

A formula can have more than one operator, such as a combination of addition and multiplication. Figure 2-5 illustrates two formulas a restaurant might use to calculate a bill for a couple who ordered the same items. The formula in cell B6 lists the additions first and multiplies by 2; the total of $24 is incorrect. The formula in cell B8 is the same except for the parentheses; the correct amount is $42.

2-5 Formulas with multiple operators

Excel follows ***mathematical order of operations***, which is the sequence of arithmetic calculations. The order in which the mathematics in a formula is carried out depends on the operator as well as left-to-right order. The basic sequence is left to right, but multiplication and division are done before addition and subtraction. This concept is also known as ***order of precedence*** or ***math hierarchy***.

You control the order of operations with parentheses. The formula in cell B8 (Figure 2-5) uses parentheses to reorder the calculation. The parentheses group the addition ($4+$10+$4+$3 = 21) and then multiplies by 2 ($21*2 = 42).

In a formula with multiple operators, references enclosed in parentheses are calculated first. If a value with an exponent exists, it is calculated next. Multiplication and division follow and finally addition and subtraction. When two operators have the same precedence, Excel calculates them from left to right.

Mathematical Order of Precedence

Operator	Operation	Order or Precedence
()	**P**arentheses	First
^	**E**xponent	Second
*	**M**ultiplication	Third
/	**D**ivision	Third
+	**A**ddition	Fourth
−	**S**ubtraction	Fourth

Exponents raise a number to a power. The formula **3^3** multiplies 3 * 3 * 3, 27. Use the caret symbol (^) to build a formula with an exponent.

Multiple Operators in a Formula

When different operators are used in a formula, you must determine how the calculation should be completed and if parentheses are necessary to set the proper order. Here are formulas with two operators. Since addition and subtraction are equal in priority, Excel calculates from left to right.

$$2 + 5 - 3 = 4 \qquad 5 + 1 - 3 = 3$$

Below are formulas with two operators with different priority. Excel calculates the multiplication first and then follows left to right order.

$$2 + 5 * 3 = 17 \qquad 2 * 5 + 3 = 13$$

Consider this formula with three different operators. Since multiplication and division are equal priority but higher than addition, the multiplication is first, followed by the division (left to right). The result of those calculations is added to 5.

$$= 2 * 5/2 + 5 = 10$$

▶**HOW TO:** Use Multiple Operators in a formula

1. Type = to start the formula.

2. Type ((left parenthesis) to start the calculation that should have priority.

 - The calculation in parentheses can occur anywhere in the formula.

3. Click the first cell for the calculation to be enclosed in parentheses.

4. Type the arithmetic operator.

5. Click the next cell for the calculation to be enclosed in parentheses.

6. Type) (right parenthesis) to end the calculation with priority (Figure 2-6).

 - You must have matching parentheses.

7. Complete the formula.

8. Press **Enter**.

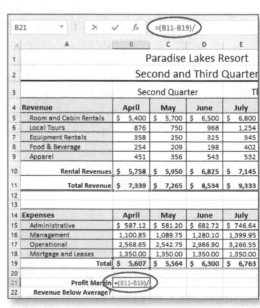

2-6 Set the order of operation with parentheses

Using Absolute, Mixed, Relative, and 3D References

Cell references in a formula are identified in different ways. How a cell reference is identified affects how the formula is adjusted when it is copied.

- A *relative cell reference* is the location of a cell, such as cell **B2**. In column B, the formula is **=B5+B7**, but when copied to column C, it is **=C5+C7**. When you copy a formula with relative references, copied references are updated to the new locations.
- An *absolute cell reference* is indicated with dollar signs as in cell **B2**. When an absolute reference is copied, it does not change. In the formula **=B6−C7**, B6 would not change when copied anywhere in the workbook. C7, on the other hand, would reflect where the copy is located. You can type the dollar signs in an absolute reference, but it is easier to use the **F4 (FN+F4)** function key. When building a formula, enter the cell address and then press **F4 (FN+F4)**.
- A *mixed cell reference* has one relative and one absolute reference. Cell **$B2** is a mixed reference. When it is copied, it always refers to column B, but the row number updates relative to where the copy is located. The formula **=$B5+C$6** has two mixed references. When copied, this formula will always show column B for the first address and row 6 for the second address.
- A *3D cell reference* is a cell located in another worksheet in the same workbook. It can be absolute, mixed, or relative. A 3D reference includes the name of the sheet as in **Sheet2!B2** or **Inventory!$B2**. The sheet name is followed by an exclamation point. When you point and click to build a 3D reference, the sheet name and exclamation point are automatically entered. When the sheet name includes special characters (@, #, &, etc.), the name is enclosed in single quotes as in **'Inventory#'!$B2**. When you type a 3D reference, you must spell the sheet name correctly and include the exclamation point and single quotes.

The following table illustrates each cell reference type:

Cell Reference Types

Cell Reference	Reference Type	Behavior When Copied
B2	Relative	Cell address updates to new location(s).
B2	Absolute	Cell address does not change.
$B2	Mixed	Column does not change; row updates to new location(s).
B$2	Mixed	Row does not change; column updates to new location(s).
Sheet2!B2	3D Relative	Cell address updates to new location(s).

> **MORE INFO**
>
> When used in a reference, the dollar sign ($) and the exclamation point (!) are identifiers. The dollar sign is not treated as a currency symbol, and the exclamation point is not considered punctuation.

Copy a Formula with a Relative Reference

When a formula with relative references is copied, the copied formulas use cell addresses that reflect their locations in the worksheet. In the Paradise Lakes worksheet shown in Figure 2-7, the formula to calculate rental revenue in cell B10 is **=B5+B7**. The formula for cell C10 is **=C5+C7**. The formula in cell B10 can be copied to cells C10:G10 and will automatically adjust for each column.

2-7 Copy a formula with a relative reference

> **HOW TO:** Copy a Formula with a Relative Reference

1. Select the cell with the formula.
 - You can select multiple adjacent cells.
2. Press **Ctrl+C** to copy the formula(s).
 - Click and drag the *Fill* pointer if the copies are adjacent to the original formula(s).
 - Use the **Copy** button on the *Home* tab if you prefer.
3. Select the destination cell or range.
 - Click the first cell in a destination range when pasting multiple cells.
4. Press **Ctrl+V** to paste the formula (see Figure 2-7).
 - The pasted formula reflects its location on the worksheet.
 - Ignore the **Paste Options** button.
 - Use the **Paste** button on the *Home* tab if you prefer.

Build and Copy a Formula with an Absolute Reference

An absolute reference in a formula maintains that address when copied. An example is a worksheet in which expenses are calculated as a percentage of revenue. You type the percentage once in a worksheet cell, use an absolute reference to that cell in the first formula, and copy the formula.

To change a cell address to an absolute reference, press the **F4 (FN+F4)** function key while keying or editing the formula. The first press of the key inserts dollar signs for the row and column reference. Another press of the **F4 (FN+F4)** key makes it a mixed reference, and each press of the key cycles through the next option.

> **HOW TO:** Build and Copy a Formula with an Absolute Reference

1. Click the cell for the formula.
2. Type an equals sign (=) to begin the formula.
3. Click the cell to be referenced in the formula.
4. Press **F4 (FN+F4)**.
 - The reference becomes absolute (Figure 2-8).
5. Complete the formula and press **Enter**.

2-8 Make a reference absolute

6. Select the cell with the formula.

7. Press **Ctrl+C** to copy the formula(s).

 - Click and drag the *Fill* pointer if the copies are adjacent to the original formula.
 - Use the **Copy** button on the *Home* tab if you prefer.

8. Select the destination cell or range.

9. Press **Ctrl+V** to paste the formula.

 - The pasted formula uses the same cell reference as the original.
 - Use the **Paste** button on the *Home* tab if you prefer.
 - Ignore the **Paste Options** button.

> **MORE INFO**
>
> When you type a constant in a formula, such as **=B7*12**, the constant (12) is treated as an absolute value.

Build and Copy a Formula with a Mixed Reference

A mixed cell reference has one relative and one absolute reference in the cell address. Part of the copied formula is unchanged and part is updated. A mixed reference has one dollar sign. You still use the **F4 (FN+F4)** function key, because each press of the key cycles through displaying the dollar signs in different combinations.

▶ **HOW TO: Build and Copy a Formula with a Mixed Reference**

1. Click the cell for the formula.

2. Type an equals sign (=) to begin the formula.

3. Click the cell to be referenced in the formula.

4. Press **F4 (FN+F4)**.

 - The reference is absolute.

5. Press **F4 (FN+F4)** again.

 - The column reference is relative and the row reference is absolute.

6. Press **F4 (FN+F4)** again (Figure 2-9).

 - The row reference is relative and the column reference is absolute.

7. Complete the formula and press **Enter**.

8. Select the formula cell.

9. Press **Ctrl+C** to copy the formula(s).

 - Drag the *Fill* pointer if copies are adjacent to the original formula.
 - You can use the **Copy** button on the *Home* tab.

10. Click the destination cell or range.

11. Press **Ctrl+V** to paste the formula.

 - The pasted formula keeps the absolute part of the reference but updates the relative part.
 - Use the **Paste** button on the *Home* tab if you prefer.

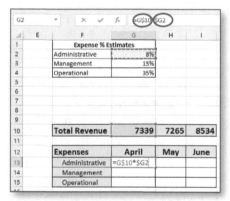

2-9 Formula with a mixed reference

Create a Formula with a 3D Reference

An important feature of an Excel workbook is that you can refer to data on any sheet in a formula. This type of formula is called a *3D reference*, because it uses more than one sheet or surface to calculate a result.

A 3D reference includes the name of the worksheet and can be absolute, mixed, or relative.

Sample 3D References

Cell on Sheet1	Formula on Sheet1	Results
B4	=B3+Sheet2!B3+Sheet3!B3	Adds the values in cell B3 on Sheet1, Sheet2, and Sheet3
B7	=SUM(B4:B6)+Sheet2!A12	Adds the values in cells B4:B6 on Sheet1 to the value in cell A12 on Sheet2
C8	=C7*Sheet2!D4	Multiplies the value in cell C7 by the value in cell D4 on Sheet2
D10	=Sheet2!B2/Sheet3!B2	Divides the value in cell B2 on Sheet2 by the value in cell B2 on Sheet3

MORE INFO

An external reference formula refers to a cell in another workbook. It can be absolute, mixed, or relative. An external reference includes the name of the workbook in square brackets as in **[PLRSales]Sheet!B$2**.

▶HOW TO: Create a Formula with a 3D Reference

1. Click the cell for the formula.
2. Type =.
3. Select the sheet tab with the cell to be used in the formula.
4. Click the required cell.
 - Press **F4 (FN+F4)** to make the reference absolute or mixed as needed.
5. Type the operator (Figure 2-10).
6. Click the next cell for the formula.
 - The next cell can be on the same or another sheet.
7. Type the next operator and complete the formula as needed.
8. Press **Enter** or any completion key.

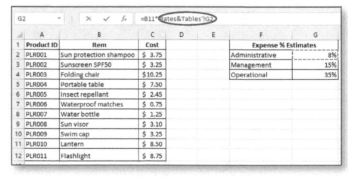

2-10 3D cell reference

Range Names and Formula AutoComplete

A *range name* is a label assigned to a single cell or a group of cells. You can use range names instead of cell references in a formula. Instead of **=B11*10%**, you can name cell B11 as "Revenue" to build the formula **=Revenue*10%**. Descriptive range names help you interpret

a formula. In addition, named cell ranges appear in the *Formula AutoComplete* list for ease in building formulas. A named cell range is an absolute reference in a formula.

You create a range name from the *Name* box or from the *Defined Names* group on the *Formulas* tab. The *Name Manager* command in this group enables you to create, edit, and delete range names. If you alter a range name, Excel automatically updates formulas that use that range name. There is also a command that enables you to name a range and apply it to existing formulas that refer to those cells.

Follow these basic rules for naming a cell range:

- Begin a range name with a letter.
- Use a short, descriptive name.
- Do not use spaces or special characters in a range name.
- Separate words in a range name with an underscore as in "First_Qtr," or use initial caps for each word such as "FirstQtr."
- Do not name a range with a single character such as "N."
- Do not name a range with a cell reference such as "B2."

To use the name in a formula, type the first character of the name when it is required to display the *Formula AutoComplete* list. You may need to type a second character to see the name in a workbook that has many range names. Select the range name in the list and press **Tab**, or double-click the name to enter it in the formula. Range names are automatically substituted in formulas when you select the named cell range in the worksheet while building a formula.

▶**HOW TO:** Name a Range and Use Formula AutoComplete

1. Select the cell or range to be named.
2. Click the **Name** box at the left of the *Formula* bar.
3. Type the name and press **Enter** (Figure 2-11).
4. Click the cell for the formula.
5. Type = to start the formula
6. Type the first one or two letters of the range name.
 - The *Formula AutoComplete* list shows range and function names.
 - The list is alphabetical, and function names are uppercase.
7. Find the range name and double-click it (Figure 2-12).
 - The name is inserted in the formula.
 - You can also click the name in the list to highlight it and press **Tab**.
8. Complete the formula.
9. Press **Enter** when the formula is complete.

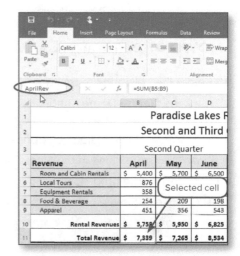

2-11 Name a range in the *Name* box

2-12 Use *Formula AutoComplete* with a range name

In addition to selecting cell ranges to name them, you can use row and column labels to create range names. The *Create from Selection* button on the *Formulas* tab automatically assigns range names based on labels in the top row, the left column, or both.

▶ HOW TO: Create Names from a Selection

1. Select the range including row or column labels (or both) (Figure 2-13).
 - Values and related labels must be adjacent.
2. Click the **Create from Selection** button [*Formulas* tab, *Defined Names* group].
 - The *Create Names from Selection* dialog box opens.
3. Select the **Top row** or **Left column** box.
 - You can choose both options if appropriate for the data.
 - There are options for the bottom row and right column.
4. Click **OK**.
5. Click the **Name box** arrow on the *Formula* bar.
 - All range names are listed.

2-13 *Create Names from Selection* dialog box

The **Define Name** button [*Formulas* tab, *Defined Names* group] opens the *New Name* dialog box. Here you can type the name, enter a comment, select the cells, and specify a *scope*. The scope determines if the range applies to a particular sheet or to the entire workbook. By default, a range name applies to the workbook. If you use the name "JanSales" on Sheet1, you cannot use it again on Sheet2, unless you scope each name to a particular sheet. When you scope names to a worksheet, you can use the name multiple times in the workbook.

▶ HOW TO: Define and Scope a Range Name

1. Select the cell range to be named.
2. Click the **Define Name** button [*Formulas* tab, *Defined Names* group].
 - The *New Name* dialog box opens.
3. Type the range name in the *Name* box.
4. Click the **Scope** drop-down list (Figure 2-14).
 - Choose the name of a worksheet as desired.
5. Select or edit the *Refers to* entry.
 - The selected cell range address displays.
 - If no cells are selected, you can type or select the range address.
6. Click **OK**.

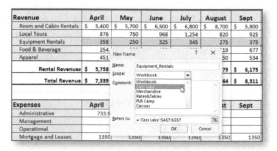

2-14 *New Name* dialog box

The *Use in Formula* button [*Formulas* tab, *Defined Names* group] displays a list of range names for insertion in a formula. You can do the same from the *Paste Name* dialog box, opened when you press the **F3 (FN+F3)** function key.

▶ HOW TO: Paste a Range Name in a Formula and Paste a List

1. Click the formula cell and type =.
2. Press **F3 (FN+F3)** to open the *Paste Name* dialog box.
 - Range names are listed in alphabetical order.

3. Find the range name and double-click it (Figure 2-15).
 - You can also highlight the range name and press **Enter** or click **OK**.
 - The range name displays in the formula.
 - The worksheet displays the highlighted range.
4. Complete the formula and press **Enter**.
5. Click a blank cell in an unused area of the worksheet.
 - You can select a cell on another worksheet.
6. Click the **Use in Formula** button [*Formulas* tab, *Defined Names* group].
7. Select **Paste Names**.
 - The *Paste Name* dialog box opens.
8. Click **Paste List**.
 - A list of range names and cell references is pasted.
 - You can edit and format these cells.

2-15 Choose a range name for the formula

Using Formula Auditing Tools

Formula auditing is the process of reviewing formulas for accuracy. Excel automatically audits formulas as you enter them and when you open a workbook based on its error checking rules [*File* tab, *Options*, *Formulas* pane]. Excel recognizes many errors, but not all of them. For example, if you type a formula that multiplies the values in two cells when it should add the values, you must find that error on your own. There are also circumstances when Excel identifies an error, but the formula is correct.

> **MORE INFO**
>
> You can set whether automatic error checking is enabled and you can select which rules are used in the *Excel Options* dialog box.

When Excel finds an error in a formula, it displays a small green error triangle in the top left corner of the cell. Click the cell to see the *Trace Error* button and point to the button to see a *ScreenTip* about the error. The *Trace Error* button has a drop-down list with options for dealing with the error.

▶ HOW TO: Trace an Error

1. Click the cell with the triangle error.
 - The *Trace Error* button appears.
2. Point to the **Trace Error** button to display a *ScreenTip*.
3. Click the **Trace Error** drop-down list (Figure 2-16).
 - Options for handling the error are listed.
4. Choose an option for the error.
 - The options depend on the type of error.
 - Select **Ignore Error** if the formula is correct.

2-16 *Trace Error* button and its drop-down list

In addition to the green triangle error, Excel functions can result in a standard error message in the cell. For example, if you create a division formula that divides by a blank cell, the result is *#DIV/0!* When you click the **Trace Error** button, it is identified as a division by zero error. Excel error messages occur for a syntax error, such as spelling a function name incorrectly, using an incorrect operator or symbol, having the wrong number of arguments, and so on. A standard error message starts with the number sign (#) and ends with an exclamation point (!).

 MORE INFO

From the *Go to Special* dialog box [**Find & Select** button, *Home* tab, *Editing* group], you can highlight cells with formula errors, blank cells, and cells with precedents and dependents. This command helps identify potential problems in a workbook.

The Formula Auditing Group

The *Formula Auditing* group on the *Formulas* tab has tools to check formulas for logic, consistency, and accuracy. These commands enable you to examine what contributes to a formula and analyze if the formula is correct. The tools are helpful but they do require that you correct the problem.

Button	Description
Trace Precedents	Displays lines with arrows to identify all cells referenced in the formula in the active cell
Trace Dependents	Displays lines with arrows to all cells that use the active cell directly or indirectly in a formula
Remove Arrows	Removes all lines and arrows from the *Trace Precedents* or *Trace Dependents* buttons
Show Formulas	Displays formulas in the cells
Error Checking	Checks data against the error rules in Excel Options
Evaluate Formula	Steps through each part of a formula and displays an outcome for each part so that an error can be isolated
Watch Window	Opens a floating window that displays selected cells and values for monitoring

Trace Precedents and Dependents

A **precedent** is a cell that contributes to the formula results. Excel displays lines from the formula cell to each precedent cell for an easy way to audit your formula. A **dependent** is a cell that is affected by the active cell. Excel displays lines from the active cell to each cell that depends on the value in that cell. When the lines and arrows are blue, the precedents or dependents do not have an error. If the lines and arrows are red, the precedents or dependents have some type of recognized error. If a precedent or dependent cell is located on a different worksheet, a black line and arrow point to a small worksheet icon, but this does not identify the actual error cell address.

▶ **HOW TO:** Use Formula Auditing Tools

1. Click the **Show Formulas** button [*Formulas* tab, *Formula Auditing* group].
 - Each formula displays in its cell.
 - Show or hide formulas by pressing **Ctrl+~**.
2. Select the formula cell.

3. Click the **Trace Precedents** button [*Formulas* tab, *Formula Auditing* group].

- Lines and arrows identify cells that contribute to the formula results (Figure 2-17).
- You can trace precedents and dependents with formulas shown or hidden.

4. Click the **Remove Arrows** button [*Formulas* tab, *Formula Auditing* group].

- Clicking the button removes all arrows.
- Click the **Remove Arrows** drop-down list to specify the type of arrow to remove.

5. Click a cell that is referenced in a formula.

- The cell need not have a formula.

6. Click the **Trace Dependents** button [*Formulas* tab, *Formula Auditing* group].

- Lines and arrows trace to cells that are affected by the active cell.

7. Click the **Remove Arrows** button [*Formulas* tab, *Formula Auditing* group].

8. Click the **Show Formulas** button [*Formulas* tab, *Formula Auditing* group].

- Formulas are hidden.
- Show or hide formulas by pressing **Ctrl+~**.

2-17 *Trace Precedents* arrows with formulas shown

> **MORE INFO**
>
> In a complex worksheet with sophisticated formulas, click the **Trace Precedents** button [*Formulas* tab, *Formula Auditing* group] once to trace the first layer of precedents. Then click the button again to trace the precedents of the precedents.

The Formula Correction Message Window

As you complete a formula with a minor error (e.g. typing "5c" as a cell address), Excel displays a message box with information about the error (Figure 2-18). For many of these types of errors, review the suggested correction and select **Yes**. For an error that Excel finds but cannot offer a solution, a message box opens with suggestions but you need to solve the problem on your own.

2-18 Formula correction message window

Circular Reference

A *circular reference* is an error that occurs when a formula includes the cell address of the formula. For example, if the formula in cell **B10** is **=B5+B10**, the reference is circular. When you try to complete such a formula, a message box opens as shown in Figure 2-19. The *Status* bar displays the location of circular references, but Excel does not correct this type of error. You can keep a circular reference in a worksheet, but the formula results are inaccurate.

2-19 Circular reference and its message window

PAUSE & PRACTICE: EXCEL 2-1

For this project, you build formulas in a Paradise Lakes Resort worksheet. You use mixed and absolute references, a 3D reference, and set order of precedence. You also name cell ranges and use auditing tools.

File Needed: *ParadiseLakes-02.xlsx* [*Student data files are available in the* Library *of your SIMnet account.*]
Completed Project File Name: ***[your initials] PP E2-1.xlsx***

1. Open the ***ParadiseLakes-02.xlsx*** workbook from your student data files.

2. Save the workbook as [your initials] PP E2-1. (If the workbook opens in *Protected View*, click **Enable Editing**.)

3. Enter and copy an addition formula.
 a. Click cell **B10** on the **Cass Lake** sheet.
 b. Type = to start a formula.
 c. Click cell **B5** to insert the first rental item in the formula.
 d. Type + as the mathematical operator.
 e. Click cell **B7** to add the second rental item. The formula is **=B5+B7** (Figure 2-20).
 f. Press **Enter** or click the **Enter** button on the *Formula* bar. The result is $5,758.
 g. Select cell **B10** and point to the *Fill* handle.
 h. Drag the *Fill* pointer to copy the formula to cells **C10:H10**. Ignore the *Auto Fill Options* button.

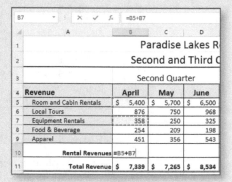

2-20 Point and click to build a formula

4. Create and copy a 3D formula with absolute cell references.
 a. Select cell **B15**. Administrative expense is calculated by multiplying the total revenue for the month by a set percentage.
 b. Type = to start the formula.
 c. Click cell **B11**, the total revenue for April.
 d. Type * to indicate multiplication.
 e. Click the **Rates&Tables** sheet tab. The sheet name is inserted in the *Formula* bar with single quotes and an exclamation point.
 f. Click cell **G2**, the percentage for administrative expenses. The cell address is added to the formula.
 g. Press **F4 (FN+F4)** to make the reference absolute (Figure 2-21).
 h. Press **Enter**. The formula is complete and the *Cass Lake* sheet is active.
 i. Select cell **B15** and drag the *Fill* pointer to copy the formula to cells **C15:G15**. The reference to cell G2 does not change, but the reference to cell B11 does (Figure 2-22).

2-21 Absolute 3D reference in the formula

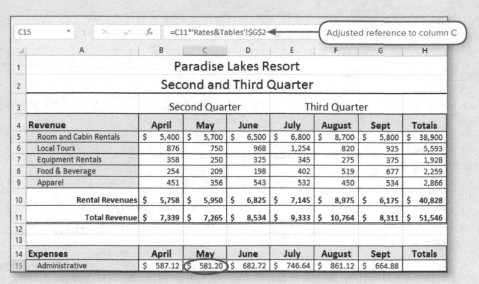

| C15 | | fx | =C11*'Rates&Tables'!G2 ← | | Adjusted reference to column C | | |

	A	B	C	D	E	F	G	H
1			Paradise Lakes Resort					
2			Second and Third Quarter					
3				Second Quarter		Third Quarter		
4	**Revenue**	**April**	**May**	**June**	**July**	**August**	**Sept**	**Totals**
5	Room and Cabin Rentals	$ 5,400	$ 5,700	$ 6,500	$ 6,800	$ 8,700	$ 5,800	$ 38,900
6	Local Tours	876	750	968	1,254	820	925	5,593
7	Equipment Rentals	358	250	325	345	275	375	1,928
8	Food & Beverage	254	209	198	402	519	677	2,259
9	Apparel	451	356	543	532	450	534	2,866
10	Rental Revenues	$ 5,758	$ 5,950	$ 6,825	$ 7,145	$ 8,975	$ 6,175	$ 40,828
11	Total Revenue	$ 7,339	$ 7,265	$ 8,534	$ 9,333	$ 10,764	$ 8,311	$ 51,546
12								
13								
14	**Expenses**	**April**	**May**	**June**	**July**	**August**	**Sept**	**Totals**
15	Administrative	$ 587.12	$ 581.20	$ 682.72	$ 746.64	$ 861.12	$ 664.88	

2-22 Copied formula with absolute reference

5. Create and copy a 3D formula with mixed references.
 a. Select cell **B16**. Management expense is calculated by multiplying the total revenue for the month by the set percentage.
 b. Type = to start the formula.
 c. Click cell **B11**, the total revenue for April.
 d. Press **F4 (FN+F4)** to make the reference absolute (B11).
 e. Press **F4 (FN+F4)** to make the reference mixed with the row reference absolute (B$11). When the formula is copied, the row will not change but the column reference will (Figure 2-23).
 f. Type * for multiplication.
 g. Click the **Rates&Tables** sheet tab. The sheet name is inserted in the *Formula* bar.
 h. Click cell **G3**, the percentage for management expenses.
 i. Press **F4 (FN+F4)** to make the reference absolute (G3).
 j. Press **F4 (FN+F4)** to make the reference mixed with the row reference absolute (G$3).
 k. Press **F4 (FN+F4)** to make the reference mixed with the column reference absolute ($G3) (Figure 2-24). When the formula is copied, the column will not change but the row will.

| B11 | | fx | =B$11 | |

	A	B	C	D
1			Paradise Lakes R	
2			Second and Third (	
3			Second Quarter	
4	**Revenue**	**April**	**May**	**June**
5	Room and Cabin Rentals	$ 5,400	$ 5,700	$ 6,500
6	Local Tours	876	750	968
7	Equipment Rentals	358	250	325
8	Food & Beverage	254	209	198
9	Apparel	451	356	543
10	Rental Revenues	$ 5,758	$ 5,950	$ 6,825
11	Total Revenue	$ 7,339	$ 7,265	$ 8,534
12				
13				
14	**Expenses**	**April**	**May**	**June**
15	Administrative	$ 587.12	$ 581.20	$ 682.72
16	Management	=B$11		

2-23 Mixed cell reference

| G3 | | fx | =B$11*'Rates&Table'!$G3 | | | | |

	A	B	C	D	E	F	G
1	**Product ID**	**Item**	**Cost**			**Expense % Estimates**	
2	PLR001	Sun protection shampoo	$ 3.75			Administrative	8%
3	PLR002	Sunscreen SPF50	$ 3.25			Management	15%
4	PLR003	Folding chair	$10.25			Operational	35%
5	PLR004	Portable table	$ 7.50				

2-24 Absolute reference to column G

l. Press **Enter**. The formula is complete and the *Cass Lake* sheet is active.

m. Select cell **B16** and drag its *Fill* pointer to cell **B17**.

n. Keep cells **B16:B17** selected and drag the *Fill* pointer for cell B17 to copy the formulas to cells **C16:G17**.

6. Use *Formula Auditing* tools.

a. Click cell **D17** to view how the mixed reference formula has been copied.

b. Click the **Trace Precedents** button [*Formulas* tab, *Formula Auditing* group]. The formula refers to cell D11 on the **Cass Lake** sheet and to the **Tables&Rates** sheet.

c. Click cell **E16** and click the **Trace Precedents** button. The formula refers to cell E11 on the **Cass Lake** sheet and to the **Tables&Rates** sheet (Figure 2-25).

d. Click the **Remove Arrows** button [*Formulas* tab, *Formula Auditing* group].

e. Click the **Show Formulas** [*Formulas* tab, *Formula Auditing* group] to see all formulas. This view does not display number formatting (Figure 2-26).

2-25 Formula precedents

2-26 Formulas displayed in worksheet

f. Click the **Show Formulas** [*Formulas* tab, *Formula Auditing* group] to hide the formulas.

7. Edit a formula and correct an error.
 a. Select cells **H15:H18** and click the **AutoSum** button [*Home* tab, *Editing* group]. The *SUM* function displays in each cell.
 b. Widen column **H** to display all data.
 c. Double-click cell **H16** to start *Edit* mode.
 d. Edit the cell range to **B15:G16** and press **Enter** to create a deliberate error. The green error triangle appears in the upper right corner of the cell.
 e. Click cell **H16** to display the **Trace Error** button and then click the button. This formula is now inconsistent with others in the column (Figure 2-27).

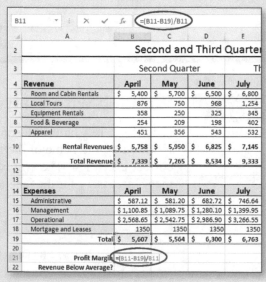

2-27 *Trace Error* button and options

 f. Select **Copy Formula from Above** to correct the error.
 g. Click cell **H16** and click the **Trace Precedents** button [*Formulas* tab, *Formula Auditing* group]. The formula refers to the correct cells in row 16.
 h. Click the **Remove Arrows** button [*Formulas* tab, *Formula Auditing* group].

8. Set mathematical order of operations.
 a. Select cell **B21**. Profit margin, as a percentage, is revenue minus expenses divided by revenue. The formula is **=(B11−B19)/B11**; the parentheses are necessary so that the subtraction is done before the division.
 b. Type **=(** to start the formula and insert the opening parenthesis.
 c. Click cell **B11**, the total revenue for April.
 d. Type **−** for subtraction.
 e. Click cell **B19**, total expenses for April.
 f. Type **)** to set the precedence with the closing parenthesis.
 g. Type **/** for division and click cell **B11** (Figure 2-28).
 h. Press **Enter**. The result is formatted as *Accounting Number* format to match the source cells and displays a zero due to rounding.

2-28 Set arithmetic order

i. Click cell **B21** and click the **Percent Style** button [*Home* tab, *Number* group].

j. Copy the formula in cell **B21** to cells **C21:G21**.

9. Name a cell range.

a. Select cell **H11** and click the **Name** box.

b. Type TotalRevenue in the *Name* box and press **Enter**.

c. Select cells **B11:G11**.

d. Click the **Define Name** button [*Formulas* tab, *Defined Names* group].

e. Type Monthly_Rev in the *Name* box and click **OK** (Figure 2-29).

f. Click cell **A1**.

g. Click the **Name box** arrow and choose **TotalRevenue**. Cell H11 is selected.

h. Click the **Name box** arrow and choose **Monthly_Rev**. Cells B11:G11 are selected.

10. Format cells **B16:H18** as **Comma Style**. Decrease the decimal two times.

11. Select cells **B15:H15** and decrease the decimal two times.

12. Press **Ctrl+Home**. Save and close the workbook (Figure 2-30).

New Name dialog box:

Name: Monthly_Rev
Scope: Workbook
Comment:
Refers to: ='Cass Lake'!B11:G11
OK Cancel

2-29 Use the *New Name* dialog box to name a range

	Paradise Lakes Resort						
	Second and Third Quarter						
	Second Quarter			Third Quarter			
Revenue	April	May	June	July	August	Sept	Totals
Room and Cabin Rentals	$ 5,400	$ 5,700	$ 6,500	$ 6,800	$ 8,700	$ 5,800	$ 38,900
Local Tours	876	750	968	1,254	820	925	5,593
Equipment Rentals	358	250	325	345	275	375	1,928
Food & Beverage	254	209	198	402	519	677	2,259
Apparel	451	356	543	532	450	534	2,866
Rental Revenues	$ 5,758	$ 5,950	$ 6,825	$ 7,145	$ 8,975	$ 6,175	$ 40,828
Total Revenue	$ 7,339	$ 7,265	$ 8,534	$ 9,333	$ 10,764	$ 8,311	$ 51,546
Expenses	April	May	June	July	August	Sept	Totals
Administrative	$ 587	$ 581	$ 683	$ 747	$ 861	$ 665	$ 4,124
Management	1,101	1,090	1,280	1,400	1,615	1,247	$ 7,732
Operational	2,569	2,543	2,987	3,267	3,767	2,909	$ 18,041
Mortgage and Leases	1350	1350	1350	1350	1350	1350	$ 8,100
Total	$ 5,607	$ 5,564	$ 6,300	$ 6,763	$ 7,593	$ 6,170	$ 37,997
Profit Margin	24%	23%	26%	28%	29%	26%	
Revenue Below Average?							

2-30 PP E2-1 completed

 SLO 2.5

Working with Statistical and Date & Time Functions

A function is a built-in formula. Like a formula, a function starts with an equals sign (=) followed by the name of the function. Each function has its own syntax, its set of rules for correct execution. The syntax includes arguments, which are cell references and other elements necessary for the function to work properly.

> **MORE INFO**
>
> A formula such as =**B2+B3−B6** is usually not called a function since it has no function name.

Excel functions are grouped into categories on the *Formulas* command tab in the *Function Library* group. This group also has an *Insert Function* button which opens the *Insert Function*

dialog box. From this dialog box, you can display an alphabetical list of all functions, a list by category, or a recently used list. You can also search for a function by name in this dialog box.

The *Statistical* function category includes calculations that determine an average, a maximum, a minimum, and a count. These common functions are options on the *AutoSum* button on the *Home* tab. The *Formulas* tab also has an *AutoSum* button with the same options.

AVERAGE Function

The *AVERAGE* function calculates the arithmetic **mean** of a range of cells. The mean is determined by adding all the values and dividing the result by the number of values. The *AVERAGE* function ignores empty cells or cells that include labels. When calculating an average, do not include total values in the range to be averaged.

The *AVERAGE* function has one argument, *numberN*. A number argument can be a range such as B11:G11. You can average up to 255 numbers (or ranges). The proper syntax for an *AVERAGE* function is:

=AVERAGE(number1, [number2], [number3], ...)

The *Number1* argument is required and others are optional.

When you choose a function from the *AutoSum* button, you will see the function name, an assumed range within parentheses, and an **Argument ScreenTip** below the cell that displays the syntax. When you choose to type a function, the *ScreenTip* shows the next argument in bold type as a guideline.

▶**HOW TO:** Use the AVERAGE Function

1. Click the cell for the function.
2. Click the **AutoSum** button arrow [*Formulas* tab, *Function Library* group].
3. Select **Average**.
 - The function and an assumed argument range display in the *Formula* bar and in the cell.
4. Select the correct cell range (Figure 2-31).
 - You can type cell addresses rather than selecting cells.
 - When the selected cells have been named, the range name is substituted in the formula.

B11 fx =AVERAGE(Monthly_Rev)

	April	May	June	July	August	Sept	Totals
Paradise Lakes Resort							
Second and Third Quarter							
	Second Quarter			Third Quarter			
Revenue	April	May	June	July	August	Sept	Totals
Room and Cabin Rentals	$ 5,400	$ 5,700	$ 6,500	$ 6,800	$ 8,700	$ 5,800	$ 38,900
Local Tours	876	750	968	1,254	820	925	5,593
Equipment Rentals	358	250	325	345	275	375	1,928
Food & Beverage	254	209	198	402	519	677	2,259
Apparel	451	356	543	532	450	534	2,866
Rental Revenues	$ 5,758	$ 5,950	$ 6,825	$ 7,145	$ 8,975	$ 6,175	$ 40,828
Total Revenue	$ 7,339	$ 7,265	$ 8,534	$ 9,333	$ 10,764	$ 8,311	$ 51,546

Expenses	April	May	June	July	August	Sept	Totals
Administrative	$ 587	$ 581	$ 683	$ 747	$ 861	$ 665	$ 4,124
Management	1,101	1,090	1,280	1,400	1,615	1,247	7,782
Operational	2,569	2,543	2,987	3,267	3,767	2,909	18,041
Mortgage and Leases	1350	1350	1350	1350	1350	1350	8,100
Total	$ 5,607	$ 5,564	$ 6,300	$ 6,763	$ 7,593	$ 6,170	$ 37,997

Total Revenue	
Average Monthly Revenue	=AVERAGE(Monthly_Rev)
Maximum Cabin Revenue	AVERAGE(number1, [number2], ...)
Minimum Tour Revenue	
Number of Months	6.00

Range name substituted for selected cells

2-31 *AVERAGE* function

5. Press **Enter**.
 - You can use any completion key.

COUNT Functions

There are five functions in the *Statistical* category that are *COUNT* functions which tally the number of items in a range. The basic *COUNT* function is an option on the *AutoSum* button, but it appears in the list as *Count Numbers*. The *COUNT* function includes only cells with values in its result.

From the *Statistical* group, you can choose *COUNTA* which includes cells with values and labels. There is a *COUNTBLANK* function that counts cells that are empty. The following table describes the *Statistical COUNT* functions.

Statistical COUNT Functions

Count Functions	Description	Example Syntax
COUNT (Count Numbers)	Counts the cells in a range that contain values	=COUNT(A1:A15)
COUNTA	Counts the cells in a range that contain any data type	=COUNTA(A1:A15)
COUNTBLANK	Counts empty cells in a range	=COUNTBLANK(A1:A15)
COUNTIF	Counts the cells in a range that meet the criteria argument	=COUNTIF(A1:A15, "Services")
COUNTIFS	Counts the cells in one or more criteria ranges that meet respective criteria arguments	=COUNTIFS(B2:B5, "=A", C2:C5, "=21")

The *COUNT* function has one argument, *valueN*. You can count up to 255 cells or ranges. The proper syntax for a *COUNT* function is:

=COUNT(value1, [value2], [value3], . . .)

The *Value1* argument is required.

▶**HOW TO:** Use the COUNT Function

1. Click the cell for the function.
2. Click the **AutoSum** button arrow [*Formulas* tab, *Function Library* group].
3. Select **Count Numbers**.
 - The *COUNT* function is inserted with an assumed range.
 - The function appears in the cell and in the *Formula* bar (Figure 2-32).

B5	× ✓ fx	=COUNT(B5:G5)											
	A	B	C	D	E	F	G	H	I	J	K	L	M

	A	B	C	D	E	F	G	H
1				Paradise Lakes Resort				
2				Second and Third Quarter				
3			Second Quarter			Third Quarter		
4	Revenue	April	May	June	July	August	Sept	Totals
5	Room and Cabin Rentals	$ 5,400	$ 5,700	$ 6,500	$ 6,800	$ 8,700	$ 5,800	$ 38,900
6	Local Tours	876	750	968	1,254	820	925	5,593
7	Equipment Rentals	358	250	325	345	275	375	1,928
8	Food & Beverage	254	209	198	402	519	677	2,259
9	Apparel	451	356	543	532	450	534	2,866
10	Rental Revenues	$ 5,758	$ 5,950	$ 6,825	$ 7,145	$ 8,975	$ 6,175	$ 40,828
11	Total Revenue	$ 7,339	$ 7,265	$ 8,534	$ 9,333	$ 10,764	$ 8,311	$ 51,546
12								
13								
14	Expenses	April	May	June	July	August	Sept	Totals
15	Administrative	$ 587	$ 581	$ 683	$ 747	$ 861	$ 665	$ 4,124
16	Management	1,101	1,090	1,280	1,400	1,615	1,247	7,732
17	Operational	2,569	2,543	2,987	3,267	3,767	2,909	18,041
18	Mortgage and Leases	1350	1350	1350	1350	1350	1350	8,100
19	Total	$ 5,607	$ 5,564	$ 6,300	$ 6,763	$ 7,593	$ 6,170	$ 37,997
20								

	J	K
Total Revenue		
Average Monthly Revenue		
Maximum Cabin Revenue	$ 6,483.33	
Minimum Tour Revenue		
Number of Months	=COUNT(B5:G5)	
	COUNT(value1, [value2], …)	

2-32 *COUNT* function

4. Select the correct cell range.
 - You can type cell addresses rather than selecting cells.
5. Press **Enter** or any completion key.

> **MORE INFO**
>
> If you use *COUNT* with a range of labels, the result is zero (0).

MAX and MIN Functions

The *MAX* function finds the largest value in a range, and the *MIN* function finds the smallest value. Both functions are options on the *AutoSum* button. Each has one argument, the cells to be evaluated.

The proper syntax for *MAX* and *MIN* functions is:

=MAX(number1, [number2], [number3], . . .)
=MIN(number1, [number2], [number3], . . .)

In many worksheets, an argument range is a group of adjacent cells such as B11:G11, but the cells need not be next to each other. You can select individual cells anywhere in the worksheet for an argument, and they are separated by commas as in =MAX(B11, B15, B18).

> **HOW TO:** Use the MAX Function with Nonadjacent Cells

1. Click the cell for the function.
2. Click the **AutoSum** button arrow [*Formulas* tab, *Function Library* group].

3. Select **Max** (Figure 2-33).

- The function displays in the cell and in the *Formula* bar.
- The *Argument ScreenTip* shows the next argument in bold **number1**.

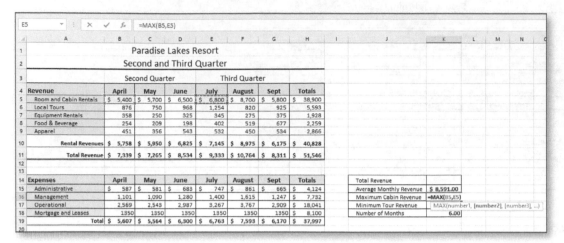

2-33 Use nonadjacent cells for *MAX*

4. Click the first cell to be evaluated.

5. Type , (a comma) to separate the arguments.

- The *Argument ScreenTip* shows the next argument in bold **number2**.

6. Click the next cell to be evaluated.

7. Type a comma , to add additional cells to the argument.

8. Press **Enter** when all the cells are listed.

AutoCalculate

The *AutoCalculate* feature is located on the right side of the *Status* bar where statistical and mathematical results are displayed for selected cells. The calculations are *Average*, *Count*, *Numerical Count*, *Maximum*, *Minimum*, and *Sum*. The *Count* calculation is the equivalent of *COUNTA*, and *Numerical Count* is the same as *COUNT*. AutoCalculate allows you to see results without inserting a function in the worksheet. You can see and change which calculations are visible by right-clicking that area of the *Status* bar to open the *Customize Status Bar* menu.

▶ HOW TO: Use AutoCalculate

1. Select the cell range or individual cells in the worksheet.

2. View the results on the *Status* bar (Figure 2-34).

- Selected options appear on the *Status* bar when appropriate; there is no *SUM* when you select labels.

3. Right-click the right side of the *Status* bar.

- The *Customize Status Bar* menu opens.
- If a function has a check mark to the left, it is active.

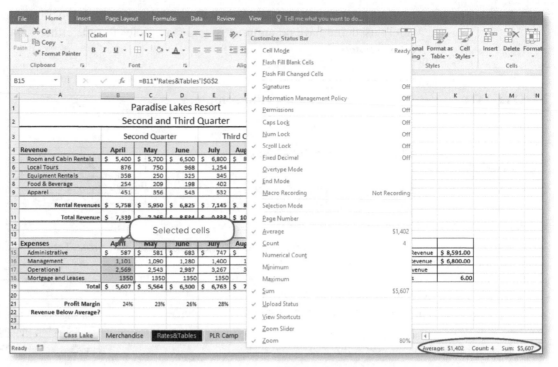

2-34 *AutoCalculate* results and other *Status* bar options

4. Select a calculation name to activate it and show it on the *Status* bar.
5. Select a calculation name with a check mark to hide it from the *Status* bar.

TODAY and NOW Functions

The *Date & Time* category has many functions for date and time arithmetic, for converting dates and times to values, and for controlling how dates and times are displayed.

The *TODAY* function inserts the current date in the cell and updates each time the workbook is opened. It uses the computer's clock, and the syntax is =TODAY(). The parentheses are necessary, but there are no arguments. The *NOW* function uses the syntax =NOW() and has no arguments. These two functions are ***volatile*** which means that the result depends on the current date, time, and computer.

After either function is inserted, you can format results to show both the date and the time. The *Format Cells* dialog box has a *Date* category and a *Time* category with many preset styles. There are also two date formats available from the *Number Format* list [*Home* tab, *Number* group], *Short Date* and *Long Date*.

In its handling of dates, Excel treats each date as a ***serial number***, a unique value assigned to each date. Excel starts by setting January 1, 1900, as number 1; January 2, 1900 is number 2, and so on. January 1, 2018, is number 43101. You can see the serial number for any date by applying the *General* format to the cell.

>
>
> MORE INFO
>
> On the *Advanced* pane in the *Excel Options* dialog box [*File* tab], you can set a 1904 date system which matches the date system in the Macintosh operating system.

You can select **TODAY** or **NOW** from the *Date & Time* function category. Since they are widely used and have no arguments, you may prefer to type either with the help of *Formula AutoComplete*.

▶HOW TO: Insert TODAY with Formula AutoComplete

1. Click the cell.

2. Type **=to** to display a filtered *Formula AutoComplete* list (Figure 2-35).

 - The list appears as soon as you type a character.
 - Each additional character further limits the list of names.

2-35 Formula AutoComplete list

3. Point to the function name and double-click.

 - Instead of double-clicking the name, point and click once to select it and press **Tab**.
 - The name and parentheses are inserted.
 - If you accidentally press **Enter** to select a name and see an error in the cell, delete the cell contents and try again.

4. Press **Enter** to complete the function (Figure 2-36).

 - Excel supplies the closing parenthesis.
 - The current date is shown in the cell.
 - The *TODAY* function has no arguments.

2-36 TODAY inserted in cell

PAUSE & PRACTICE: EXCEL 2-2

For this project, you open your Pause & Practice file and insert Excel functions to complete more of the worksheet. You insert functions from the *AutoSum* button and by typing. You also use *AutoCalculate* to check results.

File Needed: *[your initials] PP E2-1.xlsx*
Completed Project File Name: *[your initials] PP E2-2.xlsx*

1. Open the *[your initials] PP E2-1.xlsx* workbook completed in *Pause & Practice 2-1* and save it as [your initials] PP E2-2.

2. Enter functions using the *AutoSum* button.
 a. Click the **Cass Lake** worksheet tab and select cell **K14**.
 b. Click the **AutoSum** arrow button [*Formulas* tab, *Function Library* group].
 c. Choose **Sum**. The function name and parentheses are inserted, and a *Function ScreenTip* is visible.
 d. Select cells **B11:G11**. The range is highlighted on screen, and Excel has substituted the defined name that you set in *Pause & Practice 2-1* (Figure 2-37).
 e. Press **Enter**.
 f. Select cell **K15** and click the **AutoSum** arrow button [*Formulas* tab, *Function Library* group].
 g. Choose **Average**. The name and parentheses are inserted.
 h. Select cells **B11:G11**. The range is highlighted, but the range name is substituted.
 i. Press **Enter**. Average sales are $8,591.

B11 | ✕ ✓ fx | =SUM(Monthly_Rev)

	A	B	C	D	E	F	G	H	I	J	K	L	M
1	Paradise Lakes Resort												
2	Second and Third Quarter												
3			Second Quarter			Third Quarter							
4	Revenue	April	May	June	July	August	Sept	Totals					
5	Room and Cabin Rentals	$ 5,400	$ 5,700	$ 6,500	$ 6,800	$ 8,700	$ 5,800	$ 58,900					
6	Local Tours	876	750	968	1,254	820	925	5,593					
7	Equipment Rentals	358	250	325	345	275	375	1,928					
8	Food & Beverage	254	209	198	402	519	677	2,259					
9	Apparel	451	356	548	532	450	534	2,866					
10	Rental Revenues	$ 5,758	$ 5,950	$ 6,825	$ 7,145	$ 8,975	$ 6,175	$ 40,828					
11	Total Revenue	$ 7,339	$ 7,265	$ 8,534	$ 9,333	$ 10,764	$ 8,311	$ 51,546					
12													
13													
14	Expenses	April	May	June	July	August	Sept	Totals		Total Revenue	=SUM(Monthly_Rev)		
15	Administrative	$ 587	$ 581	$ 683	$ 747	$ 861	$ 665	$ 4,124		Average Monthly Revenue	SUM(number1, [number2], ...)		
16	Management	1,101	1,090	1,280	1,400	1,615	1,247	7,732		Maximum Cabin Revenue			
17	Operational	2,569	2,543	2,987	3,267	3,767	2,909	18,041		Minimum Tour Revenue			
18	Mortgage and Leases	1350	1350	1350	1350	1350	1350	8,100		Number of Months			
19	Total	$ 5,607	$ 5,564	$ 6,300	$ 6,763	$ 7,593	$ 6,170	$ 37,997					
20													

2-37 Range name substituted in formula

3. Enter the *MAX* function by typing.
 a. Select cell **K16**.
 b. Type **=ma** to display the *Formula AutoComplete* list. You only need type as many characters as necessary to see the function name.
 c. Point to **MAX** in the list, click to select it, and press **Tab** (Figure 2-38).
 d. Select cells **B5:G5** for the *number1* argument. This range is not named.
 e. Press **Enter**. Excel supplies the closing parenthesis.

2-38 Choose *MAX* from *Formula AutoComplete* list

4. Copy and edit a function.
 a. Select cell **K16** and use the *Fill* pointer to copy the formula to cell **K17**.
 b. Double-click cell **K17**. Note that the argument cell range was updated because it was a relative reference.
 c. Replace the function name *MAX* in the cell with **min** (Figure 2-39).
 d. Press **Enter**. The minimum value is $750.

2-39 Edit a function name

5. Type the *COUNT* function.
 a. Select cell **K18**.
 b. Type **=cou** to display the *Formula AutoComplete* list.
 c. Double-click **COUNTA** in the list. This function counts cells with labels and values. The *ScreenTip* shows the first argument as *value1*.
 d. Select cells **B4:G4** to count the months. The formula is =COUNTA(B4:G4).
 e. Press **Enter**. The final parenthesis is supplied, and the result is 6.00.
 f. Select cells **K14:K18** and decrease the decimal two times.
 g. Apply the **General** format to cell **K18** [*Home* tab, *Number* group, *Number Format* drop-down list].

6. Check results with *AutoCalculate*.
 a. Select cells **B11:G11**.
 b. Right-click near the middle of the *Status* bar to display the options.
 c. Verify that **Average, Count,** and **Sum** are checked.
 d. Left-click anywhere in the *Status* bar to close the menu.
 e. Compare the values shown in the *Status* bar with the results in column K.

7. Insert the *TODAY* function.
 a. Select cell **A25**.
 b. Click the **Formulas** tab.
 c. Click the **Date & Time** button [*Function Library* group].
 d. Find and select **TODAY**. A *Function Arguments* dialog box notes that this function does not have any arguments and that it is volatile (Figure 2-40).
 e. Click **OK**. The current date is inserted.
 f. Press **Ctrl+Home**.

9. Save and close the workbook (Figure 2-41).

2-40 *Function Arguments* dialog box for *TODAY*

2-41 PP E2-2 completed

Working with Financial, Logical, and Lookup Functions

The *Financial* category includes functions that determine loan payments, the amount of interest earned, the rate of return on an investment, and more. Most of the functions in the *Logical* category display TRUE or FALSE as the result, but the *IF* function is in this group. An *IF* function can test if monthly revenue is above or below average and display "Yes" or "No" in the cell. The *Lookup & Reference* category is used to find and display information from a list in the workbook. For example, you might use a *Lookup* function to insert a price from a price list.

The Function Arguments Dialog Box

Functions require arguments in a particular order. They are easy to learn and build when you use the *Function Arguments* dialog box. This dialog box opens when you choose a function name from a category on the *Formulas* tab or when you use the *Insert Function* dialog box.

The *Function Arguments* dialog box shows each argument with an entry box and an explanation (Figure 2-42). You can select cells to enter an address, or you can type directly in the entry box. In addition to doing the work for you, the *Function Arguments* dialog box helps you learn the proper syntax for a function.

Function arguments may be required or optional. Optional arguments generally add some level of refinement to the calculation. In the *Function Arguments* dialog box and the

ScreenTip, a required argument name is shown in bold. When you use *Formula AutoComplete* to build a function, the *ScreenTip* shows optional arguments in square brackets (e.g., [type]).

When you are not sure about a function's name or category, you can search for it in the *Insert Function* dialog box. Open this dialog box by clicking the **Insert Function** button on the *Formulas* tab [*Function Library* group] or the same button to the left of the *Formula* bar. In the search area, type the name of the function or a brief description of what you want the function to do. For example, you can type "rate of return" to list *Financial* functions that calculate a rate of return for an investment.

2-42 *Function Arguments* dialog box for *AVERAGE*

> ▶ **ANOTHER WAY**
>
> **Shift+F3** opens the *Insert Function* dialog box.

PMT Function

The *PMT* function is in the *Financial* category. It calculates a constant loan payment amount for a period of time at a stated interest rate. When you borrow money for tuition or to buy a car, you can use the *PMT* function to determine your monthly payment for a selected payback time.

The *PMT* function has five arguments. Three of them are required: *rate*, *nper*, and *pv*. The other arguments are optional, *fv* and *type*. The proper syntax for a *PMT* formula is:

=PMT(rate, nper, pv, [fv], [type])

- **Rate** is the interest rate, a percentage of the amount borrowed. Most rates are set at a yearly rate. To determine monthly payments, you must divide the rate by 12.
- **Nper** is the total number of periods for repayment. If you make monthly payments for five years, the *nper* argument is 60.
- **Pv** is the present value, the amount borrowed.
- **Fv** is any future value after the last payment, an amount still owed at the end of the loan. When the *fv* argument is omitted, it means zero or that you have paid back the entire amount.
- **Type** indicates if payments are made at the beginning or the end of the period. Most loan payments are at the beginning of the period, because the interest amount is less. The number *1* is used to set payment at the beginning of the period.

Figure 2-43 shows a PMT function in cell B7 **=PMT(B6/12,B5*12,B4,,1)**. In the *Formula* bar, arguments are separated by commas. Where there are two commas with nothing between them, an argument has been omitted. In this case, it is the *fv* argument.

B6/12 is the interest *rate* divided by 12 to determine a monthly payment.
B5*12 is the *nper* argument, the number of years times 12, to determine the total number of payments.
B4 is the *pv* argument, the amount of money borrowed.
1 is the *type* argument and indicates that payment occurs at the beginning of the period.

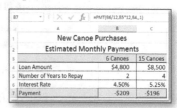

2-43 *PMT* function is in cell B7

The *PMT* result is a negative number, because the function is calculated from the borrower's point of view. It is money paid out.

▶ HOW TO: Use the PMT Function

1. Click the cell where the function results should display.
2. Click the **Insert Function** button to the left of the *Formula* bar.
 - The *Insert Function* dialog box opens.
3. Type **payment** in the *Search for a function* box.
4. Click **Go** (Figure 2-44).
 - A list of functions that include some type of payment displays.
5. Select **PMT** and click **OK**.
 - The *Function Arguments* dialog box opens.
 - The dialog box includes a description of the function.
6. Click the **Rate** box and click the cell with the interest rate.
 - You can type the rate in the entry box with the percent sign.
 - An explanation of the argument is displayed.
7. Type **/12** immediately after the address in the *Rate* box.
 - Divide by 12 for monthly payments.
 - If payments are quarterly, divide by 4.
8. Click the **Nper** box and click the cell that contains the loan term.
9. Type ***12** immediately after the address in the *Nper* box.
 - If the loan term is years and payments are quarterly, multiply by 4.
 - If the cell already displays the total number of payments, just click to enter the address.
10. Click the **Pv** box and click the cell that contains the amount of the loan.
11. Click the **Type** box.
 - The *Fv* argument is usually omitted, because loans require a zero balance at the end.
12. Type **1** in the *Type* box to set a payment at the beginning of the period (Figure 2-45).
 - Most loan payments are at the beginning, because the payment is less than if it were at the end of the period.
13. Click **OK**.

![Insert Function dialog box]

2-44 *Insert Function* dialog box

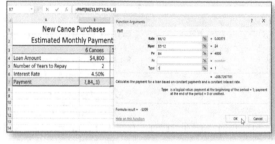

2-45 *Function Arguments* dialog box for *PMT*

> **MORE INFO**
>
> To show the payment as a positive value, type a minus sign (−) before the loan amount in the worksheet or before its cell address in the *Function Arguments* dialog box.

> **ANOTHER WAY**
>
> Choose the *PMT* function from the **Financial** button [*Formulas* tab, *Function Library* group].

IF Function

The *IF* function tests a condition or statement; if it is true, there is a specified result; if it is false, there is an alternative result. In the Paradise Lakes revenue worksheet, you can use an

IF formula to determine if each month's revenue is above average. If it is, you can display "Yes," in the cell, and if it is not, you can display "No."

> **MORE INFO**
>
> An *IF* function is similar to an *IF* statement in many programming languages.

An *IF* function has three arguments, and its syntax is:

=IF(logical_test, value_if_true, value_if_false)

- The *logical_test* is the value or statement to be evaluated.
- The *value_if_true* is the result displayed in the cell when the *logical_test* is true. You can select a cell, enter text, or use a formula for this argument.
- The *value_if_false* is the result displayed in the cell when the *logical_test* is false. You can select a cell, enter text, or use a formula for this argument.

An *IF* function can use comparison or logical operators in its arguments. The following table describes the comparison operators:

Comparison Operators

Operator	Description
=	Equal to
<>	Not equal to
>	Greater than
>=	Greater than or equal to
<	Less than
<=	Less than or equal to

Figure 2-46 has an *IF* function in cell D5 **=IF(B5>=4,18,20)**. When you use the *Function Arguments* dialog box to build a function, the commas to separate arguments are entered automatically.

B5>=4 is the *logical_test*. It determines if the value in cell B5 is equal to or greater than 4. Cell B5 is a relative reference so when the formula is copied, it will update to show the new row. The *value_if_true* argument is **18**. If the age is 4 or higher, the fee is $18. This value is a constant. It does not change when the formula is copied. The *value_if_false* argument is **20**, another constant. If the age is not 4 or higher, it must be lower and the fee is $20. The constant does not change when the formula is copied.

2-46 *IF* function in cell D5

You can insert the *IF* function from the *Logical* category on the *Formulas* tab, from the *Insert Function* button, or by typing it. When you type an *IF* function, you must type the commas to separate arguments, and you must enclose text arguments within quotation marks.

▶ HOW TO: Build an IF Function

1. Click the cell for the function.
2. Click the **Logical** button [*Formulas* tab, *Function Library* group].
 - The list of *Logical* functions opens.
3. Select **IF** in the list.
 - The *Function Arguments* dialog box for *IF* opens.
4. Click the **Logical_test** box.
5. Click the cell that will be evaluated.
 - Make the reference absolute if you know that the formula will be copied and that the reference should not change.
6. Type a comparison operator immediately after the cell address.
7. Type a value or click a cell to complete the expression to be tested.
 - You can build a statement such as B11=K15 or B11<10000.
 - Make a cell reference absolute or mixed if necessary.
8. Click the **Value_if_true** box.
9. Type the label or click a cell that contains data that should be displayed if the *logical_test* is true.
 - You can type a value in the text box.
10. Click the **Value_if_false** box.
11. Type the label or click a cell that contains data that should be displayed if the *logical_test* is false (Figure 2-47).
 - Results for the current cell are displayed in the *Function Arguments* dialog box.

2-47 *Function Arguments* dialog box for *IF*

12. Click **OK**.

 MORE INFO

The *value_if_false* argument for the *logical_test* can be another *IF* function which allows you to test for more than one possibility.

Lookup Functions

A *Lookup* function displays a piece of data from a range of cells in another part of the workbook. There are two *Lookup* functions: *VLOOKUP* (vertical) and *HLOOKUP* (horizontal). These two functions have the same syntax and similar arguments. *VLOOKUP* uses a lookup table that is organized in columns, and *HLOOKUP* uses a lookup range that is laid out in rows.

A *VLOOKUP* function has four arguments, and the syntax is:

=VLOOKUP (lookup_value, table_array, col_index_num, [range_lookup])

- The ***lookup_value*** is the data to be found or looked up. It is usually a cell address, but you can type a value or a text string. The function locates this *lookup_value* in the first column of the table array. It then displays data from the designated column in the same row as the *lookup_value*.
- The ***table_array*** is a range of cells, sorted in ascending order by the first column. The range can be located on a different worksheet or in a different workbook. It is good practice to name the range so that its reference is absolute.
- The ***col_index_num*** sets which column in the *table_array* contains the data to be displayed in the result. The columns are counted from left to right.
- The ***[range lookup]*** is optional and is often omitted. This argument is either TRUE or FALSE. TRUE means that Excel finds the closest match to the *lookup_value*, not always a good choice. If the data in the table array is sorted, TRUE will generally return the correct match. When you set this argument to FALSE, the data can be in any order.

Figure 2-48 shows a *VLOOKUP* function in cell D3 in the worksheet on the left. The result (250) is from the third column in row 6 in the table array in the worksheet on the right. These are two sheets in the same workbook.

2-48 *VLOOKUP* function in cell D3 on the left

=VLOOKUP(C3,V_Calories,3)

The *lookup_value* argument is cell C3 ("Running").

The *table_array* argument is a named cell range, *V_Calories*. The "V" is a reminder that this range is a vertical lookup table. The *V_Calories* range is cells A2:D10 in the sheet on the right. The *col_index_num* argument is *3* so that the result is from the third column, the "Calories" column, in the *V_Calories* range.

The *range_lookup* argument is omitted or TRUE. The data in the table array (on the right) is sorted so TRUE is acceptable for this argument.

You can insert the *VLOOKUP* function from the *Lookup & Reference* category on the *Formulas* tab or by searching for it in the *Insert Function* dialog box. When you are experienced using the function, you can type it in the cell and use *Formula AutoComplete*.

▶ HOW TO: Enter the VLOOKUP Function

1. Click the cell for the function.
2. Click the **Lookup & Reference** button [*Formulas* tab].
3. Select **VLOOKUP**.
 - The *Function Arguments* dialog box opens.
 - Move the dialog box if it covers data that you need to see or select.
4. Click the **Lookup_value** box.
5. Click the cell to be matched.
 - The *lookup_value* is typically a cell in the same row as the function.
 - This reference is usually relative.
6. Click the **Table_array** box.
7. Select the cell range with the lookup data.
 - When the lookup table is named, the range name is substituted.
 - The *Function Arguments* dialog box collapses while you select cells.
8. Press **F4 (FN+F4)** to make the reference absolute if cell addresses are used.
 - When a range name has been substituted, you need not do this.
9. Click the **Col_index_num** box.
10. Type the column number, counting from the left, that contains the data to be displayed (Figure 2-49).
 - The result for the current cell is displayed in the dialog box.

2-49 *Function Arguments* dialog box for *VLOOKUP*

11. Leave the *Range_lookup* argument box empty if the data in the table array is sorted.
12. Click **OK**.

The *HLOOKUP* function has a *row_index_num* argument instead of the *col_index_num* argument. *The table_array* is set up horizontally as seen in Figure 2-50, and the first row is arranged in alphabetical order from left to right. The *HLOOKUP* function is in cell C6 in the sheet on the left. The lookup table is named *H_Fees*, shown in the sheet on the right.

2-50 *HLOOKUP* in cell C6

=HLOOKUP(B6,H_Fees,2)

The *lookup_value* argument is cell B6 ("Know Your Numbers").
The *table_array* argument is a named cell range, *H_Fees*. The "H" is a visual cue for a horizontal lookup table. The *H_Fees* range is cells F2:J3 on the right.
The *row_index_num* argument is 2 so that the data shown in cell C6 is from the second row of the *H_Fees* range.
The *range_lookup* argument is omitted, because the data range is sorted alphabetically from left to right.

> ### MORE INFO
>
> The *range_lookup* argument TRUE (or omitted) finds the largest value that is less than or equal to the *lookup_value*.

▶HOW TO: Use The HLOOKUP Function

1. Click the cell for the function.
2. Click the **Lookup & Reference** button [*Formulas* tab].
3. Select **HLOOKUP**.
 - The *Function Arguments* dialog box opens.
4. Click the **Lookup_value** box.
5. Click the cell to be matched.
 - The *lookup_value* is typically a cell in the same row as the function.
 - This reference is usually relative.
6. Click the **Table_array** box.

7. Select the cell range with the lookup data.
 - When the lookup table is named, the range name is substituted.
 - The *Function Arguments* dialog box collapses while you select cells.

8. Press **F4 (FN+F4)** to make the reference absolute when cell addresses are used.

9. Click the **Row_index_num** box.

10. Type the row number, counting the first row of the *table_array* as 1 (Figure 2-51).
 - The result for the current cell is displayed in the dialog box.

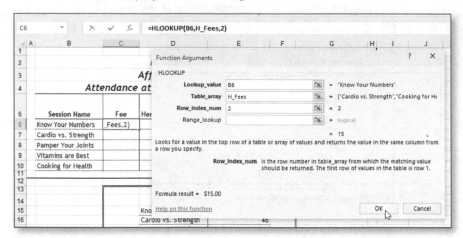

2-51 *HLOOKUP Function Arguments* dialog box

11. Leave the *Range_lookup* argument box empty if the data in the table array is sorted.

12. Click **OK**.

SLO 2.7

Using Math & Trig Functions

You have already used *SUM* from the *Math & Trig* function category. There are functions in this category to display the absolute value of data, one to calculate the cosine of an angle, or one that returns the power of a number. You might recognize the function *PI* or π from a math class. Three *Math & Trig* functions that are often used in business or personal calculations are *ROUND*, *SUMIF*, and *SUMPRODUCT*.

ROUND Function

Rounding means that a value is adjusted to display a specified number of decimal places or a whole number. You can round the numbers on your tax return in the United States which means that you need not show any cents, just dollars.

The *ROUND* function has two arguments, *number* and *num_digits*.

=ROUND(number, num_digits)

- The ***number*** is the cell or the value to be adjusted.
- The ***num_digits*** sets the number of decimal places for rounding. When this argument is zero (0), the value is displayed as the nearest whole number. When the *num_digits* argument is greater than zero, the value is rounded to that number of decimal places. You can use a negative number for the *num_digits* argument which rounds the value to the left of the decimal point. Make sure you understand the results when you round to the left of the decimal point.

When a value used in rounding is 5 or greater, results round up to the next digit. If you round 5.523 to show zero (0) decimal places, it rounds up to display as 6 because the value after the decimal point is 5. If you round 5.423 to two places, it rounds to 5.42 because the value used for rounding is 3. The *Increase Decimal* and *Decrease Decimal* buttons follow these rounding principles for displaying values in the cell as do the *Accounting Number* and *Currency* formats. These formats, however, keep the full unrounded value in the cell and use that value in calculations.

 MORE INFO

When a value is rounded, the rounded value is used in calculations, not the full unrounded number.

▶ **HOW TO:** Use the ROUND Function

1. Click the cell for the function.
2. Type =rou and press **Tab**.
 - *Formula AutoComplete* inserts the function in the cell.
 - The *number* argument is bold in the *ScreenTip*.
3. Select the cell to be rounded.
 - The cell address appears in the cell and in the *Formula* bar.
 - You can type a value if there is no cell reference.
4. Type , (a comma) to separate the arguments.
 - The *num_digits* argument is bold in the *ScreenTip*.
5. Type a number to set the number of decimal places (Figure 2-52).
6. Press **Enter**.

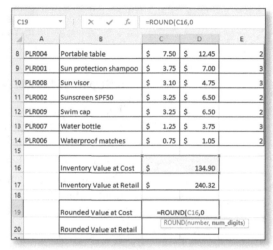

2-52 Type the *ROUND* function

 MORE INFO

Excel has a *ROUNDDOWN* function that always rounds a number down. The *ROUNDUP* function rounds a value up.

SUMIF Function

The *SUMIF* function controls which data in a range is included in the total. It allows you to eliminate cells from the calculation by criteria that you set. *Criteria* are restrictions, conditions, or rules that must be met. In a *SUMIF* function, cell values are included in the sum only if they match the criteria.

The *SUMIF* function has three arguments.

=SUMIF (range, criteria, [sum_range])

- The ***range*** is the range of cells to be evaluated or searched, the values that are compared to the criteria.
- The ***criteria*** argument defines which cells from the range should be included in the sum. You can use comparison operators, cell references, a value, or text. When you use text or a comparison operator, the criteria must be enclosed in quotation marks.

- The *[sum_range]* is the cell range to be summed. This argument is optional, because it is omitted when the range to be summed is the same as the *range* argument.

Figure 2-53 illustrates a *SUMIF* function in cell I5 that totals sales for products that have a price greater than $10.

	A	B	C	D	E	F	G	H	I	J
1		Paradise Lakes Resort								
2		Boutique Merchandise								
3	Product ID	Item	Cost	Sales Price	Quantity	Total				
4	PLR011	Flashlight	$ 8.75	$ 15.00	2	$ 30.00		Total Sales for Products > $10		
5	PLR003	Folding chair	$ 10.25	$ 15.99	3	$ 47.97			$149.37	
6	PLR005	Insect repellant	$ 2.45	$ 5.45	3	$ 16.35				
7	PLR010	Lantern	$ 8.50	$ 15.50	3	$ 46.50				
8	PLR004	Portable table	$ 7.50	$ 12.45	2	$ 24.90				
9	PLR001	Sun protection shampoo	$ 3.75	$ 7.00	3	$ 21.00				
10	PLR008	Sun visor	$ 3.10	$ 4.75	3	$ 14.25				
11	PLR002	Sunscreen SPF50	$ 3.25	$ 6.50	2	$ 13.00				
12	PLR009	Swim cap	$ 3.25	$ 6.50	2	$ 13.00				
13	PLR007	Water bottle	$ 1.25	$ 3.75	3	$ 11.25				
14	PLR006	Waterproof matches	$ 0.75	$ 1.05	2	$ 2.10				

2-53 *SUMIF* function in cell I5

=SUMIF(D4:D14,">=10",$F4:$F14)

The *range* argument is the sales price column, cells D4:D14. It is an absolute reference so that the formula can be copied.

The *criteria* argument is >=10, shown in quotation marks. The quotation marks are added automatically when you use the *Function Arguments* dialog box.

The *sum_range* argument is cells F4:F14, the cells to be added if the price is greater than 10.

> **MORE INFO**
>
> You can use wildcards (* or ?) in a criteria argument. For example, to sum sales for all items that begin with the letter S, use **s*** as the criteria. Criteria are not case-sensitive.

▶HOW TO: Build a SUMIF Function

1. Click the cell for the function.
2. Click the **Math & Trig** button [*Formulas* tab, *Function Library* group].
3. Select **SUMIF**.
4. Click the **Range** box.
5. Select the cell range to be compared against the criteria.
 - Make the reference absolute if the formula might be copied.
 - Press **F3 (FN+F3)** to paste a range name rather than selecting the range.
6. Click the **Criteria** box.
 - Type text to be compared or a value to be matched.
 - Type an expression with operators to be evaluated.
 - Quotation marks are automatically supplied.

7. Click the **Sum_range** box (Figure 2-54).
 - Select the cells to be added.
 - If the cells to be added are the same as those in the *range* argument, leave the entry blank.

2-54 *Function Arguments* dialog box for *Sumif*

8. Click **OK**.

SUMPRODUCT Function

The *SUMPRODUCT* function calculates the sum of the product of several ranges. It multiplies the cells identified in its *array* arguments and then it totals those individual products. A **product** is the result of a multiplication problem; 4 is the product of 2 times 2. An **array** is a range of cells in a row or a column. An array has a **dimension**, which is the number of columns or rows. The arrays A1:A5 and C1:C5 have the same dimension, five rows and one column.

The *SUMPRODUCT* function has the following syntax.

=SUMPRODUCT(array1, array2, [arrayN])

- The **array1** argument is the first range of cells for the multiplication.
- The **array2** argument is the range that is multiplied by the corresponding cells in the *array1* range. These two ranges must have the same number of cells, the same dimension.

It is possible to use more than two arrays so that you could have an *array3* argument or even more.

In Figure 2-55, the *SUMPRODUCT* function in cell C22 multiplies the first array C6:C20 by the corresponding values in cells F6:F20 and totals those products.

=SUMPRODUCT(C6:C20,F6:F20)

The value in cell C6 is multiplied by cell F6, cell C7 is multiplied by cell F7, and so on. Those individual products are summed, and the result is $249.15.

2-55 *SUMPRODUCT* in cell C22

▶ HOW TO: Build a SUMPRODUCT Function

1. Click the cell for the function.
2. Click the **Math & Trig** button [*Formulas* tab, *Function Library* group].
3. Select **SUMPRODUCT**.
 - The *Function Arguments* dialog box opens.
4. Click the **Array1** box.
5. Select the first cell range to be multiplied.
6. Click the **Array2** box.
7. Select the next cell range to be multiplied (Figure 2-56).
 - Both arrays must have the same number of cells and rows.
 - Use as many arrays as required for the calculation.

2-56 *Function Arguments* dialog box for *SUMPRODUCT*

8. Click **OK**.

> ▶ **MORE INFO**
>
> If an array in a *SUMPRODUCT* formula includes an empty cell, Excel treats that value as 0, but the multiplication by zero does not affect the sum.

PAUSE & PRACTICE: EXCEL 2-3

For this project, you continue working on the workbook for Paradise Lakes. You calculate totals related to camp attendance and merchandise inventory using functions from the *Math & Trig, Financial, Logical, Lookup & Reference,* and *Date & Time* categories.

File Needed: *[your initials] PP E2-2.xlsx*
Completed Project File Name: *[your initials] PP E2-3.xlsx*

1. Open the **[your initials] PP E2-2.xlsx** workbook completed in *Pause & Practice 2-2* and save it as [your initials] PP E2-3.

2. Click the **Cass Lake** worksheet tab.

3. Enter an *IF* function to determine if a month's revenue was below average.
 a. Click cell **B22** and click the **Formulas** tab.
 b. Click the **Logical** button In the *Function Library* group and select **IF**. The *Function Arguments* dialog box opens.
 c. Click the **Logical_test** text box and click cell **B11**.
 d. After "B11" in the *Logical_test* box, type < for a less than operator.
 e. Click cell **K15** and press **F4 (FN+F4)** to make this an absolute reference.
 f. Click the **Value_if_true** box and type Yes. You need not type quotation marks when you use the *Function Arguments* dialog box.
 g. Press **Tab** to move to the *Value_if_false* box. Excel supplies the quotation marks for "Yes."
 h. Type No (Figure 2-57).
 i. Click **OK**. For April, the result is *Yes*.
 j. Click cell **B22** and click the **Center** button [*Home* tab, *Font* group].
 k. Use the *Fill* pointer to copy the formula in cell **B22** to cells **C22:G22**.
 l. Press **Ctrl+Home**.

2-57 Build an *IF* function

4. Use *SUMIF* to calculate results.
 a. Click the **PLR Camp** worksheet tab. The number of attendees is tracked with the camper's ID, gender, and age.
 b. Select cell **H4**, and click the **Formulas** tab.
 c. Click the **Math & Trig** button in the *Function Library* group and select **SUMIF**.
 d. Click the **Range** text box and select cells **B4:B38**.
 e. Press **F4 (FN+F4)** to make the reference absolute.
 f. Press **Tab** and type f in the *Criteria* box. Criteria are not case-sensitive. The cells in column B will be checked to determine if they show "F."
 g. Click the **Sum_range** box, select cells **C4:C38**, and press **F4 (FN+F4)**. The values in this range will be summed for those rows in which the gender is F (Figure 2-58).
 h. Click **OK**. Female camp days are 117.
 i. Click cell **H4** and use the *Fill* pointer to copy the formula to cell **H5**.
 j. Edit the formula in cell **H5** to show m instead of "f."

2-58 Build a *SUMIF* function

5. Use *VLOOKUP* to display costs.
 a. Click the **Merchandise** sheet tab and select cell **C4**. Individual costs are missing, but they are listed on the **Rates&Tables** sheet.
 b. Click the **Lookup & Reference** button [*Formulas* tab, *Function Library* group].
 c. Select **VLOOKUP**.
 d. Click the **Lookup_value** box and select cell **A4**.
 e. Click the **Table_array** box. The table with the costs is on the **Rates&Tables** sheet.
 f. Click the **Rates&Tables** worksheet tab and select cells **A2:C12**. This array or range includes the ID, the name, and the cost. The costs are in column C, the third column from the left.

g. Press **F4 (FN+F4)** to make the array an absolute reference.

h. Click the **Col_index_num** box and type 3. The ID in cell A4 will be located in cells A2:C12 on the **Rates&Tables** sheet, and the cost in the third column will be displayed.

i. Click the **Range_lookup** box and type false (Figure 2-59).

j. Click **OK**. The cost for the first item is $8.75.

k. Copy the formula in cell **C4** to cells **C5:C14**.

6. Use *SUMPRODUCT* to calculate inventory values.

a. Click cell **C16**. This is a merged and centered cell.

b. Click the **Formulas** tab.

c. Click the **Math & Trig** button in the *Function Library* group and select **SUMPRODUCT**.

d. Click the **Array1** box and select cells **C4:C14**. There are 11 values in this range.

e. Click the **Array2** box and select cells **E4:E14**. There are 11 values in this range, and each one will be multiplied by the corresponding value in the same row in column C.

f. Click **OK**. The value of the inventory at cost is 134.9.

g. Click cell **C17**, type =sump, and press **Tab**. The function is inserted and the *ScreenTip* shows the next argument, *array1*.

h. Select cells **D4:D14** and type , (a comma) to separate the first argument from the second.

i. Select cells **E4:E14** (Figure 2-60). You need not type the closing parenthesis.

j. Press **Enter**. The value is 240.32.

k. Select cells **C16:C17** and apply the **Accounting Number** format.

7. Use the *ROUND* function.

a. Select cell **C19**.

b. Click the **Math & Trig** button [*Formulas* tab, *Function Library* group].

c. Select **ROUND**.

d. In the *Number* text box, click cell **C16**.

e. Type 0 in the *Num_digits* text box.

f. Press **Enter**. The value is rounded up to $135.00.

g. Copy the formula in cell **C19** to cell **C20**. The value from cell C17 is rounded down to $240.00.

8. Use the *PMT* function to determine payments for new canoe purchases.

a. Click the **Canoes** sheet tab and click cell **B7**.

b. Click the **Formulas** tab and the **Financial** button [*Function Library* group].

c. Select **PMT**.

d. Click the **Rate** box and click cell **B6**.

e. Immediately after "B6," type /12 to divide the rate by 12 for monthly payments.

2-59 Build a *VLOOKUP* function

2-60 Type a *SUMPRODUCT* function

f. Click the **Nper** box and click cell **B5**. Type *12 to multiply by 12 for 12 months per year.

g. Click the **Pv** box and click cell **B4**. This is the amount of the loan.

h. Click the **Fv** box. Leave this blank to indicate no balance due at the end of the loan term.

2-61 PMT function for payment at the beginning of the period

i. Click the **Type** box and type 1. The payment will made at the beginning of the month (Figure 2-61).

j. Click **OK**. The payment is −$209, a negative value because it is money paid out. This cell was formatted to show no decimal places.

9. Type the PMT function.

a. Click cell **C7**.

b. Type =pm, and press **Tab**. The *ScreenTip* shows the first argument, *rate*.

c. Click cell **C6** and type /12,. This divides the rate by 12 and enters a comma to separate the arguments (Figure 2-62).

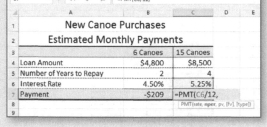

2-62 Type a PMT function

d. Click cell **C5** for the *nper* argument, type *12, to multiply by 12 and enter a comma to separate the arguments.

e. Click cell **C4** for the *pv* argument, the amount of the loan.

f. Type , (a comma) to move to the *fv* argument.

g. Type , (another comma) to move to the *type* argument. *Formula AutoComplete* lists two options for the argument (Figure 2-63).

h. Double-click **1-beginning of the period** in the *ScreenTip*.

i. Press **Enter**. The payment is −$196.

j. Press **Ctrl+Home**.

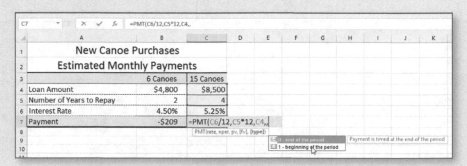

2-63 *Formula AutoComplete* for argument choices

10. Save and close the workbook (Figure 2-64).

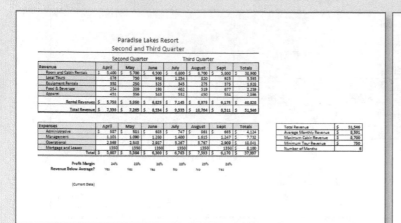

Paradise Lakes Resort
Second and Third Quarter

Revenue	April	May	June	July	August	Sept	Totals
Room and Cabin Rentals	$ 5,400	$ 5,700	$ 6,500	$ 6,600	$ 6,700	$ 5,000	35,900
Local Tours	676	730	960	1,254	820	925	5,595
Equipment Rentals	358	250	325	345	275	375	1,928
Food & Beverage	254	209	190	402	519	677	2,259
Apparel	451	356	545	552	450	554	2,386
Rental Revenues	$ 5,758	$ 5,950	$ 6,625	$ 7,145	$ 6,975	$ 6,175	40,828
Total Revenue	$ 7,339	$ 7,265	$ 8,534	$ 9,335	$ 10,764	$ 8,311	51,546

Expenses	April	May	June	July	August	Sept	Total
Administrative	$ 587	$ 591	$ 603	$ 747	$ 861	$ 665	4,124
Management	1,101	1,090	1,200	1,400	1,615	1,347	7,732
Operational	2,569	2,543	2,957	3,267	3,767	2,909	18,041
Mortgage and Leases	1350	1350	1350	1350	1350	1350	8,100
Total	5,607	5,564	6,360	6,765	7,593	6,170	37,997

Total Revenue	$ 51,546
Average Monthly Revenue	$ 8,591
Maximum Cabin Revenue	$ 8,700
Minimum Tour Revenue	$ 750
Number of Months	6

| Profit Margin | 24% | 23% | 26% | 28% | 29% | 26% |
| Revenue Below Average? | Yes | Yes | Yes | No | No | Yes |

[Current Date]

Paradise Lakes Resort
Boutique Merchandise

Product ID	Item	Cost	Sales Price	Quantity
PLR011	Flashlight	$ 8.75	$ 15.00	2
PLR003	Folding chair	$ 10.25	$ 15.39	3
PLR005	Insect repellant	$ 2.45	$ 5.45	3
PLR010	Lantern	$ 8.50	$ 15.50	3
PLR004	Portable table	$ 7.50	$ 12.45	3
PLR001	Sun protection shampoo	$ 3.75	$ 7.00	3
PLR008	Sun visor	$ 3.10	$ 4.75	3
PLR002	Sunscreen SPF50	$ 3.25	$ 6.50	2
PLR009	Swim cap	$ 3.25	$ 6.50	2
PLR007	Water bottle	$ 1.25	$ 3.75	2
PLR006	Waterproof matches	$ 0.75	$ 1.05	2

Inventory Value at Cost	$	134.90
Inventory Value at Retail	$	240.32
Rounded Value at Cost	$	135.00
Rounded Value at Retail	$	240.00

Paradise Lakes Youth Camp
Annual Attendance

Camper ID	Gender	# of Days	Age
PLR001	M	5	13
PLR002	F	6	12
PLR003	F	8	8
PLR004	F	7	11
PLR005	M	5	13
PLR006	M	3	11
PLR007	M	8	9
PLR008	F	4	11
PLR009	F	2	10
PLR010	F	8	8
PLR011	M	8	8
PLR012	F	7	12
PLR013	M	8	12
PLR014	F	7	10
PLR015	F	8	10
PLR016	M	4	10
PLR017	M	7	10
PLR018	M	1	12
PLR019	F	1	12
PLR020	F	1	12
PLR021	F	4	13
PLR022	M	10	9
PLR023	M	1	11
PLR024	F	8	11
PLR025	F	10	13
PLR026	F	8	10
PLR027	M	6	8
PLR028	M	7	9
PLR029	F	4	11
PLR030	F	4	13
PLR031	F	10	11
PLR032	F	3	10
PLR033	F	1	10
PLR034	M	3	12
PLR035	F	4	8

Total Days by Females	117
Total Days by Males	76

New Canoe Purchases
Estimated Monthly Payments

	6 Canoes	15 Canoes
Loan Amount	$4,800	$8,500
Number of Years to Repay	2	4
Interest Rate	4.50%	5.25%
Payment	-$209	-$196

2-64 PP 2-3 completed

Chapter Summary

2.1 Build and edit basic formulas (p. 497).

- A *formula* is a calculation that uses arithmetic operators, worksheet cells, and constant values. Basic arithmetic operations are addition, subtraction, multiplication, and division.
- You can type a formula in the cell or you can point and click to select cells.
- When you type a formula, *Formula AutoComplete* displays suggestions for completing the formula.
- Formulas are edited in the *Formula* bar or in the cell to change cell addresses, use a different operator, or add cells to the calculation.

2.2 Set mathematical order of operations (p. 499).

- Excel follows mathematics rules for the order in which operations are carried out when a formula has more than one operator.
- You can control the sequence of calculations by placing operations that should be done first within parentheses.
- Use the following acronym to help remember the order of arithmetic operations: **P**lease **E**xcuse **M**y **D**ear **A**unt **S**ally (**P**arentheses, **E**xponentiation, **M**ultiplication, **D**ivision, **A**ddition, **S**ubtraction).

2.3 Use absolute, mixed, relative, and 3D references in a formula (p. 501).

- A *relative cell reference* in a formula is the cell address which, when copied, updates to the address of the copy.
- An *absolute cell reference* is the cell address with dollar signs as in A5. This reference does not change when the formula is copied.
- A *mixed cell reference* contains one relative and one absolute address as in $B5 or B$5. When copied, the absolute part of the reference does not change.
- A *3D cell reference* is a cell in another worksheet in the same workbook. It includes the name of the worksheet followed by an exclamation point as in *Inventory!B2*.
- You can name a single cell or a group of cells with a defined *range name*.
- You can use range names in formulas instead of cell addresses.

- *Formula AutoComplete* displays range names so that you can paste them in a formula.
- A named range is an absolute reference.

2.4 Use formula auditing tools in a worksheet (p. 507).

- Excel highlights several types of formula errors as you work, but you still need to review errors and make corrections.
- Excel automatically error-checks formulas based on its internal rules. A potential error is marked in the upper left corner of the cell with a small triangle.
- *Formula auditing* tools include several commands to aid your review of workbook formulas and functions.
- The *Formula Auditing* group on the *Formulas* tab includes the *Trace Precedents* and *Trace Dependents* buttons.
- A *circular reference* is an error that occurs when a formula includes the address of the formula.
- Some errors are noted as you press a completion key and can be quickly corrected by accepting the suggested correction in the message window.

2.5 Use *Statistical* and *Date & Time* functions (p. 514).

- The *AVERAGE* function calculates the arithmetic mean by adding values and dividing by the number of values.
- The *COUNT* function tallies the number of cells in a range. There are different *COUNT* functions based on whether cell contents are labels, values, or blank.
- *MAX* and *MIN* functions find the largest and the smallest values, respectively, in a range.
- Commonly used statistical functions are options on the *AutoSum* button.
- The *AutoCalculate* feature displays numerical results such as *Sum*, *Average*, and *Count* on the *Status* bar for selected cells.
- The *Date & Time* category includes a *TODAY* function and a *NOW* function that display the current date and time.

2.6 Work with functions from the *Financial*, *Logical*, and *Lookup & Reference* categories. (p. 522).

- Use the *Function Arguments* dialog box for help in completing an Excel function.

539

- The *Function Arguments* dialog box includes a description of the function and an explanation of each argument.
- The *PMT* function from the *Financial* category calculates a constant payment amount for a loan.
- The *Logical* function *IF* evaluates a statement or condition and displays a particular result when the statement is true and another result when the condition is false.
- A *Lookup* function displays data from a cell located in another part of the workbook.
- Two widely used *Lookup* functions are *VLOOKUP* (vertical) and *HLOOKUP* (horizontal).

2.7 Build functions from the *Math & Trig* category (p. 530).

- The *ROUND* function adjusts a value up or down based on the number of decimal places.

- The *SUMIF* function includes cells in a total only if they meet a set criteria or condition.
- The *SUMPRODUCT* function multiplies corresponding cells from an **array** and then totals the results of each multiplication.

Check for Understanding

The SIMbook for this text (within your SIMnet account) provides the following resources for concept review:

- Multiple choice questions
- Matching exercises
- Short answer questions

Guided Project 2-1

Courtyard Medical Plaza (CMP) has doctor offices, a pharmacy, x-ray and lab services, insurance and bill-ing support, optometry and dental facilities, and onsite dining. You will complete an inventory worksheet for the pharmacy as well as insurance and payment data for the optometry group.
[Student Learning Outcomes 2.1, 2.2, 2.3, 2.4, 2.5, 2.6, 2.7]

File Needed: **CourtyardMedical-02.xlsx** *[Student data files are available in the Library of your SIMnet account.]*
Completed Project File Name: **[your initials] Excel 2-1.xlsx**

Skills Covered in This Project

- Build and copy formulas.
- Name cell ranges.
- Use *AVERAGE*, *MAX*, and *MIN*.
- Use relative, mixed, absolute, and 3D cell references in formulas.
- Use *SUMIF*.

- Check results with *AutoCalculate*.
- Use the *VLOOKUP* function.
- Set mathematical order of operations.
- Use formula auditing tools.
- Use the *PMT* and *SUMPRODUCT* functions.
- Insert the *TODAY* function.

1. Open the **CourtyardMedical-02.xlsx** workbook from your student data files and save it as [your initials] Excel 2-1.

2. Enter and copy subtraction formulas.
 a. Click cell **E2** on the **Lookup_Data** worksheet. To calculate the dollar amount of the margin, subtract the cost from the retail price.
 b. Type an equals sign (=) to start the formula.
 c. Click cell **D2**, the retail price.
 d. Type a minus sign, or hyphen (–) to subtract, and click cell **C2**, the cost.
 e. Click the **Enter** button (check mark) on the *Formula* bar. The pointer stays in the formula cell. The margin for acetaminophen is $1.49.
 f. Drag the *Fill* pointer to copy the formula in cell **E2** to cells **E3:E16**. The *Auto Fill Options* button appears near cell E16.
 g. Click the **Auto Fill Options** button and choose **Fill Without Formatting** (Figure 2-65). This option copies the formula without the top border from cell E2.
 h. Format cells **E3:E16** as **Currency**.
 i. Click the **Optometry** sheet tab and select cell **G5**.
 j. Type = to start the formula to subtract the deductible amount from the billed amount.
 k. Click cell **E5**, the billed amount.
 l. Type –, click cell **F5**, the deductible amount, and press **Enter**.
 m. Copy the formula in cell **G5** to cells **G6:G24** without formatting to maintain the fill color.

E2	▼	×	✓	fx	=D2-C2	
	A	B	C	D	E	F
1	**Product ID**	**Description**	**Cost**	**Retail**	**Margin**	
2	CMP-006	Acetaminophen	$2.50	$3.99	$1.49	
3	CMP-001	Tongue depressor	$0.55	$1.99	$1.44	
4	CMP-002	Cough drops	$0.85	$1.29	$0.44	
5	CMP-003	Nasal spray	$3.45	$5.99	$2.54	
6	CMP-004	Antiseptic wash	$2.75	$4.99	$2.24	
7	CMP-005	Disinfectant wipes	$1.25	$3.99	$2.74	
8	CMP-007	Bandage, 1 inch strips	$1.25	$3.99	$2.74	
9	CMP-008	Bandage, 2 inch strips	$1.25	$3.99	$2.74	
10	CMP-009	Bandage, assorted	$1.75	$4.99	$3.24	
11	CMP-010	Ibuprofen	$2.50	$3.99	$1.49	
12	CMP-011	Cough syrup	$2.25	$4.99	$2.74	
13	CMP-012	Antibiotic ointment	$2.25	$5.99	$3.74	
14	CMP-013	Moisture lotion	$1.55	$4.99	$3.44	
15	CMP-014	Dandruff shampoo	$2.75	$5.99	$3.24	
16	CMP-015	Insect bite gel	$3.55	$6.99	$3.44	
17						
18					○ Copy Cells	
19					○ Fill Formatting Only	
20					● Fill Without Formatting	
21					○ Flash Fill	
22						

2-65 Copy without formatting to preserve borders

3. Name cell ranges.
 a. Select cells **E5:E24**. This named range will refer to the billable amounts.
 b. Click the **Name** box.
 c. Type Billables in the *Name* box and press **Enter**.
 d. Click the **Lookup_Data** worksheet tab.
 e. Select cells **A2:D16**. This named range will not include the calculated margin.
 f. Click the **Name** box.
 g. Type Costs in the *Name* box and press **Enter**.
 h. Select cells **H2:I5** and click the **Formulas** tab.
 i. Click the **Create from Selection** button [*Defined Names* group]. Excel will create range names based on the labels in the column on the left.
 j. Select the **Left column** box and click **OK**.
 k. Click cell **A1** and click the **Name** box arrow to see the range names in the worksheet (Figure 2-66).

2-66 Range names in the worksheet

4. Use range names with *AVERAGE*, *MIN*, and *MAX*.
 a. Click the **Optometry** sheet tab and select cell **D27**.
 b. Type =aver and press **Tab**.
 c. Select cells **E5:E24** and press **Enter**. The range name is substituted in the formula when you select the cells in the worksheet.
 d. Select cell **D28**, click the **AutoSum** button arrow [*Home* tab, *Editing* group], and select **Max**.
 e. Select cells **E5:E24** and press **Enter**.
 f. Use *MIN* in cell **D29** with the same cell range.

5. Set the order of operations in a 3D formula.
 a. Click the **Insurance** sheet tab and select cell **D5**. The total with service charge is calculated by multiplying 1 plus the percentage times the billed amount. The percentages are on the **Lookup_Data** sheet in named ranges.
 b. Type = and click cell **C5**.
 c. Type *(immediately after **C5**. The next part of the formula will be calculated first.
 d. Type 1+ immediately after the left parenthesis. The calculation is (1+ the percentage).
 e. Click the **Lookup_Data** sheet tab. The sheet name is displayed in the *Formula* bar.
 f. Click cell **I2**. The range name is substituted. Because it is an absolute reference, the sheet name is removed (Figure 2-67).
 g. Press **Enter**. Because the formula refers to another sheet and a range name, the missing parenthesis is not automatically supplied (Figure 2-68).
 h. Click **Yes** to accept the suggested correction.
 i. Copy the formula to cells **D5:D9** for the Green Cross patients.

2-67 3D formula with a range name

6. Edit and copy a formula.
 a. Click cell **D9** and copy the formula to cell **D10**.
 b. Double-click cell **D10** to start *Edit* mode.
 c. Select the range name **Green_Cross** in the cell or *Formula* bar (Figure 2-69).
 d. Click the **Lookup_Data** sheet tab and select cell **I3**. The *IrisMed* range name replaces *Green_Cross*, and the parenthesis is maintained.

2-68 Formula correction message window

e. Press **Enter**. Four decimal places are shown for some results.
f. Copy the formula in cell **D10** to cells **D11:D16**.
g. Double-click cell **D16** and select **IrisMed** in the cell or in the *Formula* bar.
h. Press **F3 (FN+F3)** to open the *Paste Name* dialog box.
i. Select **Medeye** in the list and click **OK**.
j. Press **Enter**.
k. Copy the formula in cell **D16** to cells **D17:D20**.
l. Complete the formulas for Westville insurance.

7. Format cells **D5:D24** as **Currency** from the *Number Format* drop-down list. The values are rounded to two decimals places.

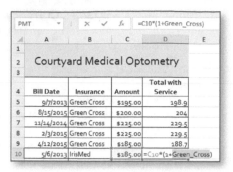

2-69 Edit the range name in a formula

8. Use the *SUMIF* function to calculate billable amounts by insurance company.
a. Click the **Optometry** worksheet tab and select cell **D31**.
b. Click the **Math & Trig** button [*Formulas* tab, *Function Library* group].
c. Select **SUMIF**.
d. Click the **Range** box and select cells **C5:C24**.
e. Click the **Criteria** box and select cell **C31** to use a relative reference to the company name.
f. Click the **Sum_range** text box and select cells **E5:E24**. The range name is substituted (Figure 2-70).
g. Click **OK**. The result is 1030, the total amount billed to Green Cross.

2-70 Different *range* and *sum_range* arguments for *SUMIF*

9. Verify results with *AutoCalculate*.
a. Select cells **E13:E15**.
b. Press **Ctrl** and select cells **E20:E21**. These are the billable amounts for the Green Cross insurance company.
c. Compare the *SUM* in the *Status* bar with the result in cell **D31** (Figure 2-71).

10. Copy the *SUMIF* function with a relative reference.
a. Select cell **D31**.
b. Drag the *Fill* pointer to copy the formula in cell **D31** to cells **D32:D34**. The *Auto Fill Options* button appears near cell D34.
c. Select cell **D32**. The reference to cell C31 in the original formula is updated to cell C32 in the copied formula (Figure 2-72).

2-71 *AutoCalculate* results in Status bar

11. Format cells **D31:D34** as **Currency** from the *Number Format* drop-down list. Press **Ctrl+Home**.

12. Use *VLOOKUP* with a range name to display costs.

 a. Click the **Pharmacy** worksheet tab and select cell **C6**. Cost and retail prices are missing.

 b. Click the **Lookup & Reference** button [*Formulas* tab, *Function Library* group] and select **VLOOKUP**.

 c. Click the **Lookup_value** box and click cell **A6**. The ID in column A will be located in the table array.

 d. Click the **Table_array** box. All prices are in the *Lookup_Data* sheet.

 e. Click the **Lookup_Data** sheet tab and select cells **A2:D16**. This range *Costs* is substituted when you select the cells; the range name is not substituted if you type the range address. Notice that the cost is in the third column.

 f. Click the **Col_index_num** box and type 3 (Figure 2-73).

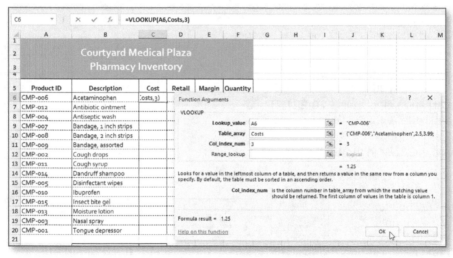

2-72 Relative reference is adjusted after copying

2-73 *VLOOKUP* and its arguments

 g. Click **OK**. The acetaminophen cost is 1.25.

 h. Copy the formula in cell **C6** to cells **C7:C20** without formatting. Format cells **C6:C20** as **Currency**.

13. Type the *VLOOKUP* function.

 a. Click cell **D6**.

 b. Type =vl and press **Tab**. The first argument is *lookup_value*.

 c. Select cell **A6** and type a comma (,) to separate the arguments. The next argument is *table_array*.

 d. Type costs,. You can type the name or select it in the *Formula AutoComplete* list (Figure 2-74).

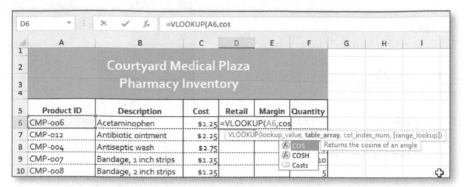

2-74 *Formula AutoComplete* shows range names

e. Type 4 for the *Col_index_num* argument, because the retail price is in the fourth column of the *Costs* range.

f. Press **Enter**. The closing parenthesis is supplied, and the retail price for acetaminophen is 3.99.

g. Copy the formula in cell **D6** to cells **D7:D20** without formatting and then format the cells as **Currency**.

14. Set order of precedence in a formula.
 a. Click cell **E6**. The formula to calculate the margin subtracts the cost from the retail price and then divides by the cost. The margin is shown as a markup percentage.
 b. Type =(to start the formula and enter the opening parenthesis.
 c. Click cell **D6** for the retail price.
 d. Type – and click cell **C6** to subtract the cost from the retail price.
 e. Type) for the closing parenthesis. This forces the subtraction to be carried out first.
 f. Type / for division and click cell **C6** to divide the results by the cost (Figure 2-75).
 g. Press **Enter**. The results are formatted as currency.
 h. Apply **Percent Style** to cell **E6**. A margin of 219% means that the retail price is more than two times the cost.
 i. Copy the formula in cell **E6** to cells **E7:E20** without formatting; then apply **Percent Style** to cells **E7:E20**.

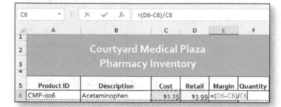

2-75 Formula with multiple operators

15. Trace precedents and dependents for formulas.
 a. Select cell **C6**.
 b. Click the **Trace Precedents** button [*Formulas* tab, *Formula Auditing* group]. The formula uses data from another worksheet and from cell **A6**.
 c. Select cell **E6** and click the **Trace Precedents** button.
 d. Select cell **D7** and click the **Trace Dependents** button. The arrow points to cell **E7**.
 e. Click the **Remove Arrows** button [*Formulas* tab, *Formula Auditing* group].

16. Enter a *SUMPRODUCT* function to calculate inventory values.
 a. Click cell **C22**.
 b. Click the **Math & Trig** button [*Formulas* tab, *Function Library* group] and select **SUMPRODUCT**.
 c. Click the *Array1* box and select cells **C6:C20**.
 d. Click the *Array2* box and select cells **F6:F20**. Both arrays have the same dimension (Figure 2-76).
 e. Click **OK**. The result in E22 is 249.15. Each value in column C is multiplied by its corresponding value in column E, and those results are summed.

2-76 Two arrays for SUMPRODUCT

17. Type the *SUMPRODUCT* function.
 a. Click cell **D23**.
 b. Type =sump and press **Tab**. The first argument is *array1*.
 c. Select cells **D6:D20** and type a comma (,) to separate the arguments. The next argument is *array2*.
 d. Select cells **F6:F20** and press **Enter** (Figure 2-77). The result is 588.29.
 e. Format cells **D22:D23** as **Currency**. Press **Ctrl+Home**.

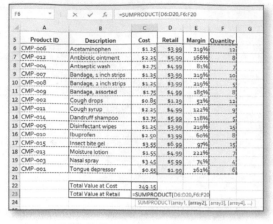

2-77 Both arrays have the same dimension

18. Use *PMT* to calculate patient payments.
 a. Click the **Payments** sheet tab and select cell **B6**.
 b. Click the **Financial** button [*Formulas* tab, *Function Library* group] and select **PMT**.
 c. Click the **Rate** box and type 2.75%/12. You can type the rate when it is not shown in a cell. Yearly rates are divided by 12 for monthly payments.
 d. Click the **Nper** box and type 24. The length of the loan is indicated in the label in cell A4. Two-year financing means 24 monthly payments.
 e. Click the **Pv** box and click cell **A6**, the amount of a loan.
 f. Press **F4 (FN+F4)** to make the reference absolute (A6). Press **F4 (FN+F4)** again to make a mixed reference A$6.
 g. Press **F4 (FN+F4)** once more to make the reference mixed $A6.
 h. Click the **Type** box and type 1 for payment at the beginning of the month. The *Fv* argument is blank (Figure 2-78).
 i. Click **OK**. The payment for financing $500 is ($21.39).
 j. Copy the formula to cells **B7:B11**. The reference to cell $A6 is mixed, and the *rate* and *nper* values that you typed are absolute.

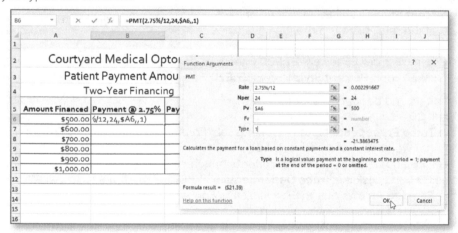

2-78 PMT arguments

19. Copy and edit a *PMT* function with a mixed reference.
 a. Copy the formula in cell **B6** to cell **C6**. The reference to cell $A6 is correct, but you need to edit the *Rate* argument.
 b. Select cell **C6** and click the **Insert Function** button in the *Formula* bar. The *Function Arguments* dialog box opens with the formula.
 c. Click the **Rate** text box and edit the calculation to 3.25%/12.
 d. Click **OK**. The payment for financing $500 at 3.25% is ($21.49).
 e. Copy the formula to cells **C7:C11**.

20. Enter the TODAY function.
 a. Select cell **A14**.
 b. Type =to, press **Tab**, and press **Enter**.
 c. Press **Ctrl+Home**.

21. Save and close the workbook (Figure 2-79).

Courtyard Medical Optometry

Patient ID	Initial Visit	Insurance	Prescription	Billable	Deductible	Patient Responsibility
CP0001	3/3/2014	Medeye	Gas Permeable	$125.00	$40.00	$75.00
CP0002	5/6/2013	IrisMed	Soft	$185.00	$50.00	$135.00
CP0003	8/12/2014	Medeye	Glasses	$225.00	$75.00	$150.00
CP0004	4/4/2014	Westville	Glasses	$125.00	$75.00	$50.00
CP0005	7/8/2014	Medeye	Soft	$245.00	$50.00	$195.00
CP0006	2/1/2015	IrisMed	Soft	$275.00	$100.00	$175.00
CP0007	3/7/2015	IrisMed	Soft	$325.00	$100.00	$225.00
CP0008	12/3/2014	Westville	Gas Permeable	$175.00	$75.00	$100.00
CP0009	9/7/2013	Green Cross	Gas Permeable	$195.00	$50.00	$145.00
CP0010	8/15/2015	Green Cross	Soft	$200.00	$75.00	$125.00
CP0011	11/14/2014	Green Cross	Soft	$225.00	$100.00	$125.00
CP0012	6/8/2015	IrisMed	Soft	$200.00	$100.00	$100.00
CP0013	5/3/2014	Medeye	Glasses	$475.00	$200.00	$275.00
CP0014	4/18/2014	IrisMed	Soft	$225.00	$75.00	$150.00
CP0015	3/17/2014	IrisMed	Soft	$225.00	$75.00	$150.00
CP0016	2/3/2015	Green Cross	Soft	$225.00	$75.00	$150.00
CP0017	4/12/2015	Green Cross	Gas Permeable	$185.00	$50.00	$135.00
CP0018	2/2/2015	Westville	Gas Permeable	$195.00	$50.00	$145.00
CP0019	2/18/2015	Westville	Soft	$225.00	$75.00	$150.00
CP0020	10/5/2014	Medeye	Glasses	$275.00	$100.00	$175.00

Average Billable	$222.50
Maximum Billable	$475.00
Minimum Billable	$125.00

Green Cross	$4,030.00
IrisMed	$4,455.00
Medeye	$4,455.00
Westville	$720.00

Courtyard Medical Optometry

Bill Date	Insurance	Amount	Total with Service Charge
9/7/2013	Green Cross	$195.00	$198.90
8/15/2015	Green Cross	$200.00	$204.00
11/14/2014	Green Cross	$225.00	$229.50
2/3/2015	Green Cross	$225.00	$229.50
4/12/2015	Green Cross	$185.00	$188.70
5/6/2013	IrisMed	$185.00	$188.98
2/1/2015	IrisMed	$275.00	$280.91
3/7/2015	IrisMed	$325.00	$331.99
6/8/2015	IrisMed	$200.00	$204.30
4/18/2014	IrisMed	$235.00	$240.05
3/17/2014	IrisMed	$235.00	$239.11
3/3/2014	Medeye	$125.00	$127.19
8/12/2014	Medeye	$235.00	$239.11
7/8/2014	Medeye	$245.00	$249.29
5/3/2014	Medeye	$475.00	$483.31
10/5/2014	Medeye	$375.00	$381.56
4/4/2014	Westville	$135.00	$137.70
12/3/2014	Westville	$175.00	$178.50
3/21/2014	Westville	$195.00	$198.90
2/18/2015	Westville	$225.00	$229.50

Courtyard Medical Optometry
Patient Payment Amounts
Two-Year Financing

Amount Financed	Payment @ 1.7%	Payment @ 3.25%
$500.00	$21.25	$21.59
$600.00	$25.68	$25.74
$700.00	$29.64	$30.02
$800.00	$34.22	$34.31
$900.00	$38.50	$38.60
$1,000.00	$42.77	$42.90

2-79 Completed Excel 2-1

Courtyard Medical Plaza
Pharmacy Inventory

Product ID	Description	Cost	Retail	Margin	Quantity
CMP-006	Acetaminophen	$1.25	$3.99	219%	12
CMP-012	Antibiotic ointment	$2.25	$5.99	166%	8
CMP-004	Antiseptic wash	$2.75	$4.99	81%	7
CMP-007	Bandage, 1 inch strips	$1.25	$3.99	219%	10
CMP-008	Bandage, 2 inch strips	$1.25	$3.99	219%	6
CMP-009	Bandage, assorted	$1.75	$4.99	185%	8
CMP-002	Cough drops	$0.85	$1.99	52%	12
CMP-011	Cough syrup	$2.25	$4.99	122%	9
CMP-014	Dandruff shampoo	$2.75	$5.99	118%	5
CMP-005	Disinfectant wipes	$1.25	$3.99	219%	16
CMP-010	Ibuprofen	$2.50	$3.99	60%	8
CMP-015	Insect bite gel	$3.55	$6.99	97%	16
CMP-013	Moisture lotion	$1.55	$4.99	222%	7
CMP-003	Nasal spray	$3.45	$5.99	74%	4
CMP-001	Tongue depressor	$0.55	$1.99	262%	6

Total Value at Cost	$249.15
Total Value at Retail	$588.29

Hamilton Civic Center (HCC) is a nonprofit community fitness center with an indoor pool, sauna, indoor track, project room, racquetball courts, meeting rooms, and a boutique. In this workbook, you complete tasks related to health seminars, a member challenge, and the daycare program.
[Student Learning Outcomes 2.1, 2.2, 2.3, 2.4, 2.5, 2.6, 2.7]

File Needed: ***HamiltonCivic-02.xlsx*** *[Student data files are available in the Library of your SIMnet account.]*
Completed Project File Name: *[your initials] Excel 2-2.xlsx*

Skills Covered in This Project

- Create and copy formulas.
- Name cell ranges.
- Use relative and absolute references.
- Set mathematical order of operations.

- Use *AutoCalculate* and formula auditing tools.
- Use *VLOOKUP* and *HLOOKUP*.
- Create an *IF* function.
- Create a *SUMIF* function.
- Use the *TODAY* function.

1. Open the ***HamiltonCivic-02.xlsx*** workbook from your student data files and save it as [your initials] Excel 2-2.

2. Name cell ranges.
 a. On the *Seminars* sheet, select cells **B6:B10**, and click the **Name** box.
 b. Type Seminars in the *Name* box and press **Enter**.
 c. Click the **Data** sheet tab. You will name the cell ranges used in the *Lookup* functions.
 d. Select cells **A2:D10** and click the **Name** box.
 e. Type V_Calories in the *Name* box and press **Enter**. This will remind you that this range is a vertical table array.
 f. Select cells **F2:J3** and click the **Name** box.
 g. Type H_Fees and press **Enter**. This range is a horizontal table array.

3. Enter and copy a division formula.
 a. Select cell **D2** on the **Data** worksheet. To calculate calories per minute, divide the total calories by the number of minutes.
 b. Type an equals sign (=) to start the formula.
 c. Click cell **C2**, the total number of calories. This formula uses relative references.
 d. Type / for division.
 e. Click cell **B2**, the number of minutes, and press **Enter**. As many decimal places as fit in the cell are displayed (Figure 2-80).

2-80 Decimal positions fill the cell

 f. Drag the *Fill* pointer to copy the formula in cell **D2** to cells **D3:D10**. Ignore the *Auto Fill Options* button.
 g. While cells **D2:D10** are selected, click the **Decrease Decimal** button [*Home* tab, *Number* group] two times. The sets the same number of decimal positions for all results.

4. Use *HLOOKUP* with a range name to display fees.
 a. Click the **Seminars** worksheet tab and select cell **C6**. Fees are in the *H_Fees* range.
 b. Click the **Lookup & Reference** button [*Formulas* tab, *Function Library* group] and select **HLOOKUP**.
 c. Click the **Lookup_value** box and click cell **B6**.
 d. Click the **Table_array** box.

e. Type **h_fees** the name of the range. It is not case sensitive, and quotation marks are not necessary.

f. Click the **Row_index_num** box and type **2** because the fees are in the second row of the *H_Fees* range (Figure 2-81).

g. Click **OK**. The fee is $15.00.

h. Copy the formula in cell **C6** to cells **C7:C10**.

5. Enter and copy an addition formula.
 a. Click cell **E15** and type an equals sign (=) to start the formula.
 b. Click cell **D6**, the number of attendees for the seminar in Hendersonville.
 c. Type + for addition.
 d. Click cell **E6** to add the number of attendees for Advocate Central.
 e. Type +, click cell **F6**, type +, and click cell **G6** (Figure 2-82).
 f. Press **Enter**.
 g. Drag the *Fill* pointer to copy the formula in cell **E15** to cells **E16:E19**. Ignore the *Auto Fill Options* button.
 h. Click cell **E20**, click the **AutoSum** button [*Home* tab, *Editing* group], and press **Enter**. The total is 209 attendees.

6. Set order of operations in a formula.
 a. Select cell **E24**. The fee is multiplied by the sum of the attendees at each hospital. Cells D6:G6 must be added first and that result is multiplied by cell C6.
 b. Type = to start the formula and click cell **C6**.
 c. Type * to multiply.
 d. Type (for the opening parenthesis. This forces the addition to be carried out first.
 e. Click cell **D6**, type +, click cell **E6**, type +, click cell **F6**, type +, and click cell **G6**.
 f. Type) for the closing parenthesis (Figure2-83).
 g. Press **Enter**. The result is 705.
 h. Format cell **E24** as **Currency** and copy the formula to cells **E25:E28**.
 i. Click cell **E29**, click the **AutoSum** button [*Home* tab, *Editing* group], and press **Enter**.

7. Use *AutoCalculate* and formula auditing tools.
 a. Select cells **E24:E28**.
 b. Compare the *SUM* in the *Status* bar with the result in cell E29.
 c. Select cell **E15**.

2-81 Arguments for *HLOOKUP*

2-82 Simple addition formula

2-83 Addition done before multiplication

d. Click the **Trace Precedents** button [*Formulas* tab, *Formula Auditing* group].
e. Click the **Trace Dependents** button. The formula in cell E15 has both precedent and dependent cells (Figure 2-84).
f. Click the **Remove Arrows** button [*Formulas* tab, *Formula Auditing* group].

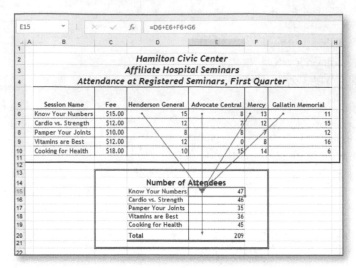

2-84 Precedent and dependent cells

8. Use *VLOOKUP* with a range name to display calories expended.
 a. Click the **Data** sheet tab.
 b. Click the **Name** box arrow and select **V_Calories**. Notice that total calories are in the third column.
 c. Click the **Calorie Tracking** sheet tab and select cell **D3**. Calories by activity are within the range *V_Calories*.
 d. Click the **Lookup & Reference** button [*Formulas* tab, *Formula Auditing* group] and select **VLOOKUP**.
 e. Click the **Lookup_value** box and click cell **C3**. The activity name in column C will be located in the table array.
 f. Click the **Table_array** box and press **F3 (FN+F3)** to open the *Paste Name* dialog box.
 g. Double-click **V_Calories** to insert it.
 h. Click the **Col_index_num** box and type 3 (Figure 2-85).
 i. Click **OK**. Calories for the first activity are 250.
 j. Copy the formula in cell **D3** to cells **D4:D23**.

2-85 Arguments for the *VLOOKUP* function

9. Build a *SUMIF* formula with absolute and relative references.
 a. Select cell **D28** on the **Calorie Tracking** sheet.
 b. Click the **Recently Used** button [*Formulas* tab, *Function Library* group].
 c. Look for and choose **SUMIF**. (If you do not see *SUMIF* in the list, click the **Math & Trig** button to find and select **SUMIF**.)
 d. Click the **Range** box and select cells **C3:C23**, the range that will be evaluated.
 e. Press **F4 (FN+F4)** to make the cell references absolute.
 f. Click the **Criteria** box and select cell **C28** to find rows with "cycling" as the activity.
 g. Click the **Sum_range** box and select cells **D3:D23**, the values to be summed if the activity is cycling.

h. Press **F4 (FN+F4)** to make the references absolute (Figure 2-86).
i. Click **OK**. The result is 795 calories.

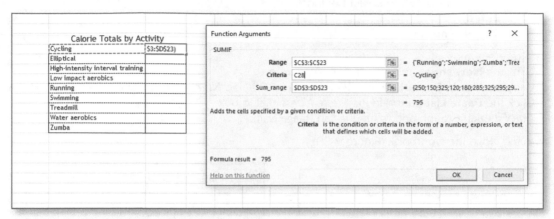

2-86 *SUMIF* **function for cycling**

10. Copy the formula in cell **D28** to cells **D29:D36** without formatting (Figure 2-87).

11. Create an *IF* function to calculate a fee based on age.
 a. Click the **Day Care** sheet tab and select cell **D5**.
 b. Click the **Logical** button [*Formulas* tab, *Function Library* group] and select **IF**.
 c. Click the **Logical_test** box and click cell **B5**.
 d. Type >=4 to test if the child is 4 years old or greater.
 e. Click the **Value_if_true** box and click cell **I9**. The fee for a child 4 years old or greater is $18.
 f. Press **F4 (FN+F4)** to make the reference absolute.
 g. Click the **Value_if_false** box and click cell **I8**. If the child is not 4 years old or greater, the child is between 1 and 3 years old.
 h. Press **F4 (FN+F4)** to make the reference absolute (Figure 2-88).
 i. Click **OK**. The fee for Mary is $18.
 j. Format the result as **Currency**.
 k. Copy the formula in cell **D5** to cells **D6:D14**.

2-87 **Copy the formula without formatting**

2-88 *IF* **function to determine the fee**

551

12. Insert the current date as a function.
 a. Click the **Data** sheet tab and click cell **A12**.
 b. Type =to and press **Tab** to select the function.
 c. Press **Enter**.
 d. Press **Ctrl+Home**.

13. Paste range names.
 a. Click the **New sheet** button in the sheet tab area.
 b. Click the **Use in Formula** button [*Formulas* tab, *Defined Names* group] and select **Paste Names**.
 c. Click the **Paste List** button in the *Paste Name* dialog box.
 d. *AutoFit* each column and name the tab **Range Names**.

14. Save and close the workbook (Figure 2-89).

Hamilton Civic Center
Affiliate Hospital Seminars
Attendance at Registered Seminars, First Quarter

Session Name	Fee	Henderson	General	Advocate	Central	Mercy	Gallatin	Memorial
Know Your Numbers	$15.00		15		8	13		11
Cardio vs. Strength	$12.00		12		7	12		15
Pamper Your Joints	$10.00		8		8	7		12
Vitamins are Best	$12.00		12		0	8		16
Cooking for Health	$18.00		10		15	14		6

Number of Attendees

Know Your Numbers	47
Cardio vs. Strength	46
Pamper Your Joints	35
Vitamins are Best	36
Cooking for Health	45
Total	209

Total Fees Collected

Know Your Numbers	$705.00
Cardio vs. Strength	$552.00
Pamper Your Joints	$350.00
Vitamins are Best	$432.00
Cooking for Health	$810.00
Total	$2,849.00

Hamilton Civic Center

Summer Day Care

Daily Fees by Child

Name	Age	Gender	Fee
Johnson, Mary	4	F	$18.00
Amed, Essa	5	M	$18.00
Jimenez, Rosa	3	F	$20.00
Femua, Valentina	3	F	$20.00
Yvea, Jeanette	2	F	$20.00
Smith, Avery	2	M	$20.00
Coonley, Evan	5	M	$18.00
Schneider, Ellery	1	F	$20.00
Lutz, Amy	4	F	$18.00
Yugio, Igor	3	M	$20.00

Age	Daily Fee
1 to 3	$20.00
4 and up	$18.00

H_Fees	=Data!F2:J3
Seminars	=Seminars!B6:B10
V_Calories	=Data!A2:D10

Member Calorie Burn Challenge

Member ID	Date	Activity	Calories
10034	2/1/2016	Running	250
10036	2/2/2016	Swimming	150
10038	2/2/2016	Zumba	325
10040	2/4/2016	Treadmill	120
10042	3/1/2016	Low impact aerobics	180
10044	3/3/2016	Elliptical	285
10046	3/5/2016	Zumba	325
10048	3/7/2016	Water aerobics	295
10050	3/9/2016	Water aerobics	295
10054	3/11/2016	Low impact aerobics	180
10036	3/13/2016	Cycling	265
10038	3/15/2016	Cycling	265
10040	3/17/2016	Water aerobics	295
10042	3/19/2016	High-intensity interval training	350
10044	3/21/2016	High-intensity interval training	350
10046	3/23/2016	Cycling	265
10048	3/25/2016	Treadmill	120
10050	3/27/2016	Zumba	325
10036	3/29/2016	High-intensity interval training	350
10054	3/31/2016	Treadmill	120
10042	4/2/2016	Running	250

Calorie Totals by Activity

Cycling	795
Elliptical	285
High-intensity interval training	1050
Low impact aerobics	360
Running	500
Swimming	150
Treadmill	360
Water aerobics	885
Zumba	975

Activity	Time	Calories	Calories per Minute
Cycling	45	265	5.889
Elliptical	30	285	9.500
High-intensity interval training	45	350	7.778
Low impact aerobics	45	180	4.000
Running	30	250	8.333
Swimming	30	150	5.000
Treadmill	30	120	4.000
Water aerobics	45	295	6.556
Zumba	45	325	7.222

Session Names and Fees

Cardio vs. Strength	Cooking for Health	Know Your Numbers	Pamper Your Joints	Vitamins are Best
$12.00	$18.00	$15.00	$10.00	$12.00

2-89 Excel 2-2 completed

Guided Project 2-3

Sierra Pacific Community College District (SPCCD) consists of four individual community colleges. The workbook for this project includes an amortization schedule for student loans and a fee and credit hour summary for several departments.
[Student Learning Outcomes 2.1, 2.2, 2.3, 2.4, 2.5, 2.6, 2.7]

File Needed: **SierraPacific-02.xlsx** [Student data files are available in the Library of your SIMnet account.]
Completed Project File Name: **[your initials] Excel 2-3.xlsx**

Skills Covered in This Project

- Name cell ranges.
- Create and copy formulas.
- Set mathematical order of operations.
- Use absolute references in formulas.
- Insert the current date as a function.
- Use the *PMT* function.
- Audit formulas.
- Use *SUMIF* and *SUMPRODUCT*.

1. Open the **SierraPacific-02.xlsx** workbook from your student data files and save it as [your initials] Excel 2-3.

2. Set range names for the workbook.
 a. On the **Student Loan** sheet, select cells **B5:C8**.
 b. Click the **Create from Selection** button [*Formulas* tab, *Defined Names* group].
 c. Verify that the **Left column** box in the *Create Names from Selection* dialog box is selected.
 d. Deselect the **Top row** box if it is checked and click **OK**.
 e. Select cells **E5:F7**. Repeat steps a–d to create range names.
 f. Click the **Name Manager** button [*Formulas* tab, *Defined Names* group] to view the names in the *Name Manager* dialog box (Figure 2-90).
 g. Click **Close**.

2-90 *Name Manager* dialog box

3. Enter a *PMT* function.
 a. Select **C8**.
 b. Click the **Financial** button [*Formulas* tab, *Function Library* group] and select **PMT**.
 c. Click the **Rate** box and click cell **C7**. The range name *Rate* is substituted.
 d. Type /12 immediately after **Rate** to divide by 12 for monthly payments.
 e. Click the **Nper** box and click cell **C6**. The substituted range name is *Loan_Term*.
 f. Type *12 after **Loan_Term** to multiply by 12.
 g. Click the **Pv** box and type a minus sign (−) to set the argument as a negative amount.
 h. Click cell **C5** (*Loan_Amount*) for the *pv* argument. A negative loan amount reflects the lender's perspective, since the money is paid out now (Figure 2-91).

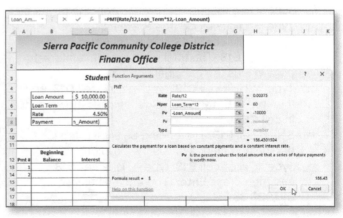

2-91 *Pv* argument is negative in the *PMT* function

i. Leave the *Fv* and *Type* boxes empty.

j. Click **OK**. The payment for a loan at this rate is $186.43, shown as a positive value.

4. Create a total interest formula.

 a. Click cell **F5** (*Total_Interest*). This value is calculated by multiplying the monthly payment by the total number of payments to determine total outlay. From this amount, you subtract the loan amount.

 b. Type = and click cell **C8** (the *Payment*).

 c. Type * to multiply and click cell **C6** (*Loan_Term*).

 d. Type *12 to multiply by 12 for monthly payments.

 e. Type – immediately after ***12** to subtract.

 f. Click cell **C5** (the *Loan_Amount*). The formula is *Payment*Loan_Term*12—Loan_Amount*. Parentheses are not required, because the multiplications are done from left to right, followed by the subtraction (Figure 2-92).

 g. Press **Enter**. The result is $1,185.81.

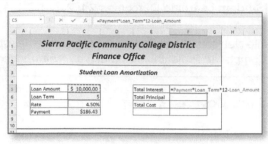

2-92 Left-to-right operations

5. Create the total principal formula and the total loan cost.

 a. Select cell **F6** (*Total_Principal*). This value is calculated by multiplying the monthly payment by the total number of payments. From this amount, subtract the total interest.

 b. Type = and click cell **C8** (the *Payment*).

 c. Type * to multiply and click cell **C6** (*Loan_Term*).

 d. Type *12 to multiply by 12 for monthly payments.

 e. Type – immediately after ***12** to subtract.

 f. Click cell **F5** (the *Total_Interest*). The formula is *Payment*Loan_Term*12—Total_Interest*.

 g. Press **Enter**. Total principal is the amount of the loan.

 h. Click cell **F7**, the *Total_Cost* of the loan. This is the total principal plus the total interest.

 i. Type =, click cell **F5**, type +, click cell **F6**, and then press **Enter**.

6. Build an amortization schedule.

 a. Click cell **B13**. The beginning balance is the total cost of the loan.

 b. Type =, click cell **F7**, and press **Enter**.

 c. Format the value as **Accounting Number Format**.

 d. Select cell **C13**. The interest for each payment is calculated by multiplying the balance in column B by the rate divided by 12.

 e. Type = and click cell **B13**.

 f. Type *(and click cell **C7**.

 g. Type /12). Parentheses are necessary so that the division is done first (Figure 2-93).

 h. Press **Enter** and format the results as **Accounting Number Format**.

 i. Select cell **D13**. The portion of the payment that is applied to the principal is calculated by subtracting the interest portion from the payment.

 j. Type =, click cell **C8** (the *Payment*).

 k. Type –, click cell **C13**, and press **Enter**.

 l. Click cell **E13**. The total payment is the interest portion plus the principal portion.

 m. Type =, click cell **C13**, type +, click cell **D13**, and then press **Enter**. The value matches the amount in cell **C8**.

 n. Select cell **F13**. The ending balance is the beginning balance minus the payment.

 o. Type =, click cell **B13**, type –, click cell **E13**, and then press **Enter**. The ending balance is $10,999.38.

2-93 The interest formula

B13	=Total_Cost
C13	=B13*(Rate/12)
D13	=Payment−C13
E13	=C13+D13
F13	=B13−E13

7. Fill data and copy formulas.
 a. Select cells **A13:A14**. This is a series with an increment of 1.
 b. Drag the *Fill* pointer to reach cell **A72**. This sets 60 payments for a five-year loan term.
 c. Select cell **B14**. The beginning balance for the second payment is the ending balance for the first payment.
 d. Type =, click cell **F13**, and press **Enter**.
 e. Double-click the *Fill* pointer for cell **B14** to fill the formula down to row **72**. The results are zero until the rest of the schedule is complete.
 f. Select cells **C13:F13**.
 g. Double-click the *Fill* pointer at cell **F13**. All of the formulas are filled (copied) to row **72** (Figure 2-94).
 h. Scroll to see the values in row **72**. The loan balance reaches 0.
 i. Press **Ctrl+Home**.

	A	B	C	D	E	F
12	Pmt #	Beginning Balance	Interest	Principal	Total Payment	Ending Balance
13	1	$ 11,185.81	$ 41.95	$ 144.48	$ 186.43	$ 10,999.38
14	2	$ 10,999.38	$ 41.25	$ 145.18	$ 186.43	$ 10,812.95
15	3	$ 10,812.95	$ 40.55	$ 145.88	$ 186.43	$ 10,626.52
16	4	$ 10,626.52	$ 39.85	$ 146.58	$ 186.43	$ 10,440.09
17	5	$ 10,440.09	$ 39.15	$ 147.28	$ 186.43	$ 10,253.66
18	6	$ 10,253.66	$ 38.45	$ 147.98	$ 186.43	$ 10,067.23
19	7	$ 10,067.23	$ 37.75	$ 148.68	$ 186.43	$ 9,880.80
20	8	$ 9,880.80	$ 37.05	$ 149.38	$ 186.43	$ 9,694.37
21	9	$ 9,694.37	$ 36.35	$ 150.08	$ 186.43	$ 9,507.94
22	10	$ 9,507.94	$ 35.65	$ 150.78	$ 186.43	$ 9,321.51
23	11	$ 9,321.51	$ 34.96	$ 151.47	$ 186.43	$ 9,135.08
24	12	$ 9,135.08	$ 34.26	$ 152.17	$ 186.43	$ 8,948.65
25	13	$ 8,948.65	$ 33.56	$ 152.87	$ 186.43	$ 8,762.22
26	14	$ 8,762.22	$ 32.86	$ 153.57	$ 186.43	$ 8,575.79
27	15	$ 8,575.79	$ 32.16	$ 154.27	$ 186.43	$ 8,389.36
28	16	$ 8,389.36	$ 31.46	$ 154.97	$ 186.43	$ 8,202.93
60	48	$ 2,423.59	$ 9.09	$ 177.34	$ 186.43	$ 2,237.16
61	49	$ 2,237.16	$ 8.39	$ 178.04	$ 186.43	$ 2,050.73
62	50	$ 2,050.73	$ 7.69	$ 178.74	$ 186.43	$ 1,864.30
63	51	$ 1,864.30	$ 6.99	$ 179.44	$ 186.43	$ 1,677.87
64	52	$ 1,677.87	$ 6.29	$ 180.14	$ 186.43	$ 1,491.44
65	53	$ 1,491.44	$ 5.59	$ 180.84	$ 186.43	$ 1,305.01
66	54	$ 1,305.01	$ 4.89	$ 181.54	$ 186.43	$ 1,118.58
67	55	$ 1,118.58	$ 4.19	$ 182.24	$ 186.43	$ 932.15
68	56	$ 932.15	$ 3.50	$ 182.93	$ 186.43	$ 745.72
69	57	$ 745.72	$ 2.80	$ 183.63	$ 186.43	$ 559.29
70	58	$ 559.29	$ 2.10	$ 184.33	$ 186.43	$ 372.86
71	59	$ 372.86	$ 1.40	$ 185.03	$ 186.43	$ 186.43
72	60	$ 186.43	$ 0.70	$ 185.73	$ 186.43	$ 0.00

2-94 Formulas copied down columns

8. Build a multiplication formula and set order of mathematical operations.
 a. Click the **Fees & Credit** sheet tab and select cell **F7**. Credit hours times number of sections times the fee calculates the total fees from a course.
 b. Type =, click cell **C7**, type *, click cell **D7**, type *, click cell **E7**, and then press **Enter**. No parentheses are necessary because multiplication is done in left to right order.
 c. Select cell **G7**. Fee collected per credit hour is determined by dividing the value in cell F7 by the number of sections times credit hours times average enrollment.
 d. Type =, click cell **F7**, and type / (. Parentheses are necessary so that left to right order is overridden.
 e. Click cell **C7**, type *, and click cell **D7**.
 f. Type *, click cell **C20**, and press **F4 (FN+F4)** to make the reference absolute (Figure 2-95).
 g. Press **Enter**. A message box notes that the closing parenthesis is missing.
 h. Click **Yes** in the message box.
 i. Select cells **F7:G7** and double-click the *Fill* pointer to copy the formulas.
 j. Format cells **G7:G18** as **Currency** and set a bottom border for cells **F18:G18**.

C20			× ✓ fx	=F7/(C7*D7*C20)				
	A	B	C	D	E	F	G	H
5								
6	Dept	Course Name	Credit Hours	# of Sections	Fees	Total Fees	Fee per Credit Hour	
7	BIO	General Biology	3	12	$125.00	$4,500.00	=F7/(C7*D7*C20)	
8	BIO	Intro to Microbiology	3	10	$135.00			
9	BIO	Anatomy & Physiology	4	8	$150.00			
10	FRL	Spanish I	3	13	$55.00			
11	FRL	French II	3	5	$55.00			
12	FRL	Mandarin I	3	5	$55.00			
13	IMS	Intro to MS Office	3	15	$75.00			
14	IMS	Intro to Excel	3	13	$75.00			
15	IMS	Access Programming	3	4	$75.00			
16	PHY	Chemistry Fundamentals	4	7	$125.00			
17	PHY	Organic Chemistry I	4	7	$150.00			
18	PHY	Fundamentals of Physics	4	8	$125.00			
19								
20		Average Enrollment	15					

2-95 Formula to calculate fee per credit hour

9. Use *SUMIF*.
 a. Select cell **D26**. Fees by department can be calculated.
 b. Click the **Math & Trig** button [*Formulas* tab, *Function Library* group] and select **SUMIF**.
 c. Click the **Range** box and select cells **A7:A18**. This range will be matched against the criteria.
 d. Press **F4 (FN+F4)** to make the reference absolute.
 e. Click the **Criteria** box and type bio.
 f. Click the **Sum_range** box, select cells **F7:F18**, and press **F4 (FN+F4)**.

g. Click **OK**. Total fees for the Biology department are 13350.

h. Format the results as **Currency**.

10. Copy a *SUMIF* function and check formula errors.

a. Click cell **D26** and drag its *Fill* pointer to copy the formula to cells **D27:D29** without formatting.

b. Double-click cell **D27**. You need to change the criteria.

c. Edit the criteria argument in the *Formula* bar or in the cell to display frl. Do not change the quotation marks or any other punctuation (Figure 2-96).

d. Press **Enter** or click the **Enter** button in the *Formula* bar. An error triangle appears in the top left corner of cell **D27**.

e. Click cell **D27** and point to its **Trace Error** button to see the *ScreenTip* (Figure 2-97). The formula has different criteria than the immediately preceding formula, but this is correct.

f. Click the **Trace Error** button and choose **Ignore Error**.

g. Double-click cell **D28** and edit the criteria argument to display ims.

h. Edit the argument in cell **D29** to show the department initials.

i. Format cells **D27:D29** as **Currency**.

2-96 Edit the SUMIF criteria in the cell or in the *Formula* bar

11. Use *SUMPRODUCT* and trace an error.

a. Select cell **E26** and click the **Formulas** tab.

b. Click the **Math & Trig** button in the *Function Library* group and select **SUMPRODUCT**.

c. Click the **Array1** box and select cells **C7:C9**, credit hours for courses in the Biology Department.

d. Click the **Array2** box and select cells **D7:D9**, the number of sections for the Biology Department.

e. Click **OK**. The Biology Department has 98 total credit hour offerings.

f. Click cell **E26** and point to its **Trace Error** button. The formula omits adjacent cells in columns C and D, which is correct.

g. Click the **Trace Error** button and select **Ignore Error**.

2-97 *Trace Error* button and its *ScreenTip*

12. Copy and edit *SUMPRODUCT*.

a. Click cell **E26** and drag its *Fill* pointer to copy the formula to cells **E27:E29** without formatting.

b. Click cell **E27** and click the **Insert Function** button in the *Formula* bar.

c. Select and highlight the range in the *Array1* box and select cells **C10:C12**. The range you select replaces the range in the dialog box (Figure 2-98).

2-98 Replace the *ArrayN* arguments

d. Select the range in the *Array2* box and select cells **D10:D12**.

e. Click **OK**.

f. Edit and complete the formulas in cells **E28:E29** and ignore errors.

13. Insert the current date as a function.

 a. Select cell **G30**.

 b. Type =to and press **Tab** to select the function.

 c. Press **Enter**.

 d. Press **Ctrl+Home**.

14. Paste range names.

 a. Click the **New sheet** button in the sheet tab area.

 b. Name the new sheet **Range Names**.

 c. Press **F3 (FN+F3)** to open the *Paste Name* dialog box.

 d. Click the **Paste List** button.

 e. *AutoFit* each column.

15. Save and close the workbook (Figure 2-99).

Sierra Pacific Community College District — Finance Office

Student Loan Amortization

Loan Amount	$10,000.00		Total Interest	$1,185.81
Loan Term	5		Total Principal	$10,000.00
Rate	4.50%		Total Cost	$11,185.81
Payment	$186.43			

Pmt #	Beginning Balance	Interest	Principal	Total Payment	Ending Balance
1	$11,185.81	$41.95	$144.48	$186.43	$10,999.38
2	$10,999.38	$41.25	$145.18	$186.43	$10,812.95
3	$10,812.95	$40.55	$145.88	$186.43	$10,626.52
4	$10,626.52	$39.85	$146.58	$186.43	$10,440.09
5	$10,440.09	$39.15	$147.28	$186.43	$10,253.66
6	$10,253.66	$38.45	$147.98	$186.43	$10,067.23
7	$10,067.23	$37.75	$148.68	$186.43	$9,880.80
8	$9,880.80	$37.05	$149.38	$186.43	$9,694.37
9	$9,694.37	$36.35	$150.08	$186.43	$9,507.94
10	$9,507.94	$35.65	$150.78	$186.43	$9,321.51
11	$9,321.51	$34.96	$151.47	$186.43	$9,135.08
12	$9,135.08	$34.26	$152.17	$186.43	$8,948.65
13	$8,948.65	$33.56	$152.87	$186.43	$8,762.22
14	$8,762.22	$32.86	$153.57	$186.43	$8,575.79
15	$8,575.79	$32.16	$154.27	$186.43	$8,389.36
16	$8,389.36	$31.46	$154.97	$186.43	$8,202.93
17	$8,202.93	$30.76	$155.67	$186.43	$8,016.50
18	$8,016.50	$30.06	$156.37	$186.43	$7,830.07
19	$7,830.07	$29.36	$157.07	$186.43	$7,643.64
20	$7,643.64	$28.66	$157.77	$186.43	$7,457.21
21	$7,457.21	$27.96	$158.47	$186.43	$7,270.78
22	$7,270.78	$27.27	$159.16	$186.43	$7,084.35
23	$7,084.35	$26.57	$159.86	$186.43	$6,897.92
24	$6,897.92	$25.87	$160.56	$186.43	$6,711.49
25	$6,711.49	$25.17	$161.26	$186.43	$6,525.06
26	$6,525.06	$24.47	$161.96	$186.43	$6,338.63
27	$6,338.63	$23.77	$162.66	$186.43	$6,152.20
28	$6,152.20	$23.07	$163.36	$186.43	$5,965.77
29	$5,965.77	$22.37	$164.06	$186.43	$5,779.84
30	$5,779.34	$21.67	$164.76	$186.43	$5,592.91
31	$5,592.91	$20.97	$165.46	$186.43	$5,406.48
32	$5,406.48	$20.27	$166.16	$186.43	$5,220.05
33	$5,220.05	$19.58	$166.86	$186.43	$5,033.62
34	$5,033.62	$18.88	$167.55	$186.43	$4,847.19
35	$4,847.19	$18.18	$168.25	$186.43	$4,660.75
36	$4,660.75	$17.48	$168.95	$186.43	$4,474.32
37	$4,474.32	$16.78	$169.65	$186.43	$4,287.89
38	$4,287.89	$16.08	$170.35	$186.43	$4,101.46
39	$4,101.46	$15.38	$171.05	$186.43	$3,915.03
40	$3,915.03	$14.68	$171.75	$186.43	$3,728.60
41	$3,728.60	$13.98	$172.45	$186.43	$3,542.17
42	$3,542.17	$13.28	$173.15	$186.43	$3,355.74
43	$3,355.74	$12.58	$173.85	$186.43	$3,169.31
44	$3,169.31	$11.88	$174.55	$186.43	$2,982.88
45	$2,982.88	$11.19	$175.24	$186.43	$2,796.45
46	$2,796.45	$10.49	$175.94	$186.43	$2,610.02
47	$2,610.02	$9.79	$176.64	$186.43	$2,423.59
48	$2,423.59	$9.09	$177.34	$186.43	$2,237.16
49	$2,237.16	$8.39	$178.04	$186.43	$2,050.73
50	$2,050.73	$7.69	$178.74	$186.43	$1,864.30
51	$1,864.30	$6.99	$179.44	$186.43	$1,677.87
52	$1,677.87	$6.29	$180.14	$186.43	$1,491.44
53	$1,491.44	$5.59	$180.84	$186.43	$1,305.01
54	$1,305.01	$4.89	$181.54	$186.43	$1,118.58
55	$1,118.58	$4.19	$182.24	$186.43	$932.15
56	$932.15	$3.50	$182.93	$186.43	$745.72
57	$745.72	$2.80	$183.63	$186.43	$559.29
58	$559.29	$2.10	$184.33	$186.43	$372.86
59	$372.86	$1.40	$185.03	$186.43	$186.43
60	$186.43	$0.70	$185.73	$186.43	$0.00

Sierra Pacific Community College District — Credit Hours and Fees by Department

Dept	Course Name	Credit Hours	# of Sections	Fees	Total Fees	Fee per Credit Hour
BIO	General Biology	3	12	$125.00	$4,500.00	$8.33
BIO	Intro to Microbiology	3	10	$135.00	$4,050.00	$9.00
BIO	Anatomy & Physiology	4	8	$150.00	$4,800.00	$10.00
FRL	Spanish I	3	13	$55.00	$2,145.00	$3.67
FRL	French II	3	5	$55.00	$825.00	$3.67
FRL	Mandarin I	3	5	$55.00	$825.00	$3.67
IMS	Intro to MS Office	3	15	$75.00	$3,375.00	$5.00
IMS	Intro to Excel	3	13	$75.00	$2,925.00	$5.00
IMS	Access Programming	3	4	$75.00	$900.00	$5.00
PHY	Chemistry Fundamentals	4	7	$125.00	$3,500.00	$8.33
PHY	Organic Chemistry I	4	7	$150.00	$4,200.00	$10.00
PHY	Fundamentals of Physics	4	8	$125.00	$4,000.00	$8.33

Average Enrollment 15

Department	Total Fees	Total Credit Hours
Biological Science	$13,350.00	98
Foreign Languages	$3,795.00	69
Information Management Systems	$7,200.00	96
Physical Science	$11,700.00	88

Loan_Amount	='Student Loan'!C5
Loan_Term	='Student Loan'!C6
Payment	='Student Loan'!C8
Rate	='Student Loan'!C7
Total_Cost	='Student Loan'!F7
Total_Interest	='Student Loan'!F5
Total_Principal	='Student Loan'!F6

2-99 Completed Excel 2-3

Independent Project 2-4

Central Sierra Insurance (CSI) sets bonus percentages based on commissions earned by each agent and calculates totals by branch office. This workbook also tracks fundraising efforts of employees for a community event.
[Student Learning Outcomes 2.1, 2.2, 2.3, 2.5, 2.6, 2.7]

File Needed: **CentralSierra-02.xlsx** *[Student data files are available in the Library of your SIMnet account.]*
Completed Project File Name: *[your initials] Excel 2-4.xlsx*

Skills Covered in This Project

- Create, copy, and edit formulas.
- Name cell ranges.
- Set mathematical order of operations.

- Set cell references to be absolute.
- Use the *NOW* function.
- Use *HLOOKUP* and *VLOOKUP* functions.
- Use the *SUMIF* function.
- Build an *IF* function.

1. Open the **CentralSierra-02.xlsx** workbook from your student data files and save it as [your initials] Excel 2-4. Review the data on each sheet.

2. On the **Tables** sheet, select cells **A6:B10** and create range names from this selection.

3. Select cells **B1:F2** and click the **Name** box. Name this as H_Rates.

4. Create an *HLOOKUP* function to display the bonus rate.
 a. Click the **Commissions** sheet tab and select cell **F5**.
 b. Start the *HLOOKUP* function and use cell **E5** as the *lookup_value*.
 c. For the *table_array* argument, use the **H_Rates** range.
 d. Use the second row for the *row_index_num* argument (Figure 2-100).

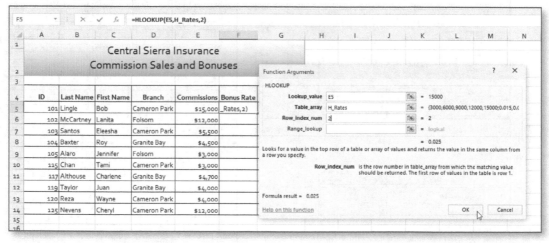

2-100 *HLOOKUP* function to display bonus rate

5. Format the results as **Percent Style** with two decimal places.

6. Copy the formula in cell **F5** to cells **F6:F14**.

7. Set order of operations to calculate total earnings.
 a. Select cell **G5**.
 b. Build a formula to add the commissions amount (E5) to the commissions amount times the rate (F5*E5). Use parentheses to set the multiplication as the first calculation.
 c. Copy the formula in cell **G5** to cells **G6:G14**.

8. Create and copy a *SUMIF* function to calculate total earnings by branch office.
 a. Select cell **E18**.
 b. Start the *SUMIF* function with cells **D5:D14** as the *Range* argument.
 c. The *Criteria* argument is a relative reference to cell **C18**.
 d. Select cells **G5:G14** for the *Sum_range* argument and make the references absolute.
 e. Copy the formula in cell **E18** to cells **E19:E20** without formatting.
 f. Format cells **E18:E20** as **Currency**.

9. Total the earnings in cell **E21**.

10. Create and format the current date.
 a. Select cell **G23** and insert the *NOW* function.
 b. Select cell **G23** and click the **Number** group launcher [*Home* tab]. On the *Number* tab, select the **Date** category.
 c. Scroll the *Type* list to find the date that displays the month spelled out, the date, a comma, and a four-digit year (Figure 2-101).
 d. Click **OK**. Press **Ctrl+Home**.

2-101 Date format selected

11. Create and copy a *VLOOKUP* function to display goals for each funding source.
 a. Click the **Family Day** sheet tab and select cell **F6**.
 b. Start the *VLOOKUP* function and use cell **E6** as the *lookup_value*.
 c. Click the **Tables** sheet tab for the *table_array* argument and use cells **A6:B10**.
 d. Use the second column as the *col_index_num* argument.
 e. Copy the formula in cell **F6** to cells **F7:F20** without formatting to preserve the fill color.
 f. Format cells **F7:F20** as **Currency** with no decimal places.

12. Create and copy an *IF* function.
 a. Select cell **H6** and start an *IF* function.
 b. Type a *logical_argument* to determine if cell **G6** is greater than or equal to (>=) cell **F6**.
 c. Type **Yes** as the *Value_if_true* argument and **No** as the *Value_if_false* argument.
 d. Copy the formula in cell **H6** to cells **H7:H20** without formatting to maintain the fill color.
 e. Center align cells **H6:H20**.
 f. Press **Ctrl+Home**.

13. Insert a new sheet at the end of the tab names and paste the range names starting in cell A1. Name the worksheet as **Range Names**.

14. Save and close the workbook (Figure 2-102).

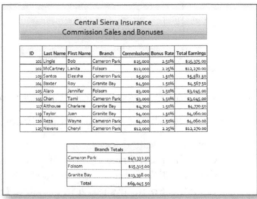

2-102 Excel 2-4 completed

Independent Project 2-5

San Diego Sailing keeps data about its fleet of rental and charter boats in a workbook. One of the sheets is missing a piece of data and another sheet has circular reference errors. You will complete work on these sheets, calculate projected rates for each boat, and build basic statistics about past rentals. [Student Learning Outcomes 2.1, 2.2, 2.3, 2.4, 2.5, 2.6, 2.7]

File Needed: **SanDiegoSailing-02.xlsx** [Student data files are available in the Library of your SIMnet account.]
Completed Project File Name: **[your initials] Excel 2-5.xlsx**

Skills Covered in This Project

- Create and copy formulas.
- Use formula auditing tools.
- Set mathematical order of operations.
- Use relative, mixed, and 3D cell references.
- Use *COUNTIF* and *SUMIF* functions.
- Build an *IF* formula.
- Insert the *TODAY* function.

1. Open the **SanDiegoSailing-02.xlsx** workbook from your student data files. When a workbook has a circular reference, a message box appears immediately as you open it (Figure 2-103).

2-103 Circular reference message

2. Click **OK** in the message box. There is a message in the *Status* bar that there are *Circular References*.

3. Save the workbook as [your initials] Excel 2-5. Review the data on each sheet.

4. Use formula auditing tools.
 a. Click the **New Prices** sheet tab and review the *Status* bar.
 b. Click cell **D5**. The formula should be 1 plus the value in cell D4.
 c. Click the **Formulas** tab and click the **Trace Precedents** button in the *Formula Auditing* group. The worksheet icon means that the formula has a 3D reference to another sheet.
 d. Click the **Evaluate Formula** button [*Formula Auditing* group]. The circular reference is identified (Figure 2-104).
 e. Click **Close** and click the **Remove Arrows** button [*Formula Auditing* group].

2-104 *Evaluate Formula* dialog box

5. Edit and copy a formula with mixed references.
 a. Edit the formula in cell **D5** to show **D$4** instead of "D5." The formula multiplies one plus the percentage value in cell D4 by the current rate on the **Fleet** sheet ($H5). With an absolute reference to row 4 and column H on the **Fleet** sheet, you can copy the formula down the column (Figure 2-105).

2-105 Mixed reference in the edited formula

 b. Copy the formula in cell **D5** to cells **D6:D19** without formatting to preserve the border. When the circular reference message box opens, click **OK**.
 c. Select cells **D5:D19** and drag the *Fill* pointer to copy the formulas to cells **E5:E19**.
 d. Click cell **E6**. The formula is adjusted to use the percentage value in cell E4. Note also that the reference on the **Fleet** sheet ($H6) is adjusted to show the correct row.

6. Build a formula with mixed references.
 a. Click cell **F5** and type =(1+ to start the formula.
 b. Select cell **F4** and make it an absolute reference to the row but not the column.
 c. Type)* for the closing parenthesis and multiplication.
 d. Click cell **I5** on the **Fleet** sheet, and make the reference absolute for the column but not the row (Figure 2-106).
 e. Copy the formula down column F without formatting to preserve the border.
 f. Format cells **F5:F19** as **Currency** and then copy cells **F5:F19** to cells **G5:G19**.

2-106 Mixed references in the new formula

7. Build an *IF* function formula.
 a. Click the **Fleet** sheet tab and select cell **G5**. Rental boats must be able to seat 8 or more people to have a stove in the galley.
 b. Create an *IF* function in which the *logical_test* argument determines if there are 8 or more seats.
 c. Use **Yes** for the *value_if_true* argument. Use **No** for the *value_if_false* argument.
 d. Copy the formula to cells **G6:G19** without formatting and then center the data in column G.

8. Insert the *TODAY* function in cell **B21**. Format the date to show the month spelled out, the date, and four digits for the year.

9. Create a division formula.
 a. Click the **Bookings** sheet tab and select cell **F5**. Average revenue per passenger can be determined by dividing the fee by the number of passengers.
 b. Build the division formula.
 c. Copy the formula in cell **F5** to cells **F6:F19**.

10. Create and copy a *COUNTIF* function to count bookings by boat type.
 a. Select cell **D27**.
 b. Start the *COUNTIF* function from the *Statistical* category by clicking the **More Functions** button in the *Function Library* group.
 c. Use cells **C5:C19** as the *Range* argument.
 d. To set a *Criteria* argument that will select all boats in the "Beneteau" group, the criteria is **ben***. If you type the formula, include quotation marks.
 e. Copy the formula in cell **D27** to cells **D28:D30**.
 f. Edit the criteria in each copied formula in cells **D28:D30** to reflect the boat type.

11. Create and copy a *SUMIF* function to calculate total revenue by boat type.
 a. Select cell **E27**.
 b. Start the *SUMIF* function with cells **C5:C19** as the *Range*.

c. The *Criteria* is ben*.
d. The *Sum_range* is cells **E5:E19**.
e. Copy the formula in cell **E27** to cells **E28:E30**.
f. Edit the criteria in each copied formula in cells **E28:E30** as needed.

12. Complete formatting.
 a. Apply the **Currency** format to all values that represent money.
 b. Format the labels in cells **A1:A2** as **18** point.
 c. Select cells **A1:F2** and center them across the selection.
 d. Merge and center the label in cell **C25** over cells C25:E25 and format it at **16** points.
 e. Bold and center the labels in rows **4** and **26**.
 f. Select cells **A4:F19** and apply **All Borders**. Do the same for cells **C25:E30**.
 g. Center the page horizontally.

13. Save and close the workbook (Figure 2-107).

San Diego Sailing Bookings
Revenue per Passenger

Date	Boat ID	Boat Type	# of Passengers	Total Fees	Revenue per Passenger
4/5/2016	1010	Catalina 270	4	$525.00	$131.25
4/8/2016	1015	Catalina 270	6	$850.00	$141.67
4/11/2016	1146	Hunter 33	6	$500.00	$83.33
4/14/2016	1150	Capri 22 Mk II	6	$525.00	$87.50
4/17/2016	1152	Capri 22 Mk II	4	$325.00	$81.25
4/20/2016	1164	Capri 22 Mk II	3	$475.00	$158.33
4/23/2016	1168	Hunter 33	6	$725.00	$120.83
4/26/2016	1175	Beneteau 40	10	$850.00	$85.00
4/29/2016	1180	Beneteau 373	8	$350.00	$43.75
5/2/2016	1185	Hunter 36	8	$650.00	$81.25
5/5/2016	1190	Beneteau 373	10	$625.00	$62.50
5/8/2016	1200	Beneteau 373	8	$725.00	$90.63
5/11/2016	1205	Beneteau 40	12	$850.00	$70.83
5/14/2016	1225	Hunter 36	8	$725.00	$90.63
5/17/2016	1230	Catalina 270	6	$675.00	$112.50

Bookings by Type

	Count	Total Revenue
Beneteau	5	$3,400.00
Capri 22 Mk II	3	$1,325.00
Catalina 270	3	$2,050.00
Hunter	4	$2,600.00

San Diego Sailing
Rental and Charter Fleet

Boat ID	Boat Type	Length	Model Year	Seats	Sleeps	Galley with Stove	Half-Day Rate	Full Day Rate
1010	Catalina 270	28'4"	2000	8	6	Yes	$375.00	$650.00
1015	Catalina 270	28'4"	2001	8	6	Yes	$425.00	$725.00
1146	Hunter 33	33'6"	2004	10	6	Yes	$350.00	$500.00
1150	Capri 22 Mk II	24'8"	2005	6	4	No	$325.00	$500.00
1152	Capri 22 Mk II	24'8"	2005	6	4	No	$325.00	$500.00
1164	Capri 22 Mk II	24'8"	2006	6	4	No	$325.00	$500.00
1168	Hunter 33	33'6"	2007	10	6	Yes	$425.00	$725.00
1175	Beneteau 40	39'10"	2008	12	6	Yes	$489.00	$750.00
1180	Beneteau 373	36'11"	2009	10	6	Yes	$369.00	$725.00
1185	Hunter 36	35'6"	2009	10	6	Yes	$349.00	$550.00
1190	Beneteau 373	36'11"	2010	10	6	Yes	$369.00	$625.00
1200	Beneteau 373	36'11"	2010	10	6	Yes	$369.00	$625.00
1205	Beneteau 40	39'10"	2012	12	6	Yes	$489.00	$750.00
1225	Hunter 36	35'6"	2012	10	6	Yes	$349.00	$725.00
1230	Catalina 270	28'4"	2012	8	6	Yes	$439.00	$675.00

2-107 Excel 2-5 completed

San Diego Sailing
New Prices at 5% and 10% Increases

Boat ID	Boat Type	Length	Half-Day 5%	Half-Day 10%	Full Day 5%	Full Day 10%
1010	Catalina 270	28'4"	$393.75	$412.50	$682.50	$715.00
1015	Catalina 270	28'4"	$446.25	$467.50	$761.25	$797.50
1146	Hunter 33	33'6"	$367.50	$385.00	$525.00	$550.00
1150	Capri 22 Mk II	24'8"	$341.25	$357.50	$525.00	$550.00
1152	Capri 22 Mk II	24'8"	$341.25	$357.50	$525.00	$550.00
1164	Capri 22 Mk II	24'8"	$341.25	$357.50	$525.00	$550.00
1168	Hunter 33	33'6"	$446.25	$467.50	$761.25	$797.50
1175	Beneteau 40	39'10"	$513.45	$537.90	$787.50	$825.00
1180	Beneteau 373	36'11"	$387.45	$405.90	$761.25	$797.50
1185	Hunter 36	35'6"	$366.45	$383.90	$577.50	$605.00
1190	Beneteau 373	36'11"	$387.45	$405.90	$656.25	$687.50
1200	Beneteau 373	36'11"	$387.45	$405.90	$656.25	$687.50
1205	Beneteau 40	39'10"	$513.45	$537.90	$787.50	$825.00
1225	Hunter 36	35'6"	$366.45	$383.90	$761.25	$797.50
1230	Catalina 270	28'4"	$460.95	$482.90	$708.75	$742.50

Independent Project 2-6

Placer Hills Real Estate has regional offices throughout central California, and each office tracks its listings and sales data. In the workbook, you need to insert agent names, calculate market days, and determine sale price as a percentage of list price. You also calculate summary statistics.
[Student Learning Outcomes 2.1, 2.3, 2.5, 2.6, 2.7]

File Needed: **PlacerHills-02.xlsx** [Student data files are available in the Library of your SIMnet account.]
Completed Project File Name: **[your initials] Excel 2-6.xlsx**

Skills Covered in This Project

- Create and copy formulas.
- Use dates in a subtraction formula.
- Name cell ranges.

- Use relative and 3D cell references in formulas.
- Use the *VLOOKUP* function.
- Use *AVERAGE, MAX, MIN*, and *COUNT*.
- Use *COUNTIF*.

1. Open the **PlacerHills-02.xlsx** workbook from your student data files and save it as [your initials] Excel 2-6. Review the data on each sheet.

2. Build a subtraction formula with dates.
 a. Select cell **N4** on the **Listings** sheet. You can subtract the older date from the later date to determine the number of days on the market.
 b. Type = and click cell **M4**, the sold date.
 c. Type − for subtraction and click cell **B4**, the listing date.
 d. Press **Enter**. The result is formatted as a date (Figure 2-108).

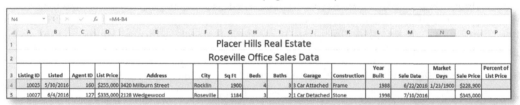

2-108 Result is formatted as a date

 e. Copy the formula in cell **N4** to cells **N5:N12** without formatting to preserve the fill color.
 f. Format cells **N4:N12** as **General**.

3. Calculate the sold price as a percentage of the list price.
 a. Select cell **P4** and type =.
 b. Build a formula to divide the selling price by the list price.
 c. Copy the formula without formatting and format the column as **Percent Style** with **two** decimal places.

4. Use the *VLOOKUP* function to insert the agent's last name in a new column.
 a. Insert a column at column **D**.
 b. Type Name in cell **D3** and click cell **D4**.
 c. Start a *VLOOKUP* function and set the agent ID (C4) as the *lookup_value* argument.
 d. Use an absolute reference to cells **A2:B7** on the **Agents** sheet for the *table_array* argument. Do not include column titles in a table array.
 e. Enter the appropriate number for the *col_index_num* argument to display the agent's last name.
 f. Copy the formula without formatting to display each agent's name and *AutoFit* the column width.

5. Name cell ranges.
 a. Select cells **E3:E12**.
 b. Press **Ctrl** and select cells **G3:G12, L3:L12**, and **P3:P12**.
 c. Click the **Create from Selection** button [*Formulas* tab, *Defined Names* group] and use the **Top row** to create range names.

d. Press **Ctrl+Home**.

e. Set this sheet to fit one page, landscape orientation.

f. Insert a footer that displays your name in the right section.

6. Calculate statistics for the agency.

 a. Click the **Statistics** sheet tab and select cell **B4**.

 b. Click the **AutoSum** button arrow and choose *Average*. There is no assumed range.

 c. Press **F3 (FN+F3)** to open the *Paste Name* dialog box.

 d. Choose **List_Price** and click **OK**. Press **Enter**.

 e. Continue on this sheet to calculate the highest and lowest list prices as well as the number of listings. Be careful to select the correct range name.

7. Use *COUNTIF* to calculate statistics.

 a. Select cell **B9**.

 b. Click the **More Functions** button in the *Function Library* group, choose **Statistical**, and select **COUNTIF**.

 c. For the *Range* argument, use the range name **Construction** (Figure 2-109).

 d. Type br* for the *Criteria* and click **OK**.

 e. Copy the formula and edit the criteria for cells **B10:B11**.

 f. Start a new *COUNTIF* function in cell **B13** with the appropriate range name. Then copy and edit the formula for cells **B14:B16**. Be sure to use criteria that will distinguish between the two city names that begin with "ro."

8. Center the sheet horizontally. Add a footer with your name in the center section.

9. Save and close the workbook (Figure 2-110).

2-109 Arguments for COUNTIF

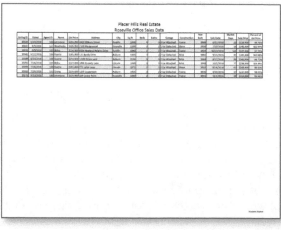

2-110 Excel 2-6 completed

Improve It Project 2-7

Mary's Rentals serves light-to-heavy equipment rental needs of contractors as well as the general public. Data has been imported from an Access database and needs to be handled for better management in Excel. Once that is done, you can calculate several statistics for the company.
[Student Learning Outcomes 2.1, 2.3, 2.4, 2.5, 2.7]

File Needed: **MarysRentals-02.xlsx** *[Student data files are available in the* Library *of your SIMnet account.]*
Completed Project File Name: *[your initials] Excel 2-7.xlsx*

Skills Covered in This Project

- Use formula auditing tools.
- Name cell ranges.
- Create, copy, and edit formulas.
- Use relative references and range names in formulas.
- Use *Statistical* functions.
- Use functions from the *Math & Trig* category.

1. Open the **MarysRentals-02.xlsx** workbook from your student data files and save it as [your initials] Excel 2-7. The *Equipment* sheet is an inventory of equipment available for rental.

2. Correct errors on the *Rentals* sheet.
 a. Click the **Rentals** tab. This data was imported from an Access database, and there are error triangles in many cells.
 b. Select cells **A2:A47** and click the **Trace Error** button near cell A2 (Figure 2-111). This data was imported as text (labels) but should be set as values.
 c. Select **Convert to Number**. The data is formatted as a value and is right-aligned.
 d. Repeat for cells **B2:C47**.
 e. Center align cells **E2:E47**. This column specifies whether the rental was daily, weekly, or monthly.
 f. Press **Ctrl+Home**.

3. Name cell ranges.
 a. Select cells **B1:B47**, press **Ctrl**, and select cells **E1:E47** and cells **I1:I47**.
 b. Create names from the selection.
 c. Press **Ctrl+Home**.

4. Create and copy a *SUMIF* function with a relative reference.
 a. Click the **Generators** sheet tab and select cell **C5**.
 b. Start the *SUMIF* function with *Equipment_ID* as the *Range* argument.
 c. The *Criteria* argument is cell **A5**.
 d. The *Sum_range* argument is the *Total_Cost* range.
 e. Copy the formula in cell **C5** to cells **C6:C7**. The relative cell reference to cell A5 is adjusted.
 f. Format cells **C5:C7** as **Currency** with no decimal places.

5. Build a custom border.
 a. Select cells **A4:C7**.
 b. Press **Ctrl+1** to open the *Format Cells* dialog box and click the **Border** tab.
 c. In the *Presets* section, click the **Outline** button.
 d. In the *Style* section, click the dotted line style (second option, first column, just below *None*).

2-111 *Trace Error* button for a selected range

e. Click the middle horizontal position in the *Border* preview area.

f. In the *Style* section, click the single solid line style (last option, first column).

g. Click the middle vertical position in the *Border* preview area (Figure 2-112).

h. Click **OK**.

6. Complete formatting.

a. Apply bold and centering to cells **A4:C4**.

b. Format cells **A1:A2** to **16** points.

c. Select cells **A1:C2** and use **Center Across Selection**.

d. Center the sheet horizontally.

e. Insert a header with your name in the right section.

2-112 Build a custom border in the *Format Cells* dialog box

7. Use *SUMIF* to calculate daily, weekly, and monthly income rentals.

a. Click the **Income Data** sheet tab and select cell **B4**.

b. Start the *SUMIF* function with **Type** as the *Range* argument.

c. Type d for daily income as the *Criteria* argument.

d. The *Total_Cost* range is the *Sum_range* argument.

e. In cells **B5:B6**, enter *SUMIF* formulas or copy and edit the formula in cell B4.

f. Use *SUM* in cell **B7**.

g. Format cells **B4:B7** as **Currency** with no decimal places.

8. Use *COUNTIF* to count rentals by type.

a. Select cell **B9** and start the *COUNTIF* function from the *Statistical* category.

b. Use the range name **Type** as the *Range* argument. The *Criteria* is d.

c. Create a separate formula in cells **B10:B11**, or copy and edit the formula in cell B9.

9. Add a border and fill.

a. Select cells **A3:B12**.

b. Click the **Font** group launcher [*Home* tab] and click the **Border** tab.

c. Click the **Outline** button in the *Presets* section.

d. In the *Style* section, click the single solid line style (last option, first column).

e. Click the middle vertical position in the *Border* preview area.

f. In the *Style* section, click the dotted line style (second option, first column).

g. Click the middle horizontal position in the *Border* preview area.

h. Click **OK**.

i. Select cells **A3:B3, A8:B8**, and **A12:B12**.

j. Click the arrow with the **Fill Color** button and choose **Black, Text 1, Lighter 50%**.

k. Select cells **A1:B2** and use **Center Across Selection**.

l. Increase the font size for cells **A1:B2** to **16**.

m. Center the sheet horizontally.

n. Insert a footer with your name in the right section.

10. Save and close the workbook (Figure 2-113).

Mary's Rentals — Income Statistics

Daily Rental Income	$4,990
Weekly Rental Income	$4,745
Monthly Rental Income	$1,440
Total	$11,175
Number of Daily Rentals	33
Number of Weekly Rentals	11
Number of Monthly Rentals	2

Student Name

Rental ID	Equipment ID	Customer ID	Date Out	Type	# of Units
2512	9863	27	04-Jan-17	D	1
2513	10235	30	04-Jan-17	D	3
2513	10289	30	04-Jan-17	D	3
2514	10236	102	05-Jan-17	D	1
2514	10237	102	05-Jan-17	D	1
2515	10283	83	05-Jan-17	W	1
2516	10047	15	06-Jan-17	D	4
2517	10103	21	06-Jan-17	W	1
2518	9863	102	07-Jan-17	W	1
2518	10015	44	07-Jan-17	D	3
2520	10868	71	07-Jan-17	D	2
2521	10426	17	08-Jan-17	D	4
2522	10237	56	09-Jan-17	W	1
2522	10425	56	09-Jan-17	W	1
2523	10428	8	09-Jan-17	D	2
2524	10015	31	10-Jan-17	D	1
2525	10868	124	10-Jan-17	D	3
2526	10235	111	10-Jan-17	D	1
2527	10015	30	12-Jan-17	D	3
2527	10047	30	12-Jan-17	D	3
2527	10235	30	12-Jan-17	D	3
2527	10283	30	12-Jan-17	D	3
2528	10236	39	12-Jan-17	W	1
2529	10289	27	13-Jan-17	D	2
2530	10235	94	13-Jan-17	D	1
2530	10427	94	13-Jan-17	D	1
2531	10283	15	15-Jan-17	W	1
2532	9863	75	15-Jan-17	D	1
2533	10103	62	15-Jan-17	M	1
2534	10426	88	15-Jan-17	D	1
2535	10428	91	16-Jan-17	D	1
2536	10047	48	17-Jan-17	W	1
2537	10235	102	17-Jan-17	D	1
2538	10237	83	17-Jan-17	D	3
2538	10289	83	17-Jan-17	D	3
2539	10868	51	17-Jan-17	D	1
2540	10426	21	17-Jan-17	D	1
2541	9863	58	17-Jan-17	D	1
2542	10015	31	18-Jan-17	M	1
2543	9863	44	18-Jan-17	W	1
2544	10868	124	18-Jan-17	W	1
2545	10235	27	18-Jan-17	D	2
2546	10425	111	20-Jan-17	D	3
2547	10426	30	20-Jan-17	W	1
2548	10427	115	20-Jan-17	D	2
2548	10236	94	20-Jan-17	D	2

Student Name

Mary's Rentals — Generator Rental Data

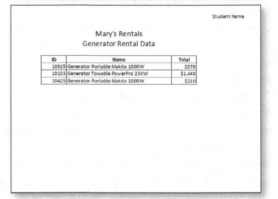

ID	Name	Total
10015	Generator Portable Makita 1000W	$570
10103	Generator Towable PowerPro 25KW	$1,440
10425	Generator Portable Makita 1000W	$210

Date Due	Rate	Total Cost
05-Jan-17	$160.00	$160.00
07-Jan-17	$10.00	$30.00
07-Jan-17	$60.00	$180.00
06-Jan-17	$25.00	$25.00
06-Jan-17	$200.00	$200.00
12-Jan-17	$480.00	$480.00
10-Jan-17	$225.00	$900.00
13-Jan-17	$360.00	$360.00
14-Jan-17	$640.00	$640.00
10-Jan-17	$30.00	$90.00
09-Jan-17	$15.00	$30.00
12-Jan-17	$35.00	$140.00
16-Jan-17	$800.00	$800.00
16-Jan-17	$120.00	$120.00
11-Jan-17	$40.00	$80.00
12-Jan-17	$30.00	$30.00
13-Jan-17	$15.00	$45.00
11-Jan-17	$10.00	$10.00
13-Jan-17	$30.00	$90.00
15-Jan-17	$225.00	$675.00
15-Jan-17	$10.00	$30.00
13-Jan-17	$120.00	$360.00
19-Jan-17	$140.00	$140.00
15-Jan-17	$60.00	$120.00
14-Jan-17	$10.00	$10.00
14-Jan-17	$120.00	$120.00
22-Jan-17	$480.00	$480.00
16-Jan-17	$160.00	$160.00
15-Feb-17	$1,080.00	$1,080.00
16-Jan-17	$25.00	$25.00
17-Jan-17	$40.00	$40.00
24-Jan-17	$900.00	$900.00
18-Jan-17	$10.00	$10.00
20-Jan-17	$200.00	$600.00
20-Jan-17	$60.00	$180.00
18-Jan-17	$15.00	$15.00
18-Jan-17	$35.00	$35.00
18-Jan-17	$160.00	$160.00
19-Feb-17	$360.00	$360.00
26-Jan-17	$640.00	$640.00
26-Jan-17	$45.00	$45.00
21-Jan-17	$10.00	$20.00
23-Jan-17	$30.00	$90.00
27-Jan-17	$140.00	$140.00
22-Jan-17	$120.00	$240.00
22-Jan-17	$35.00	$70.00

2-113 Excel 2-7 completed

Challenge Project 2-8

For this project, you create a workbook for a hair products company that includes an inventory list and an invoice form. You use *VLOOKUP* to enter the cost of the product on the invoice and then calculate a total with taxes for each product.
[Student Learning Outcomes 2.1, 2.2, 2.3, 2.5, 2.6]

File Needed: None
Completed Project File Name: *[your initials] Excel 2-8.xlsx*

Create and save a workbook as [your initials] Excel 2-8. Modify your workbook according to the following guidelines:

- In cell **A1**, type a name for the hair products company. In cell **A2**, type Customer Invoice. In cells **A4:D4**, enter these labels: Product ID, Cost, Quantity, and Total with Tax. Do not include a comma or a period. Name this sheet tab Invoice.
- Insert a new sheet and name it Stock. In cells **A1:C1**, enter labels for Product ID, Name, and Cost with no punctuation.
- In cells **A2:C11**, enter data for ten products that can be purchased from your company. Use *AutoFill* to create a series for the *Product ID*. Since this range will be used as the table array in a *VLOOKUP* function, the product IDs must be in ascending order, either A to Z or low value to high value. Name the cell range Stock (without the labels in row 1).
- Below the *Stock* range, enter Tax Rate as a label. In a cell either to the right or below the label, enter 3.75% as the rate.
- On the *Invoice* sheet, type any three of the product IDs in cells **A5:A7**. Use *VLOOKUP* in column B to display the cost. In the *Quantity* column, type three values to indicate the number ordered.
- In the *Total with Tax* column, build a formula to multiply the cost by the quantity ordered. This result should be multiplied by one plus the tax rate on the *Stock* sheet. Show a grand total in row 8.
- Use the *TODAY* function in cell **A10** on the *Invoice* sheet and format the date to show the date, the month with a three-letter abbreviation, and the year as two-digits.
- Complete formatting on the *Invoice* sheet. Select a workbook theme if desired, use cell styles, or build your own designs.
- Add a header that shows your name in the right section.
- Set document properties to show your name as the author and the company name as the title. Spell check the workbook if necessary.

Challenge Project 2-9

For this project, you create a workbook for a mobile services provider to calculate revenue from purchased mobile apps. You enter and format data and use *SUMPRODUCT* to determine revenue by category.
[Student Learning Outcomes 2.1, 2.3, 2.5, 2.7]

File Needed: None
Completed Project File Name: *[your initials] Excel 2-9.xlsx*

Create and save a workbook as [your initials] Excel 2-9. Modify your workbook according to the following guidelines:

- In cell **A1**, enter a name for your mobile services company.
- In cell **A2**, type Last Month's Activity.
- In cells **B3:D3**, enter the labels App Name, Times Downloaded, and Cost.
- In cell **A4**, type Books as the first category. In cells **A7, A10,** and **A13**, type the names of three other categories of mobile applications. Examples might be Travel, Entertainment, Games, Health, Sports, and so on.
- In cells **B5:D6**, complete data for two apps in the *Books* category. Then do the same for the other categories.
- Starting in row **18**, create a section that calculates revenue from each app category using the *SUMPRODUCT* function.
- In a cell below the data, use the *TODAY* function and format the date to show a short date.
- Select a workbook theme if desired, use cell styles, or set your own formatting.
- Add a footer that shows the current date in the left section and your name in the right section.
- Set document properties to show your name as the author and a title of your choice. Spell check the workbook if necessary.

Challenge Project 2-10

In this project, you create a workbook that calculates monthly payments for a major purchase at four possible interest rates and different payback times.
[Student Learning Outcomes 2.1, 2.3, 2.4, 2.5, 2.6]

File Needed: None
Completed Project File Name: *[your initials] Excel 2-10.xlsx*

Create and save a workbook as [your initials] Excel 2-10. Modify your workbook according to the following guidelines:

- Enter main labels that identify the worksheet and your proposed purchase.
- Build the first section for a *PMT* formula with the labels Loan, Rate, Term, and Payment. Since you plan to copy the section to show other possibilities, do not use range names.
- Fill in values for the loan amount, an interest rate, and the term. Include the percent sign when you type the interest rate. For the term, you can use the number of years or the number of months.
- Use *PMT* to calculate the payment made at the beginning of the month (*Type* argument). If you set months for the term, do not multiply the *Nper* argument by 12.
- Copy the entire section once below the current location with a blank row or two between. Then copy these two groupings one or two columns to the right. You should have four possible payment scenarios on the sheet.
- Edit the interest rate and term for each of the copied sections. Be consistent in how you indicate the term of the loan (years or months). Assume that the loan amount is the same.
- In a row below the data, use the *TODAY* function and format the date to show a short date.
- Make formatting choices to building an easy-to-read report for your possibilities.
- Add a footer with your name in the right section.
- Set document properties to show your name as the author, and spell check the workbook if necessary.

CHAPTER OVERVIEW

In addition to building formulas and functions in a worksheet, you can use Excel to graph or chart data. After selecting values and labels, you can quickly create a professional looking chart with a few clicks of the mouse. This chapter introduces you to the basics of creating, editing, and formatting Excel charts.

STUDENT LEARNING OUTCOMES (SLOs)

After completing this chapter, you will be able to:

SLO 3.1 Create Excel chart objects and chart sheets (p. 571).

SLO 3.2 Use quick layouts and chart styles to design a chart (p. 575).

SLO 3.3 Edit chart elements including titles, data labels, and source data (p. 580).

SLO 3.4 Format chart elements with shape styles, fill, outlines, and special effects (p. 587).

SLO 3.5 Use pictures, shapes, and *WordArt* in a chart (p. 591).

SLO 3.6 Build pie charts and combination charts (p. 596).

SLO 3.7 Create sunburst and waterfall charts (p. 599).

SLO 3.8 Insert and format sparklines in a worksheet (p. 602).

CASE STUDY

In the Pause & Practice projects in this chapter, you use data in a Paradise Lakes Resort workbook to build charts that compare revenue categories for two quarters. You build column and pie charts as objects and separate sheets. You also add trendlines and sparklines to further illustrate aspects of the data.

Pause & Practice 3-1: Create and edit column and bar charts.

Pause & Practice 3-2: Edit and format charts and chart elements.

Pause & Practice 3-3: Create and format pie, combo, and sunburst charts and insert sparklines.

Creating a Chart Object and a Chart Sheet

An Excel *chart* is a visual representation of numeric data in a worksheet. A chart helps you identify trends, make comparisons, and recognize patterns in the numbers. Charts are dynamic and linked to the data, so when values in the worksheet change, the chart is automatically redrawn. You can display a chart in the worksheet with its data, or you can place a chart on its own sheet.

There are different kinds of charts, and Excel can recommend the best chart type based on your selected data. It is essential, however, that you select appropriate data for a chart, because it is possible to build charts that illustrate nothing of any consequence. With experience and practice, you will learn how to create charts that have meaning to your work.

Create a Chart Object

A *chart object* is a selectable item surrounded by a square border that is separate from worksheet data. A chart object contains chart elements such as titles, axes, and gridlines, and each element is selectable, too. You can size and position a chart object in a worksheet, and you can size and position each chart element on the chart.

Source data are the cells that contain values and labels to be graphed in a chart. When you select data for a chart, you usually do not include sums, averages, or similar calculations. In Figure 3-1, the source data includes the series names in column A, the category names in row 4,

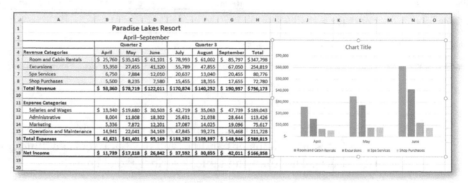

3-1 Chart object and its source data

and four values for each of three months. Each of the values is a *data point*, a cell containing a value. Each group of data points or values is a *data series*. In this example, there are four data series, one for each revenue category. Each data series has a name or label.

The text label that describes a data series is a *category label*. In Figure 3.1, the category labels are the month names.

> ► ANOTHER WAY
>
> You can create a default chart object by selecting the data and pressing **Alt+F1**.

Data for a chart is best arranged with labels and values in adjacent cells and no empty rows. If you do not include labels for the source data, there are no labels in the chart to describe the data. An empty row within the source data is graphed as a data point with a value of zero (0) and will distort the chart's ability to illustrate a comparison or trend.

When you select contiguous source data (all cells are next to each other), the **Quick Analysis** button appears in the lower right corner of the selection. The *Quick Analysis* tool

lists command groups you would be likely to use for the selected data, such as *Formatting, Charts,* or *Totals.* When you select the *Charts* command, Excel shows recommended chart types. As you point to each type, you see a preview of the chart. Click the preferred type to create the chart object in the worksheet.

▶HOW TO: Create a Chart Object from the Quick Analysis Tool

1. Select the source data range with labels and values.
 - The *Quick Analysis* button appears at the lower right corner of the range.
2. Click the **Quick Analysis** button.
 - A dialog box with command categories opens.
3. Select **Charts**.
 - Possible chart types are listed (Figure 3-2).
4. Point to a chart type.
 - A preview of the chart object is displayed.
5. Click to select the chart type.
 - The chart object displays in the worksheet.

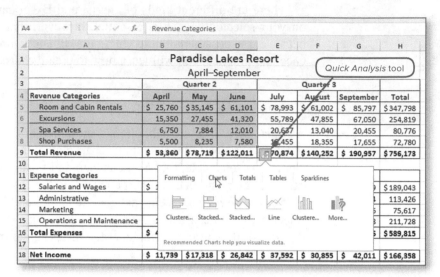

3-2 Chart options for selected data

Excel Chart Types

Excel has many chart types and most types have subtypes or variations. The most common chart types are column or bar, line, and pie, but Excel can build powerful scientific and statistical charts. The following table describes Excel chart types:

Excel Chart Types

Chart Type	Purpose	Data Example	Categories (Labels)	Values (Numbers)
Column	Illustrates data changes over a period of time or shows comparisons among items	Monthly sales data for three automobile models	Horizontal axis	Vertical axis
Bar	Displays comparisons among individual items or values at a specific period of time	Number of pairs sold for eight shoe styles	Vertical axis	Horizontal axis
Pie	Uses one data series to display each value as a percentage of the whole	Expenses or revenue by department for one quarter		One data series shown by slice size
Line	Displays trends in data over time, emphasizing the rate of change	Number of weekly web site views over a ten-week period	Horizontal axis	Vertical axis
Area	Displays the magnitude of change over time and shows the rate of change	Yearly consumption of apples, bananas, and pears over a ten-year period	Horizontal axis	Vertical axis

Continued

Chart Type	Purpose	Data Example	Categories (Labels)	Values (Numbers)
XY (Scatter) or Bubble	Displays relationships among numeric values in two or more data series; these charts do not have a category.	Number of times a patient visits a doctor, amount billed to insurance, and cost billed to patient	Horizontal axis (value 1-x)	Vertical axis (value 2-y)
Stock	Displays three series of data to show fluctuations in stock prices from high to low to close	Opening, closing, and high price for Microsoft stock each day for 30 days	Horizontal axis	Vertical axis
Surface	Displays optimum combinations of two sets of data on a surface	Perceived outside temperature at ten temperature and ten humidity levels	Horizontal axis (value 1-x)	Horizontal axis (value 1-x)
Radar	Displays the frequency of multiple data series relative to a center point. There is an axis for each category.	Style, comfort, and value ratings for three snow boot styles	NA	NA
TreeMap	Displays a hierarchical view of data with different sized and colored rectangles and sub-rectangles to compare the sizes of groups	Soda sales by product name, continent, country, and city	NA	NA
Sunburst	Displays a hierarchical view of data with concentric rings. The top hierarchy is the inner ring and each outer ring is related to its adjacent inner ring.	Tablet sales by screen size, continent, country, and city	NA	NA
Histogram	Column-style chart that shows frequencies within a distribution	Number of students in each of five grade categories for an exam	Horizontal axis	Vertical axis
Box & Whisker	Displays the distribution of data with minimum, mean, maximum, and outlier values	Sales prices of home in five suburbs during a three-week period	Horizontal axis	Vertical axis
Waterfall	Plots each element in a running total and displays negative and positive effects of each on the total	Banking or savings account register	Horizontal axis	Vertical axis
Funnel	Plots values that progressively decrease from one stage or process to the next	Job applications received, applications selected, initial interviews, team interviews, HR interview, job offer	Vertical axis	Horizontal axis
Combo Chart	Uses two types of charts to graph values that are widely different	Line chart for number of monthly web site visits and a column chart for monthly sales of online golf gloves	Either	Either

Size and Position a Chart Object

When you select a chart object, it is active and surrounded by eight selection handles. A **selection handle** is a small circle shape on each corner and in the middle of each side. To select the chart object, point to its border and click. When the chart object is selected, the *Range Finder* highlights the source data in the worksheet. When you point to a selection handle, you will see a two-pointed resize arrow. Drag a corner handle to size the height and width proportionally.

To move a chart object, point to the chart border to display a four-pointed move pointer. Then drag the chart object to the desired location.

When a chart is active or selected, the *Chart Tools Design* and *Format* tabs are available in the *Ribbon* and three *Quick Chart Tools* are available in the top right corner of the object: *Chart Elements, Chart Styles,* and *Chart Filters.*

MORE INFO

You can select individual elements or parts of the chart, and each element has its own selection handles.

▶HOW TO: Move and Size a Chart Object

1. Select the chart object.
 - Point to the border of the chart and click.
2. Point to the outside border of the chart to display a move pointer.
 - Point anywhere along the border.
3. Drag the chart object to a new location and release the pointer button (Figure 3-3).
4. Point to a corner selection handle to display a resize arrow.
5. Drag the pointer to resize the chart proportionally.

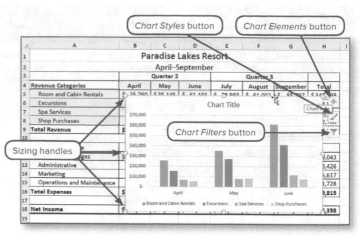

3-3 Selected chart object and move pointer

Create a Chart Sheet

A **chart sheet** is an Excel chart that is displayed on its own sheet in the workbook. A chart sheet does not have rows, columns, and cells, but the chart is linked to its data on the source worksheet.

From the *Quick Analysis* tool or the *Insert* tab, Excel creates a chart object. You must move the chart object to its own sheet with the *Move Chart* button on the *Chart Tools Design* tab. Excel uses default sheet names *Chart1, Chart2,* and so on, but you can type a descriptive name in the *Move Chart* dialog box, or you can rename the sheet at any time.

You can create an automatic column chart sheet by selecting the data and pressing the **F11** (**FN+F11**) function key.

> ### MORE INFO
>
> When the *Recommended Charts* button does not recommend a chart type, select the source data again in a left-to-right order. If there are still no suggestions, click the **All Charts** tab and choose a type.

Source data for a chart need not be contiguous. The *Quick Analysis* tool does not appear for noncontiguous data, but you can click the **Recommended Charts** button in the *Charts* group on the *Insert* tab. The *Insert Chart* dialog box opens and recommends chart types.

▶HOW TO: Create a Chart Sheet for Noncontiguous Cells

1. Select the values and labels for the chart.
 - Select the first range, press the **Ctrl** key, and select each range (Figure 3-4).
2. Click the **Recommended Charts** button [*Insert* tab, *Charts* group].
 - The *Insert Chart* dialog box opens.
 - You can click the **All Charts** tab to select any chart type.
3. Click the thumbnail for a chart type to preview the results.

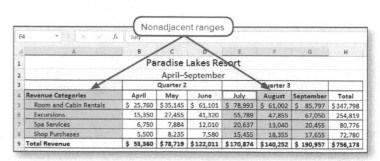

3-4 Source data ranges that are not next to each other

4. Click the preferred chart type and click **OK**.

- The chart object is active.
- The *Chart Tools* tabs are available.

5. Click the **Move Chart** button [*Chart Tools Design* tab, *Location* group].

6. Click the **New sheet** radio button (Figure 3-5).

7. Type a descriptive name for the chart sheet.

8. Click **OK**.

3-5 *Move Chart* dialog box

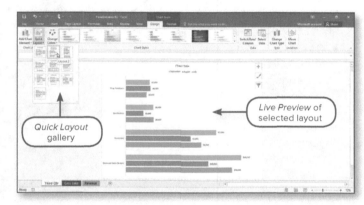

<div style="border:1px solid #888; display:inline-block; padding:4px;">SLO 3.2</div>

Using Quick Layouts and Chart Styles

A newly created chart has a default layout, color, and style. Excel has various tools to help you enhance the appearance of your chart for originality, readability, and appeal. The *Chart Tools Design* tab includes commands for selecting a chart layout, choosing a chart style, or changing the color scheme.

Apply a Quick Layout

A *chart layout* is a set of elements and the location of those elements. Elements are individual parts of a chart such as a main title, a legend, and axis titles. The *Quick Layout* button [*Chart Tools Design* tab, *Chart Layouts* group] opens a gallery of predefined layouts (Figure 3-6). As you point to an option in the gallery, *Live Preview* redraws the chart. When a chart layout adds an element such as a title, the element displays a generic label like "Chart Title." You can add or remove individual elements, as well as edit placeholder text.

3-6 *Quick Layout* gallery

▶ HOW TO: Apply a Quick Layout to a Chart

1. Select the chart object or the chart sheet tab.

2. Click the **Quick Layout** button [*Chart Tools Design* tab, *Chart Layouts* group].

- The gallery displays thumbnail images of each layout.
- Quick layouts are named *Layout 1* through the last number.

3. Point to a layout to preview it in the chart.

4. Click a thumbnail to select it.

- The chart is reformatted with the *Quick Layout* elements.

Apply a Chart Style

A ***chart style*** is a preset combination of colors and effects for a chart, its background, and its elements. The chart styles that are available for a chart are based on the current workbook theme. If you change the theme, the chart style colors are updated, and your chart reflects the new color palette. You can find chart styles in the *Chart Styles* group on the *Chart Tools Design* tab. Like a chart layout, you can preview the effects of a chart style as you point to each style in the gallery.

▶ HOW TO: Apply a Chart Style

1. Select the chart object or the chart sheet tab.
2. Click the *Chart Styles* **More** button to open the gallery or point to a *Style* thumbnail [*Chart Tools Design* tab, *Chart Styles* group].
 - The number of styles depends on the chart type (Figure 3-7).
 - Chart styles are named *Style 1* through the last number.
3. Point to a style thumbnail to see a *Live Preview* in the chart.
4. Click to select a style.
 - The chart is redrawn with the selected style.

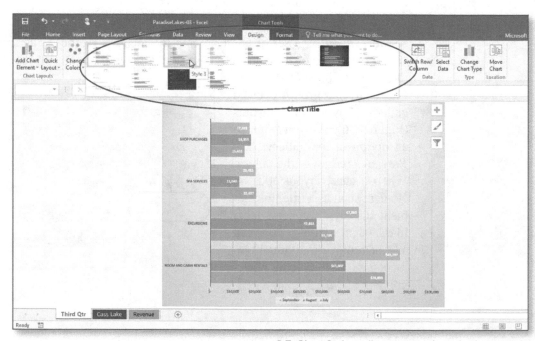

3-7 *Chart Styles* gallery and preview of selected style

Change Chart Colors

The workbook theme and the chart style form the basis for a chart's color scheme. The *Chart Styles* group [*Chart Tools Design* tab] includes a *Change Colors* button with optional color palettes. These palettes are divided into *Colorful* and *Monochromatic* groups.

▶HOW TO: Change Chart Colors

1. Select the chart object or the chart sheet tab.
2. Click the **Change Colors** button [*Chart Tools Design* tab, *Chart Styles* group].
 - A gallery of color palettes opens (Figure 3-8).
 - Color schemes are named *Color 1* through the last number.
3. Point to a palette to see a *Live Preview* in the chart.
4. Click to select a palette.
 - The chart is formatted with new colors.

3-8 *Change Colors* gallery

Print a Chart

A chart object can be printed on the page with worksheet data, or it can be printed separately. To print a chart with the data, deselect the chart object by clicking a worksheet cell. Size and position the chart and scale the sheet to fit a printed page. Then use regular *Page Setup* commands to complete the print task, such as choosing the orientation or inserting headers or footers.

> **MORE INFO**
>
> When you insert a header or footer in a selected chart object, that header or footer is not inserted on the worksheet.

To print only the chart object on its own sheet, select it and use regular *Print* and *Page Setup* options. A selected chart object, by default, prints scaled to fit a landscape page. A chart sheet also prints in landscape orientation fit to the page.

▶HOW TO: Print a Chart with Its Source Data

1. Click any cell in the worksheet.
 - Size and position the chart object as needed.
2. Click the **File** tab to open the *Backstage* view (Figure 3-9).
3. Select **Print**.

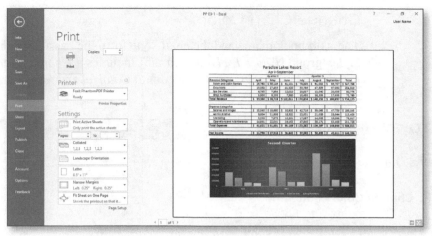

3-9 Print a chart with the data

4. Choose print settings as needed.
 - Set margins and scale the sheet to fit.
5. Click **Print**.

In this project, you insert a clustered column chart object in a worksheet that tracks revenue and expenses for Paradise Lakes Resort. You also insert a clustered bar chart sheet to highlight second quarter results.

File Needed: **ParadiseLakes-03.xlsx** [Student data files are available in the Library of your SIMnet account.]
Completed Project File Name: **[your initials] PP E3-1.xlsx**

1. Open the **ParadiseLakes-03** workbook from your student data files and save it as [your initials] PP E3-1.

2. Create a chart object.
 a. Select cells **A4:D8** on the **Cass Lake** sheet. These are labels and values for the chart.
 b. Click the **Quick Analysis** button and select **Charts**.
 c. Click **Clustered Column**.

3. Position and size the chart object.
 a. Click the chart object if it is not selected.
 b. Point to the chart border to display a move pointer.
 c. Drag the chart object so that its top left corner is at cell **A20**.
 d. Point to the lower right selection handle to display a resize arrow.
 e. Drag the pointer to reach cell **H35**.

4. Choose a quick layout.
 a. Select the chart object if necessary.
 b. Click the **Quick Layout** button [*Chart Tools Design* tab, *Chart Layouts* group].
 c. Click **Layout 3** (Figure 3-10).

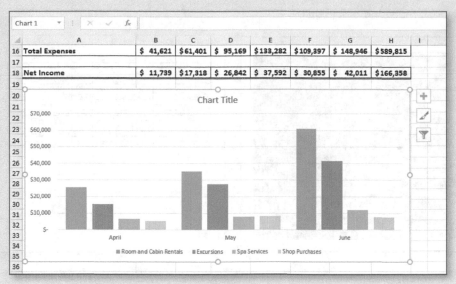

▲	A	B	C	D	E	F	G	H	I
16	Total Expenses	$ 41,621	$61,401	$ 95,169	$133,282	$109,397	$ 148,946	$589,815	
17									
18	Net Income	$ 11,739	$17,318	$ 26,842	$ 37,592	$ 30,855	$ 42,011	$166,358	

3-10 Chart object sized and positioned

5. Create a chart sheet.
 a. Select cells **A4:A8**.
 b. Press **Ctrl** and select cells **E4:G8**.
 c. Click the **Recommended Charts** button [*Insert* tab, *Charts* group].
 d. Select **Clustered Bar**.
 e. Click **OK**. The chart object is inserted and selected.
 f. Click the **Move Chart** button [*Chart Tools Design* tab, *Location* group].
 g. Click the **New sheet** radio button.
 h. Type Qtr 3 as the sheet name.
 i. Click **OK**. The chart sheet tab is active.

6. Choose a chart style.
 a. Click the **More** button to open the *Chart Styles* gallery [*Chart Tools Design* tab, *Chart Styles* group].
 b. Select **Style 7**.

7. Preview the charts.
 a. Select the **Qtr 3** sheet if necessary.
 b. Click the **File** tab to open the *Backstage* view.
 c. Choose **Print** to preview the chart sheet (Figure 3-11).
 d. Click the **Back** button to return to the worksheet.
 e. Click the **Cass Lake** worksheet tab and select cell **A1**.
 f. Click the **File** tab and select **Print**. The worksheet and chart are previewed on a single page.
 g. Click the **Back** button to return to the worksheet.

3-11 Print preview for chart sheet

8. Save and close the workbook (Figure 3-12).

3-12 PP E3-1 completed chart object and chart sheet

Editing Chart Elements and Data

A *chart element* is a separate, clickable, editable object. The chart layout and style affects which elements are initially displayed, but you can add, remove, format, size, and position elements as you design a chart. The following table describes common chart elements:

Excel Chart Elements

Element	Description
Axis	Horizontal or vertical boundary that identifies what is plotted
Axis title	Optional description for the categories or values
Chart area	Background for the chart; can be filled with a color, gradient, or pattern
Chart floor	Base or bottom for a 3D chart
Chart title	Optional description or name for the chart
Chart wall	Vertical background for a 3D chart
Data label	Optional element that displays values with the marker for each data series
Data marker	Element that represents individual values. The marker is a bar, a column, a slice, or a point on a line.
Data point	A single value or piece of data from a data series
Data series	Group of related values that are in the same column or row and translate into the columns, lines, pie slices, and other markers
Gridline	Horizontal or vertical line that extends across the plot area to help in identifying values
Horizontal (category) axis	Describes what is shown in the chart and is created from row or column headings. In a bar chart, the category axis is the vertical axis; the category axis is the horizontal axis in a column chart.

Continued

Element	Description
Legend	Element that explains symbols, textures, or colors used to differentiate data series
Plot area	Rectangular area bounded by the horizontal and vertical axes
Tick mark	Small line or marker on an axis to guide in reading values
Trendline	Line or curve that displays averages in the data and can be used to forecast future averages
Vertical (value) axis	Shows the numbers on the chart. In a bar chart, the vertical axis is along the bottom; in a column chart, the vertical axis is along the side.

> **MORE INFO**
>
> Not all charts have all elements. For example, a pie chart does not have any axes or axes titles.

Add and Remove Chart Elements

When you point to a chart element, a *ScreenTip* describes it. When you click the element, it is active and surrounded by selection handles, as shown for the legend in Figure 3-13. In addition to clicking, you can select an element from the *Chart Elements* drop-down list on the *Chart Tools Format* tab. The name of the selected element appears in the *Chart Elements* box.

You show or hide chart elements from the *Chart Elements* button in the top right corner of a chart. When you click the button, the *Chart Elements* pane opens with a list of available elements for the chart type. In this pane, select or deselect the box to show or remove an element. To hide the pane, click the **Chart Elements** button again.

3-13 Selected legend and ScreenTip for a data series

> **ANOTHER WAY**
>
> Click the **Add Chart Element** button [*Chart Tools Design* tab, *Chart Layouts* group] to show a chart element.

Chart and Axes Titles

Chart layouts may include placeholders, which are text box objects, for a main chart title and for axes titles. If the quick layout does not include titles, you can add them. In either case, you must edit the placeholder text.

A main chart title is usually positioned above the chart, but within the chart area. Once you insert the text box, you can select it and move it anywhere on the chart. You might use an axis title to clarify what is represented by the categories or the values. If the chart represents the data well, axes titles are often not necessary.

1. Click the chart object or the chart sheet tab.

2. Click the **Chart Elements** button in the top right corner of the chart.

3. Select the **Chart Title** box.

 - The *Chart Title* placeholder displays above the chart.

4. Click the **Chart Title** arrow in the *Chart Elements* pane to select a position for the title.

5. Triple-click the *Chart Title* placeholder text to select it (Figure 3-14).

 - The mini toolbar opens.

6. Type a title to replace the placeholder text.

7. Click the chart border.

 - The title object is deselected.
 - If you press **Enter** while typing in the text box, you insert a new line in the title. Press **Backspace** to remove it and then click the chart border.

3-14 Placeholder text to be edited

To edit placeholder text, you can also select the object and type text in the *Formula* bar. Then press **Enter**, or click the **Enter** button in the *Formula* bar to complete it. The label appears in the *Formula* bar as you type, and you will not see it on the chart until you press **Enter**.

All text within an object can be formatted with font attributes from the *Font* and *Alignment* groups [*Home* tab] when the element is selected. When you want to apply a format to a portion of the text, click to place an insertion point inside the element and select the characters to be changed.

> ▶ **MORE INFO**
>
> When you double-click a chart element, its *Format* pane opens with format and design choices for that element.

Removing a chart element makes more room for the actual chart. In Figure 3-15, for example, the vertical axis title "Dollars" is probably not necessary. By removing it, the chart resizes to fit the chart area. You can always show the element again if you change your mind.

To delete a chart element,

3-15 Delete an axis title to make more room for the chart

select it and press **Delete**. You can confirm which element is selected in the *Chart Elements* box on the *Chart Tools Format* tab [*Current Selection* group].

▶ HOW TO: Delete a Chart Element

1. Click the chart element.
 - The element displays selection handles.
 - Confirm which element is selected in the *Chart Elements* list box [*Chart Tools Format* tab, *Current Selection* group].
2. Press **Delete**.
 - The chart resizes to fit the area.
 - You can also right-click the chart element and choose **Delete**.

ANOTHER WAY

To remove an element, click the **Chart Elements** button in the top right corner of the chart and deselect the box for that element.

Data Labels

Data labels display the number represented by a column, bar, pie slice, or other marker on the chart. Because the value axis uses a scale, it cannot show a precise value, but a data label can display that number. Data labels should be used when there are not too many data series because they can clutter a chart. Or you can select just one or two of the data points (the individual bars or columns) and show labels for only that data.

Data labels are displayed from the *Chart Elements* button on the chart or from the same button on the *Chart Tools Design* tab [*Chart Layouts* group].

▶ HOW TO: Add Data Labels

1. Select the chart object or the chart sheet tab.
2. Click the **Chart Elements** button in the top right corner of the chart.
3. Select the **Data Labels** box.
 - *Live Preview* shows data labels for each data point in the data series
4. Point to **Data Labels** in the pane and point to its arrow (Figure 3-16).
 - Position choices for the labels are listed.
 - *Live Preview* updates as you point to each option.
5. Choose a location for the data labels.

3-16 Data labels shown outside bar markers

Data Table

A chart ***data table*** is a columnar display of the values for each data series in a chart, located just below the chart. When your readers do not have access to the source data for a chart, a data table can supply valuable information.

To include a data table below your chart, you can use the *Add Chart Element* button on the *Chart Tools Design* tab in the *Chart Layouts* group or the *Chart Elements* button on the

chart. You can show a data table with or without legend markers, a mini legend to the left of the table (Figure 3-17).

3-17 Data table element for a chart

Trendlines

A **trendline** is a chart element that plots patterns using a moving average of the current data. It uses a straight or curved line and can extend past the data to predict future averages. Some charts cannot display a trendline, such as a stacked chart, a pie chart, or a 3D chart. A basic linear trendline is appropriate for values that tend to increase or decrease as time passes. A trendline traces data for one data series as seen in

3-18 Column chart with "Total Revenue" linear trendline

Figure 3-18. If you have multiple data series, as in a typical column chart, you can add a trendline for each series.

> ### ANOTHER WAY
>
> Right-click a data series marker (its column) and choose **Add Trendline** to open the *Format Trendline* task pane and build a trendline.

▶ HOW TO: Add a Trendline to a Chart

1. Click the chart object or the chart sheet tab.
2. Click the **Chart Elements** button in the top right corner of the chart.
3. Select the **Trendline** box in the *Chart Elements* pane.
 - The *Add Trendline* dialog box lists the names of the data series.
 - When there is only one data series, the trendline is added to the chart.
4. Choose a data series for the trendline and click **OK** (Figure 3-19).
5. Point to the **Trendline** arrow in the *Chart Elements* pane.
 - Choose **Linear** to show a line for existing data.
 - Choose **Linear Forecast** to build a line for current and future data.

3-19 *Add Trendline* dialog box for chart with multiple data series

Switch Row and Column Data

Excel plots the data series based on the number of rows and columns selected in the worksheet and the chart type. Based on your choices, Excel determines if the labels are along the bottom or the side of the chart. When necessary, you can change which data series is plotted on the x-axis and which is plotted on the y-axis. In a column chart, the x-axis is along the bottom of the chart; the y-axis is along the left.

▶ HOW TO: Switch Row and Column Data

1. Click the chart object or the chart sheet tab.
2. Click the **Switch Row/Column** button [*Chart Tools Design* tab, *Data* group] (Figure 3-20).
 - The data series become the categories.
 - You can toggle between how columns and rows are plotted.

3-20 Column and row data switched

Change the Chart Type

When a chart does not depict what you intended, you need a variety of chart types for a project, or you simply prefer a different chart, you can easily change the chart type. Changing the type assumes that the source data is the same and that it can be graphed in the new chart. You should not, for example, change a column chart with three data series into a pie chart, because a pie chart has only one series. The resulting chart would not represent the data as expected.

The *Change Chart Type* button is on the *Chart Tools Design* tab in the *Type* group. For a selected chart object or sheet, you can also right-click and choose **Change Chart Type** from the context menu. The *Change Chart Type* dialog box has *Recommended Charts* and *All Charts* tabs like the *Insert Chart* dialog box.

▶ HOW TO: Change the Chart Type

1. Click the chart object or chart sheet.
2. Click the **Change Chart Type** button [*Chart Tools Design* tab, *Type* group].
 - The *Change Chart Type* dialog box opens.

3. Click the **Recommended Charts** tab.
 - Click **All Charts** tab if the recommended charts are not adequate.
4. Click a thumbnail image to preview the chart in the dialog box.
5. Select a chart type and click **OK**.

Filter Source Data

A chart displays all the categories and all the data series. You can, however, filter or refine which data is displayed by hiding categories or series. A *filter* is a requirement or condition that identifies which data is shown and which is hidden. Chart filters do not change the underlying cell range for a chart, but they enable you to focus on particular data.

You filter chart data from the *Chart Filters* button in the top right corner of the chart or in the *Select Data Source* dialog box.

▶ HOW TO: Filter Source Data

1. Select the chart object or chart sheet tab.
2. Click the **Chart Filters** button in the top right corner.
 - The *Chart Filters* pane shows a check mark for series and categories that are shown.
3. Deselect the box for a series or category to be hidden.
4. Click **Apply** (Figure 3-21).
 - The chart is redrawn.
5. Click the **Chart Filters** button to close the pane.
 - You can show the hidden data when desired.

3-21 *Chart Filters* pane

Edit Source Data

The cells used to build a chart are its source data. This data can be edited to change, add, or remove cells. In a column chart, for example, you can add a data series, or another column. To add or delete a data series in a chart object, select the chart and drag the sizing arrow in the lower right corner of the highlighted cell range to expand or shrink the data range, as shown in Figure 3-22. Removing cells from the data range deletes that data series from the chart.

3-22 The "Shop Purchases" column will be removed from chart

To edit the source data for a chart sheet, click the **Select Data** button on the *Chart Tools Design* tab [*Data* group] to open the *Select Data Source* dialog box.

> ▶ **HOW TO: Add a Data Series in a Chart Sheet**

1. Click the chart sheet tab.

2. Click the **Select Data** button [*Chart Tools Design* tab, *Data* group].

 - The *Select Data Source* dialog box opens.
 - The worksheet is active, and the source cells are highlighted.

3. Select the new cell range in the worksheet (Figure 3-23).

 - If the cell ranges are not adjacent, select the first one, type a comma, and select the next range.
 - You can type cell addresses in the *Chart data range* box rather than selecting cells.

4. Click **OK**.

 - The chart sheet is active and redrawn with the edited source data range.

3-23 *Select Data Source* dialog box for a chart sheet

> ▶ **ANOTHER WAY**
>
> You can open the *Select Data Source* dialog box by clicking **Select Data** at the bottom of the *Chart Filters* pane. You can define filters from this dialog box by selecting or deselecting a series or category name box.

SLO 3.4

Formatting Chart Elements

Quick Layout and *Chart Styles* apply formatting, but you can change most attributes to personalize your work. Making your own format choices enables you to distinguish your charts from those of other Excel users. You can also use company, association, or school colors and images to further differentiate your charts.

Some chart elements consist of a group of related elements. A data series, for example, is the group of values for a particular item. Within each data series, there are data points. You can format the entire data series or an individual data point.

When you select a chart element, certain options on the *Chart Tools Design* tab apply to only that element. When the chart area (background) is selected, for example, you can change only its fill or border color.

Apply a Shape Style

A **shape style** is a predesigned set of borders, fill colors, and effects for a chart element. **Shape fill** is the background color, and **shape outline** is the border around the element. **Shape effects** include shadows, glows, bevels, or soft edges. All of these commands are available in the *Shape Styles* group on the *Chart Tools Format* tab.

Shape styles are shown in a gallery and are grouped as *Theme Styles* or *Presets*. Point to an icon to see a *ScreenTip* with a descriptive name and click an icon to apply it to the selected element. *Live Preview* is available for a chart object but not for a chart sheet.

HOW TO: Apply a Shape Style

1. Select the chart element.
 - Confirm or select a chart element by clicking the **Chart Elements** drop-down arrow [*Chart Tools Format* tab, *Current Selection* group] and choosing the name.
 - If you accidentally open the *Format* task pane for a chart element, close it.
2. Click the **More** button [*Chart Tools Format* tab, *Shape Styles* group].
 - Each icon in the *Shape Styles* gallery displays fill, outline, and effects (Figure 3-24).
 - Point to an icon to see its name and *Live Preview* in a chart object.
3. Click a shape style icon.
 - The chart element is reformatted.

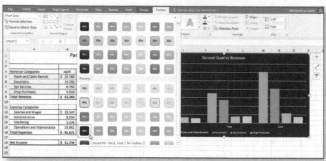

3-24 *Shape Style* gallery for the chart area

Apply Shape Fill, Outline, and Effects

Fill color, outline width and color, and special effects are available separately, and your choices override shape style settings already applied.

For fill color, you choose from the gallery, standard colors, or a custom color. After you choose a color, you can refine it to use a gradient, a variegated blend of the color.

HOW TO: Apply Gradient Fill to a Chart Element

1. Select the chart element.
 - Confirm or select a chart element from the **Chart Elements** list [*Chart Tools Format* tab, *Current Selection* group].
2. Click the **Shape Fill** button [*Chart Tools Format* tab, *Shape Styles* group].
 - The gallery and menu options are listed.
3. Point to a color tile to see its name in a *ScreenTip*.
 - *Live Preview* applies the color to an element in a chart object.
4. Select a color tile to apply the color.
5. Click the **Shape Fill** [*Chart Tools Format* tab, *Shape Styles* group].
6. Choose **Gradient** to open the gallery (Figure 3-25).
7. Point to a tile to see its description.
8. Click the preferred gradient.

3-25 *Shape Fill* and *Gradient* galleries

The outline for a shape is a border that surrounds or encircles the element. Not all chart elements are suited to an outline, but elements such as the chart or plot area often benefit from the use of an outline. When you add an outline to a chart element, you can select a weight or thickness for the line as well as a color. The thickness of an outline is measured in points, like fonts. Excel provides a gallery of weights to help you visualize the width. After you apply an outline, it is easier to see the effect if you deselect the chart object.

HOW TO: Apply an Outline to a Chart Element

1. Select the chart element.
2. Click the **Shape Outline** button [*Chart Tools Format* tab, *Shape Styles* group].
 - The gallery and menu options are listed.
3. Choose a color.
4. Click the **Shape Outline** button [*Chart Tools Format* tab, *Shape Styles* group].
5. Click **Weight** to open its gallery.
6. Choose a width for the outline (Figure 3-26).
7. Click a worksheet cell or another chart element to see the outline.

3-26 *Outline color* and *Weight* galleries

Special effects that are commonly used are bevels and shadows, because they give an element a realistic, three-dimensional look. These effects are best used on larger elements, such as the chart area, because they can overwhelm smaller elements.

To remove an effect, select the element and click the **Shape Effects** button. Choose the effect group to select the first option such as **No Shadow** or **No Bevel**.

HOW TO: Apply an Effect to a Chart Element

1. Select the chart element.
2. Click the **Shape Effects** button [*Chart Tools Format* tab, *Shape Styles* group].
 - The gallery lists effect groups and then variations for each group.
3. Select a group for the effect (Figure 3-27).
 - If a group name is grayed out, it is not available for the selected element.
4. Point to an icon to see its name.
5. Click to choose an effect.
6. Click a worksheet cell or another chart element to see the outline.

3-27 *Shape Effects* gallery for the plot area

The Format Task Pane

Every chart element has a *Format* task pane that consolidates shape, fill, and color options and provides custom commands for the element. To open the *Format* pane for a chart element, double-click the element or right-click it and choose **Format** [*Element Name*] from the menu. The *Format* pane opens to the right of the workbook window and automatically updates to reflect the selected element.

> **ANOTHER WAY**
>
> Open a *Format* task pane for a selected object by clicking the **Format Selection** button [*Chart Tools Format* tab, *Selection* group].

A task pane lists command options at the top of the pane. In Figure 3-28, *Title Options* and *Text Options* are available because the selected element is a chart title. The small triangle next to the first *Options* name enables you to choose a different chart element.

For each options group, most *Format* task panes have at least two buttons. The *Fill & Line*, *Effects*, and *Options* buttons are common, but there are other buttons for selected elements. Point to a button to see its *ScreenTip*. When you click a button, the pane displays relevant commands.

3-28 *Format Chart Title* pane

> **MORE INFO**
>
> Expand or collapse a command group in the *Format* task pane by clicking the command name.

▶ HOW TO: Use the Format Task Pane to Change Shape Fill

1. Double-click the chart element.
 - The *Format* task pane for the element opens on the right.
 - Select another element in the chart to see its task pane.
 - You can also select an element and click the **Format Selection** button [*Chart Tools Format* tab, *Current Selection* group] to open the task pane.
2. Click the name of the *Options* group at the top of task pane.
 - For some chart elements, there is only one group.
3. Click the **Fill & Line** button in the *Format* task pane.
4. Click **Fill** to expand the group.
5. Click the **Fill Color** button to open the gallery (Figure 3-29).
6. Choose the desired color.

3-29 *Fill & Line* command in the *Format Plot Area* task pane

While the *Fill & Line* and *Effects* buttons offer similar commands for all elements, the *Options* button in a *Format* task pane is specific to the element. For a data series in a column chart, for example, these commands determine whether numbers are shown to the right or left of the chart (secondary or primary axis), or whether the columns overlap. A pie chart, on the other hand, has options that allow you to rotate the pie or explode slices.

▶ HOW TO: Use the Format Task Pane to Format Data Labels

1. Double-click a data label element in the chart.
 - Right-click an element and choose **Format Data Labels**.
 - All data labels for one series are selected.
2. Choose **Label Options** at the top of the task pane.
 - Point to a button to see a *ScreenTip*.
 - *Text Options* are also available.
3. Click the **Label Options** button.
4. Click **Label Options** or **Number** to expand the command group.
5. Select format options for the labels (Figure 3-30).
 - Formats are applied as you select them.
6. Close the task pane.

3-30 *Format Data Labels* pane

Using Pictures, Shapes, and WordArt in a Chart

A chart can be enhanced with pictures, shapes, or *WordArt*. Pictures can be inserted as separate design objects on the chart, or they can be used as fill for a chart element. You can draw a shape such as an arrow or a lightning bolt to highlight a particular data point on a chart. *WordArt* is often applied to a chart title for a distinctive look.

Use a Picture as Shape Fill

An image can be used to fill the chart area, the plot area, or a marker, especially bars, columns, or pie slices. You have probably seen bar charts with stick figures to illustrate population numbers or column charts with tiny automobile images to show auto sales. You can use an image file from your computer, from external media, or from an online source. And always verify that you have permission to use an image in your work.

The size and design of the picture is important, and you should guard against making the chart appear busy. You can edit some attributes of a picture in Excel, but this depends on the picture format.

A picture is inserted from the **Fill** command on the *Format* task pane for the element. After you have inserted a picture, the task pane displays **Stretch** and **Stack** options. *Stretch* enlarges and elongates a single copy of a picture to fill the element. The *Stack* choice sizes and repeats the image to fill the area. There is also a **Stack and Scale** setting for precise matching of the number of images used per unit of value.

▶ HOW TO: Use a Picture as Fill

1. Double-click the chart element for the fill.
 - The *Format* task pane opens.
 - You can also right-click the element and choose **Format [*Element Name*]**.
2. Click the **Fill & Line** button in the *Format* task pane.
3. Click **Fill** to expand the group.
4. Select the **Picture or texture fill** radio button.
 - If the last-used picture or texture displays in the chart element, ignore it. It will be replaced.

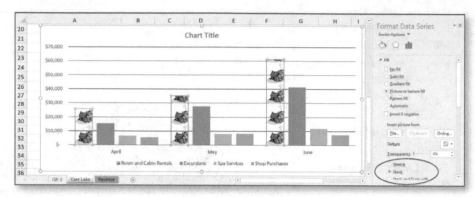

3-31 Image used as fill for data series

5. Click **Online** to search for an image or click **File** to choose a stored image.
6. Find and insert the image.
 - The picture is placed in the chart element.
7. Click the **Stack** button in the task pane (Figure 3-31).
 - Copies of the picture fill the element.

Insert Shapes

The *Shapes* gallery is located in the *Insert Shapes* group on the *Chart Tools Format* tab. These predefined shapes include arrows, lines, circles, and other basic figures. Shapes can be used to highlight or emphasize a point in the chart. They can be drawn anywhere on the chart, but are usually placed on the background or the plot area so they do not obscure any data. A shape, once drawn, is a clickable, selectable object. When it is selected, the *Picture Tools Format* tab is available with commands for altering the appearance of the shape and there is also the *Format Shape* task pane.

▶ HOW TO: Insert a Shape in a Chart

1. Select the chart object or the chart sheet tab.
2. Click the **More** button [*Chart Tools Format* tab, *Insert Shapes* group].

3. Select the shape.
4. Click and drag to draw the shape on the chart (Figure 3-32).

 - The shape is selected.

5. Type text for the shape.

 - Text is optional.
 - Some shapes cannot display text.

6. Click the **Drawing Tools Format** tab to format the shape.

 - You can also apply formatting from the *Format Shape* task pane.

7. Click a worksheet cell or another chart element to deselect the shape.

3-32 Shape inserted in chart

ANOTHER WAY

Insert a shape from the *Shapes* button on the *Insert* tab [*Illustrations* group].

Use WordArt in a Chart

WordArt is a text box with preset font style, fill, and effects. *WordArt* is best used for main titles, because it can make smaller elements unreadable. You apply a *WordArt* style from the *Chart Tools Format* tab, *WordArt Styles* group. You can further design a *WordArt* style by individually changing its fill, outline, and effects.

> MORE INFO
>
> You can insert a *WordArt* text box from the *Insert* tab [*Text* group] and position it on the chart.

▶ HOW TO: Use WordArt in a Chart

1. Select the chart title object.

 - You can also apply *WordArt* to an axis title, a data label, or the legend.

2. Click the **More** button to open the *WordArt Styles* gallery [*Chart Tools Format* tab, *WordArt Styles* group].

3. Point to a style icon to see a *ScreenTip* with a description.

 - The styles use colors and effects from the workbook theme.
 - *Live Preview* works in a chart object but not on a chart sheet.

4. Click the preferred style (Figure 3-33).

3-33 *WordArt Style* gallery for selected chart title

For this project, you open your Pause & Practice file to edit and format the Paradise Lakes Resort charts. You switch row and column data, remove chart elements, and change the chart type. Finally, you format the charts for increased visual appeal.

File Needed: ***[your initials] PP E3-1.xlsx***
Completed Project File Name: ***[your initials] PP E3-2.xlsx***

1. Open the **[your initials] PP E3-1** workbook completed in *Pause & Practice 3-1* and save it as [your initials] PP E3-2.

2. Switch the row and column data in the chart object.
 a. Click the **Cass Lake** worksheet tab.
 b. Point to the border or edge of the chart object and click to select it.
 c. Click the **Switch/Row Column** button [*Chart Tools Design* tab, *Data* group].

3. Edit, add, and remove chart elements.
 a. Click to select the chart title box.
 b. Point to the placeholder text and triple-click to select all of it.
 c. Type Second Quarter Activity.
 d. Click the chart border to deselect the title.
 e. Click the **Chart Elements** button in the top right corner of the chart.
 f. Select the **Axis Titles** box.
 g. Select the horizontal *Axis Title* placeholder below the columns and press **Delete**.
 h. Select the vertical *Axis Title* placeholder.
 i. Click the *Formula* bar, type Revenue, and press **Enter** (Figure 3-34).
 j. Click a worksheet cell to deselect the chart object.

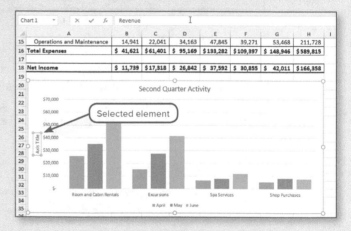

3-34 Edit the text in the *Formula* bar

4. Change the chart type.
 a. Click the **Qtr 3** sheet tab.
 b. Click the **Change Chart Type** button [*Chart Tools Design* tab, *Type* group].
 c. Click the **Recommended Charts** tab.
 d. Find and select the first **Clustered Column** in the pane on the left.
 e. Click **OK**.

5. Filter the source data.
 a. Click the **Chart Filters** button at the top right corner of the chart.
 b. Deselect the **Excursions** box in the *Series* area.
 c. Click **Apply**.
 d. Click the **Chart Filters** button to close the pane (Figure 3-35).

3-35 Filtered data in chart

594

6. Apply shape styles and outlines to chart elements.
 a. Click the **Cass Lake** tab and select the chart object.
 b. Click the **Chart Elements** drop-down arrow [*Chart Tools Format* tab, *Current Selection* group].
 c. Choose **Plot Area** to select the plot area of the chart.
 d. Click the **More** button [*Chart Tools Format* tab, *Shape Styles* group].
 e. Click **Subtle Effect – Gold**, **Accent 4** in the fourth row in the *Theme Styles* group.
 f. Click the drop-down arrow for the **Shape Outline** button [*Chart Tools Format* tab, *Shape Styles* group].
 g. Choose **Black**, **Text 1** in the top row of the *Theme Colors*.
 h. Click the **Chart Elements** drop-down arrow [*Chart Tools Format* tab, *Current Selection* group].
 i. Choose **Vertical (Value) Axis Major Gridlines** to select the major gridlines in the plot area.
 j. Click the icon with the **Shape Outline** button [*Chart Tools Format* tab, *Shape Styles* group] to apply the last-used color (**Black**, **Text 1**).
 k. Click the **Chart Elements** drop-down arrow [*Chart Tools Format* tab, *Current Selection* group] and choose **Chart Area**.
 l. Apply **Black**, **Text 1** for the outline (Figure 3-36).
 m. Click a worksheet cell.

3-36 Plot area formatted

7. Use a picture as fill.
 a. Click the **Qtr 3** tab.
 b. Double-click one of the "Room and Cabin Rentals" columns to open the *Format Data Series* task pane.
 c. Click the **Fill & Line** button.
 d. Click **Fill** to expand the command group.
 e. Select the **Picture or texture fill** button.
 f. Click **Online**, type log cabin in the *Bing Image Search* box, and press **Enter**.
 g. Choose an image and insert it (Figure 3-37). If you choose an image that cannot be used as fill, a message appears in the columns; just select a different picture.
 h. Select the **Stack** radio button in the *Format Data Series* task pane.
 i. Click **Fill** to collapse the command group and click **Border** to expand its group.
 j. Select the **Solid line** button.
 k. Click the **Color** button and choose **Black**, **Text 1**.
 l. Close the task pane.

3-37 Online search for a picture as fill

8. Use *WordArt* in a chart.
 a. Triple-click the **Chart Title** placeholder text to select the text.
 b. Type Third Quarter Activity.
 c. Triple-click the new label and change the font size to **32 pt**.
 d. Click the border area of the chart title to display the selection handles.
 e. Click the **More** button [*Chart Tools Format* tab, *WordArt Styles* group].
 f. Choose **Fill – Gray-25%**, **Background 2**, **Inner Shadow** (third row).

9. Format the legend.
 a. Click to select the legend.
 b. Click the **Home** tab and change the font size to **12 pt**.
 c. Click the chart border to deselect the legend.
 d. Click a worksheet cell and press **Ctrl+Home**.

10. Save and close the workbook (Figure 3-38).

3-38 PP E3-2 completed worksheet and chart sheet

SLO 3.6

Building Pie and Combination Charts

A pie chart represents one set of related values and shows the proportion of each value to the total. A combination chart uses at least two sets of values and plots each data series with a different chart type. A combination chart can also have two value axes, one on the left and one on the right.

Create a 3-D Pie Chart

A pie chart graphs one data series and illustrates how each number relates to the whole. Be cautious about the number of categories, because a pie chart with hundreds of slices is difficult to interpret and does not depict the relationship among the values.

As you develop chart-building skills, you can choose a type from the *Charts* group on the *Insert* tab. When you select a chart type button, you see a gallery with available subtypes. As you point to each subtype, *Live Preview* previews the chart.

From the *Insert Pie or Doughnut Chart* button on the *Insert* tab, you can select from a gallery of 2-D or 3-D pie types as well as a doughnut shape (Figure 3-39). A doughnut chart is a pie chart with a hollow center. There are also options for a pie chart with a bar or another pie chart.

3-39 Selected data series and categories for a pie chart

1. Select the cells that include the values and the category labels.
 - The labels and values need not be adjacent.
2. Click the **Insert Pie or Doughnut Chart** button [*Insert* tab, *Charts* group].
3. Choose **3-D Pie**.
 - A pie chart object is placed in the worksheet.
4. Click the **Move Chart** button [*Chart Tools Design* tab, *Location* group].
5. Click the **New sheet** button.
6. Type a name for the chart sheet.
7. Click **OK**.

Pie Chart Elements and Options

In a pie chart, the data series is represented by the whole pie. A data point is a slice of the pie. You can format the data series as a whole, or you can format individual slices.

A pie chart can display a legend and a title. It does not, however, have axes and does not use axes titles. Data labels can be used in place of a legend, because they show the same information.

Custom commands for a pie chart are the angle of the first slice and the percent of explosion. These commands are available on the *Format* task pane for the data series (the whole pie) or for a selected data point (one slice). The angle of the first slice allows you to rotate the pie. The first slice starts at the top of the chart at 0° (zero degrees). As you increase that value, the slice arcs to the right. *Live Preview* displays the results, too.

Exploding a pie slice emphasizes that slice, because it moves the slice away from the rest of the pie. This uses more white space in the chart, and the pie gets smaller. You set explosion as a percentage.

▶ **HOW TO:** **Rotate a Pie Chart and Explode a Slice**

1. Double-click the pie shape.
 - The *Format Data Series* task pane opens.
 - You can also right-click the pie shape and choose **Format Data Series**.
2. Click the **Series Options** button.
3. Drag the vertical slider to set the *Angle of first slice*.
 - The percentage is shown in the entry box.
 - You can also type a percentage or use the spinner arrows to set a value.
4. Click the data point (slice) to explode.
 - The *Format Data Point* task pane opens.
5. Drag the vertical slider to set the *Pie Explosion* (Figure 3-40).
 - The percentage is shown in the entry box.
 - The larger the percentage, the farther the slice is from the rest of the pie.
 - You can type a percentage or use the spinner arrows to set a value.

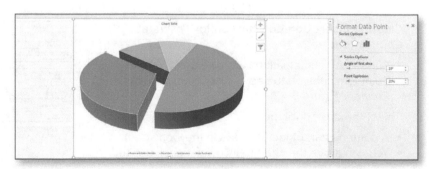

3-40 **Exploded pie slice with angle of first slice changed**

Create a Combination Chart

A combination chart includes at least two chart types such as a line chart and a column chart. Paradise Lakes Resort can use a combination chart to compare revenue from cabin and room rentals to total revenue. These two values reflect a different scale of numbers, so showing one series as a line and the other as a column focuses the comparison (Figure 3-41).

> **MORE INFO**
>
> A line and column combination chart resembles a column chart with a trendline, but the combination chart uses actual values. The trendline predicts values.

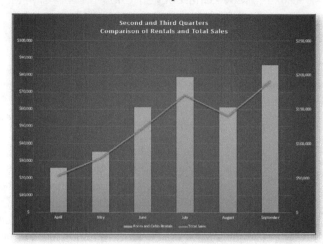

3-41 Line-Column combination chart

The most common combination of chart types is line and column, but you can also use a line and area combination. Excel offers an option to create a custom combination, but it is best to use this only after you have experience charting your data.

> **MORE INFO**
>
> Not all chart types can be combined. If you try to do so, Excel opens a message box to inform you.

Create a combination chart from the *Insert Combo Chart* button in the *Charts* group on the *Insert* tab as well as from the *All Charts* tab in the *Insert Chart* dialog box.

▶ **HOW TO:** Create a Combination Chart

1. Select the cell ranges for the chart.
 - The cell ranges need not be contiguous.
2. Click the **Insert Combo Chart** button [*Insert* tab, *Charts* group].
 - Suggested combinations are displayed.
 - Point to a subtype to see a description and a *Live Preview* (Figure 3-42).
3. Select the chart subtype.
 - A combo chart object displays in the worksheet.
 - You can move the chart to its own sheet if desired.

3-42 Insert Combo Chart button options

Combination Chart Elements and Options

A combination chart has at least two data series, each graphed in its own chart type. Keep this type of chart relatively simple, because its purpose is to compare unlike items and too many data series complicate what viewers see.

In a combination chart, you can display values on two vertical axes. The axis on the left is the primary

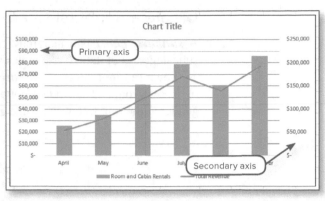

3-43 Secondary axis for a combo chart

axis; the one on the right is secondary (Figure 3-43). This option is best when the values are very different or use a different scale.

For the secondary axis, Excel builds the number scale based on the data. Select the data series to be plotted on the secondary axis and choose the option from the *Series Options* command group in the *Format* task pane. You can also define a secondary axis in the *Insert Chart* or the *Change Chart Type* dialog boxes.

A combination chart has the same elements and commands as a regular column or line chart. You can apply chart styles and layouts, as well as shape fill, outline, effects, pictures, shapes, and *WordArt*.

▶HOW TO: Display a Secondary Axis on a Combination Chart

1. Select the chart object or the chart sheet tab.
2. Select the data series to be shown on the secondary axis.
 - Select the line or any column in a line-column combo chart.
 - You can also choose the data series from the *Chart Elements* box [*Chart Tools Format* tab, *Current Selection* group].
3. Click the **Format Selection** button [*Chart Tools Format* tab, *Current Selection* group].
4. Click the **Series Options** button in the task pane (Figure 3-44).
5. Click the **Secondary Axis** radio button.
 - Additional options for the axis depend on the chart type.
6. Close the *Format Data Series* task pane.

3-44 *Format Data Series* task pane to define a secondary axis

Creating Sunburst and Waterfall Charts

New chart types in Excel 2016 visualize data in ways that previously required engineering or similar specialized software. With a sunburst chart, you can show relationships between multiple categories of data. A waterfall chart depicts a running total for financial data so that you can assess the impact of negative and positive cash flows. These charts have many characteristics of standard Excel charts, but they have a few limitations related to requirements for the data they plot.

Create a Sunburst Chart

A **sunburst chart** is a hierarchy chart that illustrates the relationship among categories and subcategories of data. It resembles a doughnut chart with concentric rings for each layer of data as shown in Figure 3-45. A **hierarchy** is a division of data that identifies a top group followed by lesser groups. The student population at your college can be illustrated in a hierarchy with gender at the top, followed by age group, then home city, followed by area of study, and so on.

3-45 Sunburst chart for third quarter revenue for two locations

Paradise Lakes Resort keeps a record of revenue by location, category, and month. The inner ring in Figure 3-45 is the top level of the hierarchy, the location. The second level is the revenue category (Rentals, Excursions, etc.), and the outside ring is the month's revenue. From the chart, you can see that Baudette contributed slightly more than half of the total revenue and that the boutique purchases at Cass Lake were high.

A sunburst chart has one data series and no axes. It can display a title, data labels, and a legend. The *Chart Tools Design* and *Format* tabs provide basic options for fine-tuning the appearance of the chart.

The *Insert Hierarchy Chart* button [*Insert* tab, *Charts* group] has two subtypes, *Sunburst* and *TreeMap*. These subtypes can handle large amounts of data, but be careful not to build charts that are difficult to interpret due to their size.

> **MORE INFO**
>
> A *TreeMap* chart illustrates hierarchical data using rectangles of various sizes and colors to represent the divisions and subdivisions.

 HOW TO: Create a Sunburst Chart

1. Select the source data with labels and values.
 - The **Quick Analysis** button appears, but the *Charts* group does not include the *Sunburst* chart type.
2. Click the **Insert Hierarchy Chart** button [*Insert* tab, *Charts* group].
 - A menu lists the subtypes.
3. Point to **Sunburst** to see a *Live Preview*.

4. Click **Sunburst** to select it.
 - A chart object is placed in the worksheet.
5. Click the **Move Chart** button [*Chart Tools Design* tab, *Location* group].
6. Select **New sheet**.
7. Type a name for the chart sheet and click **OK**.
 - The *Chart Tools Design* and *Format* tabs are available.
8. Click the sunburst shape to select the circle.
9. Point to a category name in the inner ring and click to select the data point.
 - The category and its related items are selected (Figure 3-46).

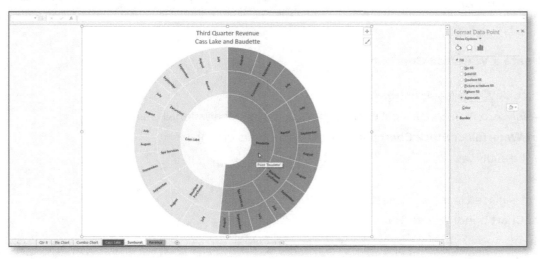

3-46 Sunburst chart sheet with selected data point

10. Format the data point as desired.
 - If the *Format Data Point* task pane is not open, click the **Format Selection** button [*Chart Tools Format* tab, *Current Selection* group].
11. Click outside the chart background to deselect the chart.

> ▶ **MORE INFO**
>
> The *Hierarchy* charts do not appear in any *Recommended Charts* list, but they are listed on the *All Charts* tab.

Create a Waterfall Chart

A **waterfall chart** is a financial chart that displays a moving total for positive and negative values. A waterfall chart graphs how each expense or outlay affects the account. You might, for example, build a waterfall chart to visualize your monthly income sources (inflows) and expenditures (outlays) to watch how you spend your resources.

In Figure 3-47, it is obvious that payroll consumes most of the cash account for Paradise Lakes Resort. In a waterfall chart, the depth or height of the marker indicates the value. In the figure, the beginning balance and ending total markers rest on the bottom axis. The other amounts are described as floating.

A waterfall chart plots one data series and has a legend that clarifies the increase, decrease, and total colors. A waterfall chart can also include axes, titles, gridlines, and data labels.

The *Insert Waterfall or Stock Chart* button is in the *Charts* group on the *Insert* tab. These charts do not appear in the *Recommended Charts* list, but they are available on the *All Charts* tab.

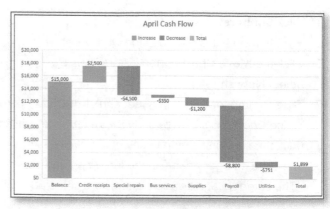

3-47 Waterfall chart for cash flow

▶ **HOW TO:** Create a Waterfall Chart Sheet

1. Select the source data with labels and values.
 - The *Quick Analysis* button appears but does not have an option for a waterfall chart.
2. Click the **Insert Waterfall or Stock Chart** button [*Insert* tab, *Charts* group].
 - A menu lists the subtypes.
3. Click **Waterfall**.
 - A chart object is placed in the worksheet.
4. Click the **Move Chart** button [*Chart Tools Design* tab, *Location* group].
5. Select **New sheet**.
6. Type a name for the chart sheet and click **OK**.
 - The *Chart Tools Design* and *Format* tabs are available.
7. Click a column marker to select the data series.
8. Click the ending marker to select only it.
9. Click the **Format Selection** button [*Chart Tools Format* tab, *Current Selection* group].
10. Click the **Series Options** button in the task pane.
11. Expand the *Series Options* group.
12. Select the **Set as total** box (Figure 3-48).
 - The marker rests on the bottom axis and is no longer floating.
13. Close the task pane and click outside the chart to deselect it.

3-48 Set a marker as a total

SLO 3.8

Inserting and Formatting Sparklines

Sparklines are miniature charts in a cell or cell range. They can be used to illustrate trends and patterns without adding a separate chart object or sheet. They do not have the same characteristics as an Excel chart.

Sparklines are created from a selected data range and placed in a location range, usually next to the data (Figure 3-49). They are embedded in the cell, almost like a background. If you enter a label or value in a cell with a sparkline, that data appears on top of the sparkline.

3-49 Column sparklines in a worksheet

Insert Sparklines

There are three sparkline types: **Line**, **Column**, and **Win/Loss**. The *Sparklines* commands are located on the *Insert* tab of the worksheet. The *Data Range* is the range of cells to be graphed, and the *Location Range* is the cell or range for the sparklines. The **Sparkline Tools Design** tab opens when you select the sparkline group.

▶ HOW TO: Insert Column Sparklines in a Worksheet

1. Select the cell range of data to be graphed.
2. Click the **Column Sparkline** button [*Insert* tab, *Sparklines* group].
 - The selected range address is shown in the *Data Range* entry box.
 - You can select or edit the data range here.
3. Click the *Location Range* box.
4. Select the cell or range for the sparklines (Figure 3-50).
5. Click **OK**.

3-50 *Create Sparklines* dialog box

Sparkline Design Tools

When sparklines are selected, the *Sparkline Tools Design* tab opens. This context-sensitive tab includes several options for changing the appearance of the sparklines. There is a *Sparkline Style* option that changes the color scheme for the sparkline group, but you can also change colors with the *Sparkline Color* command. The *Marker Color* command enables you to choose a different color for identified values. A **marker** for a sparkline is the data point value. You can use different colors to highlight the high, low, first, or last value as well as negative values.

When you define a location range for sparklines, they are embedded as a group. If you select any cell in the sparkline range, the entire group is selected. Subsequent commands affect all sparklines in the group. From the *Group* section on the *Sparkline Tools Design* tab, you can ungroup the sparklines so that you can format them individually.

From the *Sparkline Tools Design* tab, you can also change the type of sparkline, such as making a column sparkline into a line sparkline. The *Show* group lists the marker values that can be highlighted. When you select one of these options, that marker in the sparkline is formatted with a different color.

▶ HOW TO: Format Sparklines

1. Click a cell with a sparkline.
 - The sparkline group is selected.
2. Click the *Sparkline Line Tools Design* tab.
3. Click the **More** button [*Sparkline Tools Design* tab, *Style* group].
4. Choose a sparkline style.
 - The sparkline group is recolored.
5. Select the **High Point** box in the *Show* group (Figure 3-51).
 - A default color based on the sparkline style is applied to the highest value in the sparkline for each row.
6. Click the **Sparkline Color** button [*Sparkline Tools Design* tab, *Style* group].
7. Choose a color for the sparkline group.
 - The sparkline group is recolored, and the color from the *Sparkline Style* is overridden.
8. Click the **Marker Color** button [*Sparkline Tools Design* tab, *Style* group].
9. Choose **High Point** and select a color.
 - The color for the highest value is reset.

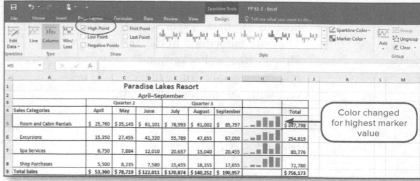

3-51 *High Point* **marker selected for sparklines**

Clear Sparklines

You can remove sparklines from a worksheet with the *Clear* command in the *Group* group on the *Sparkline Tools Design* tab. After sparklines are cleared, you may also need to delete the column where they were located or reset row heights and column widths.

▶ HOW TO: Clear Sparklines

1. Select any cell in the sparklines range.
2. Click the arrow with **Clear Selected Sparklines** button [*Sparkline Tools Design* tab, *Group* group].
3. Choose **Clear Selected Sparklines Groups**.

▶ MORE INFO

When you ungroup sparklines, you can select a single sparkline cell and clear it.

PAUSE & PRACTICE: EXCEL 3-3

For this project, you complete Paradise Lakes' revenue report by inserting a pie chart that shows the proportion of each revenue category. You also insert a combination chart sheet to compare rentals with total revenue and a sunburst chart to analyze third quarter revenue. Finally, you insert sparklines in the worksheet.

File Needed: *[your initials] PP E3-2.xlsx*
Completed Project File Name: *[your initials] PP E3-3.xlsx*

1. Open the *[your initials] PP E3-2* workbook completed in *Pause & Practice 3-2* and save it as [your initials] PP E3-3.

2. Create a pie chart for total sales revenue.
 a. Select the **Cass Lake** tab.
 b. Select cells **A5:A8** as the category.
 c. Press **Ctrl** and select cells **H5:H8** as the data series.
 d. Click the **Insert Pie or Doughnut Chart** button [*Insert* tab, *Charts* group].
 e. Choose **3-D Pie**.
 f. Click the **Move Chart** button [*Chart Tools Design* tab, *Location* group].
 g. Click the **New sheet** button and type Pie Chart as the sheet name.
 h. Click **OK**.

3. Format a pie chart.
 a. Select the **Pie Chart** tab.
 b. Click the **Chart Title** placeholder to select it and then triple-click the **Chart Title** placeholder text.
 c. Type Second and Third Quarters and press **Enter**.
 d. Type Sources of Revenue on the second line.
 e. Drag to select the first line of the title.
 f. Use the mini toolbar to change the font size to **24 pt**.
 g. Drag to select the second line of the title.
 h. Use the mini toolbar to change the font size to **18 pt**. (Figure 3-52).

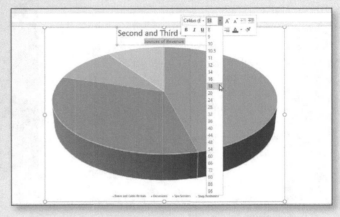

3-52 Chart titles typed and font size changed

 i. Click the chart border to deselect the title.
 j. Double-click the pie to open the *Format Data Series* task pane.
 k. Click the **Series Options** button in the *Format Data Series* task pane.
 l. Click the **Room and Cabin Rentals** slice to change to the *Format Data Point* task pane.
 m. Set the pie explosion percentage at **10%**.
 n. Close the task pane.
 o. Select the legend at the bottom of the chart to display selection handles.
 p. Click the **Home** tab and change the font size to **14 pt** (Figure 3-53).

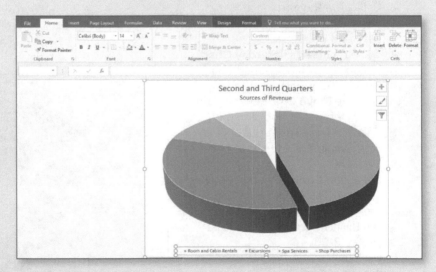

3-53 Selected legend with new font size

4. Create a combination chart for total sales revenue and room and cabin rentals.
 a. Select the **Cass Lake** tab.
 b. Select cells **A4:G5** as one data series and category.

c. Press **Ctrl** and select cells **A9:G9** as another data series and category.

d. Click the **Insert Combo Chart** button [*Insert* tab, *Charts* group].

e. Choose **Clustered Column – Line on Secondary Axis**.

f. Click the **Move Chart** button [*Chart Tools Design* tab, *Location* group].

g. Click the **New sheet** button and type Combo Chart as the sheet name.

h. Click **OK**.

5. Format a combination chart.

a. Select the **Combo Chart** tab, select the **Chart Title** placeholder, and then triple-click the placeholder text.

b. Type Second and Third Quarters and press **Enter**.

c. Type Comparison of Rentals and Total Revenue on the second line.

d. Click the chart border to deselect the chart title.

e. Choose **Style 6** [*Chart Tools Design* tab, *Chart Styles* group] (Figure 3-54).

f. Click the background to deselect the chart.

3-54 Combo chart with Style 6

6. Create a sunburst chart for third quarter revenue analysis.

a. Select the **Revenue** tab.

b. Select cells **A5:D28** as the data series and categories. This chart will illustrate revenue for Cass Lake and Baudette.

c. Click the **Insert Hierarchy Chart** button [*Insert* tab, *Charts* group].

d. Choose **Sunburst**.

e. Click the **Move Chart** button [*Chart Tools Design* tab, *Location* group].

f. Click the **New sheet** button and type Sunburst as the sheet name.

g. Click **OK**.

h. Select the **Chart Title** placeholder and type Third Quarter Revenue.

i. Press **Enter** and type Cass Lake and Baudette on the second line (Figure 3-55).

j. Click the chart border to deselect the title object.

k. Click to select the title object and change its font size to **16 pt**.

l. Click the background to deselect the chart.

3-55 Sunburst chart with edited title

7. Insert sparklines in a worksheet.
 a. Select the **Cass Lake** tab.
 b. Right-click the column **H** heading and choose **Insert** to insert a new column.
 c. Select the cell range **B5:G8** as the data to be charted with sparklines.
 d. Click the **Column Sparkline** button [*Insert* tab, *Sparklines* group].
 e. Click the **Location Range** box, and select cells **H5:H8**.
 f. Click **OK**.

8. Format sparklines.
 a. Click the **Sparkline Color** button [*Sparkline Tools Design* tab, *Style* group] and select **Green**, **Accent 6**, **Darker 25%**.
 b. Select the sparkline group if necessary, click the **Format** button [*Home* tab, *Cells* group], and change the **Row Height** to **30 (40 pixels)**.
 c. Format column **H** to a width of **16.00 (117 pixels)**.
 d. Press **Ctrl+Home**.

9. Save and close the workbook (Figure 3-56).

Paradise Lakes Resort									
April–September									
	Quarter 2			Quarter 3					
Revenue Categories	April	May	June	July	August	September			Total
Room and Cabin Rentals	$ 25,760	$35,145	$ 61,101	$ 78,993	$ 61,002	$ 85,797			$347,798
Excursions	15,350	27,455	41,320	55,789	47,855	67,050			254,819
Spa Services	6,750	7,884	12,010	20,637	13,040	20,455			80,776
Shop Purchases	5,500	8,235	7,580	15,455	18,355	17,655			72,780
Total Revenue	$ 53,360	$78,719	$122,011	$170,874	$140,252	$ 190,957			$756,173
Expense Categories									
Salaries and Wages	$ 13,340	$19,680	$ 30,503	$ 42,719	$ 35,063	$ 47,739			$189,043
Administrative	8,004	11,808	18,302	25,631	21,038	28,644			113,426
Marketing	5,336	7,872	12,201	17,087	14,025	19,096			75,617
Operations and Maintenance	14,941	22,041	34,163	47,845	39,271	53,468			211,728
Total Expenses	$ 41,621	$61,401	$ 95,169	$133,282	$109,397	$ 148,946			$589,815

3-56 PP E3-3 completed worksheet

Chapter Summary

3.1 Create Excel chart objects and chart sheets (p. 571).

- A **chart** is a visual representation of worksheet data.
- A **chart object** is a selectable item or element in a worksheet.
- A **chart sheet** is an Excel chart on its own tab in the workbook.
- The cells with values and labels used to build a chart are its **source data**.
- Chart objects and sheets are linked to their source data and contain editable chart elements such as data labels or a chart title.
- Commonly used chart types are *Column, Line, Pie,* and *Bar,* and Excel can build sophisticated statistical, financial, and scientific charts.
- You can size and position a chart object in a worksheet, or move it to its own sheet using the *Move Chart* button in the *Location* group on the *Chart Tools Design* tab.
- The *Quick Analysis* tool includes a command group for charts, and it appears when the selected source data is contiguous.

3.2 Use Quick layouts and chart styles to design a chart (p. 575).

- A **chart layout** is a set of elements and their locations in a chart.
- The *Quick Layout* button [*Chart Tools Design* tab, *Chart Layouts* group] includes predefined layouts for the current chart type.
- A **chart style** is a predefined combination of colors and effects for chart elements.
- Chart styles are based on the current workbook theme.
- The *Change Colors* command [*Chart Tools Design* tab, *Chart Styles* group] provides quick color palettes for customizing a chart.
- A chart object can be printed with its worksheet data or on its own sheet.
- A chart sheet prints on its own page in landscape orientation.

3.3 Edit chart elements including titles, data labels, and source data (p. 580).

- A **chart element** is a selectable and editable part or item in the chart.

- Chart elements include chart and axes titles, data labels, legends, gridlines, and more, depending on the type of chart.
- Excel plots data based on the number of rows and columns selected and the chart type, but you can switch the row and column data.
- You can change some chart types into another type using the *Change Chart Type* button on the *Chart Tools Design* tab.
- Chart data can be filtered to hide and display values or categories without changing the source data.
- Source data for a chart can be edited to use a different cell range or to add or remove a data series.

3.4 Format chart elements with shape styles, fill, outlines, and special effects (p. 587).

- A **shape style** is a predesigned set of fill colors, borders, and effects.
- **Shape fill**, **outline**, and **effects** can also be applied to a chart element from the *Chart Tools Format* tab.
- A chart element has a *Format* task pane that includes fill, outline, and effects commands as well as specific options for the element.
- Most formats can also be applied to a selected chart element from the *Home* tab.

3.5 Use pictures, shapes, and *WordArt* in a chart (p. 591).

- For chart shapes that have a fill color, you can use a picture as fill.
- Images used as fill can be from your own or online sources, but not all pictures work well as fill.
- Shapes are predefined outline drawings available from the *Insert Shapes* group on the *Chart Tools Format* tab or from the *Illustrations* group on the *Insert* tab.
- Shapes can be placed on a chart to highlight or draw attention to a particular element.
- **WordArt** is a text box with a preset design, often used to format a chart title.

3.6 Build pie charts and combination charts (p. 596).

- A pie chart has one data series and shows each data point as a slice of the pie.

- A pie chart does not have axes, but it does have options to rotate or explode slices.
- A combination chart uses at least two chart types to highlight, compare, or contrast differences in data or values.
- You can format a combination chart to show a secondary axis when values are widely different or use different scales.

3.7 Create sunburst and waterfall charts (p. 599).

- A *sunburst chart* has one data series that is grouped in a *hierarchy*.
- A sunburst chart illustrates the relationship among the hierarchies in a pie-like chart with concentric rings.
- A *waterfall chart* depicts a running total for positive and negative values.
- A waterfall chart is used for financial or other data that shows inflows and outlays of resources.

- A waterfall chart resembles a column chart and has category and value axes.
- You can place a sunburst chart or a waterfall chart as an object or on a separate sheet.

3.8 Insert and format sparklines in a worksheet (p. 602).

- A *sparkline* is a miniature chart in a cell or range of cells in the worksheet.
- Three sparkline types are available: *Line*, *Column*, and *Win/Loss*.
- When inserted in a range of cells, sparklines are grouped and can be ungrouped.
- The *Sparkline Tools Design* tab is visible when a sparkline is selected and includes formatting options such as setting the color or identifying high and low values.

Check for Understanding

The SIMbook for this text (within your SIMnet account) provides the following resources for concept review:

- Multiple choice questions
- Matching exercises
- Short answer questions

Guided Project 3-1

Life's Animal Shelter (LAS) is an animal care and adoption agency that accepts unwanted and abandoned domestic animals. For this project, you create expense charts and insert sparklines to help the agency track expenses for the first six months of the year. You also build a waterfall chart to graph cash flow for a month.
[Student Learning Outcomes 3.1, 3.2, 3.3, 3.4, 3.5, 3.6, 3.7, 3.8]

File Needed: **LAS-03.xlsx** [Student data files are available in the Library of your SIMnet account.]
Completed Project File Name: **[your initials] Excel 3-1.xlsx**

Skills Covered in This Project

- Create a chart object.
- Create a chart sheet.
- Apply *Quick Layout* and chart styles.
- Add and format chart elements.
- Change the chart type.
- Filter the data series.
- Insert a shape in a chart.
- Create and format a combination chart.
- Insert and format sparklines in a worksheet.
- Create and format a waterfall chart.

1. Open the **LAS-03** workbook from your student data files and save it as [your initials] Excel 3-1.

2. Create a pie chart object.
 a. Select the **Jan-June** sheet and select cells **A5:A10**. Press **Ctrl** and select cells **I5:I10**.
 b. Click the **Insert Pie or Doughnut Chart** button [*Insert* tab, *Charts* group].
 c. Select the **2D-Pie** chart subtype.

3. Create a chart sheet.
 a. Select the pie chart object.
 b. Click the **Move Chart** button [*Chart Tools Design* tab, *Location* group].
 c. Click the **New sheet** button.
 d. Type Pie Chart in the text box.
 e. Click **OK**.

4. Apply a chart style.
 a. Click the **More** button [*Chart Tools Design* tab, *Chart Styles* group].
 b. Select **Style 12**.

5. Edit and format chart elements.
 a. Click the chart title element.
 b. Click the *Formula* bar, type January through June Expenses, and press **Enter**.
 c. Triple-click the new label in the chart and change the font size to **28 pt**.
 d. Click the legend element to select it and to deselect the title element.
 e. Click the **Font Size** arrow [*Home* tab, *Font* group] and change the legend size to **12 pt**.
 f. Select the *Chart Area* element, the chart background.
 g. Click the **Shape Outline** button [*Chart Tools Format* tab, *Shape Styles* group].
 h. Choose **Black, Text 1** as the color.
 i. Click the **Shape Outline** button again.

j. Choose **Weight** and select **1 pt**.

k. Click outside the chart background to see the outline (Figure 3-57).

6. Create a bar chart object.
 a. Click the **Jan-June** sheet tab.
 b. Select cells **A4:G9** as source data, omitting the *Rent* expense.
 c. Click the **Quick Analysis** button and select **Charts**.
 d. Select **Clustered Bar**.
 e. Point to the chart border to display a move pointer.
 f. Drag the chart object so that its top left corner is at cell **A13**.
 g. Point to the bottom right selection handle to display a resize arrow.
 h. Drag the pointer to reach cell **I30** (Figure 3-58).

7. Change the chart type.
 a. Click the bar chart object.
 b. Click the **Change Chart Type** button [*Chart Tools Design* tab, *Type* group].
 c. Click the **Recommended Charts** tab.
 d. Choose **Clustered Column** in the left pane.
 e. Click **OK**.

8. Filter the source data.
 a. Click the column chart object.
 b. Click the **Chart Filters** button in the top right corner of the chart.
 c. Deselect the **January**, **February**, and **March** boxes.
 d. Click **Apply** in the *Chart Filters* pane (Figure 3-59).
 e. Click the **Chart Filters** button to close the pane.

9. Edit, format, and add chart elements.
 a. Click the chart title object.
 b. Click the *Formula* bar.
 c. Type Second Quarter Variable Expenses and press **Enter**.
 d. Click the **Chart Elements** arrow [*Chart Tools Format* tab, *Current Selection* group] and choose **Chart Area**.
 e. Click the **Shape Outline** button [*Chart Tools Format* tab, *Shape Styles* group].
 f. Choose **Black**, **Text 1** as the color.
 g. Click the **Shape Outline** button again and choose **Weight** and **1 pt**.

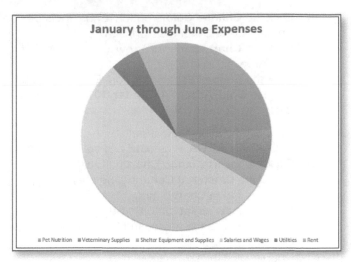

January through June Expenses

■ Pet Nutrition ■ Veterinary Supplies ■ Shelter Equipment and Supplies ■ Salaries and Wages ■ Utilities ■ Rent

3-57 Pie Chart sheet with format changes

3-58 Bar chart object sized and positioned

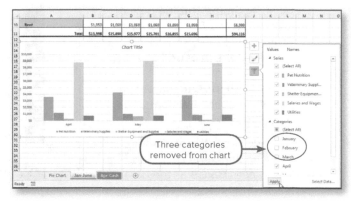

Three categories removed from chart

3-59 Chart filters applied

h. Click the **Change Colors** button [*Chart Tools Design* tab, *Chart Styles* group].

i. Choose **Color 3** in the *Colorful* group.

j. Click the **Chart Elements** arrow [*Chart Tools Format* tab, *Current Selection* group] and choose **Plot Area**.

k. Click the **Shape Fill** button [*Chart Tools Format* tab, *Shape Styles* group].

l. Choose **Gold**, **Accent 4**, **Lighter 80%** as the color.

m. Click a worksheet cell.

10. Create a combination chart sheet.

a. Select cells **A9:G9**. Press **Ctrl** and select cells **A11:G11**.

b. Click the **Insert Combo Chart** button [*Insert* tab, *Charts* group].

c. Select the **Clustered Column-Line** chart subtype.

d. Click the **Move Chart** button [*Chart Tools Design* tab, *Location* group].

e. Click the **New sheet** button, type Combo Chart as the name, and click **OK**.

f. Double-click the line marker in the chart.

g. Click the **Series Options** button in the *Format Data Series* task pane.

h. Select the **Secondary Axis** box in the task pane (Figure 3-60).

i. Close the task pane.

Toggle display of secondary axis

3-60 Combo chart and a secondary axis

11. Edit and format chart elements.

a. Edit the chart title placeholder to Utilities Expense and Total Expenses.

b. Select the chart area.

c. Apply a **1 pt**. **Black, Text 1** outline to the chart area.

d. Click one of the column markers to select the data series.

e. Click the **More** button [*Chart Tools Format* tab, *Shape Styles* group].

f. Select **Moderate Effect – Black**, **Dark 1** in the *Theme Styles* group.

g. Click the line marker.

h. Click the **Shape Outline** button [*Chart Tools Format* tab, *Shape Styles* group].

i. Choose **Gold**, **Accent 4** as the color.

j. Click the **Shape Outline** button again and choose **Weight** and **3 pt** (Figure 3-61).

12. Insert sparklines in the worksheet.

a. Click the **Jan-June** sheet tab.

b. Select cells **B5:G9** as the data range.

c. Click the **Column Sparkline** button [*Insert* tab, *Sparklines* group].

d. Select cells **H5:H9** for the *Location Range* and click **OK**.

e. Click the **Sparkline Color** button [*Sparkline Tools Design* tab, *Style* group].

f. Choose **White, Background 1, Darker 50%**.

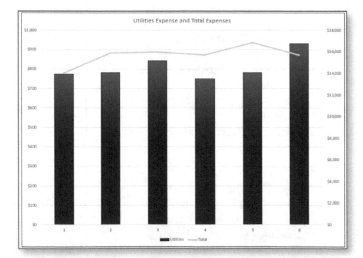

3-61 Line and column formatted in combo chart

13. Insert a shape in a chart.
 a. Select the column chart object.
 b. Click the **More** button [*Chart Tools Format* tab, *Insert Shapes* group].
 c. Select the **Text Box** shape [*Basic Shapes* group].
 d. Draw a text box like the one shown in Figure 3-62.
 e. Type Utilities are to be removed from an updated chart per management request.
 f. Drag a selection handle to size the text box shape if necessary.
 g. Point to a border of the *Text Box* shape to display a four-pointed arrow and position it if needed.

3-62 Text box shape inserted in chart

14. Click a worksheet cell and press **Ctrl+Home**.

15. Create a waterfall chart object.
 a. Select the **Apr Cash** sheet tab.
 b. Select cells **A5:B14**. This data represents cash coming in and going out for April.
 c. Click the **Insert Waterfall or Stock Chart** button [*Insert* tab, *Charts* group].
 d. Select **Waterfall**.

16. Size and position a chart object.
 a. Point to the chart border to display the move pointer.
 b. Drag the chart object so that its top left corner is at cell **C1**.
 c. Point to the bottom right selection handle to display the resize arrow.
 d. Drag the pointer to cell **L20**.

17. Format chart elements.
 a. Double-click the Net Cash column marker and then click the marker again to open the *Format Data Point* pane.
 b. Click the **Series Options** button in the task pane and expand the *Series Options* group.
 c. Select the **Set as total** box.
 d. Triple-click the chart title placeholder text and type April Cash Flow.
 e. Select the chart area and apply a **1 pt**. black outline.
 f. Click a worksheet cell and press **Ctrl+Home**.

18. Save and close the workbook (Figure 3-63).

3-63 Excel 3-1 completed worksheets and charts

Guided Project 3-2

Wear-Ever Shoes is a shoe outlet with several locations. In a worksheet that tracks sales of popular items for the past six months, you create a bar chart to compare the number of pairs sold by style. You also create a combination chart to compare number of pairs sold and unit cost for each style. For another set of data, you create a sunburst chart to illustrate sales by shoe style, gender, and color.
[Student Learning Outcomes 3.1, 3.2, 3.3, 3.4, 3.5, 3.6, 3.7]

File Needed: **WearEverShoes-03.xlsx** [Student data files are available in the Library of your SIMnet account.]
Completed Project File Name: **[your initials] Excel 3-2.xlsx**

Skills Covered in This Project

- Create a chart sheet.
- Change the chart type.
- Apply a chart style.

- Add and format chart elements.
- Use a picture as fill.
- Create and format a combination chart.
- Use *WordArt* in a chart.
- Create and format a sunburst chart.

1. Open the **WearEverShoes-03** workbook from your student data files and save it as [your initials] Excel 3-2.

2. Create a column chart sheet.
 a. Select cells **A5:B16** on the **Unit Sales** sheet.
 b. Click the **Quick Analysis** button and choose **Charts**.
 c. Select **Clustered Column**.
 d. Click the **Move Chart** button [*Chart Tools Design* tab, *Location* group].
 e. Click the **New sheet** button.
 f. Type Sales Chart and click **OK**.

3. Change the chart type.
 a. Click the **Sales Chart** sheet tab if necessary.
 b. Click the **Change Chart Type** button [*Chart Tools Design* tab, *Type* group].
 c. Click the **Recommended Charts** tab.
 d. Choose **Clustered Bar** in the left pane and click **OK**.

4. Apply a chart style.
 a. Click the **Chart Styles** button in the top right corner of the chart.
 b. Select **Style 7**.
 c. Click the **Chart Styles** button to close the pane.

5. Add fill color to a data series.
 a. Double-click one of the bars to open the *Format Data Series* task pane.
 b. Click the **Fill & Line** button in the task pane.
 c. Click **Fill** to expand the command group.
 d. Select the **Vary colors by point** box.

6. Use a picture as fill for a data point.
 a. Click the "Classy Pumps" bar to display its *Format Data Point* task pane.
 b. Click the **Fill & Line** button in the task pane.
 c. Click **Fill** to expand the command group.
 d. Click the **Picture or texture fill** button.
 e. Click **Online** to open the *Insert Pictures* dialog box.
 f. Type heels in the *Bing Image Search* box and press **Enter** (Figure 3-64).

g. Select an image and click **Insert**.

h. Click the **Stack** radio button in the task pane.

i. Close the task pane and click the chart border.

3-64 Online image search for fill in a data point

7. Create a combination chart sheet.

 a. Click the **Unit Sales** sheet tab.

 b. Select cells **A5:A16**. Press **Ctrl** and select cells **E5:F16**.

 c. Click the **Insert Combo Chart** button [*Insert* tab, *Charts* group].

 d. Select the **Clustered Column-Line on Secondary Axis** chart subtype.

 e. Click the **Move Chart** button [*Chart Tools Design* tab, *Location* group].

 f. Click the **New sheet** button.

 g. Type Cost&Retail and click **OK**.

8. Edit chart elements.

 a. Click the chart title placeholder.

 b. Type Cost and Selling Price Comparison in the *Formula* bar and press **Enter**.

 c. Select the chart title box.

 d. Click the **Home** tab and change the font size to **20 pt**.

 e. Select the chart area and apply a **¾ pt**. **black** outline.

 f. Select one of the column shapes.

 g. Click the **More** button [*Chart Tools Format* tab, *Shapes Styles* group].

 h. Choose **Intense Effect - Blue**, **Accent 1** in the bottom row of the *Theme Styles* gallery.

 i. Select the line marker.

 j. Click the **Shape Outline** button [*Chart Tools Format* tab, *Shape Styles* group] and choose **Black**, **Text 1** as the color.

 k. Change the weight of the line to **3 pt**.

9. Use *WordArt* in a chart.

 a. Click the chart title.

 b. Click the **More** button [*Chart Tools Format* tab, *WordArt Styles* group].

 c. Choose **Fill - Black**, **Text 1**, **Shadow** in the first row of the gallery.

 d. Click the chart border to deselect the title.

10. Create a sunburst chart.

 a. Click the **Grouped Sales** sheet tab.

 b. Select cells **A5:D24**.

 c. Click the **Insert Hierarchy Chart** button [*Insert* tab, *Charts* group].

 d. Click **Sunburst** to select it.

 e. Click the **Move Chart** button [*Chart Tools Design* tab, *Location* group].

 f. Select **New sheet**, type Sunburst, and click **OK**.

11. Format a sunburst chart.

 a. Click the chart title element.

 b. Triple-click the placeholder text to select it.

 c. Type Sales by Style, Color, and Gender.

 d. Click the sunburst shape to select the circle.

e. Point to the **Comfy Walking Shoes** arc in the inner ring and click twice to select the data point. The data point is the wedge that represents two colors of the style. You can confirm your selection on the *Chart Tools Format* tab in the *Current Selection* group. It should display "Branch Comfy Walking."

f. Click the **Format Selection** button [*Chart Tools Format* tab, *Current Selection* group].

g. Click the **Fill & Line** button.

h. Click **Fill** to expand the command group.

i. Choose **Solid fill** and click the **Color** button.

j. Choose **Orange**, **Accent 6**, **Lighter 40%**.

k. Close the task pane.

l. Click outside the chart background to deselect the chart.

12. Save and close the workbook (Figure 3-65).

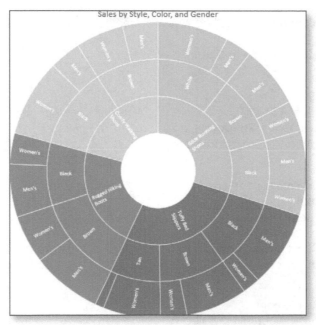

3-65 Excel 3-2 completed chart sheets

Guided Project 3-3

Blue Lake Sports has locations in several major cities and tracks sales by department in each store. For this project, you create a pie chart that shows each store's share of golf-related sales for the first quarter. You also create a line chart to illustrate week-to-week sales for specific departments in one of the stores and insert sparklines in the data.
[Student Learning Outcomes 3.1, 3.2, 3.3, 3.4, 3.6, 3.8]

File Needed: **BlueLakeSports-03.xlsx** [Student data files are available in the Library of your SIMnet account.]
Completed Project File Name: **[your initials] Excel 3-3.xlsx**

Skills Covered in This Project

- Create, size, and position a pie chart object.
- Apply a chart style.
- Change the chart type.
- Add and format chart elements.
- Create a line chart sheet.
- Apply a chart layout.
- Insert and format sparklines in a worksheet.

1. Open the **BlueLakeSports-03** workbook from your student data files and save it as [your initials] Excel 3-3.

2. Create a pie chart object.
 a. Select the **Revenue by Department** sheet, select cells **A4:F4**, press **Ctrl**, and select cells **A13:F13**.
 b. Click the **Recommended Charts** button [Insert tab, Charts group].
 c. Choose **Pie** and click **OK**.

3. Apply a chart style.
 a. Select the chart object.
 b. Click the **More** button [Chart Tools Design tab, Chart Styles group].
 c. Select **Style 12**.

4. Size and position a chart object.
 a. Point to the chart object border to display the move pointer.
 b. Drag the chart object so its top left corner is at cell **A21**.
 c. Point to the bottom right selection handle to display the resize arrow.
 d. Drag the pointer to cell **G36**.

5. Change the chart type.
 a. Select the pie chart object and click the **Change Chart Type** button [Chart Tools Design tab, Type group].
 b. Select the **All Charts** tab and choose **Pie** in the left pane.
 c. Choose **3-D Pie** and click **OK**.

6. Format pie chart elements.
 a. Double-click the pie to open its Format Data Series task pane.
 b. Click the **Atlanta** slice to update the pane to the Format Data Point task pane. (Rest the pointer on a slice to see its identifying ScreenTip.)
 c. Click the **Series Options** button in the Format Data Series task pane.
 d. Set the pie explosion percentage at **10%**.
 e. Close the task pane.
 f. Click the chart object border to deselect the **Atlanta** slice.

7. Add and format chart elements in a pie chart.
 a. Click the **Chart Elements** button in the top right corner of the chart.
 b. Select the **Data Labels** box.

c. Click the **Data Labels** arrow to open its submenu and choose **More Options**.

d. Click the **Label Options** button In the *Format Data Labels* pane.

e. Click **Label Options** to expand the group.

f. Select the **Percentage** box.

3-66 *Format Data Point* task pane for data labels

g. Deselect the **Value** box (Figure 3-66).

h. Press **Ctrl+B** to apply bold.

i. Change the font size to **12 pt** [*Home* tab, *Font* group].

j. Click the chart object border to select it.

k. Click the **Shape Outline** button [*Chart Tools Format* tab, *Shape Styles* group] and choose **Purple**, **Accent 4**, **Darker 50%**.

l. Click the **Shape Outline** button and choose **Weight** and **1 pt**.

m. Click a worksheet cell.

8. Create a line chart sheet.

a. Select the **Atlanta Revenue** sheet tab.

b. Select cells **A4:E7**.

c. Click the **Quick Analysis** button and choose **Charts**.

d. Select **Line**.

e. Click the **Move Chart** button [*Chart Tools Design* tab, *Location* group].

f. Click the **New sheet** button.

g. Type Promo Depts and click **OK**.

9. Apply a chart layout.

a. Click the **Quick Layout** button [*Chart Tools Design* tab, *Chart Layouts* group].

b. Select **Layout 5** to add a data table to the chart sheet (Figure 3-67).

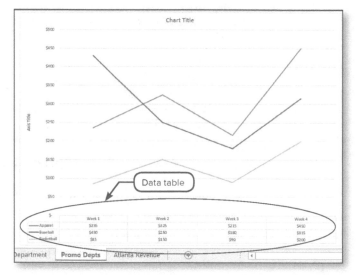

3-67 Data table added by *Quick Layout*

10. Change the chart type.

a. Click the **Change Chart Type** button [*Chart Tools Design* tab, *Type* group].

b. Select the **All Charts** tab and choose **Line with Markers** in the *Line* category.

c. Click **OK**.

11. Edit chart elements in a line chart.
 a. Click the chart title placeholder.
 b. Type **Special Promotion Departments** in the formula bar and press **Enter**.
 c. Click the vertical axis title placeholder.
 d. Type **Dollar Sales** in the formula bar and press **Enter**.
 e. Click the **Chart Elements** drop-down arrow [*Chart Tools Format* tab, *Current Selection* group].
 f. Choose **Series "Apparel"** to select the line in the chart.

3-68 Marker options for the data series

 g. Click the **Format Selection** button [*Chart Tools Format* tab, *Current Selection* group].
 h. Click the **Fill & Line** button in the *Format Data Series* task pane.
 i. Click **Marker** and then click **Marker Options** to expand the group (Figure 3-68).
 j. Choose **Built-in** and select **10 pt**.
 k. Click the *Series Options* triangle at the top of the task pane and choose **Series "Baseball"** (Figure 3-69).
 l. Apply the same marker changes for the baseball series.
 m. Select the basketball series and make the same marker changes.
 n. Close the task pane and click outside the chart.

12. Insert sparklines in the worksheet.
 a. Click the **Atlanta Revenue** tab.
 b. Right-click the column **F** heading and choose **Insert**.
 c. Select cells **B5:E18** as the data range.
 d. Click the **Line Sparkline** button [*Insert* tab, *Sparklines* group].
 e. Select cells **F5:F18** in the *Location Range* box.
 f. Click **OK**.

13. Format sparklines in worksheet.
 a. Click the **Format** button [*Home* tab, *Cells* group] and change the **Row Height** to **24**.
 b. Click the **Format** button [*Home* tab, *Cells* group] and set the **Column Width** to **35**.
 c. Select the **Markers** box in the *Show* group in the *Sparkline Tools Design* tab.
 d. Click the **Sparkline Color** button [*Sparkline Tools Design* tab, *Style* group].
 e. Choose **Black, Text 1** for the line color.
 f. Click cell **A1**.

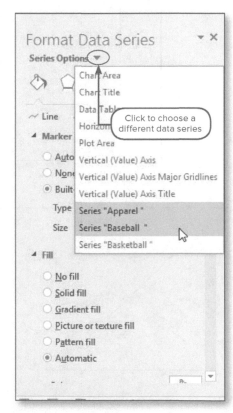

3-69 New data series selected

14. Change the page orientation to landscape.

15. Save and close the workbook (Figure 3-70).

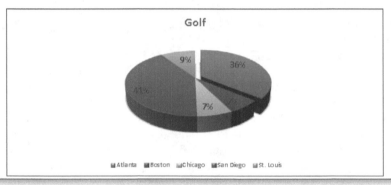

Blue Lake Sports
First Quarter Sales by City

Department	Atlanta	Boston	Chicago	San Diego	St. Louis	Total
Apparel	$ 2,600	$ 3,200	$ 3,800	$ 3,700	$ 3,200	$ 16,500
Baseball	$ 3,500	$ 1,200	$ 1,350	$ 2,100	$ 2,475	$ 10,625
Basketball	$ 1,800	$ 1,800	$ 2,250	$ 1,400	$ 1,750	$ 9,000
Bike & Skate	$ 1,500	$ 1,325	$ 1,225	$ 2,450	$ 1,650	$ 8,150
Exercise	$ 2,650	$ 2,875	$ 3,250	$ 3,775	$ 2,950	$ 15,500
Fishing	$ 2,350	$ 1,035	$ 1,250	$ 2,750	$ 1,450	$ 8,835
Footwear	$ 1,875	$ 2,675	$ 3,575	$ 3,250	$ 2,950	$ 14,325
Game Room	$ 1,300	$ 1,500	$ 1,900	$ 1,050	$ 1,275	$ 7,025
Golf	$ 4,750	$ 875	$ 925	$ 5,400	$ 1,250	$ 13,200
Hockey	$ 850	$ 1,875	$ 1,950	$ 750	$ 1,650	$ 7,075
Hunting	$ 2,000	$ 1,000	$ 650	$ 725	$ 950	$ 5,325
Lacrosse	$ 1,750	$ 1,800	$ 1,750	$ 1,375	$ 1,150	$ 7,825
Running	$ 1,925	$ 2,400	$ 2,800	$ 2,650	$ 2,000	$ 11,775
Winter Sports	$ 1,250	$ 34,350	$ 2,750	$ 550	$ 1,550	$ 40,450
Total	$ 30,100	$ 57,910	$ 29,425	$ 31,925	$ 26,250	$ 175,610

Golf

(Pie chart: Atlanta 36%, 7%, 41%, 9% with legend: Atlanta, Boston, Chicago, San Diego, St. Louis)

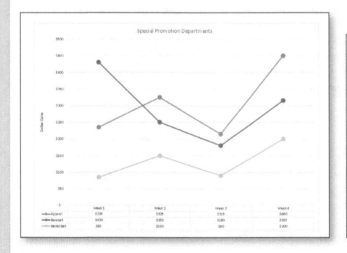

3-70 Excel 3-3 completed worksheet and charts

Independent Project 3-4

For this project, you create a column chart to illustrate April–September revenue for Classic Gardens and Landscapes. You also build a pie chart sheet to graph the proportion that each category contributes to total revenue.
[Student Learning Outcomes 3.1, 3.2, 3.3, 3.4, 3.5, 3.6]

File Needed: **ClassicGardens-03.xlsx** [Student data files are available in the Library of your SIMnet account.]
Completed Project File Name: **[your initials] Excel 3-4.xlsx**

Skills Covered in This Project

- Create a chart object.
- Size and position a chart object.
- Edit and format chart elements.
- Edit the source data for a chart.
- Build a pie chart sheet.
- Use texture as fill.
- Add and format data labels in a chart.

1. Open the **ClassicGardens-03** workbook from your student data files and save it as [your initials] Excel 3-4.

2. Create a **Clustered Column** chart object for cells **A4:G9**.

3. Move the chart object so that its top left corner is at cell **A12**. Size the bottom of the chart to reach cell **H30**.

4. Edit the chart title to display CGL Major Sales Revenue on one line and Second and Third Quarters on the second line.

5. Apply chart **Style 14** to the chart.

6. Format the first line of the chart title to a font size of **20 pt**. Format the second title line as **16 pt**.

7. Apply a ½ **point Black**, **Text 1** outline to the chart area.

8. Verify that the chart is still selected. In the highlighted range in the worksheet, drag the resize pointer to remove the *Design Consulting* data series from the chart (Figure 3-71).

9. Create a *3-D Pie* chart for cells **A4:A9** and cells **H4:H9**. Move the chart to its own sheet named **Revenue Breakdown**.

3-71 Resize the chart by dragging the resize pointer

10. Edit the chart title to display Revenue by Category. Change the font size to **32**.

11. Select the legend and change the font size to **12**.

12. Apply the **Woven mat** texture fill to the *Patio and Furniture* slice.

13. Add data labels to display in the center of each slice.
 a. Display the *Format Data Labels* task pane, choose the **Accounting** format, and set **0** decimal places.
 b. While the data labels are selected, change the font size to **14 pt** and apply **bold** [*Home* tab, *Font* group].

14. Deselect the chart.

15. Save and close the workbook (Figure 3-72).

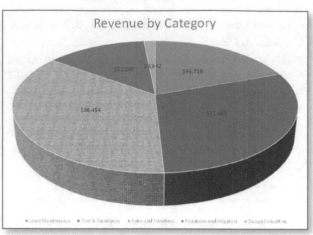

3-72 Excel 3-4 completed chart sheets

Independent Project 3-5

For this project, you create a stacked bar chart to illustrate projected tuition and fee amounts for Sierra Pacific Community College District (SPCCD). You also create a pie chart to show total projected revenue for the time period and add sparklines to the worksheet.
[**Student Learning Outcomes 3.1, 3.2, 3.3, 3.4, 3.6, 3.8**]

File Needed: **SierraPacific-03.xlsx** [Student data files are available in the Library of your SIMnet account.]
Completed Project File Name: **[your initials] Excel 3-5.xlsx**

Skills Covered in This Project

- Create a chart object.
- Size and position a chart object.
- Apply a chart style.
- Switch row and column data.

- Edit chart source data.
- Create a pie chart sheet.
- Edit and format chart elements.
- Insert and format sparklines in a sheet.

1. Open the **SierraPacific-03** workbook from your student data files and save it as [your initials] Excel 3-5.

2. Select cells **A3:E7** and use the *Quick Analysis* tool to create a stacked bar chart object.

3. Size and position the chart below the worksheet data in cells **A10:G28**.

4. Apply **Chart Style 6**.

5. Edit the chart title to display Tuition Revenue Projection.

6. Apply a **½ pt Dark Blue**, **Text 2** outline to the chart object.

7. Edit the source data to remove the utilization and facilities fees from the chart.

8. Switch the row and column data for the chart so that semester names are shown on the vertical axis.

9. Create a 3-D pie chart sheet for cells **A4:A7** and cells **F4:F7**. Move the chart to a new sheet named Total Revenue.

10. Apply **Chart Style 3** and a **black ½ pt** outline.

11. Edit the chart title to Projected Revenue Sources.

12. Format the legend font size to **12 pt**.

13. Create a column sparkline with cell **G8** as the location range for cells **B8:E8**. Format cell **G8** with an **Outside Border** [*Home* tab, *Font* group].

14. Save and close the workbook (Figure 3-73).

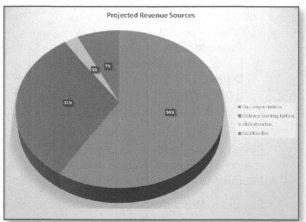

3-73 Excel 3-5 completed worksheet and chart

Independent Project 3-6

Courtyard Medical Plaza (CMP) is a full-service medical office complex providing customers with a variety of medical services in one location. For this project, you create charts to illustrate data about the number of procedures performed at CMP as well as how patients came to the facility. Your final task is to prepare a waterfall chart for the operations account.
[Student Learning Outcomes 3.1, 3.2, 3.3, 3.4, 3.5, 3.7]

File Needed: ***CourtyardMedical-03.xlsx*** [*Student data files are available in the* Library *of your SIMnet account.*]
Completed Project File Name: *[your initials] Excel 3-6.xlsx*

Skills Covered in This Project

- Create a column chart sheet.
- Add and edit chart elements.
- Add and format a trendline in a chart.
- Insert a text box shape in a chart.
- Display gridlines in a chart.
- Use gradient fill for a chart object.
- Create a waterfall chart.

1. Open the **CourtyardMedical-03** workbook from your student data files and save it as [your initials] Excel 3-6.

2. Select the **Patient Arrivals** worksheet. Create a clustered column chart sheet for cells **A5:M5** and cells **A7:M7**. Move the chart to its own sheet named Immed Care.

3. Edit the chart title to display Immediate Care Patient Count.

4. Click the **Chart Elements** button and select **Trendline**.

5. Click the options arrow next to **Trendline** and select **More Options** to open the *Format Trendline* task pane.
 a. In the *Forecast* group, set the **Forward** value to **12**.
 b. Choose **Olive Green, Accent 3, Darker 50%** for the line color.
 c. Set the **Width** of the trendline to **4 pt**.

6. Draw a *Text Box* shape between the 300 and 400 gridlines and type The number of patients who come in for Immediate Care services will continue to grow. (Figure 3-74).

3-74 Text box shape in a chart

7. Select the **Procedures Count** worksheet and use the *Quick Analysis* tool to create a clustered column chart for cells **A5:D16** on its own sheet named Procedures Chart.

8. Edit the chart title to Number of Procedures on the first line and Three-Month Period on the second line.

9. Change the chart type to a clustered bar chart.

10. Click the **Chart Elements** button. Show **Primary Major Vertical**, **Primary Major Horizontal** and **Primary Minor Vertical** gridlines. Format each gridline element to use **Black, Text 1, Lighter 50%**.

11. Use the **Shape Fill** button to format the plot area to **Tan, Background 2**.

12. Select the **Operations** sheet tab and create a waterfall chart object for cells **A3:B9**.

13. Position the waterfall chart object so that its top left corner is at cell **A11**. Size the object to reach cell **I28**.

14. Select the ending balance marker and set it as a total.

15. Edit the chart title placeholder to CMP Operations Account.

16. Select the chart area and apply a **1 pt black** outline.

17. Click a worksheet cell and press **Ctrl+Home**.

18. Save and close the workbook (Figure 3-75).

3-75 Excel 3-6 completed worksheet and charts

Improve It Project 3-7

Central Sierra Insurance is a multi-office insurance company that handles commercial and personal insurance products. In this project, you add missing data and verify that the charts are updated.
[Student Learning Outcomes 3.2, 3.3, 3.4]

File Needed: **CentralSierra-03.xlsx** *[Student data files are available in the* Library *of your SIMnet account.]*
Completed Project File Name: **[your initials] Excel 3-7.xlsx**

Skills Covered in This Project

- Edit source data.
- Switch row and column data.
- Change chart colors.
- Apply a chart style.
- Add and format elements in a chart.
- Change the chart type.

1. Open the **CentralSierra-03** workbook from your student data files and save it as [your initials] Excel 3-7. There are two chart objects on the worksheet.

2. Insert a new row at row 8.

3. Type Motorcycle in cell **A8**. In cells **B8:D8**, type these values: 15, 82, and 24.

4. Change the pie chart object to a **3-D Pie** and apply **Chart Style 3**. Notice that a data series for "Motorcycle" has been added.

5. Switch the row and column data for the column chart. The data series for "Motorcycle" is not included.

6. Click the **Select Data** button [*Chart Tools Design* tab, *Data* group] and reset the source data to show cells **A5:D10**.

7. Change the column chart color scheme to **Color 11** in the *Monochromatic* list.

8. Format chart elements.
 a. Use the **Shape Fill** button [*Chart Tools Format* tab, *Shape Styles* group] to apply **Olive Green, Accent 3** fill for the **Side Wall** of the column chart.
 b. Use the **Shape Fill** button to apply the **Linear Down** gradient in the *Light Variations* group to the side wall.

c. Apply the same fill and gradient to the **Walls** element.

d. Apply the **Olive Green**, **Accent 3**, **Lighter 60%** with no gradient to the **Floor** element.

e. Select the horizontal gridlines and use the **Shape Outline** button to format them with **Black**, **Text 1**, **Lighter 50%**.

9. Select the pie chart object and change the colors to **Color 11** in the *Monochromatic* group.

10. Use **Olive Green**, **Accent 3** as shape fill for the pie chart area with a **Linear Down** gradient from the light variations.

11. Apply a **½ pt Olive Green**, **Accent 3**, **Darker 25%** outline to both chart objects.

12. Save and close the workbook (Figure 3-76).

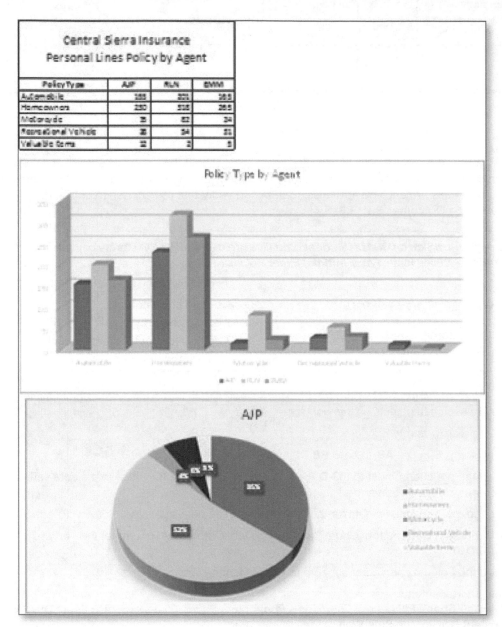

3-76 Excel 3-7 Completed worksheet with charts

Challenge Project 3-8

For this project, you build a worksheet by copying a worksheet from one of the student data files, editing data, and creating a TreeMap chart.
[Student Learning Outcomes 3.1, 3.2, 3.3, 3.7]

File Needed: ***WearEverShoes-03.xlsx*** [Student data files are available in the Library of your SIMnet account.]
Completed Project File Name: ***[your initials] Excel 3-8.xlsx***

Create a new workbook and save it as [your initials] Excel 3-8. Modify your workbook according to the following guidelines:

- Open the ***WearEverShoes-03*** workbook from your student data files.
- Copy the **Grouped Sales** sheet to ***[your initials] Excel 3-8***. Close ***WearEverShoes-03***.
- Rename the *Grouped Sales* sheet as My Groups.
- Delete column **C** to create two levels in the hierarchy, the style name and the color. Each item has a value.
- Select a topic of interest or relevance to you that can be placed in a two-level hierarchy like the worksheet. Examples are college department and course name; company name and functional area; state and city; music type and song title. Assign different values if appropriate to your data.
- Edit the data in the worksheet to reflect your groups and subgroups. Edit the title labels also.
- Type a main and secondary title for your data. Format your worksheet.
- Select the appropriate data and create a *TreeMap* hierarchy chart on its own sheet.
- Edit the chart title and apply a chart style.
- Edit the source data to increase or decrease values and see how the *TreeMap* is adjusted.

Challenge Project 3-9

For this project, you create a worksheet and accompanying charts to track daily usage of your smartphone, tablet, or smart watch.
[Student Learning Outcomes 3.1, 3.2, 3.3, 3.4, 3.5, 3.6]

File Needed: None
Completed Project File Name: ***[your initials] Excel 3-9.xlsx***

Create a new workbook and save it as [your initials] Excel 3-9. Modify your workbook according to the following guidelines:

- Enter the days of the week as column headings, starting in cell B2.
- As row headings starting in cell A3, type the names of five daily tasks or activities for your device. Examples are "Send text," "Receive phone call," "Use GPS," "View video," or similar tasks.
- Enter a value for the number of times you perform each task on each day.
- Type a main title for your data in row 1. Format your data.
- Create a column chart object that compares the number of times for each task on Monday.

- Size and position the chart object below the worksheet data.
- Change the layout or apply a chart style.
- Edit the chart title placeholder to display an appropriate title.
- Format chart elements to create an attractive, easy-to-understand chart of your data.
- For the task with the greatest Monday value, create another column chart that displays daily numbers for that one task.
- Size and position this chart object below the first chart.
- Format the second chart to complement the first chart.

Challenge Project 3-10

For this project, you create a worksheet with a column/line combo chart that compares air temperature and humidity level in your city or town for 10 days. You also insert a single sparkline in the data.
[**Student Learning Outcomes 3.1, 3.2, 3.3, 3.4, 3.6, 3.8**]

File Needed: None
Completed Project File Name: *[your initials] Excel 3-10.xlsx*

Create a new workbook and save it as [your initials] Excel 3-10. Modify your workbook according to the following guidelines:

- In a worksheet, enter dates in cells **A4:A13** for each of the last 10 days or each of the next 10 days.
- In column B, enter a recorded or predicted temperature in degrees for each date at 12 noon. Use an online weather reference or a weather app.
- In column C, enter corresponding humidity levels as percentages. Use the same weather reference or make an estimate.
- Type a main title for the data as well as column labels.
- Create a clustered column/line combo chart with a secondary axis for the percentages. Move the chart to its own sheet.
- Change the layout or apply a chart style.
- Edit and format the chart elements as needed.
- In the worksheet, select the range of temperature values as the data range for a line sparkline. As the location range, select cell **D14**. Format column D as **32.00 (229 pixels)** wide.
- Format the sparkline and adjust row heights to better display the data and the sparkline.

POWERPOINT

Microsoft® Office

IN PRACTICE

powerpoint

Creating and Editing Presentations

POWERPOINT

CHAPTER OVERVIEW

Microsoft PowerPoint is the leading presentation software. Whether you need to create a quick display or a very polished presentation with dazzling graphics, creative animation effects, and video, PowerPoint has all the tools you need. You can use PowerPoint for slide shows with computer projection equipment in meeting rooms, for self-running presentations viewed by individuals, or for presentations shown on the web. This chapter covers the basics of starting and editing a PowerPoint presentation.

STUDENT LEARNING OUTCOMES (SLOs)

After completing this chapter, you will be able to:

SLO 1.1 Create, open, and save a presentation (p. 633).

SLO 1.2 Work with slides, layouts, placeholders, and text (p. 644).

SLO 1.3 Navigate between slides and organize content by reproducing and rearranging slides (p. 653).

SLO 1.4 Change theme colors and fonts (p. 659).

SLO 1.5 Insert headers and footers to add identifying information (p. 663).

SLO 1.6 Insert, resize, and align a picture from a file (p. 667).

SLO 1.7 Apply and modify transition effects to add visual interest (p. 670).

SLO 1.8 Preview a presentation and print slides, handouts, and outlines (p. 672).

SLO 1.9 Apply presentation properties (p. 675).

CASE STUDY

Throughout this book you have the opportunity to put into practice the application features that you are learning. Each chapter begins with a case study that introduces you to the Pause & Practice projects in the chapter. These Pause & Practice projects give you a chance to apply and practice key skills. Each chapter contains three to five Pause & Practice projects.

Hamilton Civic Center (HCC) is a nonprofit community fitness center that partners with the local hospital for educational events. Doctors and nurses provide classes on a variety of health and wellness issues for adults. HCC also works with local schools to support their academic programs and sponsors events for children.

In this chapter, you develop a presentation about training for an upcoming marathon that is being promoted to HCC members.

Pause & Practice 1-1: Create a presentation and develop text content.

Pause & Practice 1-2: Apply a presentation theme, change theme colors and fonts, and edit content.

Pause & Practice 1-3: Add interest with pictures and apply transitions, and print supplements.

SLO 1.1

Creating, Opening, and Saving Presentations

PowerPoint provides several ways to start, view, and save a presentation. Always save your presentation if you will need to access it again. If you close the presentation before saving it, your content is lost.

Create a Presentation

When PowerPoint first opens, you can start a new presentation or open an existing presentation that is listed on the left. Clickable images called *thumbnails* have a name below each one. If you prefer to work on text content only, click the **Blank Presentation** thumbnail to go directly to your first slide so you can begin developing content.

Other thumbnails represent built-in *Themes* that provide a unified look for all the slides in a presentation. Most themes have color or graphic treatments that create a background design. When you click a theme, a dialog box opens where you can choose from four or more *Variants* showing different color combinations. Variants may have different graphics, too. Once these choices are made, you can start developing content.

The following three How-to Boxes explain several different ways to start a presentation.

▶**HOW TO:** Create a Presentation When First Opening PowerPoint

1. Open PowerPoint and you will see the *Backstage* view (Figure 1-1).

2. Click **Blank Presentation** to go directly to your first slide.

Or

3. Click a **Theme** to open a dialog box (Figure 1-2).

4. Click the arrow buttons below the slide example to see how colors are applied to different layouts.

1-1 PowerPoint *Backstage* view

5. Select one of four *Variants* on the right that provide different color combinations.

6. Click **Create**.

1-2 Theme *Variants*

When you create a new presentation, PowerPoint assigns a generic name, such as *Presentation1*, that appears in the title bar. Additional new presentations are named in the same way. When you save the presentation with a new name, that name appears in the title bar.

> **MORE INFO**
>
> When your content is complete, save your presentation (discussed on pages P1-10 – P1-12) and then close it by clicking the **File** tab and then clicking **Close**. To close PowerPoint, click the **Close** button (an **X**) in the upper right corner of the title bar. If you click the **Close** button before saving, your presentation will automatically close or you will be asked if you want to save your presentation if changes have been made.

▶ HOW TO: Create a New Presentation When PowerPoint Is Open

1. Click the **File** tab to open the *Backstage* view.
2. Click **New** and use one of these methods to start a presentation:
 - Select a *Theme*, select a *Variant*, and click **Create** to open the presentation with the selected theme and colors.
 - Double-click a *Theme* to open the presentation with that theme and the default *Variant* colors.
 - Double-click **Blank Presentation** to go directly to your first slide.

Or

3. Press **Ctrl+N** to open a new blank presentation.

A theme simplifies the process of creating professional looking presentations by providing consistent background graphics, colors, and font settings. A ***template*** contains the characteristics of a theme and usually provides sample content you can edit or delete if you want only the background a template provides. Many themes and templates are available in PowerPoint by searching online when you start a new presentation, or they can be downloaded at Office.com. You can save downloaded themes and templates so they are available for future use. *SLO 1.4: Changing Theme Colors and Fonts* provides information about searching within PowerPoint and customizing theme settings.

> **MORE INFO**
>
> Your computer must be connected to the Internet to download themes and templates.

▶ HOW TO: Create a New Presentation from Online Templates and Themes

1. Click the **File** tab to open the *Backstage* view.

2. Click **New**. In the search box, type a word, such as small business, and click the **Start searching** button (Figure 1-3). Available templates and themes appear.

 - Filter your results by typing the word and and then typing a second search word such as travel.
 - Click the **Start searching** button to search again.

1-3 Search for online themes and templates

Or

3. Click one of the *Suggested searches* for general topics and available templates and themes will appear.

 - Filter your results by clicking one of the terms in the *Category* list on the right (Figure 1-4).
 - Filter your results by typing the word or before another search word and searching again.

1-4 Search results for online themes and templates

4. Click a thumbnail to open a dialog box to review other slides in addition to the title slide. Some templates include a description (Figure 1-5).

5. Click **Create** and the presentation opens.

 - The presentation may contain sample content that you need to delete before adding your content.

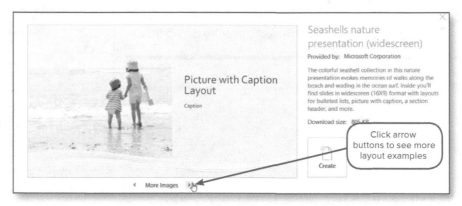

1-5 Template with description and sample content

You can use an existing presentation to start a new presentation. To do this, open a presentation file from a source such as your computer, USB drive, local network, cloud space such as *OneDrive*, or an email attachment.

▶ HOW TO: Open a Recent Presentation

1. Start PowerPoint and click the **File** tab to open the *Backstage* view.

2. Click **Open** to display the *Open* area on the *Backstage* view.

3. Select **Recent** and click a presentation name on the right to open it.

- If you open a presentation frequently, you can pin it.
- Click the **Pin** icon to the right of the presentation name (Figure 1-6) and the presentation name moves to the top in a *Pinned* area.

Or

1-6 Pin a presentation in the *Open* area on the *Backstage* view

4. Select **OneDrive** or **This PC** to open folders and files from these locations (Figure 1-7). Click the presentation name to open it.

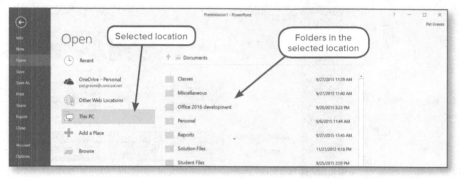

1-7 Folders in *This PC*

Or

5. Click **Browse** and the *Open* dialog box appears where you can find folders and files from other locations (Figure 1-8). Select the file and click **Open** to display the presentation and close the dialog box.

1-8 *Open* dialog box

▶ MORE INFO

For instructions to set up a *OneDrive* account, refer to *SLO Intro.1: Using Windows 10* in *Intro Chapter 1: Windows 10, Office 2016, and File Management*.

▶ ANOTHER WAY

Ctrl+O opens the *Backstage* view where you can open a presentation. **Ctrl+F12** opens the *Open* dialog box. Some laptops require **Fn+Ctrl+F12**.

Views

PowerPoint provides different views to help you create slides, organize them, and display them in a slide show. When you start a new presentation, it opens in **Normal** view. The *Ribbon* displays across the top of the window and has nine tabs with commands organized in groups (Figure 1-9). Additional tabs, such as the *Drawing Tools Format* tab, open depending on what you are doing. Several tabs contain commands similar to those in Word, whereas other tabs display features that are unique to PowerPoint.

1-9 PowerPoint *Ribbon* with *Home* tab displayed

The area below the *Ribbon* is divided into panes where you create and work on slides: A *Thumbnail* pane is on the left and a *Slide* pane is on the right. A *Notes* pane may display below the slide. You can change views using commands on the *View* tab [*Presentation Views* group] (Figure 1-10) or the *View* buttons on the *Status* bar at the bottom of the window.

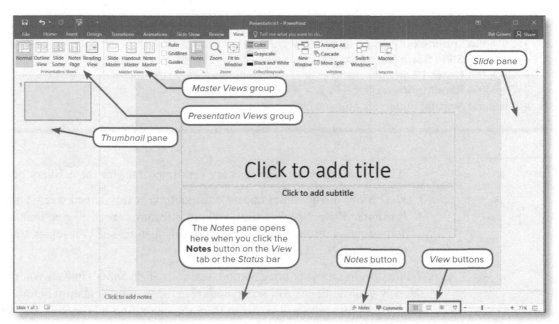

1-10 *Normal* view with *View* tab and *Notes* pane displayed

The *View* tab has five *Presentation Views* that include the following:

- **Normal View**: The default view where you enter content and move between slides as you develop them. Click the *Normal* button or the *Notes* button to open a *Notes* pane below the slide to add speaker notes for individual slides.
- **Outline View**: The left pane displays slide titles and bulleted text instead of slide thumbnails.

- *Slide Sorter View*: Slides appear as thumbnails so it is easy to reorganize slides and apply transition effects to control how the slides advance.
- *Notes Page View*: Each slide appears at the top of a page with space below the slide where you can type speaker notes.
- *Reading View*: The slide show displays at full-screen or another window size controlled by the viewer. Navigation controls are in the *Status* bar at the bottom of the window.

The *Master Views* group includes the following: **Slide Master**, **Handout Master**, and **Notes Master**. These views are used to change formatting that affects the whole presentation.

The *View* buttons located on the *Status* bar provide easy access to different PowerPoint views regardless of which *Ribbon* tab is currently open (Figure 1-11).

1-11 *View* buttons

▶HOW TO: Change Views

1. Click the **View** tab. Note that *Normal* is selected in the *Presentation Views* group and you can see the *Slide* and *Thumbnail* panes.
2. Observe the changes as you access each different view using buttons on the *View* tab or *Status* bar:
 - Click the **Outline** button and text appears on the left instead of slide thumbnails.
 - Click the **Slide Sorter** button to display all slide thumbnails in your presentation.
 - Click the **Notes Page** button and your current slide appears at the top of a page.
 - Click the **Reading View** button to see your slides in a window.
 - Click the **Normal** button to return to *Normal* view.

The following two more views are very important for the delivery of your presentation:

- *Slide Show View*: Slides appear one at a time at full-screen size for audience viewing.
- *Presenter View*: Speaker notes and other features are displayed that are helpful for delivering a presentation. For more on this feature, see "Presenter View" in *SLO 3.5: Controlling Display Options*.

While developing your presentation, test it in *Slide Show* view so you can see the content in the way your audience will see it, and rehearse your presentation before using it.

Start a presentation slide show from the beginning by pressing **F5**; start with the current slide by clicking the **Slide Show** button on the *Status* bar. You may also use buttons on the *Slide Show* tab (Figure 1-12).

1-12 *Slide Show* tab

1. Click the **Slide Show** tab.
2. Click the **From Beginning** button [*Start Slide Show* group] to display slides from the beginning, regardless of which slide is the current slide.
3. Click the **From Current Slide** button to display slides starting with the current slide.
4. Move through the slides by clicking the screen or pressing one of several keys on the keyboard: **spacebar, Enter, Page Down, Down** arrow, or **N**.

Adjusting pane sizes can help you better focus on one aspect of your presentation. For example, thumbnails become larger when you increase the size of the thumbnail pane and you have more room to write when you increase the size of the notes pane. In each case, the slide becomes a little smaller.

▶ **HOW TO:** Adjust Pane Sizes

1. Point to the pane border separating the *Thumbnail* pane and the *Slide* pane until your pointer turns into a sizing pointer with two arrows (Figure 1-13).
2. Click and drag the pane border to the right to increase thumbnail size and to the left to decrease thumbnail size.
3. If the *Notes* pane is not open, click the **Notes** button [*View* tab, *Show* group or *Status* bar].
4. Point to the pane border separating the *Slide* pane and the *Notes* pane.

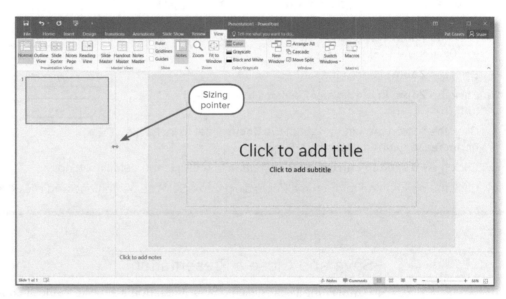

1-13 *Thumbnail* pane and *Notes* pane size is increased

5. Click and drag the *Notes* pane border up or down to increase or decrease the *Notes* pane size.
6. Click and drag the *Notes* pane border down to the bottom of the window or click the **Notes** button on the *Status* bar to remove this pane.

Use ***Zoom*** to increase the current slide size in *Normal* view when you need to see more detail. Use the *Zoom* dialog box to set a specific magnification level or adjust the magnification by using the *Zoom* slider. You can use *Zoom* on the *Slide Sorter* view also.

► **HOW TO:** Use the Zoom Dialog Box

1. Click the **Zoom** button [*View* tab, *Zoom* group] and the *Zoom* dialog box opens.
2. Select a preset zoom percentage such as 200% (Figure 1-14) or enter a percentage number, such as 150%.
3. Click **OK**. The slide size is increased and you can see only a portion of the slide.
4. Click the **Zoom** button again, select **Fit**, and click **OK** to return to the default setting so the entire slide displays.

1-14 *Zoom* dialog box

The *Zoom* controls are located on the right side of the *Status* bar and the current slide size percentage is shown. At 100%, the slider is in the center. Drag the slider or click the **Zoom** buttons to adjust the slide size.

► **HOW TO:** Use the Zoom Controls

1. Click the **Zoom Out** button several times to decrease the view to 50% (Figure 1-15).
2. Drag the **Zoom** slider to the center.
3. Click the **Zoom In** button several times to increase the view to 150%.
4. Click the line on the left or right of the **Zoom** slider to increase or decrease the percentage.
5. Click the **Fit slide to current window** button to return to the default setting.
6. Click the percentage to open the *Zoom* dialog box. Select a percentage and click **OK** to close the dialog box.

1-15 *Zoom* controls

Save and Close a Presentation

PowerPoint assigns each new presentation a generic name such as *Presentation1*. When you save the presentation for the first time, change the generic name to a more meaningful name.

► **HOW TO:** Save a Presentation

1. Click the **File** tab to open the *Backstage* view.
2. Click **Save** or **Save As** to display the *Save As* area (Figure 1-16).
3. Select the location where you want to save your presentation: *OneDrive, Other Web Locations,* or *This PC.*
 - Select an appropriate folder. If you select the wrong folder, click the blue **Up** arrow and select again.
 - Type a file name in the box that appears at the top and click the **Save** button

1-16 *Save As* area on the *Backstage* view

4. Click the **Browse** button to open the *Save As* dialog box (Figure 1-17).

- Browse to the appropriate folder to save the file.
- Type the presentation name in the *File name* area and click the **Save** button.

1-17 *Save As* dialog box

When saving for the first time, you can also click the **Save** button on the *Quick Access* toolbar, or press **Ctrl+S**, to open the *Save As* area on the *Backstage* view. As you revise your presentation, simply clicking the **Save** button on the *Quick Access* toolbar will resave it with the same name in the same location.

If you want to create a second version of that file, then click the **File** tab and then click **Save As** to resave it with a different name in the same or different location. The original presentation is not affected by any changes you make to the second presentation.

> **ANOTHER WAY**
> Press **F12** to open the *Save As* dialog box.

You can save PowerPoint presentations in a variety of formats. By default, PowerPoint 2016 presentations are saved with the .pptx file extension. To change the type of presentation format, select the format of your choice from the *Save as type* area in the *Save As* dialog box (Figure 1-18).

1-18 *Save As* file types

The following table lists available formats that are most commonly used for PowerPoint:

Save Formats

Type of Presentation	File Extension	Uses of This Format
PowerPoint Presentation	.pptx	PowerPoint presentation compatible with 2007–2016 software versions that use an XML-enabled file format. This is the default file format.
PowerPoint 97-2003 Presentation	.ppt	PowerPoint presentation compatible with 1997–2003 software versions. Newer software features are not supported.
PDF (Portable Document Format)	.pdf	Similar to pictures of slides, with each slide shown as a separate page. The file size may be smaller than the original presentation, so this format often works well for presentations distributed electronically.
PowerPoint Template	.potx	PowerPoint template that can be used to format presentations.
Windows Media Video or Mpeg-P4 Video	.wmv or .mp4	PowerPoint presentation saved as a video that will play on many media players. Three resolution sizes are available, and all create large file sizes.
Outline/RTF	.rtf	A presentation text-only outline with a small file size for easy sharing.
PowerPoint Picture Presentation	.pptx	PowerPoint presentation that converts each slide into an image. It helps to reduce file size or create images for inclusion in other documents.
Open Document Presentation	.odp	PowerPoint presentation that can be opened in applications that use the Open Document Presentation format, such as Google.Docs or OpenOffice.org.

> **MORE INFO**
>
> Other file formats are used to save individual slides or images on slides. These graphic file formats include .jpg, .png, .tif, .bmp, .wmf, or .emf. These formats are explained on page P1-38.

When you are finished with a presentation, save your final version and then close the presentation by clicking the **File** tab, and then clicking **Close** or clicking the **Close** button [**X**] in the upper right corner of the title bar.

Share and Export Options

From the *Backstage* view you have options for *sharing* (Figure 1-19) or *exporting* (Figure 1-20) your presentation using different file formats. Not all classroom computer lab configurations permit access to shared online sites or network locations.

1-19 *Share* options

Share

- *Share with People*: Saves your presentation to a *OneDrive* location so you can share it with others.
- *Email*: Sends your presentation as an attachment in the file type you choose.
- *Present Online*: Requires a Microsoft Account so people can link to your slide show through a web browser.
- *Publish Slides*: Sends presentation files to a shared library or SharePoint site.

1-20 *Export* options

Export

- *Create PDF/XPS Document*: Preserves formatting and reduces file size for easier distribution.
- *Create a Video*: Saves your presentation as a video.
- *Package Presentation for CD*: Saves your presentation and all linked or embedded files.
- *Create Handouts*: Transfers slides and notes to a Word document that you can re-format.
- *Change File Type*: Saves your presentation or individual slides in different file formats.

While working on a presentation in *Normal* view, you can share it with others. Click the **Share** button on the upper right of your PowerPoint window (Figure 1-21). Click **Save to Cloud** and then select the online location for your files.

1-21 *Share* button

Working with Slides, Layouts, Placeholders, and Text

Using *Normal* view, you will frequently enter slide text and other objects using *placeholders*. By default, these placeholders have no fill color or border, but you may choose to emphasize them by adding color. You can resize placeholders as needed to fit content. The available placeholders and their positions are controlled by the particular *layout* that you choose.

When PowerPoint first opens or when you start a blank presentation, the first slide has a *Title Slide* layout with two placeholders: a presentation title and a subtitle. You can add text directly into these placeholders or you can type slide titles and bulleted text in *Outline* view. The font, font size, and alignment are preset, but you can change them as you develop your presentation. Keep in mind that text should be brief, straight to the point, and easy to read.

Add Slides and Choose Layouts

To insert additional slides, you click the **New Slide** button on the *Home* tab. After a title slide, PowerPoint automatically inserts a *Title and Content* layout. This layout is used for developing most slides; it has a placeholder for the slide title and a placeholder for inserting bulleted text or content such as pictures, tables, or charts. From that point forward, each time you click the top of the **New Slide** button, you add a new slide with the same layout as the previous one (unless you use the *Title Slide* layout again). If you click the **New Slide** drop-down arrow (bottom half), you see a gallery of layouts, such as the ones shown in Figure 1-22, for a blank presentation using the *Office Theme*.

Layouts provide a starting point for your slide designs. You can change

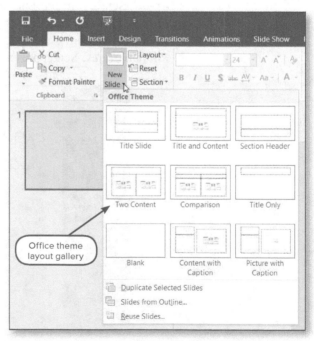

1-22 Slide layouts

layouts or customize each slide for the content you are developing. The available layouts vary based on the current theme. The most common layouts are described in the following table:

Slide Layouts

Layout Name	Layout Description
Title Slide	A layout used for a presentation's opening slide. It contains a title and a subtitle placeholder.
Title and Content	A layout used for the body of a presentation. It contains a placeholder for the slide title and a larger placeholder for many different kinds of content.
Section Header	This layout is similar to a Title Slide layout and usually has a slightly different appearance. It can divide a lengthy presentation or introduce different topics or speakers.
Two Content	This layout has a slide title placeholder and two smaller content placeholders to display either two brief lists or a list and a graphic object, such as a picture or chart.
Comparison	A layout that is similar to the Two Content layout, but it works better for comparing two lists because it provides a heading area above each content placeholder.
Title Only	A layout with only one placeholder for the title (usually at the top) of the slide.
Blank	This layout has no placeholders.
Content with Caption	A layout that is similar to the Two Content layout, but one area is designated for content, such as a table or chart, while the other area is meant for descriptive text.
Picture with Caption	This layout has a large area for a picture and another area for descriptive text.

▶HOW TO: Choose and Change Slide Layouts

1. Choose a layout for a new slide using one of these methods:
 - Click the **New Slide** button [*Home* tab, *Slides* group] to insert a slide with the default layout.
 - Click the **New Slide** drop-down arrow [*Home* tab, *Slides* group] and select a layout from the layout gallery. The current theme name will appear at the top.
2. Change the layout of a selected slide by following these steps:
 - Click the **Layout** button [*Home* tab, *Slides* group].
 - From the layout gallery, select a different layout.
 - Repeat this process to try another layout.
3. Click the **Undo** button [*Quick Access* toolbar] to remove the layout change.

Enter Text in Placeholders

When you first see placeholders on slides, they appear as boxes with a thin, dotted border. When you click inside the placeholder, it becomes active with a blinking insertion point where you can type or edit text (Figure 1-23). Click the border to select the placeholder and the line becomes solid (Figure 1-24). In both cases, *sizing handles* that are small white circles appear on the corners and sides. A *rotation handle* that is a circular arrow appears at the top.

Dotted line border as it first appears

Click to add title

Click to make the placeholder active with an insertion point

1-23 Placeholders for text

By default, PowerPoint automatically fits text in a placeholder. Therefore, keep the wording of titles concise so the text does not become too small. Depending on the font that is used, title text for individual slides is usually 36–44 points. When using the *Title Slide* layout, the title text is usually 54–72 points.

Sizing handle

Rotation handle

Solid line border shows placeholder can be moved or sized

1-24 Selected placeholder to move or resize

> **MORE INFO**
>
> A point is a unit of measurement in typography used to represent the height of text characters and the space between lines. The number of points in one inch is 72. The widescreen slide size is 13.33" × 7.5" (*Width* × *Height*).

In body placeholders, a bullet (a small symbol such as a circle or square) automatically appears when you type text and press **Enter**. Bullets help mark the beginning of a line, so people recognize items as separate. You can also add subpoints that are indented below a bulleted item. Be sure your list is very concise, usually no more than six items, and the text size is 20–28 points. Larger font sizes are very important if you are presenting in a large room so your audience can read slide text from a distance. However, if you are preparing a presentation to be viewed on a computer or online, you can use smaller font sizes.

Bulleted lists are appropriate when items require no particular order. If you need to show items in order, use a numbered list instead.

▶HOW TO: Work with Lists

Increase List Level button

1. Click after the first bullet in the body placeholder and type text.

2. Press **Enter** to type another bulleted item using the same list level.

3. Press **Tab** or click the **Increase List Level** button [*Home* tab, *Paragraph* group] (Figure 1-25) to indent a bulleted item to the right (Figure 1-26).

1-25 Paragraph group on the *Home* tab

4. Use *Outline View* to enter several text slides. *Outline View* displays all slide titles and bulleted text in the left pane.

 - Click the **Outline View** button [*View* tab, *Presentation Views* group].
 - Position your insertion point at the beginning of a bulleted item and press **Shift+Tab** or click the **Decrease List Level** button [*Home* tab, *Paragraph* group] (Figure 1-27) to move a bulleted item to the left to create a slide title.
 - Change text capitalization as needed for a title (Figure 1-28).

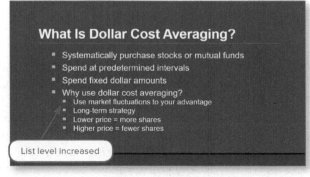

What Is Dollar Cost Averaging?

- Systematically purchase stocks or mutual funds
- Spend at predetermined intervals
- Spend fixed dollar amounts
- Why use dollar cost averaging?
 - Use market fluctuations to your advantage
 - Long-term strategy
 - Lower price = more shares
 - Higher price = fewer shares

List level increased

1-26 Bulleted list slide

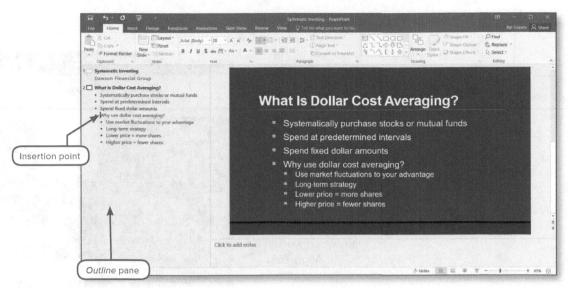

1-27 Slide with bulleted text before list level changes

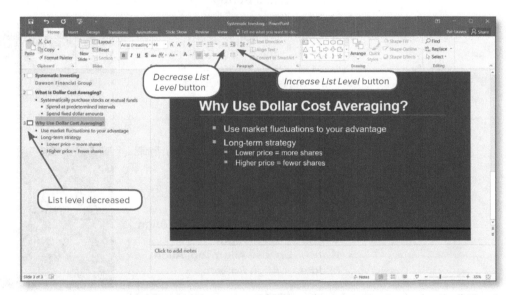

1-28 New slide created by decreasing the list level

5. Convert a bulleted list to a numbered list by selecting the text to be changed and then clicking the **Numbering** button [*Home* tab, *Paragraph* group].

> **MORE INFO**
>
> To move from the title to the body placeholder, press **Ctrl+Enter**. If you are in the last placeholder, press **Ctrl+Enter** to create a new slide.

Align, Move, and Resize Placeholders

How text is positioned within placeholders is controlled by *horizontal alignment* and *vertical alignment*. A small margin automatically appears in placeholders so the text within them does not touch the border.

▶HOW TO: Align Text and Placeholders

1. Align selected text within placeholders horizontally or vertically using these options:

 - *Horizontal*: Choose **Align Left**, **Center**, **Align Right**, or **Justify** (aligns text on both the left and right) [*Home* tab, *Paragraph* group]. *Justify* is rarely used on slides because it can cause irregular spacing between words.
 - *Vertical*: Click **Align Text** [*Home* tab, *Paragraph* group] and then choose **Top**, **Middle**, or **Bottom** (See Figure 1-29).

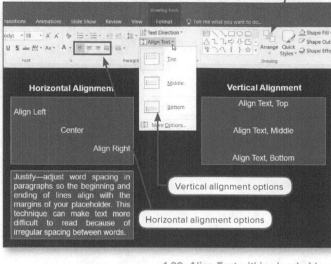

1-29 *Align Text* within placeholders

2. Align selected placeholders with one another. The same drop-down list of options appears on two tabs, so use the tab that is most convenient to you.

 - Click the **Arrange** button [*Home* tab, *Drawing* group] and then choose **Align**.
 - Click the **Align** button [*Drawing Tools Format* tab, *Arrange* group].

3. Choose an alignment option from the drop-down list (Figure 1-30):

 - *Horizontal*: Choose **Align Left**, **Align Center**, or **Align Right**.
 - *Vertical*: Choose **Align Top**, **Align Middle**, or **Align Bottom**.

1-30 *Align* options

Move a placeholder by pointing to its border so your pointer changes to a move arrow (with four points) (Figure 1-31). Click to select the placeholder and drag it to a new position. Use the same technique for moving other objects such as shapes and pictures.

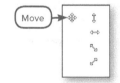

1-31 Move and resize pointers

To increase or decrease placeholder size, point to a corner or side *sizing handle* until your pointer changes to a *resize pointer* (with two points) (see Figure 1-31). As you drag to resize, your pointer changes to a crosshair and the area you will keep is grayed out (Figure 1-32). When you release the pointer, the circle handles appear again. Drag a corner sizing handle (with a diagonal resize pointer) to change both the horizontal and vertical dimensions at the same time.

1-32 Resize a placeholder

648

You can control the way placeholders and other objects are resized by pressing one of three keys as you drag:

- *Ctrl*: The placeholder size changes from a fixed center point.
- *Shift*: The height and width proportions are maintained as the size changes.
- *Ctrl+Shift*: The placeholder resizes from the center and remains in proportion.

Another way to precisely resize a placeholder is to enter the exact dimensions in the *Size* group on the *Drawing Tools Format* tab (Figure 1-33).

All of these techniques for moving, aligning, and resizing also apply to pictures and other objects. If you don't like a change that you made, click the **Reset** button in the *Slides* group on the *Home* tab.

1-33 *Size* group

Edit Text

Notice that your pointer changes when you are working with text. When you see a blinking insertion point, PowerPoint is waiting for you to type text. When you point to text, your pointer changes to a text selection tool so you can click and drag to select text.

Much like Word, commands for editing text are on the *Home* tab in the following groups (from left to right) (Figure 1-34):

- *Clipboard group*: **Cut**, **Copy**, **Paste**, and **Format Painter**.
- *Font group*: Character formatting commands such as **Bold**, **Italic**, **Underline**, **Case**, **Font**, and **Font Size**.

1-34 *Clipboard*, *Font*, and *Paragraph* groups on the *Home* tab

- *Paragraph group*: Paragraph formatting commands such as **Align**, **Bullets**, **Numbering**, and **Increase List Level**.

Also, many text formatting options are available on the mini toolbar (Figure 1-35), which appears when text is selected. You can undo or redo actions using commands on the *Quick Access* toolbar.

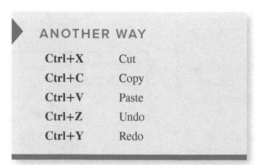

ANOTHER WAY

Ctrl+X	Cut
Ctrl+C	Copy
Ctrl+V	Paste
Ctrl+Z	Undo
Ctrl+Y	Redo

1-35 Mini toolbar

▶**HOW TO: Delete Text**

1. Press **Delete** to remove text to the right of the insertion point.
2. Press **Backspace** to remove text to the left of the insertion point.
3. Select text and press **Delete** to remove several words at one time.

Click outside a text placeholder to deselect it. Handles no longer appear.

Change Text Case

Text *case* refers to how text is capitalized. In several themes, text appears in a placeholder in uppercase (all capital) letters. Be careful when using uppercase letters, because they may not be as easy to read as text with initial caps (the first letter only is capitalized). People can generally read lowercase text faster than uppercase text. Also, uppercase words in email are thought to represent shouting, and this negative connotation might carry over to your presentation if you overuse capital letters. Use uppercase letters when you really want to emphasize selected words or brief phrases.

▶ HOW TO: Change Case

1. Select the text to be changed.
2. Click the **Change Case** button [*Home* tab, *Font* group].
3. Choose from the options **Sentence case.**, **lowercase**, **UPPERCASE**, **Capitalize Each Word**, or **tOGGLE cASE** (Figure 1-36).

1-36 *Change Case* options

Change List Bullet Symbols

You can change the bullet symbol in a placeholder if it seems inappropriate or if its color blends too much with the slide background.

▶ HOW TO: Change Bullet Symbols

1. Select the text or placeholder where you want to change the bullet.
 - Select text in the placeholder to change the bullet for one or more bulleted items.
 - Select the bulleted placeholder to change all bullets in the placeholder.
2. Click the **Bullets** drop-down arrow [*Home* tab, *Paragraph* group] and then select **Bullets and Numbering** to open the *Bullets and Numbering* dialog box (Figure 1-37).
3. Select one of the pre-defined bullets.
4. Enter a different number in the *Size* box to increase or decrease the bullet size.
5. Click the **Color** button to select a different bullet color.
6. Click the **Customize** button to open the *Symbol* dialog box (Figure 1-38), where you can select from many symbols displayed in several fonts.

1-37 *Bullets and Numbering* dialog box

7. Select a symbol and a *Character code* appears. This is a unique number that your computer uses to identify the symbol you have chosen.
8. Click **OK** to add that symbol to the *Bullets and Numbering* dialog box.
9. Select the bullet and click **OK** to change the bullets on selected text.

Character code for the selected symbol

1-38 *Symbol* dialog box

The three **Wingdings** fonts have most of the available character bullets from the *Symbols* dialog box. You can also select picture bullets that are more decorative from the *Bullets and Numbering* dialog box.

The Format Painter

To copy formatting from text, shapes, or pictures and apply these settings to another selection, use the **Format Painter**. You can apply the changes on the same slide or on different slides.

▶**HOW TO:** Use the Format Painter

1. Select the text or other object with the format that you want to copy.
2. Click **Format Painter** [*Home* tab, *Clipboard* group] (see Figure 1-34). Your pointer changes to a paintbrush.
3. Move the paintbrush over the text or other object that you want to change and click to apply the formatting.
4. Apply the change to multiple selections by double-clicking the **Format Painter** button.
5. Press **Esc** to stop formatting.

Reuse Slides from Another Presentation

You can add slides from another presentation without opening it as long as you can access the location where it is stored.

▶**HOW TO:** Reuse Slides

1. Click between two slides in the thumbnail area where you want one or more new slides inserted. A red line between the slides indicates your insertion point.
2. Click the **New Slide** drop-down arrow [*Home* tab, *Slides* group] and select **Reuse Slides** from the bottom of the layout gallery. The *Reuse Slides* pane automatically opens.
3. Click the **Browse** button in the *Reuse Slides* pane and then click **Browse File** (Figure 1-39).

1-39 *Reuse Slides* pane

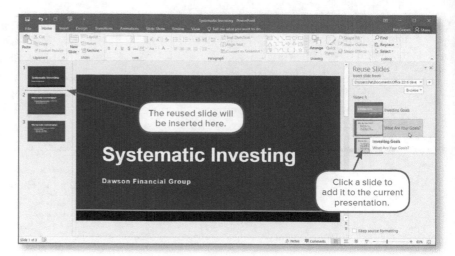

1-40 *Reuse slides*

4. Find the location where your presentation with the slides you need is saved and select the file name.

5. Click **Open**. The slides in this second presentation appear in the *Reuse Slides* pane with text showing their titles (Figure 1-40).

6. Click the slides you want to insert in your current presentation.
 - By default, the reused slides will appear with the formatting of your current presentation.
 - If you want the inserted slides to retain their design from the original presentation, select the **Keep source formatting** checkbox at the bottom of the *Reuse Slides* pane before inserting them.

7. Click the **Close** button at the top of the *Reuse Slides* pane.

> **MORE INFO**
>
> When task panes open, they are docked on the right side of the PowerPoint window. If you have a wide computer screen and you are using PowerPoint in a window size that does not fill the screen, you can drag a pane away from the window so your slide size becomes larger. Double-click the pane to dock it on the right of the window again.

Check Spelling and Word Usage

PowerPoint's *AutoCorrect* feature repairs many simple errors such as changing "teh" to "the" or "recieve" to "receive" as you enter text on your slides. You can customize *AutoCorrect* options to include words that you frequently misspell or abbreviate when the word should be spelled.

PowerPoint will automatically add a red, wavy line below words it does not recognize. Use the *Spelling* feature to correct errors at any time during a presentation but always when you are making your final adjustments. You still need to carefully read the content to find any words that may have been missed, such as names or words that might not be in the spelling dictionary. If your audience sees mistakes when viewing your slide show, your credibility is undermined.

▶ HOW TO: Check Spelling

1. Click the **Spelling** button [*Review* tab, *Proofing* group] (Figure 1-41). The *Spelling* pane opens on the right (Figure 1-42).
2. Consider each word that is identified and whether or not the suggested spelling is correct.
3. Click the **Audio** button on the *Spelling* pane to hear the word pronounced.
4. Click the **Change** button to insert a suggested spelling; click the **Ignore** button if you want to skip the suggestion.
5. Click **OK** when the spell check is complete. The *Spelling* pane automatically closes.

1-41 *Spelling* button on the *Review* tab

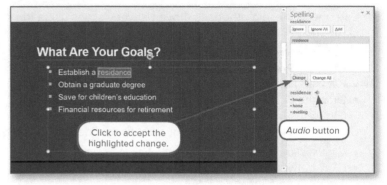

1-42 *Spelling* pane

If you want to replace an awkward word or one that is used too frequently, use PowerPoint's ***Thesaurus*** to find a more appropriate word.

▶ HOW TO: Use the Thesaurus

1. Click the word you want to change.
2. Click the **Thesaurus** button [*Review* tab, *Proofing* group]. The *Thesaurus* pane opens and the selected word appears in the search box (Figure 1-43). Words with similar meanings appear below it.
3. Click a word in this list to see more options; click the **Back** arrow to return to the original list.
4. Click the **Down** arrow on the right of a word in this list and choose **Insert**. The selected word on your slide is replaced with the new word.
5. Click the **Close** button at the top of the *Thesaurus* pane.

1-43 *Thesaurus* word choices

SLO 1.3

Navigating between Slides and Organizing Content

When developing a presentation, you might need to move between slides as ideas occur to you or when you have new information to add. You can rearrange slides at any time. Always examine your sequence carefully when all slides are complete. The final order must be logical to you and to your audience.

Navigate between Slides

In *Normal* view, you can move between slides by clicking the **Next Slide** and **Previous Slide** buttons, clicking scroll arrows, or dragging the scroll box to the right of the window. You can also click thumbnails or use keyboard shortcuts.

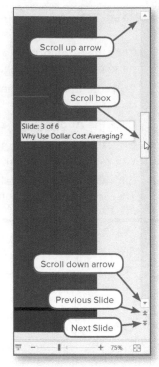

▶ HOW TO: Navigate between Slides

1. Use one of these methods to move between slides using the scroll bar and buttons on the right:
 - Click the **Next Slide** button or the **Scroll Down** arrow to go to the next slide.
 - Click the **Previous Slide** button or **Scroll Up** arrow to go to the previous slide.
 - Click above or below the scroll box to move between slides one at a time.
 - Drag the *Scroll* box up or down to move to a specific slide, using the slide indicator (Figure 1-44).
2. Use one of these methods to move between slides using the *Thumbnail* pane.
 - Click a slide thumbnail to make that slide active.
 - Click between slide thumbnails to select a position for a new slide. A red line indicates your insertion point.
3. Press the following shortcut keys:

First slide	**Home**
Last slide	**End**
Next slide	**Page Down** or **Down** arrow
Previous slide	**Page Up** or **Up** arrow

1-44 Navigate between slides

Copy, Paste, and Duplicate Slides

To reuse a slide's content or format, copy the thumbnail. It is stored in your computer's temporary storage area called the ***Clipboard***. The original slide remains in its position. Paste the copied slide where you need it and edit the text.

▶ HOW TO: Copy and Paste Slides

1. Select the thumbnail of the slide to be copied (Figure 1-45).
2. Press **Ctrl+C** or click the **Copy** button [*Home* tab, *Clipboard* group] to copy the slide.
 - You can also right-click a slide thumbnail and select **Copy** from the context menu.
3. Move the insertion point to the place between slides where you want the copied slide to appear. A red line indicates your insertion point.
4. Press **Ctrl+V** or click the **Paste** button [*Home* tab, *Clipboard* group].
 - You can also right-click a slide thumbnail and select **Paste** from the context menu.
5. Edit the text on the new slide as needed.

1-45 Copy and paste a selected slide

Duplicating also creates a second copy of a slide. You can drag the second slide to a different position.

▶ HOW TO: Duplicate Slides

1. Select the thumbnail of the slide to be duplicated.
2. Press **Ctrl+D** to duplicate the slide. The second slide appears immediately after the original slide and the new slide is selected.
 - You can also right-click a slide thumbnail and select **Duplicate Slide** from the context menu.

Select Multiple Slides

If you need to make the same changes to more than one slide, you can select more than one slide thumbnail.

▶ HOW TO: Select Multiple Slides

1. Select multiple adjacent slides (in order) by selecting the first slide and then pressing **Shift** while you click the last slide (Figure 1-46).
2. Select multiple nonadjacent slides (not in order) by selecting the first slide and then pressing **Ctrl** while you click each of the slides you need to select (Figure 1-47).

Selected slides

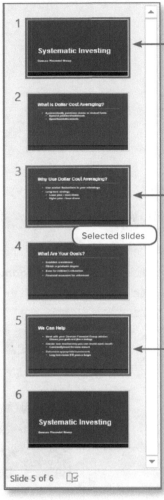

Selected slides

Slide 1 of 6

Slide 5 of 6

1-46 Adjacent slides selected **1-47** Nonadjacent slides selected

Rearrange Slide Order

You can rearrange slides at any time while developing a presentation. In the *Thumbnail* pane you can drag slide thumbnails up or down. On the *Outline* view, you can drag the slide icons. You can also cut slides and paste them into different positions. However, when your presentation has more slides than can be seen in the *Thumbnail* pane, it is best to rearrange slides using *Slide Sorter* view (Figure 1-48).

The *Slide Sorter* view enables you to see your presentation as a whole. The thumbnails are arranged from left to right in rows. By default, they are shown at a 100% size. Click buttons on the *Status* bar to change this percentage. The **Zoom In** button will increase the slide thumbnail size if you need to see the slide content better; the **Zoom Out** button will decrease the slide thumbnail size and you see more slides at one time.

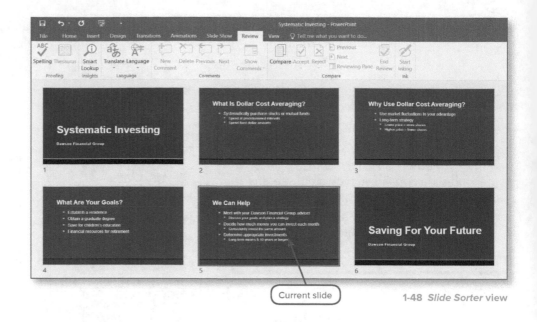

1-48 *Slide Sorter* view

Current slide

▶ HOW TO: Rearrange Slides in Slide Sorter View

1. Click the **Slide Sorter** button on the *Status* bar.
2. Click the **Zoom In** or **Zoom Out** buttons to adjust the size of the thumbnails.
3. Click and drag the slide thumbnails into their new positions (Figure 1-49).

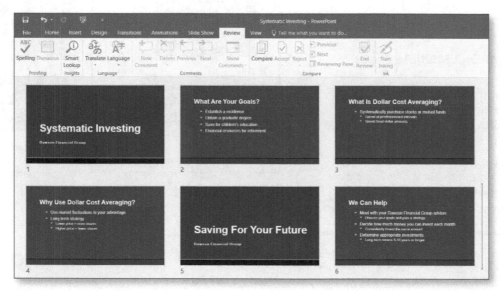

1-49 Slides rearranged

Delete Slides

Remove slides by deleting slide thumbnails in *Normal* view and *Slide Sorter* view or by deleting the slide icon in *Outline* view. You can also use the **Cut** button on the *Home* tab in the *Clipboard* group. This method is helpful because if you change your mind about the deletion later, you can paste the deleted slides back into the presentation from the *Clipboard*.

▶HOW TO: Delete Slides

1. Right-click the slide thumbnail (or the *Slide* icon in *Outline* view). Click **Delete Slide** from the context menu.

Or

2. Select the slide thumbnail (or the *Slide* icon in *Outline* view). Press **Delete** or click **Cut** [*Home* tab, *Clipboard* group].

PAUSE & PRACTICE: POWERPOINT 1-1

For this project, you develop the text for a presentation about upcoming marathon events at the Hamilton Civic Center. This presentation promotes event preparation for participants. You start with a blank presentation, add slides, reuse slides from another presentation, and change formatting.

File Needed: *Marathon Info-01.pptx* *(Student data files are available in the* Library *of your SIMnet account.)*
Completed Project File Name: *[your initials] PP P1-1.pptx*

1. Open PowerPoint and click **Blank Presentation** to start a new presentation.
 a. If PowerPoint is already open, press **Ctrl+N** or click the **File** tab, click **New**, and then click **Blank Presentation**.

2. Name and save the presentation.
 a. Press **F12** to open the *Save As* dialog box.
 b. Browse to the location where you want to save your files and double-click to open the appropriate folder (Figure 1-50). If necessary, click the **New Folder** button, type a name for the new folder, and then double-click to open it.
 c. Type [your initials] PP P1-1 in the *File name* area.
 d. Verify that the *Save as type* area says "PowerPoint Presentation."
 e. Click **Save**. The *Save As* dialog box closes.

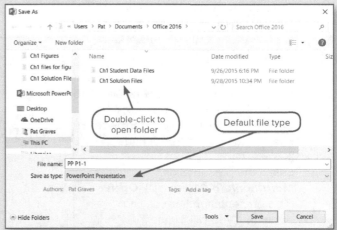

1-50 *Save As* dialog box

3. Display slide 1. Type the following text in the placeholders:

 Title: Take the Right Steps

 Subtitle: Train for a Marathon

4. Click the **New Slide** button [*Home* tab, *Slides* group] twice to add two new slides. The slide thumbnails will appear blank, but the slides have the *Title and Content* layout with two placeholders. Type the following text on slides 2 and 3:

Slide 2 Title:	What Is Your Goal?
Bulleted items:	• Run the second half faster
	• Beat a time you've run before
	• Or
	• Finish the marathon
Slide 3 Title:	Start Early to Be Ready
Bulleted items:	• Begin 5-16 weeks in advance
	• Get a physical check up
	• Prepare gear for running
	• Join a training group
	• Enjoy camaraderie
	• Be accountable
	• Run 3-4 times a week

5. Change a slide layout and adjust the text.
 a. Display slide 3 and click the **Layout** button [*Home* tab, *Slides* group]. Next, select the **Two Content** layout.
 b. Select the last four bulleted items on the left placeholder and press **Ctrl+X** to cut them.
 c. Click the right placeholder and press **Ctrl+V** to paste them.
 d. Delete any extra bullets by placing your insertion point on that line and pressing **Backspace**.
 e. Select the middle two bulleted items on the right placeholder and press **Tab** or click the **Increase List Level** button [*Home* tab, *Paragraph* group] to format them as indented subpoints under the first-level item (Figure 1-51).

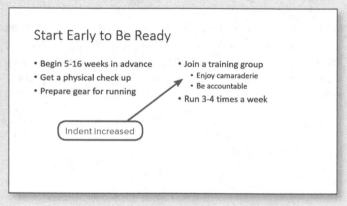

1-51 *Two Content* layout

6. Insert three slides from another presentation.
 a. Display slide 3. Click the **New Slide** drop-down arrow and select **Reuse Slides**.
 b. On the *Reuse Slides* pane, click the **Browse** button; then select **Browse File** and locate your student data files.
 c. Select the presentation ***MarathonInfo-01*** and click **Open**. (This presentation has spelling errors that you will fix later.)
 d. Click three slides (Figure 1-52) to insert them: "Practice Runs," "Eat Energy Foods," and "Get Running Apparel."
 e. Close the *Reuse Slides* pane.

1-52 Reuse slides

7. Rearrange slides.
 a. Click the thumbnails and drag them up or down so the six slides are in this order: "Take the Right Steps," "What is Your Goal?," "Start Early to Be Ready," "Get Running Apparel," "Eat Energy Foods,"and "Practice Runs."

8. Insert and duplicate a new slide.
 a. Display slide 6. Click the **New Slide** drop-down arrow and select the **Title Only** layout.
 b. Type Look It UP! in the title placeholder on slide 7. (Figure 1-53).
 c. Select the title text and change the font size to **72 pt**.
 d. Select this slide thumbnail and press **Ctrl+D** to duplicate it to create slide 8.

9. Edit and duplicate a slide.
 a. Display slide 8. Replace the title with the text Mark It DOWN!.
 b. Select this slide thumbnail and press **Ctrl+D** to duplicate it to create slide 9.

10. Display slide 9. Change the title text to See You THERE!

11. Click the **Spelling** button [*Review* tab, *Proofing* group] and correct each of the spelling errors ("performance," "soreness," "banana," and "yogurt").

12. Save and close the presentation (Figure 1-54). You will continue to work on this presentation for *Pause & Practice 1-2* and *Pause & Practice 1-3*.

> **Look It UP!**
>
> **1-53** Placeholder text resized

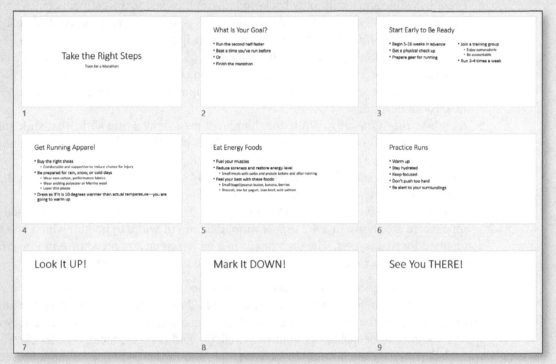

1-54 PP P1-1 completed

SLO 1.4

Changing Theme Colors and Fonts

In PowerPoint, you can quickly change theme colors and fonts using the *Design* tab. If you want to make additional theme changes, use the *Slide Master* tab. The **Slide Master** stores information about slide backgrounds, layouts, colors, and fonts for each theme. In this section, you change theme colors and fonts using both of these tabs so you can learn to choose the method that is most efficient for what you need to change.

When you start a new presentation and search online for templates and themes, you may find backgrounds with artwork or pictures that match your topic perfectly. The file names you see below each thumbnail do not distinguish between themes and templates. Many of the

presentations that appear in a search will have the PowerPoint default file extension (.*pptx*). Those saved as template files will have a different file extension (.*potx*). Depending on how your software is set up, you may not see these file extensions when you open files.

You can search through general categories or enter a specific search word to get more targeted results. Themes and templates are provided by Microsoft and other companies.

Your searches will provide results that include the following:

- *Theme*: A slide show with only background graphics and text treatments but no content. Different layouts control where slide objects are positioned. You can control design elements with the *Slide Master* to create custom designs.
- *Template*: A slide show with the characteristics of a theme but also with sample content on several slides. You can edit the content or remove individual slides that you do not need for your presentation. You can control design elements with the *Slide Master* to create custom designs.
- *Template, title slide only*: While the thumbnail may show a title slide, that slide might be the only content in the presentation. Other slides may be blank or have no related graphic background. The *Slide Master* has not been used.
- *Template, individual slide only*: Thumbnails may show only a diagram or chart that can be revised for a new presentation. Usually, the *Slide Master* has not been used.
- *Different slide sizes*: Two slide sizes will appear. The thumbnails that have an almost square appearance are shown in a 4:3 ***aspect ratio***, the ratio of width to height, which was the standard for many years. The thumbnails in a wide-screen size are shown in PowerPoint's default 16:9 aspect ratio, which reflects the shape of current computer screens.

People who frequently see presentations become very familiar with the slide show designs that appear in common software. So seeing a slide show with a contemporary looking design that truly matches the topic is refreshing. Caring enough to match your theme to your topic speaks volumes to people about your preparedness and competence. Consider carefully what you select so the design is suitable for your topic and for how your slide show is used.

▶ HOW TO: Apply a Theme to an Existing Presentation

1. Click the **Design** tab.
2. Click the **More** button in the *Themes* gallery to see additional themes.
3. Point to a thumbnail to see a live preview of that theme on the current slide (Figure 1-55).
4. Click the thumbnail to apply the theme.

1-55 *Design* tab and *Themes* gallery

Change Theme Colors

When changing theme colors, select colors that are appropriate for your topic. Also consider where you will present. Because of room lighting, colors for a slide show projected on a large screen are not as clear or vibrant as what you see on a computer screen directly in front of you. These differences can influence your color choices. Be sure your text is easy to read with a high contrast between the text and background colors (dark on light or light on dark).

Every presentation, even a blank one, begins with a set of colors that have been chosen to work well together. With each built-in theme, PowerPoint provides *Variants* on the *Design* tab that show different theme colors and some variants have different graphics. Many more theme colors are available.

▶**HOW TO:** Change Theme Colors Using the Design Tab

1. Click the **Design** tab.
2. Click the **More** button [*Variants* group].
3. Select **Colors** and a drop-down list appears showing theme colors (Figure 1-56).
4. Point to a set of theme colors and you see a live preview of those colors on your current slide. The blank, Office theme will show a live preview only if the background colors have changed.
5. Click the colors or a theme name to apply it to all slides.

1-56 *Design* tab and *Theme Colors*

The first two colors in each color theme represent the background and text colors; the remaining six show accent colors. Once you select theme colors, you can apply a *Background Style* to change to a light or dark variation of background and text colors. Click the **More** button [*Design* tab, *Variants* group] and select **Background Styles**. Point to a color in the gallery to see a live preview; click a color to apply it.

Not all of the themes you find online permit color changes in the same way. It depends on how the background design was created. For more on customizing theme colors, see *SLO 3.1: Creating Custom Theme and Background Colors*.

Change Theme Fonts

Select your fonts carefully. Some fonts seem very traditional and serious; others appear more playful and flamboyant. Use fonts that are appropriate for your presentation topic.

Consider how legible the font is with the background color you are using. Letters can appear very thin and are not easy to read unless you apply bold. Also consider issues related

to where you present. The lighting and room size affect how readable the text is on a large screen and you must use large font sizes. If you are designing a presentation to be displayed for a single person on your notebook or tablet computer, you can use smaller font sizes.

Every presentation, even a blank one, begins with a pair of *Theme Fonts*. The heading font is used for slide titles and the body font is used for all other text. Sometimes the same font is used for both. You can view or change *Theme Fonts* from the *Design* tab or from the *Slide Master* tab.

▶ HOW TO: Change Theme Fonts Using the Design Tab

1. Click the **Design** tab.

2. Click the **More** button [*Variants* group].

3. Select **Fonts** and a drop-down list appears showing theme fonts (Figure 1-57).

4. Point to a pair of theme fonts and you see a live preview of those fonts applied to the current slide.

5. Click a theme font pair to apply it to all slides.

1-57 *Design* tab and *Theme Fonts*

Use the Slide Master to Change Theme Colors and Fonts

It is best to use the *Slide Master* tab to change theme colors or theme fonts when you are also changing other design elements. For example, you could customize slide layouts or background graphics by adding a company logo to all slides in a presentation. Each *Slide Master* has a variety of layouts, shown in the pane at the left, that control positioning of different types of content. If you are adding graphics or changing only specific layout colors, then select only the layout you want to change. Changes made on the first layout at the top of this pane generally apply to all other layouts.

▶ HOW TO: Change Theme Colors and Fonts Using the Slide Master

1. Click the **View** tab.

2. Click the Slide Master button [*Master Views* group] (Figure 1-58) to open the *Slide Master* tab.

3. Scroll up to select the first layout, the *Slide Master* layout, at the top of the *Thumbnails* pane so your changes will affect all layouts.

4. Click the **Colors** button [*Background* group] and a drop-down list appears showing theme colors (Figure 1-59).

5. Point to a set of theme colors and you see a live preview of those colors on your current *Slide Master* layout.

6. Click the colors or a theme color name to apply it to all *Slide Master* layouts.

1-58 *Slide Master* button on the *View* tab

7. Click the **Background Styles** button [*Slide Master* tab, *Background* group] to change the background to light or dark variations (Figure 1-60).

 - You can apply different *Background Styles* to various *Slide Master* layouts.
 - This feature is available on the *Design* tab, also.

8. Click the **Fonts** button [*Slide Master* tab, *Background* group] and a drop-down list appears showing theme fonts.

9. Point to a pair of theme fonts and you see a live preview of those fonts applied to the current layout.

10. Click a theme font pair to apply it to all layouts.

11. Click the **Close Master View** button [*Slide Master* tab, *Close* group].

1-59 *Slide Master* tab and *Theme Colors*

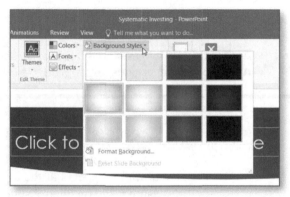

1-60 *Background Styles*

Inserting Headers and Footers

If you want to include identifying information on all slides of a presentation, use the *Header & Footer* command on the *Insert* tab (Figure 1-61). **Footers** are displayed on every slide with placeholders for the date and time, slide number, and footer text. These placeholders often appear across the bottom of the slide, but they may appear in different places depending on the theme. You can choose to show footers on all slides or only on selected slides.

1-61 *Insert* tab

Create a Slide Footer

When you enter information using the *Header and Footer* dialog box, placeholders appear on the slides. You can move these placeholders if you wish.

1. Click the **Insert** tab.

2. Click the **Header & Footer** button [*Text* group]. The *Header and Footer* dialog box displays.

3. Click the **Slide** tab (Figure 1-62).

4. Click the check boxes to select the following as needed:

 • **Date and time**: Choose between **Update automatically** to show the current date or **Fixed** to enter a specific date.
 • **Slide number**: Each slide is numbered.
 • **Footer**: Type text you want to appear on each slide.

5. Check the box for **Don't show on title slide** if you do not want footer information to appear on any slide created with the *Title Slide* layout.

6. Apply your choices by clicking one of these buttons:

 • **Apply:** the settings are applied to the current slide only.
 • **Apply to All:** the settings are applied to all slides.

1-62 *Slide* tab in the *Header and Footer* dialog box

Create a Notes and Handouts Header

Because notes and handouts are usually printed documents, they can include *header* information that appears at the top of each page. Control all settings for notes and handouts in the same way you control slide footers.

1. Click the **Insert** tab.

2. Click the **Header & Footer** button [*Text* group]. The *Header and Footer* dialog box displays.

3. Click the **Notes and Handouts** tab (Figure 1-63).

4. Click the check boxes to select the following as needed:

 • **Date and time**: Choose between **Update automatically** to show the current date or **Fixed** to enter a specific date.
 • **Page number**: Each page is numbered.
 • **Header**: Type text you want to appear on each page.
 • **Footer**: Type text you want to appear on each page.

5. Click the **Apply to All** button to apply your settings to all pages.

1-63 *Notes and Handouts* tab in the *Header and Footer* dialog box

If you leave items blank in the *Header and Footer* dialog box, empty placeholders show on your slide, but no information appears in *Slide Show* view.

For this project, you continue working on the presentation about training for a marathon. You add a theme then change theme colors and fonts to revise two individual slides. Finally, you add a footer to your slides and add page numbering to the notes and handout pages.

File Needed: *[your initials] PP P1-1.pptx*
Completed Project File Name: *[your initials] PP P1-2.pptx*

1. Open the presentation you completed in *Pause & Practice 1-1*.
 a. Click the **File** tab to open the *Backstage* view and click **Open** on the left.
 b. Click **Browse** to open the *Open* dialog box.
 c. Locate the folder where you want to save this file.
 d. Select the **[your initials] PP P1-1** presentation and click **Open**.

2. Rename and save the presentation.
 a. Click the **File** tab to open the *Backstage* view and select **Save As** on the left.
 b. Click **Browse** to open the *Save As* dialog box.
 c. Locate the folder where your files are saved.
 d. Change the file name to [your initials] PP P1-2.
 e. Click **Save** to save the presentation and close the *Save As* dialog box.

3. Apply a theme.
 a. Click the **Design** tab.
 b. Click the **More** button [*Themes* group] to open the *Themes* gallery (Figure 1-64).
 c. Click the **Facet** theme so it is applied to all slides.

1-64 *Themes* gallery

4. Change theme colors and the background style.
 a. Click the **More** button [*Design* tab, *Variants* group] and select **Colors**.
 b. Scroll down the list and select the **Aspect** theme.
 c. Click the **More** button again and select **Background Styles**.
 d. Select **Style 4**, which applies a solid black background (Figure 1-65).

5. Change theme fonts.
 a. Click the **More** button [*Design* tab, *Variants* group] and select **Fonts**.
 b. Scroll down the list and click the **TrebuchetMS** font pair (Figure 1-66).

1-65 *Background Styles*

6. Modify and move the title.
 a. Display slide 1. Select the title placeholder and apply these font changes: **60 pt.**, **Bold** [*Home* tab, *Font* group], and **Align Left** [*Home* tab, *Paragraph* group].
 b. Click the **Arrange** button [*Home* tab, *Drawing* group], select **Align**, and select **Align Top**.
 c. Select the word **Right**. Click the **Change Case** button [*Home* tab, *Font* group] and select **UPPERCASE**.
 d. Resize the placeholder by dragging the right horizontal sizing handle so the text fits on one line.

7. Modify and move the subtitle.
 a. Select the subtitle placeholder on slide 1 and apply these font changes: **36 pt.**, **Bold** [*Home* tab, *Font* group], and **Align Left** [*Home* tab, *Paragraph* group].
 b. Move the subtitle placeholder below the title and select both placeholders.
 c. Click the **Arrange** button [*Home* tab, *Drawing* group], select **Align**, and then select **Align Left**.

8. Change the bullet.
 a. Display slide 2. Select the bulleted text and click the **Bullets** drop-down arrow [*Home* tab, *Font* group].
 b. Select **Bullets and Numbering**.
 c. Change the *Size* to **100%** of text.
 d. Click the **Color** button and select **Red, Accent 2** (Figure 1-67).
 e. Click the **Customize** button to open the *Symbol* dialog box.
 f. Change the *Subset* to **Geometric Shapes** (Figure 1-68). Select the **Black Square** (Character code 25A0).
 - If the **Wingdings** font is available, select a similar symbol (Character code 110).
 g. Click **OK** to insert the symbol and close the *Symbol* dialog box. Click **OK** again to close the *Bullets and Numbering* dialog box.
 h. Click to position your insertion point before the word "**Or**" on the third bulleted item.
 i. Press **Backspace** to remove the bullet from this item only. Apply **bold**.

9. Add a slide footer.
 a. Display slide 2 and click the **Header & Footer** button [*Insert* tab, *Text* group].
 b. On the *Slide* tab, select **Slide number** and **Footer** (Figure 1-69).

1-66 Change *Theme* font

1-67 Change bullet size and color

1-68 *Symbol* dialog box

c. In the *Footer* text box, type Take the Right Steps, Train for a Marathon.
d. Select **Don't show on title slide**.
e. Click the **Apply** button. The dialog box closes and the footer appears only on this slide.
f. Press **Shift** and click the footer and the page number placeholders to select them both. Increase the font size to **18 pt**. [*Home* tab, *Font* group].

10. Save and close the presentation (Figure 1-70).

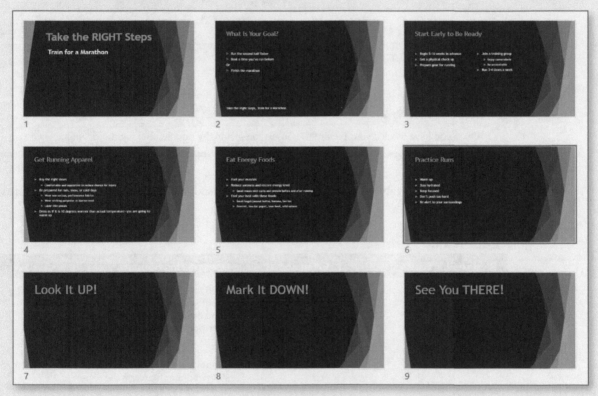

1-69 *Header and Footer* dialog box with changes

1-70 PP P1-2 completed

Working with a Picture from a File

SLO 1.6

An old adage says "A picture is worth a thousand words." That saying is still true today, because pictures bring a sense of realism to a presentation. Select pictures appropriate for your topic. Include pictures obtained from web sites only if you have the permission of the image owner to avoid copyright infringement. For academic purposes, you may include images if you reference their sources as you would any other research citation.

Insert a Picture

PowerPoint supports different graphic file types, so you can insert almost any digital image from a camera, or one created by scanning a document, into a slide show. To insert a picture, click the **Picture** button in the *Images* group on the *Insert* tab. Be aware that pictures can increase the file size of your presentation dramatically.

> **HOW TO:** Insert a Picture

1. Click the **Insert** tab.
2. Click the **Pictures** button.
3. Select the drive and folder where your picture is saved.
4. Select the file you want to insert (Figure 1-71).
5. Click **Insert**.

1-71 *Insert Picture* dialog box

> **ANOTHER WAY**
>
> Once you have located your picture file, insert the picture by double-clicking the file name.

The following table lists the more commonly used graphic file formats for pictures and illustrations.

Graphic File Formats

Picture File Type	Extension	Uses of This Format
JPEG (Joint Photographic Experts Group)	.jpg	Used for photographs and complex graphics. Handles gradual color blending well. Produces a smaller file size than most other formats. Transparency is not supported.
PNG (Portable Network Graphics)	.png	Used for photographs and complex graphics. Supports transparency so areas removed from the image appear blank on the slide.
GIF (Graphics Interchange Format)	.gif	Suited for line art and simple drawings because it is limited to 256 colors. Used for simple animated graphics. Does not handle gradual color blending well. Supports transparency.
Windows Metafile and Enhanced Windows Metafile	.wmf and .emf	Used for simple 16-bit or 32-bit graphics.
Device Independent Bitmap	.bmp	Images usually display well in their original size, but if you increase size, the image will be distorted.
TIFF (Tagged Image File Format)	.tiff	Designed for print publications. Produces high-quality images with large file sizes. Supports transparency.

Resize a Picture

To resize a picture, point to a sizing handle (white circle on the border) and drag it. Dragging the corner sizing handles will maintain correct proportions because they move diagonally to change both horizontal and vertical dimensions at the same time. Dragging the side handles can cause distortion because the height or width is changed independently.

You can precisely resize a picture by entering dimensions in the *Size* group on the *Picture Tools Format* tab (Figure 1-72) that appears when a picture is selected. When you change the *Height* or *Width* measurement [*Size* group], the other measurement will automatically adjust.

Reset Picture button Enter sizes **1-72** *Picture Tools Format* tab

Maintain the correct ratio between height and width to avoid distorting the image. You can make a picture smaller and still retain its clarity, but some pictures cannot be made larger without becoming blurred or distorted. If you change the size incorrectly, restore the picture's original dimensions by clicking the **Reset Picture** button [*Picture Tools Format* tab, *Adjust* group] and selecting **Reset Picture & Size**. Depending on the picture's resolution, you may need to resize it again to fit your slide.

Align a Picture

As you place pictures and other graphic objects on slides, consider how they are aligned. Everything on the slide should align in some way. You can align selected pictures and other objects with each other or on the slide in the same way you align placeholders (see *Align, Move, and Resize Placeholders* in *SLO 1:2 Working with Slides, Layouts, Placeholders, and Text*.) Click the **Align** button [*Picture Tools Format* tab, *Arrange* group] and select the alignment from the drop-down list (Figure 1-73):

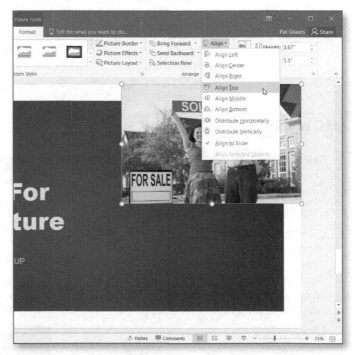

1-73 *Align Top* and *Align Right*

- *Horizontal alignment*: **Align Left**, **Align Center**, or **Align Right**
- *Vertical alignment*: **Align Top**, **Align Middle**, or **Align Bottom**

The picture shown in Figure 1-73 displays the following alignment: **Align Right**, **Align Top**, and **Align to Slide**.

Applying and Modifying Transitions

A *transition* is the visual effect of movement that occurs when one slide changes to the next slide. Each transition effect in PowerPoint provides a different type of movement. You can find these in the *Transition to This Slide* gallery on the *Transitions* tab (Figure 1-74).

1-74 *Transitions* tab

Each slide can have only one transition. You can set transitions for one slide at a time in *Normal* view or apply the same transition to all slides. If you want to use different transitions, select thumbnails in *Normal* view or *Slide Sorter* view and click a transition to apply it to those slides. Once a transition has been applied, an icon symbolizing movement appears with the slide thumbnail.

Although it is possible to apply different transitions on every slide in a presentation, it is neither practical nor advisable. People are very accustomed to PowerPoint use today and know that slides are going to change. Random movements using many different transitions do not entertain an audience and may be distracting or even annoying. Control movement skillfully to reinforce your message. For example, you could apply a "quiet" transition for most of your presentation (sort of like turning pages in a book or an e-reader) and then apply a more "energetic" transition to key slides to grab attention or signal the beginning of a new topic. Use the *Slide Sorter* view to see more slides at once and decide which slides might benefit from a different movement.

In the *Timing* group, the **Advance Slide** options control whether slides advance **On Mouse Click** (the default) or after the number of seconds that you specify. You can also add sound to a transition using the *Timing* group.

▶ HOW TO: Apply Transitions

1. Select the slide thumbnail where you want a transition to appear.

2. Click the **Transitions** tab.

3. Click the **More** button [*Transition to This Slide* group] to see additional transitions (Figure 1-75) organized by the following categories:

 - *Subtle*
 - *Exciting*
 - *Dynamic Content*

4. Apply one transition to all slides in the presentation.

 - Select a transition effect.

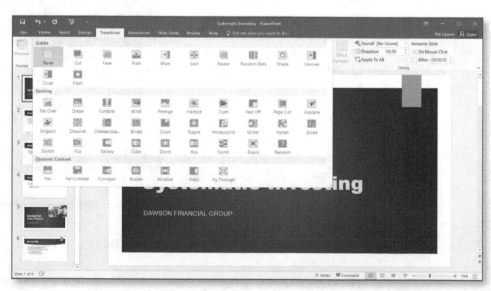

1-75 *Transitions* gallery

- Select **On Mouse Click** [*Timing* group] if it is not already selected.
- Click the **Apply to All** button [*Timing* group].

5. Apply a different transition to selected slides.
- Click the **Slide Sorter** button on the *Status* bar.
- Press **Ctrl** as you click to select one or more slides that should have a different transition.
- Click to apply a different transition effect and the movement is displayed on the selected slides.
- Select **On Mouse Click** [*Timing* group] if it is not already selected. (Figure 1-76).

1-76 Change transitions on selected slides in *Slide Sorter* view

6. Preview slides in different views to test the movement.
- *Slide Sorter* view: Click the **Slide Sorter** button on the *Status* bar. Select a slide thumbnail and click **Preview** [*Transitions* tab, *Preview* group]. Repeat for other slides.
- *Normal* view: Click the **Normal View** button on the *Status* bar. Select a slide and click **Preview**. Click the **Next Slide** button to advance from slide to slide.
- *Slide Show* view: Click the **Slide Show** tab and press **N** to advance from slide to slide.
- Click the **From Beginning** button [*Start Slide Show* group] to view the slide show from the first slide. Click to advance from slide to slide.

Duration, shown in seconds, controls how fast the slides change. Duration seconds vary based on the selected transition effect. Movement might be barely visible if the duration is fast; a slower duration of five or more seconds will cause the movement to be much more noticeable. Enter a different number to change the duration and experiment to see what works best for your content.

Select Effect Options

Effect Options control the direction of transition movement. Each transition can have only one effect option, but most transitions provide two or more options from which you can choose. You can apply these options as you are setting up your transitions or later when you are editing your presentation.

▶ **HOW TO:** Select Effect Options

1. Select a slide with a transition.
2. Click the **Effect Options** button [*Transition* tab, *Transition to This Slide* group] to see a drop-down list showing directional movements (Figure 1-77).
3. Select an effect option to apply it.

4. Apply the effect option to multiple transitions if appropriate:

- Click **Apply To All** [*Transition* tab, *Timing* group] if this movement is appropriate for all slides.
- If different transitions have been applied, select the slide thumbnails in *Slide Sorter* view with the same transition and then apply the appropriate effect option.

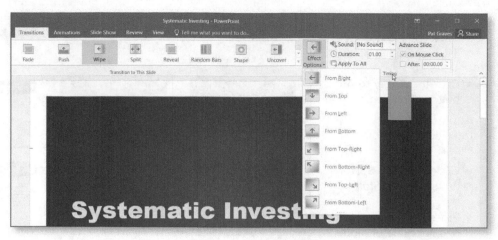

1-77 Transition *Effect Options*

5. Preview the slides in *Slide Show* view to test all transitions and effect options.

Exploring Print Options

You may want to proofread your presentation content on paper or review the slides with a colleague. Or you may want to prepare audience handouts or your own printed materials to use while you are giving the presentation. PowerPoint 2016 provides convenient ways to preview and print presentation slides, handouts, notes pages, or outlines.

Preview a Presentation

Before printing, check your slides to ensure everything looks as you intended. The *Backstage* view [*File* tab, *Print* button] displays each slide or handout page in your presentation as it will look when printed. Use the navigation controls at the bottom of the window to go through the slides or pages one at a time. You can also use the scroll bar on the right. Adjust slide or page size using the *Zoom* controls on the lower right.

The look of your slides in *Backstage* view is influenced by the selected printer. The preview image shows in color if you are printing with a color printer or in **grayscale** (shades of black) if you are printing with a printer that prints only black. In a work setting, you may have a small desktop printer for printing rough draft copies with black print and a network printer for printing more expensive, high-quality color pages.

If you design slides in color and plan to print slides or handouts in grayscale, preview your slides in grayscale to confirm that all text is readable. You may need to adjust a few colors to get good results.

In *Backstage* view, select a printer from the available list of local and network printers. **Print Settings** are shown as buttons with the current setting displayed. Click the list arrow for a list of the following options:

- *Which Slides to Print*: Choose *Print All Slides*, *Print Selection*, *Print Current Slide*, or *Custom Range* using slide numbers entered in the *Slides* box (slides 1–3 or slides 1–3, 5, 8)
- *What to Print*: Choose *Full Page Slides*, *Notes Pages*, *Outline*, or *Handouts*. You can print handouts with 1, 2, 3, 4, 6, or 9 slides on a page with the sequence of slides arranged horizontally or vertically. You can also specify *Frame Slides*, *Scale to Fit Paper* (increases slide size), or *High Quality*.

- *Print Side*: Choose between *Print One Sided* or *Print on Both Sides*. You can choose to *Flip pages on long edge* or *Flip pages on short edge* to control how pages will turn if they are bound together at the top or side like a book. However, not all printers can print on both sides, so you may not see these options.
- *Print Order*: Choose between *Collated* and *Uncollated*. Usually slides print in order (collated), but you may want to print multiple copies page by page (uncollated).
- *Orientation*: Choose between *Landscape* and *Portrait*. By default, slides print in landscape orientation; notes and handouts print in portrait orientation. This option is not available if you are printing full-size slides.
- *Color Range*: Choose among *Color*, *Grayscale*, or *Pure Black and White*.

Below the print *Settings* in *Backstage* view, you can click the **Edit Header & Footer** link to open the *Header and Footer* dialog box and then enter or revise information on the *Notes and Handouts* tab.

Print a Slide

The default print settings print each slide on letter-size paper. Adjust print settings as needed to print the current or selected slides.

▶HOW TO: Print a Slide in Grayscale

1. Click the **File** tab.
2. Click **Print** on the left.
3. Select an appropriate printer.
4. Locate the *Settings* area. Click the list arrow for each box and choose options from the drop-down list, such as the following:
 - *Which Slides to Print*: **Print Current Slide**
 - *What to Print*: **Full Page Slides**
 - *Print Order*: **Collated**
 - *Color Range*: **Grayscale** (Figure 1-78)
5. Enter the number of copies, if you need more than one.
6. Click the **Print** button at the top.

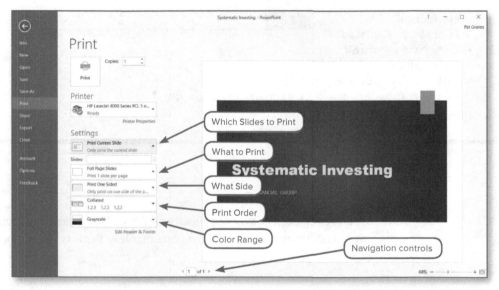

1-78 Print settings for a full-size slide

Print a Handout

Handouts print one to nine slides on a page. You can use these pages as audience handouts or for your own reference during a presentation. Selecting *Scale to Fit Paper* increases the slide size. *Framing* shows the shape of slides, which is helpful when printing slides with a white

background on white paper. Depending on the number of slides, changing the page orientation to landscape may increase slide size.

When preparing handouts for an audience, consider which slides will be important for the audience to have. You can specify which slides to include and perhaps reduce the number of pages required for printing.

▶ HOW TO: Print a Handout for Selected Slides in Color

1. Click the **File** tab.
2. Click **Print** on the left.
3. Select a color printer.
4. Locate the *Settings* area. Click the list arrow for each box and choose options from the drop-down list, such as the following:
 - *Which Slides to Print*: Type the specific slides needed (1, 3–4, 6) in the *Slides* box to print a *Custom Range*.
 - *What to Print*: **6 Slides Horizontal**
 - *Print Order*: **Collated**
 - *Orientation*: **Portrait Orientation**
 - *Color Range*: **Color** (Figure 1-79)
5. Type the number of copies, if you need more than one.
6. Click the **Print** button at the top.

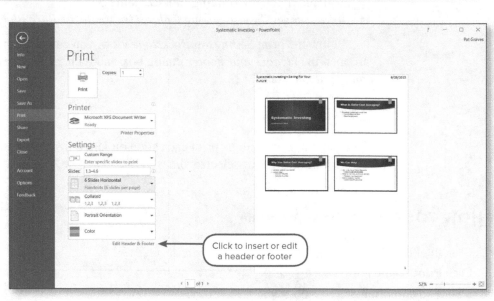

1-79 Print settings for a handout

Print an Outline

If a presentation consists of mostly slides with titles and bulleted lists, printing an outline is a very concise way to display the content. Only the text is shown.

▶ HOW TO: Print an Outline in Pure Black and White

1. Click the **File** tab.
2. Click the **Print** button on the left.
3. Select an appropriate printer.
4. Locate the *Settings* area. Click the list arrow and choose options from the drop-down list, such as the following:
 - *Which Slides to Print*: **Print All Slides**
 - *What to Print*: **Outline**
 - *What Side*: **Print One Sided**
 - *Print Order*: **Collated**

- *Orientation*: **Portrait Orientation**
- *Color Range*: **Pure Black and White**
 (Figure 1-80)

5. Enter the number of copies, if you need more than one.

6. Click the **Print** button at the top.

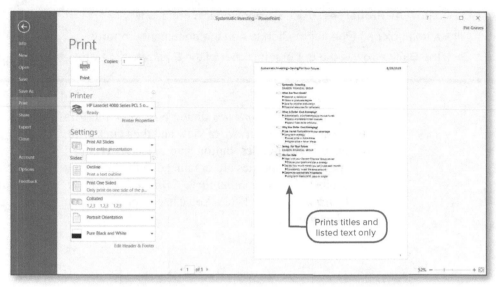

1-80 Print settings for an outline

Applying Properties

PowerPoint automatically records information called ***properties***, or ***metadata***, that identify details of your presentation to help you manage and track files. Some information is generated automatically such as the file size, creation date, and number of slides. These details are not visible in the presentation; they appear on the *Backstage* view or the *Properties* dialog box. Items shown with fields can be edited by inserting your own content such as title and author. Properties can be viewed by others who use the presentation.

▶ HOW TO: Add Properties Using Backstage View

1. Click the **File** tab to display the *Backstage* view.

2. Click **Info** if it is not already selected.

3. Point to the properties listed on the right. The property field names are followed by the information for the current presentation.

 - Some properties cannot be changed because they are automatically generated.
 - A text box with a red border indicates a property field where the information can be edited (Figure 1-81). Click the box to add your content.

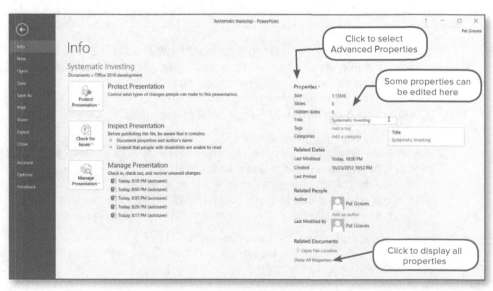

1-81 Document properties on the *Backstage* view

4. Click **Show All Properties** to access additional information.

5. Click a text box and type information to edit the document property.

6. Click the **Back** arrow in the upper left corner of the *Backstage* view to return to your presentation.

To open the *Properties* dialog box, click the **File** tab to display the *Backstage* view and then click **Info**. Click the **Properties** button and select **Advanced Properties**. Properties are organized in the following five tabs: *General*, *Summary*, *Statistics*, *Contents*, and *Custom* (Figure 1-82). You can edit properties on the *Summary* tab.

1-82 *Properties* dialog box

PAUSE & PRACTICE: POWERPOINT 1-3

For this final Pause & Practice project, you finish the presentation about training for a marathon. You insert, resize, and align several pictures, apply transitions, change the presentation properties, and print a handout.

Files Needed: *[your initials] PP P1-2.pptx, RunnersGroup-01.jpg, RunnerWoman-01.jpg*, and *MarathonSchedule-01.jpg (Student data files are available in the Library of your SIMnet account.)*
Completed Project File Name: *[your initials] PP P1-3.pptx*

1. Open the presentation you completed in *Pause & Practice 1-2*.
 a. Click the **File** tab to open the *Backstage* view and click **Open** on the left.
 b. Click **Browse** to open the *Open* dialog box.
 c. Locate the folder where your files are saved.
 d. Select the *[your initials] PP P1-2* presentation and click **Open**.

2. Rename and save the presentation.
 a. Click the **File** tab to open the *Backstage* view and select **Save As** on the left.
 b. Click **Browse** to open the **Save As** dialog box.
 c. Locate the folder where you want to save this file.
 d. Change the file name to [your initials] PP P1-3.
 e. Click **Save** to save the presentation and close the *Save As* dialog box.

3. Insert, resize, and align a picture on the slide.
 a. Display slide 1. Click the **Insert** tab, and then click the **Pictures** button [*Images* group].
 b. Locate your student data files.

c. Select **RunnersGroup-01** and click **Insert** (or double-click the file name) to insert the picture (Figure 1-83).

d. With the picture selected, click the **Align** button [*Picture Tools Format* tab, *Arrange* group].
 - Select **Align Bottom**.
 - Repeat to select **Align Right**.

e. Drag the picture's left horizontal sizing arrow to resize the picture so the *Width* is **8.5"** (Figure 1-84).
 - Because the picture is already blurred to reflect the speed of running, it looks fine when you stretch the picture.
 - If necessary, move the subtitle so it is between the title and picture.

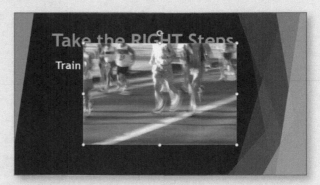

1-83 Picture of runners inserted

4. Insert and align a picture.
 a. Display slide 6. Click the **Insert** tab and click the **Pictures** button.
 b. Locate your student data files.
 c. Select **RunnerWoman-01** and click **Insert** (or double-click the file name) to insert the picture.
 - No resizing is required for this picture.
 d. Select the picture and click the **Align** button [*Picture Tools Format* tab, *Arrange* group] and select **Align Right**.

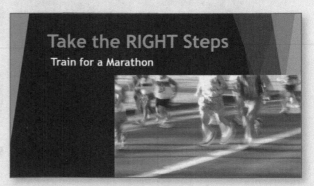

1-84 Picture resized and aligned

5. Add a new slide and insert a picture of a table.
 a. With slide 6 displayed. Click the **New Slide** drop-down arrow [*Home* tab, *Slides* group].
 b. Select the **Title Only** layout.
 c. Type the title Upcoming Marathons.
 d. Click the **Insert** tab, and then click the **Pictures** button [*Images* group].
 e. Locate your student data files.
 f. Select **MarathonSchedule-01** and click **Insert** (or double-click the file name) to insert the picture.
 g. Increase the picture *Width* to **8.5"** (*Picture Tools Format* tab, *Size* group).
 h. Move the table so it is approximately centered in the black area (Figure 1-85).

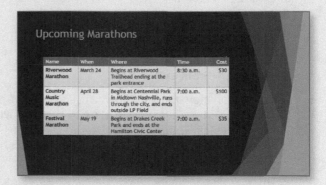

1-85 Picture of a table inserted and positioned

6. Adjust placeholder size and alignment.
 a. Display slide 8. Select the title placeholder and resize it horizontally on the right side so the text fits in the placeholder without extra horizontal space or word wrapping.
 b. Click the **Align** button [*Drawing Tools Format* tab, *Arrange* group] and select **Align Left**. Repeat to select **Align Top** (Figure 1-86).
 c. Display slide 9. Repeat steps 6a and 6b using **Align Center** and **Align Bottom**.

1-86 Title placeholder aligned top and left

 d. Display slide 10. Repeat steps 6a and 6b using **Align Right** and **Align Middle**.

 e. Change the font color for the word "THERE!" on slide 10 to **Tan, Text 2** [*Home* tab, *Font* group].

7. Apply one transition to all slides.

 a. Click the **Slide Sorter** button [*Status* bar].

 b. Click the **Transitions** tab.

 c. Click the **Wipe** transition from the gallery.

 d. Click **Effect Options** [*Transition* tab, *Transition to This Slide* group].

 e. Select **From Left** (Figure 1-87).

1-87 Transition *Effect Options*

 f. Click **Apply To All** [*Transition* tab, *Timing* group].

8. Select each of the following slides and apply different transitions (listed first) and effect options to emphasize the content.

 Slide 2: **Zoom**, **In**
 Slide 7: **Doors**, **Vertical**
 Slide 8: **Pan**, **From Bottom**
 Slide 9: **Pan**, **From Top**
 Slide 10: **Pan**, **From Left**

9. Test transition movements.

 a. In *Slide Sorter* view, press **Ctrl+A** to select all slides.

 b. Click **Preview** [*Transitions* tab] to see the movements.

 c. Select the first slide and click the **Slide Show** button [*Status* bar].

 d. Click to advance each slide so you can see the movements in *Slide Show* view. At the end, click or press **Esc** to exit *Slide Show* view.

10. Change presentation properties.

 a. Click the **File** tab to open the *Backstage* view.

 b. Click **Info** on the left if it is not already selected. The properties display on the right.

 c. Click the *Title* field and type Train for a Marathon.

 d. Click the **Properties** button, then select **Advanced Properties** to open the *Properties* dialog box (Figure 1-88).

1-88 *Properties* dialog box

e. Click the **Summary** tab and type the following information in the respective fields:

Title: Train for a Marathon (already entered)
Subject: Athletic Event Promotion
Author: Your Name *(unless it already appears)*
Comments: This presentation will be shown at the Civic Center to explain how to get ready for upcoming marathon events.

f. Click **OK** to close the *Properties* dialog box and return to *Backstage* view.

11. Print slides as a handout. If your computer is not connected to a printer, skip step e.
 a. Click the **Print** button on the left.
 b. Select the appropriate printer.
 c. Change the following *Settings* by clicking the list arrow for each option (repeat as necessary for more than one change) (Figure 1-89):
 Which Slides to Print: **Print All Slides**
 What to Print: **Handouts, 6 Slides Horizontal, Frame Slides, Scale to Fit Paper**
 Print Order: **Collated**
 Orientation: **Portrait**
 Color Range: **Grayscale** (or **Color** if you prefer)

1-89 *Print* settings

 d. Preview the handout by clicking the navigation buttons to see both pages.
 e. Click the **Print** button at the top of the *Backstage* view.
 f. If necessary, click the **Back** button to close *Backstage* view.

12. Press **Ctrl+S** to save the presentation (or click **Save** on the *File* tab or the *Quick Access* toolbar). Close the presentation (Figure 1-90).

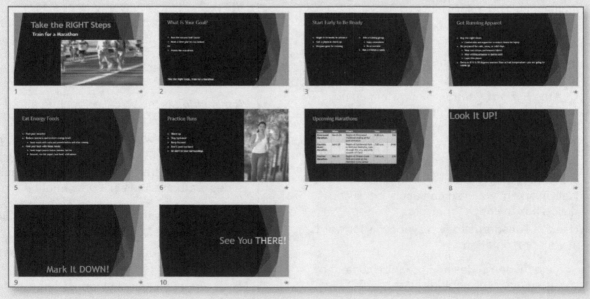

1-90 PP P1-3 completed

Chapter Summary

1.1 Create, open, and save a presentation (p. 633).

- You can start developing presentation content with a blank presentation, a **Theme**, an existing presentation, or a **Template**.
- PowerPoint views enable you to look at your content in different ways.
- The **Zoom** feature allows you to adjust the size of the current slide.
- The standard file format for presentation files has an extension of *.pptx*.
- In *Backstage* view, PowerPoint provides a variety of save and send options. For example, you can save a presentation as a PDF file or email a presentation file as an attachment.
- Additional themes and templates are available by searching online through PowerPoint or downloading them at Office.com.

1.2 Work with slides, layouts, placeholders, and text (p. 644).

- Use **placeholders** for presentation text and objects such as pictures, tables, and charts. You can resize, reposition, and align text placeholders on slides.
- The *New Slide* button displays a gallery of slide layouts with placeholders arranged for different content.
- You can change fonts using commands on the *Home* tab or the mini toolbar.
- *Change Case* changes the way words are capitalized.
- In bulleted lists, you can change the bullet symbol, size, and color.
- Use the **Format Painter** to copy formatting from one object and apply it to another object.
- The *Reuse Slides* feature enables you to insert slides from another presentation.
- Although potential spelling errors are automatically marked, you also can use the *Spelling* dialog box to check for errors.
- Use the **Thesaurus** to find synonyms for words in your presentation.

1.3 Navigate between slides and organize content by reproducing and rearranging slides (p. 653).

- You can move selected slides using a variety of methods to rearrange their sequence.

- Copy, paste, duplicate, and delete slides using the *Slides* pane or *Slide Sorter* view.

1.4 Change theme colors and fonts (p. 659).

- Presentation themes provide a cohesive look through the consistent use of background designs, colors, and font treatments.
- Consider the topic and tone of your presentation when choosing theme colors and fonts.

1.5 Insert headers and footers to add identifying information (p. 663)

- Both headers and footers are used for notes pages and handouts. They are applied to all pages or to individual pages.
- Footers usually appear at the bottom of slides but can appear in other locations. They are applied to all slides, all slides except the title slide, or to individual slides.

1.6 Insert, resize, and align a picture from a file (p. 667).

- PowerPoint supports different graphic file types; you can insert almost any digital image into slide shows.
- Use **sizing handles** or enter exact dimensions to increase or decrease a picture's size.
- Avoid distortion when resizing pictures by maintaining accurate height and width ratios.
- You can align pictures with one another or with the slide.

1.7 Apply and modify transition effects to add visual interest (p. 670).

- A **transition** is the visual effect that appears when one slide changes into another slide.
- The **Effect Options** command enables you to control the direction of transition movement.
- You can apply transitions to one slide, multiple slides, or to all slides in a presentation.

1.8 Preview a presentation and print slides, handouts, and outlines (p. 672).

- *Backstage* view allows you to examine each slide in your presentation before printing.
- The printer you select influences how slides appear in *Backstage* view.
- **Grayscale** shows shades of black.

- **Print Settings** control which slides to print, what to print, and the print order, orientation, and color range.

1.9 Apply presentation properties (p. 675).

- **Properties** are automatically recorded in your presentation file.
- You can add properties such as subject, keywords, or category to help manage and track files.
- Edit properties in *Backstage* view under *Info* or by opening the *Properties* dialog box.

Check for Understanding

The SIMbook for this text (within your SIMnet account) provides the following resources for concept review:

- Multiple choice questions
- Matching exercises
- Short answer questions

Guided Project 1-1

Jason Andrews is a sales associate for Classic Gardens and Landscaping (CGL) and frequently talks to customers when they visit the CGL showroom. For this project, you prepare a presentation he can use when introducing customers to CGL services.
[Student Learning Outcomes 1.1, 1.2, 1.3, 1.4, 1.5, 1.6]

Files Needed: ***GardenView-01.jpg*** and ***CGLLogo-01.png*** *(Student data files are available in the* Library *of your SIMnet account.)*
Completed Project File Name: ***[your initials] PowerPoint 1-1.pptx***

Skills Covered in This Project

- Create a new presentation using a theme.
- Change theme colors and background style.
- Change theme fonts.
- Add slides.
- Change font size.

- Rearrange slides.
- Use the *Format Painter*.
- Insert a footer.
- Check spelling.
- Adjust placeholder position.
- Insert, align, and resize a picture.
- Save a presentation.

1. Create a new presentation using a theme.
 a. Click the **File** tab, and then click **New**.
 b. Double-click the **Ion** theme (Figure 1-91).

2. Save the presentation as [your initials] PowerPoint 1-1.

3. Change the theme colors.
 a. Click the **Design** tab.
 b. Click the **More** button [*Variants* group] to select each of the following options:
 Colors: Scroll down the list and select the **Paper** theme.
 Background Styles: Select **Style 3** from the gallery (Figure 1-92).
 Fonts: Select the **Candara** font group.

1-91 *Ion* theme selected

4. Type the following text in the placeholders on slide 1. Press **Ctrl+Enter** to move between placeholders.
 Title: Creating Beautiful Outdoor Spaces
 Subtitle: Jason Andrews, Sales Associate

5. Format the title and subtitle.
 a. Apply **bold** and **shadow** [*Home* tab, *Font* group] format to both the title and subtitle.
 b. Change the title font size to **66 pt**. and resize the title placeholder to remove extra space at the top.
 c. Change the subtitle font size to **28 pt**.

6. Add slides.
 a. Click the **New Slide** button [*Home* tab, *Slides* group] to add a new slide that automatically has the **Title and Content** layout. Type the following text for slide 2:

Title	Our Services
Bulleted items	• Garden center
	• Tree nursery
	• Gift shop
	• Delivery and installation
	• Patios and irrigation systems

1-92 *Background Styles*

b. Repeat this process to create three new slides with the following text:

Slide 3 title	Available Products
Bulleted items	• Shrubs, perennials, annuals
	• Soils and mulches
	• Garden décor including fountains
	• Shade trees and evergreen screening trees
	• Flowering or ornamental trees
	• Trees and plants for Christmas
Slide 4 title	Why Sustainable Design?
Bulleted items	• Energy efficiency increased
	• Water efficiency increased
	• Dependency on chemicals decreased
	• Vigor assured through native and hardy plants
Slide 5 title	We Make It Easy
Bulleted items	• We can do the entire project or we can assist
	• You can do as much, or as little, as you like
	• We will provide:
	• Landscape design planning or just advice
	• Soil testing
	• Low-cost delivery
	• Fountain set up

c. Click the **New Slide** drop-down arrow [*Home* tab, *Slides* group] and click the **Title Slide** layout. Type this text in the placeholders:

Title	Call for a Consultation
Subtitle	615-792-8833

d. Increase the font size for the subtitle phone number to **32 pt**.

7. Move the slide 5 thumbnail before slide 4.

8. Apply **bold** and use the *Format Painter*.
 a. Display slide 2, select the title text, and apply **bold** [*Home* tab, *Font* group].
 b. Double-click the **Format Painter** button [*Home* tab, *Clipboard* group] so you can apply this change more than one time.
 c. Press **Page Down** and click the title text on slide 3 to apply the same change.
 d. Repeat for slides 4 and 5.
 e. Click the **Format Painter** button or press **Esc** to stop applying formatting.

9. Create a footer with the company name in the footer text.
 a. Click the **Header & Footer** button [*Insert* tab, *Text* group] to open the *Header and Footer* dialog box.
 b. On the *Slide* tab, check the following options: **Date and time** with **Update automatically**, **Slide number**, and **Footer** (Figure 1-93).

1-93 *Header and Footer dialog box*

c. In the *Footer* text box, type Classic
 Gardens and Landscaping.
d. Select **Don't show on title slide**.
e. Click the **Apply to All** button.

10. Click the **Spelling** button [*Review* tab,
 Proofing group] and correct any spelling
 errors you find.

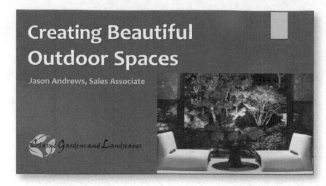

1-94 Completed title slide

11. Format the title slide so it is more distinctive.
 a. Display slide 1.
 b. Select the subtitle and click the **Change
 Case** button [*Home* tab, *Font* group].
 Select **Capitalize Each Word**.
 c. Resize the title and subtitle placeholders to fit the text.
 d. Click the **Insert** tab, and then click the **Pictures** button to open the *Insert Pictures* dialog box.
 e. Locate your student data files.
 f. Select **GardenView-01** and **CGL Logo-01**. Click **Insert**.
 g. Resize the logo *Width* to **5.5"** [*Picture Tools Format* tab, *Size* group] and the *Height* will
 automatically adjust.
 h. Align the text and pictures as shown in Figure 1-94.

12. Save and close the presentation (Figure 1-95).

1-95 PowerPoint 1-1 completed

Guided Project 1-2

Solution Seekers, Inc., a management consulting firm, is preparing a series of brief presentations to be
used in a training program for new hires. For this project, you develop a presentation about how to get
better results when writing email messages.
[Student Learning Outcomes 1.1, 1.2, 1.3, 1.6, 1.7, 1.8, 1.9]

Files Needed: ***EmailResults-01.pptx**, **EmailContent-01.pptx***, and ***AtSymbol-01.jpg*** (Student data files are
available in the Library of your SIMnet account.)
Completed Project File Name: ***[your initials] PowerPoint 1-2.pptx***

Skills Covered in This Project

- Open a presentation.
- Change bullets.
- Reuse slides from another presentation.
- Rearrange slides.
- Check spelling.
- Adjust placeholder position.
- Insert a picture.
- Apply transitions.
- Preview a presentation.
- Change presentation properties.
- Print a handout.
- Save a presentation.

1. Open and resave a presentation.
 a. Click the **File** tab, select **Open**, and click **Browse**.
 b. Locate your student data files and double-click **EmailResults-01** to open the presentation.
 c. Press **F12** to open the *Save As* dialog box and save this presentation as [your initials] PowerPoint 1-2 in the appropriate location.

2. Change the bullets for additional emphasis.
 a. Display slide 2 and select the bulleted text.
 b. Click the **Bullets** drop-down arrow [*Home* tab, *Paragraph* group].
 c. Select **Bullets and Numbering**.
 d. Click the **Color** button and select **Orange, Accent 6** (Figure 1-96).
 e. Change the size to **90%** of text.
 f. Click the **Customize** button to open the *Symbol* dialog box.
 g. Change the *Subset* to **Geometric Shapes** (Figure 1-97). Select the **Black Right-Pointing Pointer** (Character code 25BA)
 - If the font **Wingdings 3** is available, select a similar symbol (Character code 117).
 h. Click **OK** to close the *Symbol* dialog box. Click **OK** again to close the *Bullets and Numbering* dialog box.

1-96 Change bullet color

3. Reuse slides from another presentation.
 a. Display slide 2. Click the **New Slide** drop-down arrow and select **Reuse Slides**.
 b. Click **Browse** on the *Reuse Slides* pane and then select **Browse file**. Locate your student data files.
 c. Select the presentation **EmailContent-01** and click **Open**. (This presentation has spelling errors that you will correct later.)
 d. Click all four slides on the *Reuse* Slides pane to insert them (Figure 1-98).
 e. Close the *Reuse Slides* pane.

1-97 Change bullet symbol

4. Use the *Slides* pane to rearrange the six slides in this order: "Getting Results with Email," "Ask These Questions," "Why?," "Write a Meaningful Subject Line," "Organize It!," and "Keep It Short."

5. Click the **Spelling** button [*Review* tab, *Proofing* group] and correct all of the spelling errors: receive, Careless, organized, capture, response, and separate. The spelling of Email on slide 1 is correct and can be ignored.

6. Use the *Format Painter* to change bullets.
 a. Display slide 2 and select the body placeholder with the bulleted text.
 b. Double-click the **Format Painter** button [*Home* tab, *Clipboard* group] so you can apply what you have copied more than one time.
 c. Press **Page Down** and click the list on slide 3 to apply the change for the first-level bullets.
 d. Repeat for slides 4 and 5.
 e. Press **Esc** to end formatting.

7. Change and position text.
 a. Display slide 6 and delete the picture on the right.
 b. Select the subtitle text, "Keep It Meaningful," and resize the placeholder to fit the text.
 c. Select the title text, "Keep It Short," change the font size to **24 pt**., and resize the placeholder to fit the text.
 d. Position the title text above the subtitle text on the orange shape at the right. Change the font color to **Black, Text 1**.
 e. Select both placeholders and click **Arrange** [*Home* tab, *Drawing* group], select **Align**, and select **Align Right** (Figure 1-99).

1-98 *Reuse Slides* pane

8. Insert and align a picture.
 a. Click the **Insert** tab, and then click the **Pictures** button.
 b. Locate your student data files.
 c. Select **AtSymbol-01** and click **Insert**.
 d. Click **Align** [*Picture Tools Format* tab, *Arrange* group] and select **Align Left**.

9. Apply one transition and effect option to all slides.
 a. Click the **Transitions** tab.
 b. Click the **Switch** transition from the gallery.
 c. Click **Effect Options** [*Transition to This Slide* group] and select **Left**.
 d. Click **Apply To All** [*Timing* group].

1-99 *Completed ending slide*

10. Preview the presentation.
 a. Click the **Slide Sorter** button [*Status* bar].
 b. Press **Ctrl+A** to select all slides. Click **Preview** [*Transitions* tab] to examine the movements in *Slide Sorter* view.
 c. Click the first slide and click the **Slide Show** button [*Status* bar]. Advance through the slides to see the movements in *Slide Show* view.

11. Change presentation properties.
 a. Click the **File** tab to open *Backstage* view, and then click **Info**.
 b. Click the **Properties** button and select **Advanced Properties**. Click the **Summary** tab and type this information as needed in the respective fields:

Title:	Getting Results with Email
Subject:	Writing
Author:	Your Name (unless it already appears)
Comments:	This presentation is for the new hire seminar.

 c. Click **OK** to close the *Properties* dialog box.

12. Print slides as a handout.
 a. Click the **Print** button on the left of the *Backstage* view.
 b. Select the appropriate printer.
 c. Change the following *Settings* by clicking the button list arrow for each option:

Which Slides to Print:	**Print All Slides**
What to Print:	**Handouts, 6 Slides Horizontal, Frame Slides, Scale to Fit Paper**
Print Order:	**Collated**
Orientation:	**Portrait**
Color Range:	**Grayscale** (or **Color** if you prefer)

 d. Click the **Print** button at the top of the *Backstage* view.

13. Save and close the presentation (Figure 1-100).

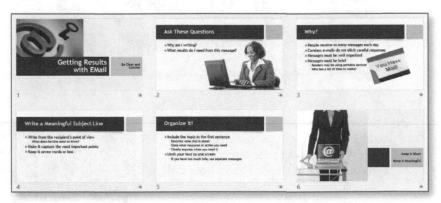

1-100 PowerPoint 1-2 completed

Guided Project 1-3

At Placer Hills Real Estate, realtors are always thinking of ways to help sellers make their homes more marketable and help buyers find the right home. For this project, you prepare a presentation for realtors to use when they speak with individual clients to explain how sellers can provide an added-value benefit by offering a home warranty.
[**Student Learning Outcomes 1.1, 1.2, 1.5, 1.6, 1.7, 1.9**]

Files Needed: *PHRELogo-01.png* and *BuyerIncentive-01.pptx* (*Student data files are available in the Library of your SIMnet account.*)
Completed Project File Name: *[your initials] PowerPoint 1-3.pptx*

Skills Covered in This Project

- Create a new presentation using an online template.
- Change font size.
- Adjust picture position.
- Insert a picture.
- Reuse slides from another presentation.
- Check spelling.
- Insert a footer.
- Apply transitions.
- Change presentation properties.
- Save a presentation.

1. Create a new presentation using an online template.
 a. Click the **File** tab, and then click **New**.
 b. Type the word marketing in the search box and click the **Start Searching** button or press **Enter**.

c. Select the **Business sales strategy proposal presentation** (Figure 1-101) and click **Create** to download the presentation. (If you are unable to download the file, it is available as the presentation **BusinessSalesStrategy-01** in your student data files.)

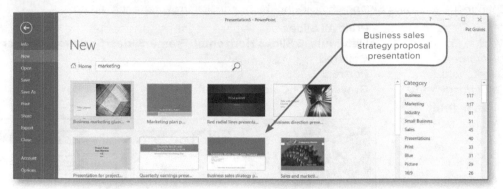

1-101 Online marketing themes and templates

d. Remove the presentation content. Select slide 1 in the *Thumbnail* pane, press **Ctrl+A** to select all slides, and press **Delete**. The slides are deleted from the presentation.

2. Click the **New Slide** button [*Home* tab, *Slides* group] and the slide that appears automatically has a *Title Slide* layout. Type the following text in the placeholders:
 Title: Compete with New Homes
 Subtitle: Angie O'Connor Sales Associate

3. Save the presentation as [your initials] PowerPoint 1-3 in the appropriate location.

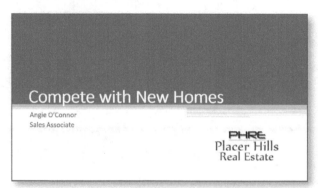

1-102 Completed title slide

4. Increase the title font size to **60 pt**. and apply **bold** [*Home* tab, *Font* group].

5. Insert the PHRE company logo.
 a. Click the **Pictures** button [*Insert* tab, *Images* group] and locate your student data files.
 b. Select **PHRELogo-01** and click **Insert** (or double-click the file name) to insert the picture.
 c. Increase the logo size (*Width* **3"** and the *Height* automatically adjusts).
 d. Position this logo in the lower right as shown in Figure 1-102.

6. Reuse slides from another presentation.
 a. Click the **New Slide** drop-down arrow and select **Reuse Slides**.
 b. Click **Browse** on the *Reuse Slides* pane. Select **Browse file** and locate your student data files.
 c. Select the presentation **BuyerIncentive-01** and click **Open**.
 d. Click slides **2–6** (starting with the "Seller Needs" slide) on the *Reuse Slides* pane to insert them (Figure 1-103).
 e. Close the *Reuse Slides* pane.

7. Click the **Spelling** button [*Review* tab, *Proofing* group] and correct the following spelling errors: Competitive, maintained, replacement, and deductible.

1-103 *Reuse Slides* pane

8. Display slide 6. Resize the picture using the center sizing handle to stretch it to the bottom of the slide.

9. Add a footer.
 a. Click the **Header & Footer** button [*Insert* tab, *Text* group].
 b. On the *Slide* tab, select **Slide number** and **Footer**.
 c. In the *Footer* text box, type Placer Hills Real Estate.
 d. Select **Don't show on title slide**.
 e. Click the **Apply to All** button. The footer appears in small text on the upper right.
 f. Delete the footer that is over the picture on slide 6.

1-104 Transition *Effect Options*

10. Apply one transition to all slides.
 a. Click the **More** button [*Transitions* tab, *Transition to This Slide* group] to open the gallery. Click the **Box** effect.
 b. Click **Effect Options** [*Transitions* tab, *Transition to This Slide* group]. Select **From Bottom** (Figure 1-104).
 c. Click **Apply To All** [*Transitions* tab, *Timing* group].
 d. Select slide 1. Click the **Slide Show** button [*Status* bar] and advance through the slides to see the movements in *Slide Show* view.

11. Change presentation properties.
 a. Click the **File** tab, then click **Info**.
 b. Click the **Properties** button and select **Advanced Properties** to open the *Properties* dialog box. Type the following information as needed in the respective fields:
 Title: Compete with New Homes
 Subject: Sales Strategies
 Author: Angie O'Connor
 Comments: Seller can offer a home warranty to encourage buyer purchase.
 c. Click the **OK** to close the *Properties* dialog box.

12. Save and close the presentation (Figure 1-105).

1-105 PowerPoint 1-3 completed

Independent Project 1-4

Wilson Home Entertainment Systems (WHES) assists customers with everything from a single television purchase to a home network installation to the design and construction of an elaborate home theater. For this project, you work on a presentation that sales representatives can use to describe the capabilities of WHES to potential customers.
[**Student Learning Outcomes 1.1, 1.2, 1.4, 1.6, 1.7, 1.9**]

Files Needed: ***SpecialEnvironment-01.pptx***, ***WHESLogo-01.png***, ***Family-01.jpg***, and ***Theater1-01.jpg*** (*Student data files are available in the* Library *of your SIMnet account.*)
Completed Project File Name: ***[your initials] PowerPoint 1-4.pptx***

689

Skills Covered in This Project

- Open a presentation.
- Add slides.
- Apply a theme.
- Change theme colors.
- Insert a picture.
- Adjust placeholders.
- Check spelling.
- Apply transitions.
- Change presentation properties.
- Save a presentation.

1. Open the presentation **SpecialEnvironment-01**.

2. Save the presentation as [your initials] PowerPoint 1-4.

3. After slide 1, insert two new slides with the *Title and Content* slide layout. Type the following text for slides 2 and 3:

 Slide 2 title: Our Residential Services
 Bulleted items:
 - Design
 - Sales
 - Installation
 - Maintenance

 Slide 3 title: Sales
 Bulleted items:
 - Authorized dealer for the highest-quality home theater technology in the industry
 - Televisions
 - Projectors
 - Blu-Ray Players
 - Cables

4. Apply a theme and change theme colors.
 a. Select the **Integral** theme and the third **Variant** (Figure 1-106).
 b. Select the **Orange Red** theme colors.

5. Insert different pictures.
 a. Display slide 1 and delete the popcorn picture.
 b. Delete the subtitle placeholder.
 c. Insert **Family-01** and **WHESLogo-01** from your student data files.
 d. Increase the family picture size (*Height* **5"** and *Width* **7.52"**) and align it on the top right (Figure 1-107).
 e. Align the logo on the bottom right.
 f. Change the title placeholder font color to **White, Background 1**, apply **bold**, increase the font size to **66 pt.**, and apply a **Shadow**.
 g. Resize the title placeholder so it word wraps as shown. Move it to the red area on the left.

6. Click the **Spelling** button and correct the following spelling errors: cabling, television, and calibration.

7. Increase the text size and insert a picture.
 a. Display slide 2. Select the bulleted text placeholder and change the font size to **40 pt**.
 b. Insert **Theater1-01** from your student data files.
 c. Increase the picture size (*Height* **5"** and *Width* **7.52"**) and align it on the bottom right.

8. Display slide 6. Increase the picture size (*Height* **2.18"** and *Width* **9"**) and center it horizontally in the space below the text.

1-106 Change variant

1-107 Completed title slide

9. Apply one transition to all slides.
 a. Select the **Cube** transition.
 b. Apply the **From Bottom** effect option.
 c. Click **Apply To All**.

10. Open the *Properties* dialog box and insert the following presentation properties as needed on the *Summary* tab:

 Title: Create Your Special Environment
 Subject: Residential Services
 Author: Liam Martin

11. Close the *Properties* dialog box.

12. Save and close the presentation (Figure 1-108).

1-108 PowerPoint 1-4 completed

Independent Project 1-5

The Advising Offices in the Sierra Pacific Community College (SPCC) District work to assist students throughout the completion of their academic programs. Because SPCC has a large population of students who are retraining themselves for different types of employment, job-related information is especially important. For this project, you prepare a presentation about writing resumes.
[**Student Learning Outcomes 1.1, 1.2, 1.3, 1.4, 1.7, 1.8**]

Files Needed: ***ResumeUpdates-01*** and ***ResumeContent-01.pptx*** *(Student data files are available in the Library of your SIMnet account.)*
Completed Project File Name: *[your initials] PowerPoint 1-5.pptx*

Skills Covered in This Project

- Open a presentation.
- Change theme background style and fonts.
- Change case.
- Adjust sizing and alignment.
- Add slides.
- Reuse slides from another presentation.
- Check spelling.
- Apply transitions.
- Print a handout.
- Save a presentation.

1. Open the **ResumeUpdates-01** presentation from your student data files.

2. Save the presentation as [your initials] PowerPoint 1-5.

3. Change theme style and font.
 a. Change the *Background Style* to **Style 4** (Figure 1-109).
 b. Change the *Theme Fonts* to **Georgia**.

4. Adjust placeholder sizing and text.
 a. Display slide 1 and select the title placeholder. Change text alignment to **Align Left**.
 b. Resize the placeholder so the text word wraps on two lines.
 c. Select the subtitle placeholder and change text alignment to **Align Left** (Figure 1-110).

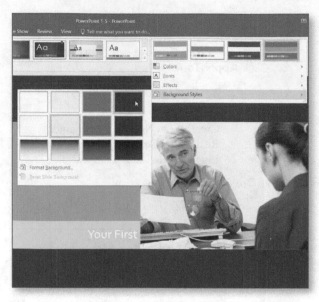

1-109 *Background Styles*

5. Insert two new slides after slide 2 with the *Title and Content* layout. Type the following text for slides 3 and 4:

Slide 3 title:	Accomplishments, Not Duties
Bulleted items:	• Include only the most impressive details about your career
	• Quantify your day-to-day tasks
	• How many times?
	• What was the result?
	• How much money was saved?
Slide 4 title:	Proofread
Bulleted items:	• Employers take spelling and grammar errors as signs of carelessness
	• Ask a trusted friend or colleague to look at your resume

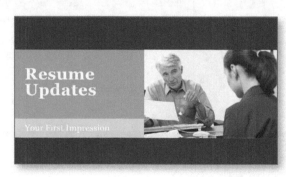

1-110 *Completed title slide*

6. Reuse slides from another presentation.
 a. Move your insertion point after slide 3.
 b. Open the *Reuse Slides* pane and browse to find **ResumeContent-01** from your student data files.
 c. Insert all three slides and close the *Reuse Slides* pane.

7. Display slide 8.
 a. Select the title placeholder and change text alignment to **Align Left**. Type Success!.
 b. Resize the title placeholder to fit the text.
 c. Delete the subtitle placeholder.

8. Correct the following spelling errors: Improve, redundant, achievements, and any other errors you find.

9. Apply the **Reveal** transition with the **Through Black from Right** effect option to all slides.

10. Print slides as an outline (Figure 1-111).

11. Save and close the presentation (Figure 1-112).

1-111 Outline

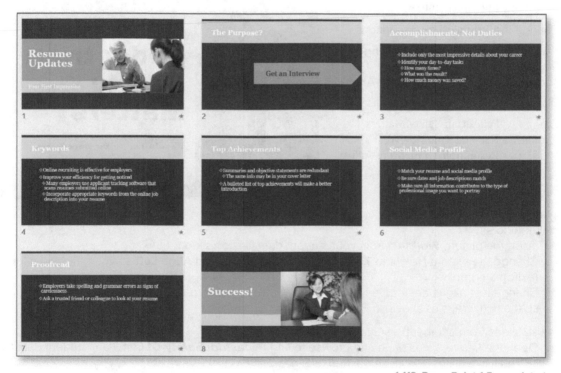

1-112 PowerPoint 1-5 completed

Independent Project 1-6

At the Hamilton Civic Center, workshops are offered to the community to address fitness, health, and wellness issues. For this project, you develop a presentation for an upcoming series about helping families become more active.

[Student Learning Outcomes 1.1, 1.2, 1.3, 1.4, 1.5, 1.6, 1.7, 1.9]

Files Needed: ***PedestrianSafety-01.pptx***, ***Walk1-01.jpg***, and ***Walk2-01.jpg*** *(Student data files are available in the* Library *of your SIMnet account.)*
Completed Project File Name: ***[your initials] PowerPoint 1-6.pptx***

Skills Covered in This Project

- Create a new presentation using a theme.
- Change theme colors and fonts.
- Change case.
- Reuse slides from another presentation.
- Check spelling.

- Rearrange slides.
- Insert a picture.
- Adjust placeholders.
- Insert a footer.
- Apply transitions.
- Add presentation properties.
- Save a presentation.

1. Create a new presentation and select the **Retrospect** theme.

2. Save the presentation as [your initials] PowerPoint 1-6.

3. Change the following theme options:

Theme Colors:	**Yellow Orange**
Background Styles:	**Style 6**
Theme Fonts:	**Arial Black-Arial**

4. Display slide 1 and type the following text:

Title:	Pedestrian Safety Matters
Subtitle:	Keeping That New Year's Resolution To Be More Active

5. Select the subtitle text and change the case to **Capitalize Each Word**.

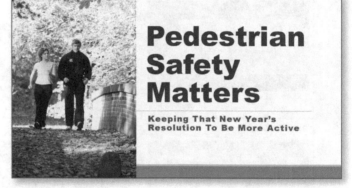

1-113 **Completed title slide**

6. Insert a picture and resize the placeholders.
 a. Insert the picture ***Walk1-01*** from your student data files on slide 1.
 b. Change the picture *Height* to **7.5"** and choose **Align Top** and **Align Left** so you have room for text on the right.
 c. Change text alignment for the title and subtitle placeholders to **Align Left**. Resize the placeholders so the text wraps as shown in Figure 1-113.

7. Reuse slides from another presentation.
 a. Open the *Reuse Slides* pane and browse to find ***PedestrianSafety-01*** from your student data files.
 b. Insert all five slides and close the *Reuse Slides* pane.

8. Display slide 2. Put your insertion point in front of the word "Guard" and press **Enter** to show this text as the last item in the list.

9. Correct the following spelling errors: pedestrians, aggressive, Remember, traffic, Regardless, and cloudy.

10. Adjust slide order to match the sequence shown in Figure 1-114.

11. Add a footer with the text Pedestrian Safety Matters. Apply it to all slides except the title slide.

12. Insert and position a picture.
 a. Display slide 6. From your student data files, insert the picture ***Walk2-01***.
 b. Change the picture *Height* to **7.5"**.
 c. Position the picture with **Align Top** and **Align Right**.

13. Apply the **Push** transition with the **From Right** effect option to all slides.

14. Preview the transitions in *Slide Show* view.

15. Open the *Properties* dialog box and insert the following presentation properties on the *Summary* tab:

Title: Pedestrian Safety Matters
Subject: Active Lifestyle
Author: Anna Lorenzo

16. Close the *Properties* dialog box.

17. Save and close the presentation (Figure 1-115).

1-114 Slide order

1-115 PowerPoint 1-6 completed

Improve It Project 1-7

For this project, you revise a presentation for Margaret Jepson, insurance agent at Central Sierra Insurance. You adjust theme colors and fonts, and add other information to the slide show, including a picture.
[**Student Learning Outcomes 1.1, 1.2, 1.3, 1.4, 1.5, 1.6, 1.7, 1.8, 1.9**]

Files Needed: ***TotaledCar-01.pptx***, ***Travel-01.jpg***, and ***CSILogo-01.png*** *(Student data files are available in the Library of your SIMnet account.)*
Completed Project File Name: ***[your initials] PowerPoint 1-7.pptx***

- Open a presentation.
- Change theme colors.
- Check spelling.
- Insert a picture.
- Adjust placeholders.
- Insert a footer.
- Apply transitions.
- Change presentation properties.
- Print a handout.
- Save a presentation.

1. Open the presentation *TotaledCar-01* from your student data files.

2. Save the presentation as [your initials] PowerPoint 1-7.

3. Change the following theme options:

Theme Colors:	**Blue Green**
Background Style:	**Style 3**
Theme Font:	**Trebuchet MS**

4. Format text and insert a picture logo.
 a. Display slide 1 and change the title font size to **66 pt**.
 b. Delete the subtitle placeholder.
 c. Insert the picture *CSILogo-01* from your student data files, change the *Width* to **5"**. Position the logo below the title on the shape across the bottom of the slide (Figure 1-116).

5. Change a layout and insert a picture.
 a. Display slide 5. Change the slide layout to **Section Header**.
 b. Type the following text on two lines in the placeholder near the top of the slide. The text is right aligned and this placeholder right aligns with the title placeholder below.

 780-886-2400
 Margaret Jepson

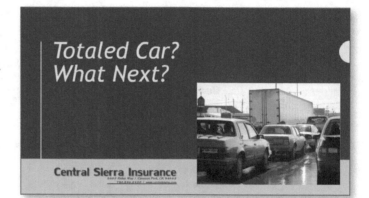

1-116 Completed title slide

 c. Insert the picture *Travel-01*, and change the *Width* to **7"**. Position it on the left as shown in Figure 1-117.

6. Add footer text and slide numbering to all slides except the title slide.

 Slide footer text: The Totaled Car

7. Add header text and page numbering.

 Handout header text: Central Sierra Insurance

8. Apply and preview transitions.
 a. Select the **Clock** transition with the **Counterclockwise** effect option.
 b. Apply this transition to all slides.
 c. Preview the transitions.

9. Open the *Properties* dialog box and insert the following presentation properties as needed on the *Summary* tab.

Title:	Totaled Car? What Next?
Subject:	Accident Insurance
Author:	Margaret Jepson

10. Print a handout with the following options: **6 Slides Horizontal**, **Frame Slides**, and **Scale to Fit Paper** (Figure 1-117).

11. Save and close the presentation.

1-117 PowerPoint 1-7 completed, printed as a handout

Challenge Project 1-8

For this project, tell the story of your favorite vacation. Create six slides that introduce the topic and describe your main points with bulleted lists. Insert photographs to illustrate locations and resize them to fit with related text.
[Student Learning Outcomes 1.1, 1.2, 1.4, 1.5, 1.6, 1.7, 1.8, 1.9]

File Needed: None
Completed Project File Name: *[your initials] PowerPoint 1-8.pptx*

Create a new presentation and save it as [your initials] PowerPoint 1-8. Modify your presentation according to the following guidelines:

- Search for an online theme that is appropriate for your topic. Apply it to your presentation.
- Use different slide layouts for variety.
- Insert three or more pictures.
- Add a footer.
- Apply transitions.
- Check spelling and include presentation properties.
- Print a handout.

Challenge Project 1-9

Think about different jobs for which you are qualified. On the Internet, research four different jobs and identify several characteristics and requirements for each job. Many online resources provide job-related information, such as www.careerbuilder.com or the *Occupational Outlook Handbook* at www.bls.gov/ooh/. **[Student Learning Outcomes 1.1, 1.2, 1.3, 1.4, 1.5, 1.6, 1.7, 1.8, 1.9]**

File Needed: None
Completed Project File Name: ***[your initials] PowerPoint 1-9.pptx***

Create a new presentation and save it as [your initials] PowerPoint 1-9. Modify your presentation according to the following guidelines:

- Select an appropriate theme and use the *Design* tab to change colors and fonts as needed for your topic.
- Create a distinctive title slide.
- Write bulleted lists describing the characteristics and requirements of each different job with no more than six lines of bulleted text on each slide.
- Apply transitions.
- Check spelling and include presentation properties.
- Print handouts with six slides on a page.

Challenge Project 1-10

For this project, develop a presentation about how a presenter can manage nervous tendencies when presenting in front of an audience. Include information from your own experiences and refer to online resources, such as www.presentationmagazine.com. **[Student Learning Outcomes 1.1, 1.2, 1.3, 1.4, 1.5, 1.6, 1.7, 1.8, 1.9]**

File Needed: None
Completed Project File Name: ***[your initials] PowerPoint 1-10.pptx***

Create a new presentation and save it as [your initials] PowerPoint 1-10. Modify your presentation according to the following guidelines:

- Select an appropriate theme and use the *Design* tab to change colors and fonts as needed for your topic.
- Create a distinctive title slide.
- Write bulleted lists describing typical causes of nervousness and suggest ways to control nervousness when presenting.
- Insert pictures to illustrate concepts.
- Apply transitions.
- Check spelling and include presentation properties.
- Print an outline of the presentation.

Illustrating with Pictures and Information Graphics

CHAPTER OVERVIEW

In our world today, we are surrounded by information graphics. We see them in television programming, web sites, and published material of all kinds. We interpret signage that helps us get from place to place and readily recognize many iconic images that help us with everyday tasks. These graphics communicate visually and can be more effective than long passages of text.

PowerPoint gives you the ability to create information graphics—to visually display information in ways that help an audience quickly grasp the concepts you are presenting. You can choose from many options, such as adding shapes or color for emphasis, pictures to illustrate, diagrams to show processes, and charts to show data relationships.

STUDENT LEARNING OUTCOMES (SLOs)

After completing this chapter, you will be able to:

SLO 2.1 Work with shapes, select theme colors and standard colors, and apply styles (p. 701).

SLO 2.2 Create interesting and eye-catching text effects with *WordArt* styles and text effects (p. 710).

SLO 2.3 Search for pictures and illustrations, modify picture appearance, and compress picture file size (p. 712).

SLO 2.4 Organize information in a grid format using tables and customize the arrangement of columns and rows (p. 721).

SLO 2.5 Format portions of a table by applying styles, colors, and effects (p. 726).

SLO 2.6 Show processes and relationships with *SmartArt* graphics (p. 731).

SLO 2.7 Improve the appearance of *SmartArt* graphics by applying styles, colors, and effects (p. 734).

SLO 2.8 Create charts that show relationships between data values and emphasize data in different ways based on the chart type and chart elements (p. 738).

SLO 2.9 Format a chart by applying preset styles or manually customizing individual chart elements (p. 743).

CASE STUDY

Classic Gardens and Landscapes (CGL) is a landscape design company that creates beautiful and low-maintenance landscapes for outdoor living spaces. Frank and Sandra Hunter recently bought a new home from a builder. It has minimal landscaping, so they contacted Gerod Sunderland, a landscape designer for CGL, to discuss improvements.

Gerod visited the property and designed plans with several options for trees, shrubs, and plants. You have been asked to prepare a

presentation illustrating his key points for his meeting with the Hunters.

Pause & Practice 2-1: Add visual interest with picture enhancements and creative text designs.

Pause & Practice 2-2: Prepare a table.

Pause & Practice 2-3: Create an organization chart and convert text to a *SmartArt* graphic.

Pause & Practice 2-4: Create column and pie charts with an enhanced appearance.

SLO 2.1

Working with Shapes, Colors, and Styles

Shapes can emphasize key points. For example, an arrow can point to an object, or a line can connect two related objects. You can draw a variety of shapes using drawing tools from PowerPoint's **Shapes** gallery; each shape has both an outline and fill color. The **Shape Styles** galleries make it easy to apply preset colors and shape effects or you can customize shape effects as you illustrate your slides.

Shapes and Text Boxes

The *Shapes* gallery (Figure 2-1) is on the *Home* tab [*Drawing* group], the *Insert* tab [*Illustrations* group], and the *Drawing Tools Format* tab [*Insert Shapes* group]. Shapes are grouped in the following categories:

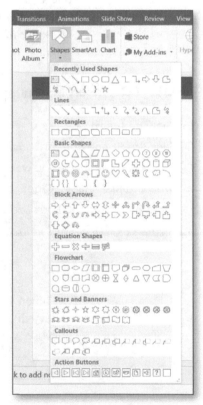

- *Recently Used Shapes*
- *Lines*
- *Rectangles*
- *Basic Shapes*
- *Block Arrows*
- *Equation Shapes*
- *Flowchart*
- *Stars and Banners*
- *Callouts*
- *Action Buttons*

To insert a shape, select the shape you want from the *Shapes* gallery and use the following features to draw and adjust your shape:

- *Crosshair:* A large plus sign used to draw the shape
- *Sizing handles:* White circles on the corners and sides of the shapes used to change shape size
- *Rotation handle:* A circular arrow on the top used to make shapes angle
- *Adjustment handle:* Yellow circles used to change curves or points

2-1 *Shapes gallery*

 You can add text to shapes and format the text as you do text in a placeholder or in a text box. However, the text in shapes or in text boxes does not appear in *Outline* view.

▶ HOW TO: Insert a Shape

1. Click the **Insert** tab.
2. Click the **Shapes** button [*Illustrations* group] to display the *Shapes* gallery.
3. Select the shape you want and your pointer becomes a crosshair (Figure 2-2).
4. Click and drag to draw the shape in the approximate size you need (Figure 2-3). The shape appears with sizing handles and a rotation handle. It may have adjustment handles.
5. Click and drag an adjustment handle to change areas within a shape such as the tip of an arrow or star, the corners of a rounded rectangle, or the line used with a callout.
6. Add text, if needed, by typing in the selected shape as you would type in a placeholder.
7. Resize the shape if necessary and move it to the appropriate position on the slide.

Crosshair

2-2 Crosshair drawing a shape

Rotation handle
Adjustment handle
Sizing handle

2-3 Shape with handles

When you need more than one of the same shape, you can efficiently draw them using *Lock Drawing Mode*.

▶ MORE INFO

Press the **Shift** key while you drag to constrain shapes. The oval becomes round, the rectangle becomes square, and lines are straight.

▶ HOW TO: Insert Multiple Shapes

1. Click the **Insert** tab.
2. Click the **Shapes** button [*Illustrations* group] to display the *Shapes* gallery.
3. Right-click the shape you want, and click **Lock Drawing Mode** (Figure 2-4).
4. Draw the first shape. Repeat to draw more of the same shape.
5. Press **Esc** to turn off *Lock Drawing Mode* when you are finished.

2-4 *Lock Drawing Mode*

When you select an existing shape, the *Drawing Tools Format* tab opens and the *Shapes* gallery displays on the left in the *Insert Shapes* group. If the existing shape does not fit your purpose, you can easily change the shape.

▶ HOW TO: Change a Shape

1. Select the shape to be changed.
2. Click the **Edit Shape** drop-down arrow [*Drawing Tools Format* tab, *Insert Shapes* group] (Figure 2-5).

2-5 *Change Shape*

3. Select **Change Shape** and click a different shape from the *Shapes* gallery.
4. Click a blank area of the slide to deselect the shape.
5. Click **Undo** to return to your original shape.

Using ***text boxes***, you can add text anywhere on a slide without using placeholders. For example, you can add notations to identify slide objects or insert brief phrases you want to emphasize. Text boxes can be sized and moved around like any other shape.

▶ HOW TO: Insert a Text Box

1. Click the **Insert** tab.
2. Click the **Text Box** button [*Text* group] and your pointer changes to an insertion point. Create a text box using one of the following methods:
 - Click the slide background to place your insertion point where you want the text to appear. Begin typing and the text box expands as you enter text. The *Home* tab opens.
 - Click and drag to change the pointer to a crosshair and draw a text box (Figure 2-6) in the approximate width you need. The *Home* tab opens. The text box height adjusts as you type text.
3. Resize if necessary by dragging sizing handles or entering *Height* and *Width* sizes [*Drawing Tools Format* tab, *Size* group] (Figure 2-7).
4. Click and drag the text box to move it to an appropriate position on the slide.

2-6 Draw a text box

2-7 Size measurements

Style Galleries and Effect Options

Different *Style* galleries provide collections of preset effects for shapes, pictures, or other objects. You can customize all effects using the related button such as ***Shape Effects, Picture Effects***, or ***Text Effects*** to access drop-down galleries. You can choose from *Shadow, Reflection, Glow, Soft Edges, Bevel, 3D Rotation,* or *Transform*. These options are described in the following table. You can also apply one or more effects without first using styles from a gallery.

Effect Options

Effect	Options
Shadow	**Shadow** effects appear in three groupings. An **Outer** shadow shows behind an object from different directions. An **Inner** shadow makes part of the object looked raised. A **Perspective** shadow shows below so the object appears to float.
Reflection	A **Reflection** shows a mirror image below an object, like a reflection on a shiny surface or on water. You can control how close the reflection is to the object.
Glow	**Glow** provides a colored area around an object that fades into the background color on your slide. Glow colors by default are based on the current theme colors, but you can use other colors. The size of the *Glow* is measured in points.

Continued

Effect	Options
Soft Edges	Shapes and other objects have either straight edges or well-defined curves. **Soft Edges** creates a feathered edge that gradually blends into the background color. The size of the blending area is measured in points from the edge of the object inward. The larger the point size, the less you see of the object.
Bevel	**Bevel** effects add light and dark areas to create a dimensional appearance. Objects or text can look raised or inset.
3D Rotation	**3D Rotation** effects include **Parallel**, **Perspective**, and **Oblique** options that create an illusion of depth by rotating an object from front to back.
Transform	**Transform** is a *Text Effect* used to change the shape of words. It is not available for shapes or pictures.

The width of your PowerPoint window affects how galleries are displayed on the various tabs. If you have a narrow PowerPoint window, you need to click a **Quick Style** button to open a gallery. If your window is wide, part of a gallery displays, and you click the **More** button to open the complete gallery.

Adjust Outline Weight and Style

Emphasize a shape outline by making it wider with a contrasting color; deemphasize a shape outline by making it thinner. You can choose to show no outline or match its color to the shape to make the outline disappear. Many of the options for shape outlines also apply to lines (straight or curved) that you draw.

Select a shape or line and click the **Shape Outline** button [*Drawing Tools Format* tab, *Shape Styles* group]. Click one of the following options to choose from additional variations in a drop-down list (Figure 2-8):

- **Weight:** Displays line thickness measured in points
- **Dashes:** Displays lines made with various combinations of dots and dashes (Figure 2-9)
- **Arrows:** Displays arrowheads or other shapes for both ends of a line

2-8 Shape Outline Weight

At the bottom of these three drop-down lists, select **More Lines** to open the *Format Shape* pane (Figure 2-10) where you can customize the following *Line* options:

- **Color:** Provides color choices
- **Transparency:** Adjusts transparency percentages
- **Width:** Controls the thickness of lines measured in points
- **Compound type:** Provides outlines with two or more lines in different thicknesses
- **Dash type:** Displays lines made with various combinations of dots and dashes

2-9 Shape Outline Dashes

2-10 Format Shape pane

- **Cap type:** Controls the look (*Square*, *Round*, or *Flat*) of the ends of lines; it is usually applied to single lines or arrows
- **Join type:** Controls the look (*Round*, *Bevel*, *Miter*) for the connection point where two lines meet (for example, at the corner of a rectangle or square)
- **Begin and End Arrow type:** Controls the shape for both ends of an arrow
- **Begin and End Arrow size:** Controls the size of the shape at both ends of an arrow

The *Format Shape* pane is a convenient place to change many options. Figure 2-10 shows the *Fill & Line* tab with *Line* options displayed because a line was selected when the pane opened. Different options appear if you have a shape selected or if you choose a *Gradient* line. Above *Line* you can select *Fill* to change shape colors. You can click the arrow in front of these options to expand or collapse each list.

Additional tabs under *Shape Options* on the *Format Shape* pane include *Effects* and *Size & Properties* with related options on each tab. Click the icons at the top of the pane to select different tabs.

> **ANOTHER WAY**
>
> Right-click a shape and then select **Format Shape** from the context menu to open the *Format Shape* pane.

Themes and Standard Colors

As you learned in Chapter 1, each PowerPoint *Theme* starts with a set of *Theme Colors* that provide background and accent colors. When you apply *Theme Colors* for shapes and text, these colors automatically change when you select a different set of *Theme Colors*.

Consider all of the colors used throughout your presentation when you select colors because some are more appropriate than others. This section explains how colors are arranged in PowerPoint and describes different ways to "mix" custom colors. The same techniques for choosing colors apply to color fills or outline colors.

Change Solid and Gradient Fill Colors

To change the color of a selected shape, click the **Shape Fill** button [*Drawing Tools Format* tab, *Shape Styles* group] to open the **Theme Colors** gallery (Figure 2-11). Notice the colors arranged in the first row. The first four colors represent background and text colors; however, you can use these colors for other slide objects as well. The remaining six colors represent accent colors. These colors appear when viewing gallery styles and some effect options such as *Glow*. Beneath each color on the first row is a column of lighter and darker shades (shown as percentages) of that color. When you point to any color, a *ScreenTip* shows its name.

Below the *Theme Colors* is a single row of **Standard Colors** arranged in the order of a rainbow. When standard colors are used, they remain in effect even if *Theme Colors* change.

2-11 *Theme Colors* gallery

Gradient colors blend two or more colors together. Using the *Format Shape* pane, you can select from preset colors or customize your own gradient color by changing the colors and how they blend.

▶ **HOW TO:** Change Gradient Colors Using the Format Shape Pane

1. Select a shape and click the **Shape Fill** button [*Drawing Tools Format* tab, *Shape Styles* group].

2. Select **Gradient** to select from a gallery of light and dark variations of the current fill color that blend the colors in different directions (Figure 2-12).

3. Click **More Gradients** at the bottom of the gallery to open the *Format Shape* pane to customize the colors.

4. Choose **Gradient fill** and make selections under *Fill* options from the following:

 • *Preset gradients:* Theme color variations (Figure 2-13)
 • *Type: Linear, Radial, Rectangular,* or *Path*
 • *Direction:* Options change based on the selected *Type*.
 • *Angle:* The percentage changes with each *Type* and *Direction*.
 • *Gradient stops:* Shapes on the gradient bar that you can move to control where colors change (Figure 2-14)

5. Select a *Gradient stop* and change its settings to control color blending:

 • *Delete a stop:* Click the **Remove Gradient Stop** button or drag the stop down to remove it from the gradient bar.
 • *Add a stop:* Click the **Add Gradient Stop** button or click the gradient bar where you want the stop to appear.
 • *Color:* Select the stop, and then change the color.
 • *Position:* Enter a different percentage or drag the stop on the gradient bar to change its position.
 • *Transparency:* Click the arrows to change the percentage. When *Transparency* is 0%, the color is opaque (solid). As the percentage increases, the color becomes increasingly transparent and more of the background color shows through.
 • *Brightness:* Click the arrows to change the percentage. As the percentage decreases from 100%, the color softens.

2-12 Gradient color variations for the selected color

2-13 Preset gradients based on theme colors

2-14 Gradient stops

6. Check **Rotate with shape** to maintain the color settings when a shape or text is rotated so it angles on the slide.

7. Select **No line** or **Solid line** under *Line* options to control whether or not an outline shows around a shape or text.

8. Click the **X** at the top of the pane to close the *Format Shape* pane.

Select Custom Colors

The *Colors* dialog box provides many solid color options on two tabs so you can either pick from displayed colors or mix a custom color. The new color appears in the lower right corner so you can compare it to the original color. Custom colors are not affected by any changes made to theme colors.

> **HOW TO: Use the Standard Tab to Select a Color**

1. Select a shape and click the **Shape Fill** button [*Home* tab, *Drawing* group or *Drawing Tools Format* tab, *Shape Styles* group].
2. Click **More Fill Colors** to open the *Colors* dialog box.
 - Select the *Standard* tab (Figure 2-15).
 - Colors are arranged in a honeycomb shape with colors blending from white to black below.
3. Click a color to apply it and notice the *New* color that appears on the right above the *Current* color.
4. Adjust the *Transparency* as needed.
5. Click **OK** to apply the new color.

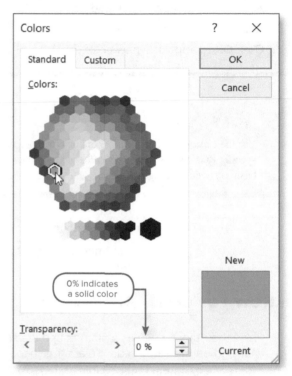

2-15 *Standard* tab in *Colors* dialog box

When you need more precision in selecting a color, use the *Custom* tab on the *Colors* dialog box. Colors are arranged like a rainbow, and you drag a crosshair to select a different color. You drag the crosshair up or down to change the color intensity and then move a slider to adjust how light or dark the color appears. Color model information is shown on the *Custom* tab also. The ***RGB model*** is typically used for computer displays and colors are formed by blending values of the three numbers for *Red*, *Green*, and *Blue*. Highly saturated colors at the top have higher number values (255 maximum). You can use these numbers to match colors in different shapes and in different presentations.

> **HOW TO: Use the Custom Tab to Mix a Color**

1. Select a shape and click the **Shape Fill** button [*Home* tab, *Drawing* group or *Drawing Tools Format* tab, *Shape Styles* group].
2. Click **More Fill Colors** to open the *Colors* dialog box.

3. Click the *Custom* tab (Figure 2-16) and a crosshair is positioned for the *Current* color.

- Drag the crosshair horizontally to select a different color. Notice the new color that appears on the right above the *Current* color.
- When the crosshair is at the top, colors are highly **saturated** (intense and vibrant).
- As you move the crosshair down, colors become less saturated (duller and less intense).

4. Drag the slider on the right to adjust the **luminosity** (lightness or brightness).

- Drag up to add white and increase the luminosity.
- Drag down to add black and decrease the luminosity.

5. Adjust the *Transparency* as needed.

6. Click **OK** to apply the new color.

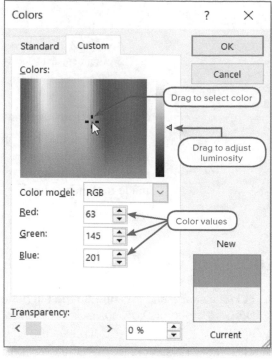

2-16 *Custom* tab in *Colors* dialog box

> **MORE INFO**
>
> Use the *Custom* tab in the *Colors* dialog box if you need to enter specific RGB values to match a color such as a color used for a business or college logo.

Use the Eyedropper for Color Matching

You can match the exact color of an object in PowerPoint with the **Eyedropper** and apply it to a shape.

> **HOW TO:** Use the Eyedropper

1. Place the object, such as a picture, and the shape to be changed on the same slide. Select the shape.

2. Click the **Shape Fill** button [*Home* tab, *Drawing* group or *Drawing Tools Format* tab, *Shape Styles* group] and select **Eyedropper**.

3. Move your pointer (now an Eyedropper) around in the picture and a live preview of each color appears. Pause to see a *ScreenTip* showing the *RGB* (Red Green Blue) values (Figure 2-17).

4. Click to select a color and it is applied to your selected shape.

Or

5. Press **Esc** to cancel the *Eyedropper* without selecting a color.

2-17 *Eyedropper* live preview and *RGB* colors

To match a color anywhere on your computer screen, left-click and hold as you drag the Eyedropper to other areas of the screen outside of PowerPoint.

Apply Picture, Texture, or Pattern Fills

You can fill shapes with more than colors. The following options are available by clicking the **Shape Fill** button [*Drawing Tools Format* tab, *Shape Styles* group] or from the *Format Shape* pane. With *WordArt*, the *Text Fill* button [*Drawing Tools Format* tab, *WordArt Styles* group] is used.

- *Picture fill:* Fills the shape with a picture from a file or from an online search
- *Texture fill:* Applies an image such as woven fabric or wood
- *Pattern fill:* Applies a mixture of two colors in various dotted or crosshatch designs

▶ HOW TO: Apply Picture, Texture, or Pattern Fills

1. Select a shape and click the **Shape Fill** button [*Home* tab, *Drawing* group or *Drawing Tools Format* tab, *Shape Styles* group].

2. From the drop-down list, select **Picture** to open the *Insert Pictures* dialog box. Browse or search for a picture and click **Insert**. The picture fills the shape.

Or

3. From the drop-down list, select **Texture** to open the gallery (Figure 2-18). Click a texture to fill the shape or click **More Textures** to open the *Format Shape* pane.

 - Select **Picture or texture fill** and then click the **File** button or the **Online** button to search for textures that are saved as a picture.

Or

4. Select a shape and right-click. Select **Format Shape** from the callout menu to open the *Format Shape* pane.

 - Click **Fill**, if necessary, to display *Fill* options.
 - Select **Pattern fill** (Figure 2-19).
 - Click a pattern to fill the shape.
 - Change *Foreground* and *Background* colors as needed.
 - Click other patterns to see how different these colors look in different patterns.

5. Close the *Format Shape* pane.

2-18 *Texture* fills

2-19 *Pattern* fills on the *Format Shape* pane

Applying WordArt Styles and Text Effects

You can apply interesting *text effects* for many purposes. For example, you can make slide titles more attractive and easier to read, or you can provide a bold focal point on a slide. One way is to start by inserting *WordArt*.

▶ HOW TO: Apply WordArt Styles

1. Click the **WordArt** button [*Insert* tab, *Text* group] to open the *WordArt Styles* gallery (Figure 2-20).

 - The gallery has preset text effects showing a variety of solid, gradient, and pattern fill colors.

2. Click to select a *WordArt* style.

 - A text box displays on your slide with sample text that you edit to create a *WordArt* object (Figure 2-21).

3. Use the *Font* group [*Home* tab] to apply the following character formatting:

 - Select a different font or attribute such as bold or italic.
 - Change the font size by entering a point size or using the **Increase Font Size** and **Decrease Font Size** buttons.
 - Click the **Character Spacing** button to control the distance between letters. You can expand or condense the spacing.

2-20 *WordArt Styles* gallery

2-21 *WordArt* as it first appears

▶ MORE INFO

When using text in a large size, *Tight* character spacing conserves space yet keeps the text easy to read.

You can also start with text in a placeholder or text box and then apply text effects. With either method, you use commands on the *WordArt Styles* group [*Drawing Tools Format* tab] (Figure 2-22) to customize your text. These commands—*Text Fill, Text Outline, and Text Effects*—are similar to the *Shape* commands.

2-22 *WordArt Styles* group

▶ HOW TO: Apply Text Effects to Existing Text

1. Select a *WordArt* object or text in a placeholder or text box.

 - Click the **More** button [*Drawing Tools Format* tab, *WordArt Styles* group] to open the *Styles* gallery.
 - Point to a style to see a live preview applied to your text (Figure 2-23).
 - Click a style to apply it.

2. Use the *WordArt Styles* group [*Drawing Tools Format* tab] to change colors and add special effects:

- Click the **Text Fill** button to select **Theme** or other color options.
- Click the **Text Outline** button to select **Theme** or other color options as well as line weight and style.
- Click the **Text Effects** button and select from *Shadow, Reflection, Glow, Bevel, 3D Rotation,* or *Transform* effects and then choose the option you prefer.

Or

3. Select a *WordArt* object or text box and right-click to open the context menu. Click **Format Shape** to open the *Format Shape* pane.

- Select **Shape Options** to change *Fill* or *Line* options.
- Select **Text Options** to change *Text Fill* or *Text Outline* options.

2-23 *WordArt* object with a style applied

> **MORE INFO**
>
> If the *WordArt Styles* gallery is not open on your *Drawing Tools Format* tab, click the **Quick Styles** button.

Changing the text outline color and increasing line weight emphasizes the outline just as it does on shapes. Different line styles can create interesting effects. Using pictures or patterns as fill colors can add a creative touch when text is shown in a large size. A variety of different colors and effects are shown in Figure 2-24.

2-24 Sample fill and line effects

> **ANOTHER WAY**
>
> Select the text in a *WordArt* object and right-click. Click **Format Text Effects** from the context menu to open the *Format Shape* pane with *Text Options* listed.

Transform effects are unique to text and are used to warp a word or phrase to different shapes or to follow a path. For example, text can angle, flow in a circle, and arc up or down. As you point to different *Transform* effects, a live preview shows how your text will look in that shape. Once a *Transform* effect has been applied, text size is not limited to the font size because you can drag the *WordArt* sizing handles. *Transform* effects also provide one or more yellow adjustment handles that control the slant of letters or the curve of text.

2-25 *Transform Fade Up* effect applied

▶ HOW TO: Apply a Transform Effect

1. Select a *WordArt* object.
2. Click the **Text Effects** button [*Format* tab, *WordArt Styles* group].
3. Select **Transform** from the drop-down list (Figure 2-25) to open the *Transform* gallery.
4. Point to an effect to see a live preview applied to your text.
5. Click an effect to apply it.
6. Adjust as needed using sizing and adjustment handles.

SLO 2.3

Working with Pictures

In Chapter 1, you learned how to insert pictures from files, change their size, and align them on the slide. In this section, you use a variety of photo editing techniques to enhance a picture's appearance. You will also use PowerPoint's search capabilities to find images to help illustrate presentation concepts and consider various licensing requirements for the use of images available online.

Apply Picture Styles

When you select a picture on a slide, the *Picture Tools Format* tab becomes available. Different *Styles* allow you to frame pictures, give them a 3D appearance, add a reflection, or apply other treatments. You can choose from preset options using the *Picture Effects* drop-down galleries.

When you use multiple pictures in a presentation, try to maintain consistency and use the same or a similar style for each of them. If you use different styles, be sure you have a reason for making them look different so the effects do not appear random.

▶ HOW TO: Apply a Picture Style

1. Select a picture and click the **Picture Tools Format** tab.
2. Click the **More** button on the gallery [*Picture Styles* group] to see the predefined effects (Figure 2-26).

3. Drag your pointer over the styles to see a live preview applied to your picture. A *ScreenTip* showing the style name appears.

4. Click a style to apply it to your picture.

5. Change to a different style by selecting a new style from the gallery.

2-26 Picture style applied

Picture Effects are similar to *Shape Effects*. Each different effect has many options you can adjust.

▶ HOW TO: Apply or Modify Picture Effects

1. Select a picture and click the **Picture Effects** button [*Picture Tools Format* tab, *Picture Styles* group].

2. Point to each effect in the drop-down list to see a gallery (Figure 2-27) that provides many different options.

3. Select **Options** at the bottom of each gallery to open the *Format Picture* pane where you can make changes to fine-tune a specific effect.

 • Right-click the picture and select **Format Picture** from the context menu to open the *Format Picture* pane.

4. Remove a picture style by selecting the picture and clicking the **Reset Picture** button [*Picture Tools Format* tab, *Adjust* group].

2-27 Picture Effects

Crop a Picture

You can *crop* (trim) unwanted areas of a selected picture by dragging black *cropping handles* on the corners and sides of the picture that appear when you click the **Crop** button. When you point to these handles, your pointer changes to a black shape that resembles the cropping handle. Be careful when dragging to be sure you are moving a cropping handle and not a sizing handle.

▶ HOW TO: Crop a Picture

1. Select a picture and click the **Crop** button [*Picture Tools Format* tab, *Size* group].

2. Drag one or more cropping handles toward the center of the picture; the area to be removed from the edges is grayed out (Figure 2-28).

3. Click the **Crop** button again to accept this change.

2-28 Cropped area of a picture

Always check your pictures and crop them as needed to be sure they have a strong focal point. Excess detail clutters a picture and does not help your viewers quickly grasp what you want them to see.

Change Picture Colors

Pictures are digital photographs usually made up of many colors to achieve the realism that they portray. PowerPoint's *Color* feature allows you to vary picture colors. For example, you might want to make a picture look old, or fade the picture so text over the picture is easy to read.

▶**HOW TO:** Change Picture Colors

1. Select a picture you want to change.
2. Click the **Color** button [*Picture Tools Format* tab, *Adjust* group] to open a gallery showing different color options (Figure 2-29).
 - The current option within each group is highlighted.
3. Select one or more options to customize your picture colors:
 - *Color Saturation:* Colors are more muted as you move from the center to the left as saturation becomes lower; colors are more intense as you move from the center to the right as saturation increases.
 - *Color Tone:* Colors on the left have cool tones and lower temperature values; colors on the right have warm tones and higher values.
 - *Recolor:* Options on the first row include *Grayscale, Sepia, Washout,* and percentages of *Black and White.* The second and third rows display dark and light monotone variations of accent colors.

2-29 *Color* gallery

4. Click **Picture Color Options** at the bottom of the gallery to open the *Format Picture* pane with the **Picture Color** options displayed.

Set a Transparent Color

An image with a white background works well on a slide with a white background (or on a typical Word document) because you see just the image. However, a white background can detract from an image if you place it on a slide background with a contrasting color.

Use the ***Set Transparent Color*** feature to remove a single-color background. Because this feature removes only one color, it does not work well for pictures that have a lot of detail and many colors.

▶**HOW TO:** Set a Transparent Color

1. Select a picture.
2. Click the **Color** button [*Picture Tools Format* tab, *Adjust* group].

3. Click **Set Transparent Color** and your pointer changes to a pen tool.

4. Point to the area of the picture you want to remove and click.

 - All of the pixels with that color value disappear, revealing what is behind the picture (Figure 2-30).

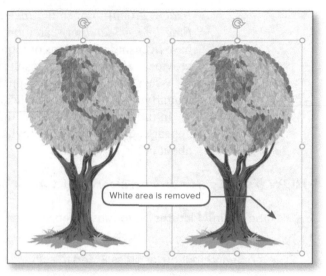

White area is removed

2-30 *Set Transparent Color* applied

Compress Pictures

Pictures can greatly increase your presentation file size. You can **compress** single pictures or all pictures at one time to reduce the picture resolution depending on the quality you need. For print you generally need a higher resolution, and for on-screen viewing a lower resolution is usually fine. Resolution options are expressed in *pixels per inch (ppi)* and are based on *Target output* such as *Print (220 ppi)* or *Web (150 ppi)*. The ppi measurement for viewing on screen is very different from the *dots per inch (dpi)* print measurement for printing on paper. An inexpensive printer can produce 1,200 or more dpi, which produces crisp, clear letterforms that are easy to read on paper.

Deleting cropped areas of pictures removes unused information and, therefore, reduces file size. Compression only affects how the pictures display in the presentation file and not the original picture files.

▶ **HOW TO:** Compress Picture File Size

1. Select a picture.

2. Click the **Compress Picture** button [*Picture Tools Format* tab, *Adjust* group] to open the *Compress Pictures* dialog box (Figure 2-31).

3. Deselect **Apply only to this picture** if you want the compression to apply to all pictures in the presentation.

4. Select **Delete cropped areas of pictures** if you have cropped pictures.

5. Select the appropriate *Target output*. Some options will be grayed out if they are not available for your selected picture.

6. Click **OK** to close the dialog box.

2-31 *Compress Pictures* dialog box

Insert Online Pictures and Illustrations

Click the **Picture** button [*Insert* tab, *Images* group] to open the *Insert Pictures* dialog box where you can search for pictures (digital photographs or illustrations) that you have saved in folders on your computer or any other location. Click the **Online Picture** button [*Insert* tab,

Images group] to open the *Insert Pictures* dialog box where you can search the web using *Bing Image Search* or search on your *OneDrive* location. Pictures you find on the web may have licensing restrictions or require fees to use them. The *Insert Pictures* dialog box does not provide a way to filter the results based on your intended use.

When the search results appear, each picture has a *ScreenTip* identifying its name and a magnifying button you can click to temporarily increase the thumbnail size.

In the lower left corner of the dialog box, the picture name, pixel size, and web source appears. A *pixel* is an abbreviated term for *picture element*, a single unit of information about color.

> ▶ **HOW TO:** Search for and Insert a Picture or Illustration

1. Click the **Online Pictures** button [*Insert* tab, *Images* group] (Figure 2-32) to open the *Insert Pictures* dialog box.
2. Type the search word In the *Bing Image Search* box (Figure 2-33).
3. Click the **Search** button (or press **Enter**) to activate the search.
 - Thumbnails of all the pictures that match your search word appear that are licensed under Creative Commons (Figure 2-34). **CC Only** shows in the search box.
4. Click the drop-down arrow by **CC Only** and select **All Images** to expand your search.
5. Click to select the picture you want.
6. Press **Ctrl** while you click to select more than one picture.
7. Click the **Insert** button. The picture downloads and the *Insert Pictures* dialog box closes.

2-32 *Online Pictures* button

2-33 *Insert Pictures* dialog box

2-34 Pictures from search

> ▶ MORE INFO
>
> Open the *Insert Pictures* dialog box when creating a new slide by clicking the **Online Pictures** icon on the content placeholder.

> ▶ MORE INFO
>
> Be careful to select images that are appropriate for your topic. Some cartoon-like illustrations look amateurish and may not be appropriate for academic or business presentations.

Creative Commons Licensing

A Creative Commons (CC) license enables the free distribution of copyrighted work when the creator wants to give people the right to copy, use, or remix by building upon the work. This right is usually for non-commercial purposes. The creator can make requirements for attribution so the creator is credited for the work. You can read more about these requirements at https://creativecommons.org.

You can activate a search on the Creative Commons site for images, music, and video using Google, Google Images, or other search engines to locate work listed with the CC license. However, the results cannot be guaranteed because no registration is required to use a CC license. You still need to contact the creator (copyright holder) directly or contact the web site where you found the content.

Another way to find images that you can save for future use is through Microsoft's *Bing* search engine at www.bing.com. Select an **Images** search, type a word in the search box, press **Enter**, and the results display. Click the link for **License** (Figure 2-35) to filter your results to one of the following criteria:

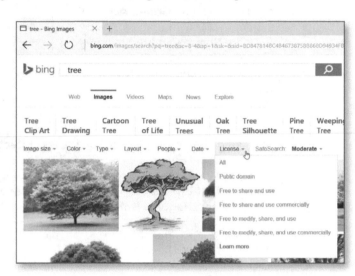

2-35 Image search at Bing.com

- Public Domain
- Free to share and use
- Free to share and use commercially
- Free to modify, share, and use
- Free to modify, share, and use commercially

Bing does not verify CC licensing; you still need to go to the image's web site to determine the actual licensing being used.

PAUSE & PRACTICE: POWERPOINT 2-1

When Gerod Sunderland shares his landscaping proposal with homeowners, he provides detailed printed information and uses a presentation to illustrate concepts. For this project, you add pictures and other objects to his presentation and apply a variety of styles and colors to enhance the content.

File Needed: ***LandscapingProposal-02.pptx*** *(Student data files are available in the Library of your SIMnet account.)*
Completed Project File Name: ***[your initials] PP P2-1.pptx***

1. Open the presentation ***LandscapingProposal-02***.
2. Save the presentation as [your initials] PP P2-1.

3. Add a rectangle.
 a. Display slide 1 and click the **Shapes** button [*Insert* tab, *Illustrations* group].
 b. Select the **Rectangle** shape.
 c. Click and drag to draw a rectangle across the top of the slide.
 d. Change the rectangle *Height* to **.4"** and *Width* to **13.33"** [*Drawing Tools Format* tab, *Size* group].
 e. Click the **Shape Fill** button [*Drawing Tools Format* tab, *Shape Styles* group] and select **Green, Accent 6** (Figure 2-36).
 f. Click the **Shape Outline** button [*Drawing Tools Format* tab, *Shape Styles* group] and select **No Outline**.

2-36 Change *Shape Fill* color

 g. Position the rectangle below the orange line.

4. Add text effects.
 a. Select the title on slide 1 and click the **Text Effects** button [*Drawing Tools Format* tab, *WordArt Styles* group].
 b. Select **Bevel** and then **Circle** (Figure 2-37).
 c. Click the **Text Effects** button again, select **Shadow**, and then select **Offset Diagonal Bottom Right**.

5. Make a picture color transparent.
 a. Select the picture of a leaf on slide 1.
 b. Click **Color** [*Picture Tools Format* tab, *Adjust* group].
 c. Select **Set Transparent Color** and your pointer changes to a pen tool.
 d. Click the white area around the leaf so it becomes transparent (Figure 2-38).

2-37 Apply *Text Effects*

6. Apply effects and use the *Format Painter*.
 a. Display slide 2 and select the left list heading placeholder.
 b. Click the **Shape Fill** button [*Drawing Tools Format* tab, *Shape Styles* group] and select **Texture**.
 c. Click the **Papyrus** option (first row).
 d. Apply **Bold** [*Home* tab, *Font* group].
 e. With the placeholder still selected, click the **Format Painter** button [*Home* tab, *Clipboard* group]. Click the list heading placeholder on the right to apply the copied format.

2-38 Completed slide 1

7. Add a frame shape.
 a. Display slide 3. Click the **Shape** button [*Insert* tab, *Illustrations* group] and select the **Frame** shape under the *Basic Shapes* heading.
 b. Click and drag to draw a frame.
 c. Adjust the frame size (*Height* **1"** and *Width* **3.3"**) [*Drawing Tools Format* tab, *Size* group].
 d. With the frame selected, type Allow three days.
 e. Change the font size to **24 pt**.

8. Change to a different shape and color.
 a. Select the frame shape on slide 3. Click the **Edit Shape** button [*Drawing Tools Format* tab, *Insert Shapes* group] and select **Change Shape**.
 b. Click the **Bevel** shape under the *Basic Shapes* heading.
 c. Change the *Shape Fill* [*Drawing Tools Format* tab, *Shape Styles* group] to **Gold, Accent 4**.
 d. Position this shape below the bulleted text (Figure 2-39).

9. Search for and insert an online picture on slide 3.
 a. Click the **Online Pictures** button [*Insert* tab, *Images* group] to open the *Insert Pictures* dialog box.
 b. Type the word soil in the *Bing Image Search* box.
 c. Click **Search** (or press **Enter**) to activate the search. Results will be similar to Figure 2-40.
 d. Locate a picture of a plant in soil similar to the one in Figure 2-41.
 e. Point to the picture and text appears at the bottom. Point to that area to see the picture's size information and its web address. Make a note of this web address for step 10. Click **Insert**.

10. Resize and crop a picture.
 a. Select the picture on slide 3 and change its size as needed to fit in the blank area on the right of the slide.
 b. Click the **Crop** button [*Picture Tools Format* tab, *Size* group] and crop a little space from all four edges to focus more on the plant.
 c. Click the **Crop** button again to accept the crop.
 d. Click the **More** button [*Picture Tools Format* tab, *Picture Styles* group] and select the **Rotated White** picture style.
 e. Insert a text box [*Insert* tab, *Text* group] and type the picture's source information.
 f. Position the text box below the picture (see Figure 2-41).

11. Compress a picture to reduce presentation file size.
 a. Select the picture on slide 3 and click **Compress Pictures** [*Picture Tools Format* tab, *Adjust* group].
 b. Deselect **Apply only to this picture**.
 c. Select **Use document resolution** for the *Target output*.
 d. Click **OK**.

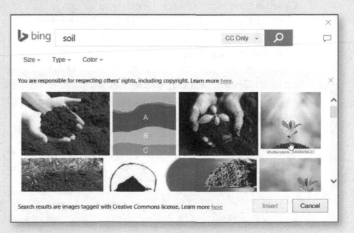

2-39 Text box positioned below list

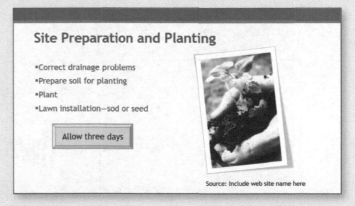

2-40 *Online Pictures* search results

Site Preparation and Planting

- Correct drainage problems
- Prepare soil for planting
- Plant
- Lawn installation—sod or seed

Allow three days

Source: Include web site name here

2-41 Completed slide 3

12. Add *WordArt* text.
 a. Display slide 8. Click the **WordArt** button [*Insert* tab, *Text* group].
 b. Select the **Gradient Fill – Gold, Accent 4, Outline – Accent 4** style from the style gallery.
 c. Type Thank you for your business! in the *WordArt* text box.
 d. Move the *WordArt* object so it is at the top of the picture (Figure 2-42).
 e. Change the *Character Spacing* [*Home* tab, *Font* group] to **Tight**.

2-42 *WordArt* with gradient fill applied

13. Change the *WordArt* gradient fill and outline colors.
 a. Select the *WordArt* object, if necessary, and click the **Text Fill** button [*Drawing Tools Format* tab, *WordArt Styles* group]. Select **Gradient** and click **More Gradients** to open the *Format Shape* pane. All gradient options appear in the pane.
 b. Select the second gradient stop (at Position **4%**) and click the **Remove gradient stop** button.
 c. Select the left gradient stop (at Position **0%**) and change the color to **Green, Accent 6, Lighter 40%**.
 d. Select the right gradient stop and change the color to **Green, Accent 6, Darker 50%** (Figure 2-43).
 e. Close the *Format Shape* pane.
 f. Select the *WordArt* object, if necessary, and click the **Text Outline** button [*Drawing Tools Format* tab, *WordArt Styles* group]. Change the outline color to **Black, Text 1**.

14. Apply a *Transform* effect to the *WordArt*.
 a. Click the **Text Effects** button [*Drawing Tools Format* tab, *WordArt Styles* group]. From the drop-down list, select **Transform**. On the *Transform* gallery, click the **Deflate Bottom** effect (Figure 2-44).
 b. Resize the *WordArt* (*Height* **2"** and *Width* **10"**). Click **Align** [*Drawing Tools Format* tab, *Arrange* group] and click **Align Center** so the *WordArt* fits across the top of the picture (Figure 2-45).

Two gradient stops blend two colors

2-43 *Format Shape* pane

2-44 *WordArt Transform* gallery

2-45 *Deflate Bottom Transform* effect applied and adjusted

15. Save and close your presentation (Figure 2-46).

2-46 PP P2-1 completed

Creating a Table

Tables show data in an organized and easy-to-read format because information is arranged in **columns** (vertical) and **rows** (horizontal). The intersection of a column and row is a **cell**. **Border** lines and **shading** show the table structure. Working with PowerPoint tables is much like working with tables in Word. You can create a table from a content placeholder when you create a new slide or by using options on the *Insert* tab.

Once you create a table, you can change its size as well as column width and row height. Use table formatting to emphasize the contents in different ways and help your audience interpret the data. If you plan to project your slides on a large screen, be sure your table information is concise so you can use a minimum font size of 20 points. If a table requires a lot of detailed information, then prepare the table as a full-page handout with body text at an 11–12 point size. You could prepare a PowerPoint slide to reference the handout as you explain the table, or perhaps show only a portion of the table on a slide.

Insert and Draw Methods

You can create the columns and rows of a table in different ways. Click the **Table** button [*Insert* tab, *Tables* group] to visually select columns and rows by dragging over them. The table dimensions (such as *3×4 Table* meaning three columns by four rows) are shown at the top of the drop-down list. By default, columns and rows appear on the slide with even sizing, but you can adjust column width and row height as you add information.

▶**HOW TO:** Insert a Table and Select Columns and Rows

1. Display the slide where you want the table.
2. Click the **Insert** tab.
3. Click the **Table** button [*Tables* group] to open the drop-down list.
4. Drag across and down to select the number of columns and rows you need (Figure 2-47).

2-47 Table cells selected

5. Release the pointer to insert the table.

Use the **Insert Table** command [*Insert* tab, *Tables* group] to create a table by entering a specific number of columns and rows.

> ▶ **HOW TO:** Insert a Table and Enter the Number
> of Columns and Rows

1. Display the slide where you want to insert the table.
2. Click the **Insert** tab.
3. Click the **Table** button [*Tables* group] to open the drop-down list.
4. Click **Insert Table** and the *Insert Table* dialog box opens (Figure 2-48).
5. Specify the number of columns and rows you need.
6. Click **OK** to close the *Insert Table* dialog box and insert the table.

2-48 *Insert Table* dialog box

To insert a table on a new slide, click the **Table** icon in the empty content placeholder to open the *Insert Table* dialog box. Enter the number of columns and rows to create the table. Because of the placeholder size, the table width will be slightly wider than when you click the **Insert** button to create a table.

The final way to create a table is by drawing the table area and dividing it into columns and rows. This method works well when space is limited on the slide because of other content.

> ▶ **HOW TO:** Draw a Table

1. Display the slide where you want the table.
2. Click the **Insert** tab.
3. Click the **Table** button [*Tables* group] to open the drop-down list.
4. Click **Draw Table** and your pointer changes to a pen.
5. Drag the pen to draw the outside border of the table in the size you want.
6. Click the **Draw Table** button [*Table Tools Design* tab, *Draw Borders* group] to activate the pen again.

7. Drag the pen inside the table to insert horizontal and vertical lines that divide the table into rows and columns (Figure 2-49).

 • Start dragging near but not touching the outside border and the lines will expand on both ends to reach the borders.

8. Press **Esc** to turn off the pen tool.

Pen tool

2-49 *Draw Table*

Regardless of the method you use to create a table, the *Table Tools Design* tab (Figure 2-50) and *Table Tools Layout* tab (Figure 2-51) are available when the table is active.

2-50 *Table Tools Design tab*

2-51 *Table Tools Layout tab*

Move and Select

Your insertion point indicates where you are within a table to add text. To move from cell to cell, use one of the following methods:

• Press **Tab** to move to the next cell on the right (or the first cell in the next row).
• Press **Shift+Tab** to move to the previous cell on the left.
• Press arrow keys to move in different directions from the current cell.
• Click a cell to move the insertion point to that cell.

Where you point within a table influences whether you select individual cells, columns, rows, or the entire table. Your pointer changes to a selection pointer (a black arrow that points in different directions based on what you are selecting).

▶**HOW TO:** Select Cells, Columns, Rows, and the Table

1. Select a cell by pointing inside the left border and clicking when your pointer turns into a black arrow that angles.
2. Select a column by using one of the following methods:

 • Point above the column's top border and click when your pointer turns into a downward-pointing black arrow (Figure 2-52).
 • Move your insertion point to any cell in the column. Click the **Select** button [*Table Tools Layout* tab, *Table* group] and click **Select Column.**

Pointer and selected column

2-52 *Select table column*

3. Select a row by using one of the following methods:

- Point outside the table to the left of a row and click when your pointer turns into a right-pointing black arrow (Figure 2-53).
- Move your insertion point to any cell in the row. Click the **Select** button [*Table Tools Layout* tab, *Table* group] and click **Select Row**.

Pointer and selected row

2-53 *Select table row*

4. Select multiple cells, columns, or rows by using one of the following methods:

- Drag across adjacent cells.
- Press **Shift** as you click additional adjacent cells.

5. Select an entire table by using one of the following methods:

- Drag across all cells in the table.
- Move your insertion point to any cell in the table. Click the **Select** button [*Table Tools Layout* tab, *Table* group] and click **Select Table**.

Insert and Delete Rows and Columns

After you begin entering table content, you may need to add rows or columns. You can change a table's structure in several ways:

- Insert rows above or below the current row.
- Insert columns to the left or right of the current column.
- Delete rows and columns.

▶ HOW TO: Insert and Delete Rows and Columns

1. Click inside the table.
2. Click the **Table Tools Layout** tab.
3. Insert a row or column.

- Click a table cell next to where you want to add a column or row.
- Click the **Insert Above** or **Insert Below** buttons [*Rows & Columns* group] to add rows.
- Click the **Insert Left** or **Insert Right** buttons [*Rows & Columns* group] to add columns.

4. Delete a row or column.

- Click a table cell where you want to delete a column or row.
- Click the **Delete** button and select **Delete Columns** or **Delete Rows** [*Rows & Columns* group] (Figure 2-54).

2-54 *Delete* button

> ### ▶ ANOTHER WAY
>
> Right-click a row or column and insert or delete rows and columns by selecting the appropriate option from the mini toolbar.

Merge and Split Cells

Use the ***Merge Cells*** command to combine two or more cells in a row or column. For example, you can merge all the cells in the top row of a table so a title will span all columns. Use the ***Split Cells*** command to divide any single cell into two or more cells.

▶ HOW TO: Merge and Split Cells

1. Select the cells to be merged.
2. Click the *Table Tools Layout* tab.
3. Click the **Merge Cells** button [*Merge* group] to combine those cells into one cell.
4. Select the cell (or cells) to be split.
5. Click the *Table Tools Layout* tab.
6. Click the **Split Cells** button [*Merge* group] to open the *Split Cells* dialog box and enter the number of columns and rows that you need.
7. Click **OK** to close the dialog box.

> **▶ ANOTHER WAY**
>
> Click the **Eraser** button [*Table Tools Design* tab, *Draw Borders* group] and your pointer turns into an eraser. Click a border within the table to remove it and merge cells. Press **Esc** to turn off the **Eraser**.

Adjust Sizing

You often need to resize tables to display information appropriately. Column widths will vary based on content, but row height should usually be consistent.

▶ HOW TO: Resize a Table, Cells, Columns, and Rows

1. Resize a table.
 - Enter sizes in the *Height* and *Width* boxes [*Table Tools Layout* tab, *Table Size* group].
 - Click and drag table sizing handles as you would to resize a shape.
2. Resize a cell, column, or row.
 - Point to a cell, column, or row border. When your pointer changes to a splitter (Figure 2-55), click and drag to increase or decrease the size of the cell, column, or row.
 - Select the cell, column, or row to change; then enter the size you want in the *Height* and *Width* boxes [*Table Tools Layout* tab, *Cell Size* group].
3. Resize a column to fit the text within it.
 - Point to a column border and double-click when your pointer changes to a splitter.
4. Distribute column width or row height evenly.
 - Select the columns or rows to be changed.
 - Click the **Distribute Rows** or **Distribute Columns** buttons [*Table Tools Layout* tab, *Cell Size* group].

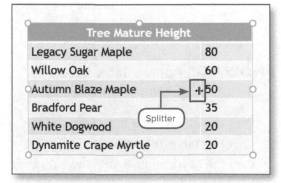

2-55 Change column width

SLO 2.5

Formatting a Table

You can format text in a table as you can any other text such as changing fonts and text effects. You can also change cell margins and text direction. While shading and borders may appear decorative, these effects can make a table easier to interpret. For example, shading on rows can make the text easier to read across rows; shading on a column can draw attention to the text displayed there. PowerPoint provides many preset styles using color combinations derived from theme colors. You can customize effects to create a unique design.

Table Style Options and Effects

On the *Table Tools Design* tab, the ***Table Styles*** gallery provides options for a table's design. The first style on each row of options is shown in black and white while the other six styles are in theme accent colors. Table styles are arranged in the following categories:

- *Best Match for Document*
- *Light*
- *Medium*
- *Dark*

Each table style is influenced by the features checked for ***Table Style Options*** [*Table Tools Design* tab]. Fill colors that emphasize table cells vary depending on which of the following options you select:

- ***Header Row*** or ***Total Row:*** The first or last row has a darker color and has bold text in a contrasting color.
- ***First Column*** or ***Last Column:*** The first or last column has a darker color and has bold text in a contrasting color.
- ***Banded Rows*** or ***Banded Columns:*** The rows or columns have alternating colors. *Banded Rows* makes reading across the table easier. *Banded Columns* emphasizes the separate columns.

> *Table Styles* are arranged by category

> Medium Style 2 - Accent 6

▶**HOW TO: Apply a Table Style and Change Options**

1. Click anywhere in the table you want to change.
2. Click the **Table Tools Design** tab.
3. Click the **More** button in the *Table Styles* group to see the complete gallery (Figure 2-56). The current style is highlighted.
4. Point to a style to see a live preview. *ScreenTips* identify each style name.

2-56 *Table Styles*

5. Click a style to apply it.

6. Adjust the *Table Style Options* as needed.
 - Check **Header Row** and **Banded Rows** [*Table Style Options* group].
 - Deselect **Banded Rows** and select **Banded Columns** [*Table Style Options* group].

If you want to remove table formatting, click the **More** button [*Table Tools Design* tab, *Table Styles* group] and click **Clear Table**. To emphasize the table or cells within the table, such as a heading row, you can apply effects to selected areas.

▶ **HOW TO:** Apply Table Effects

1. Select the table, or the cells, to be changed.

2. Click the **Effects** button [*Table Tools Design* tab, *Table Styles* group (Figure 2-57).

3. Select one of the following effects:
 - **Cell Bevel**
 - **Shadow**
 - **Reflection**

4. Point to an option to see a live preview. *ScreenTips* identify each option name.

5. Click an option to apply it.

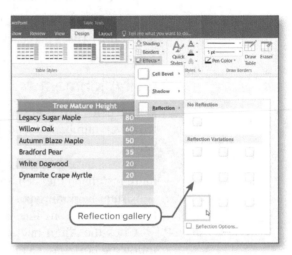

2-57 *Reflection Effects*

Shading and Border Colors

After you apply a built-in table style, you can change colors to emphasize your content or better match other aspects of your presentation. Select the cells you want to change and use the *Shading* button [*Table Tools Design* tab, *Table Styles* group] to select a different color (Figure 2-58). The icon for this button is the same as a *Shape Fill* button.

Border lines separate cells and outline the edge of the table, but not all table styles show border lines. To add lines, use the *Borders* button [*Table Tools Design* tab, *Table Styles* group] and each available option shows where the border line will be applied when that option is selected (Figure 2-59).

2-59 *Pen Weight* changed and *Outside Borders* applied

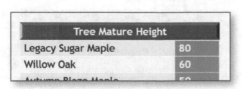

2-58 Shading emphasizes content

Select the appropriate area before you apply the border change. If you want the border lines thicker, increase the *Pen Weight* [*Table Tools Design* tab, *Draw Borders* group] before you apply the border change. You can remove borders from selected cells by clicking the **Borders** button and selecting **No Border**.

Also, you can apply, change, and remove borders using the ***Pen*** tools [*Table Tools Design* tab, *Draw Borders* group]:

- ***Pen Color:*** Change line color.
- ***Pen Style:*** Choose a different line style.
- ***Pen Weight:*** Change line thickness.
- ***Draw Table:*** Draw table area as well as column and row border lines.
- ***Eraser:*** Remove border lines.

It may take a little practice to use the pen to change table lines and not start a new table. Select the **Eraser** and click each border line you need to remove.

Cell Alignment

Within cells, text is aligned on the left by default, which is appropriate for words and phrases. However, numbers should usually be right-aligned so your audience can more easily interpret values.

If cells have a single line of text, center the text vertically in the cells. If some cells contain more text than other cells, top alignment generally works best because reading is easier with a consistent beginning position. Bottom alignment works well for column headings when they have more than one line of text.

Click the **Align** buttons [*Table Tools Layout* tab, *Alignment* group] and choose from the following horizontal and vertical alignment options:

- *Horizontal alignment:* **Align Left, Center, Align Right**
- *Vertical alignment:* **Align Top, Center Vertically, Align Bottom**

Cell Margins and Text Direction

Space is needed between the border lines of a cell and the text in the cell. The default internal margin spacing is *Normal*. You can change the spacing by clicking the **Cell Margins** button [*Table Tools Layout* tab, *Alignment* group] and choose from one of the following options (Figure 2-60):

- *Normal:* Top/Bottom **.05"** and Left/Right **.1"**
- *None:* All Sides **0"**
- *Narrow:* All Sides **0.05"**
- *Wide:* All Sides **0.15"**

Click **Custom Margins** to open the *Cell Text Layout* dialog box to enter other measurements.

2-60 *Cell Margins* options

Text is, by default, arranged horizontally in each cell. Be careful when changing text direction because your text may not be as easy to read. Click **Text Direction** and choose one of the following four options (Figure 2-61):

- *Horizontal*
- *Rotate all text 90°*
- *Rotate all text 270°*
- *Stacked*

2-61 *Text Direction* options

PAUSE & PRACTICE: POWERPOINT 2-2

For this project you create a table of costs, insert a row of data, and format the table to blend with other colors used in the landscaping presentation. You also add a text box to show an alternative cost.

File Needed: **[your initials] PP P2-1.pptx** (Student data files are available in the Library of your SIMnet account.)

Completed Project File Name: **[your initials] PP P2-2.pptx**

1. Open the presentation **[your initials] PP P2-1** and save it as [your initials] PP P2-2.
2. Create a table.
 a. Display slide 4 and click the **Insert Table** icon on the content placeholder to open the *Insert Table* dialog box.
 b. Enter 4 columns and 5 rows on the *Insert Table* dialog box. Click **OK** to close the dialog box and create the table.
 c. Type the following table text: (Note: PowerPoint does not recognize Hydroseeding, but this is the correct spelling.)

Item	Quantity	Cost Each	Totals
Trees–shade	3	500	1,500
Trees–ornamental	3	150	450
Perennials	30	12	360
Hydroseeding sq. ft.	8,000	.10	800

 d. Click and drag across the table to select all cells. Change the *Font Size* to **20 pt**. [*Home* tab, *Font* group] (Figure 2-62).
3. Adjust table sizing and alignment.
 a. Adjust column width by pointing to each border separating the columns and double-clicking when your pointer changes to a splitter.
 - For the right side of the "Totals" column, the pointer will change to a splitter if you deselect the table and then point just inside the right border. Drag to make the column fit the text.

Costs Include Planting/Installation

Item	Quantity	Cost Each	Totals
Trees–shade	3	500	1,500
Trees–ornamental	3	150	450
Perennials	30	12	360
Hydroseeding sq. ft.	8,000	.10	800

2-62 Table as it first appears with font size change

b. Point above the "**Quantity**" column and click when your pointer turns into a black arrow. Drag across the "**Cost Each**" and "**Totals**" columns to select all cells in those columns. Click the **Align Right** button [*Table Tools Layout* tab, *Alignment* group].

4. Insert rows and add text.
 a. Click the "**Perennials**" cell and click the **Insert Above** button [*Table Tools Layout* tab, *Rows & Columns* group].
 b. Add the following text to the newly inserted row:
 Shrubs 10 40 400
 c. Click in the "**Hydroseeding**" cell and click the **Insert Below** button [*Table Tools Layout* tab, *Rows & Columns* group].
 d. Select the last three cells on the new row and click the **Merge Cells** button [*Table Tools Layout* tab, *Merge* group].
 e. Add the following text:
 Total 3,510

5. Select table styles, options, and shading.
 a. Click the **More** button [*Tables Tools Design* tab, *Table Styles* group] and select the **Medium Style 3, Accent 6** style.
 b. Check **Header Row, Total Row,** and **Banded Rows** [*Tables Tools Design* tab, *Table Style Options* group] if they are not already checked.
 c. Select a row with gray shading. Click the **Shading** button [*Table Tools Design* tab, *Table Styles* group] and select **Green, Accent 6, Lighter 80%**. Repeat for the remaining two gray rows.
 d. Select the last row. Click the **Shading** button and select **Green, Accent 6, Lighter 60%**.
 e. Select the first row. Click the **Effects** button [*Table Tools Design* tab, *Table Styles* group], click **Cell Bevel**, and select **Cool Slant** (Figure 2-63).

Item	Quantity	Cost Each	Totals
Trees—shade	3	500	1,500
Trees—ornamental	3	150	450
Shrubs	10	40	400
Perennials	30	12	360
Hydroseeding sq. ft.	8,000	.10	800
Total			3,510

2-63 Style, row shading, and *Bevel* effect applied

6. Add borders and a shadow effect.
 a. Select the table.
 b. Click the **Pen Color** button [*Table Tools Design* tab, *Draw Borders* group] and select **Green, Accent 6, Darker 50%**.
 c. Click the **Pen Weight** button [*Table Tools Design* tab, *Draw Borders* group] and select **6 pt**.
 d. Click the **Borders** drop-down arrow [*Table Tools Design* tab, *Table Styles* group] and select **Outside Borders**.
 e. Select the table and click the **Effects** button [*Table Tools Design* tab, *Table Styles* group]. Click **Shadow** and select **Offset Diagonal Bottom Right** in the *Outer* category.

7. Center the table so it is centered on the slide.
 a. Click **Align** [*Table Tools Layout* tab, *Arrange* group] and select **Align Center**. Click **Align** again and select **Align Middle**.

8. Insert a text box.
 a. Click the **Text Box** button [*Insert* tab, *Text* group] and click the slide below the table to start a text box. Type the following text:
 Sod cost for 8,000 sq. ft. @ .60 = $4,800

b. Change the font size to **20 pt**. [*Home* tab, *Font* group].

c. Click the **Shape Fill** button [*Home* tab, *Drawing* group] and select **Green, Accent 6, Lighter 60%**.

d. Resize the text box as necessary so the text fits on one line. Move it to the lower right of the slide (Figure 2-64).

9. Save and close your presentation (Figure 2-65).

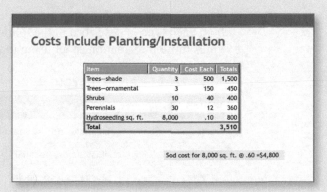

Costs Include Planting/Installation

Item	Quantity	Cost Each	Totals
Trees—shade	3	500	1,500
Trees—ornamental	3	150	450
Shrubs	10	40	400
Perennials	30	12	360
Hydroseeding sq. ft.	8,000	.10	800
Total			3,510

Sod cost for 8,000 sq. ft. @ .60 =$4,800

2-64 Completed table on slide 4

2-65 PP P2-2 completed

Creating a SmartArt Graphic

To clearly illustrate concepts such as processes, cycles, or relationships, you can create a diagram using *SmartArt graphics* to help your audience see connections or sequences. This is a very important communication strategy; the shapes of the diagram are concisely labeled for each concept and the shapes are connected in various ways. For example, you can show subtopics radiating from a central topic or sequential steps in a work flow.

The *SmartArt Tools Design* tab (Figure 2-66) provides options for the overall layout and styles of the *SmartArt* graphics. You can add shapes and rearrange the order of shapes.

The *SmartArt Tools Format* tab (Figure 2-67) provides options to customize shape and text styles, fill colors, outline colors, and effects.

2-66 *SmartArt Tools Design* tab

2-67 *SmartArt Tools Format* tab

SmartArt Layouts

SmartArt layouts (diagrams) are organized by type in the *Choose a SmartArt Graphic* dialog box; each type is described in the following table. When you select a layout, PowerPoint provides more information about using that specific layout.

SmartArt Graphic Layout Types and Purposes

Type	Purpose
List	Illustrates non-sequential or grouped information
Process	Illustrates sequential steps in a process or workflow
Cycle	Illustrates a continuing sequence or concepts related to a central idea
Hierarchy	Illustrates a decision tree or top-to-bottom relationship such as an organizational chart
Relationship	Illustrates concepts that are connected such as contrasting, opposing, or converging
Matrix	Illustrates the relationship of four parts to the whole
Pyramid	Illustrates proportional or interconnected relationships
Picture	Shows pictures as integral parts of many different diagrams
Office.com	Shows diagrams from layouts on Office.com

▶ HOW TO: Create a SmartArt Graphic

1. Click the **Insert SmartArt Graphic** icon on the content placeholder to open the *Choose a SmartArt Graphic* dialog box.

Or

2. Display the slide where you want to insert the *SmartArt* graphic and click the **Insert** tab.

3. Click the **SmartArt** button [*Illustrations* group] to open the *Choose a SmartArt Graphic* dialog box.

4. Select a type from the list on the left (Figure 2-68).

5. Click a layout in the gallery to select it.

6. Click **OK** to close the dialog box. The *SmartArt* graphic appears on the slide with sample text.

2-68 *Choose a SmartArt Graphic* dialog box

When you insert a *SmartArt* graphic using the *SmartArt* button on the *Insert* tab, the initial size of the *SmartArt* frame may be different than if you inserted the *SmartArt* graphic using the content placeholder on a new slide with a *Title and Content* layout. You may need to resize the frame for your content to fit appropriately on your slide.

If the layout you choose has picture placeholders on the shapes, such as the *Continuous Picture List* layout shown in Figure 2-69, click each picture icon to open the *Insert Pictures* dialog box. Locate the picture you want to use and click **Insert**. The picture is sized automatically and shaped to fit the current picture placeholder.

2-69 *SmartArt Continuous Picture List* layout

Add Text

Click the **Text Pane** button [*SmartArt Tools Design* tab, *Create Graphic* group] to open a pane beside your layout. As you type in the pane, *SmartArt* text appears as a bulleted list and also in the *SmartArt* shapes. Text becomes smaller in the shapes as you enter more text, so it is important to use only a few words. You can resize or move the *Text pane*.

 List layouts often work well if you have two levels of bulleted text: Level 1 (the first line) and Level 2 (text indented to a sublevel). How text is arranged when using two levels of information varies based on the selected layout. Notice in Figure 2-70 that Level 1 text is in a shape and Level 2 text is in a bulleted list below the shape.

▶ HOW TO: Type SmartArt Text Using the Text Pane

1. Open the *Text pane*, if necessary, by using one of the following methods:
 - Click the **Text Pane** button [*SmartArt Tools Design* tab, *Create Graphic* group].
 - Click the smaller **Text Pane** button on the left side of the *SmartArt* frame.
2. Type text after the first bullet to add Level 1 text.
3. Press **Enter** to add a new item. Another shape appears in your *SmartArt* layout, and shape sizes automatically adjust.
4. Press **Tab** to indent for Level 2 text (Figure 2-70).
5. Press **Shift + Tab** to go from Level 2 text to Level 1 text.
6. Use arrow keys to move through the listed items.
7. Remove a shape by deleting the related bulleted text in the *Text pane*.
 - The *Text pane* automatically closes when you click outside the *SmartArt* layout.
 - If you want to keep the current *SmartArt* layout active, click the pane's **Close** button or the **Text Pane** button to close the pane.

2-70 *SmartArt Text Pane*

Another way to add text is to type directly into each *SmartArt* shape so you can easily see how your text fits without becoming too small. Pressing **Tab** does not move your insertion point between shapes. You can paste copied text but you cannot drag text into a *SmartArt* shape.

▶ HOW TO: Type Text in SmartArt Shapes

1. Close the *Text Pane*, if open, by clicking the **Close** button in the top-right corner of the pane.
2. Click each *SmartArt* shape to select it and type your text. A dashed border appears on the shape as you type or edit your text.
3. Click outside the *SmartArt* frame, or press **Esc**, when you are finished (Figure 2-71).

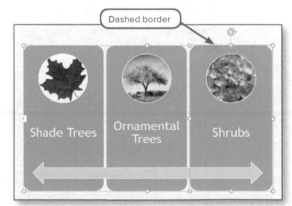

2-71 Add text in the *SmartArt Continuous Picture List* layout

If you already have listed information on your slide, you can quickly change bulleted text to a *SmartArt* graphic. The gallery layouts that first appear are designed for listed information, but you can access all of the other layouts, too.

1. Select the bulleted text placeholder or the text within the placeholder that you want to convert to a *SmartArt* graphic.
2. Click the **Home** tab.
3. Click the **Convert to SmartArt Graphic** button [*Paragraph* group] (Figure 2-72). The gallery displays layouts that are designed to show listed information.
4. Click a layout to apply it.

Or

5. Click **More SmartArt Graphics** to open the *Choose a SmartArt Graphic* dialog box.
6. Select from all layouts and then click **OK** to close the dialog box and insert the *SmartArt* graphic.

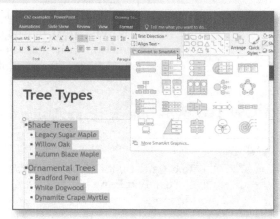

2-72 Convert to *SmartArt* graphic

SLO 2.7

Formatting a SmartArt Graphic

When you create a *SmartArt* graphic, by default it appears using the first accent color in the current color theme. You can customize many style options and colors using the *SmartArt Tools Design* tab as well as rearrange shape order, add shapes, or change layouts.

SmartArt Styles

The **SmartArt Styles** gallery provides different effects for emphasizing the diagram shapes. In the **3-D** category, the styles have a dimensional effect. When choosing these styles, be sure that your diagram is not distorted or difficult to interpret.

1. Select the *SmartArt* graphic.
2. Click the **SmartArt Tools Design** tab.
3. Click the **More** button [*SmartArt Styles* group] to open the *SmartArt Styles* gallery (Figure 2-73).
4. Point to a style to see a live preview.
5. Click a style to apply it.

2-73 *SmartArt* graphic styles

Change Colors

The **Change Colors** gallery provides a quick way to change all the colors in a *SmartArt* graphic at the same time. Color options are arranged in categories using theme accent colors; some show variations of the same color while others have different colors.

Individual shape colors within a *SmartArt* graphic can be changed as you would any other shape.

▶ **HOW TO:** Change SmartArt Colors

1. Select the *SmartArt* graphic.
2. Change colors for the entire diagram by clicking the **Change Colors** button [*SmartArt Tools Design* tab, *SmartArt Styles* group] and selecting a gallery option (Figure 2-74).
3. Change the color of a selected shape within a diagram by clicking the **Shape Fill** button or the **Shape Outline** button [*SmartArt Tools Format* tab, *Shape Styles* group] and choosing an appropriate color.

2-74 *SmartArt* graphic *Change Colors* options

Change Layouts

You may find that the *SmartArt* graphic layout you have chosen is not appropriate for the particular process or relationship you are trying to show. Or you might need a layout that displays two levels of information.

▶ **HOW TO:** Change Layouts

1. Select the *SmartArt* graphic.
2. Click the **SmartArt Tools Design** tab, and click the **More** button [*Layouts* group] to open the *Layouts* gallery (Figure 2-75).
3. Point to a layout to see a live preview of that layout.
4. Click a layout to apply it.

Or

5. Click **More Layouts** to open the *Choose a SmartArt Graphic* dialog box.
6. Select from all layouts and then click **OK** to close the dialog box and apply the new layout.

2-75 *SmartArt* graphic layouts

Add Shapes

The ***Add Shape*** button on the *SmartArt Tools Design* tab inserts shapes in relation to the selected shape. The available options include the following:

- *Add Shape After*
- *Add Shape Before*
- *Add Shape Above*
- *Add Shape Below*
- *Add Assistant*

Being able to control where a new shape appears is important. For example, you can add shapes to an organization chart as new employees are hired. An assistant shape is only available for organization charts.

2-76 *Add Shape* options

▶ HOW TO: Add Shapes

1. Select the shape closest to where you want to add a shape.
2. Click the **SmartArt Tools Design** tab.
3. Click the **Add Shape** drop-down arrow [*Create Graphic* group] (Figure 2-76) and select the position where you want to add the new shape.

To change the flow of a diagram, click the **Right to Left** button [*SmartArt Tools Design* tab, *Create Graphic* group].

PAUSE & PRACTICE: POWERPOINT 2-3

For this project you create an organization chart showing the CGL employees who will be managing various aspects of the landscaping for Frank and Sandra Hunter. You also convert one of the existing lists to a *SmartArt* graphic and rearrange slide objects for an interesting appearance. The *SmartArt* styles applied blend with other colors in the presentation.

File Needed: ***[your initials] PP P2-2.pptx*** *(Student data files are available in the* Library *of your SIMnet account.)*
Completed Project File Name: ***[your initials] PP P2-3.pptx***

1. Open the presentation ***[your initials] PP P2-2*** and save it as [your initials] PP P2-3.
2. Create a new slide and insert a *SmartArt* graphic.
 a. Display slide 1. Click the **New Slide** drop-down arrow and select the **Title and Content** layout.
 b. Type the slide title Your CGL Team.
 c. Click the **Insert a SmartArt Graphic** icon on the content placeholder to open the *Choose a SmartArt Graphic* dialog box.
 d. Select the *Hierarchy* type from the list on the left.
 e. Click the **Organization Chart** layout and click **OK** to close the dialog box and insert the *SmartArt* graphic.

3. Insert text.
 a. Select each *SmartArt* shape and type the text displayed in Figure 2-77.

2-77 Organization chart

b. Press **Enter** after each name within a shape. Let the job titles word wrap as needed.

4. Change the organization chart using the *SmartArt Tools Design* tab.
 a. Change the flow by clicking the **Right to Left** button [*Create Graphic* group].
 b. Click the **More** button [*SmartArt Styles* group] and select the **Inset** effect (Figure 2-78).
 c. Click the **Change Colors** button [*SmartArt Styles* group] and scroll down to select **Gradient Loop, Accent 6** (Figure 2-79).

2-79 New colors applied

2-78 *SmartArt* graphic styles

5. Change bulleted text to a *SmartArt* graphic.
 a. Display slide 4. Select the bulleted text and click the **Convert to SmartArt** button [*Home* tab, *Paragraph* group].
 b. Click the **Vertical Bullet List**. The *SmartArt* list fills the slide and is too large since other objects are already on the slide (Figure 2-80).

6. Change the *SmartArt* graphic so it fits on the slide with the other objects.
 a. Press **Ctrl** while you click each *SmartArt* shape to select them all. Change the font to **24 pt**.
 b. Select the *SmartArt* frame (not individual shapes) and resize it (*Height* **3"** and *Width* **5"**) [*SmartArt Tools Format* tab, *Size* group] to better fit the text and other objects on the slide.
 c. Change the style to **Inset** [*SmartArt Tools Design* tab, *SmartArt Styles* group].
 d. Click the **Change Colors** button [*SmartArt Tools Design* tab, *SmartArt Styles* group] and select **Gradient Range – Accent 6**.
 e. Rearrange slide objects as displayed in Figure 2-81. Be careful to point to the *SmartArt* frame when moving it so the whole diagram moves and not just an individual shape within the frame.

2-80 *SmartArt* graphic shapes as they originally appear

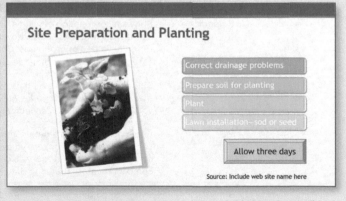

2-81 Completed slide 4

7. Save and close your presentation (Figure 2-82).

2-82 PP P-3 completed

Creating a Chart

Charts help viewers interpret data and make comparisons. If you have lots of data, then create your chart in Excel and copy it to a PowerPoint slide. However, for most situations, PowerPoint's *Chart* feature will provide all the options you need.

To insert a chart in PowerPoint 2016, click the **Insert Chart** icon on a new slide content placeholder or click the **Insert** tab and click the **Chart** button [*Illustrations* group] to add a chart to an existing slide. You can choose a chart type to control how data is represented such as with columns, bars, lines, or pie slices. The following table lists chart types and describes their purposes:

Chart Types and Purposes

Type	Purpose
Column	Shows a comparison of values or data changes over time. Categories are shown on the horizontal axis and values are shown on the vertical axis. Columns may be clustered to show a range of values or groupings. Columns in a category may be stacked to emphasize the total category value rather than the subsections that make up the category.
Line	Shows data changes over time; works well to show trends with multiple data series plotted at even intervals. Categories are shown on the horizontal axis and values are shown on the vertical axis. Markers can indicate individual values.
Pie	Shows the values in a data series in proportional sizes that make up a whole pie. Values cannot be negative or zero values. Percentages or actual values can be displayed near or on pie slices. This category also includes *Doughnut* charts that show parts of a whole but can contain more than one data series as rings.
Bar	Similar to column charts except bars are horizontal; works well for comparison of values. Categories are shown on the vertical axis and values are shown on the horizontal axis.

Continued

Type	Purpose
Area	Shows data changes over time; emphasizes the total values across a trend.
X Y (Scatter)	Shows the relationships between data using values on both the X and Y axes to plot data points; works well to emphasize where data sets have similar values. This category also includes *Bubble* charts.
Stock	Shows fluctuation of stock prices with high, low, and close values displayed over time.
Surface	Shows the differences between two sets of data. Instead of values, color bands represent the same range of values as in a topographic map showing land elevations.
Radar	Shows the combined values of several data series with values relative to a center point.
Treemap	Displays categories by color arranged in a structure that helps to compare proportions within a hierarchy.
Sunburst	Displays data in a circular pattern of rings that create a hierarchy with the highest level in the center. With multiple categories, this chart shows how the outer rings relate to the inner rings.
Histogram	Shows the distribution of data grouped by frequencies. Can include a cumulative total.
Box & Whisker	Shows multiple data sets organized by quartiles (ranked data divided into four equal groups) and shown as proportional boxes. Variability is shown as lines above or below the boxes. Outliers are plotted as individual points.
Waterfall	Shows how an initial value is affected by the addition of positive and negative values with columns that reflect a running total.
Combo	Combines two charts such as a column chart with a line chart displayed over it.

> ### MORE INFO
> Use *Help* to search for "chart types" to see examples and get tips on how to arrange data in a worksheet.

The *Chart Tools Design* tab (Figure 2-83) and the *Chart Tools Format* tab (Figure 2-84) are available when a chart is active.

2-83 *Chart Tools Design* tab

2-84 *Chart Tools Format* tab

When you insert a chart in PowerPoint, a **spreadsheet** opens with sample data in rows and columns. A group of data values from each column is a **data series;** a group of data values from each row is a **category**. You can edit the sample data by entering your own information or you could copy and paste data from Excel, Word, or Access. If you need to revise the data in Excel, click the **Excel** button in the spreadsheet title bar.

Because the spreadsheet and PowerPoint chart are linked, the changes you make to the spreadsheet are automatically reflected in the chart.

▶ HOW TO: Insert a Chart

1. Click the **Insert** tab; then click the **Chart** button [*Illustrations* group]. You can also click the **Insert Chart** icon on a new slide content placeholder.
 - In the *Insert Chart* dialog box (Figure 2-85), chart types are listed on the left and a variety of chart layouts for each type appear on the right.
 - A *ScreenTip* identifies chart names.
2. Click a layout to select a chart.
3. Click **OK** to close the dialog box and insert the chart.
 - A spreadsheet automatically opens showing sample data that you edit (Figure 2-86).

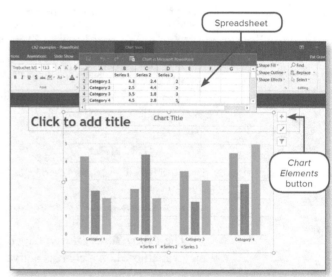

2-85 *Insert Chart* dialog box 2-86 *Spreadsheet linked to a chart*

▶ MORE INFO

When you insert a chart using the *Insert* tab, the size of the chart frame will be different than when you insert a chart from the *Title and Content* placeholder as you create a new slide. Resize the chart frames as needed.

The chart frame displays ***chart elements,*** the objects that make up the chart. Chart elements vary based on the type of chart used. You can see which chart elements are shown by clicking the **Chart Elements** button, the top button (with a green plus sign) on the right of the chart frame. You can add or remove elements by changing selections from the list. Other chart elements appear in the drop-down list box in the *Current Selection* group on the *Chart*

Tools Format tab and in the *Format* pane when you are working on the chart. The following table defines chart elements:

Chart Elements and Definitions

Element	Definition
Y-Axis (Vertical)	Also called the *Value Axis*; displayed vertically with numbers usually arranged on the left of a chart
X-Axis (Horizontal)	Also called the *Category Axis;* displayed horizontally with word or number labels across the bottom of the chart
Axis Titles	Both the Y-Axis and the X-Axis can include titles to name values or categories
Chart Area	The background area where the entire chart is displayed in a frame
Chart Title	A chart may include a title
Data Labels	Used to identify data series or its individual points; may include values
Data Markers	The graphical representation of values shown as columns, bars, slices, or data points
Data Table	The data that creates the chart is shown in table format below the chart
Error Bars	Used to show margins of error or standard deviation amounts
Floor	Area at the bottom of a 3-D chart that creates an illusion of depth
Gridlines	Lines that appear behind a chart to help the viewer judge values
Legend	The key that identifies each data series by color
Plot Area	The rectangle between the vertical and horizontal axes that appears behind the data markers
Tick Marks	Lines of measurement on an axis that help to interpret values on each axis
Trendline	Shows averages on 2-D charts that are not stacked and can extend beyond actual data to predict future values
Walls	Areas, including Back Walls and Side Walls, of a 3-D chart behind the data markers that help to create an illusion of depth

Enter Data and Edit

After you replace the spreadsheet sample data with your data, you can close the spreadsheet. If you need to revise the data as you work on the chart in PowerPoint, you can open the spreadsheet again.

▶ HOW TO: Edit Data in the Spreadsheet

1. Select the chart you want to modify.
2. Click the top of the **Edit Data** button [*Chart Tools Design* tab, *Data* group] to display the spreadsheet (Figure 2-87).
 - If you need to modify the data in Excel, click the **Edit Data** drop-down arrow and choose **Edit Data in Excel** to display the Excel worksheet.
 - You can click and drag the Excel window to a different location or resize it if more or less space is needed.

2-87 *Edit Data* button

3. Replace cell contents (Figure 2-88) by clicking in the **cell** and typing your data.

4. Move around in the spreadsheet by clicking your pointer or using keyboard shortcuts as follows:

 • Press **Enter** to move the insertion point down one row.
 • Press **Shift+Enter** to move the insertion point up one row.
 • Press **Tab** to move the insertion point to the next cell on the right.
 • Press **Shift+Tab** to move to the previous cell on the left.
 • Press arrow keys to move in any direction.

5. Click the spreadsheet **Close** button to return to the PowerPoint chart.

2-88 Default spreadsheet data

> ▶ **MORE INFO**
>
> Remove the sample data on the spreadsheet by clicking the **Select All** button (above the row 1 heading and to the left of the column A heading) and then pressing **Delete**.

Spreadsheet columns may need adjustments to show all data. If a cell displays number signs (#) rather than the data you entered, the cell is not wide enough to display cell contents.

• Change column width by pointing to the top of the column and dragging the splitter or double-click the line between columns to auto fit the contents.
• Be sure the shading of the selected rows and columns (see Figure 2-88) correctly identifies the category, series, and data cells. Drag a corner sizing handle to adjust.
• Columns in a spreadsheet with blank cells must be deleted so the related chart displays without a blank space.
• You can add new columns or rows in the spreadsheet or edit the spreadsheet in Excel.

▶**HOW TO: Modify the Spreadsheet**

1. Select the chart you want to modify.

2. Click the top of the **Edit Data** button [*Chart Tools Design* tab, *Data* group].

3. Adjust column width. Position your pointer on the vertical line to the right of the column heading (Figure 2-89); then use one of these methods:

 • Drag to the correct width.
 • Double-click and the column automatically adjusts to fit the widest data entered in that column.
 • Right-click to open the context menu and select **Column Width**, then type the width number on the *Column Width* dialog box. Click **OK** to close the dialog box.

4. Use Excel to modify data.

 • Click the **Edit Data** drop-down arrow [*Chart Tools Design* tab, *Data* group] and choose **Edit Data in Excel**. The Excel window displays.

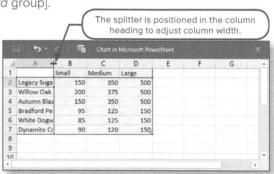

2-89 Adjust column width

- Click a cell where you need to add a cell, row, or column. Click the **Insert** drop-down arrow [*Home* tab, *Cells* group] and select the option you need.
- Adjust column width or edit titles and data values as you normally would within Excel.
- Close Excel to return to the chart on your slide.

In PowerPoint, switch the data series by clicking the **Switch Row/Column** button [*Chart Tools Design* tab, *Data* group]. In a column chart, for example, data displayed on the X-axis (bottom) and Y-axis (left) will be reversed.

Change Chart Type

Click the **Change Chart Type** button [*Chart Tools Design* tab, *Type* group] to open the *Change Chart Type* gallery where you can choose from the many different layouts. For example, Figure 2-90 shows data in a line chart and Figure 2-91 shows the same data in a clustered column chart.

2-90 Line chart

2-91 Clustered column chart

Formatting a Chart

You can change the look of a chart by applying preset styles or manually customizing individual chart elements.

Chart Styles and Colors

The **Chart Styles** gallery [*Chart Tools Design* tab] provides preset effects for chart elements including the chart background. Click the **More** button to see styles arranged by number. Click a style to apply it (Figure 2-92).

2-92 *Chart Styles* gallery

Click the **Change Colors** button [*Chart Tools Design* tab] to select *Colorful* or *Monochromatic* (shades of one color) combinations based on theme colors (Figure 2-93). The colors you choose then show in all the available chart styles. Be careful when selecting colors so the chart shapes (columns, bars, lines, or pie slices) are easy to distinguish for value comparisons. The colors also need to coordinate with your overall presentation (Figure 2-94).

If possible, avoid arranging red and green colors together. People who have difficulty recognizing different colors are most likely to have problems with red and green because they can look beige or gray.

2-93 *Chart Colors gallery*

2-94 *Chart style applied and colors changed*

Format Chart Elements

You can select chart elements (objects) and apply formatting in several ways.

▶ HOW TO: Format a Chart Element

1. Change colors and effects for a selected chart element using the Chart Tools Format tab:
 - Click the **Chart Tools Format** tab, click the **Shape Fill**, **Shape Outline**, or **Shape Effects** buttons [*Shape Styles* group] and choose appropriate colors and effects (Figure 2-95).
 - When text is selected, click the **Text Fill**, **Text Outline**, or **Text Effects** buttons [*WordArt Styles* group] and choose appropriate colors and effects.
2. Use one of these methods to open the *Format* pane (displayed on the right) and change options as needed:
 - Click the **Chart Tools Format** tab, select the element you need to change in the *Current Selection* drop-down list box. Click **Format Selection** [*Chart Tools Format* tab, *Current Selection* group] to open the *Format* pane for that element.
 - Double-click to open the appropriate *Format* pane or right-click and choose the **Format** option for that element to open the appropriate *Format* pane.
 - Click the **Chart Elements** button beside the chart and select a particular element. Click the triangle beside each element to select from different options. Click **More Options** to open the appropriate *Format* pane.

2-95 *Colors changed on data series*

To change the chart area size, point to any sizing handle (the white circles on the chart frame) and resize by dragging. You can resize chart elements, but be careful not to distort size relationships.

You can fill elements of a chart with pictures. While a chart area picture might provide an interesting background, be careful when using pictures to avoid making the chart cluttered or the text difficult to read. The goal is always to create a chart that is easy to interpret.

In Figure 2-96, the chart area has a solid fill. The plot area has a gradient fill with the darkest color at the bottom which helps to emphasize the height of the columns. In Figure 2-97, the chart type is a *3-D Column Chart*. The column heights (especially for the shorter columns) are not as easy to compare in this chart as they are in Figure 2-96.

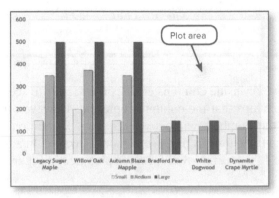

2-96 Chart plot area with gradient fill

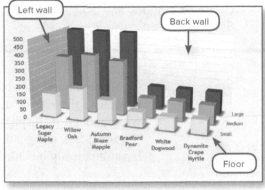

2-97 Chart with *3-D Rotation*

Legends and Labels

The *legend* identifies each data series by color. It is usually displayed on the right, but you can move it to other positions, display it horizontally above or below the plot area, or delete it.

▶ **HOW TO: Change Legend Position and Colors**

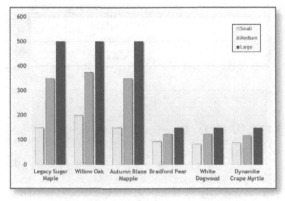

2-98 Legend moved and recolored

1. Change the selected legend's position by using one of the following methods:
 - Click the **Chart Tools Format** tab, select **Legend** in the *Current Selection* drop-down list box, and click **Format Selection** [*Chart Tools Format* tab, *Current Selection* group] to open the *Format Legend* pane. Select a position. Deselect **Show the legend without overlapping the chart** if you want the legend to appear over the plot area (Figure 2-98).
 - Double-click to open the *Format Legend* pane or right-click and choose **Format Legend** to open the *Format Legend* pane. Select a position.
 - Click the **Chart Elements** button beside the chart, click the **Legend** triangle, and then select a position or choose **More Options** to open the *Format Legend* pane.
 - Select the legend and drag it to another position within the chart area. Resize it as needed.
2. Change the selected legend's colors by using one of the following methods:
 - Click the **Chart Tools Format** tab, click the **Shape Fill** or **Shape Outline** buttons, and select different colors.
 - Right-click the legend and choose **Format Legend** to open the *Format Legend* pane. Click the **Fill & Line** tab and then select appropriate fill and border colors.
3. Remove a selected legend by using one of the following methods:
 - Click the **Chart Elements** button beside the chart and deselect the **Legend**.
 - Select the legend and press **Delete**.

Data labels display values for each data series. These labels appear in different places based on the chart style. Use the *Format Data Labels* pane to customize labels.

▶ HOW TO: Display Data Labels

1. Select the chart and then click the **Chart Element** button beside the chart to open the list of *Chart Elements*.
2. Click **Data Labels** and select a position or click **More Options** to open the *Format Data Labels* pane.
 - Change *Label Options* to control the display and position of the value as well as *File & Line, Effects, Size & Properties* options.
 - Click **Text Options** and then select icons at the top of the pane to control *Text Fill & Outline* colors, apply *Text Effects,* and add a *Text Box.*

Using data labels above or inside columns enables the viewer to see the exact data value as well as the size relationships that the columns represent. However, the columns must be wide enough to display the numbers without overlapping. If the columns are too narrow (Figure 2-99), using a data table for this purpose is more effective. In a data table, the legend is automatically included, so it was removed from the plot area in Figure 2-100.

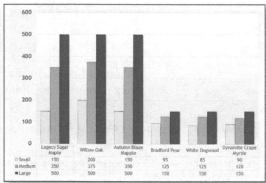

2-99 Data labels 2-100 Data table

▶ HOW TO: Display a Data Table

1. Select the chart and then click the **Chart Element** button beside the chart to open the list of *Chart Elements*.
2. Deselect **Data Labels** and **Legend** if these elements are selected. They will automatically display in the table.
3. Click **Data Table** and the table appears below the chart.
4. Point to any number in the data table, right-click to open the context menu, and select **Format Data Table** to open the *Format Data Table* pane. **Table Options** are displayed with three icons at the top of the pane.
 - Change *Data Table Options* (column icon) to control table borders and the legend key (the color that identifies each data series).
 - Click the *Fill & Line* icon (paint bucket) or the *Effects* icon (pentagon) to make color and effect changes.
 - Click **Text Options** and then select icons at the top of the pane to change *Text Fill & Outline Colors,* apply *Text Effects,* or add a *Text Box.*

A pie chart has one data series. Each slice represents a value and the size of the slice illustrates its relationship to the whole. The number of slices is best limited to six or seven slices; too many slices make a pie chart difficult to interpret.

Unlike a column or line chart, a pie chart does not have axes or axes titles. Data labels are often used instead of a legend because they are easier to interpret. You have several options for where data labels appear, either on the slices or outside the slices (Figure 2-101). Be sure to select an option that makes it easy for the viewer to match the number with the related slice. Usually the label font size must be increased. The *Format Data Labels* pane has many options you can explore (Figure 2-102).

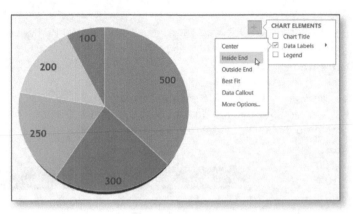

2-101 Pie chart data label positions

2-102 *Format Data Labels* pane

Explode a Pie Slice

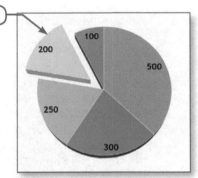

2-103 3-D pie chart with exploded slice

You can **explode** (separate) pie chart slices by dragging the pie slices away from the center. However, when all slices are separated, no single slice is emphasized. To emphasize just one slice, it is best to first design a pie chart as you want it to look and then drag that one slice away from the pie. Consider, also, how your colors are applied so the most noticeable or brightest color is used for the slice that you want to emphasize (Figure 2-103).

▶ HOW TO: Explode a Pie Slice

1. Click a pie to select the pie object.
2. Click again to select just one pie slice. Check the handles to be sure you have selected the correct slice and not a label on the slice.
3. Click and drag slightly away from the center of the pie so the slice is emphasized.

As you drag a pie slice away from the center, the entire pie becomes smaller. You can make the whole pie larger by resizing the plot area. Removing the legend creates more space for the pie, too.

For this project, you create a pie and two clustered column charts showing the cost distribution for CGL landscaping, cost comparisons for tree sizes, and the height of mature trees being considered for the new landscape.

Files Needed: *[your initials] PP P2-3.pptx* and *Trees-02.jpg (Student data files are available in the Library of your SIMnet account.)*
Completed Project File Name: *[your initials] PP 2-4.pptx*

1. Open the presentation file *[your initials] PP P2-3* and save it as [your initials] PP P2-4.
2. Create a 3-D pie chart.
 a. Select slide 6, "**Cost Distribution**."
 b. Click the **Insert Chart** icon on the content placeholder.
 c. Select the **Pie** chart type then select the **3-D Pie** layout. Click **OK**.
 d. Replace the spreadsheet sample data with the data in the following list. Point to the top of the column and then click and drag the splitter to resize columns.

	Cost
Trees—Shade	1,500
Trees—Ornamental	450
Shrubs	400
Perennials	360
Hydroseeding sq. ft.	800

3. Resize the spreadsheet window so you can proof all entries. Be sure all chart data is selected (Figure 2-104).

4. Close the spreadsheet.

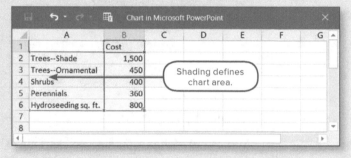

2-104 Spreadsheet linked to a chart

5. Format the 3-D pie chart.
 a. Delete the **Cost** chart title in the chart area because it duplicates the slide title.
 b. Click **Style 3** [*Chart Tools Design* tab, *Chart Styles* group].
 c. Verify that **Chart Area** [*Chart Tools Format* tab, *Current Selection* group] is selected. Click the **Shape Fill** button [*Chart Tools Format* tab, *Shape Styles* group]. Select **No Fill**.
 d. Click the **Shape Outline** button [*Chart Tools Format* tab, *Shape Styles* group] and select **No Outline**.
 e. From the drop-down list, select the **Series "Cost" Data Labels** [*Chart Tools Format* tab, *Current Selection* group]. Increase the font size to **20 pt.** [*Home* tab, *Font* group].
 f. Click the **Legend** and increase the font size to **20 pt.** [*Home* tab, *Font* group].
 g. Click and drag the legend to the upper right of the **Chart Area**.
 h. From the drop-down list, select the **Plot Area** [*Chart Tools Format* tab, *Current Selection* group]. Drag the center sizing handles to increase the plot area height so it matches the chart area height. The pie will be larger (Figure 2-105).
 i. Select the single slice for "**Trees—Ornamental**" and explode that slice by dragging it down slightly.

2-105 Slice exploded and legend repositioned

6. Create a clustered column chart.
 a. Select slide 7, "**Tree Size Cost Comparisons**." Click the **Insert Chart** icon on the content placeholder.
 b. Click the **Clustered Column** layout and click **OK**.
 c. Replace the spreadsheet data with the following data:

	Small	Medium	Large
Legacy Sugar Maple	150	350	500
Willow Oak	200	375	500
Autumn Blaze Maple	150	350	500
Bradford Pear	95	125	150
White Dogwood	85	115	150
Dynamite Crape Myrtle	90	120	150

 d. Close the spreadsheet. If you need to check the data, click the **Edit Data** button [*Chart Tools Design* tab, *Data* group].
 e. Delete the chart title in the chart area.
 f. Change the chart style to **Style 8** [*Chart Tools Design* tab, *Chart Styles* group] which has a dark fill for the chart area.

7. Add chart elements.
 a. Click the **Chart Elements** button on the right side of the chart to display the list of elements (Figure 2-106).
 b. Select the following **Axes**, **Axis Titles**, **Data Table**, **Gridlines**, and **Legend** if they are not already selected.
 - The **Data Table** automatically appears below the columns.

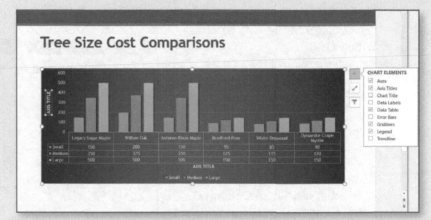

2-106 Clustered column chart with *Style 8* applied and chart elements listed on the right

8. Adjust chart formatting by selecting the following elements in the chart area. If necessary, confirm that you have the correct element selected [*Chart Tools Format* tab, *Current Selection* group].
 a. Select the *Vertical (Value) Axis Title* (rotated text on the Y-axis) and edit the text by typing Tree Cost.
 b. Select the *Horizontal (Category) Axis Title* (X-axis) below the data table and press **Delete**.
 c. Select the **Legend** and press **Delete**.
 d. Drag the chart area center sizing handle up to increase the height. Adjust the chart area size (*Height* **5"** and *Width* **11.5"**) [*Chart Tools Format* tab, *Size* group].
 e. Move the chart area up slightly so the blank space above and below the chart is even.
 f. Select each of the following chart elements and click **Shape Fill** [*Chart Tools Format* tab, *Shape Styles* group] to change the colors (Figure 2-107):
 - *Chart Area:* **Gold, Accent 4, Lighter 60%**

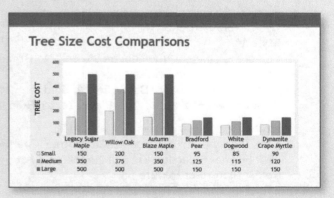

2-107 Completed chart

- *Plot Area:* **White, Background 1**
- *Large Series:* **Green, Accent 6, Darker 50%**
- *Medium Series:* **Green, Accent 6**
- *Small Series:* **Green, Accent 6, Lighter 60%**

g. Change text color and sizes.
 - Select each text element and change the font color to **Black, Text 1**.
 - Increase the font size on the axis title to **20 pt**.
 - Increase the table text and axis numbers to **18 pt**.

9. Create another clustered column chart.
 a. Select slide 8, "**Growth Potential**." Click **Chart** [*Insert* tab, *Illustrations* group] because this slide does not have a content placeholder.
 b. Click the **Clustered Column** layout and click **OK** to close the dialog box.
 c. Replace the spreadsheet data with the following data:

	Height
Legacy Sugar Maple	80
Willow Oak	60
Autumn Blaze Maple	50
Bradford Pear	35
White Dogwood	20
Dynamite Crape Myrtle	20

 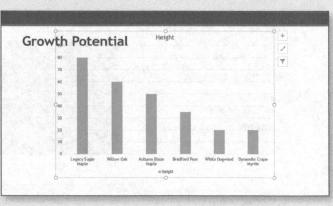

 2-108 Column chart as it first appears

 d. Delete the extra columns in the spreadsheet so the chart columns on the slide can expand in the available space (Figure 2-108).
 - Select spreadsheet **Column C** and **Column D** headings and the entire columns are selected.
 - Right-click, then select **Delete**. The columns are empty and the remaining columns fill the chart area.
 - Verify that data is correctly selected and adjust spreadsheet borders if necessary.
 e. Close the spreadsheet.
 - The chart area is not as wide as in the previous chart because you inserted the chart directly on the slide rather than inserting it through a content placeholder that had different proportions.

10. Format the chart.
 a. Delete the chart title and the legend.
 b. Resize the chart area (*Height* of **5.5"** and *Width* **10"**) [*Chart Tools Format* tab, *Size* group].
 c. Position the chart evenly on the slide.
 d. Click the **More** button [*Chart Tools Design* tab, *Chart Styles* group] and change the chart style to **Style 14**.
 e. Select the columns and change the color to **Green, Accent 6**.
 f. Change font colors and sizes as follows:
 - *Vertical (Value) Axis:* **Black, Text 1, Bold**, and **20 pt**.
 - *Horizontal (Category) Axis:* **Black, Text 1, Bold**, and **18 pt**.

11. Select the *Chart Area* and apply a picture fill.
 a. From the drop-down list, select **Chart Area** [*Chart Tools Format* tab, *Current Selection* group] and click **Format Selection** to open the *Format Chart Area* pane.
 b. Select **Picture or texture fill**.
 c. Click **File** and browse to your student data files. Select **Trees-02** and click **Insert**.

d. Change the *Transparency* percentage to **60%** (by dragging the slider or typing the percentage) to soften the picture's colors since it is behind the columns and text (Figure 2-109).

e. Close the Format Chart Area pane.

12. Click the **Transitions** tab and then select the **Wipe** transition with the **From Left** *Effect Options.* Click **Apply to All** [*Timing* group].

13. Save and close your presentation (Figure 2-110).

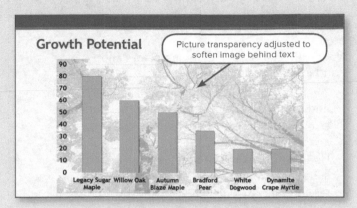

2-109 Chart resized, colors changed, and picture fill

2-110 PP P2-4 completed

Chapter Summary

2.1 Work with shapes, select theme colors and standard colors, and apply styles (p. 701).

- Change shape size by entering exact height and width sizes or by dragging sizing handles.
- Use *Lock Drawing Mode* to draw the same shape multiple times.
- Use *text boxes* to position text anywhere on a slide.
- PowerPoint's various *style* galleries provide collections of preset effects for shapes, pictures, or other objects.
- Line *Weight* is the line thickness measured in points.
- *Dashes* show lines with a combination of dots and dashes.
- When you apply *Theme Colors* to shapes, the colors change when a different theme is applied.
- *Standard Colors* do not change when a different theme is applied.
- Computer screens use the *RGB model* that displays colors by blending values for *red, green,* and *blue.*
- Highly *saturated* colors are intense and vibrant; colors that are not saturated are muddy and dull.
- *Luminosity* is a measure of lightness that is adjusted by the amount of white or black in the color.
- The *Eyedropper* is used to match any color on your computer screen.

2.2 Create interesting and eye-catching text effects with *WordArt* styles and text effects (p. 710).

- The *WordArt* styles gallery shows a collection of preset text effects.
- The *Transform* effect warps text into different shapes or follows a path.
- You can fill *WordArt* with solid or gradient colors, textures, patterns, or pictures.
- Use the *Line Style* option in the *Format Shape* dialog box to customize line styles.

2.3 Search for pictures and illustrations, modify picture appearance, and compress picture file size (p. 712).

- Use the *Insert Pictures* dialog box to search for online pictures and illustrations.

- The *Picture Styles* gallery shows a collection of preset picture effects.
- To remove a picture style, click the *Reset Picture* button.
- Use *Crop* to trim unwanted areas of a selected picture.
- Increase *Color Saturation* to make picture colors more vibrant; decrease color saturation to make picture colors more muted.
- *Color Tone* changes a picture's cool or warm tones.
- Select *Color* and then *Recolor* to change a picture's color to a monotone color.
- The *Set Transparent Color* feature can make one color in a picture transparent. This feature works well to remove white backgrounds.
- Use *Compress Pictures* to reduce the file size of your presentation.

2.4 Organize information in a grid format using tables and customize the arrangement of columns and rows (p. 721).

- You can insert and delete table *columns* and *rows.*
- *Merge* table cells to join them; *split* table cells to create multiple cells.
- Column width usually varies based on content; row height is usually a consistent size.

2.5 Format a table by applying styles, colors, and effects (p. 726).

- You can apply *WordArt Styles* to table text.
- *Table Styles* provide options for a table's design using theme accent colors.
- *Table Style Options* control how columns and rows are emphasized to feature areas of the table.
- Border lines can separate cells and shading can emphasize cells.
- Horizontal cell alignment options include *Align Left, Center,* or *Align Right;* vertical cell alignment options include *Align Top, Center Vertically,* or *Align Bottom.*

2.6 Show processes and relationships with *SmartArt* graphics (p. 731).

- Use *SmartArt graphics* to create diagrams that illustrate concepts such as processes, cycles, or relationships.

- **SmartArt layouts** are organized by categories.
- Each layout includes information about how you can use it or the meaning it conveys.
- Type text directly in each *SmartArt* shape or type text in the *Text Pane*.
- Change bulleted text to a *SmartArt* graphic by clicking the **Convert to SmartArt Graphic** button.

2.7 Improve the appearance of *SmartArt* graphics by applying styles, colors, and effects (p. 734).

- **SmartArt Styles** provide a gallery of *Effect Options*.
- The **Change Colors** button provides a gallery of color options arranged in categories.
- The **Add Shape** button inserts shapes in relation to the selected shape.
- You can format or individually resize shapes within a *SmartArt* graphic.

2.8 Create charts that show relationships between data values and emphasize data in different ways based on the chart type and chart elements (p. 738).

- Charts in PowerPoint are linked to spreadsheets where data is entered. Changes made to the data will automatically appear in the chart.

- Charts created in Excel can be edited in PowerPoint because they are linked.
- A group of data values is a **data series**.
- *Chart Layouts* are arranged in categories including *Column, Line, Pie, Bar,* and *Area*.
- The **Chart Area** displays the entire chart including all **chart elements**.
- The *Plot Area* provides a background for *Data Markers,* the columns, bars, or slices that represent data.

2.9 Format a chart by applying preset styles or manually customizing individual chart elements (p. 743).

- **Chart Styles** provide a gallery of preset effects for chart elements.
- The **Legend** is a key that identifies each data series by color.
- The *Change Colors* button provides a gallery of colorful or monochromatic colors for chart elements.
- You can customize chart elements individually to enhance their appearance.
- To emphasize a pie slice, you can **explode** it by separating the slice from the rest of the pie chart.

Check for Understanding

The SIMbook for this text (within your SIMnet account) provides the following resources for concept review:

- Multiple choice questions
- Matching exercises
- Short answer questions

Guided Project 2-1

Guest satisfaction has always been important to the success of Paradise Lakes Resort (PLR) in Minnesota. The general manager plans to use feedback from social media to identify problems and to guide improvements at the resort. In this project you illustrate a presentation the general manager will use to explain these concepts to employees at PLR.
[Student Learning Outcomes 2.1, 2.2, 2.3, 2.6, 2.7]

File Needed: *SocialMedia-02.pptx (Student data files are available in the Library of your SIMnet account.)*
Completed Project File Name: *[your initials] PowerPoint 2-1.pptx*

Skills Covered in This Project

- Apply a picture style.
- Adjust size dimensions.
- Apply text effects.
- Insert a text box.
- Create a *SmartArt* graphic.
- Apply a *SmartArt* style and effects.

1. Open the presentation *SocialMedia-02*. This design theme shows slide titles at the bottom of all slides except the title slide.

2. Save the presentation as [your initials] PowerPoint 2-1.

3. Resize a picture and apply a style.
 a. Select the lake picture on slide 1.
 b. Change the picture *Width* to **6"** [*Picture Tools Format* tab, *Size* group]. The *Height* automatically adjusts.
 c. Apply the **Metal Oval** picture style [*Picture Tools Format* tab, *Picture Styles* group].
 d. Position the picture on the left (Figure 2-111).

4. Adjust the title text to complement the wood decking shown in the picture.
 a. Select the title text "Improving Guest Satisfaction" on slide 1 and increase the font size to **60 pt**.
 b. Adjust the placeholder so it fits the text and move it down slightly.
 c. Select the title text and click the **Text Fill** button [*Drawing Tools Format* tab, *WordArt Styles* group], select **Texture**, and select **Medium Wood**.
 d. With the title text selected, click the **Text Effects** button, select **Shadow**, and select **Shadow Options**. The *Format Shape* pane opens. Change the following settings:
 Transparency: **20%**
 Blur: **5 pt**.
 Angle: **50°**
 Distance: **5 pt**.
 f. Close the *Format Shape* pane.

5. Insert a new slide with a *Title and Content* layout after slide 1.

2-111 Title slide

6. Add text and a shape.
 a. Display slide 2 and type the slide title **Why Social Media?** In this theme, the title placeholder is at the bottom of the slide.
 b. Type the following bulleted text:

 Revenue
 Market Share
 Guest Satisfaction
 Guest Loyalty

 c. Resize the bulleted list placeholder so it fits the text and move the text to the right (Figure 2-112).
 d. Click the **Shapes** button [*Insert* tab, *Illustrations* group] to open the gallery. Select the **Up Arrow** shape (*Block Arrow* category).
 e. Draw an arrow (*Height* **3.5"** and *Width* **2.5"**). Then position the arrow to the left of the text.
 f. With the arrow selected, click the **More** button [*Drawing Tools Format* tab, *Shape Styles* group] and apply the **Intense Effect, Orange, Accent 1**.

2-112 Slide 3 with a shape

7. Insert a new slide with a *Blank* layout after slide 4.

8. Create a *SmartArt* graphic and insert an additional shape on slide 5.
 a. Click the **Insert** tab.
 b. Click the **SmartArt** button and select the **Cycle** type.
 c. Select the **Continuous Cycle** layout and click **OK**.
 d. Add the following text to each shape starting with the top shape and continuing in a clockwise direction around the circle:

 More Rentals
 Rentals
 Social Media Comments
 Improvements
 Better Social Media Comments

 e. Select the "**Better Social Media Comments**" shape, click the **Add Shape** drop-down arrow [*SmartArt Tools Design* tab, *Create Graphic* group] and select **Add Shape After**.
 f. Type **Higher Ratings** in the new shape.
 g. Click the **Intense Effect** style [*SmartArt Tools Design* tab, *SmartArt Styles* group].
 h. Select all shapes with text by pressing **Ctrl** while you click each one. Change the font size to **20 pt**. and apply **bold** [*Home* tab, *Font* group].
 i. With all the shapes selected, resize the shapes horizontally (*Width* **2.75"**) so the word "Improvements" fits on one line (Figure 2-113).

9. Insert a text box.
 a. Click the **Text Box** button [*Insert* tab, *Text* group] and click inside the cycle layout.
 b. Type the following text and resize the text box so that the text wraps on two lines as shown in Figure 2-113:

 With the help of NewMediaMarketing.com

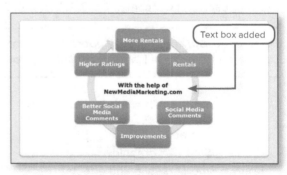

2-113 Slide 4 with *SmartArt* graphic and effects added

c. Change the font size to **20 pt.**, apply **bold**, and center the text [*Home* tab, *Font* group].

d. Adjust the text box size, if necessary, and center it in the middle of the cycle layout as shown in Figure 2-113.

10. Apply a transition.

a. Click the **Reveal** transition effect [*Transitions* tab, *Transition to This Slide* group].

b. Click **Apply To All** [*Transitions* tab, *Timing* group].

11. Save and close the presentation (Figure 2-114).

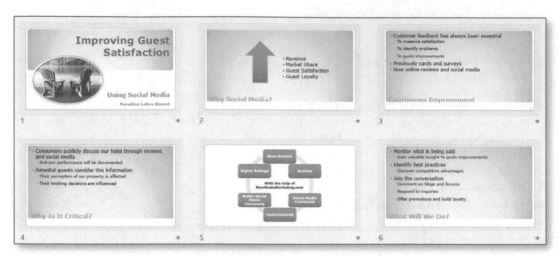

2-114 PowerPoint 2-1 completed

Guided Project 2-2

For this project, you prepare a presentation with key points essential to maintain a healthy lifestyle and show examples of weight loss calorie requirements for men and women at different ages. The doctors at Courtyard Medical Plaza will use this presentation to encourage clients to be more active.
[**Student Learning Outcomes 2.1, 2.2, 2.3, 2.4, 2.5, 2.6, 2.7**]

File Needed: ***StayingActive-02.pptx*** *(Student data files are available in the* Library *of your SIMnet account.)*
Completed Project File Name: *[your initials] **PowerPoint 2-2.pptx***

Skills Covered in This Project

- Apply text effects.
- Create a *SmartArt* graphic.
- Apply a *SmartArt* style and effects.
- Insert an online picture.
- Crop a picture.
- Apply a picture style.
- Adjust size dimensions.
- Insert a text box.
- Insert and format a table.

1. Open the presentation ***StayingActive-02***.

2. Save the presentation as [your initials] PowerPoint 2-2.

3. Format the presentation title.
 a. Select the title placeholder on slide 1.
 b. Click the **Text Effects** button [*Drawing Tools Format* tab, *WordArt Styles* group], click **Transform**, and select **Square** (*Square* is the first style under *Warp*). The text fills the title placeholder.
 c. Click the **Bring Forward** drop-down arrow [*Drawing Tools Format* tab, *Arrange* group], and select **Bring to Front** so the green triangle is behind the text.
 d. Click the **Text Fill** button [*Drawing Tools Format* tab, *WordArt Styles* group], select **Texture**, and click **More Textures** to open the *Format Shape* pane.
 e. Select **Pattern fill** and then choose the **Large checker board** pattern.
 f. Change the *Foreground Color* to **Aqua, Accent 1, Lighter 40%** and the *Background Color* to **White, Text 1**.
 g. Click **Text Fill** to close those options on the *Format Shape* pane. Click **Text Outline** to open outline options. Select **Solid line** and change the color to **Black, Background 1**.
 h. Click the **Text Effects** icon at the top of the pane. Select **Glow**.
 i. Change the *Color* to **Green, Accent 2, Lighter 60%** and the *Transparency* to **20%**. Verify the *Size* is **10 pt**. (Figure 2-115).
 j. Close the *Format Shape* pane.

2-115 Text Effects for presentation title

4. Insert a *SmartArt* graphic, apply a style, and change colors using the *SmartArt Tools Design* tab.
 a. Display slide 2 and click the **SmartArt** icon on the content placeholder to open the *Choose a SmartArt Graphic* dialog box.
 b. Select the **Hierarchy** type and the **Horizontal Hierarchy** layout. Click **OK** to close the dialog box and insert the SmartArt graphic.
 c. Delete the three shapes on the right.
 d. Click the **Text Pane** button on the left of the *SmartArt* frame, if necessary, to open the *Text Pane*.
 e. Type Keep Moving after the first bullet. Type the following items after the indented bullets:

 Moderate Intensity Activity
 Count Steps (Press **Enter** to add another bullet.)
 Combine Aerobic and Strengthening

 f. Click the *Text Pane* **Close** button.
 g. Select the **Subtle Effect** *SmartArt* style [*SmartArt Tools Design* tab, *SmartArt Styles* group].
 h. Click the **Change Colors** button [*SmartArt Tools Design* tab, *SmartArt Styles* group] and select **Colorful Range, Accent Colors 4 to 5** (Figure 2-116).

2-116 *SmartArt* graphic with style and colors changed

5. Search for a picture and apply a picture style.
 a. Display slide 3. Click the **Online Pictures** button [*Insert* tab, *Images* group] to open *the Insert Pictures* dialog box.
 b. Search for an online picture using the search word gardening.
 c. On the search results dialog box, click the list arrow by the *Search* button to select **All Images**. Select an appropriate picture and click **Insert**.
 d. Select the **Rotated White** picture style [*Picture Tools Format* tab, *Picture Styles* group].
 e. Resize the picture as needed so it fits on the right of the slide.

6. Crop a picture and apply a picture style.
 a. Display slide 5 and select the picture. Click the **Crop** button [*Picture Tools Format* tab, *Size* group] and crop the picture to focus only on the family. Click **Crop** again to accept your change.
 b. Select the **Rotated White** picture style [*Picture Tools Format* tab, *Picture Styles* group] to match the other picture.
 c. Move the picture to the right of the slide.

7. Insert a new slide after slide 6 with a *Title and Content* layout.

8. Add text.
 a. On slide 7, type the title text **Calorie Examples**.
 b. Click the **Text Box** button [*Insert* tab, *Text* group], click below the title, and type **Gaining 5 pounds a year**.
 c. Apply **Bold** and change the font size to **20 pt**. [*Home* tab, *Font* group].
 d. Resize the text box as needed. Right-align the text box and the slide title.

9. Insert a table, add text, and modify formatting.
 a. Click the **Table** icon on the content placeholder on slide 7.
 b. Enter **6** columns and **5** rows on the *Insert Table* dialog box. Click **OK** to close the dialog box.
 c. Type the text shown in Figure 2-117.

Shading reflects the same person at two ages.

Age	Height	Weight	Maintain	Fat Loss	Extreme Fat Loss
20	5 ft 10 in	200	2,647	2,118	1,600
25	5 ft 10 in	225	2,769	2,215	1,800
30	6 ft 2 in	240	2,916	2,333	1,920
35	6 ft 2 in	265	3,038	2,430	2,120

2-117 Table with formatting changes

 d. Select all cells and change the font size to **20 pt**. [*Home* tab, *Font* group]. Change to **Center** alignment [*Table Tools Layout* tab, *Alignment* group].
 e. Adjust column width by double-clicking the border line between columns. Deselect the table, if necessary, so your pointer changes to a splitter to adjust the right border of the last column so the text fits on one line. When you stop dragging, the table is selected again.
 f. Change the *Pen Color* to **Black, Background 1** and verify the *Pen Weight* is **1 pt**. [*Table Tools Design* tab, *Draw Borders* group].
 g. Click the **Borders** button, and select **All Borders** [*Table Tools Design* tab, *Table Styles* group].
 h. Select the second and third rows. Click the **Shading** button [*Table Tools Design* tab, *Table Styles* group] and select **Aqua, Accent 1, Lighter 80%**.
 i. Select the fourth and fifth rows. Click the **Shading** button [*Table Tools Design* tab, *Table Styles* group] and select **Aqua, Accent 1, Lighter 60%**.
 j. Center the table on the slide.

10. Duplicate the table and edit the text in the second table.
 a. Select the table on slide 7 and press **Ctrl+D** to duplicate it.
 b. Position the second table centered near the bottom of the slide.
 c. Edit the table content to match the text shown in Figure 2-118.

Age	Height	Weight	Maintain	Fat Loss	Extreme Fat Loss
20	5 ft 7 in	150	2,041	1,633	1,225
25	5 ft 7 in	175	2,163	1,730	1,400
30	5 ft 9 in	180	2,204	1,763	1,440
35	5 ft 9 in	205	2,325	1,860	1,640

2-118 Table with text edits

11. Insert and format a shape to identify table contents on slide 7.
 a. Click the **Shapes** button [*Insert* tab, *Illustrations* group] and select the **Oval**. Draw an oval shape and adjust its size (*Height* **0.9"** and *Width* **2"**) [*Drawing Tools Format* tab, *Size* group].
 b. Click the **Shape Fill** button [*Drawing Tools Format* tab, *Shape Styles* group] and change the color to **Gold, Accent 5, Lighter 40%**.
 c. Click the **Shape Outline** button [*Drawing Tools Format* tab, *Shape Styles* group] and change the color to **Green, Accent 2**. Repeat to change the *Weight* to **3 pt**.

d. Type the word Female. Change the font color to **Black, Background 1** and apply **Bold**.
e. Click the **Edit Shape** button [*Drawing Tools Format* tab, *Insert Shapes* group] and select **Change Shape**. Select **Explosion 1** in the *Stars and Banners* category.
f. Position this shape at the left corner of the bottom table (Figure 2-119).

12. Duplicate and edit a shape.
 a. Select the "**Female**" shape and press **Ctrl+D** to duplicate it.
 b. Position the second shape at the left corner of the top table.
 c. Change the text to Male.

13. Format the table:
 a. Display slide 8 and select the table. If necessary, change the *Pen Color* to **Black, Background 1** and the *Pen Weight* to **1 pt**. [*Table Tools Design* tab, *Draw Borders* group].
 b. Click **Borders** [*Table Tools Design* tab, *Table Styles* group] and select **All Borders**.
 c. Change the font size for all text to **20 pt**.
 d. Select all cells and click the **Center Vertically** button [*Table Tools Layout* tab, *Alignment* group].
 e. Change the table size (*Height* **4.5"** and *Width* **9"**) and click the **Center** button [*Table Tools Layout* tab, *Alignment* group] to center it horizontally on the slide.

14. Apply a transition.
 a. Click the **Cube** transition effect [*Transitions* tab, *Transition to This Slide* group].
 b. Click **Apply To All** [*Transitions* tab, *Timing* group].

15. Save and close the presentation (Figure 2-120).

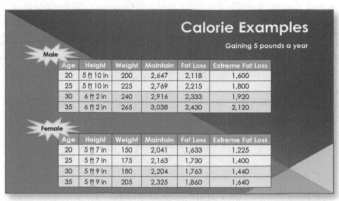

2-119 Slide 7 completed tables

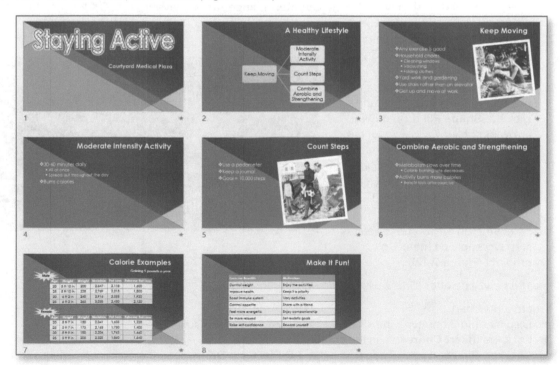

2-120 PowerPoint 2-2 completed

Guided Project 2-3

Solution Seekers, Inc., has been asked to develop a presentation for a meeting of personnel managers about salary trends for information technology workers. For this project, you modify tables and prepare charts showing average salaries and salaries for selected jobs.
[Student Learning Outcomes 2.1, 2.2, 2.3, 2.5, 2.6, 2.7, 2.8]

File Needed: *InfoTechSalaries-02.pptx (Student data files are available in the Library of your SIMnet account.)*
Completed Project File Name: *[your initials] PowerPoint 2-3.pptx*

Skills Covered in This Project

- Convert text to a *SmartArt* graphic.
- Apply a *SmartArt* style and effects.
- Create a pie chart.
- Format a table.
- Create a column chart.

- Apply chart styles.
- Format chart elements.
- Insert *WordArt* and apply effects.
- Apply a picture style.
- Insert and align text boxes.

1. Open the presentation *InfoTechSalaries-02*.

2. Save the presentation as [your initials] PowerPoint 2-3.

3. Convert bulleted text to a *SmartArt* graphic and modify the style and colors.
 a. Display slide 2. Select the bulleted text and click the **Convert to SmartArt** button [*Home* tab, *Paragraph* group].
 b. Select **More SmartArt Graphics** to open the *Choose a SmartArt Graphic* dialog box.
 c. Select the **Relationship** type and the **Counterbalance Arrows** layout. Click **OK** to close the dialog box.
 d. Apply the **Cartoon** style [*SmartArt Tools Design* tab, *SmartArt Styles* group].
 e. Select the down arrow shape pointing to "Fewer Layoffs" and click the **Shape Fill** drop-down arrow [*SmartArt Tools Format* tab, *Shape Styles* group].
 f. Select **Gradient** and under *Dark Variations,* click **Linear Down** to emphasize the downward movement.
 g. Select the up arrow and repeat step f to apply a **Linear Up** gradient (Figure 2-121).

2-121 Slide 2 *SmartArt* graphic with color changes

4. Insert a new slide after slide 2 with a *Title and Content* layout.

5. Create a pie chart.
 a. Display slide 3 and type the slide title Employee Salary Satisfaction.
 b. Click the **Insert Chart** icon in the content placeholder.
 c. Click the **Pie** chart type. Then select the **3-D Pie**. Click **OK** to close the dialog box and insert the chart.

d. Replace the spreadsheet data with the data shown in Figure 2-122. Close the spreadsheet.

6. Modify a pie chart.
 a. Drag the chart title "**Satisfaction%**," to the top left of the chart area. Increase the font size to **24 pt**. [*Home* tab, *Font* group].
 b. Click the **Chart Elements** button on the right side of the slide and select **Legend**. Select **Right**.
 c. Increase the font size to **20 pt**. [*Home* tab, *Font* group] and drag the legend to the bottom right of the chart area.
 d. Click the **Chart Elements** button again and select **Data Labels**. Select **Inside End**.
 e. Click the **Chart Elements** list box arrow [*Chart Tools Format* tab, *Current Selection* group] and select **Series "Satisfaction %" Data Labels**. Increase the font size to **24 pt**. and apply **Bold** [*Home* tab, *Font* group] (Figure 2-123).

7. Modify table formatting.
 a. Display slide 4 and select the table. Increase the font size to **20 pt**. [*Home* tab, *Font* group].
 b. Select **Header Row** and **Banded Rows** [*Table Tools Design* tab, *Table Style Options* group].
 c. Apply the **Themed Style 1, Accent 2** style [*Table Tools Design* tab, *Table Styles* group].
 d. Increase the table size (*Height* **4"**) [*Table Tools Layout* tab, *Table Size* group].
 e. Click the **Center Vertically** button [*Table Tools Layout* tab, *Alignment* group].
 f. Select columns 2–5 and click **Align Right** [*Table Tools Layout* tab, *Alignment* group].

8. After slide 4, insert a new slide with a *Title and Content* layout.

9. Create a column chart.
 a. Select slide 5 and type the slide title Salary Change, Selected Jobs.
 b. Click the **Insert Chart** button on the content placeholder.
 c. Select the **Clustered Column** chart and click **OK**.
 d. Replace the spreadsheet data with the data shown in Figure 2-124. Select **Column D**, right-click, and select **Delete**. By removing the blank column, the chart displays correctly with no blank space. Close the spreadsheet.

10. Modify a column chart.
 a. Delete the "**Chart Title**" placeholder.
 b. Click the **Chart Elements** button on the right side of the chart, select **Legend**, and then click **More Options** to open the *Format Legend* pane.

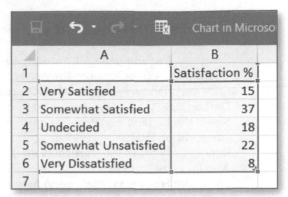

	A	B
1		Satisfaction %
2	Very Satisfied	15
3	Somewhat Satisfied	37
4	Undecided	18
5	Somewhat Unsatisfied	22
6	Very Dissatisfied	8
7		

2-122 Spreadsheet linked to a chart

2-123 Slide 3 completed pie chart

	A	B	C
1		2016	2017
2	Project Manager	107,331	110,550
3	Applications Developer	91,989	94,750
4	Security Analyst	84,267	89,950
5	Network Specialist	64,920	67,000
6	Technical Support	56,590	57,288
7	Help Desk	44,365	46,950
8			

2-124 Spreadsheet linked to a chart

c. Click the **Legend Options** heading, if necessary, to open the list of options. Select **Top Right** and deselect **Show the legend without overlapping the chart**.

d. Close the *Format Chart Area* pane.

e. Select the **Legend** and click the **Shape Fill** button [*Chart Tools Format* tab, *Shape Styles* group]. Change the legend color to **Brown, Accent 2, Darker 50%**.

f. Click the chart frame to select the **Chart Area** and change the **Shape Fill** color to **Teal, Accent 1, Darker 50%**.

g. Select the **Legend** and increase the font size to **18 pt**. [*Home* tab, *Font* group]. Repeat to increase the **Vertical (Value) Axis** font size to **18 pt**.

h. Select the **Horizontal (Category) Axis** and increase the font size to **20 pt**. (Figure 2-125).

11. Select the picture on slide 6 and apply the **Moderate Frame, Black** picture style [*Picture Tools Format* tab, *Picture Styles* group].

12. Insert *WordArt* text on slide 6.

a. Click the **WordArt** button [*Insert* tab, *Text* group] and select the **Fill – White, Text 1, Outline – Background 1, Hard Shadow – Accent 1** style.

b. Type Employees Are Valuable in the *WordArt* placeholder and move this text above the picture.

c. With the *WordArt* placeholder selected, click the **Text Effects** button [*Drawing Tools Format* tab, *WordArt Styles* group], select **Shadow**, and click **Offset Diagonal Bottom Right**.

d. Click the **Text Outline** button [*Drawing Tools Format* tab, *WordArt Styles* group] and select **Black, Background 2**.

e. Deselect the *WordArt* text (Figure 2-126).

13. Insert text boxes on slide 6 for salary numbers.

a. Click the **Text Box** button [*Insert* tab, *Text* group], click below the picture, and type $75,270. Change the font color to **Black, Background 2**, increase the font size to **20 pt.**, and apply **Bold**.

b. Position this salary below the first person on the left in the picture.

c. With the salary text box selected, press **Ctrl+D** and position the duplicated text box below the second person in the picture. Repeat for the remaining two people in the picture.

d. Edit the text boxes to change the three duplicated salaries to $64,644, $55,340, and $49,982.

e. Select all of the salary text boxes and click the **Arrange** button [*Home* tab, *Drawing* group]. Select **Align** and click **Align Selected Objects** if necessary. Repeat to click **Align Bottom** (see Figure 2-126).

2-125 Slide 5 completed clustered column chart

2-126 Slide 6 picture style, text effects, and text boxes

14. Apply transitions.
 a. Click the **Blinds** transition effect [*Transitions* tab, *Transition to This Slide* group].
 b. Click **Apply To All** [*Transitions* tab, *Timing* group].
 c. Apply the **Zoom** transition to slide 6.

15. Save and close the presentation (Figure 2-127).

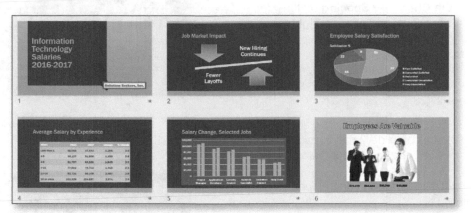

2-127 PowerPoint 2-3 completed

Independent Project 2-4

At Pool & Spa Oasis, sales associates must educate new spa owners about keeping spa water safe with proper maintenance. For this project, you prepare a presentation that emphasizes the routine to follow, explains pH level numbers, and lists available products that are typically used to balance water.
[**Student Learning Outcomes 2.1, 2.2, 2.3, 2.4, 2.5, 2.6, 2.7**]

File Needed: ***Balancing-02.pptx*** (*Student data files are available in the* Library *of your SIMnet account.*)
Completed Project File Name: *[your initials]* ***PowerPoint 2-4.pptx***

Skills Covered in This Project

- Insert *WordArt* and apply effects.
- Adjust size dimensions.
- Insert an online picture.
- Apply a picture style.
- Create a *SmartArt* graphic.
- Apply a *SmartArt* style and effects.
- Insert and format a table.
- Insert a text box.
- Change solid and gradient colors.

1. Open the presentation ***Balancing-02***.

2. Save the presentation as [your initials] PowerPoint 2-4.

3. Change the title text arrangement.
 a. Display slide 1. Delete the title text "**Balancing Act**," but leave the word "**The**" as shown.
 b. Insert *WordArt* with the style **Fill – White, Outline – Accent 1, Glow – Accent 1**.
 c. Type Balancing Act.
 d. Apply a **Shadow, Offset Right** *Text Effect*.
 e. Click the **Character Spacing** button [*Home* tab, *Font* group] and choose **Tight**.
 f. Apply the *Transform* text effect of **Cascade Up**.
 g. Increase the *WordArt* size (*Height* **3"** and *Width* **9"**) and position it as shown in Figure 2-128.

2-128 Slide 1 with *WordArt*

4. Insert a picture and adjust text spacing. The bulleted list placeholder on slide 2 has a gradient fill color so it cannot be resized without distorting the slide.
 a. Display slide 2. On the first indented line in the bulleted list, place your insertion point in front of the word "correct." Press **Shift+Enter** to insert a line break so the remaining text go to the next line without starting a new paragraph. Repeat to split the next line twice: before "microorganisms" and "Bromine."
 b. Search for an online picture using the words hot tub and insert a picture similar to the one shown in Figure 2-129.
 c. Resize the picture as needed to fit on the right side of the slide.
 d. Apply the **Bevel Rectangle** picture style.
 e. Position the picture as shown.

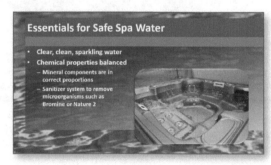

2-129 Slide 2 with inserted picture and picture style

5. Insert a *SmartArt* graphic, add text, and change formatting.
 a. Display slide 4. Insert a *SmartArt* graphic from the *Process* category with the **Continuous Block Process** layout.
 b. Type Test Water, Add Necessary Products, and Enjoy! in the three shapes.
 c. Resize the *SmartArt* graphic (*Height* **5"** and *Width* **9.5"**).
 d. Apply the **Polished** *SmartArt* style.
 e. Select the **arrow** and apply **Gradient** colors. Select **More Gradient** to open the *Format Shape* pane.
 f. Select a *Preset gradient* of **Light Gradient – Accent 2**. The *Type* is **Linear** and change the *Direction* to **Linear Left**.
 g. Modify the gradient stops:
 - *First stop:* Color **Light Blue, Background 2**; Position **0%**
 - *Second stop:* Color **Light Turquoise, Accent 2, Lighter 80%**; Position **40%**; Brightness **80%**
 - *Third stop:* Remove
 - *Fourth stop:* Color **Turquoise, Accent 2, Lighter 40%**; Position **100%**; Brightness **40%**

h. Close the *Format Shape* pane.
i. Apply **Bold** to all *SmartArt* text.
j. Position the *SmartArt* graphic as shown in Figure 2-130.

6. Insert a table, add text, and change formatting.
 a. Display slide 5. Insert a table with **3** columns and **4** rows.
 b. Select **Header Row** and **Banded Rows**.
 c. Type the following text:

Level	Numbers	Results
High	8.0	Alkaline, Scale
Good	7.2 – 7.6	Ideal pH Range
Low	6.0	Acidic, Corrosion

 d. Change the font size to **20 pt**. for all table text.
 e. Apply the **Themed Style 1, Accent 1** table style.
 f. Select each column and adjust the *Cell Width* as follows: left column is **1.5"**, middle column is **2.8"**, and right column is **2.8"**.
 g. Change the alignment on the middle column to **Center**.
 h. Center the table on the slide.

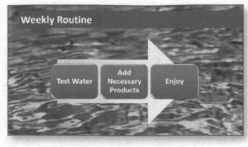

2-130 Slide 4 *SmartArt* graphic with style and color changes

7. Insert a text box.
 a. Insert a text box below the table on slide 5. Type Drain and replace spa water every 60-90 days.
 b. Change the font size to **20 pt**.
 c. Change the shape fill to **Turquoise, Accent 2, Lighter 80%**.
 d. Resize the text box, if necessary, so the text fits on one line. Position it below the table aligned with the right of the table.

8. Copy and format a table.
 a. Select the table on slide 5 and copy it.
 b. Display slide 6 and paste the table.
 c. Delete the middle column and size the table so it is **9"** wide.
 d. Delete the table text and add three rows.
 e. Type the following text:

Products	Purpose
Sanitizer	Type needed depends on sanitizer system
Test Strips	Measures chemical levels
Shock Treatment	Breaks down organic or unfiltered material
Total Alkalinity	Increases or decreases to balance pH levels
Calcium Increaser	Balances dissolved calcium
Stain and Scale Prevention	Removes metallic impurities

 f. Adjust the column width as needed to avoid word wrapping.
 g. Center the table on the slide.

9. Apply the **Ripple** transition with the **From Top-Left** effect option to all slides.

765

10. Save and close the presentation (Figure 2-131).

2-131 PowerPoint 2-4 completed

Independent Project 2-5

Prospective home buyers need to understand mortgage requirements and how to prepare to apply for a mortgage. Angie O'Connor at Placer Hills Real Estate wants to use a presentation on her notebook computer to help guide her discussions about these concepts with clients. For this project, you develop the presentation.
[Student Learning Outcomes 2.1, 2.3, 2.4, 2.5, 2.6, 2.7, 2.8]

Files Needed: ***PreparetoBuy-02.pptx*** and ***PlacerHillsSold-02.jpg*** (*Student data files are available in the Library of your SIMnet account.*)
Completed Project File Name: *[your initials] PowerPoint 2-5.pptx*

Skills Covered in This Project

- Insert a picture.
- Crop a picture.
- Apply a picture style.
- Adjust size dimensions.
- Insert a chart and edit data.

- Apply chart styles.
- Format chart elements.
- Insert text boxes.
- Insert and format a table.
- Convert text to a *SmartArt* graphic.
- Apply a *SmartArt* style and effects.

1. Open the presentation ***PreparetoBuy-02***.
2. Save the presentation as [your initials] PowerPoint 2-5.

3. Insert and modify a picture.
 a. On slide 1, insert the **PlacerHillsSold-02** picture from your student data files.
 b. Crop the picture on the left and right as shown in Figure 2-132.
 c. Resize the picture (*Height* **5.5"** and the *Width* automatically adjusts).
 d. Apply the **Rounded Diagonal Corner, White** picture style.
 e. Position the picture on the right side of the slide as shown in Figure 2-132.

2-132 Slide 1 with inserted picture and picture style

4. Insert a chart showing how fixed mortgage rates have changed over time.
 a. Display slide 4. Click the **Insert Chart** button on the content placeholder.
 b. Select the **Line** chart type and then select the **Line with Markers** chart layout. Click **OK**.
 c. Replace the spreadsheet data with the data shown in Figure 2-133.
 • Be sure the selection area includes row 10 to avoid error messages.
 • Delete **Column D** so the corresponding chart area is correct with no blank space.
 • Close the spreadsheet.

5. Examine the line chart as it first appears (Figure 2-134).
 • It is accurate, but the data series lines are too thin and data markers too small.
 • The following changes (steps 6–13) will make the chart easier to interpret.

6. Delete the chart title.

7. Change the chart area *Shape Fill* to **Brown, Background 2**.

8. Format the line and markers on the "Rate" series.
 a. Select the "Rate" line and right-click. Select **Format Data Series** to open the *Format Data Series* pane (Figure 2-135).
 b. Click the **Fill & Line** icon at the top of the pane.
 c. Click **Line** options at the top of the pane below the icons and change the *Width* to **3 pt**.
 d. Click **Marker** options below the icons and select the following:
 • *Marker Options:* **Built-in**; *Type:* **Square**, and *Size:* **15** (Figure 2-136)
 • *Fill:* **Solid fill**; *Color:* **Orange, Accent 2**

9. Format the line and markers on the "Points" series.
 a. Select the "Points" line. Click **Line** options and select the following:
 • *Line:* **Solid line**; *Color:* **Orange, Accent 4**
 • *Width:* **3 pt**.

	A	B	C
1		Rate	Points
2	1974	9.19	1.2
3	1979	11.2	1.6
4	1984	13.88	2.5
5	1989	10.32	2.1
6	1994	8.38	1.8
7	1999	7.44	1
8	2004	5.84	0.7
9	2009	5.04	0.7
10	2014	4.17	0.6
11			

2-133 Spreadsheet linked to a chart

2-134 Line chart as it first appears

Click to open *Fill & Line* tab

2-135 *Format Data Series* pane

b. Select **Marker** options and select the following:
- *Marker Options:* **Built-in**; *Type:* **Diamond**; *Size:* **20**
- *Marker Fill:* **Solid fill**; *Color:* **Red, Accent 5**

10. Close the *Format Data Series* pane.

11. Select the *Horizontal (Category) axis* and increase the font size to **16 pt**. and apply **bold**. Repeat for the *Vertical (Value) axis*.

12. Select the **Chart Area**, change the *Width* to **11"**, and center the chart horizontally.

13. Move the chart up slightly to make room for a source notation at the bottom of the slide.
 a. Insert a text box and type the following:

 Information based on Freddie Mac survey data
 http://www.freddiemac.com/pmms/pmms30.htm

 b. Position the text box as displayed in Figure 2-137.

14. Insert and format a table:
 a. Display slide 5 and insert a table with **5** columns and **3** rows.
 b. Type the text shown in Figure 2-138.
 c. Select all text and change the font size to **24 pt**. Adjust column width as needed.
 d. Select columns **2–5** and change to **Center** alignment.
 e. Change to **Bottom** alignment in the first row and change the row *Shading* to **Gold, Accent 1, Darker 25%**.
 f. Align the table in the horizontal and vertical center on the slide.

15. Insert a text box above the table on the left.
 a. Type **$250,000**.
 b. Change the font to **40 pt**. and **bold**.

16. Insert a text box below the table on the right.
 a. Type the following text on three lines:

 Lender rates are influenced by credit scores.
 Plan for a 20% down payment to avoid cost of points.
 Add taxes and insurance premiums.

17. Convert a list to a *SmartArt* graphic.
 a. Display slide 6. Select the bulleted text and convert it to a *SmartArt* graphic with the **Vertical Curved List** layout.
 b. Resize the *SmartArt* frame on the right so it fits the longest line of text.

18. Apply the following changes to the *SmartArt* graphic:
 a. Change the colors to **Colorful Range, Accent Colors 2 to 3**.
 b. Apply the **Moderate Effect** *SmartArt* style.
 c. Select all of the white circles and change the *Shape Fill* to **Red, Accent 5, Darker 25%** and apply the *Bevel* effect of **Cool Slant**.
 d. Center the *SmartArt* graphic horizontally on the slide (Figure 2-139).

This square will mark the data points on the line

2-136 *Format Data Series* pane with *Marker* options

Markers are emphasized and resource information is added.

2-137 Slide 4 completed line chart

Loan Product	Rate	Number of Payments	Monthly Payments	Total Paid
15 Year Fixed	3.11%	180	$1,739.71	$313,147.80
30 Year Fixed	3.88%	360	$1,176.31	$423,471.60

2-138 Table for slide 5

2-139 Slide 6 *SmartArt* graphic with style and effects changed

768

19. Apply the **Shape** transition with the **Out** effect option to all slides.

20. Save and close the presentation (Figure 2-140).

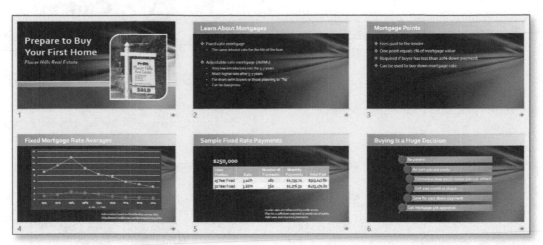

2-140 PowerPoint 2-5 completed

Independent Project 2-6

Kathy Sung, Director of Services at Life's Animal Shelter (LAS), will talk to a luncheon group of business-people. For this project, you develop the presentation she will use to explain the needs of LAS and describe ways people can contribute through donations or by volunteering their time.
[Student Learning Outcomes 2.1, 2.2, 2.3, 2.4, 2.5, 2.6, 2.7]

Files Needed: *YouCanHelp-02.pptx, CountryStroll-02.jpg, DayCare-02.jpg, Food-02.jpg, Groom-02.jpg,* and *RoyalTreatment-02.jpg* (*Student data files are available in the* Library *of your SIMnet account.*)
Completed Project File Name: *[your initials] PowerPoint 2-6.pptx*

Skills Covered in This Project

- Apply text effects.
- Apply a picture style.
- Set transparent color.
- Recolor a picture.
- Adjust size dimensions.
- Insert a text box.
- Insert and format a table.
- Convert text to a *SmartArt* graphic.
- Create a *SmartArt* graphic with pictures.
- Apply a *SmartArt* style and effects.

1. Open the presentation *YouCanHelp-02*.

2. Save the presentation as [your initials] PowerPoint 2-6.

3. Display slide 1. Change the title *Text Fill* color to **Dark Red, Accent 1, Darker 25%**. Apply the *Bevel* text effect of **Angle**.

4. Change the font size to **80 pt**. and resize the placeholder on the right so one word is on each line.

5. Resize a picture and remove a background color.
 a. Select the dog picture on slide 1.
 b. Increase the picture size (*Height* **5.9"** and *Width* **4.7"**).
 c. Use *Set Transparent Color* to remove the white area in the picture.
 d. Position the dog picture as shown in Figure 2-141.

2-141 Slide 1 with picture added, white background removed

6. Apply a picture style.
 a. Display slide 2 and increase the picture size (*Height* **5.84"** and *Width* **8"**).
 b. Apply the **Moderate Frame, Black** picture style.
 c. Center the picture horizontally and position it near the top of the slide.

7. Insert a text box and apply formatting:
 a. Insert a text box below the picture and type the following text:
 Our operating funds come through donations and pet adoption fees.
 b. Change the *Font Color* to **White, Background 1** and *Font Size* to **20 pt**.
 c. Resize the text box so the text wraps on two lines as shown in Figure 2-142.
 d. Change the *Shape Outline* to **White, Background 1** and the *Weight* to **3 pt**.
 e. Change the *Shape Fill* to **Black, Text 1**.
 f. Center the text box horizontally below the picture.

2-142 Slide 2 with picture and text box inserted

8. Copy and paste a slide.
 a. Select the slide 2 thumbnail and press **Ctrl+C**.
 b. Move your insertion point after slide 3 and press **Ctrl+V**.

9. Format the new slide 4.
 a. Replace the text in the text box below the picture with the words We Need Your Help!
 b. Resize the text box to fit the text and center it horizontally under the picture.
 c. Select the picture and change the *Color* to **Orange, Accent color 2 Dark** (Figure 2-143).

2-143 Slide 4 with picture recolored

10. Convert a list to a *SmartArt* graphic.
 a. Display slide 5 and convert the list to a **Vertical Bullet List** *SmartArt* graphic.
 b. Increase the *SmartArt* frame height to **4.7"** so the text size increases.
 c. Reduce the width to **9"**.
 d. Apply the **Cartoon** *SmartArt* style.

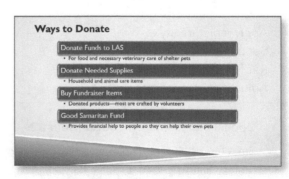

2-144 Slide 5 *SmartArt* graphic converted from bulleted text

e. Move the *SmartArt* up and center it horizontally as displayed in Figure 2-144.

11. Convert a list to a picture type *SmartArt* graphic.

a. Display slide 6 and convert the list to a **Picture Lineup** *SmartArt* graphic.

b. Click the **Picture** icon on each shape to open the *Insert Pictures* dialog box.

c. Browse to locate your student data files and insert the following pictures going from left to right (Figure 2-145):

1 *DayCare-02*
2 *CountryStroll-02*
3 *RoyalTreatment-02*
4 *Food-02*
5 *Groom-02*

Each picture is automatically resized.

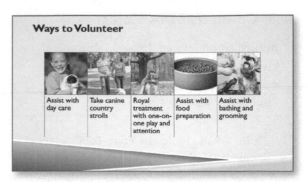

2-145 Slide 6 *SmartArt* graphic picture layout

12. Insert a new slide after slide 6 with a *Title and Content* layout.

a. Type the title Items We Need

b. Insert a table with **3** columns and **5** rows.

c. Type the table text shown in Figure 2-146.

d. Increase the font size to **20 pt**.

e. Adjust column width so each column fits the longest line of text.

f. Center the table on the slide.

13. Apply the *Gallery* transition to all slides.

14. Save and close the presentation (Figure 2-147).

Cleaning	Paper Products and Bedding	Dog and Cat Play
Bleach	Paper Towels	Dog and Cat Treats
Pine Sol	Paper Plates	Chewies
Mop Heads	Plastic Containers with Lids	Collars
Towels	Blankets	Leashes

2-146 Table text

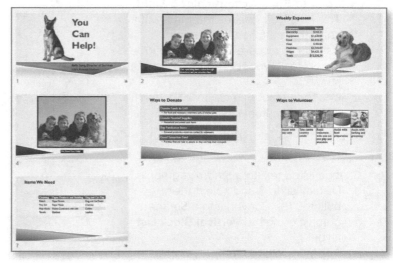

2-147 PowerPoint 2-6 completed

Improve It Project 2-7

The Hamilton Civic Center needs a presentation to explain benefits of yoga and encourage members to join yoga classes. For this project, you revise a presentation to add pictures, create a *SmartArt* graphic and apply various styles and effects for a contemporary appearance.
[Student Learning Outcomes 2.2, 2.3, 2.4, 2.5, 2.6, 2.7]

File Needed: *Yoga-02.pptx* (*Student data files are available in the* Library *of your SIMnet account.*)
Completed Project File Name: *[your initials] PowerPoint 2-7.pptx*

771

- Apply text effects.
- Insert an online picture.
- Apply a picture style.
- Reposition slide objects.

- Convert text to a *SmartArt* graphic.
- Apply a *SmartArt* style and effects.
- Format a table.
- Compress pictures.

1. Open the presentation *Yoga-02* that has a *Standard* size (4:3 aspect ratio). The slide size is 10"×7.5" compared to the slide size of 13.33"×7.5" for the default Widescreen size (16:9 aspect ratio).

2. Save the presentation as [your initials] PowerPoint 2-7.

3. Format the title slide for a more dynamic appearance.
 a. Search online and insert a yoga picture similar to the one shown in Figure 2-148.
 b. Resize the picture as needed.
 c. Apply a **Bevel Rectangle** picture style.
 d. Select the title placeholder and apply the **Wave 1** *Transform text effect*.

4. Recolor the logo picture.
 a. Select the logo and change the picture *Color* to **Blue, Accent color 5 Light**. This change replaces the black with a color that matches theme colors.
 b. Use *Set Transparent Color* to remove the white so your background color shows.
 c. Change the logo *Width* to **2.5"** and the *Height* will automatically adjust.

5. Arrange title slide objects as shown in Figure 2-148.

6. Change listed text to a *SmartArt* graphic.
 a. Display slide 3 and select the bulleted list. Convert it to a *SmartArt* graphic using the **Vertical Block List** layout.
 b. Apply the **White Outline** *SmartArt* style.
 c. Apply the **Colorful Range – Accent Colors 4 to 5** *SmartArt* colors (Figure 2-149).

7. Insert, position, and compress pictures.
 a. Display slide 4. Search online and insert an appropriate yoga picture.
 b. Resize the picture if needed and position it on the right.
 c. Apply a **Bevel Rectangle** picture style.
 d. Resize the bulleted text placeholder as needed to fit with the picture.

2-148 Title slide

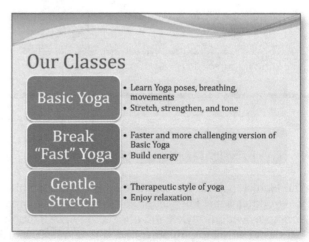

2-149 *SmartArt* graphic *Vertical Block List* layout

e. Display slide 5. Repeat steps 7a–d.

f. Select the picture, and click **Compress Pictures**. Use document resolution, delete cropped areas of pictures, and apply compression to all pictures.

8. Modify the table.

a. Display slide 6. Select the table text and increase the font size to **20 pt**.

b. Apply the **Medium Style 2 – Accent 4** table style.

c. Select the title row and apply the **Riblet** *Bevel* effect.

d. Increase the table *Height* to **2.5"**.

e. Center the text vertically in all cells.

f. Add a **1 pt**. border to all cells using the **Blue, Accent 4, Darker 50%** pen color (Figure 2-150).

g. Align the table vertically in the middle of the slide.

Classes	Days	Hours
Basic Yoga	Mon/Wed	4:15 – 5:15 p.m.
Break "Fast" Yoga	Tues/Thurs	7:00 – 8:10 a.m.
Gentle Stretch	Fri	10:00 – 11:30 a.m.

2-150 Slide 6 table

9. Apply the **Dissolve** transition to all slides.

10. Save and close your presentation (Figure 2-151).

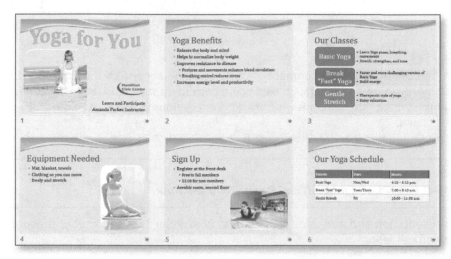

2-151 PowerPoint 2-7 completed

Challenge Project 2-8

For this project, do online comparison shopping for items you would be likely to buy such as clothing, household products, or automotive supplies. Prepare slides describing the products and apply text effects to the slide titles. Prepare a chart that shows costs either for the same product at several web sites or similar products at the same site.

[Student Learning Outcomes 2.1, 2.2, 2.3, 2.4, 2.5, 2.6, 2.7, 2.8, 2.9]

File Needed: None
Completed Project File Name: *[your initials] PowerPoint 2-8.pptx*

Create a new presentation and save it as [your initials] PowerPoint 2-8. Modify your presentation according to the following guidelines:

- Select an appropriate theme and apply color and font changes as needed for your topic.
- Prepare a title slide and product description slides.
- Search online for a related image and insert it on the title slide.
- Add one or more shapes to emphasize a slide object.
- Insert a *SmartArt* graphic to illustrate a process or relationship.
- Create a table summarizing some of your findings.
- Create two charts to compare specific items.

Challenge Project 2-9

Using data from the United States Department of Labor published online by the Bureau of Labor Statistics (http://www.bls.gov), prepare a presentation explaining current trends in the labor force. For example, you could show unemployment rate comparisons from different regions or wage estimates for various occupations in different states.
Student Learning Outcomes 2.1, 2.2, 2.3, 2.4, 2.5, 2.6, 2.7, 2.8, 2.9]

File Needed: None
Completed Project File Name: *[your initials] PowerPoint 2-9.pptx*

Create a new presentation and save it as [your initials] PowerPoint 2-9. Modify your presentation according to the following guidelines:

- Select an appropriate theme and apply color and font changes as needed for your topic.
- Create a title slide using a *Transform* text effect.
- Include several bulleted slides describing current trends.
- Search for appropriate pictures, resize as needed, and apply a picture style to each one.
- Add one or more shapes to emphasize a slide object.
- Insert a *SmartArt* graphic to illustrate a process or relationship.
- Prepare a table showing salaries for several jobs in different locations or for data changing over time.
- Prepare a chart comparing employment statistics from your state or region.

Challenge Project 2-10

Using information from one of your favorite coffee or soft drink manufacturers, such as the facts you can find at www.thecoca-colacompany.com or www.pepsico.com, prepare a presentation comparing different products. You could show the diversity of the product line or list promotional products with pricing. From financial information provided on the sites, you could feature total revenue, total profits, or other interesting performance data in your presentation.
[Student Learning Outcomes 2.1, 2.2, 2.3, 2.4, 2.5, 2.6, 2.7, 2.8, 2.9]

File Needed: None
Completed Project File Name: *[your initials] PowerPoint 2-10.pptx*

Create a new presentation and save it as [your initials] PowerPoint 2-10. Modify your presentation according to the following guidelines:

- Select an appropriate theme and apply color and font changes as needed for your topic.
- Create a distinctive title slide using *WordArt* combined with a shape to create interest.
- Search online for appropriate pictures and insert three or more.
- Adjust picture sizes and apply picture styles.
- Prepare slides listing key factors contributing to the company's growth.
- Feature selected financial information in a table.
- Prepare a *SmartArt* graphic illustrating a specific process or relationship from historical or operational information.
- Create a chart showing comparisons for data such as net revenue, operating profit, or growth over a period of time.